M000222753

GRIFFON
GUN DOG SUPREME

Joan Bailey

SWAN VALLEY PRESS
HILLSBORO, OREGON

Other books by Joan Bailey:

How To Help Gun Dogs Train Themselves

Published by: Swan Valley Press
9601 NW Leahy Rd.
Portland, OR 97229

Library of Congress Catalog Card Number: 96-67220

Publisher's Cataloging in Publication
(Prepared by Quality Books Inc.)

Bailey, Joan
Griffon: gun dog supreme: the history and the story of how to save a breed/ Joan Bailey. — Hillsboro, OR: Swan Valley Press, 1996.
p. cm.
ISBN 0-9630127-2-X

1. Hunting dogs. 2. Wirehaired pointing griffon.
I. Title.
SF428.5.B28 1996 636.7'52
QBI95-20013

Credit Card Orders: 1-800-356-9315

Cover Photograph: Larry Mueller
Cover Design: Chris Silva

WARNING—DISCLAIMER

DEDICATED TO

JOSEF J NADEKER

CONTENTS

Acknowledgments ix
Foreword by Larry Mueller x
Introduction xi

PART ONE - THE HISTORY OF THE GRIFFON

Chapter 1. Before the 19th Century 1
Jean Castaing

Chapter 2. The Korthals Era (1850-1900) 5
Eduard Karel Korthals
The Patriarchs

Chapter 3. End of the 19th Century and the Korthals Era 21
"The Pointer Blood in the Korthals Griffons"
Who Was Hegewald?

Chapter 4. Early 20th Century (Europe) 31

Chapter 5. Early 20th Century (North America) 39
Key to Pedigrees

Chapter 6. WPGCA Founded 1951 53
The Second Griffon Club
Who Were the Rest of These Charter Members?

Chapter 7. The Sixties, A Period of Transition 69
Marg Allen
1963: Marg Allen and Joan Bailey Meet

Chapter 8. 1969, A Pivotal Year for Griffons 83
France
Germany
First Versatile Hunting Dog Test in North America

Chapter 9. The Early Years of NAVHDA (1969-1972) Part I 99
"The Green Book"

Chapter 10. The Early Years of NAVHDA (1973-1976) Part II 111

Chapter 11. Griffon Club Begins Own Testing Program (1976) 125
Yesterday, Today, Tomorrow

Chapter 12. Griffon Breeding Program—1974-1982 129
Let's Stop the Deterioration of the Griffon
WPGCA Breeder's Agreement
People Count Too: Let's Meet the Challenge

Chapter 13. First Intermediate Hunting Dog Test Maine & California 143
Once More to Wolferszell

Chapter 14. Griffon Breeding Program—1980-1983 155
First Judges Seminar—Nebraska
For Roy A. Speece

Chapter 15. Restoration of the Griffon Breed in North America—1984 165
WPGCA Breeding Program
Facing the Truth
Solving the Problem
Research for Injection of Foreign Blood
Methods of Restoration
The Cesky Fousek
Opinions About the Origin of the Cesky Fousek (1995)
Explanation of the Scarcity of Documents
Immediate Plans
Implementation of the Restoration Program
Expected Results
Conclusion

Chapter 16. The Beginning of the Second Phase of WPGCA Approved Breeding Program—1984 179
End of a Year, The Beginning of a New Decade for Our Griffons
Realistic Approach to the "Fousek" Injection
December 1985—ERIK OD JEZERAK Arrives in America

Chapter 17. The Last Half of the '80s 187
The Third Fousek Arrives—HELA Z DOBROWSKA

Chapter 18. 1988, 100th Anniversary of Original Korthals Griffon Club in Germany 197
100th Celebrations Across America
The Rocky Mountain Griffon Club
Looking Back, By Dick Austin

Chapter 19. End of the '80s, Beginning of the '90s 211
Heartland Griffon Club Formed

Chapter 20. Turning the Bend into the '90s 227
March 1991, Two More Fouseks Arrive
Disappointments

Chapter 21. Heading for Home 239
Dick Austin Steps Down from the Board of Directors
Joan Bailey Steps Down from Editor of the GDS
Waiting for a Puppy? By Richard Bovard
The Laurent Frileux Award
The General Rogers Award
WPGCA BOD Changes Qualification Requirements for Gen. Rogers Award
In Memory: Don Nicholson †

Chapter 22. Past, Present, Future 253
Dr. Carl Tabel †
Tribute from the Large Munsterlander Club of North America
"Saul's Lament"
From the Nederlandse Griffonclub

1995
WPGCA Officers for 1995-1997
John Lundberg
A Look To the Future

PART TWO TESTING, JUDGING, AND BREEDING VERSATILE HUNTING DOGS 271
"I Just Want A Good Hunting Dog"

Chapter 23. Why and How We Test Versatile Hunting Dogs 273
Natural Ability, Intermediate Hunting Dog & Utility Field Tests

Chapter 24. Judging 279
Requirements for Judges
Apprentice Judging
Judging Teams
Judges Seminars
Dogs Are A Combination Of Their Genetic Predisposition and Their Environment

Chapter 25. Griffon Registry Book (GRB) 287
Why The Need For Breed Club Registry
AKC and Other Mass Registration Bodies

Chapter 26. Breeding Part I 291
Kynology
Genetics
Inbreeding and Line Breeding
How Korthals Used In-Breeding and Line Breeding With the Eight Patriarchs To Stabilize the Griffon Breed

Chapter 27. Breeding Part II 307
A Further Look at Inbreeding
Dogs That Don't Qualify for Breeding are Not Bad Dogs
Control of Breeding in Germany
How To Read A Pedigree
Short Resume of Cesky Fousek Breeding History
Developing a Line
How To Start & Maintain a Line Within a Breed
How a Dog Becomes a Foundation Male or a Foundation Female of a Line
No Mathematical Formula For Breeding Dogs
Progeny Testing
What About Griffon Breeders Outside the WPGCA Breeding Program?
Proposed Standard of the Breed - A Working Document

Chapter 28. Hip Dysplasia and its Relationship in Breeding Griffons 323
What is it and How Does it Affect Griffons?
Why Should I Radiograph My Dog's Hips If I Don't Intend to Breed?
Hip Dysplasia in Griffons, Part I
Hip Dysplasia in Griffons, Part II

Chapter 29. Reducing Hip Dysplasia and How it Relates to WPGCA Approved Breeding Program 341
Hip Dysplasia, by Dr. E.A. Corley
How Dr. Corley's Breeding Program Applies to WPGCA Breeding Program
Latest Breaking News Updating Present Research on Diagnosing Hip Dysplasia
OFA Responds to the PennHIP Announcement
WPGCA Board of Directors Responds
Latest Data From OFA on HD In Griffons

Chapter 30. The Future 349
Keeping the Korthals Griffon "Pure"
Are We On the Right Track?
Griffons That Have Qualified in IHDT That May Be Used for Breeding in 1996-1997
Results of Spring Field Tests 1995
Dr. Thomas Mintscheff †

Epilogues 357
Joe Nadeker
"Wintering Quail" By Roy Speece

Appendix 363
A. Tabulation of results of all Griffons tested since 1969 in tests recognized by the WPGCA and, all Griffons tested in NAVHDA since 1976
B. Original Constitution (1951) WPGCA.
C. Constitution WPGCA (Revised 1994).
D. Breeding Rules, WPGCA Breeding Program.
E. WPGCA Breeder's Agreement.
F. Griffon Registry Book (GRB).
G. Breed Standards (French, German, AKC).
H. Awards From the Dog Writers of America Association.
I. "Hello Wired Dog - Goodbye, Cooperation."

Bibliography 463

ACKNOWLEDGMENTS

This is my book. But many people played a part in making the book happen, and in making it the best it could be. Five people did critical readings of the manuscript, which is tedious, and requires long hours. They are **Joe Nadeker** (see Epilogues), who began reading at least one year before anyone else. Those were the rough, terrible first drafts, what I call the early part of labor. Then **Glenn Lehrer** did several critical readings, with tremendous input of energy and time. **Ed Bailey** read an early version and gave advice that was critical in getting the manuscript properly organized. **Brad Meyen** read, not just from the view point of a long-time member of the Griffon club, but also from a legal point of view and gave me vital guidance. **Larry Mueller** read, gave suggestions. Then he read some rewrites and came up with key points that needed clarification.

Other people who read for me were **Bill Tarrant, Jim Seibel**, **Dennis Carlson**, **John Lundberg**, **Jack Dallimore**, **Charlie Miller**, and **Rick Molt**.

Of special mention is **John Pitlo**, who proof read the entire tabulation of test results in the appendix, which is a tremendous amount of work—hours and hours. Then towards the end of the entire process I sent John that part of the index on disks and he transposed them into a readable format. I'm greatly indebted to his input in this regard.

Mike and **Kathi Rackouski** came to my rescue at the "eleventh hour," when the computer program for pedigrees failed. They retyped all the pedigrees in this book, a particularly difficult task when you get to the Czech names.

Many other people, mostly Griffonniers, helped in varying capacities with different aspects of the book and I thank them. They were:

Rick & Tina Molt
Ralph & Dorothy Nodine
Kohel Haver (copyright law)
Dennis & Linny Stovall (Blue Heron Publishing)
Bob Hinckley
Warren Webster
Sandy Cushman
Silke Alberts
Tom Whitley
Martha Wagoner (editing)
Kirk Streit
Russell Ward
Barbara Koessler

Grateful appreciation is extended to the **North American Versatile Hunting Dog Association** for permission to print the test results of all Griffons tested in their sanctioned tests from 1971 through 1995.

FOREWORD

By Larry Mueller

This is a work of tough love.

I've read a great number of breed books. Most are pure fiction—fairy tales about perfect dogs in perfect breeds. They commonly express great sentimental love, little in-depth understanding, a strong desire to please others in their group, and a political willingness to cover up faults and failures if this promotes their aims or the aims of their tribe.

Joan's book fails this criteria in every respect. While average breed books are about "pure" breeds that supposedly need no improvement; Joan writes about a breed in creation. And her's is the fact of life. No breed is static. It rises or falls with the creativity of its breeders.

The following truism seems so simple, but in the emotionally attached world of dogs it's not: "Problem solving begins by seeing the problems." Quite unlike most breed aficionados, Joan Bailey demonstrates uncommonly clear, tough love vision. Political correctness would have been safer. Considerable risks accompany full truth and disclosure about people and their dogs. But Joan courageously documents with great detail the best and the worst in Wirehaired Pointing Griffons. As she often says about judging dogs in tests, "Do it right because this information is on the records forever." Because of her truth and honesty, Griffons and their breeders will benefit from this book for all time.

It goes far beyond that, however. At some point in the manuscript, I recognized that I was reading on two levels. It does, of course, tell us the origin and history of the Wirehaired Pointing Griffon. But if we read carefully and honestly, and forget legend and hype, we find the how-it-was-done origin and up-and-down history of most breeds. The Griffon problems, if we swallow hard and admit it, are the problems of all breeds. So are the solutions. The tests for identifying superior Griffons work for any gun dog breed. And the methods and the plan for holding the genes of superior Griffons into perpetuity works for any dogs. On its second level, this is THE breed book for ALL breeds.

Larry Mueller,
Hunting Dogs Editor,
OUTDOOR LIFE March, 1995

Author

***MAINE, Spring 1995, Northeast Griffon Club Intermediate Hunting Dog Test: PRAIRIE STORM'S ABBY** with owner Jim Hughes, and senior judge Joan Bailey, just before the start of the track of the live pheasant. **ABBY** (Prize I) is typical of the fine young Griffons being produced by the Griffon Club's Approved Breeding Program. **ABBY's** story is special though. One year before this test, just one month after her Natural Ability Test, she contracted distemper despite having had her shots. Jim and his wife nursed this fine dog back to health, and she will be used in the Breeding Program. (Compliments Karen Hurtig)*

Introduction

What is the Griffon

During the twentieth century the Griffon has been described by numerous North American outdoor writers in as many different terms as there are writers. Most of them never owned a Griffon and few ever hunted over one. In Europe in the late nineteenth century and the early 20th century sports writers were saying a great deal about the Griffons, especially that strain known then as the *Korthals Griffon,* extolling its virtues.

In North America, where the game of field trials for pointers and setters was invented and promoted, the Griffon early on was often described by outdoor writers as a good dog for an old man. He was a shoe polisher, a meat dog. This description was often garnered from the trialer's intellect, not from the hunter's desire for a sound dog that hunted always for the gun.

The real truth is the *well-bred Griffon is a practical, wire-coated, versatile hunting dog for the on-foot hunter.* He covers all areas likely to hold game, leaving the impression that nothing has been missed. He does his job joyfully, eager for game contact, in a cooperative manner with his master, who is also his hunting partner.

This means he is not a self-hunter. If he has been brought along properly he will become the other half of an efficient hunting team. Without hesitation he will go into heavy cover and track wounded game on land as well as in the marsh or in a brome grass field. He will cover large fields for Hungarian partridge with great efficiency. At the end of the day he goes home with his master and slips into his role of family dog.

All of the above is true, but it is also true of the other versatile breeds: the German Wirehair, German Shorthair, Brittany spaniel, Pudelpointer, Cesky Fousek, Munsterlander (large and small), Vizsla, Weimaraner, German Longhair and the rest. Yet, every breed is slightly different from its cousins.

Griffon development happened a little more than 100 years ago, about the time of the Industrial Revolution in Europe that produced a middle class. Until then there had been only the extremely wealthy (landed aristocracy) and the masses of very poor peasants.

The wealthy could afford to have a kennel full of dogs, plus the necessary people to care for and train these dogs. They had pointers and retrievers; some even had tracking dogs and coursing hounds (Greyhounds, etc.).

When history produced this new middle class—doctors, lawyers, merchants, and others—these people lived mostly in or very close to the city. They could have only one dog. They had neither space nor money for an entire kennel. It was at this point that most of the versatile breeds we know today, were developed by private breeders to fill this need.

People wanted a dog that could search, point, track wounded game (both feather and fur), retrieve from land and water, and could adapt to living in or at his master's home. In other words, this dog had to have the temperament to be a good family dog, though not exactly as we would mean it today, as most dogs in those days did not live inside the home.

What should you expect from a versatile hunting dog? First, as with any breed, you want sound temperament. This is *the number one consideration.* Unsound temperament, or, as some of us call it, mental instability, is the number one enemy of every dog breed today. So, no matter which breed you choose, or which kennel, the best advice is to research temperament thoroughly. With sound temperament comes a high degree of reliability in all areas.

If your Griffon is from sound hunting stock, he will search the fields thoroughly, leaving the impression that no game has been bypassed. In the grouse woods you can expect the same thing, though he will naturally shorten his range. Throughout his hunting he will always be *hunting for the gun.* Griffons form a strong partnership with their master. The hunt becomes a team effort.

The Griffon can switch from hunting upland birds in the morning, to jump shooting ducks in the late afternoon, or vice versa. Or, quite often, the dog may do both at the same time.

You might be hunting the edge of a corn field. Close by is a ditch with running water. You're hunting for pheasants. As you walk along you notice that a few mallards have landed in the ditch up ahead. You put your dog at heel and the two of you sneak up on the ducks. As they take off, you knock one down and it falls back into the ditch. In a moment your dog is in the water, about to catch the duck and retrieve it to you. Now you have a pheasant and a duck in your bag.

You go a bit further and old Griff points a rabbit. Have you ever tasted cottontail rabbit? Well, let me tell you, it's tastier than pheasant! With a versatile dog you can shoot rabbits if you wish, and even large hares. These dogs will point rabbits and hares and love to retrieve any kind of furred game.

The differences between the versatile breeds are not great. Easy to distinguish are the smooth-coated dogs from the rough or long-coated ones. Yet there are more similarities between the Griffon and German Shorthair than there are differences. The best we can say is that all these breeds were developed to do the same job. What differentiates one breed from another is the unique style or manner, in which the dogs do their job, and, of course, outward physical appearance.

Some people prefer a smooth-coated dog. Others prefer a long-coated; and still others like the wirehaired coat. Many believe that the hard, wire coat is more protective, both in cold, wet conditions, as well as in thick, dry cover.

For the Griffon devotee, perhaps it is the dog's strong desire to please his master that wins the hunter's heart. Or, it's the easygoing, family dog who possesses a unique sense of humor. Maybe it's the moustache and beard. Probably it's a combination of all these.

In 1976, John Falk, writing in his ***The Complete Guide to Bird Dog Training***, said about the Griffon, "By and large, the griff is so eager to please that he will practically knock himself out for a few words of praise, a pat on the head, and a bit of affectionate encouragement. Finding a hunting breed that seeks a closer relationship with master and family would be difficult, indeed."

If one were to write about the unique personality of the Griffon, one might as well just quote John Falk, because the well bred, properly bred Griffon does have a strong desire to please his or her master or mistress. This is his job in life, whether in the field, or in the home. In the field he becomes an intense dog that has a strong desire for game contact, but wants to please you by putting the game in your pocket. Then he switches when you get home, and becomes a laid back member of the family, cuddling with the kids on the floor, or lying quietly in his corner when company is there, or riding in the car to the store. He is indeed the old handle given to him when he first arrived in America—a jack of all trades.

He is a practical hunting dog, always hunting to produce game for the bag. This is part of his strong desire to please, to cooperate, which makes him easy to train. He is just as happy working in a marsh as in a thick grouse woods or a large alfalfa field. He will work a covey of bobwhites, then work the singles, and move on to handle a moving cock pheasant. He will retrieve your duck and work just about any other game bird you desire. If you want him to point rabbits he will do so and retrieve them to you proudly and with joy.

The trick is to obtain a well-bred pup and develop this young dog into what you want. In order for you to obtain such a dog it will help if you understand his history.

One cannot write the history of the Griffon without also writing about the people who have owned and bred them. It is *both* the dogs and their masters that shaped the Griffon destiny.

*"**HIGHLAND TOD**," painted by Richard Ansdell around the early 1800's. The two dogs in the center certainly look like forerunners of our modern Griffons. All the other dogs look like forerunners of other modern breeds too.*

__MOUSTACHE__, a painting of one of Korthals' early Griffons—not one of the patriarchs. __MOUSTACHE__ was used extensively for breeding by Korthals. (See Part Two.) The original painting hangs in the Institute of Wildlife in Hannover, Germany.

PART ONE

THE HISTORY OF THE GRIFFON

CHAPTER ONE

BEFORE THE NINETEENTH CENTURY

No one can say with absolute certainty exactly where, when, or how the Griffon originated. Very few breeds can be traced to one specific origin. What we do know about the Griffon is that, for centuries, a wirehaired, or rough-haired hunting dog was mentioned and sometimes described by hunting writers from all over Europe. The actual name "Griffon" is first recorded in a letter by Henry IV of France to de Montmorency, dated April 12, 1596, where he speaks about his little "Griffon." In 1616 Coler wrote about dogs with "long shags all over their bodies, originating in Norway and Iceland."

In 1598 Charles d'Arcussia wrote in a book about falconry that the Griffons and Bracques (shorthaired pointing dogs) were not much good for the flights of partridge. J. E. de Selincourt, in his book *Le Parfait Chasseur*, published in 1683, classifies the different breeds of dogs, putting the pointing dogs under the heading of gundogs to distinguish them from hounds.

He divided gundogs into three breeds: the Bracque (the forerunner of the shorthaired pointing dog that we have today), the spaniel, and the Griffon. He stated that the Griffons were used both as pointing dogs and as hounds, and that the best Griffons came from Piedmont in Italy.

One should not confuse the Griffon we are talking about with two very ancient breeds—the French Vendeen hounds. One was called griffon de la vendee and resembled an English Otterhound. The other hound was the Griffon Nivernais. Before the concept of "pure breeds," writers used a person's name, or a geographical location to distinguish one strain of dog from another. Hence the griffon de la vendee came from the name of Vendeen, who was the breeder. Much, much later came the Korthals Griffon.

NOTE: If you have never owned a Griffon, you may want to skip most of the chapters on the early history and go on to the chapters dealing with more recent history. For long-time Griffons owners, I have presented the history in detail, knowing that most of you want to learn about the fascinating story of our breed.

JEAN CASTAING

Monsieur Castaing is the author of the only known book about Griffons: *Le Griffon d'arret, Historique, Standard, Elevage* (The Pointing Griffon, History, Standard, Breeding). The first edition was published in France in 1949. Two of the three copies in my possession came to me as part of the Griffon Club records when I took over the position of secretary from Douglas Feathers in 1967. One of them is a 1949 paperback edition, and written on the cover in General Roger's (founder of our present day Griffon Club) handwriting is: Col. T. Def. Rogers, Qtrs 75, Ft Bragg, N.C.

As far as I know, there were five editions. We have three editions in the club. We have a second edition, published in 1963, with the title changed to *Le Griffon d'Arret A Poil Dur Korthals.*

The fifth and most recent edition was published in 1987, to mark the 100th jubilee of the Korthals Griffon Club in 1988. It is much better done than previous editions, with a painting of a Griffon head on the cover. It was sent to me from the French Griffon Club late in 1988, and was autographed by Monsieur Castaing as follows:

> Respectful homage by the author to Madame Bailey, Presidente du Club American du Griffon d'Arret a Poil Dur, for the development, competence, devotion, illuminating the worth of this excellent breed on the American continent.
>
> J. Castaing

Monsieur Castaing is well known for his many articles and books about hunting, hunting dogs, training, and breeding. For Griffon devotees in France *Le Griffon d'Arret A Poil Dur Korthals* has been like a bible. It contains an in-depth, well-researched history, divided into pre-history; the Cherville Griffon and the Guerlain Griffon; the Korthals Era (1873-1914); the Critical Era (1919-1939); and the Contemporary era. The remainder of the book deals with: preserving and improving the characteristics, the standard, and the future of the Griffon.

In the pre-history section, Castaing quotes a famous French novelist and hunter from the early part of the nineteenth century, Ponson du Terrail, who wrote:

> He is cindery grey, spotted with white and orange, his hair is long and rough, his round head resembles a hedgehog. But through this formless ball shines an eye sparkling with intelligence—he is brave, ardent and clever—the Griffon will always be the preferred dog of the true hunter—it is the Zouave Warrior among dogs. If France wants to put a dog on its coat of arms, as a symbol of valor and faithfulness, she would wisely choose the Griffon. Oh the valiant beast that nothing stops, which continues always.

In eighteenth century England Griffons were known as Russian Pointer or Russian Retriever. According to Castaing, this was so because the English seemed to consider the bearded dogs as products of the Siberian area.

There was also the Griffon de Bresse, one of the most ancient breeds of France, a favorite with sportsmen for centuries. It closely resembled the English Otterhound and had a hard, wiry coat.

Artists such as van der Stealen in 1590, Riedinger around 1650, and Gessner in 1770 used rough-coated dogs in their paintings, sometimes calling them Griffons. Their appearance was as different as their names in the languages of different countries. In earlier times the Griffon is mentioned as Polish and Hungarian Water Dog; Icelandic Pudel; Barbet; Hessian Shaggy Head; Spinone in Italy; in England Russian Pointer, Smousbart in Holland (Korthals called his rough-coated dogs Smousbart until he moved to Germany. There he began calling them Griffons.) In Alsace-Lorraine, Rhineland,

France, and Belgium the breed was known as Griffon. *It would seem these rough-haired dogs existed in many European countries for centuries.*

As to the origin of the word "griffon" and its relation to the rough-haired, bearded hunting dog, the likely origins include the Latin "gryphus (hawk), and "gryphium" (hook, claw); old German "grif" (hook); and in French "griffe" (claw). In mythology there is an animal with an eagle's head and wings, and a lion's body. It is called "gryfon."

In the twelfth century, a peasant festival was called a Griffon. Later, the word came to be synonymous with "uncivilized." In 1652 Rabelais called the mountain people of Savoyln, Piedmont and the Alps Griffons. When the Protestants in Waldensen returned to their villages after their flight to the Alps in 1545-1689, they brought with them from those Alpine lands rough-coated dogs which had originated in Italy and which had been bred for hunting purposes. They named the dogs Griffons, after the mountain people from whom they came. *That name was used for all rough-haired dogs of that time.* Probably the name Griffon just stuck because it described the dog quite well. Even today the Griffon looks rough and uncivilized.

When the long history of the Griffon is brought to light it is obvious that the rough-haired hunting dog was bred many centuries ago in different European countries, under different names. And it is impossible to say it originated in any one country.

An interesting historical aside concerning the word "Griffon" is that the first ship ever to sail the upper Great Lakes was the "Griffon." The ship was built in 1679 near Niagara Falls on the Canadian side. Her construction was supervised by Moyse Hillaret, a master shipbuilder brought especially from France for the job. The ship was named the "Griffon" in honor of Count Frontenac, governor of Canada, whose coat of arms bore the mythical animal with an eagle's head and wings, and a lion's body.

By the middle of the nineteenth century one could loosely classify five different groups of rough-haired dogs:

1) The Spinone in Italy, probably from mixed breeding of old Italian Spinone and long-haired Griffons (or Barbets, as they were sometimes called) later infused with Korthals blood. Earlier this dog was mostly white with brown or lemon patches; this gradually changed to a bluish-gray with the addition of the Korthals blood. However, many white strains can still be found today. (Unfortunate for the Spinone—in North America today there are a few puppy factories producing poor quality dogs.)

2) In France there was a long-haired group which was bred by Monsieur Emanuel Boulet of Elbeut through a mixed breeding of the old Griffon and his own Griffon Boulet. It was popular for some time as a water specialist.

3) Also in France was the Griffon Guerlain strain. This strain was first established in 1847 by the Marquis de Clerville and was known then as the Griffon d'arret Picard, later becoming known as the griffon Guerlain after Monsieur A. Guerlain of Crotoy, who was the successor to the Marquis de Clerville's kennel. This dog is reported to have developed from mixed breedings between Griffon and Pointer and was mostly white with lemon patches.

4) In Germany about 1865 there was a breed called Stickelhaar (bristly-hair), bred partly from the old Hessian shaggy beard, the German setter, other rough-haired dogs (including probably Cesky Fousek), and possibly the Bracque (forerunner of the German Shorthair). These dogs were bred by Mr. H. Bontant of Frankfurt.

5) The old rough-haired group scattered over all the Continent, called by the

collective name Griffon. At that time this rather neglected group was in danger of being forgotten.

It is important to remind ourselves that at this time the word "Griffon" was used loosely all over Europe to describe dogs that had a shaggy, rough-haired appearance.

And now we arrive at that point in history when the name Korthals enters the picture. As Mr. W. Kantz wrote in Volume 25 of the *Griffonstammbuch* (Griffon Stud Book) (GSB), "It is to E.K. Korthals' great merit to have saved the Griffon from oblivion, *recreated* (emphasis added) him, and made him highly appreciated as a uniform race. Korthals' name will always be inseparably connected with the Griffon breed."

EDUARD KAREL KORTHALS. Born November 16, 1851 in Amsterdam; Died July 4, 1896 in Frankfurt, age 45*. Photo taken circa 1882. (Compliments of The Nederlandse Griffonclub Historical Archives.)*

CHAPTER TWO
THE KORTHALS ERA (1850-1900)

From childhood, Korthals was a dog lover and passionate hunter. He had all possible breeds of dogs on his father's estate in Holland, including rough-haired dogs that some people called Griffons, but in Holland they called them Smousbard. According to Korthals' kennel book, by about 1873 he already had begun breeding his strain of Griffons. He found the dogs to be very effective in the marsh and dune country where he lived.

Korthals was the son of a rich munitions manufacturer in Amsterdam. He and his father were fascinated by breeding. By using selective breeding, Korthals' father succeeded in breeding a strangely marked herd of cattle at the family estate. So it was natural that the son had similar interests, and no doubt developed some knowledge of breeding by observing his father's work.

But as Castaing put it, "his taste for breeding being greater than his taste for business, Eduard Korthals preferred to quit the family business and native country in 1873 at the age of 23." Provided with a small income, Castaing recounts,

> Korthals settled in Germany in the hunting country of Hesse, where he had friends. It was near one of them, the prince of Solms-Braunfels at Bibesheim (a great fan of hunting dogs, especially pointers) that Korthals settled down in 1877 as kennel master to the Prince. Paralleling the raising of Pointers, he created for himself a breed of Griffon Pointers that he had already begun to raise in Holland for swamp hunting.
>
> Until his death in 1896, he devoted himself to this breeding with a persistence and intelligence which have easily classed him among the great breeders of history.

I agree emphatically with Castaing's emphasis that Korthals was an ardent hunter and that this passion was combined with a keen interest and knowledge in breeding. In his early years in Holland he lived near the Polder country (a term used to describe the swamps behind the dikes in Holland). So it was natural that Korthals' first interest was in dogs that could hunt in that kind of terrain, mostly for waterfowl. But, as he used his Griffons to hunt other game as well, he realized these dogs' talents were not limited to the swamps.

Writing further on Korthals, Castaing said:

> The particular qualities of the Griffons, their intelligence, their robustness, their resistance to all weather changes must have induced this hunter to assemble all these elements in them while adding those traits which they might lack in order to make a hunting dog for all terrains, in all climates, for all game; in a word, the ideal help for the practical country hunter. [Today we might say—"practical on-foot hunter.] On the other hand, the fad for English dogs, who were much more imaginative than the continental dogs of that time, and with better noses, was beginning to catch on; but the English couldn't satisfy the tastes of a well-rounded hunter like Korthals. Their qualities were obvious in open country, but were balanced by too many faults, such as fra-

> gility, aversion to thorns and water, and too independent a character. We mustn't forget that Korthals was in Germany and German hunters demanded from their dogs more than a spectacularly long point and useless chase....
>
> The German hunter demands of his hunting dog enterprise and a firm point, a good nose, tracking and finding wounded game—including large animals—a biting of attack, retrieving in deep water, and besides—the work of a watch dog. These are, of course partly training—but all breeds do lend themselves equally well to training and the old continental breeds excelled in this flexibility. Outdistanced by the English dogs in liveliness and sometimes nose, between the Europeans and the newcomers something was lacking—it was up to Korthals to unite the traits.
>
> From there his goal was set—to create a dog having more initiative and speed than the current continental dog—with a sensitive nose, flexible and intelligent enough to adapt to training by anyone, robust enough to hunt all day and go out again the next, resistant to cold or heat, covered with a water repellent coat. All these qualities were found, of course, spread through several breeds. To unite them in one dog seemed a gamble—to stabilize them and make them genetically transmittable seemed impossible.

A friend of Korthals, C. Hacke van Myden, shared Korthals' interest in the breed and joined him in a breeding program for Griffons. Later Mr. Hacke von Myden withdrew from the partnership and left his dogs to Korthals. Those dogs were **HANS, PLUTO** and **BELLO**.

According to his kennel book (a photocopy of Korthals' original handwritten kennel book was given to me for our club by Mr. V. Gessel of the Dutch Griffon Club), between 1863 to 1876 Korthals purchased about 20 dogs, and was given the three mentioned above. Some of these dogs were:

BRESTOR	*Spaniel*, female, cost: 10 florins.
SPOT	*Retriever*, male, whelped in 1873—a gift.
JUNO	*3/4 Pointer*, female, light lemon, whelped in 1873, purchased for 80 florins. (Do not confuse this dog with the patriarch **JUNON GSB 125**.)
CASTOR	*Spaniel*, male, purchased for 75 florins.
BRUNO	*German Spaniel*, male, cost 45 florins.
DIAAN	*Spaniel,* female, cost 75 florins.
HANS	*Griffon*, female, black with white spot on the chest, about 4 years old, purchased in November 1874 for 75 florins; she was shown at Utrecht in 1875, as a Griffon nivernais.
PLUTO	*Barbet,* male, white and brown, about 2 1/2 years, (purchased in 1875 for 25 florins), won a bronze medal at the show in Utrecht in 1875.
FINETTE	*French Shorthair,* female, (purchased in Paris for 35 francs).
RUSTAN	*German Shorthair.*
BELLO	Griffon female, white and brown, about 7 years old, (purchased for 60 florins).

LADY	*Pointer x German Shorthair* cross, female, (price 150 florins).
CHASSEUR	*1/4 Pointer x 3/4 German Shorthair,* male (price 150 florins).
TOM	*Griffon,* male, white with lemon colored ears, (purchased in Paris for 150 florins); in 1876 he won a silver medal at Lay Haye, and a bronze medal in 1877 in Amsterdam.

(**TOM, HANS** and **FINETTE** were the only dogs from Korthals kennel that can be traced to France with certainty. None of the three were known to be allowed in breeding.)

The Patriarchs

Castaing took these descriptions of the patriarchs, from the Griffon Staumbuch (GSB) circa 1889:

BANCO (GSB 2): male, steel gray and brown, bought in The Hague, at about 2 and 1/2 in 1876. Known by a drawing in Volume 1 GSB [German Stud Book]...with untrimmed feathers. This dog seemed to be of above average size, although a Griffon—still a little different from the type we know today [1949]. His coat seemed dense and hard, the ear flat and not very long, an expressive eye, the beard and moustache not very developed (which goes with a hard coat). The entirety gave the impression of a robust dog, perhaps a little heavy. He was an excellent hunter with a good nose and lots of endurance.

HECTOR (GSB 30): male Griffon of white and brown, bought in Amsterdam in 1874, about 3 years old. We don't know anything more of him except he produced with **MOUCHE, MADAME ANGOT**, famous bitch who had a tremendous influence.

JANUS (GSB 33): male, gray and brown, bought in Amsterdam in 1874, resold in 1875. This dog was a Barbet. Korthals did not yet distinguish between Barbet and Griffon. With **MOUCHE** he had one descendant, **HUZAAR.**

SATAN (GSB 67): male, black Griffon with a white spot on the chest and some beige marks. Bred with **MADAME ANGOT** he produced **ZAMPA (GSB 171).**

DONNA (GSB 190): female, long-haired Griffon Boulet type, bought in Germany in 1879. Bred twice with **MOUSTACHE I,** she produced only two pups: **ANGOT** (not **MADAME ANGOT**), and **CLAIRETTE (GSB 100).**

JUNON (GSB 129): female, half-blood German Shorthair, brown color, belonging to an Amsterdam amateur breeder, that he [Korthals] used around 1875, when she was 6 years old. Let's underline the unorthodox type of this bitch, more or less half-breed and remember only for the moment the influences she had on the whole family of Korthals Griffons.

MOUCHE (GSB 143): female, gray and brown Griffon. Bought in Amsterdam in 1874, about 7 years old…A sketch of her appearing in Volume 1 of the GSB doesn't look at all like the photo and was probably done after her death by someone who didn't know her. Very good hunter, especially in the woods and swamps. Mother of **MADAME ANGOT,** by **HECTOR,** and **HUZAAR** by **ANUS.**

These were the seven patriarchs, but just as the three musketeers were really four, so the seven patriarchs were really eight. In effect everyone agrees to give the title to **VESTA**, who, like **JUNON**, didn't belong to Korthals.

VESTA, female, wasn't inscribed in the GSB and that's why she doesn't appear officially in the list of patriarchs, but two of her offspring are listed in the GSB (**FAUST GSB 21** and **FLORA GSB 15**) with the mention "origin unknown." **VESTA** belonged to a forester named Schneider, who loaned her to Korthals. The offspring of this bitch...were very prized by Korthals and we know by photos and accounts of trials and shows that many of her grandchildren contributed to making the breed famous (**FAUST GSB 21, TASSO GSB 77, MIRALDA GSB 782**) and others).

Here is how Korthals listed the six patriarchs that he purchased in his kennel book. The other two, remember, he never owned, but borrowed.

MOUCHE	*Griffon* bitch, purchased for 60 florins, and the promise of a pup.
JANUS	*Barbet*, male, purchased for 50 florins.
HECTOR	*Griffon*, male, white [emphasis added] and brown,purchased in 1874 for 25 florins and another dog.
SATAN	*Griffon*, male, purchased in 1875 for 150 florins.
BANCO	*Griffon*, male, purchased in 1876 for 100 florins. (GSB 2)
JUNON	(GSB 125).

In addition to these dogs, Korthals also listed the following dogs in his kennel:

BELLINE	*Griffon* bitch, *white* [emphasis added] and

	brown, by **HECTOR** out of **MOUCHE,** whelped Sepember 1874, died January 1875.
PHANOR	*Griffon*, male, *white* [emphasis added]and yel low, whelped April 1875.

In 1873, Korthals left Holland and moved to Germany where Prince Albrecht zu Solms-Braunfels became his friend and patron. Solms was a wealthy man with a passionate hobby for hunting and hunting dogs. It is the prestigious field test in Germany for German Shorthairs that is called "the Solmes," in honor of this man.

Korthals trained the prince's dogs and continued the breeding of Griffons. In 1881 the Prince leased the hunting grounds of Biebesheim in the Hessian marsh and installed Korthals there. At Biebesheim Korthals concentrated solely on breeding Griffons. Many fine dogs were raised there and sold throughout Holland, France, Belgium, and Germany. It was at this time that he obtained **DONNA** and **VESTA,** which became the seventh and eighth patriarchs of the Korthals Griffon.

(Today we would not refer to the female dogs as "patriarchs," but the eight progenitors have always been called the eight patriarchs and I see no reason to change this bit of history.)

The ideal toward which Korthals worked was the correct anatomy for a hunting dog, medium size, one that runs close to the ground, coarse hair with wooly (down) undercoat and the characteristic beard. The color was blue-gray with liver patches, or solid liver with a sprinkling of white hair (ticked). Today the proper terms are liver-ticked, dark liver-ticked, light liver-ticked, white and instead of using "patches" we say "plates." Through careful selection and breeding and mainly through ruthless culling of all products which did not come up to his standards of type and hunting performance, Korthals succeeded in a relatively short time of twelve years in creating a uniform breed. By 1886, they were able to set a breed standard and in 1888 Korthals and 140 Griffon friends founded the Griffon Club, which was an international club with headquarters in Germany. The Griffon Stud Book (GSB) is one of the oldest stud books, if not the oldest.

People ask "What nationality is the Griffon?" The answer is that it is not a breed of dog from one country, but from several countries and is thus an international breed, which existed for several hundred years throughout Europe. From all the documents available to us today we can say with certainty that of the eight dogs Korthals used to "fix" (to make a breed able to reproduce itself with consistency) the Griffon breed, or his *strain* (Korthals Griffon), six of the eight dogs were obtained while Korthals was in Holland. These would be **MOUCHE, JANUS, HECTOR, SATAN, JUNON** and **BANCO.** The seventh, **DONNA,** was purchased in Germany and the eighth, **VESTA**, was loaned to him by a German forester.

Korthals, the "Master of Biebesheim" (He was called this title by many kynologists of the day, and for decades after his death.), allowed only the name "Griffon d'Arret a Poil Dur" (Wirehaired Pointing Griffon) for this breed. It was only after his death that the breed became known also as Korthals Griffon. *He was adamant that the Griffon was an international breed, that it did not belong to any one country.*

Castaing makes a very important point that has been missed by nearly everyone else regarding Korthals' development of the Griffon and how the eight patriarchs became the foundation. Somehow a false legend about Korthals' work spread all over

A PAGE FROM KORTHALS' KENNEL BOOK.
The names begin to sound familiar, such as
YANKA, NANON, BECASSE II, KENAU.

Baguette

geboren: 17 Mei 1885
van „Médoc-Moustache" uit Angot.

II Pr. Rotterdam 1886.

Verkocht aan H. M. Lichte.
Rozendaal.

„Niniche" (R. Solms's)
door Chasseur-Moustache
op 21 Januari 1888.

„Jessy" (Völsing)
door Beaujolais
op 22 & 24 Januari 1888
nest gestorven.

„Yanka" (Clausius)
belegt vom „Chasseur-Moustache"
in August
am 29 October 1887
5 jongen (daarvan 1 dood)

„Ballade" (Clausius)
belegt vom „Faust II"
am 20 & 27 Februar 1888.
27 April jongen.

„Nanon" belegt vom
„Beaujolais" am 17 & 20 März 1888

„Bécasse II" belegt vom
„Cavour" am 19 März 1888.

Kermès

geboren: 24 Januari 1885
van „Chasseur-Moustache" uit Bécasse
Verk. aan Baron di Moffart

„Hexe" (Hansult's)
belegt vom Tambour
op 15 Septb. 1887

„Tosca"
belegt vom „Gessler"
op 2 & 3 Octbr. 87

„Becasse II"
belegt vom „Cavour"
op 9 & 12 Octbr 87.

„Cane" (v. Gienanth)
belegt vom „Chasseur-Moustache"
op 17 & 20 Octbr. 87.

„Kenau"
belegt vom Chasseur-Moustache
op 12 Dezember 1887

„Cara" (v Gienanth)
belegt vom Cavour
op 10 Januar 1888

Europe and even across the Atlantic. The legend, as it has been told for decades, is that Korthals searched all over Europe for the ideal dogs to develop his Griffon. And wherever he found one he bought it, and when he had the eight dogs he began breeding and developing the Griffon.

In reality, it was later, when Korthals realized the great influence these seven or eight dogs had had in bringing the development of the Griffon to such a solid peak, that he could point out which ones had been outstanding in their prepotency. That was when he created the GSB—the Griffon Staumbuch (Griffon Stud Book), and wrote in it the names of those dogs he considered to be the patriarchs of his work. At that time in history only those dogs tracing back directly to one or more of the eight patriarchs could be called "pure blood Korthals."

Therefore, Castaing believes that there are many Griffons improperly called Korthals Griffon, which do not trace back to the eight patriarchs, *yet they are Griffons,* and the official designation for them should be "griffon d'arret a poil dur" (wirehaired pointing griffon). Castaing was right in saying that the Korthals Griffon was only *one line* or strain *in the Griffon breed.*

It was only in 1889, fifteen years *after* the first of the patriarchs was used for breeding that the GSB was created, and only then that those eight dogs were given the status of patriarch. In fact a couple of those patriarchs only stayed in Korthals' kennel a short time (**BANCO** and **JANUS**). He sold them after having them only one year, not realizing the importance their blood would be to his strain of dogs until much later.

Korthals began his work with a goal, but he did not have some preconceived plan; i.e., if I breed dog A to dog B the results will be A,B,C,D. He used the method of selection (choosing the best dogs for breedings, see part II, Chapters 26 and 27 on Breeding), and culled ruthlessly.

Castaing explains that the fame of the Korthals Griffons was attained by success in field trials. Some of those early dogs, direct descendants of the eight patriarchs were: **MOUSTACHE II(GSB 45), BATTA (GSB 89), CHASSEUR-MOUSTACHE (GSB 13), PASSO (GSB 77), KENAU (GSB 131), MADAME AUGOT (GSB 137), ROBIN-MOUSTACHE (GSB 24), PASSE-PARTOUT (GSB 54), MIRALDA (GSB 792), CADEAU (GSB 901), CACHOU (GSB 913), CAPITAINE FRACASSE (GSB 1916)** and many others that Castaing says "...have acquired the right to immortality."

Castaing quotes from the summary of field trials of the era thus:

> **KENAU**, born the 12th of March, 1886 to Mr. Korthals: Her style is lively, her nose marvelous, her sureness perfect; She stops partridge from afar, lies down by herself while waiting the arrival of her handler.

These would have been Hungarian partridge, and the "lies down" refers to the dogs going on point and immediately lying down so as to make the shooting safer. Most hunters of the day, especially owners of versatile dogs, trained them to drop after the point.

In 1897, the Griffons were being praised by sports-writers, who up to then had been skeptical. One writer (*Le Chasseur Pratique*, April 16, 1897) stated:

> ...I'm happy to be able to give full justice to Mr. Korthals' breed. These Griffons, brought from several countries, have a very good nose. Certainly these Griffons are good field dogs as well as good for forest and swamp—hav-

MOUCHE (G.S.B. 143)

TWO OF THE PATRIARCHS.

BANCO (G.S.B. 2)

ing all that is needed for that. They hunt with intelligence and prudence and still they are full of enthusiasm. Ah! They are not sleepy dogs. They run quickly, the nose in the air, they don't take as much space and haven't the speed of pointers and setters (although **CACHOU** can match some of them), but their range is broad, their hunt well sustained. They are the alert and rigorous workers that their appearance implies. In the afternoon, in warm weather, they constantly beat freshly plowed fields, running there with the same ease as on firm ground.

Castaing sums up this high point in the history of Griffons with:

Here we are thus at the culmination of the triumphal era. These notes sum it all up. In two decades, the Griffon of short range, and limited nose, became the bridge dreamed of by Korthals between the old Continental dog and the English dog while at the same time keeping its own characteristics and its aptitude for hunting in all weather and on all terrains. Other resumes of field trials of that period (in water, swamps, forest, rocky trails, etc.) shows them as perfect and at ease in all the circumstances that a hunter could demand of a hunting dog.

Then Castaing gives us another commentary of the day from a sporting magazine:

All these dogs hunted at a gallop and stopped abruptly at a good distance; their swift running astonished the men of the time, used to seeing the continental dogs at a slow trot sometimes even walking. Their resistance to heat, the maintenance of their pace on all terrains (including swamp ones), their vigor, their ardor, their love of hunting—all stupefied the spectators. What astonished them the most was the majority of these dogs had a tendency to follow rabbits—and their handlers didn't get upset—nor were they penalized as long as they returned to the hunt in a short time.

Castaing comments on the above quote with his own excellent insight:

Their indulgence (still in force today) [that would be 1949] was, I must say, fairly badly seen by the purists, especially the French ones whose ideas (often a little narrow) have not helped the progress in breeding...because there is a reason for considering this sin as minor: Korthals himself had praised the pursuit of hares to give agility and speed. Most of them were, besides, trained the German way, that is to say on the trail of wounded animals; finally the dogs presented at the field trials were not dogs trained and raised only for this purpose, but working dogs used to hunting, on plains, in swamps, in woods—used to seeing the game fall, to look for it when it was wounded and retrieve it, in a word these were hunting dogs not circus dogs, it was just that which made their fame.

So Castaing understood completely what a Griffon should be! He says that the reader shouldn't think that the Griffon took off after every hare or rabbit that popped up, that it was an occasional occurrence, not the rule, and "...this instinct wasn't at all incompatible with practical training, it was only a manifestation of an instinct without which they wouldn't be hunting dogs." Mr. Castaing knows practical hunting and hunting dogs, otherwise he could not have written this. He goes on to tell a lovely anecdote as a perfect example:

At the Field Trial of the Griffon Club in 1908, **FRACASSE** followed a hare for about 6 miles, and on his return went back to a magnificent hunt not even looking at numerous hares that he raised after that—doing splendid

Above: Famous drawing of ***CHASSEUR MOUSTACHE (GSB 13)****.*

Below: ***CAPITAINE FRACASSEE (GSB 1916)****, owned and bred by Baron von Gingins.*

*Famous drawing of **CHASSEUR MOUSTACHE** performing Totverbeller, which means that the dog has tracked and found the deer and is now barking in a special manner to summon the master to the dead deer.*

> work, making beautiful points on partridge, without making another single mistake "As if," said the judge, "he wanted to have a little fun before settling down to work." A just judgment equal to the intelligence of the animal.

Castaing tells about field trials organized by the Griffon Club in 1903. The trials consisted of the field portion with the usual rules for pointers and setters, followed by retrieving tests from a track where game had been killed at the end (300 meters). (This is what we call today retrieve of dead game from a track, or for short we say "drag track.") The next day would be a blood track, and they had the choice of doing it two ways: 1) the dog follows the track and comes back and leads the handler to the dead game (In Germany they call this Totverweisser.), or 2) the dog follows the track and when he reaches the dead game he barks in a special manner to summon his master (In Germany it is Totverbeller).

After this there were several other obedience tests: stay at the spot, search thick brush, search without game, kill a fox, track a duck, retrieve a duck from deep water. Except for killing the fox, this is what our utility test is today, a little more than 90 years later.

Castaing says that to neglect any of this work in testing the dogs (swamps, heavy cover, water, tracking) "is equal to atrophying or making disappear his inborn aptitudes. And one might as well use a pointer whose ideal destiny is to work open fields. It is varied trials that have won the Griffons their nickname 'Maid of all Work,' which certain breeders have carelessly denied their dogs."

He emphasizes again that the Korthals Griffon was only one of several different strains of Griffons, but that the Korthals strain was "pure." I think the term "pure" to him meant stabilized, able to reproduce itself. In fact he used the word stabilization, saying that it was from the Korthals bloodlines that other Griffon breeders were able to incorporate Korthals blood, thus raising all the Griffons to "the rank of a single breed." Elaborating further, Castaing says,

> ...[I]t would be a mistake to think that the improvement of the Griffon and the stabilization of its characteristics were propagated outside of Korthals kennels only by using bloodlines from his dogs. Korthals himself knew that such a system is rapidly ruined by inbreeding. In reality, paralleling the judicious use of his dogs, breeders were using his methods on their own dogs. And it is because those breeders were imbued with a sporting attitude, not from commercialism, and because they were numerous and spread out in many countries, that the breed stabilized so quickly and in such a definitive way. However, so that each man could, in the same spirit, carry his tone to the common building project, it was necessary that all these builders be united by the same doctrine, solidly united across the frontiers. This unity of purpose and method completed the work of the master.

As Castaing said of the Korthals family:

> ...[It] was the bed of coals which spread with the speed and relentlessness of a conflagration, like the ancestral hearth where dying families come to be revitalized. From Bibesheim, the blood of Korthals Griffons spread to Southern Germany, than all Germany—then to Dutch Griffons, Belgian, Swiss and French. The patriarchs were scarcely dead before their blood, more or less mixed with indigenous Griffons, was running across the whole continent.

Above: ***LA HESSE (GSB 3255),*** *bred by Baron von Gingins, whelped June 6, 1908* ***(Le Capitaine Fracasse x Claudine).*** *Below:* ***MABEL URIAN (GSB 2401),*** whelped September 11, 1905 ***(Le Capitaine Fracasse x Claudine).*** *There's more about* ***MABEL*** *in chapter 26. These dogs, along with others such as* ***CARCASS, MISS URIAN, POLDER,*** *were very well known in their time and used extensively for breeding. Photos taken circa 1911.*

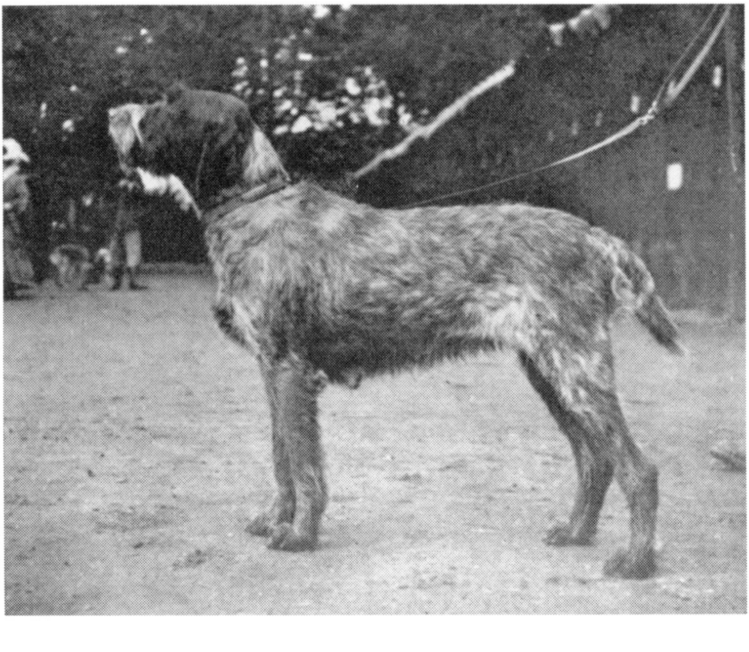

A group of owners at a field test in The Netherlands in the fall of 1911. Compliments GSB.

Above: ***CLOWN DE FISMES (GSB 189)****, circa 1920. This dog had a lot of field test prizes and was considered to be an outstanding dog of his time. Below:* ***RATZ-WOLFF (GSB 816)****, a female highly regarded and used for breeding. She would be of a later time as indicated by the much higher registration number.*

Famous photo of Korthals, taken in 1890 in Berlin, with four of his dogs when he was awarded a special medal by the German Emperor for conspicuous results as a breeder. This was about 20 years after he had begun his task of re-establishing and stabilizing the Griffon. The dog in the left front is said to have been ***PARTOUT***.

CHAPTER THREE
END OF THE NINETEENTH CENTURY AND THE KORTHALS ERA

As we head toward the end of the nineteenth century in the history of our Griffons, it is impossible for most of us to comprehend the difficulties that Korthals encountered. At that time stud books were unknown in Europe. In 1870 there were no registration papers, no field trials. France had just lost the 1871 war against Germany. Because of the animosity between the two countries, the German Canine Board refused to acknowledge Korthals' breed as long as he called it "Griffon." The French-sounding name evidently displeased the German authorities. If he had consented to call his dogs wirehaired German pointers things would have been different. But he refused to do so, maintaining that the Griffon was an international breed and not of specific German origin.

Korthals maintained this position and continued his work. When dogs such as **CHASSEUR MOUSTACHE, GUERRE, TAMBOUR, KENAU, PASSEPARTOUT, CAPTAIN FRACASSE, CRACK de MERLIMONT**, and others showed their merits in field trials and exhibitions, and when the Count of Flanders and the Grand Duke of Russia bought Korthals Griffons, the tide had turned. In 1890 Korthals was awarded a medal by the German Emperor for conspicuous results as a breeder. (See photo.)

There was continued controversy during the late 1800s and into the early part of the twentieth century as to what was a "true" Griffon, what was a "true" Pricklyhair (wirehair). Some people, in support of a national breed in Germany, maintained there was only a German rough-haired (wirehair) breed and that so-called Griffons (Korthals) were merely a mixture of all sorts of breeds.

Other people felt there were no significant differences between Korthals Griffons and the dogs being bred in Germany at that time by other breeders, with wirehaired coats, and that *all* the rough-coated dogs should be classified as one breed. This point of view said that there were slight differences between Korthals' dogs, Bontant's dogs, and dogs from other breeders, and that these differences were merely different strains of the same breed resulting from the personal preferences of each breeder, and hence his selection of dogs to be used for breeding. At any rate, for a short time all the wirehaired breeds were classified as one breed—rough-coated dogs.

Later, however, some breeders made crosses with German Shorthair and a short time later the Griffon Club was formed, and the breed maintained as *pure*.

Korthals was one of the earliest kynologists to instigate field testing for versatile hunting dogs for the purpose of selective breeding. In the course of the 22 years that he was a breeder, his Griffons were so successful and caused so much of a stir at expositions and field trials that his kennels became the object of a rigorous campaign of disparagement by those who declared his successes were due only to the continual infusion of other blood. Korthals replied in several different hunting magazines of the day, as follows:

"The Pointer Blood in the Korthals Griffons"

(This was the title of the article, written by Korthals, responding to the attacks being made about his breeding.)

> The suspicion has been expressed several times recently that the Korthals Griffons owe their refinement in respect to hunting qualities to the introduction of pointer blood. This opinion, which originally showed up only here and there and which can only have been started by persons far from this kennel, appears to be finding an increasing number of adherents, for one now encounters it more and more frequently in various journals in the field. Hence the undersigned now feels himself forced to counter it before it grows into a superstition hard to destroy. Just how oddly criticism of breeds and their qualities is often times practiced is evident in some passages from the article entitled "New Crityerria are necessary in the Breeding of Working Dogs" (***Deutzchen Jager-Zeitung***).
>
> After Mr........ states in No. 3, October 11, that he does not know the Griffons exactly but that one may assume that 95% of them have "insufficient, short" noses and after Dr. Hans Von Kadich contradicts this assertion in No. 8 then he, Mr.......simply finishes this breed off in No. 9 as follows, "I should like to mention with regard to the Korthals Griffons alluded to by Dr. von Kadich that Korthals is said to have used pointer blood in the breeding of his dogs!"
>
> I consider it unnecessary to enter upon an exchange of opinions with Mr.... about the hunting value of the breed, but I should like to explain in the interest of my line [strain] that from the beginning up to today, i.e. 18 years, I have bred only with Griffons without the aid of a foreign breed. The refinement undergone by the strain can only be attributed to careful selective breeding, breeding for specific purpose and the type and manner of training.
>
> E.K. Korthals
> Biebesheim am Rhein, November 1888

Prominent people came to Korthals' defense in this matter. Among them was A.P.B. Albrecht, Prince of Solms-Braunfels, who in 1890 spoke out in hunting journals about the purity and quality of Korthals' dogs:

> As far as the controversial question is concerned, I must declare dogs were bred pure and inherited with consistency without which cardinal point one cannot even speak of the breed.... In the judgement of a single individual for the value of its breeding, only that experience can guide us which shows proof of pure hereditary transmission.
>
> If, however, the breeder finds no individuals which reproduce purely, then he can be certain that he is not dealing with the descendants of a pure breed.
>
> If he *still* desires to achieve his goal and create a constant breed from the given stock material, i.e. dogs which do not with consistency transmit hereditary traits, then he must follow the difficult path of imprinting upon and establishing in his strain the prototype he envisions by careful selective breeding. Thus have all breeds originated and thus too, has Mr. Korthals (Ipenwoud Kennels) brought his strain of roughhaired pointers to their present degree of perfection, which surely no one will deny and longer since his dogs display great harmony in form and coat, great capability of achievement and very satisfactory consistency of hereditary transmission.
>
> Not long ago I visited this kennel and was most satisfied to find his scarcely twelve year old breeding attempts crowned with such success. From this breeder who has done so much for this breed I learned much about its origin, which was interesting and completely new to me. He began his strain

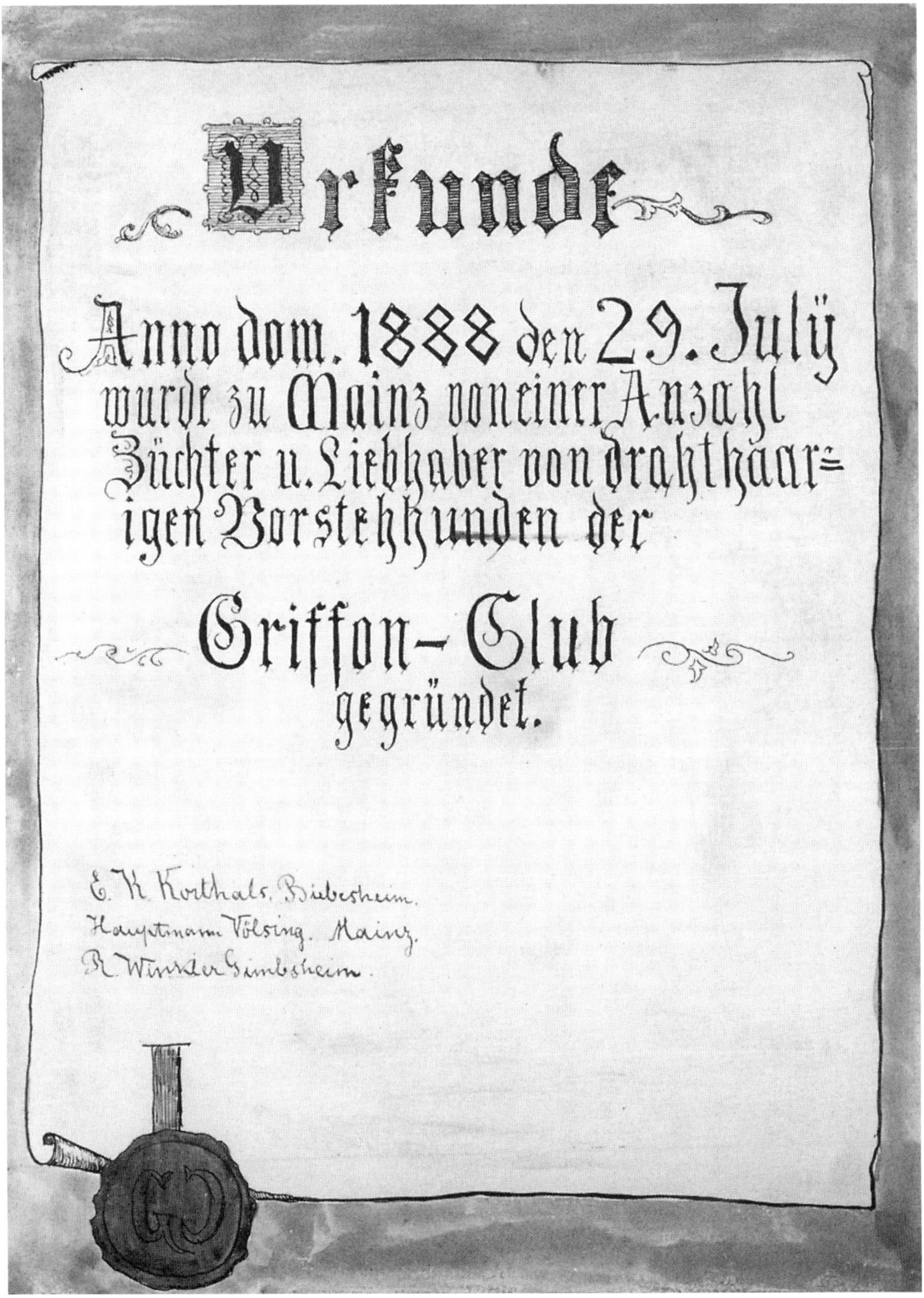

Vrkunde

Anno dom. 1888 den 29. Julÿ
wurde zu Mainz von einer Anzahl
Züchter u. Liebhaber von drahthaar=
igen Vorstehhunden der

Griffon-Club
gegründet.

E. K. Korthals. Biebesheim.
Hauptmann Völsing. Mainz.
R. Winkler Gimbsheim.

This is a photo of the original charter of the first Griffon Club, formed by Korthals and his followers on July 29, 1888, signed by him and Mr. Winkler. (Compliments Griffon-Club e.V.)

with dogs which he saw and procured in Holland and which he esteemed especially for their hunting qualities and many sided usefulness. For these reasons he decided to breed them. He then had to set up the points himself, choose his ideal and then work step-by-step toward the desired goal.

The ideal he set up for a roughhaired, multi-gifted [versatile] working dog was an anatomical structure suited to the intended use, including good medium size without being long-legged, hard and wiry hair with woolly underhair, on the snout the characteristic moustache and over the eyes bristly bushes of hair, blue-gray color with brown [liver] patches or monotone brown [liver], often shot through with white hairs [ticked]. One of his best breeding products and a true representative of his strain was **RATIZ** whose excellent portrait painted by Sperling is known everywhere and so greatly enthused the ***Allgemeine Sportzeitung*** [German Sports Magazine] that **RATIZ** was presented in one of their articles as the prototype of the roughhaired *German* pointer.

Naturally in the beginning, Mr. Korthals, like everyone who begins breeding with inconsistent blood, had in his litters pups of greatly varying appearance and deviating coat, many too shorthaired, others too woolly or long-haired. These were all killed and only those raised and used for continued breeding which came closest to the ideal. The strain is now very well balanced and those members I saw had without exception hard hair of the right length and were either brown with white hairs or bluish-gray with brown patches.

*[**NOTE:** Remember that one of the patriarchs (**JUNON**) was half German Shorthair. She was a short-haired pointer type dog, or what today we would call a German Shorthair. This accounts in part for some Griffons that are born with a completely short coat, i.e., smooth-coated, no furnishings, like a German Shorthair.]*

Some of his dogs seemed to me somewhat too tall; one can certainly not reproach them with lack of size. As long as he was in Holland, the breeder called these dogs 'Smousbaarden' the customary name in Holland for such dogs because of their moustache. Since that name is unknown in this country, Mr. Korthals, when he moved to Germany, used the comfortable short name "Griffon" for his dogs since *they seemed to him identical with the dogs known in France by that name.* (Emphasis added.)

In any case, however, the widespread view that the Korthals dogs are of French origin is false, for there is not a single dog in the pedigrees of the five generations of his sires which Master Vollrath had done beautifully in life-size since they were all still alive at that time. I also encountered frequently the false opinion that Mr. Korthals' dogs have long, woolly hair which may stem from the fact that he calls them "Griffons" and this name usually signifies the "Griffon a Poil long," while in France one knows the much more highly esteemed "Griffon a Poil dur" with which Mr. Korthals' dogs have in common the prickly hair and the color. There is no doubt, however, that the Korthals dogs possess already great consistency in hereditary transmission and Mr. B undoubtedly means these dogs in his article in the ***Deutschen Jager*** when he warns against crossbreeding the Griffons since they transmit their characteristics like a weed.

The gentleman named could scarcely give this breed (strain) greater praise, for it is precisely this consistency in hereditary transmission for which every breeder strives, and which is *the* test for the purity of a breed.

*[**NOTE:** Today we call this pre-potency, the ability of a dog to pass on his characteristics to his or her progeny.]*

> In France Griffon breeding does not appear to be at its peak as one so often assumes here, for when Mr. Korthals dogs were shown at the Belgian show and carried off all the major awards, the ***Chasse Illustree*** greeted this success with the remark that one had to go from France to a Belgian exhibition to see..."Griffons a Poil dur" sent from Germany and more beautiful than any existing in France.
>
> It was also Mr. Boulet, who ranked as the top Griffon breeder in France, who recently picked out three young dogs, two of them simply brown [liver] because he prizes this color most highly, in the Ipenwoud Kennels [Korthals' kennel name]. This gentleman stated to me that he now wanted to breed this line pure and not cross it with his line, although he has bred his line for twenty years, because his dogs are too long and soft haired as a result of crossbreeding with Epagneuls [spaniels] and he wants only pricklyhaired dogs. Thus he wishes to breed Griffons in France and imports for that purpose dogs from Germany which notoriously possess not a drop of French blood.
>
> That only proves the practical sense of this breeder who takes the good where he finds it and is not subject to the ban of a principle of nationality which would view such a procedure as a crime. One appears thus now in all countries, to desire to give recognition solely to the pricklyhaired dog among the rough-haired dogs because for utility this hair is the most practical.
>
> Prince Albrecht vom Solms

At the time of Korthals' death in 1896, he had achieved international acclaim as a breeder. Articles appeared in sporting magazines in Germany, France, Belgium, Holland, and England. In the GSB Volume IV, 1894-97 page 137 appears the following: Even before his death, the eminent writer, Hegewald, wrote in March 1883:

> From reports coming in from all over about presently available versatile utility dogs, it seems that **MOUSTACHE II** (GSB 34) (color blue-gray with brown head, disks and dots, whelped January 9, 1881, by **MOUSTACHE I** out of **ZAMPA**) is the firmest and best qualified dog for the task at the present time. His nose is excellent thus having the quality which is the basic requirement of all kinds of performances. In spite of his wirehaired coat he rarely needs water even in the hottest summer, much less than the pointer.
>
> **MOUSTACHE II** is an excellent bird dog who if rabbits are fairly scarce firmly points and follows, retrieves everything, hunts loudly in the woods [this means the dog "gives tongue", or bays while on a track], works firmly after blood track and is reliable in barking dead [barks at the end of a track of wounded big game].
>
> In winter he is absolutely insensitive against frost and cold, he can stay quiet for hours and sits motionlessly and attentively beside his master on the battue [waiting quietly for driven game]. He is full of temperament [means full of desire, passion for the hunt, for game contact] while searching, as well as retrieving in gallop and together with this he is extremely obedient. When in the first of my books I presented this dog as the ideal one next to the elegant field trial dog for the German hunter, I frequently encountered skepticism on the part of the non-hunters and butchers as if I would strive for something that could never be attained. Gentlemen, Hegewald's utility dog is no longer an illusion, he now exists really and truly, one and a half years after my book left the press.
>
> In view of this fact and because of this success which in Germany, Austria, Switzerland and wherever German is spoken assures us the best and most useful dogs in the world because we have the required material, it only has to be handled and trained after the model of **MOUSTACHE II**, I offer you my apologies for many a strong word that might have been said in the course of the controversy in defense of the cause but never with the intent to hurt.

> Mr. E. K. Korthals, the enviable owner of **MOUSTACHE II** and the famous kennel IPENWOUD at Biebesheim near Darmstadt, lives only for dogs, kynology and hunting. Nothing else exists for him. His knowledge of the subject, his kynological practical routine so to speak, is clearly phenomenal. With the same mastery that he showed at the Darmstadt Field Trials that **RODERICK,** the English setter, was to be the unchallenged winner of field trials, so this tireless, successful expert shows in **MOUSTACHE II** the versatile utility dog for the German hunter as he should be according to Hegewald.
>
> ...His nose is excellent thus having the quality which is the basic requirement of all kinds of performances. In spite of his wirehaired coat he rarely needs water even in the hottest summer, much less than the pointer...The utility dog and his further development would not be taken care of by more competent and careful hands. As far as I am concerned, I am satisfied and consider the task I have set myself as fully accomplished.

And five years later, Hegewald wrote:

> I have received questions from Bavaria about the Korthals Griffon and what I think of the usefulness of this breed. I expressed myself on this subject five years ago in ***Waidmann*** [Hunter] in detail. My opinion has not altered in the meantime and I consider the Korthals Griffon one of the best working dogs in Germany at this time...One praises especially the "trainability" of the Korthals Griffon for all the natural talents for their also many sidedness [versatility] are already present in the blood of these dogs.
>
> Hegewald
> Cynologist

[Kynologist can be spelled with a K or a C.] "What Counts In Judging Working Dogs," Hegewald. D.J.Z, Vol. XI, No. 12.

Who Was Hegewald?

"Hegewald" was a pen name for Baron von Zedlitz, born in 1838 and died in 1903. A part of the Neukirch forest where he grew up was called Hegewald, and he took that as his pen name. Along with Korthals, Hegewald worked hard to develop the field testing of versatile dogs and to base breeding decisions mainly on performance (testing) results. He was well known and respected in his day as a sportsman, outdoor writer, and kynologist.

According to Bodo Winterhelt in "The German Wirehair," ***Pointing Dog Journal***, July/August 1993, Hegewald spent most of his time pursuing his passion for wildlife and hunting, and wrote countless essays and articles in support of the need for a truly versatile hunting dog. This work opened the road for the German versatile hunting dog movement. He is remembered and honored as the creator of the German Wirehair, or Deutsch Drahthaar as he is properly called in Germany.

Winterhelt said, Hegewald "...believed that all versatile breeds are in their roots related through the pointer and the hound and the pudel. No doubt the [German] Wirehair had a tremendous genetic pool to draw from. If there was an outstanding wirehair, it would be used for breeding. If there was an outstanding pudelpointer or griffon, they would be used respectively."

More insight on Hegewald is offered by Horst Detert ("Altmeister Hegewald zum Gedaechtnis," translated by Hans Klein, *56 Hegewald Zuchtpruefung, VDD, September/October 1988):* Detert wrote,

> He paved the way for the test structure used today. In 1925 Friedrich

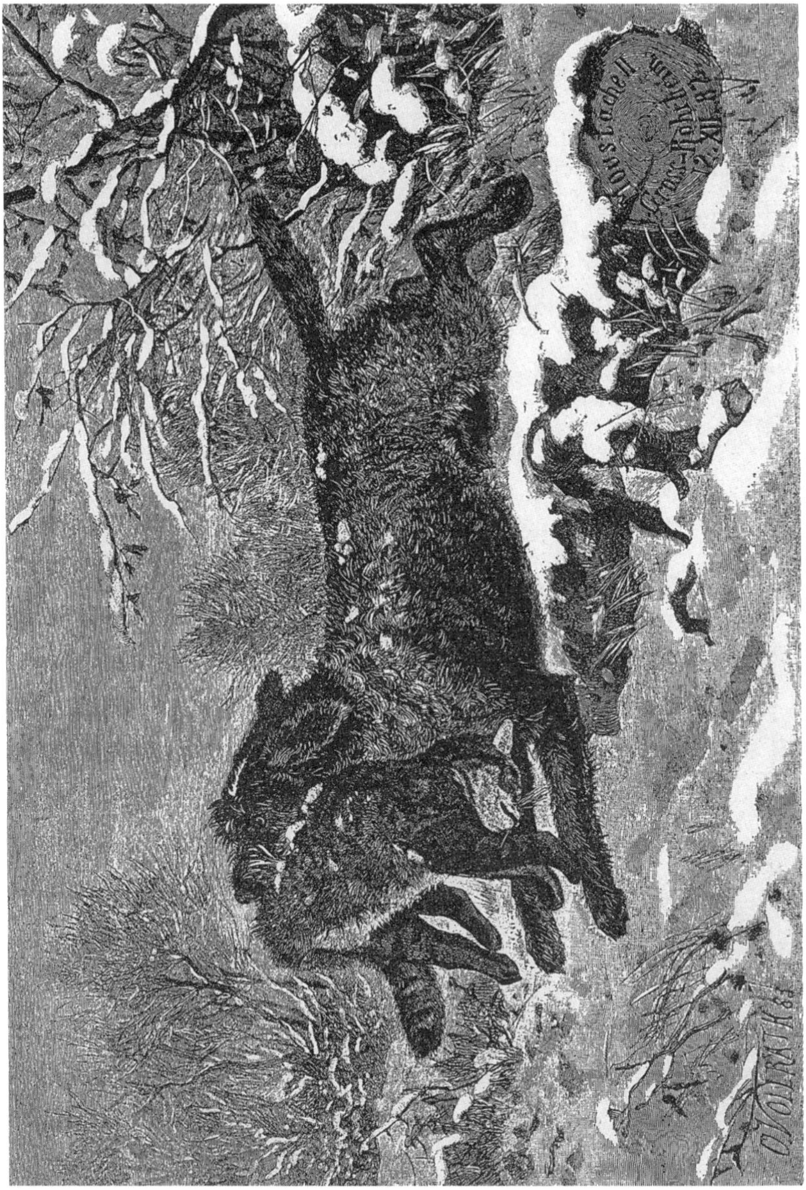

MOUSTACHE II (G.S.B. 45).

> Ostermann wrote in the *Drahthaar Blaetter* that Hegewald's work aided in the founding of the JGHV (Jagdegebrauchshundverband) and that the DGstB (Deutsches Gebrauchshundstammbuch) was established through his work. The DGstB is utilized to collectively publish test data of all hunting dog breeds in one performance book. It is based on his ideas and work. Now each year the DGstB is published by the JGHV. Hegewald is known as the father of the German utility hunting dog performance breeding test. He pioneered the tests to further [promote, encourage] performance breeding. The HZP (Herbstzucht Pruefung) [This is the fall breeding test, which we call here Intermediate Hunting Dog Test. See Part II] was initiated exclusively through his efforts. He stressed testing of dogs during the main hunting season in the fall and winter. Before, these tests were performed only in the spring. Even if Hegewald's writings often missed the mark, his vision that only properly bred and trained dogs are useful for a successful hunt, was accepted by the breeders and hunters of German hunting dogs.
>
> What were Hegewald's aims? An article by Friedrich Ostermann, an honorary member of the JGHV, describes them as follows: He was a leader of German hunting ethics. 1. He stressed a humane hunt, a fair chase and the use of trained blood tracking dogs. 2. He worked for the development of useful hunting dogs through performance breeding programs and public performance testing...

Hegewald and Korthals lived during the same era. Hegewald was the elder, born in 1838, Korthals was born 13 years later in 1851. Both had a strong passion for hunting dogs. However, Korthals was passionately interested in breeding, as well as hunting, whereas Hegewald was primarily a writer.

When Korthals died (at the early age of 45 in 1896) Hegewald was 58 and would live six more years. At the time of Korthals' death, obituaries appeared in all the hunting magazines and publications of that time. Here is Hegewald's obituary tribute to Korthals:

E. K. KORTHALS †

Just now arrived by Telegraph a sorrowful message, that the Master of Biebesheim, E.K. Korthals departed (left us) peacefully in his sleep.

Even so we were afraid for some time about the life of the dear departed, still we stand deeply in shock, admitting openly at the grave site our deep sorrow for the loss of this energetic man, to whom the hunting fraternity is forever indebted.

The Master's accomplishments will survive and memory of him shall never perish in the hearts of the true hunters.

So much for today, this troubled message to our dear readers.

In deep Mourning
Hegewald

***(Der Waidmann, XXVII. Band, Nr. 42.** Translated by Joe Nadeker.)*

***Korthals** in his hunting area at Biebesheim with two of his Griffons.*

From an exhibition in Mainz, 1911, a prize for the best collection of a breeding group. The dogs were bred by Baron von Gingins, who died that year. Notice the good substance, and also the loose leashes, the relaxed manner of the dogs, denoting calm temperaments.

CHAPTER FOUR
EARLY TWENTIETH CENTURY (EUROPE)

Thus as Korthals passes out of the picture, we find the following people in charge of the Griffon Club:

Honorary President	Prince Albrecht of Solms-Braunfels
President	Baron A. von Gingins, Cronberg i Taunus
Secretary	R. Winkler, Gimbsheim, Rheinhessen
Membership	G.F. Leliman, Holland (close friend of Korthals)

The club was international and the GSB (Griffon Stammbuch-Griffon Stud Book) was maintained in Germany, but reports and articles appearing in the GSB were written in German, in French and sometimes in Dutch. Other countries began their own Griffon clubs (France, Belgium, Holland) but the "mother" club was in Germany and it was there that the official publication, the GSB, was published. Field trials were held in all these countries and results were reported in the GSB.

Before Korthals' death he and other prominent breeders of rough-haired dogs agreed that these dogs were all of one breed and therefore could be bred together if a breeder so desired. But after his death some breeders began breeding their Griffons, or rough-haired dogs, with German Shorthair. The proponents of the Korthals Griffon felt this was weakening the breed and would lose much of what Korthals had accomplished in "fixing" his strain. It was about this time that the break came and the Griffon Club became a club only for Korthals Griffons.

In 1897 the Pudelpointers formed their own club. Not long after that the other proponents of the other rough-haired dogs eventually formed the Deutsch Drahthaar Club (German Wirehair) and took as their motto, "Zucht Nach Leistun," which translates roughly, "Breed after (from) performance." Later the Deutsch Drahthaar Club used as their policy, "Breed as you like but tell what you breed." The Deutsch Drahthaar followers then began to develop their breed by breeding Griffons, or rough-haired dogs, to other breeds, as well as to other rough-haired dogs, but careful records were kept and nothing was hidden.

The dogs were bred for their hunting qualities, regardless of the breed.

There were both nationalistic reasons, as well as purely dog-breeding reasons for this split. First, remember that relations between France and Germany at this time were strained. Germany had defeated France in 1871. The official German dog registry wanted Korthals to call his dogs German Rough-Haired Pointers. But Korthals was adamant and would not do this, maintaining that his strain of dogs did not originate in any one country and it was therefore a continental breed.

The word "griffon" is not French, but it does *sound* French. This annoyed some Germans. In addition to political reasons there were simply differences of opinions among breeders whether or not to outcross the rough-haired breeds with other breeds such as German Shorthair and Pudelpointer.

Taking all these factors into consideration one can then have a better understanding of why and how certain developments came about regarding the Griffon and the Deutsch Drahthaar. The Drahthaar became Germany's wirehaired hunting dog, almost their national hunting dog. World War I, of course, emphasized these nationalistic ideas, as did World War II. Hermann Goering was an avid hunter and championed the cause of the Deutsch Drahthaar. Today the Deutsch Drahthaar is by far the most popular wirehaired versatile hunting dog in Germany, as well as the most popular wirehaired versatile dog in North America. With such a high number of dogs there is a huge gene pool to draw from.

When Korthals died a few men carried on his work and gradually became more prominent in the Griffon Club. Baron de Gingins became president. Mr. Winkler remained as secretary and he took some dogs from Korthals' kennel and exhibited them in field trials throughout Europe. He also did quite a bit of breeding.

When Gingins died in 1911, Mr. Leliman became president. This demonstrates how international the Korthals Griffon people were even 15 years after Korthals' death. Leliman was from The Netherlands, and another member of the executive

Baron von Gingins with ***GIROUETTE (GSB 1594)****, whelped in 1900.*

committee, G.C.W.F. O'Breen, from Belgian, who was a well-known outdoor writer of that era. That year Griffon devotees in The Netherlands formed their own Griffon Club.

Social history about the people involved with Griffons and other versatile breeds at this time is important, for it helps us to grasp a more accurate understanding of the history of the breed. As with most other hunting breeds of this era, the handful of men involved with the Griffon were well-to-do. Some were more than well-to-do. They had money to spend on care (kennel men), purchasing, and on travel. Equally as important, they had leisure time.

We know that Korthals came from a wealthy family in Holland. But when he moved to Germany his family's wealth was no longer available to him. What would have happened if Prince Albrecht zu Solms had not become his patron, is hard to say.

When historical records are studied it would be difficult for anyone to dispute the truth that Korthals developed a true strain of Griffon—a wirehaired dog, sound of mind and body with excellent abilities to produce game in field, forest, and water.

When he died in 1896, well-known sports writers of the time from several countries extolled the virtues of the Korthals Griffon. Korthals sold dogs to people in Germany, France, Belgium, Holland, and other countries, including some to Prince Ezerhazy of Hungary.

By 1911, fifteen years after Korthals death, the Griffon had spread even as far as the United States. But the first Griffon to reach America came much earlier, in 1887, from England, and was registered with the American Kennel Club as a Russian Setter (Griffon), **ZOLETTE 6773 (Guerre x Tambour)**, because that's what the English called a Griffon in those times. (*Volume 4, American Kennel Club Publication.*)

Despite the interest and dedication evidenced by such men as Gingins, Leliman, Winkler, and others after Korthals' death, the exacting control of breeding that Korthals must have maintained during his lifetime would have gradually eroded. The breed became more numerous and popular. People were breeding Griffons in many countries, without any type of controls, even in the United States, where the *first* Griffon Club in America was founded in 1916.

Then came World War I. In 1919, after the war ended, the French Griffon Club published the first volume of their own Griffon Registry called "Livre des Origines du Griffon a Poil Dur." It was abbreviated to LOG and listed 201 Griffons registered in 1919 and the early part of 1920. Belgium followed and also formed their club after the War I.

In Germany after World War I, the Drahthaar, Pudelpointer, Stichelhaar and Griffon clubs merged to form a club for the wirehaired breeds. Around 1936, due to the political situation in Germany, this club was forced to break apart due to "orders from above." After World War II the Pudelpointer, Stickelhaar and Griffon clubs began to publish one news bulletin to serve all three clubs. This lasted well into the 1960s. The Drahthaar Club became large and strong and stayed on its on.

Following is an excerpt from a history of the breed written by an old friend of mine, Frau Paula Pohl, who was the Studbook Keeper of the German Griffon Club for many years. This history was included in a special publication commemorating the 90th anniversary of the Griffon Club in 1978. She is speaking about the era of World War II.

> Fate interfered and made the distribution of volume XXVIII of the GSB possible only after the unfortunate World War II, in 1949. After the hardest war of all, and the separation of Germany, it was strongly believed that it was hopeless to bring the Griffon Club back to life. But here again the "old faithful" members, such as Mr. Albert Schneider, and Mr. Wilhelm Kantz, stood by the rules of Korthals. Mr. Kantz had joined the Griffon Club in 1898. Ever since World War I he was on the committee for the Stud Book and was known for his breeding successes in his kennel "Wetterau." Through painful work he gathered the old accounts and after several letters he managed to bring a few faithful members back together.
>
> The times after the war did not allow any firearms, which added to the loss of interest in breeding. But it was joyful to find out that the 77th annual field trials would be held in the "Revier Bensheim an der Gergstrasse" on September 26, 1948. The last trials had been held on May 3, 1942 in the "revier Neider-Wollstadt by Freidberg." The 1948 trials showed that the existing material was scanty. The call to the surviving female dog owners to breed was crowned with success.

In an article from The Netherlands Griffon Club news-letter, December 1985, translated by John Pitlo (a member of the board of directors of WPGCA, judge, breeder, and founder of the Heartland Griffon Club), we get more details of the history of our breed:

> The Korthals Griffon, mostly shortened to Griffon, is a rough-coated pointing dog for the hunting of small game (pheasants, Hungarian partridge, duck, rabbit and hare). However, in Germany he is also used to hunt deer. He is an optimal work dog. The dog is also a cheerful and affectionate house pet [we would say "family dog"], a permanent warden of house and field.
>
> The breed traits of the Griffon have existed since October 1887, when 16 recognized breeders met in Mainz, Germany and established breed characteristics and these have not been altered since that time. This breed is therefore one of the oldest, maybe the oldest, hunting dog breed on the continent.
>
> The Griffon is supposed to be an efficient all around [versatile] hunting dog, both before and after the shot. A dog with an excellent nose, points solid as a rock, and retrieves everything from land and water. He must then have no fear of the water. During the winter, he must furthermore be able to withstand the cold and frost and in spite of his temperament which has a passion for the hunt, he must be able to lie down for long periods and stay at his post (i.e. duck blind)....
>
> ...[Korthals'] first Kennelbook, which is still in possession of our club [WPGCA has a photocopy of the kennel book] has dates beginning in January 1872. In 1874 he began the building of a consistently bred rough-coated hunting dog breed. In that year he bought from his friend Amand, a seven year old bitch named **MOUCHE** and a three year old male named **HECTOR**. From this combination, the first Korthals Griffons were born in September of that same year [1874]. Through careful breeding and continuous selection, he wanted to fix certain breed characteristics.
>
> The task he was facing was to breed consistently dogs that were bold, that would hunt diligently with a sharp [keen, excellent] nose, that were solid on the track and liked to enter water. Between 1874 and 1886 he achieved success, thanks to a tremendous *practical knowledge, a rich experience with hunting dogs, good insight into the hereditary possibilities* [emphasis added], strong determination and resolution of financial problems.
>
> He called this dog the Griffon. This was a name that had been used for centuries in west Europe for all types of rough-coated dogs of different sorts.
>
> On July 29, 1888, he, and a large number of other Griffon lovers, organized a European purebred dog association which was called the Griffon

L. O. G.

LIVRE DES

ORIGINES

DU

GRIFFON A POIL DUR

VOLUME I. — 1919

N°s 1 - 201

ÉDITÉ SOUS LE PATRONAGE DU
CLUB FRANÇAIS DU GRIFFON A POIL DUR
et du GRIFFON-CLUB BELGE

Reconnu par
la *Société Centrale pour l'Amélioration des Races de Chiens en France,*
la *Société Royale Saint-Hubert de Belgique*
et le *Real Societad de Fomento de las Razas Caninas,* en Espagne.

BRUXELLES
IMPRIMERIE J.-E. GOOSSENS, S. A.
1920

Copy of the front page from the first volume of the French Griffon Club's stud book (1911).

Rauhhaar-Blätter

Mitteilungsblatt des Rauhhaar-Reinzucht-Verbandes
Griffon-Club e. V. — Club Stichelhaar — Verein Pudelpointer e. V.
im Jagdgebrauchshund-Verband

Einzelpreis 50 Dpfg.	**Folge 30 / Juli 1965**	Verlagsort: Friedberg i. H.

Aus dem Inhalt:

Mitteilungen des Vereins Griffon-Club e. V. . . . Seite 1—8
Mitteilungen des Vereins Pudelpointer e. V. . . . Seite 9—30
Mitteilungen des Club Stichelhaar . . . . Seite 31—32

„Amsel v. Kastanienhain"
Griffon-Hündin
GSB 10716
gew. 24. 6. 1964
Züchter u. Besitzer:
Walter Geisel,
Kronberg/Ts.

Copy of the cover from the newsletter for the three wirehaired breeds

Club. The club started with two new ideas for those times. They organized field tests in the spring and fall and they printed a Griffon registry, which contained the names of all the purebred Korthals Griffons.

This club did not survive World War II. Today there are Griffon clubs in The Netherlands, Germany, Belgium, France, Italy, United States.

More details come from another article in the same issue of the Dutch news-letter, titled "When Was The Netherlands Griffon Club Founded?

...On July 29, 1888, Korthals and a large number of other Griffon lovers met in Mainz and founded a European purebred hunting dog association, which was called the Griffon Club. This organization had members in Germany, France, Netherlands, Belgium, Switzerland, Italy, Sweden, Denmark and several in Russia. Because members lived so far from each other, the club experienced severe organizational problems, i.e. long distances between members. There were two solutions. On one side one had the Griffon registry and on the other side the founding of individual Griffon clubs in those areas where many Griffon owners lived....

...The binding element between these clubs was not only the authority of the mother club, but especially the Griffon registry [GSB] which resided in Germany.

In 1911, the first real divisions occurred. After plenty of back and forth conversations between the Netherlands members of the European Griffon Club, it was decided to establish a special division. The driving force behind this effort was O'Breen. So, on May 17, 1911, in Arnheim, the Netherlands Division of the European Griffon Club with self rule was founded.

The President was Leliman, who, following the death of Baron de Gingins in that same year, also became the President of the European Club. Secretary/Treasurer was O'Breen. The division had 27 members. The contribution (dues) were 2.50 guilders per year.

In 1918, the French and Belgian clubs severed ties with the European club because they believed the European club was too strongly influenced by German members. Furthermore, the French club began their own Griffon registry and were joined in this effort by the Belgian club. The Netherlands division cut the tie with the European club in 1940. The European club did not survive World War II.

After 1945 many of the old and faithful founded the German Griffon Club, who inherited the Griffon registry of the mother club. This registry has become a German affair, which mentions only Griffons bred in Germany.

What are we actually going to celebrate in 1988? We are going to commemorate that 100 years ago the European Griffon Club was founded, that it is the mother club of all now existing Griffon clubs in Western Europe and North America. [See Chapter 18, for the coverage of the 100th anniversary.]

But, it is simultaneously a commemoration of the 100 year existence of our roughbeards, our Griffon breed, that lies so close to all our hearts. I hope that 1988 is a memorable year for all Griffoniers...."

This brings us to the post World War II time in the history of our breed, in Europe. Let's go back now and see where and when our whiskered friends crossed the ocean and began life in the new world.

BOLERO VOM GIMBSHEIM (GSB 4492)*, one of the earliest Griffons imported to the United States; he was brought in by Dr. Ilyus of Pennsylvania, circa 1916.* ***BOLERO,*** *whelped in 1912, was bred by Mr.W inkler, secretary of the German (Korthals) Griffon Club, and a personal friend of Korthals.* ***BOLERO****'s grandfather was* ***CAPITAINE FRACASSE****.*

CHAPTER FIVE
EARLY TWENTIETH CENTURY (NORTH AMERICA)

NOTE: *If you are new to Griffons and not yet caught up in their bloodlines, you can skip past the pedigrees that appear throughout most of the remaining chapters. The text will tell the story and you need not stop to pour over the pedigrees. They have been included in the text to document and to instruct, and to make them more accessible to readers, rather than putting them in the appendix.*

As stated earlier, the first known Griffon arrived in the United States in 1887. Then, in 1907 Mr. Louis A. Thebaud imported some Griffons, followed soon by Dr. E.B. Ilyus. The Griffon Club of America, the first club, was founded on August 16, 1916, by Dr. E.B. Ilyus, of Lancaster, Pennsylvania. The officers were: president: Mr. Louis A. Thebaud, Morristown, New Jersey; vice-president: Mr. Arthur Duane, Sharon, Connecticut; treasury: Mr. W.N. Gilbert Clark, West Medway, Massachusetts; and secretary, Dr. Ilyus.

Dr. Ilyus gave the real credit to Mr. Thebaud for bringing the Griffon to the United States. Mr. Thebaud discovered the Griffon while on a hunting trip to France, and imported several in 1907, and more later. He was also very active in bringing the Brittany spaniel to the United States.

In an article from the French Griffon Club Stud Book (LOG Volume II, 1920), the author says,

> ...Little by little the Griffon has become appreciated in the United States, thanks to imported dogs, and a reputation began to be established and quality was improved.
>
> The initiative was laid by Dr. Ilyus in 1916...he and others in the U.S. who had good hunting areas, imported several good Griffons before the War, with the aid of Mr. Thebaud. Some of these Griffons were: **FILEUSE DE MERLIMONT, KOB DE MERLIMONT, HOMERE**.
>
> Unfortunately these dogs, placed in the home of a trainer, were used for some random breeding, without knowledge [of the bloodlines, nor of principles of breeding]. The result was that the dogs from these breedings became the only models of kinds of hair and colors. They were represented as the typical Griffon without being true to type. One of these products is **KOB'S JOE**, a white and liver dog that was reported to have succeeded in the Dog Show in New York [city] in 1920.
>
> Later, Dr. Ilyus imported **MICHE DE MOULIGNON (GSB 5385), MAMZELLE DE MOULIGNON (GSB 5384), MARQUIS DE MERLIMONT (GSB) 5459), KAME DE MERLIMONT (GSB 4305), BOLERO VOM GIMBSHEIM (GSB 4492), FLAMBEAU (GSB 3999),** and lastly **BANCO VOM FISCHSEE (GSB 6306).**

Passepartout
Arlequin (F)
Miralda
Le Capitaine Fracasse (F)
Passepartout
Riposte (F)
Kate Bella
Rabot (F)
Faust de Baccara (F)
Claudine (F)
Ironie (F)

PEDIGREE 1
Bolero von Gimbsheim (G)

Picco Gen: Heck (G)
Bandit von Gimbsheim (G)
Kordi (F)
Diana von Gimbsheim (G)
Flock Campana (G)
Hele Campana (G)
Struppia vom Vogelsburg (G)

Sans Souci (F)
Gribouille d'Amiens (F)
Coquette I de Merlimont (F)
Homere (F)
Delateur d'Amiens (F)
Frimousse d'Amiens (F)
Dugazon (F)
Homere's George (A)
Cavour de Merlimont (F)
Crack de Merlimont (F)
Coquette I de Merlimont (F)
Fileuse de Merlimont (F)
Stop d'Amiens (F)
Diane d'Amiens (F)
Mirette d'Amiens (F)

PEDIGREE 2
Stag de Greylock

Rock (F)
Cob (F)
Diane de Merlimont (F)
Kob de Merlimont (F)
Crack de Merlimont (F)
Jonquille de Merlimont (F)
Phane de Merlimont (F)
Miss Greylock (F)
Figaro de Bruges (F)
Cosaque de Merlimont (F)
Rita de Merlimont (F)
Charmonte de Merlimont (F)
Nougat (F)
Coquette I de Merlimont (F)
Cora de Merlimont (F)

Right: This is a poor quality reproduction of an old photo of Louis Thebaud, the president of the first Griffon club in America, who brought so many Griffons to this country.

Below: ***CRACK DE MERLIMONT (GSB 2070)*** *and* ***CIGARETTE DE MERLIMONT (GSB 2156).*** *They were from the same kennel, but were not littermates.* ***CRACK*** *was in the 5th generation of* ***STICK DE MERLIMONT,*** *imported to the U.S. by Mr. Thebaud, and used for breeding here.*

[LE CAPTAINE FRACASSE is in several of these pedigrees and through him you can trace back directly to one of the eight patriarchs. See Part Two, Chapter 26. The author continues:]

> These were of good blood and it is hoped that these new ones will repair the damage that took place at the beginning. Unfortunately, the American breeders are not able to have a little more frequent (or closer) relationship with their European colleagues...

Perhaps if proper knowledge, guidance, and control had existed during the short years of that first Griffon Club, the history of the Griffon in North America might have been much different.

KEY TO PEDIGREES

(A) after a dog's name indicates it was bred in America; (B) Belgium; (F) France; (G) Germany; (H) Holland; FQ (Quebec, Canada, dogs are of French bloodlines, bred in Quebec.); (CF) Cesky Fousek, bred in Czechoslovakia or 100% Cesky Fousek bred in the U.S. from Fouseks imported to the U.S. by WPGCA *ONLY*.

Dogs in bold type have qualified in a field test.

In addition to the men who founded the first Griffon club, and who were the officers, there were a few other affluent outdoorsmen who brought more Griffons to America during the same period, or who bought dogs from Thebaud and Ilyus and their friends during this period.

A Mr. E.D. Emson, Hightstown, New Jersey, owned a Griffon **STAG DE GREYLOCK** (FDSB 41116). The dog was whelped August 12, 1916, bred by a kennel in Gardner, Massachusetts, GREYLOCK GRIFFON KENNELS. See the pedigree below. **STAG** was directly out of the dogs imported by Thebaud and Ilyus. By selling the first generation offspring to any hunter and not testing progeny, not keeping any control of the breeding, dogs were destined to fall into some wrong hands along the way. (See Part Two, chapters 26 and 27, on breeding.)

Emson advertised **STAG DE GREYLOCK** for stud services. He also had him in dog shows. No doubt **STAG** sired a number of litters. **STAG** traces back through **CRACK DE MERLIMONT** to one of the patriarchs. (Pedigrees illustrating this connection are in Part Two.)

In a long article about Griffons, written by A.F. Hochwalt and published in the 1922 Sportsman's Digest from Cincinnati, after comparing their "slow" working manner to the faster, classy work of setters and pointers, the author says, "One significant thing is, the extraordinary demand that is being constantly maintained for the Griffon, and very young puppies bring prices that are entirely out of proportion to the intrinsic value or merit of the dog, but in certain spheres the griffon has become a fad and it is quite likely that breeders will reap the benefit."

By 1929 Griffons were being registered in FDSB (Field Dog Stud Book, the registry for American Field, which sponsors trials for pointers and setters.). There were two breeders in Klamath Falls, Oregon, a Mr. C.A. Evans and Mr. H.W. Middleton. There were two breeders in Connecticut: Mr. J.P. Mannion in Ridgefield and Mr. C.E. Danforth in Norwalk. Mannion was using for stud **STICK DE MERLIMONT**, who was imported from France by Mr. Thebaud.

Other breeders included Mr. & Mrs. Erastus T. Tefft, from Tarrytown, New York (a suburb of New York City) whose kennel name was STARIDGE. Many of their Griffons were registered in AKC in the 1930s. One has only to look at some of the pedigrees from their kennels to see that they bought their stock from dogs out of the ones imported by Thebaud and Ilyus.

Famous Griffons in the pedigrees of their dogs included: **STICK DE MERLIMONT, UNE DE MERLIMONT, CAPITAINE FRICASSE, CRACK DE MERLIMONT, BOLERO VOM GIMBSHEIM.** (Pedigress of **STICK, FRICASSE,** and **CRACK** are in Chapter 26.) Mr. & Mrs. Tefft were long-time friends of WPGCA charter members David and Henriette Barbieri. The Teffts bred over 200 Griffons between 1925 and 1935 and were sponsors of the first Griffon Club, along with Mr. Ilyus and Mr. Theband. The distances between these Northeastern breeders were not great, so they could have easily been in close contact during these years.

But important in the early part of the century is Griffon activity in other parts of America. One name synonymous with Griffons in the Northwest is Bob Ward. Bob lived in Missoula, Montana, and opened a sporting goods store still known today—not only in Missoula, but with branches in other major cities of Montana—as simply *Bob Ward's & Sons*. Today his children and grand children run the stores. Bob died in 1985 at the age of 100. I remember going to the original *Bob Ward's* in Missoula many times during the 1950s, primarily for fishing gear. One of his sons could always tell you where the fish were biting that week.

With the help of Dr. Charles R. Thornton of Missoula, Bob brought a few Griffons of French blood from the East to Montana. Thornton was also instrumental in bringing German Shorthairs to the United States in 1925. Another man who helped bring Griffons into Bob's hands was Dr. Dratz of Missoula. And Walter McLeod, a prominent citizen of Missoula, was interested enough to purchase **STARIDGE CLIVE** from Mrs. Tefft so that this male could be used for stud by Bob.

In an interview with Marg Allen circa 1966, published in the November 1966 ***The Gun Dog Supreme (GDS)***, Bob said,

> In the year of 1928 I bought Doctor Dratz's imported Griffons. I raised one fine litter from them, and from there on I had quite a time getting a good stud. There was only one breeder in this country at that time, who had good imported stock. That was Mr. Tefft in New York. He asked $500 for a male pup. That was beyond me in those days, as raising my family of six boys and two girls kept me pretty busy.
>
> A few years later, however, Mr. Tefft passed away and Walter McLeod of this city, and owner of the Missoula Mercantile Company bought **STARIDGE CLIVE** from Mrs. Tefft. Then Walter McLeod gave **STARIDGE CLIVE** to my kennels and from there on we produced some fine Griffons. I bred very selectively to natural workers and type also. During World War II I had to go out of the dog business, as the army had taken five of my sons, and I had a store to run with no help. I have been out of a gun dog ever since until now [1966] and have missed years of real pleasure. There is no dog to take the place of a Griffon. Once you know them they do get under your skin. Some writers claim there is no such thing as an all-round strain of dog. I do believe they have never owned a....Griffon.

Bob took as his kennel name HARDROCK MONTANA and this name is still honored and protected by our own Griffon Registry Book (GRB). The name should

PEDIGREE 3
Hardrock Montana Dan (A)

Parents	Grandparents	Great-grandparents	Great-great-grandparents
Homere's Ned (A)	Louis de Merlimont (F)	Marquis de Merlimont (F)	
		Homere's Cigale (A)	
	Lottie de Greylock (A)	Homere's George (A)	Homere (F)
			Fileuse de Merlimont (F)
		Miss Greylock (F)	Kob de Merlimont (F)
			Charmante de Merlimont (F)
Dulcy (A)	Banko v Fisch See (G)	Semper Whist (A)	
		Diane v Seebach (G)	
	Bolero's Belle (A)	Bolero von Gimbsheim (G)	Rabot (F)
			Diana von Gimbsheim (G)
		Mamzelle de Moulignon (A)	

PEDIGREE 4
Stouthearted Rex (A)

Parents	Grandparents	Great-grandparents	Great-great-grandparents
Staunchdown (A)	Hardrock Montana Dan (A)	Homere's Ned (A)	Louis de Merlimont (F)
			Lottie de Greylock (A)
		Dulcy (A)	Banko v Fisch See (G)
			Bolero's Belle (A)
	Hardrock Montana Birdie (A)	Staridge Clive (A)	Staridge Medoc (A)
			Staridge Cleo (A)
		Hardrock Montana Queen (A)	Homere's Ned (A)
			Dulcy (A)
Hardrock Montana Birdie (A)	Staridge Clive (A)	Staridge Medoc (A)	Suffield Hector (A)
			Staridge Pixie (A)
		Staridge Cleo (A)	Stick de Merlimont (F)
			Cigale de Greylock (A)
	Hardrock Montana Queen (A)	Homere's Ned (A)	Louis de Merlimont (F)
			Lottie de Greylock (A)
		Dulcy (A)	Banko v Fisch See (G)
			Bolero's Belle (A)

never be used by anyone with the exception of a member of Bob's family. Unfortunately, we can not protect any kennel name used in registering a dog with AKC, or other registries and HARDROCK MONTANA has been misused at least ten times, if not more, in the past twenty years.

When you study the pedigrees of **HARDROCK MONTANA DAN**, realize **DAN** and **QUEEN** were of the same breeding, but different litters. Technically **QUEEN** was bred by Mr. Dratz, but he used Bob's kennel name.

In the April 7, 1980 issue of *The Missoulian (Missoula, Montana)*, a full page profile about Bob told how he had come to Montana from Minnesota when he was 16, and stepped off the train with 10 cents in his pocket. Here is part of what appeared in that article, dealing with the time when his family was growing up in Missoula:

> Ward's rigorous outdoor life was not simply recreation, though. "A lot of his hunting and fishing was to put food on the table for us," said his daughter, Mary Jane. "I can remember him telling about taking the street car up to Marshall Canyon to go and get us meat to eat..."
>
> Ward explained that he would ride the Missoula-to-Bonner street car as far as Marshall Grade, walk into the canyon, shoot a deer or two, return to Missoula on the street car, and go back for the deer with pack horses.
>
> "I had a good bunch of hungry kids," he said, "but they never went to bed hungry." ...Ward, who said his sons started "carrying a gun as soon as they could walk good," added, "My kids was all good shots."
>
> Hunting, however, got Ward into trouble with a long-time principal of Missoula County High School, a man named Ketchum.
>
> "I took my boys on the opening day of duck season every year," Ward said. "And Ketchum said to me one time, 'Do you know your boys were absent day before yesterday?' I said, 'Ya, I took 'em hunting ducks.' 'Well,' he said, 'you shouldn't do that.' And I said, 'Well, that's what I'm gonna do as long as I live. I'm gonna take 'em hunting ducks on the opening day; my boys get that day, and nobody else is going to butt in.'"
>
> How did Mr. Ketchum respond to Ward's pronouncement?
>
> "He didn't like it," Ward said. "But 20 years later he was in my store on Higgins Avenue, and he came up to me and said, 'Remember when I used to bawl you out about taking your kids hunting?' I said, 'Ya, I remember.' And he said, 'Well, I was wrong. I can see that now. Your boys are all good boys.'"
>
> ...But fishing and hunting were only part of Ward's outdoor-related activities. For years he raised and sold bird dogs, including English pointers and setters and wirehaired griffons. He also consistently won area turkey shoots and rifle matches, and he became an accomplished photographer.
>
> ...Ward's son, Irvine, thinks his father fished until he was about 88.
>
> He also continued to hunt—he killed a male brown bear near Evaro Hill with a bow and arrow when in his 70s, thus making Ripley's Believe It or Not column—and he won a national rifle-shooting competition in Kalispell at age 66.

You can easily see how Bob's early dogs traced back to the dogs imported from France by Thebaud and Ilyus, especially through **HARDROCK MONTANA DAN.**

About the same time as Bob Ward, or possibly a few years later, another important name for Griffons in Montana appears—H. G. Kirkelie from Whitefish (near Kalispell). Some how Kirkelie ended up with a famous French import, **KADINE DE GAGNY** (Pedigree in Chapter 26). We do know, from a handwritten letter, dated

***STARIDGE CLIVE**, owned by Bob Ward. (Compliments Bob Ward, via Marg Allen.)*

***HARDROCK MONTANA DAN**, owned by Bob Ward. (Compliments Marg Allen.)*

June 26, 1951 that the breeder in France with the kennel name DE GAGNY sent **KADINE DE GAGNY** (LOG 6833) to a Mr. Conover in Chicago in 1939. He also mentions in the same letter that he recommended that **KADINE** be bred to another dog that had been imported to the United States—**STOP DE FORT MANOIR (LOG 8233)**.

Thanks to Kirkelie's grandson, Robert "Kirk" Streit presently of Kalispell, Montana (and a member of WPGCA), we have a photocopy of Kirkelie's kennel book. On page 7, Kirkelie writes about **KADINE:** "Acquired from H.C. Conover, Chicago, Ill." This was early in 1944. **KADINE** produced four litters.

What makes it difficult to trace the progeny and further generations is that in those days they did not know how to name dogs properly. Some of **KADINE's** pups were given the DE GAGNY kennel name. But if one is careful, lines can still be traced. Just don't assume that because a dog has a kennel name from France or Germany, that the dog is from that country. Many people in America improperly used kennel names that did not belong to them when they named their dogs.

Kirkelie called his kennels SPORTSMEN'S KENNELS, but he didn't have a "kennel name." Bob Ward called his kennels ORCHARD HOMES KENNELS, and after some years began using the kennel name HARDROCK MONTANA.

It's pretty obvious that Bob Ward and Kirkelie (or "Kirk") bought dogs from one another. **STOUT-HEARTED REX,** whelped Jan. 25, 1941, was bred by Ward but was owned by Kirkelie and used as a stud by him eight times, four of those with **KADINE**.

Existing records and photographs indicate that there was a lot of Griffon activity going on in western Montana in the 40s and into the 50s. There are still fragments of the descendants of these dogs existing today. You'll see some of the descendants when we get into Part II, especially Chapter 26, for example **CAPTAIN HARP GRADY.**

And this brings us to yet another important name in Montana: Marg Allen**.** Marg and her husband migrated from Minnesota to western Montana. Being enthusiastic hunters they built a motel near Nine Pipes Waterfowl Refuge, some 70 miles south of Kalispell and 50 miles north of Missoula. They were located in the magnificent, fertile Flathead Valley, with the Mission Mountains to the east and the vast valley spreading out to the west. Upland birds and waterfowl were abundant, not to mention big game.

The Allens had a couple of Griffons at this time (circa early 1950s), of what lineage is unknown, but I would imagine they were from Kirkilee or Ward. Tragedy struck during the early 50s when Mr. Allen was killed in a car accident. Marg sold the motel (which is still called "Allentown") and moved to Missoula with her two dogs.

KADINE DE GAGNEY.

KADINE, *taken from the other side, from a different angle. (Compliments the Kirkelies, via Marg Allen.)*

STOUTHEARTED REX*, in the Flathead Valley, Montana. (Compliments the Kirkelies, via Marg Allen.)*

X, some pups, and probably Mrs. Kirkelie, 1947. (Compliments, her grandson, Robert "Kirk" Streit.)

*Kirkelie puppies. Above, **KADINE** doing the dam's work, **REX**, behind the wire fence. (Compliments "Kirk" Streit.)*

Below, a different litter. Looks like all will have good coats, and some will have short coats, if scarcity of whiskers is any sign. (Compliments Marg Allen.)

*Below: **MARG ALLEN** (on the right),a hunting friend, and Marg's Griffons, on a goose hunt in the Flathead Valley of Montana, circa 1950. She said the dogs were 8 months, and that they should have had a shorter "chassis...however our two dogs worked beautifully, retrieving ducks, pointing Chinese pheasants and even helped hunt deer and antelope." Obviously the dogs helped with the geese too. Right: a photo of the same dogs at 15 months, taken in Missoula.*

CHAPTER SIX
WIREHAIRED POINTING GRIFFON CLUB OF AMERICA 1951

Founded in 1951 by Brigadeer General Thomas DeForth Rogers

While all the Griffon activity—breeding and lots of hunting—was taking place in the Northwest, things were happening in other parts of the United States. Remnants of those dogs from the first three decades in the eastern United States had reproduced many times. More Griffons were in the hands of hunters.

People just bred Griffons. There was no program, no plan, no controls. Additional breeders from those times were: Roger Hora, Iowa City, Iowa; Dr. G.F. Biebesheimer, Mason City, Iowa; Charles Van Studdiford, Warrenton, Missouri (who had stock both from Kirkelie and the breeders on the East Coast); Ethel Garcia from Massachusetts; Howard Cunningham from Reno, Nevada.

In 1949 General Rogers (who at that time was "Lt. Colonel" Rogers) was stationed in Germany. While there he came into contact with Griffons and bought **CISA V.D. HOHEN LINDE**. When General Rogers was sent home, **CISA** came with him to America.

General Rogers was a man of great enthusiasm and leadership. By August 29, 1951, he had managed to gather to his fold 19 charter members to form the Wirehaired Pointing Griffon Club of America (WPGCA). These charter members were:

Mrs. Marg M. Allen, Missoula, Montana
Mr. Harvey Buckridge, Hot Springs, Montana
Mr. David Barbieri, Thornwood, New York
Lt. Col. J.P. Brown, Fort Bragg, North Carolina
Dr. J.F. Biebesheimer, Mason City, Iowa
Mr. Joesph Chandler, Silver Springs, Maryland
Mrs. Daphne Cianchini, Rockville, Maryland
Mrs. Helen Inez Clark, Dickerson, Maryland
Mrs. Ethel C. Garcia, Marshfield, Massachusetts
Mr. & Mrs. Roger Hora, Iowa City, Iowa
Miss Barbara Kefauver, Frederick, Maryland
Mr. H.G. Kirkelie, Kalispell, Montana
Mr. Horace Koessler, Missoula, Montana

*Left: General Rogers son, Tom Jr., with **CISA VON DER HOHEN LINDE** on the left: **VALOUR D'ARGENT**, center, and **ELFIN D'ARGENT** on the right. **VALOUR** and **ELFIN** were bred by General Rogers.(Photo probably by Gen. Rogers.)*

Mr. Frank Ludwick, Washington, D.C.
Mr. Delbert Marshall, Kalamazoo, Michigan
Mr. John G. Martin, Hartford, Connecticut
Lt. Col. T. DeF. Rogers, Fort Belvoir, Virginia
Mr. Thomas DeF. Rogers Jr, Fort Bragg, North Carolina
Mr. J.A. Rudy, Toledo, Ohio

***Marg Allen*:** Although Marg is at the top of the list of charter members, technically she was not a charter member. But indirectly she had a great deal to do with the formation of the WPGCA. She was in touch with General Rogers and gave her support and encouragement of the breed which helped him to start the club. The reason she was not a charter member is that sadly her husband was killed at about the time the club was being formed. But, by 1957 she was running the thriving sportsman's motel in the heart of a hunting paradise in the Flathead Valley, and she joined the WPGCA.

Marg played such an important role in the promotion of Griffons and keeping them alive in the United States, that, just because of a technicality she should not be left off the list of people who were charter members.

In the club files is a typed copy of a proposed revision of the club constitution for 1964. It is accompanied by a covering letter from General Rogers to Doug Fethers, the secretary at that time. A copy of the *original* constitution (1951) and a copy of our present day one (1994) appear in the appendix.

Here is what General Rogers wrote to Fethers in 1963:

Brig. General T. DeF. Rogers, Ret.
c/o Adrian Wilson & Associates
APO #301, San Francisco, CA

Mr. Douglas A. Fethers
1633 Woodworth St, NE
Grand Rapids, MI

Dear Doug,

The continued success and growth of the Wirehaired Pointing Griffon Club of America is a tribute *not* to the exact wording of its constitution, but to the unselfish dedication of members such as yourself to the objectives set forth in its constitution. To those members, and particularly to you, the club owes a heartfelt vote of thanks.

As a matter of interest to our members, the original WPGCA constitution was drafted and approved by our charter members after consulting with and receiving suggestions from AKC. These suggestions were incorporated in the constitution. Eventually WPGCA hopes to become a full-fledged member of AKC (members of which are clubs—not individual persons), and consequently several provisions of our Constitution were specifically drafted to conform with the membership requirements of AKC—the designation of Missoula, Montana as the place for conducting official AKC shows, matches, and trials is no serious limitation on the activities of WPGCA. I'm sure that under appropriate circumstances AKC would permit a change of designated location. Missoula was selected in 1951 because the greatest concentration of Hunting Griffons was then in the Missoula area.

Benefiting from experience, the WPGCA has adopted a parliamentary procedure much simpler and more effective than the formal procedures set forth in the original constitution. In essence, ***The Gun Dog Supreme*** has become the medium for submitting motions, resolutions, nominations for office, treasurer's reports, etc. to our members; and for obtaining the consensus of the members. I believe that it would be proper at this time for the WPGCA to adopt a revised constitution reflecting the improvements that we have learned from experience and I therefore move that the following be adopted:

What followed immediately after this section of General Rogers' letter is the 1964 revised constitution (which was not very different from the original one), and was approved by the membership and stayed in effect until 1970 when we felt revisions needed to be made.

If you turn to the appendix and look over the original constitution, you'll see that General Rogers relied heavily on AKC input and approval. Today we steer completely away from AKC, and have a constitution that, above all else, protects the dogs. Even so, today's constitution is not that different in general content from the original one.

General Rogers incorporated his proposed revision as part of his letter to Fethers, signed it:

Sincerely,

Tom Rogers

And added this important P.S.:

P.S. I sincerely hope Marg Allen accepts your nomination. She was truly the founder of WPGCA.

They must have wanted her to be secretary or president, but she declined. I remember her telling me that she did not want to hold any office.

Who Were the Rest of These Charter Members?

***David Barbieri*:** Mr. Barbieri was a highly skilled gunsmith who was kept busy by Abercrombie & Fitch, that unique and wonderful store in New York City that catered to wealthy sportsmen and sportswomen in the East. I remember going to the gun department in the late 1950s and seeing more of the finest shotguns in one place at one time than I ever will again. Mr. Barbieri was vice-president of our club in 1958. He owned **VIGOUR D'ARGENT,** bred by General Rogers.

***J.F. Biebesheimer*:** He was from Mason City, Iowa—in the heart of the some of the best quail and pheasant hunting in the United States. Doctor Biebesheimer (His name is very similar to the place in Germany where Korthals did his breeding and from which his kennel name came, but this is just a coincidence.) had two bitches from the **DE GAGNY** line, one sired by Kirkelie's **STOUTHEARTED REX** and the other by a **MERLIMONT** stud. He also owned a male **THIEL OF BIEBESHEIM** sired by Mr. Conover's imported **STOP DE FORT MANOIR.** In 1952 Dr. Biebesheimer became vice-president of the WPGCA.

J.P. Brown: He was a paratrooper with the 28th Airborne out of Fort Bragg and owned **GRIS PERLE.**

Harvey Buckridge: was from Hot Springs, Montana, not far from Kallispell, so his bitch, **GINGER,** probably came from Kirkelies. He bred one known litter (of three pups) out of **GINGER.**

Daphne Cianchini: She had been breeding Griffons for a number of years and owned **CIAN'S BOYOU BON BON,** whose color portrait appeared in National Geographic Magazine in 1947. In the 50s she owned **WYCHINGWIND MICHELIN**, sire of **VALOUR D'ARGENT.**

Ethel Garcia: Mrs. Garcia, from Massachusetts, chose the kennel name GARCENDA. More information follows in a later chapter.

Roger Hora and his wife. He and his wife were also in Iowa, in fact from Iowa City, where today our Heartland Griffon Club holds a field test every year. No doubt they obtained their Griffons from Dr. Biebesheimer in nearby Mason City.

Barbara Kefauver. She was from the Washington D.C. area and quite active in the club, and was alternate secretary at one time. (There used to be an office of alternate secretary in the event that General Rogers would be sent overseas.)

H.G. Kirkelie and his wife: As noted earlier, the Kirkelies played a very important role in promoting and breeding Griffons in the United States, and they brought the name Bob Ward to the attention of General Rogers, who finally traced him through the help of Marg Allen.

Horace "Shorty" Koessler: He was a prominent and well-known resident of Missoula, Montana, had Griffons for quite some years and was the final charter member of our club. In the 1950s he owned **MAIS OUI D'ARGENT** and **BEAUCOUP D'ARGENT.** He later sold **BEAUCOUP** to another early club member, Howard Cunningham of Reno, Nevada. These dogs were out of some of the Kirkelie and Bob Ward stock. In the late sixties and early seventies, Marg Allen managed to get some Griffons from Europe for "Shorty," as he was known by his friends. Shorty was killed in 1987, when his plane went down in the mountains of Idaho. His wife, Barbara, still lives and works in Missoula.

Frank M. LudwicK: He was a successful corporate lawyer in Washington, D.C., and owned **SILVER FIZZ** (bred by John Martin) and **CHASSEUR d'ARGENT** (bred by General Rogers).

John G. Martin: Mr. Martin was our first club president and quite a remarkable man. He imported from France **UNICO DE NADILAC** and renamed him **MILLSHIRE POTSTILL**, MILLSHIRE being his kennel name. He had a gorgeous gentleman's farm, Johnny Cake Farm, atop Johnny Cake Mountain in a small, rural town near Hartford, Connecticut. One of the first early tests for versatile hunting dogs in Connecticut was held at his farm in November 1972. Mr. Martin owned the great Heublein's import business (A-1 sauce, Harvey's Bristol Cream, Smirnoff Vodka). During World War II he served as an officer in North Africa.

Lt. Col. Thomas DeForth Rogers: Not our first president, but the founder of our club, (though he gives that title to Marg Allen), and the first secretary and first editor of ***The Gun Dog Supreme***.

***Thomas DeForth Rogers Jr*:** This was General Rogers' son, appointed by our vice president in 1969 to serve as our President for the unexpired term after his father died that year.

* * * * *

Quite an impressive list of people. What a grand beginning! Even more exciting for history buffs, is that just as General Rogers was getting our club underway, Dr. Thomas Mintscheff, of Germany, moved with his wife to a suburb of New York City, Croton-On-Hudson, and with them from Germany came their famous griffon **SIEGFRIED V.D. KREUZEICHE,** and a female Griffon, **UTE V.D. KREUZEICHE. SIEGFRIED** had earned many prizes in field tests in Germany and was considered to be an outstanding Griffon of his time. He was eight years old when he arrived in America, so was only used for stud here a few times.

Dr. Mintscheff is a very gifted, talented dog person. He has the magic touch and is a superb trainer. For many years he was also the Breed Warden of the German Griffon Club. In Germany the Breed Warden gives advice to would-be breeders on who they should breed their bitches to. He was, of course, also a judge for many years in Germany. More about Dr. Mintscheff later in our history.

Also in 1952 a kennel in Massachusetts, GARCENDA KENNELS was breeding a lot of Griffons. They were putting many Griffons into the show ring. Most of these dogs resulted from close inbreeding. It is doubtful these dogs were hunted. It is from these lines that some of our trouble was to erupt a few years later, both in temperament and in hip dysplasia.

Look at the pedigree of **GARCENDA'S VICTORIA** (Part Two, Chap. 28, and also Ped 11, in this chapter). In correspondence from General Rogers in 1967 he mentions to me that **GARCENDA'S VICTORIA** was suspected to be dysplastic (no OFA in those days, just a term used at the time for "loose hip sockets.") He also told me that this bitch was manshy, which translates to poor temperament. Unfortunately a fine dog, **KADINE DE GAGNY,** was in this pedigree. A case of indiscriminate breeding, causing even a dog with fairly good genes to appear in a negative light.

An interesting sidelight at this point in the early history of the WPGCA is that in 1951 a Dr. Gigante from Detroit, Michigan, was importing and breeding Spinoni (and according to General Rogers "a breed practically identical in every way to our Wirehaired Pointing Griffon") and a breeding was planned with one of Gigante's bitches to **VALOUR D'ARGENT.** In the September 1953 GDS, General Rogers writes that the membership had accepted the Spinoni to be considered identical to the Wirehaired Pointing Griffon. This meant they would be considered the same breed and could be bred interchangeably. There is nothing further in the records to indicate that these breedings took place, nor how they might have overcome the problems of registering resulting progeny.

There appears to be only one slim connection between the first Griffon Club, formed in 1920 in the Northeast, with the second one, the Wirehaired Pointing Griffon Club of America, founded in 1951. The one tie was that of Mrs. Erasus Tefft selling some of her STAR RIDGE Griffons to Dr. Dratz in Missoula, thus putting some of that blood into the hands of Bob Ward, who along with the Kirkelies and Marg Allen kept the breed going. Marg's encouragement to General Rogers to form a club, and General Rogers' initial contact with Mrs Tefft were also factors in the slim connection. And at least, through our bearded friends, we do connect, which is a nice concept to hold and to give us a feeling of continuity.

PEDIGREE 5

Cisa v.d. Hohen Linde (G)

- **Siegfried v.d. Kruezeiche (G)**
  - **Donnar v Waldhaus (G)**
    - **Flink v.d. Blauen Donau (G)**
      - **Jago Aigner (G)**
      - **Lore Moguntia (G)**
    - **Berga v.d. Blauen Donau (G)**
      - **Unkas v.d. Wetterau (G)**
      - **Lorra v.d. Juralp (G)**
  - **Bianka vom Pfahlof (G)**
    - **Haldo v.d. Lerchenheid (G)**
      - **Tyras Haagen (G)**
      - **Becasse v.d. Lerchenheid (G)**
    - **Fix v.d. Kreuzeiche (G)**
      - **Nero v.d. Juralp (G)**
      - **Pussy v.d. Kreuzeiche (G)**
- **Elena v Barental (G)**
  - **Benno vom Meckartal (G)**
    - **Blitz vom Wendelstein (G)**
      - **Nero v.d. Juralp (G)**
      - **Asta vom Barental (G)**
    - **Asta vom Barental (G)**
      - **Jago Aigner (G)**
      - **Cora v.d. Mindelburg (G)**
  - **Alma vom Barental (G)**
    - **Jago Aigner (G)**
      - **Hermansky v Geiseigasteig (G)**
      - **Ida Urian (F)**
    - **Cora v.d. Mindelburg (G)**
      - **Cato v.d. Kreuzeiche (G)**
      - **Adda vom Steinreisach (G)**

PEDIGREE 6

Beaucoup d'Argent (A)

- Silver Fizz (A)
  - Unico de Nadillac (F)
    - Sloop des Picards (F)
      - Itom des Sommaire (F)
      - Jina d'Artagnan (F)
    - Sybel des Gatines (F)
      - Hurf de la Haule (F)
      - Poulette de Gatines (F)
  - Milshire Orris (A)
    - Junior of Warrenville (A)
      - Mickey of Warrenville (A)
      - Kadine de Gagny (F)
    - Cian's Bayou Bon Bon (A)
      - Bonaparte (A)
      - Milisande (A)
- Cisa v.d. Hohen Linde (G)
  - **Siegfried v.d. Kruezeiche (G)**
    - **Donnar v Waldhaus (G)**
      - **Flink v.d. Blauen Donau (G)**
      - **Berga v.d. Blauen Donau (G)**
    - **Bianka vom Pfahlof (G)**
      - **Haldo v.d. Lerchenheid (G)**
      - **Fix v.d. Kreuzeiche (G)**
  - **Elena v Barental (G)**
    - **Benno vom Meckartal (G)**
      - **Blitz vom Wendelstein (G)**
      - **Asta vom Barental (G)**
    - **Alma vom Barental (G)**
      - **Jago Aigner (G)**
      - **Cora v.d. Mindelburg (G)**

PEDIGREE 7
Unico de Nadillac (F)

- Sloop des Picards (F)
  - Itom des Sommaire (F)
    - Pick des Erans (F)
      - Pack d'Orville (F)
      - Alerte des Ebans (F)
    - Dora de la Ruelle (F)
      - Casse cou des Diss (F)
      - Vera de Faverolles (F)
  - Jina d'Artagnan (F)
    - Galop des Ronces Vives (F)
      - Estoc de Gagny (F)
      - Datte du Pigeonnier (F)
    - Godille de la Dernade (F)
      - Cab de la Fauconnie (F)
      - Cigale de la Dernade (F)
- Sybel des Gatines (F)
  - Hurf de la Haule (F)
    - Zimas de Gagny (F)
      - Caillou des Diss (F)
      - Tulipe de Gagny (F)
    - Eymiss de Patroa (F)
      - Clown de Patroa (F)
      - Arlette de Patroa (F)
  - Poulette de Gatines (F)
    - Hurf de la Haule (F)
      - Zimas de Gagny (F)
      - Eymiss de Patroa (F)
    - Margot de la Croix Tempez (F)
      - Fiston de la Croix Tempez (F)
      - Java de la Croix Tempez (F)

PEDIGREE 8
Brynhilde of Biebesheim (A)

- Stouthearted Rex (A)
  - Staunchdown (A)
    - Hardrock Montana Dan (A)
      - Homere's Ned (A)
      - Dulcy (A)
    - Hardrock Montana Birdie (A)
      - Staridge Clive (A)
      - Hardrock Montana Queen (A)
  - Hardrock Montana Birdie (A)
    - Staridge Clive (A)
      - Staridge Medoc (A)
      - Staridge Cleo (A)
    - Hardrock Montana Queen (A)
      - Homere's Ned (A)
      - Dulcy (A)
- Bernadette de Gagny (A)
  - Stouthearted Rex (A)
    - Staunchdown (A)
      - Hardrock Montana Dan (A)
      - Hardrock Montana Birdie (A)
    - Hardrock Montana Birdie (A)
      - Staridge Clive (A)
      - Hardrock Montana Queen (A)
  - Kadine de Gagny (F)
    - Estoc de Gagny (F)
      - Alto de le Dernade (F)
      - Babette de Gagny (F)
    - Helda de Merlimont (F)
      - Ardent de Gagny (F)
      - Done de Marquetaire (F)

PEDIGREE 9

John's Nevada George (A)

Sloop des Picards (F)
Unico de Nadillac (F)
Sybel des Gatines (F)
Silver Fizz (A)
Junior of Warrenville (A)
Milshire Orris (A)
Cian's Bayou Bon Bon (A)
Beaucoup d'Argent (A)
Donnar v Waldhaus (G)
Siegfried v.d. Kruezeiche (G)
Bianka vom Pfahlof (G)
Cisa v.d. Hohen Linde (G)
Benno vom Meckartal (G)
Elena v Barental (G)
Alma vom Barental (G)

Haxo de Sagrolle (F)
Stop de Fort Manoir (F)
Jockasse de Fort Manoir (F)
Theil of Biebesheim (A)
Stouthearted Rex (A)
Pago of Biebesheim (A)
Bernadette de Gagny (F)
Nevada Queen (A)
Mickey of Warrenville (A)
Trouble of Warrenville (A)
Kadine de Gagny (F)
Trientje of Biebesheim (A)
Stouthearted Rex (A)
Pago of Biebesheim (A)
Bernadette de Gagny (F)

PEDIGREE 10

Alf vom Niddertal (G)

Tommy de la Courette (B)
Wisky du Mandarin (F)
Ultra (B)
Ipo vom Welleseind (G)
Crack v Wiesenheim (H)
Guuka vom Welleseind (H)
Farra von Welleseind (H)
Blucher v.d. Altenburg (G)
Putti vom Wedelstein (G)
Argus vom Kynast (G)
Sturmur Meguntia (G)
Astrid v.d. Michelherd (G)
Siegfried v.d. Kruezeiche (G)
Brinka v.d. Hohen Linde (G)
Elma vom Barental (G)

Donnar v Waldhaus (G)
Siegfried v.d. Kruezeiche (G)
Bianka vom Pfahlof (G)
Cato v.d. Hohen Linde (G)
Benno vom Meckartal (G)
Elma vom Barental (G)
Alma vom Barental (G)
Frigga v.d. rauhen Gracht (G)
Argus v Schlobzwinger (G)
Arntrae v.d. rauhen Gracht (G)
Cora v.d. Blauen Donau (G)
Colja v.d. rauhen Gracht (G)
Basse v.d. Blauen Donau (G)
Emir v.d. rauhen Gracht (G)
Cora v.d. Blauen Donau (G)

The dog on the left is ***SIEGFRIED V.D. KREUZEICHE*** *(GSB 9642), the one on the right,* ***HILKA V.D. RAUHEN GRACHT****. Both dogs qualified in all three field tests, and* ***SIEGFRIED*** *won many more prizes. A lot of the dogs that came to us from Germany in the 1950s and 1960s had these dogs in their pedigrees.*

In 1952 Charles Van Studdiford of Missouri joined the club. Over the years he had many Griffons, bred quite a few and hunted over many of them. He was more a pointer man and left the tails undocked. He took his string of Griffons to the Canadian prairies to work them on the sharptail grouse and get them to move out more like the pointers he was used to.

One of his bitches should be noted, **BRYNHILDE OF BIEBESHEIM**, obviously from Dr. Biebesheimer's kennel in Iowa. Later, in the section on breeding, we'll get into pedigrees, and talk about earlier breedings that took place, such as the use of this bitch. We'll show how she, and a few other Griffons of that era, were the result of close inbreeding, without strict monitoring, and is where much of our troubles began—in the 1950s.

In 1954 we hear about hip dysplasia again, but at that time, as mentioned earlier, it was called "loose hip sockets." General Rogers wrote in the GDS, "...With the help of these two breeders it has been possible for the club to identify beyond serious doubt the particular strain responsible for the few cases of faulty hip sockets that have occurred in our breed. Moreover, these breeders have eliminated that strain from the breeding program, a step which should go far to completely wipe out the fault among Griffons in America...." He didn't say who these two breeders were.

As we know, it did not wipe out hip dysplasia in Griffons, partially, I suspect, because they were only able to identify one or two strains and missed several others. (See Chapters 28 and 29, on hip dysplasia for additional information.)

Also in 1954 Douglas Fethers of Grand Rapids, Michigan joined the club after purchasing several dogs from Mrs. Garcia (GARCENDA'S) kennel (see above). Later he would get more Griffons and be appointed Secretary in 1959.

About this same time there was a new club member in Vancouver, British Columbia, who imported a Griffon **FANNE NIMRODSKA DORA** from Yugoslavia, whelped behind the Iron Curtain. When you see the photo of **FANNE** it makes you wonder if this wasn't a cousin of our present day Cesky Fousek? But, I'm getting ahead of the story. She was bred to **BEAUCOUP D'ARGENT** and produced a litter from which came **SPORT D'ARGENT.**

In 1955—with support from General Rogers—a small group of Griffonniers in the Reno, Nevada area organized a field trial for Griffons. It was held under the rules and sanction of the American Field. It was not a *test* for versatile hunting dogs as we know it today, but it was a beginning to get our dogs in the testing field. It was a typical field trial with the dogs run in braces, a bird field, and judges on horseback. There were over 40 entries which included Brittanies, German Shorthairs, Weimaraners, German Wirehairs, Vizslas and Griffons. The winning dog was **JOHN'S NEVADA GEORGE**, a Griffon, with second place going to his sire, **BEAUCOUP D'ARGENT.** (See pedigre 9.)

In 1956 Raymond Bergeron, who had been stationed in Germany during his stint in the army, brought back **ASTOR V.D. ALTENBURG** who was used for breeding. About eight years later Sam Herndon purchased a pup from Germany, **ERWIN V.D. BRECH**, which came from Franz Kroninger's kennel. Kroninger was president of the Germany Griffon Club for many years, including the times some of us visited the Griffonniers in Germany.

Also in 1956 a new club member, George Foreman of Buffalo, New York, imported a male from france, **ELOI DES GRANDES ROSEAUX.** In the same year another member, Albert Schneider of White Plains, New York imported a bitch from

On the left is ***FANNE NIMRODSKA DORA*** *and on the right* ***GYPSY D'ARGENT (Beaucoup D'Argent x Fanne Nimrodska Dora)****. Below is* ***ERWIN V.D. BRECH (Cato v Kochertal x Cora v.d. Altenburg)****.*

Belgium, **ELZA DU MOULIN A VENT**, who was bred to **VIGOUR D'ARGENT** (owned by David Barbieri), and pups whelped November 1957.

General Rogers and his wife, Doris, became friends with Dr. Mintscheff and his wife. General Rogers' first Griffon, **CISA V.D. HOHEN LINDE,** had been sired by Mintscheff's famous **SIEGFRIED V.D. KREUZEICHE**, so they had that personal connection that so many of us in the dog world have—our dogs are related, so we feel a special bond. One of the reasons **SIEGFRIED** became so famous is that Dr. Mintscheff, an excellent trainer, ran him in many field tests, so there are many wins behind his name.

In 1957 Dr. Mintscheff brought over a pup from Germany, **ALF VOM NIDDERTAL,** for new club member Henry Felton of Lewiston, Idaho. **ALF** was used for breeding a number of times in the Northwest, first by Marg Allen, then by others. So **ALF** left his stamp on the breed in the United States. My first Griffon was sired by **ALF.**

Dr. Mintscheff bred his bitch, **UTE V.D. KREUZICHE**, to **SIEGFRIED.** This resulted in the "C" litter **VOM LUDA JANA** (Mintscheff's kennel name). Only three dogs resulted from this breeding: **CAYUSE**, **CHICO** and **COSSET.**

Marcus Nalley, of Tacoma, Washington, President of Nalley Foods, became our club president in 1958. Serving as vice-president was Henriette Barbieri, and Barbara Kefauver served as alternate secretary. General Rogers remained as secretary/treasurer and editor of ***The Gun Dog Supreme***.

In the September 1958 issue of ***Field & Stream***, Joe Stetson, Gun Dog Editor, wrote "The Continental Way." He suggested setting up field trials which would stress the versatility of the continental dogs. From what he had observed, he was impressed with their "joy of working." Dr. Mintscheff and Joe Stetson became acquaintances when they were neighbors in a suburb of New York City, in the Hudson River Valley. Later Stetson wrote about the Griffon in another article for ***Field & Stream***, "All Purpose Hunter."

Volume 17, December 1958, was the last issue of the GDS written and edited by General Rogers. In 1959 he turned these chores over to Douglas Fethers of Grand Rapids, Michigan, and finally accepted the well earned title of president of the Wirehaired Pointing Griffon Club of America.

Douglas Fethers was secretary from 1959 until July 1967. He had obtained a griffon, **GARCENDA'S VICTORIA,** from the GARCENDA kennel in Massachusetts. **VICTORIA** was the product of inbreeding, half brother to half sister. That she was manshy, as reported by General Rogers, is no surprise after studying her pedigree. (See Chapter 28.) Fethers bred her to **DE JON D'ARGENT,** not a field-tested dog, because in those days we didn't have any testing program. But, according to General Rogers, this was a good male. Out of this came a male, **ZIMAS D'ARGENT.** (See Ped 12.)

ASTOR V.D. ALTENBURG stayed at Fethers', for quite some time, and while he was there, Fethers bred **GARCENDA'S VICTORIA** to **ASTOR.** Fethers kept one of the pups from this litter, **CRISSI VOM ALTENBURG** (improperly named). **CRISSI** was manshy. I visited Fethers one day and saw **CRISSI,** one of the worst cases of a manshy dog I've ever seen. Eventually he bred **CRISSI** to **ZIMAS**—half brother to half sister. And remember, on **CRISSI**'s side, there was already close in-breeding in the third generation.

So this was close inbreeding to weak temperament. One of the dogs from this breeding, **ARTEMIS VOM ALTENBURG D'ARGENT**, was owned by Louise

PEDIGREE 11
Crissi vom Altenburg (A)

- Sire: **Astor v.d. Altenburg (G)**
  - **Siegfried v.d. Kruezeiche (G)**
    - **Donnar v Waldhaus (G)**
      - **Flink v.d. Blauen Donau (G)**
      - **Berga v.d. Blauen Donau (G)**
    - **Bianka vom Pfahlof (G)**
      - **Haldo v.d Lerchenheid (G)**
      - **Fix v.d. Kreuzeiche (G)**
  - **Astrid v.d. Michelherd (G)**
    - **Argus vom Kynast (G)**
      - **Putti vom Wedelstein (G)**
      - **Sturmer Meguntia (G)**
    - **Brinka v.d. Hohen Linde (G)**
      - **Siegfried v.d. Kruezeiche (G)**
      - **Elma vom Barental (G)**
- Dam: Garcenda's Victoria (A)
  - Garcenda's Jacque (A)
    - Bonaparte (A)
      - Mickey of Warrenville (A)
      - Kadine de Gagny (F)
    - Milisande (A)
      - Staunchdown (A)
      - Hardrock Montana Birdie (A)
  - Garcenda's Collette (A)
    - Bonaparte (A)
      - Mickey of Warrenville (A)
      - Kadine de Gagny (F)
    - Nanon d'Argent (A)
      - Bonaparte (A)
      - Milisande (A)

PEDIGREE 12
Artemis v Altenburg d'Argent (A)

- Sire: Zimas d'Argent (A)
  - De Jon d'Argent (A)
    - Beaucoup d'Argent (A)
      - Silver Fizz (A)
      - Cisa v.d. Hohen Linde (G)
    - Babe of Helda's Rex (A)
      - Stouthearted Rex (A)
      - Helda's Dreamer (A)
  - Garcenda's Victoria (A)
    - Garcenda's Jacque (A)
      - Bonaparte (A)
      - Milisande (A)
    - Garcenda's Collette (A)
      - Bonaparte (A)
      - Nanon d'Argent (A)
- Dam: Crissi vom Altenburg (A)
  - **Astor v.d. Altenburg (G)**
    - **Siegfried v.d. Kruezeiche (G)**
      - **Donnar v Waldhaus (G)**
      - **Bianka vom Pfahlof (G)**
    - **Astrid v.d. Michelherd (G)**
      - **Argus vom Kynast (G)**
      - **Brinka v.d. Hohen Linde (G)**
  - Garcenda's Victoria (A)
    - Garcenda's Jacque (A)
      - Bonaparte (A)
      - Milisande (A)
    - Garcenda's Collette (A)
      - Bonaparte (A)
      - Nanon d'Argent (A)

Wisky du Mandarin (F)
Ipo vom Welleseind (G)
Guuka von Welleseind (H)
Blucher v.d. Altenburg (G)
Argus vom Kynast (G)
Astrid v.d. Michelherd (G)
Brinka v.d. Hohen Linde (G)
Alf vom Niddertal (G)
Siegfried v.d. Kruezeiche (G)
Cato v.d. Hohen Linde (G)
Elma vom Barental (G)
Frigga v.d. rauhen Gracht (G)
Arntrae v.d. rauhen Gracht (G)
Colja v.d. rauhen Gracht (G)
PEDIGREE 13
Emir v.d. rauhen Gracht (G)
Miss Tempest Nellagram (A)
De Jon d'Argent (A)
Zimas d'Argent (A)
Garcenda's Victoria (A)
Tim vom Altenburg (A)
Astor v.d. Altenburg (G)
Crissi vom Altenburg (A)
Garcenda's Victoria (A)
Tammy de la Oakes Heuvel (A)
Houdoe v Welleseind (H)
Golo (H)
Cadi of Gerbert (H)
Gerta Deufer de la Oakes Heuvel (H)
Houdoe v Welleseind (H)
Astrah (H)
Itanja v Weisenheim (H)

Siegfried v.d. Kruezeiche (G)
Ali von Luda Jane (G)
Ute v.d. Kruezeiche (G)
Cato vom Kochertal (G)
Siegfried v.d. Kruezeiche (G)
Ella vom Marienheim (G)
Dolde vom Karental (G)
Erwin v.d. Brech (G)
Argus vom Kynast (G)
Barri vom Tannenberg (G)
Cara v.d. Hohen Linde (G)
Cora v.d. Altenburg (G)
Argus vom Kynast (G)
Astrid v.d. Michelherd (G)
PEDIGREE 14
Brinka v.d. Hohen Linde (G)
Hansel Zu Den Bergen Gehen (A)
Donnar v Waldhaus (G)
Siegfried v.d. Kruezeiche (G)
Bianka vom Pfahlof (G)
Astor v.d. Altenburg (G)
Argus vom Kynast (G)
Astrid v.d. Michelherd (G)
Brinka v.d. Hohen Linde (G)
Crissi vom Altenburg (A)
Bonaparte (A)
Garcenda's Jacque (A)
Milisande (A)
Garcenda's Victoria (A)
Bonaparte (A)
Garcenda's Collette (A)
Nanon d'Argent (A)

Barclay of Brevard, North Carolina, a long time club member. She reported that the bitch was shy of temperament with soft, wooly coat (Ped 12, same breeding as **ZIMAS DE ARGENT**).

During this period, a male pup, **ERWIN V.D. BRECH,** was brought here from Germany. Like all dogs in those days, he was never field tested. Fethers bred **CRISSI** to **ERWIN.** I don't know about the rest of the litter, but I can tell you about one: **HANSEL ZU DEN BERGEN GEHEN.** He was my second Griffon and at about four months of age he began exhibiting all the signs of being manshy, which he never recovered from during his entire life. Despite the field-tested blood on his sire's side, and field-tested blood on his grandfather's side, **ASTOR**, the weak blood of his dam, **CRISSI,** came to the fore.

Above: ***ARTEMIS VOM ALTENBURG D'ARGENT.***

Below: ***ALF VOM NIDDERTAL****, with* ***ZORIE****, a pup by him, out of* ***TAMMY DE L'OAKES HEUVEL****, bred by Marg Allen. (Compliments Marg Allen)*

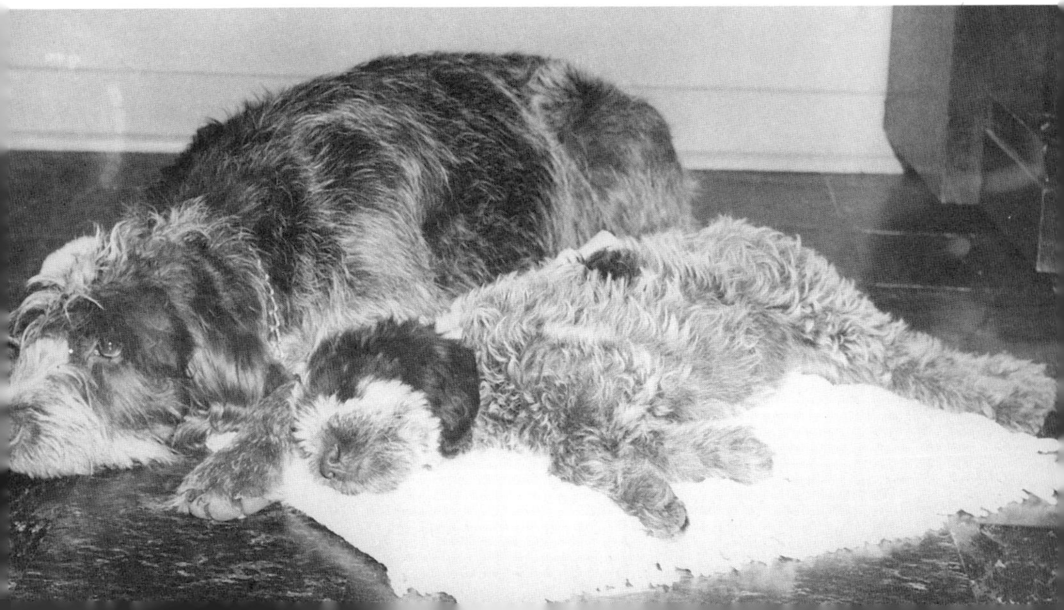

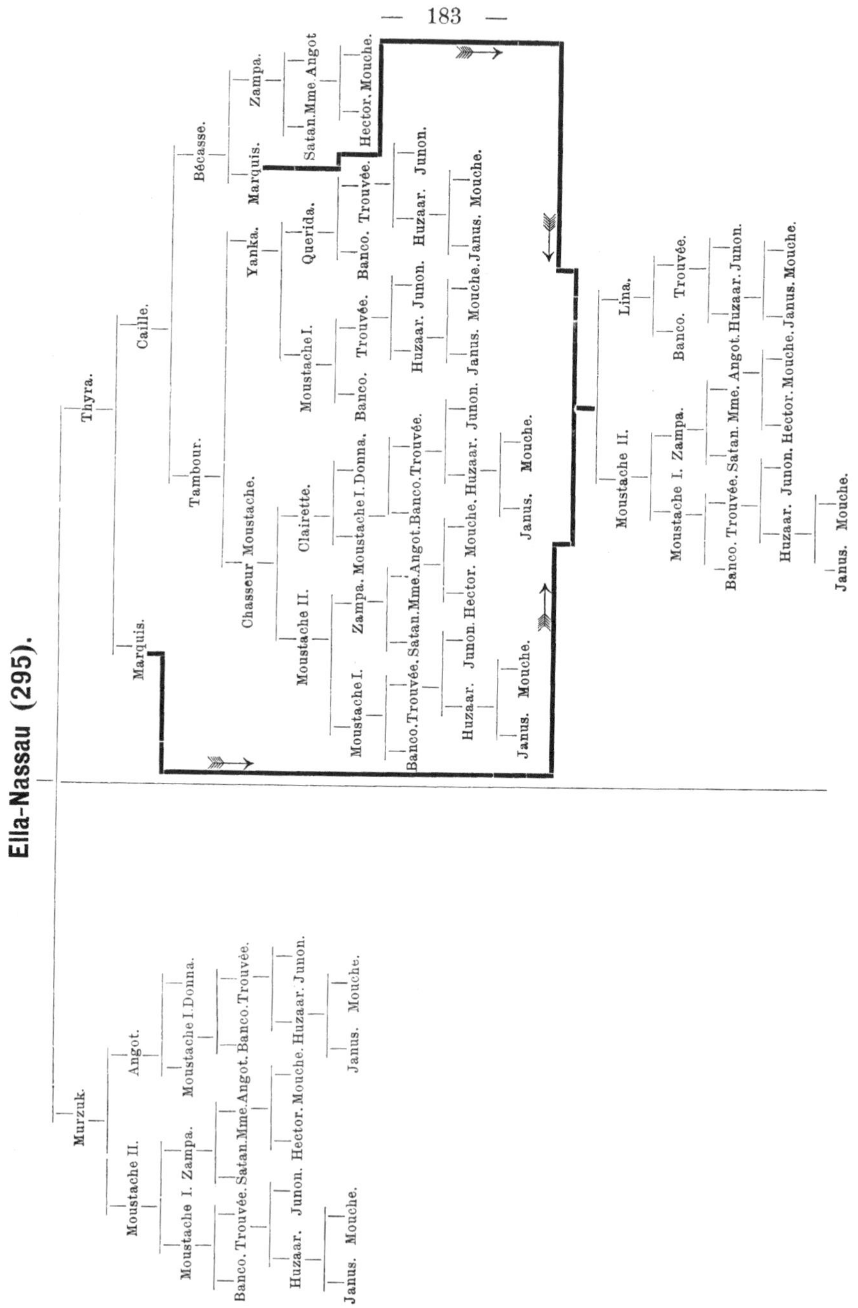

Pedigree from 1890 German stud book (GSB), Volume II. (See Part Two, Chapter 26, for more about ELLA-NASSAU.)

CHAPTER SEVEN
THE SIXTIES
A PERIOD OF TRANSITION

Marg Allen

In the early 1960s General Rogers was president and Douglas Fethers was secretary and editor of ***The Gun Dog Supreme*** (GDS). Marg Allen was very active as a breeder and promoter of the breed. These were the years when she was running ads for Griffons in the major outdoor magazines, telling people who called her, "These dogs just about train themselves. They go into heavy cover, and they retrieve ducks and geese from our fast flowing rivers here in Montana." She was a good sell and hunters bought dogs from her.

Not so many years ago there was hardly a Griffon owner in North America who did not know of Marg Allen. Today most members of our club do not know who Marg was, or what she did for the Griffons in North America. I don't know the exact year that Marg got her first Griffon, but when I met her, in 1963 in Missoula, she had those two very old Griffons and I believe they were her first ones. (See photo, Chapter 5.)

In those years of the sixties Marg bred a lot of dogs and sent them to people all over the United States. At that time we did not have tests for versatile hunting dogs, so none of Marg's dogs were tested. In hindsight, and with a lot more knowledge than I had in those days, I would have to say that Marg's biggest fault was that she loved the Griffons too much—she could hardly ever see a fault in ANY Griffon. On the other hand, who of us is perfect?

What Marg did for our breed was to create and maintain an interest for a number of years. This helped us to be in a holding pattern until valid testing came along in the seventies. Her enthusiasm and love for the breed stirred everyone who met her and was responsible for many of us deciding to get a Griffon. There was definitely a time for Marg Allen, and I really don't know where the breed would be today if Marg had not become involved.

She hunted her dogs hard, witness the photo with all the geese from the Flathead. In the 1950s Marg had a lot of contact with the Kirkelies in Kalispell and they hunted together occasionally. Here's a letter (hand written) to Marg from Kirk Kirkelie, dated November 25, 1970:

> Dear Marg:
>
> My conscience finally caught up with me, so there is only one thing to do, and that's to drop you a few lines. You have been so wonderful about writing me, I'll never forget that, and want you to know I think about [you] every day. I have no excuse, it's just neglect. (Forgive please)
>
> Now about **KADINE**, will enclose some snaps, keep them if you wish as I have others.
>
> Hope you are in good health so you could get out and hunt.
>
> Have hunted some, not much luck. No ducks yet. Am hoping this storm

up north will kick them out. Had a few flakes here this a.m., but it melted at once.

Bob, David and I took a trip up the Southfork and camped a week. Saw some elk. No chance for a shot, but a good time any how. Mack came up later. It's such a beautiful day. If it's like this Saturday will go see about ducks. Mack has a larger boat then I, so talked to him about you coming up for a duck hunt out to the blinds on Flathead Lake. It gets rough out there at times. That's why I like a boat like Mack's. But, I don't want you to take any chances on bad roads.

There are so many things to talk about, so keep hoping.

Two of my sisters are here now. They will be leaving for the coast in a few days.

Well Marg, I hope with all my heart that you stay well. The way you are working on the book, it will be good.

Sincerely,
Kirk

The return address on the envelope was: Kirkelie, 40 La Salle Rd., Kalispell, MT 59901. And it took a six cent stamp to mail it! Sounds like Marg had decided to write a book. Marg gave me this letter, along with many other documents, to preserve for the history of our breed.

In the early sixties she made contact with Bob Ward, which is how I came to meet Bob in 1964. ***The Gun Dog Supreme*** was telling members and would-be members/owners that Griffons were just about perfect and they all were great dogs. With no testing going on, who was to say what the dogs were like. It wasn't too many years later that we did start testing the dogs and found out something was lacking. The GDS came out about twice a year, usually four pages, in the same format we have today.

Another active club member and Griffon owner at this time was Marcus Nalley of Tacoma, Washington. He was very involved with Ducks Unlimited and was a regional chairman for Washington state. I think Marg Allen may have been instrumental in getting him interested in Griffons.

About 1963 or 1964 we began to hear about Cliff Morton of Portland, Maine, who had just purchased **TIM VOM ALTENBURG** (littermate to Barclay's **ARTEMIS** in previous chapter) from Mr. Fethers. And in Albany, New York, Dr. William Milner owned **COSSETT VON LUDA JANA.** This would be the "C" litter bred by Dr. Mintscheff. At the same time Mr. Louis Bueti, a gun smith from Mount Kisco, New York, was breeding a litter of Griffons.

Mr. Karel J.J. Brouwers of Newark, Delaware imported a bred bitch, **ASTRAH**, from Holland. The sire she had been bred to was **GOLO**. They produced **GEE GEE GOLO** (HD2, Chapter 28), who turned out to be dysplastic, but was used for breeding long before hip dysplasia had been discovered.

An active breeder in the Northwest in the sixties was Fred Falk who used the kennel name THREEACRES. He bred a litter out of **THREEACRES NEVADA JEEP** by **ALF VOM NIDDERTAL.** (See Ped 15, **THREE ACRES BOBO J.**)

In 1963 someone in Michigan, only interested in the show ring and not a hunter, began breeding Griffons. The kennel name was VAL DE TONNERREE, and from there came many Griffons with poor temperament. (See Ped 16, **CACHE CACHE DU VAL TONNERRE**). Notice the line-breeding to **GARCENDA'S VICTORIA**.

Doug Fethers bred a litter out of **GARCENDA'S VICTORIA** by **ASTOR V.D. ALTENBURG**, a field tested/qualified male imported from Germany. There were three pups. A male, **CEDARVIEW CHIEF**, went to Mr. Louis Bueti. A littermate, **CRISSI VOM ALTENBURG**, was kept by Fethers and used for breeding, as mentioned previously.

Reno, Nevada, became an area of interest for Griffonniers. **BEAUCOUP D'ARGENT (Silver Fizz x Cisa v.d. Hohen Linde)**, bred by General Rogers, was purchased by John Hickok, from "Shorty" Koessler in Missoula.

During the early sixties, General Rogers made contact with Douglas Hume of Islington, Ontario (near Toronto). Some years later I was to meet Doug. He was instrumental in helping Bodo Winterhelt bring the first Pudelpointers into Canada. He helped to translate from German the test rules for the Vollgrebrauchshund Prufung (VGP, full Utility Field Test for versatile hunting dogs in Germany). Doug Fethers issued this translation in a special printing of ***The Gun Dog Supreme*** (Special Edition 1964 with a photograph of **CORA V.D. ALTENBURG** on the cover). Unfortunately, no acknowledgment or credit was given to Doug Hume for his translation. At least we can belatedly thank him for this valuable work. Doug's translations were the basis for the original versatile hunting dog rules in North America when they were written in 1969.

1963, Marg Allen and Joan Bailey Meet

In September 1963 Ed Bailey and I moved into a house in Missoula, Montana, on Jackson Drive, up in the Rattlesnake Canyon. Our next door neighbor was Marg Allen. Chance - or serendipity? From our dining room we could look directly into Marg's fenced in back yard. On moving day I glanced into that yard and said to Ed, "Look at those funny-looking dogs." Unknowingly, with utter innocence, my destiny had been set.

How could I have known that those "funny-looking dogs" would change my life so profoundly? We had an old Springer Spaniel and were looking to start a new pup and wanted a pointing breed. We had never heard of a Griffon, though we had heard of German Wirehair. The following spring Marg bred her **TAMMY DE L'OAKES HEUVEL** to **ALF VOM NIDDERTAL** and we got our first Griffon, a female pup, **MISS TEMPEST NELLAGRAM**.

Ed was on a temporary, one-year assignment, so we left Missoula that August (1964), with a three-months-old puppy, and headed for eastern Canada, where Ed had accepted a permanent position to teach animal behavior at the University of Guelph. Like many neophytes, we knew nothing about breeding dogs, but Marg encouraged us to get a male and to breed the female, **TEMPY**, to the new male. That fall we ordered a male pup from Doug Fethers.

Remember, this was a time in our Griffon history where most owners knew little about the breed, less about bloodlines, almost nothing about genetics and breeding principles, and *there was no field-testing of dogs.* People just bought puppies and when the puppies grew up some of the owners bred the bitches to whatever male they could find. Joan and Ed Bailey were no different.

So in January 1965 my **HANSEL ZU DEN BERGEN GEHEN** arrived by plane from Michigan. In 1966 we bred the two dogs and in March a litter of 10 puppies arrived. They were sold to hunters from all different parts of the country.

Despite my ignorance, I was very curious about the origin of all the different dogs. Who were their sires and dams, grandparents, great grandparents?

***BEAUCOUP 'ARGENT**, and his young hunter friend is probably John Hickok's daughter.*

This information was not available in the GDS. My curiosity grew to wanting to know what field tests the German ancestors had qualified in. What did all the abbreviations on the pedigrees, like "Pr.I", and "D.G.St.B.," mean? I really wanted to know more about these dogs. Not just the Bailey dogs, but all the dogs I was reading about in the GDS.

In January 1965 Ed met a young man from Germany, Henry Tabel, a graduate student in the Veterinary College at the University of Guelph. One day Ed happened to mention to Henry that he had to go home early to take the dogs for a run. Henry (real name Hinrich) asked what breed of dogs? Griffons. It turned out that Henry's father was none other than *the* Carl Tabel in Germany. Serendipity again? Luck? I don't think so.

Dr. Tabel was highly respected in Germany as a modern day "father" of the Deutsch Drahthaar, or German Wirehair, and also well known among ALL the versatile hunting dog clubs in Germany as a field judge, trainer, author of many books, and editor of one of the versatile hunting dog magazines. He wrote a book on training versatile hunting dogs, which became a classic in Germany.

Well, that cold winter afternoon when Ed came home, he had Henry in tow. The three of us took the two dogs (one just a pup of about four months) out for a short run, and Henry stayed for dinner. WE TALKED DOGS.

For the first time we learned that these dogs of ours were "versatile" hunting dogs. We didn't use the word "versatile," because Henry didn't know how to translate jagdgebrauchshund into English. He simply explained to us that these

			Wisky du Mandarin (F)
		Ipo vom Welleseind (G)	
			Guuka von Welleseind (H)
	Blucher v.d. Altenburg (G)		
			Argus vom Kynast (G)
		Astrid v.d. Michelherd (G)	
			Brinka v.d. Hohen Linde (G)
	Alf vom Niddertal (G)		
			Siegfried v.d. Kruezeiche (G)
		Cato v.d. Hohen Linde (G)	
			Elma vom Barental (G)
	Frigga v.d. rauhen Gracht (G)		
			Arntrae v.d. rauhen Gracht (G)
		Colja v.d. rauhen Gracht (G)	
PEDIGREE 15			**Emir v.d. rauhen Gracht (G)**
Three Acres Bobo J (A)			
			Silver Fizz (A)
		Beaucoup d'Argent (A)	
			Cisa v.d. Hohen Linde (G)
	Bruce's Ripsnorter (A)		
			Theil of Biebesheim (A)
		Nevada Queen (A)	
			Trientje of Biebesheim (A)
	Three Acres Nevada Jeep (A)		
			Silver Fizz (A)
		Beaucoup d'Argent (A)	
			Cisa v.d. Hohen Linde (G)
	Chukar Lady Reeva (A)		
			Theil of Biebesheim (A)
		Nevada Queen (A)	
			Trientje of Biebesheim (A)

			Beaucoup d'Argent (A)
		De Jon d'Argent (A)	
			Babe of Helda's Rex (A)
	Zimas d'Argent (A)		
			Garcenda's Jacque (A)
		Garcenda's Victoria (A)	
			Garcenda's Collette (A)
	Siegbert v.d. Altenburg (A)		
			Siegfried v.d. Kruezeiche (G)
		Astor v.d. Altenburg (A)	
			Astrid v.d. Michelherd (G)
	Crissi vom Altenburg (A)		
			Garcenda's Jacque (A)
		Garcenda's Victoria (A)	
PEDIGREE 16			Garcenda's Collette (A)
Cache-Cache du Val de Tonnerre (A)			
			Bonaparte (A)
		Garcenda's Jacque (A)	
			Milisande (A)
	Rusty of Grand Haven (A)		
			Garcenda's Jacque (A)
		Garcenda's Victoria (A)	
			Garcenda's Collette (A)
	Gigi Girl (A)		
			Stop de Fort Manoir (F)
		Theil of Biebesheim (A)	
			Pago of Biebesheim (A)
	The Hare (A)		
			Trouble of Warrenville (A)
		Trientje of Biebesheim (A)	
			Pago of Biebesheim (A)

dogs—Griffons, Drahthaars, and other breeds—did many different things: searched, tracked, worked in water, pointed, retrieved, etc.

Next he brought us a copy of his father's book, ***Der Jagdgebrauchshund*** (*The Versatile Hunting Dog*). Ed had his German lab technician at the university, Marian Wilke, translate most of the book for us. We smoothed out the translation, with help from Henry. I immediately began using this new book to train my new dog, **HANSEL**.

And it worked! Oh, I made some mistakes of course, but basically I was able to use Tabel's methods, which are the methods of training versatile hunting dogs that most dog owners in Germany use even today.

All the things that Henry told us and showed us provided a wonderful education. He could explain what the various abbreviations on German pedigrees meant. So now we knew something about our dogs.

While all this was going on in our neck of the woods, we were still in close contact with Marg Allen in Montana, who continued to breed more litters. In 1967 Doug Fethers, club secretary/treasurer, became quite ill and Marg suggested to General Rogers that he appoint Joan Bailey to fill out Doug's term of office. I accepted and put out my first issue of ***The Gun Dog Supreme*** in August 1967.

About this time Maurice Packer of Willows, California, imported a male from Germany. The dog was **ARTUS VOM KASTANIENHAIN**, a male puppy, so not field-tested. Littermates **ADDA** and another male littermate were brought in at the same time for other people. Packer ran a hunting preserve. He also owned **GEE GEE GOLO**, who much later was diagnosed dysplastic. He bred this bitch to **ARTUS** and a high number of dogs from that breeding turned out to be dysplastic, although most became good hunting dogs, from all reports. (See Part Two, Chapter 28 for pedigrees of **ARTUS, GEE GEE GOLO** and other dysplastic dogs.) Packer was vice-president of the Griffon Club in the late sixties.

One of the dysplastic dogs from this breeding was **DUTCH MASTER'S GENERAL** (See Chapter 28.), owned by Roy Speece of York, Nebraska, who became one of our finest presidents. More about Roy and **THE GENERAL** later in the epilogues, but here's a letter to the Griffon Club general membership from Roy which appeared in the August 1966 GDS. It is the first time in many years that we hear about breeding principles, and the criteria that make up a real breeder:

An Open Letter to the Wirehaired Pointing Griffon Breeders of America, By Roy Speece

Dear Sirs:

It takes a man who can be a cruel critic of his own dogs, a man who can see without prejudice the faults of his favorites to be a successful dog breeder. Such a man can be a credit to the business.

....Gunshyness is a negative example of inheritance (nervousness) and environment (poor training). Most of the things about a dog that we first notice except for size and color are really combinations of inherited qualities and environmental conditions. It is the inherited qualities only that we can partly control in selective breeding....

Some important inherited characteristics can be almost completely destroyed by ruthless and ignorant handlers. The "bidability" of a dog or the instinct for a dog to point can certainly be kicked out of any dog. These are only examples of bad environment shaping a dog with good inheritance....

Deeper of course than the evaluation of each dog to a conscientious breeder is the study of the family pedigree. The pedigree of a dog should be

> scrutinized with a wary and searching eye. The strengths and weaknesses of the entire family line should be noted and weighed and studied....
>
> For a dog breeder to simply breed a He to a She and then to sell puppies should be considered a crime and a sin among dog men. Each of you should breed for better dogs. Each of you should breed for great dogs.
>
> And now for the final point of this paper. The seller should offer for sale only those puppies that meet the standards. To be able to cull and destroy from a litter you have planned is the acid test but this must be done if you are to improve the breed. Perhaps it could be excusable to sell as "pets only" the culls of a litter if you first made them incapable of reproduction. But you should never allow the poor of a litter to be registered and land in the hands of the ignorant or selfish. It would be bad enough to create puppy factories from select stock but to allow such from culls would certainly be the destruction of the breed as working dogs.
>
> Great dogs come from great dogs. Great dogs are the product of fortunate matings...."

Roy was to play an important part in our club, and with our breed in the years ahead.

Coming back into the Griffon world in the 1960s was Bob Ward. Marg Allen gave Bob a pup from one of her litters and they used Bob's kennel name instead of Marg's, naming this pup **HARDROCK MONTANA TOMMY (Mike von Hessling x Tammy de l'Oakes Heuvel).**

In the last part of the sixties we began to hear more about Cliff Morton in Portland, Maine. Later, Cliff would become our vice-president and in 1971 would spearhead the forming of the Northeast Griffon Club, which is still very active in Maine and New England.

In 1966 one of our new members was Harold Baskin from California, who would become one of our presidents in the years ahead. By 1968 Harold had already organized the Sierra Griffon Club, our first regional chapter club, and in that year Harold and his small group organized a ***field trial***, run according to American Field rules. It was a field trial for pointing dogs, not a field test for versatile hunting dogs. *But it was a beginning.*

In 1967 Marg Allen imported from Germany two female puppies from Walter Geisel's kennel, **CORA** and **CIRA VOM KASTANIENHAIN**. They were a repeat breeding of the "A" VOM KASTANIENHAIN litter. Marg kept **CORA** and gave **CIRA** to Bob Ward. Bob bred **CIRA** to his **HARDROCK MONTANA TOMMY**, and from that breeding he shipped a puppy to Alaska. From all known records this dog was the first Griffon in Alaska.

In 1968, one week before the Sierra Griffon Club's first field trial, General Rogers died suddenly of a heart attack. From my letter to the membership reporting on his death I wrote, "...Without General Rogers there would be no Griffon Club today. He worked hard to build a club that would promote Griffons, the breed of dog so dear to his heart. He always referred to any work for the club as a 'labor of love.' He labored longer and harder than anyone. Since 1951 General Rogers *was* the Griffon club...."

Upon my request, Tom Jr. took over the unexpired term of president that his father had held.

At that first field trial in March 1968, the highest scoring dog was **ATTILA D'ARGENT** (D'ARGENT is the Rogers' kennel name). He was bred by General

Above: ***GEE GEE GOLO****, April 1961, so she probably was around 12 months.*

Below: Cover picture of my first edition of the GDS, August 1967: ***GERI VANTAGE HOME (Mike v Hessling x Tammy de l'Oakes Heuvel)*** *and the caption read:* ***Fall...Early Morning...The Big Sky Country****.*

Rogers son, Tom Jr. (See Chapter 28). Incidentally, the test was held on Grizzly Island, near Fairfield, California, which is where, in the 1990s we have tested our dogs with the Klub Deutsch Kurzhaar-USA (KDK-USA).

Other Griffons in the 1968 trial were: **A.J. VOM KASTANIENHAIN** (improperly named, not from the KASTANIENHAIN kennel in Germany), **BLUCHER VOM BARENTAL, BUFF, HAPPY DOLLY, MATADOR, DUCHESS VON HEDEL** (owned by Harold Baskin), **ALLEN'S LACY VON BITTERROOT, BARON VON DUNKEL, BERTHA, DIRK VOM DOENITZ (Cedarview Garcenda's Mickey x Bonanza's First Lady Lisa), AGATE D'ARGENT** (littermate to **ATTILA), ARTUS VOM KASTANIENHAIN** (who was now owned by T.K. Meredith of Reno), **ABEILLE D'ARGENT** (another **D'ARGENT** littermate), **JOHANN GOLO, PRINCESSAN BRIGIT VON ALLEN, HANSIE DINGO GOLO,** and **HAPPY DOLLY.**

Hip dysplasia came to our attention in 1968. We heard about the Orthopedic Foundation for Animals (OFA) and started urging Griffon owners to x-ray their dogs. The OFA fee was $10.00! The first dysplastic Griffon discovered was **DUTCH MASTERS GENERAL (Artus v Kastanienhain x Gee Gee Golo)**, owned by Roy Speece, and then in a littermate, **DUCHESS VON HEDEL**, owned by Harold Baskin. It was then diagnosed in **ATTILA D'ARGENT**.

At the same time the first two Griffons to be certified by OFA as being clear of hip dysplasia (HD) were **TAMMY DE L'OAKES HEUVEL** and **CORA VOM KASTANIENHAIN**, owned by Marg Allen.

And in 1968 contact was made with the Quebec Griffon Club (Quebecoise du Griffon d'Arret A Poil Dur Korthals), through Jacques Biberon their club president.

In the August 1968 GDS we urge "...If we are to approach the standards of the Germans, we must have regional clubs to hold trials, judge conformation and coat, and thereby encourage a higher standard in our breeding stock. We have some breeders in North America breeding some fine Griffs. But, we also have some who are not breeding the quality we should demand. In most cases the breeders who produce dogs that do not meet the standards do so from lack of experience and lack of knowledge of the breed. Our job then is also to educate..."

In the same issue the following puppies were listed for sale:

Mr. & Mrs. Vince Richardson, Illinois:

FALK VOM WALDPARK (imported from Germany as a pup, not field tested) x **TAMMY'S RAGGETY ANN**.

Mr. Lawrence Giard, Massachusetts:

POP DE LA REOTE (imported from France, not field tested) x **CHER CHER LE BEC**.

Mr. A.J. Taff, Wisconsin:

PETER TUFFY x FANNY VOM WALDPARK (imported from Germany, not field-tested).

Mr. Harold Knapp, Montana:

BINIFI ZUMERF FILDE x GERI VANTAGE HOME.

Miss Mary Busser, Ohio:

TRACY'S MARELU OF CHERRY HILL x **GRETAL OF CHERRY HILL**.

Above, ***CORA V KASTANIENHAIN*** *and right, her dam,* ***DIANA V.D. ALTENBURG.***

Mr. Robert Mitchell, Michigan:

POP DE LA REOTE x **PEARL DU VAL.**

Mrs. John Pauwels, Pennsylvania:

FRITZ HEINRICH VON HESS x **BLUETTE DU VAL DE TONNERRE.**

Mr. James Clegg, Washington:

HARDROCK MONTANA TOMMY x **BRUNHILDE VOM NIDDERTAL** (improperly named).

Mr. Charles Van Studdiford, Missouri:

PLATINUM PRINCE x **TEAK.**

PLATINUM PRINCE x **ZIP**. (See Ped 18.)

Mrs. R.E. Lambert, Alabama:

VIKING LAD x **BON BON.**

Mr. Jacques Biberon, Quebec:

QUICK DU KIAMIKA x **POLKA DU HAUT LEON.**

HELLO DE PORT GIRAUD x **KETTY DU COURTIL BISSIEUX.**

That's a pile of Griffon puppies, and all sold with no breeding controls, no sire and dam field tested, no hips x-rayed. That was another world. A few dogs today can be traced back to some of those breedings, i.e., DE LA REOTE, VANTAGE HOME, DE L'OAKES HEUVEL, etc.

HANS VOM NIDDERTAL *(improperly named)* ***(Alf v Niddertal x Jill of Nally Dale)*** *on the left.* ***JACQUE DE L'NELLAGRAM (Alf v Niddertal x Tammy de l'Oakes Heuvel)****, right.*

***BOB WARD** with **HARDROCK MONTANA KING (Tommy x Cira)**, circa 1966, taken at Marg Allen's home. Next page: Bob with the litter out of **CIRA** by **TOMMY**. On the back of the photo Bob wrote: "First lesson sit."*

PEDIGREE 17
Mike von Hessling (A)

Duke v Kirchdorf (A)	Capt. Harp Grady (A)	Capt. Punch	Staunchdown (A)
			Hardrock Montana Princess (A)
		La Belle Cherrie (A)	Stouthearted Rex (A)
			Kadine de Gagny (F)
	Mais Qui d'Argent (A)	Silver Fizz (A)	Unico de Nadillac (F)
			Milshire Orris (A)
		Cisa v.d. Hohen Linde (G)	**Siegfried v.d. Kruezeiche (G)**
			Elena v Barental (G)
Gee Gee Golo (A)	Golo (H)	**Houdoe v Welleseind (H)**	**Wisky du Mandarin (F)**
			Guuka von Welleseind (H)
		Cadi of Gerbert (H)	**Aras of Gerbert (B)**
			Adickie of Gerbert (B)
	Astrah (H)	**Houdoe v Welleseind (H)**	**Wisky du Mandarin (F)**
			Guuka von Welleseind (H)
		Itanja v Weisenheim (H)	**Wisky du Mandarin (F)**
			Attie (H)

PEDIGREE 18
Platinum Princess (A)

Platinum Prince (A)	Platinum (A)	Grouse King (A)	Elfin d'Argent (A)
			Brynhilde of Biebesheim (A)
		Gold (A)	Trouble of Warrenville (A)
			Brynhilde of Biebesheim (A)
	Grouse Queen (A)	Grouse King (A)	Elfin d'Argent (A)
			Brynhilde of Biebesheim (A)
		Silver (A)	Trouble of Warrenville (A)
			Brynhilde of Biebesheim (A)
Zip (A)	Samson v.d. Altenburg (G)	Artus vom Kastanienhain (G)	**Dingo v Teufelstein (G)**
			Diana v.d. Altenburg (G)
		Allen's Lacy v Bitterroot (A)	Alf vom Niddertal (G)
			Tammy de la Oakes Heuvel (A)
	Crissi v.d. Brech (A)	Erwin v.d. Brech (G)	**Cato vom Kochertal (G)**
			Cora v.d. Altenburg (G)
		Crissi vom Altenburg (A)	**Astor v.d. Altenburg (G)**
			Garcenda's Victoria (A)

CHAPTER EIGHT
1969 - A PIVOTAL YEAR FOR GRIFFONS

Many events took place during 1969 that were to have momentous, positive effects upon our breed. Harold Baskin, with help from members of the Sierra Griffon Club, again organized another *field trial* that was held in March. This time I was determined to fly to California and attend this trial. Looking back with the advantage of so many years, I have to chuckle. Harold and Sally Baskin had invited me to stay at their home in South San Francisco. I accepted with great appreciation. We had never met, but Harold and I recognized each other at the airport. (In those days he wore a cowboy hat, so he was easy to pick out of the crowd.)

The day before the trial I checked into the motel in Fairfield where most participants would be staying. I will never forget the following morning, stepping outside of my room and seeing all those Griffons in one place at the same time. What a thrill. The next thrill was more shock than thrill. Upon my arrival at the site on Grizzly Island I was told that I would be a judge, along with John Rickman of Stockton. I had never judged before, nor had John. On top of that it was a "field trial," and we were to actually judge from horseback.

We just didn't know any better at the time, and we did the best we could do, and as was said earlier, it was a beginning. And, just as important, I got to see about 20 Griffons working in the field and in the water. That was valuable knowledge.

The annual dues in 1969 were $5.00. Puppies listed for sale in the April 1969 GDS:

Gary Whiting, Washington:
DIRK VON DOENITZ x MISKA VOM SCHLEMM KREIDE.

Paul Ewald, Missouri:
SAMSON V.D. ALTENBURG x CRISSI V.D. BRECH (both dogs improperly named, using kennel names belonging to breeders in Germany).

John Voland, Pennsylvania:
BUCK'S MOSE AQUA RANGE x BABBETTE VON FAIRFIELD.

Bob Ward, Montana:
HARDROCK MONTANA TOMMY x CIRA VOM KASTANIENHAIN.

Harold Newby, Washington:
DIRK VON DOENITZ x ALLURE D'ARGENT.

Marg Allen, Montana:
GUSTAVE VOM NELLAGRAM x CORA VOM KASTANIENHAIN.

MIKE VOM HESSLING x TAMMY DE L'OAKES HEUVEL.

Harold Knapp, Montana:
MIKE VOM HESSLING x GERI VANTAGE HOME.

Dwight Felton, Washington:
ALDERLANE TURK x RENA BON ZOR ZOR.

Charles Van Studdiford, Missouri:
PLATINUM PRINCE x ZIP.

Joan Bailey, "Judge," Grizzly Island, California, 1969.

*Below, **AGATE D'ARGENT**, during the test in California. She was one of the high scorers.*

Phew, another passel of untested parents and puppies.

In June 1969 a meeting was held in Portland, Maine between Griffon owners from New England and Griffonniers from the Quebec Griffon Club. A report of that meeting appeared in the August 1969 GDS. Here are a couple of excerpts from that report: "The love and dedication to Griffons bridged all cultural gaps, removed language barriers and spanned international borders at the organizational meeting of the Northeast Griffon Club. On the evening of June 21, 1969, the Sebago Room of the Sheraton Hotel in Portland, Maine bulged with good fellowship and amiable bragging about bewhiskered Griffons and super dog deeds of hunting prowess."

The group included Jacques Biberon (president Quebec Griffon Club) and Claude Rosquin (vice president, Quebec Griffon Club), Cliff Morton from Portland (then vice-president WPGCA), Ed and Joan Bailey, and a few others. In the June 1969 GDS we wrote:

> If enthusiasm is any indication of potential, the Northeast Griffon Club holds it all. A magnificent thing to behold was the stolid 'downeaster' and the excitable 'Quebecer' radiating friendship and unity of purpose and all of it for the best interest of the breed, whether its called Wirehaired Pointing Griffon or Griffon d'Arret a Poil dur or just plain Griffon!

Out of this weekend came a significant learning experience for me. The Quebec Griffonniers had brought several of their dogs with them. *It was the first time I had ever seen a Griffon with a hard coat.* Yes, I had now been involved with these dogs since 1963, owned and hunted over three of them, and had raised a litter, but *I had never seen a hard coat.* But, I was not the only one that weekend, who was looking at and feeling hard coats for the first time. Nearly every American Griffonnier there that weekend was having a similar experience.

Of course the message that we received was that we MUST start breeding for proper coats.

Then later that same month, the Quebec Griffon Club held a field trial near Montreal. Ed Bailey and I attended, and once again, without any notice, I was asked to be a judge. This time, however, it was on foot, not horseback, so that was one step in the right direction. Here's what Ed Bailey wrote for the August 1969 GDS, about this trial:

> Perched behind an old stump, its roots washed clean by spring floods, I could see a 2 pound walleye lazing with the swirl in the clear Richelieu River. Mr. Courville with 11 month old **RICKY** sitting expectantly at his leg waited for the duck to be thrown and the shot. Then the minimum hold of 3 seconds and **RICKY** hit the water. But the duck slipped its shackles, splashed flightlessly across the water and dove—under RICKY. That manoeuvre will confuse a seasoned dog. The duck paddled to shore, headed into the brush up the hill toward the gallery of spectators. But **RICKY** is a clever little girl and she used her nose to follow and she captured and retrieved the wayward waddler. (At this point it was probably good that I didn't understand French because I had done the tying of the wings and feet of that miserable mallard). All the ducks were brought in for a better job of shackling and the trial started over again....
>
> The trial then moved from the water to the field. The weather that started out warm 3 hours earlier was now fast approaching 90. A 20 mile an hour wind swept down the hot bird field and gallant dogs worked. Remarkable judges—Joan Bailey, Raymond Platiau, Jacque Tougas, and Claude Rosquin....followed 14 dogs through their tests. They were a sunburned, wind blown foursome measuring each dog's performance with complete objectivity....

In late June club member Mary Busser, and her sister and brother-in-law, all from Ohio, made a trip to France and Germany. By this time I was in contact with a number of Griffonniers in both countries and had been able to supply Mary with many names. Here's part of Mary's report as printed in the October 1969 GDS: As soon as they landed at Orly, outside of Paris, they got their little rental car and:

> ...entered the race on the freeway and drove to Montlucon....That evening Monsieur Henry Lempereur [kennel name DES ZAZINES] met us at our hotel and took us to his home to meet his lovely wife and see his dogs. M. Lempereur had at his home kennel 8 bitches, 3 males, and two litters of pups. All his adult Griffons looked alike! [Mary was seeing uniformity in Griffons for the first time!] They all had good pigment [meaning dark liver color]..., straight hard coats with hair about 1" to 2" long, and all were medium size. Collectively they looked like one breed....

They then went on to Germany and visited several breeders—Josef Mayer, Joseph Ade, and, in Munich Fritz Wurtenburger (I would dance with Herr Wurtenburger in 1988 at the 100th Jubilee) and finally in Cologne, Frau Paula Pohl. Mary's report ended with this observation:

> I hope I learned something from this visit. Possibly the most important thing was a realization that we must impose some restrictions on ourselves in our breedings. We must stop this "backyard" breeding. I know what a temp-

***PLATINUM PRINCE**, whelped in 1950, photo circa 1966, on quail in Missouri. (See Ped 18.) He was own by Charles van Studdiford, who did not dock the tails of his Griffons.*

tation it is to do this—I did it and I will not do it again. We must be selective in our breeding stock or we will continue to throw out big, shaggy Griffons in America...I now plan to be a very selective breeder.

Later that summer Jerry Knap, a Canadian outdoor writer who had an interest in Griffons mentioned that a meeting was to be held in Orono, Ontario, about a two hour drive from our home near Guelph. We were told that a man from Germany named Bodo Winterhelt, who bred Pudelpointers (whatever they were), would be in charge of the meeting and that the purpose was to form a testing organization for "all purpose" hunting dogs.

We went to that meeting, which was held in Bodo's home. Most of the people present owned Pudelpointers, and a few owned German shorthairs. There were no other Griffon owners present. Generally speaking we were impressed with the concept of such an organization, but doubtful if it could be pulled off.

A few months later another meeting was held, which we were not able to attend, because we were in Germany and France. At this meeting the North American Versatile Hunting Dog Association (NAVHDA) was formed and plans were made to hold a Utility Field Test in October.

During the summer of 1969, sometime after the field trial near Montreal, we met Laurent Frileux. His mother, Dominique, then secretary of the French Griffon Club, had written to me, telling me that Laurent was moving to Montreal, and that he could bring a puppy for the American Griffon Club with him (Most people in Europe refer to the WPGCA as the "American Griffon Club".).

So we followed up on this, found someone who would take the pup, and Laurent flew into Toronto, where we met him. He had carried this puppy on his lap all the way from Paris. We took the puppy to air cargo, where it was shipped on to Ohio to its new owner.

I'll always remember how Laurent, who loved to cook, opened his suitcase at air cargo and took out his white chef's apron and put it in the shipping crate for the puppy. We brought Laurent home, he spent the night with us and we took him back to the airport in the morning and put him on a plane for Montreal.

In the meantime, towards the end of September Ed and I had a chance to go to France and Germany. Ed was invited to give a paper at the International Ethology (animal behavior) Conference in France, and his transportation would be paid by the University of Guelph. We scraped up airfare for me, and away we went, after writing letters to the various Griffon people in France and Germany.

France

After flying all night, we landed at Orly, and went to our hotel in Paris and rested for a few hours. Then Madame Frileux, who became our good friend, Dominique, came to fetch us and took us to one of the big department stores. She had with her a four month-old Griffon, **SCARLETT DE SAINT LANDRY**, and **SCARLETT's** grandmother, **LYDIE DU LINGOND.** Both dogs accompanied us into the department store, rode the escalators, and **SCARLETT,** in all the excitement, had an "accident" on the carpet, but all was taken in stride.

Then Dominique insisted we check out of the hotel and come and stay "at home" with her and her husband, Claude, in their lovely apartment. That evening, in their white Mercedes convertible, the four of us and the puppy went to a private bistro. The puppy was attended to first by the waiter, who brought her a little dish of milk. While we ate our first dinner in Paris, puppy slept contentedly under the table.

This was followed with a drive up the Champs Elyse in the white convertible, with puppy sitting at my feet, and Ed and Claude sitting up on the back of the car, because there was no back seat. From there we took a short cruise on a river boat along the Seine. Not bad for a Griffonnier's first day in Paris.

After one more day of shopping in Paris we were off to Chalo, the Frileux' beautiful country home. There with **LYDIE** and her daughter, **OONA DE SAINT LANDRY**, we went to the field. The hunting season was not open yet, and game was not plentiful, but the dogs found enough partridge to demonstrate good noses, excellent searching, and strong pointing instinct.

We were very impressed with the dogs' conformation and coat, especially **LYDIE**. One of **SCARLETT's** eyes was ectropic, but had been surgically corrected.

A few days later, near Paris, we went to visit Madame Loiseau, whose kennel name is DU BOIS FOLLET. This kennel name is familiar to many of us, because three dogs from her kennel came to North America. **TONIK DU BOIS FOLLET** was the first to come. Shortly after our trip to Europe, I was able to arrange for this male pup to be shipped to John Martin in Connecticut. Mr. Martin, you will recall, was the first president of the WPGCA. Unfortunately **TONIK** was not hunted very much and lived in a kennel. A few years later, when **TONIK** was four, Ed and I were able to buy him from Mr. Martin and bring him home to Canada.

Next to come was **TAQUIN DU BOIS FOLLET** to Jacques Biberon in Que-

***LYDIE DU LINGOND**, Owned by Madame Dominique Frileux, Paris, former secretary of the French Griffon Club. **LYDIE** was Champion Trialer on Shot Game, and International Champion of Beauty. She is a prototype for a Griffon. (Compliments DIM, France)*

bec. The French system of naming dogs is different from the system used in most other parts of Europe, and from the one we use in our club. The French system assigns a different letter of the alphabet to each year. Therefore, if a breeder has more than one litter in the same year, the dogs from both litters have names that start with the same letter. **TONIK** and **TAQUIN** were born in the same year. They were both bred by Madame Loiseau and had the same sire, **PIPO DE VIEILLES ROUCHES**, but they had different dams. **TONIK's** dam was **LORENE DES RONCIERS DE CLAVIERIES**, **TAQUIN's** dam was **OUCHKA DU BOIS FOLLET**.

The third dog from Madame Loiseau was **VICTORIA DU BOIS FOLLET** (**Pipo x Lorene**), a repeat breeding of **TONIK's** litter. **VICTORIA** went to Dick Austin in California in 1972 and she became the foundation bitch for the first phase of the WPGCA Approved Breeding Program.

At Madame Loiseau's we also got to meet a well known Griffonnier from France, M. Henri Mongrenier, and two of his dogs, **NICK DES VIEILLES ROUCHES** and **PYRAM**.

Germany

From Paris we flew to Cologne, Germany where after many years of corresponding, we were to meet Frau Paula Pohl, the Stammbuchfurerin for the German Griffon Club. That translates to "registrar," or keeper of the records. Once we were settled, we called at the Pohl home and were warmly welcomed.

The next day we hunted on the outskirts of Cologne with the Pohls and some of their hunting friends. The pheasant season was not yet open, but Hungarian partridge was open. We hunted over **ALAN** and a littermate, **ATOUT**, in wheat stubble and beet fields, finding more than a hundred pheasants and four good coveys of partridge. Ed earned a "well done" from the others, for his marksmanship on the partridge. They had loaned us beautiful guns for this day. It was quite amazing to me, to be hunting and finding all this game, yet we were just across the river from the city of Cologne and I could see the top of the famous cathedral. This was made possible by the intense game management used in Germany. I would learn more about this later, but that was the reason that we could find game and hunt on the edge of a huge city.

From Cologne we flew to Frankfurt and were taken by car to Walter Geisel's home in the beautiful town of Kronberg am Taunus. By that time Mr. Geisel had already sent seven dogs to the United States: **ARTUS** and two littermates, **BIRKA** and a littermate, and **CORA** and **CIRA VOM KASTANIENHAIN**, all of the same breeding, but three different litters.

The next day we flew on to Munich and met Franz Kroninger, President of the German Griffon Club, and a protege of Dr. Thomas Mintscheff, who at that time was the breed warden. Franz took us that day to see several different Griffons in the Munich area. One was **ARTUS V.D. NEUBURG (Ali v.d. Brech x Doinah v.d. Brech).** (See Part Two.) **ARTUS** had done very well in field tests. I remember him as being very large and well put together.

That evening we had dinner at the Kroningers' home with Dr. Mintscheff and his wife. After dinner the Mintscheffs took us to their village of Baumenheim, where we stayed for a few days. Here's what I wrote about our time in Baumenheim in the December 1969 GDS:

Athos de la Courette (F)
Sing Sing de la Guillaumie (F)
Negrita de Marysette (F)
Erick de l'Apocalypse (F)
Usky de la Veyle (F)
Caresse dite Candy du Grand (F)
Yole de Rascagne (F)
Iso du Lingond (F)
Ueno de L'Etoile D'Heudicourt (F
Yo (F)
Tanie de la Galvaude (F)
Grace (F)
Yockey des Vieux Grisards (F)
Bobette (F)
PEDIGREE 19
Lydie du Lingond (F)
Xola (F)
Nicky de la Broussaille (F)
Ulysse de la Grand Terre (F)
Stella de la Fontaine Cuvier (F)
Yockey des Vieux Grisards (F)
Igor de la Galvaude (F)
Tael de Galvaude (F)
Myrrhe de la Galvaude (F)
Jolie du Lingond (F)
Ueno de L'Etoile D'Heudicourt (F
Yo (F)
Tanie de la Galvaude (F)
Grace (F)
Yockey des Vieux Grisards (F)
Bobette (F)
Xola (F)

Van de la Crove St Cyr (F)
Athos de Ya Ka Keui (F)
Hadjah de Galrande (F)
Hirsute de Ya Ka Keui (F)
Xol des Gatines (F)
Edda du Val de Creuse (F)
Xiane de Viner de Cour (F)
Olaf du Bois Follet (F)
Vickings (F)
Dacier du Vivier de Cour (F)
Uckie du Grand Piquey (F)
Lorene des Ronciers de Clavieres (F)
Atila de la Noi Cado (F)
Cyta de Vrainville (F)
Ardente de Vrainville (F)
PEDIGREE 20
Scarlett de Saint Landry (F)
Vickings (F)
Dacier du Vivier de Cour (F)
Uckie du Grand Piquey (F)
Jody des Zizaines (F)
Xico de Meltine (F)
Elfie des Zizaines (F)
Brigande de Nadaillac (F)
Oona de Saint Landry (F)
Erick de l'Apocalypse (F)
Iso du Lingond (F)
Grace (F)
Lydie du Lingond (F)
Yockey des Vieux Grisards (F)
Jolie du Lingond (F)
Grace (F)

The next afternoon with Dr. Mintscheff's **HEXE V.D. ALTENBURG** and her two 4 month old male puppies, we went to the field. [See Part Two for Pedigree.] **HEXE** is a phenomenon. She retrieved a duck she had marked an hour earlier, from 400 yards, having made 4 blind retrieves in the interval. She pointed some 20 or 30 pheasants that afternoon. The pups made their first water retrieves and blind retrieves. **HEXE** took a 500 yard drag track of a duck and retrieved it. We then visited many Griffons of all ages in the area.

We had just seen 5 hours of fantastic dog work with an amazing man dedicated to Griffons. We talked at great length on breeding and tests...and training.

With the hindsight of 25 years, what we saw that afternoon was not spectacular dog work, but good dog work. I witnessed a man who was gifted in the ability to work with dogs, who spends far more time with his dogs than most of us. There is no doubt that the dogs were good and that they had excellent natural abilities. Today I know that what those dogs did that day is what we expect our versatile dogs to always do, every day.

When you see versatile dogs perform in all the tasks they are bred to do, *for the first time*, it is very impressive. How many of us can remember the first time we saw a dog do an ordinary drag track? Remember? You thought wow! Then over time you learned that this is no big deal, that nearly ANY dog can be taught to do a drag track. So, over the years I've been able to put things in a better perspective, which helps in making breeding decisions. The following day we all drove to the "Brech," Franz Kroninger's hunting lodge in southern Germany, not far from the Czech border. VON DER BRECH is Mr. Kroninger's kennel name. Over the next few days we hunted partridge and watched as Dr. Mintscheff prepared **HEXE** for the Utility Field Test, and Mr. Kroninger prepared **BIRGA VON DER CULM** for the Fall Breeding Test (what we call here the Intermediate Hunting Dog Test). I worked with Dr. Mintscheff, learning how to lay a 500-meter blood track, so that he could work **HEXE** on it.

Later we went to the water to prepare **BIRGA** for the "tracking of the wounded duck" portion of the test. It was several years later before I realized the significance of what had happened that day. **BIRGA** did not want to go in the water, so Mr. Kroninger rigged up a pulley system with ropes, he on one side of the water, Dr. Mintscheff on the other. They forced **BIRGA** into the water and used the pulleys to drag her back and forth across the water, until finally the dog would do it on her own.

At the time we were upset with these harsh methods we witnessed. Only later did I realize that this bitch passed the *breeding* test, though she was extremely weak in water, which probably meant there was a weakness (defect) in her temperament. Nevertheless, **BIRGA** was bred a number of times. Particularly unfortunate for us here in the United States was/is that ALL the Griffons which we brought over from Germany after that time—after 1969—had **BIRGA** in the pedigree, and a lot of the mental instability that occurred in our Griffons here, since 1969, can be traced back to this dog. That is not to say that she was the only cause, but that she had a very strong genetic influence on the breed.

One can see that **BIRGA** was the result of too much close inbreeding. (For a more detailed discussion of **BIRGA** and inbreeding, see Part II, Chapter 26 and 27.)

The two pups of Dr. Mintscheffs that we saw, **DAVY** and **DIA**, were the result of similar breeding. (See Part Two.) **DAVY** was sent to the United States, was never tested, and sired at least two litters. Neither litter was tested.

We learned a great deal from this trip. We got to see first hand how these dogs are used in a versatile manner. And we learned some training tips, especially from Dr. Mintscheff. Now we had a much better understanding of what our dogs were about. Most of all we learned about individual dogs, good characteristics as well as bad ones.

First Versatile Hunting Dog Test in North America
October 19, 1969

A short time after our return from Europe we participated in the first field test of the North American Versatile Hunting Dog Association (NAVHDA). The judges were Bodo Winterhelt, Jerry Knap, and Ed Bailey. None of the three were experienced judges, but we had to start somewhere. Bodo had at least participated in trials in Germany.

There were Pudelpointers, German Shorthairs, and perhaps one German Wirehair. I remember vividly how excited I was, standing on top of a knoll in the rain, sharing an umbrella with Alyson Knap, realizing that this was the proper way to test our dogs. I could envision the future and the ability we would now have to test all our Griffons. The flutter of expectation beat gently in my heart.

So 1969 comes to a close and for our Griffons many events had taken place which would have a lasting impact on the breed in the years ahead.

ARTHUS V.D. NEUBURG (Ali v.d. Brech x Doinah v.d. Brech) *(Compliments Paul Schneider.) Circa 1969.*

Vickings (F)

Dacier du Vivier de Cour (F)

Uckie du Grand Piquey (F)

Joke des Zizaines

Xico de Meltine (F)

Elfie des Zizaines (F)

Brigande de Nadaillac (F)

Pipo des Vieilles Rouches (F)

Yo (F)

Gef (F)

Bobette (F)

Kety de la Fontaine St. Germain

Diamant de Nouste Lotge (F)

Flora de la Fontaine St Martin (F)

PEDIGREE 21

Edel des Zizaines (F)

Victoria du Bois Follet (F)

Tarzan de la Montagne des Moulins (F)

Vickings (F)

Tina de Lasheid (B)

Dacier du Vivier de Cour (F)

Rif de la Courette (F)

Uckie du Grand Piquey (F)

Quety de Giray Beaute (F)

Lorene des Ronciers de Clavieres (F)

Xacha du Roselier (A)

Atila de la Noi Cado (F)

Xeres de Drolibrille (F)

Cyta de Vrainville (F)

Xico de Meltine (F)

Ardente de Vrainville (F)

Wiskie (F)

Vickings (F)

Dacier du Vivier de Cour (F)

Uckie du Grand Piquey (F)

Joke des Zizaines

Xico de Meltine (F)

Elfie des Zizaines (F)

Brigande de Nadaillac (F)

Pipo des Vieilles Rouches (F)

Yo (F)

Gef (F)

Bobette (F)

Kety de la Fontaine St. Germain

Diamant de Nouste Lotge (F)

Flora de la Fontaine St Martin (F)

PEDIGREE 22

Edel des Zizaines (F)

Taquin du Bois Follet (F)

Van de la Crove St Cyr (F)

Athos de Ya Ka Keui (F)

Hadjah de Galrande (F)

Hirsute de Ya Ka Keui (F)

Xol des Gatines (F)

Edda du Val de Creuse (F)

Xiane de Viner de Cour (F)

Ouchka du Bois Follet (F)

Vickings (F)

Dacier du Vivier de Cour (F)

Uckie du Grand Piquey (F)

Lorene des Ronciers de Clavieres (F)

Atila de la Noi Cado (F)

Cyta de Vrainville (F)

Ardente de Vrainville (F)

Alarich vom Mornbach (G)
Blitz vom Bibertal (G)
Geissa vom Marienheim (G)
Caro vom Waldpark (G)
Alban v.d. Brech (G)
Brinka vom Waldpark (G)
Astrid von Malepartus (G)
Ajax v.d. Culm (G)
Greif vom Marienheim (G)
Alarich vom Mornbach (G)
Citty vom Kochertal (G)
Gitta v.d. Brech (G)
Barri vom Tannenberg (G)
Cora v.d. Altenburg (G)
PEDIGREE 23
Boss vom Wolfsberg (G)
Astrid v.d. Michelherd (G)
Dacier de Vivier de Cour (F)
Joke des Zizaines (F)
Elfie des Zizaines (F)
Pipo des Vieilles Rouches (F)
Gef (F)
Kety de la Fontaine St. Germain
Flora de la Fontaine St. Martin (F
Diana v.d. Neuburg (G)
Alarich vom Mornbach (G)
Ali v.d. Brech (G)
Cora v.d. Altenburg (G)
Arda v.d. Neuburg (G)
Ajax vom Waldpark (G)
Doinah v.d. Brech (G)
Arda v.d. Brech (G)

Athos de Ya Ka Keui (F)
Hirsute Ya Ka Keui (F)
Edda du Val de Creuse (F)
Olaf du Bois Follet (F)
Dacier du Vivier de Cour (F)
Lorene des Ronciers de Clavieres (F)
Cyta de Vrainville (F)
Sacha de Saint Landry (F)
Dacier du Vivier de Cour (F)
Jody des Zizaines (F)
Elfie des Zizaines (F)
Oona de Saint Landry (F)
Iso du Lingond (F)
Lydie du Lingond (F)
PEDIGREE 24
Fancy Queue Blanc (A)
Jolie du Lingond (F)
Dingo v Teufelstein (G)
Artus vom Kastanienhain (G)
Diana v.d. Altenburg (G)
Hauptling Laufendes Pferd (A)
Bob's Nevada Don Juan (A)
Viking Girl (A)
Muffet d'Argent (A)
Agate d'Argent (A)
Blucher v.d. Altenburg (G)
Alf vom Niddertal (G)
Frigga v.d. rauhen Gracht (G)
Jauntie d'Argent (A)
Tim vom Altenburg (A)
Tammy de la Oakes Heuvel (A)
Gerta Deufer de l'Oakes Heuvel (H)

Above: 1949, Dr. Mintscheff with: ***UTE V.D. KREUZEICHE, SIEGFRIED V.D. KREUZEICHE****, and* ***HILKA V.D. RAUEHN GRACHT****, Germany. Below:* ***HEXE V.D. ALTENBURG****, pointing a pheasant in 1966.*

Above: ***CORA V.D. ALTENBURG****, owned by Franz Kroninger, President of the German Griffon Club.* ***CORA*** *was used extensively for breeding. (Compliments MUNCH, Germany) Below:* ***ALI V.D. BRECH****, out of* ***CORA*** *by* ***ALARICH V MORNBACH****,* ***ALI*** *was also used a great deal for breeding.*

Below: ***JAGO AIGNER****, a well known dog in Germany back several decades, used for breeding.* ***(Hermansky vom Geiselgasteig x Ida Urian)***

CHAPTER NINE
THE EARLY YEARS OF NAVHDA (1969 TO 1972) PART ONE

We cannot write our history without telling about the influence of NAVHDA on our breed. After the first NAVHDA test in October 1969, NAVHDA was off and running.

In the spring of 1970 we held our first Natural Ability Test at Bodo's home in Orono, Ontario, situated on a private hunting preserve run by Bodo. Judges were Doug Hume, Rudi Lorra (vice-president of NAVHDA), Jerry Knap (board of directors, NAVHDA), and Ed Bailey. We had a big announcement in the April GDS, urging members with young dogs to enter, but none did.

At the same time the Sierra Griffon Club held their 3rd *field trial* in California. They were still holding field trials and hadn't yet been convinced to switch to versatile field tests. In the fall of 1970 the Quebec Griffon Club and the Northeast Griffon Club held a joint field test in Quebec, run under the rules of NAVHDA, though it was not sanctioned by NAVHDA, but was certainly sanctioned by the WPGCA. Judges were Ed Bailey and Jerry Knap.

We did get to see some good dogs this weekend, and it turned out to be quite a gathering of Griffonniers from the United States. Lou Taxiarchis brought Cliff Morton and Carl Wibe all the way from Portland, Maine. At this time Cliff and Carl were "old timers" and Lou reported that the conversations during the drive back to Portland should have been recorded. Cliff just kept talking up a storm, to the point where Carl, in desperation, finally turned off his hearing aid.

These two old timers were just thrilled to death to see all these Griffons, and enjoyed all the wonderful French food, even managing to talk one of the women into giving them loaves of freshly baked bread to take home. Field tests in Quebec were absolutely unique. Here's am excerpt of what I wrote in the October 1970 GDS about this test: "Sunday morning found us again eating, as the Quebec Griffon Club hosted a breakfast on the test grounds [under a pavilion]....Once again we downed red wine, wonderful French bread, cold cuts, followed by French omelets! After that we dragged ourselves to the water work then back to the fields where the blind retrieves were conducted."

That fall NAVHDA held another Utility Field Test. By this time Ed Bailey had been appointed director of judging, and at this test he served as senior judge. Another judge was Laurent Frileux, who had been with us at the field test in Quebec the previous month, and a third judge was Henry Tabel. Fifteen dogs were entered, but only two qualified, due mostly to lack of preparation and training.

*Left: **HEXE V.D. ALTENBURG**, 1969, at the "Brech," training for the full Utility Test, the blood track portion. Shown here at the conclusion of the track. (Compliments, Ed Bailey)*

The following spring, 1971, Jerry Knap (member of the Griffon Club) was now acting secretary of NAVHDA (replacing John Kegel who had been secretary/treasurer, and who now became just the treasurer). Three NAVHDA Natural Ability Tests were held: Suffield, Connecticut; McHenry, Illinois; and Orono, Ontario. Griffons and Griffon owners were prominent in every test.

In Connecticut Lou Taxiarchis brought with him from Maine, his **ROLF VOM PHILOHELA**, Cliff Morton, and Carl Wibe, breeder of **ROLF**. In Ontario a littermate to **ROLF**, **GHOST'S SHADOW**, owned by Hugh Stark, was highest scoring dog for the day, as was **ROLF** in Connecticut. (For pedigree of **ROLF** and **SHADOW**, see Chapter 28.) In Illinois one Griffon was entered and managed to qualify with a Prize III. We started riding a "high," though unknowingly it was a false high.

Important for our Griffons is that it was the beginning of valid testing of our dogs, *for the first time*, just as it was for the other versatile breeds.

In June of that year the Quebec Griffon Club held another field test. Laurent Frileux's mother, Dominique was coming to visit him and would be there for the field test. Judges that weekend were: Madame Frileux, Laurent, Ed Bailey, Claude Rosquin, Jerry Knap and Joan Bailey. We used two judging groups. Again, the NAVHDA rules were used, but the test could not be sanctioned by NAVHDA, because we were not using all official NAVHDA judges. But the WPGCA recognized the test.

Except for Hugh Stark's **GHOST'S SHADOW**, all the dogs in this test were of French blood, either imported directly from France, or bred in Quebec of French blood. An important dog in our history was tested that weekend in Natural Ability—**TAQUIN DU BOIS FOLLET** (Ped 22.) Very important are the scores **TAQUIN** received. He was 16 months old (which is old for NAT—16 months is the absolute limit for NAT). He received: nose-4, search-4, water-4, pointing-3, tracking-3, attitude-4, cooperation-2.

His sire, **PIPO DES VIEILLES ROUCHES**, was a very independent dog, though he had many field trial wins. **PIPO** had strong desire for game and manifested this desire in a very aggressive search in the field, which is undoubtedly why he had so many field trial wins. **TAQUIN** was much the same. He was not cooperative, and was difficult to control. Yet he had some wonderful qualities, specifically his intense desire for game, which meant that he found a lot of game, and he also had great love of water. The problems came in his inability to hunt for the gun, and inability to be a cooperative partner in a hunting team.

A year later, at 28 months, **TAQUIN** was entered in a Utility Field Test in Quebec (there was no IHDT in those days) and scores were: attitude-4, stamina-4, nose-4, search-4, pointing-1 (his uncooperative temperament is showing up here in pointing, though he had a strong pointing instinct.), steady to wing and shot-0, retrieve of bird-1, retrieve from drag-2, Cooperation-2, retrieve of duck-4, behavior in blind-3, walk at heel-2, remaining at blind-2.

Perhaps a gifted, talented handler, with plenty of time could have presented **TAQUIN** differently, or made him be a more useful hunting dog. *But that is not the kind of dog we want to produce.* We want to produce dogs that are easy to train for the average hunter. Most of us are not gifted, talented trainers. We are just average.

At any rate, we only used **TAQUIN** one time in our breeding program, and then realized he was not what we were looking for, despite his positive characteris-

Above, Laurent crouches down with his hand resting on ***SHEILA DE NOREBIB*** *and gives advice to the handler. (Quebec June, 1971) (Compliments Andre Lecoz) Left,* ***TAQUIN DU BOIS FOLLET****, 16 months, retrieving a duck to Jacque Biberon. (Quebec June, 1971) (Compliments Alyson Knap)*

tics. Other people did use him for breeding, and his uncooperative temperament was manifested in different ways in many of his progeny and descendants.

That weekend in Quebec provided valuable, objective information on some of our Griffons. It was also a happy, lovely time with Dominique Frileux, Laurent and all the other Griffonniers. All our happiness was to turn to tragedy a few days later, when young Laurent was killed while taking his mother on a fly-in fishing trip in the wilds of Quebec. When the plane landed on the water, Laurent stepped out and walked too close to the propeller and was killed. The pain of his death is with me these many years later.

That fall, NAVHDA held three field tests: one in Illinois, another in Connecticut, and the third one in Ontario. Jerry Knap was still secretary, and Ed Bailey still director of judging. Bodo Winterhelt remained president.

A fourth test, sanctioned by NAVHDA, was put on in Maine by the Northeast Griffon Club. Those of us who were there will not forget that weekend. It was quite special and quite humorous. There was a training clinic on Saturday, led by Bodo Winterhelt. Sunday there was a Natural Ability Test in 90-degree, humid weather. Judges were Bodo Winterhelt, Steve Babine, Ed Bailey, Don Smith, and Clayton Pilz.

The two littermates, **ROLF VON PHILOHELA** and **GHOST'S SHADOW** were again entered and each got a Prize I.

By this time Ed Bailey and I were working with NAVHDA and trying to promote the NAVDHA concept within the Griffon Club. I knew how important it was that as many Griffons as possible be tested.

Around this time a male pup, **BARRY V.D. NEUBURG (Phebus de Celibuty x Doinah v.d. brech),** was imported to New England and was used for quite a few breedings, though he was never field tested.

"The Green Book"

Sometime in 1971, or possibly into 1972, we began to talk about the need for a training book. With all the training clinics we were holding at Natural Ability Tests, we could easily see that most owners of these young versatile hunting dogs had no idea how to train their dogs. At first we assumed that Jerry Knap, an outdoor writer, would write this book, and we talked to Jerry concerning this. He told us he would do it.

Although NAVHDA was expanding, the board of directors could see that even more expansion was apparent for the near future. The board also realized that there would have to be funds if this expansion was to happen. In fact money was becoming more and more critical. Jerry hadn't started the book at this point, and I remember saying to Bodo and Ed something like, "You two can write this book." They both stared at me. "Yes, you can, and the money from the sale of the book can go to NAVHDA."

Once they were convinced, the next question was, "How can we finance the printing of the book?" Someone, I don't remember who it was, suggested that we print 25 or 30 numbered, leather-bound copies of the book, at a significantly higher price than the regular books, and offer these to members of NAVHDA whom we thought would be interested.

Well, that is exactly what we did. I took on the job of keeping on Ed's and Bodo's backs, to write. I became an expert nagger. They would talk and decide which one was going to write which chapters. Every month or two I would organize a meeting between the three of us, so they could see what the other was doing.

Above, ***BARRY V.D. NEUBURG****, imported from Germany as a pup, but never tested.*

Below, littermate ***BASKO****, who did very well in all his field tests in Germany.*

Once we got the first rough draft finished, there was enough material to work with so that I could start dealing with printers, getting quotes, etc. At the same time I was gathering many photos for the book and when I couldn't find a photo to illustrate a particular training step I tried to take photos, or asked others to take them. We even organized a professional photo shoot in upstate New York, and about a third of the photos used in the book were taken in a studio. I must say that neither Bodo, Ed nor I liked the unnatural look of those photos, but they did the job.

Of course, I was doing all the typing (pre-computer days) for both Ed and Bodo. Once the final draft of the book was finished, I began the layout on the dining room table. My years of experience with doing the layout of ***The Gun Dog Supreme*** served me well for doing a book layout. As I placed each photo in the text I wrote its caption.

There are a couple of sections in the book that were taken, or reprinted from old issues of ***The Gun Dog Supreme***. In Chapter 1, the section on heeling came from the June 1971 issue, including the photos of me and my Griffon, **HANS**. The entire last chapter, Chapter 9, The Down, is reprinted from the October 1971 **GDS**. All of these photos were taken by Ed Bailey, and again the Bailey Griffons were the subjects. Both the section on heeling and the chapter on down were translated from Dr. Carl Tabel's book, for previous use in ***The Gun Dog Supreme.***

Each of the authors got one leather-bound, numbered copy, and each autographed the other's book. In those days most people called me by the nickname of "Pete." Bodo wrote in Ed's copy, "Pete, your name should appear on top of this book. You did most of the work while we had our fun. Love, Bodo." It was nice to have the acknowledgment of all the hours I put in to make this book happen. We all like being acknowledged.

The first edition of ***The Training and Care of the Versatile Hunting Dog*** came out in August 1973. The book did exactly what we had intended: it helped people to train their versatile dogs, and it raised money, a lot of money, to fund NAVHDA. It has been reprinted roughly ten times, and I would estimate has probably sold at least 30,000 copies to date. Because of it's bright green cover it became known as "The Green Book." I still recommend it as a companion to my ***How To Help Gun Dogs Train Themselves***. It is the best step-by-step book available in North America for fully training a versatile hunting dog.

In the spring of 1972 NAVHDA offered four Natural Ability Tests. Virginia (judges were: Bodo Winterhelt, Ed Bailey and Don Smith); Connecticut (judges were: Milo Jones, Jerry Knap, George Adolph, Steve Babine); Minnesota (judges were: Ed Bailey and Don Smith); Puslinch, Ontario (judges were: Ed Bailey, Jerry Knap, Don Smith, and Henry Tabel).

The Ontario test was once again held on the Bailey farm and one of the spectators was Jack Dallimore, who lived in Rochester, New York, at the time. Jack is another person who would play an important role in the history of the WPGCA and breed.

About this time some people imported a pup from Germany, **DON V.D. NEUBURG,** and according to Marg Allen, they let the dog sit in a kennel for a couple of years. So Marg bought **DON,** and said when she found him that he was timid and scared. After keeping him with her for awhile, she placed him with a Mr. Crookshanks in Missoula. The dog was used for breeding several times, and at age 4 he was evaluated in NAT at a test near Spokane in 1974 or 1975. This was around the same time that Marg imported **CORA VOM KASTANIENHAIN.**

At the NAVHDA utility field test in October 1971, conformation evaluation. We used to line up in the morning before any of the field work, to do the conformation. This often wasted the cooler, early morning temperatures, so eventually this was changed to judging after the water so that coats got properly assessed as well. On the left is Joan Bailey with her dog ***HANS****, and next to her Alyson Knap with her wonderful German Wirehair,* ***ARDA****. And on the far right is Henry Tabel, whose dog is being checked by Bodo Winterhelt. Below, Bodo checks* ***HANS'*** *bite. (Compliments Ed Bailey)*

During this period, another outdoor writer had been in touch with me—Larry Mueller, who would become a true friend to our club, and a personal friend of mine. Larry and I enjoy talking and learning about dogs, and over the years we do this, mostly by phone, but occasionally we meet at a field test and continue our dialogue in person. Back in 1972 I told Larry about the Minnesota test and he came. He wrote about NAVHDA and the Griffon Club in one of his books, ***Bird Dog Guide***, first published in 1973:

> NAVHDA is in very capable hands. Dr. Edward Bailey, Puslinch, Ontario, is a professor of animal behavior and is currently the director of judging as well as secretary of the association. Dr. Bailey's wife, Joan, is secretary-treasurer of the Wirehaired Pointing Griffon Club of America and the gifted editor of ***The Gun Dog Supreme***, the Griffon club's news bulletin which the Dog Writer's Association of America voted best of its kind in 1971....NAVHDA president until April 1, 1974, Sigbot "Bodo" Winterhelt, is a Pudelpointer breeder in Orono, Ontario who had been a trainer and breeder of versatile dogs in Germany for 30 years.

Fifteen Griffons were evaluated in these four spring tests. That was quite an accomplishment for us. Just as important were the Griffonniers that played pivotal positions in each test. Ed Bailey traveled 650 miles to get to the Virginia test. John Martin, first president of the Griffon Club, offered the use of his Johnny Cake Farm for the Connecticut test. Lou Taxiarchis and Jerry Knap served as judges. In Ontario the test was held on the Bailey farm. In Minnesota Bill and Barbara Jensen, members of the Griffon Club since about 1968, organized that test. Whether or not these four tests would have happened without help from Griffonniers is something to ponder.

In the fall of 1972 there were four NAVHDA sanctioned tests, plus one with the Quebec Griffon Club, using the NAVHDA rules, but not sanctioned by NAVHDA.

The Quebec test took place early in September with emphasis on the older dogs in Utility. That's the same test where **TAQUIN DU BOIS FOLLET** was tested. I also ran my **HANSEL ZU DEN BERGEN GEHEN** in preparation for running him a month later in Ontario in NAVHDA, where he qualified for a Prize III in Utility at the age of 8 years.

Of major importance for the Griffon Club was the NAVHDA test in Maine that fall. The Sierra Griffon Club in California was still holding an annual trial under American Field Rules. I kept trying to convince them to switch over to the versatile dog system being used by NAVHDA. I managed to talk Harold Baskin and Dick Austin into flying to the Maine test to watch firsthand what we were doing.

They brought their wives, Sally and Joanne. Joanne was kept busy that weekend, trudging through the fields, taking movies (this was before camcorders) to show to the other members of the Sierra Griffon Club back in California. Harold and Dick served as apprentice judges, which put them in optimum positions for learning this new system.

As a result of their visit to Maine, plus my persistence, Harold and Dick were able to persuade members of the Sierra Griffon Club to try the NAVHDA way of testing. This paved the way the following spring for the first test of versatile dogs in California.

Marg Allen with ***DON .D. NEUBURG****, the German import she rescued from someone and resold to a man in Missoula.He used* ***DON*** *for breeding several times.*

This is the Marg Allen that I remember, and it even looks like the photo was taken in her front yard, next door to the Bailey house.

Above: ***DUCKPOND BRUNEHILDE (Barry v.d. Neuburg x Tina de la Reote)****,* *owned by Ralph Nodine. She scored all 4's in Natural Ability, with a 4H in Search. She was Ralph's first Griffon, and a great many dogs that Ralph has bred can be traced back to her. (Compliments Vern Brand)*

Below: ***ULRICH DE ST LANDRY****, owned by Bill and Barbara Jensen.* ***ULRICH*** *was given to the American Griffon Club by Dominique Frileux, in memory of her son, Laurent. We asked the Jensens if they would take him. They did, were never sorry, and loved him dearly, though he was dysplastic and could not be used for breeding. Here he is in one of his two Natural Ability Tests, this one in Ontario on the Bailey farm (1972), entering the water to get the dummy during the test for love of water. (Compliments Joan Bailey)*

SHAD D'OASIS *(Compliments, Brand)*

CHAPTER TEN
THE EARLY YEARS OF NAVHDA (1973 TO 1976) PART TWO

By January 1, 1973, Ed Bailey had been elected secretary of NAVHDA, and also retained his appointed position of director of judging. This can be translated to its real meaning. Joan Bailey now did the secretarial work for NAVHDA, took care of a good part of the director of judging duties, and was still secretary of the Griffon Club. And I had also been appointed director of promotion for NAVHDA.

After much persuasion and cajoling, Ed and I managed to bring the Sierra Griffon Club and the rest of the NAVHDA board of directors into agreement to hold a test in California in March 1973. It was quite a weekend. A three-day event with a training clinic on Saturday, which had to be split into two groups because there were so many people that wanted to enter their dogs in the clinic. Bodo took one group, and Ed and Don Smith took the other. There was a training table set up for each group. They worked all day with 38 dogs.

The next day we divided into three judging groups in order to accommodate the 26 dogs entered in Natural Ability. We were short on judges, but did the best we could. Bodo Winterhelt and Bill Jensen took one group. (Bill had never judged before but, like most of the early NAVHDA judges, they had to start somewhere.) Don Smith and Joan Bailey took another group (I had been apprentice judging, attended judges seminars, and in 1972 qualified my dog in Utility, and was given official judge status prior to this trip.) Ed Bailey took the third group, without any other help. Of course today we would never allow only one judge, but those were the early years, we were spread too thin, and did the best we could.

About a year earlier, before the California test, as director of promotion for NAVHDA, I had been in touch with Dave Duffey, who was then the gun dog editor for ***Field & Stream***. He came to a judges clinic in Ontario and shortly thereafter, wrote a column on NAVHDA, which resulted in about 200 letters to the secretary of NAVHDA. That meant that I answered those letters. One of those letters was written by Joe Nadeker.

So on that Sunday morning in California, at the water, came a man walking towards me with a rust-colored Vizsla on a lead. I knew this was Joe Nadeker. We

*On page 109, **SHAD D'OASIS**, see Chapter 28. **SHAD** was a wonderful Griffon with all the attributes we desire. Sadly he turned out to be dysplastic and could not be used for breeding.He died tragically when someone shot him, leaving **SHAD** to crawl home where he died with his owner, George Robinson. Left: In October 1972, Orono, Ontario, **HANSEL ZU DEN BERGEN GEHEN** and Joan Bailey during the steady at the blind work in Utility Field Test, where they qualified (Pr. III), **HANS** being the first Griffon in North America to do so. (Compliments, Vern Brand)*

Above: ***GUS T. WINDS**: **Sacha de St. Landry (Olaf du Bois Follet x Oona de St. Landry) x Barrie v Nellagram (Gustave v Nellagram x Cora v Kastanienhain)**, during the training clinic, learning "Whoa." In the conformation evaluation, **GUS** got "1" in Coat with the comments: (soft, 6 inches long). See appendix for scores. A littermate, **RINGO VON BARRIE**, also got "1" in coat, with comments: (soft, 7 inches long.) (Compliments, Jim Lohr) Left: **DER JAGER VON SCHMIDTSHAUSEN (Al's Ledaren von Bitterroot x Auben vom Nellagram)**. He was entered in UFT, did not qualify, conformation was "2" (pinchers bite, open eye, too long in back, 2 inches over standard. Coat "1" (very soft, curly.) (Compliments, Barbara Jensen)*

met, shook hands, talked. Again, not knowing at the time, my life had been changed. Joe Nadeker. Well, that is another chapter.

But also that weekend, I met for the first time Rolf Benseler, with his German Shorthair, and Silke Alberts and her German Wirehair. Not too many years later a chapter of NAVHDA formed in Northern California, with Joe as President, and they sponsored field tests in California for a decade or more.

That weekend in California there were a few Griffons tested that would play a part in our breeding program in the coming years. Of great importance that weekend was **VICTORIA DU BOIS FOLLET,** who was tested in Natural Ability, ending up with a Prize III, because she only got a "1" in tracking the live pheasant. Today in the Griffon Club that would not be a qualifying score, as we require a "2" to qualify.

The other dog of importance was **BOSS VOM WOLFSBERG**. When we were in Germany in 1969, Griffonniers there knew we had just come from France and they asked us about the French Griffons. We gave them our honest answers including our opinion that the French dogs had excellent, hard coats, something we saw little evidence of in Germany. They also knew that we had recently brought over several dogs from France.

So Franz Kroninger, president of the German Griffon Club, suggested to us that we do a puppy exchange: They would send us a puppy if we would send them a puppy from our breeding program provided it had at least 50 percent French blood. They wanted French blood, but were too proud to go next door for it. Instead they got a puppy from us clear across the ocean in California. We ended up sending to them **FANCY QUE BLANC**, and we got **BOSS VOM WOLFSBERG**.

An interesting side note here is that when we were in France, the Griffonniers there told us that the Germans were not breeding "pure Korthals Griffons." When we got to Germany, they told us, the French are not breeding "pure Korthals Griffons." Yet by this time, one breeder from Germany had taken his bitch to France and bred her to a French male. This was Fritz Wurtenburger (kennel name V.D. NEUBURG), whom I met in 1988 at the 100th. He bred his **ARDA V.D. NEUBURG** to **PIPO DES VIEILLES ROUCHES**, and the year before that he bred his **DOINAH V.D. BRECH** to a French male **PHEBUS DE CELIBUTY** (parents of **BARRY V.D. NEUBURG**). He didn't wait for "French blood" to come via America. From the "D" v.d. Neuburg breeding two males came to the United States. They were **DON** and **DAGO V.D. NEUBURG.** Both were used for breeding and you'll read more about them. Remember, **DON** is the dog Marg Allen rescued.

We did use **BOSS** for a couple of breedings, but the results were not outstanding and we didn't use him any more.

Following that first NAVHDA test in California, members of the Sierra Griffon Club became a vital element for testing versatile dogs on the west coast.

That same spring (1973) there were also NAVHDA tests in W. Virginia, Oklahoma, and Ontario, and in the fall we went to a new area, Iowa.

It was at this first Iowa test that I met most of the Don Nicholson family. Don couldn't come, but Elaine brought the two boys, Dave and Mike, who ran their dogs in Natural Ability. They are now grown men, Dave with children of his own, is a vital part of our Heartland Griffon Club.

Earlier, in September, a test was held near Syracuse, New York. Luckily—very luckily, Dr. Carl Tabel was visiting his son, Henry, so that Henry was able to

Near Syracuse, New York in September 1973, listening to scores being read are left to right: Ed Bailey, Henry Tabel, Dr. Carl Tabel. (Compliments Joan Bailey)

bring his father to the New York test. He served as an honorary judge. What a thrill it was for us to have him with us. Just prior to his trip to North America, the German government awarded him the Iron Cross First Class for his work for versatile hunting dogs.

In the spring of 1974 there were nine NAVHDA tests: Washington, D.C.; Spokane, Washington; Sacramento, California; Buffalo, New York; Toronto, Canada; Minnesota; Iowa; Maine; and Manitoba.

I've always encouraged ALL griffon owners to enter their dogs in Natural Ability, *even if I, or they, don't think the dog will do well.* Having only half the information cripples us in making breeding decisions. Over the years I've watched people in leadership positions in other breed clubs encourage owners of poor dogs *not* to enter those dogs. By doing this it makes their breed *look* better than it really is. But it surely doesn't help the breed in the long run.

In those early years of NAVHDA the Griffons did not look so good. For example, in the spring test in Washington, near Spokane, in 1974, 11 of the dogs entered in Natural Ability were Griffons. Out of the 11, only two qualified. That's pretty poor. Out of all the Griffons entered in all spring tests that year, only 6 out of 22 qualified and 3 of the 6 only made a Prize III.

I judged in the Washington test and saw all those Griffons, most of them poor, though there was a spark of brilliance in a few of them. I was very discouraged, so much so that I felt like quitting. I remember clearly walking across a field beside Bodo and asking, "What's the use?" It was out of that experience, plus the records we had, that my idea for a breeding program was born.

In 1974 Joe Nadeker, upon the recommendations of Ed Bailey and Joan Bailey, was appointed to the NAVHDA board of directors. That year NAVHDA held their first international judges clinic near Buffalo, New York. Of the 20 some judges attending, at least five were from the Griffon world: Joe Nadeker, Jack Dallimore, Ed Bailey, Joan Bailey, Bill Jensen, and a few more.

In December of that year NAVHDA held their annual board of directors meeting at the Bailey home in Ontario, and Joe was there, coming all the way from California. One cold, bright, wintry day we took Joe and one of our Griffons for a walk through one of our grouse woods and managed to get up one or two ruffed grouse for him.

In the spring of 1975, 11 Natural Ability Tests were held throughout North America. Below is a list of test locations and judges. All names in italics were/are people who have either owned Griffons or played significant roles in the betterment of our Griffons:

SOUTHERN CALIFORNIA (judges were: ***Bodo Winterhelt***, Bob Singler, ***Joe Nadeker***, and Johnnie Shulkey).

WASHINGTON, D.C. (judges were: ***Floyd Shikoski, Joan Bailey,*** George Adolph, Jack Throckmorton).

SPOKANE, WASHINGTON (judges: ***Bodo Winterhelt***, ***Joe Nadeker.)***

PROVIDENCE, RHODE ISLAND (judges: John Kegel, ***Paul Bouchard***, Steve Babine, Don Smith, Gerry Guay).

Above: In Oklahoma, spring 1973, during the training clinic, Bodo Winterhelt explains retrieving training to L Strong, as he works with ***ULLA DE ST LANDRY****. She was overage for the NAT, but Bodo and I took her out f unofficial evaluation. Out of that we decided to breed her, to* ***TONIK DU BOIS FOLLET****. Left below: Bodo w with* ***ULLA****, steadying her in the presence of game. Note far to the right, a live quail in a net is being lowerec raised by an assistant, while Bodo steadies the dog. These two photos give the reader an opportunity to see the e lent conformation on this bitch. She passed on this conformation, especially her head, to her progeny which inc* ***LUCAS OF HUNTER'S CREEK****, who passed it on, and,* ***AVAJ OF IAMONIA****, who passed it on, and they now passed it to one more generation. That's prepotency. (Compliments Joan Bailey)*

'EDIGREE 25
per Heather Hen (A)

- Arapaho of Windy Hills (H)
  - Butty (H)
    - Appollo v Batavia-Dodewero (H)
    - Trix (H)
      - Oscar (H)
      - Zalka (H)
  - Freya (H)
    - Tell (H)
      - Berna (H)
      - Trix (H)
    - Cita (H)
      - Oscar (H)
      - Britta v Hermannsberg (G)
- Mickie vom Freidrichtal (A)
  - Graf vom Griff (A)
    - Tracys Marelu of Cherry Hill (A)
      - Artus vom Kastanienhain (G)
      - Allen's Lacy v Bitterroot (A)
    - Gretal of Cherry Hill (A)
      - **Hansel Zu Den Bergen Gehen (A)**
      - Miss Tempest Nellagram (A)
  - Auben vom Nellagram (A)
    - Alf vom Niddertal (G)
      - **Blucher v.d. Altenburg (G)**
      - **Frigga v.d. rauhen Gracht (G)**
    - Cora vom Kastanienhain (G)
      - **Dingo v Teufelstein (G)**
      - **Diana v.d. Altenburg (G)**

'EDIGREE 26
yoming's Lucky

- Don v.d. Neuburg (G)
  - **Pipo des Vieilles Rouches (F)**
    - **Joke des Zizaines**
      - **Dacier du Vivier de Cour (F)**
      - **Elfie des Zizaines (F)**
    - **Kety de la Fontaine St. Germain**
      - Gef (F)
      - **Flora de la Fontaine St Martin (F)**
  - **Arda v.d. Neuburg (G)**
    - **Ali v.d. Brech (G)**
      - **Alarich vom Mornbach (G)**
      - **Cora v.d. Altenburg (G)**
    - **Doinah v.d. Brech (G)**
      - **Ajax vom Waldpark (G)**
      - **Arda v.d. Brech (G)**
- Juniper Heather Hen (A)
  - Arapaho of Windy Hills (H)
    - Butty (H)
      - Appollo v Batavia-Dodewero (H)
      - Trix (H)
    - Freya (H)
      - Tell (H)
      - Cita (H)
  - Mickie vom Freidrichtal (A)
    - Graf vom Griff (A)
      - Tracys Marelu of Cherry Hill (A)
      - Gretal of Cherry Hill (A)
    - Auben vom Nellagram (A)
      - Alf vom Niddertal (G)
      - Cora vom Kastanienhain (G)

GUELPH, ONTARIO (judges: ***Ed Bailey***, Rudy Lorra, Don Smith, ***Joan Bailey***, John Kegel, ***Clem Walton***).

MANHATTAN, KANSAS (judges: ***Ed Bailey, Floyd Shikoski***).

BUFFALO, NEW YORK (judges: ***Ed Bailey***, Rudy Lorra, George Adolph, ***Jack Dallimore***).

MINNEAPOLIS, MINNESOTA (judges: ***Floyd Shikoski, Bill Jensen***, Noel Christenson).

CHICAGO, ILLINOIS (judges: Don Smith, ***Bill Jensen***, Rudy Lorra).

BOISE, IDAHO (judges: ***Bodo Winterhelt, Joe Nadeker, Ed Bailey***).

HARTFORD, CONNECTICUT (judges: Don Smith, Steve Babine, ***Joan Bailey, Floyd Shikoski***, Art Belisle, ***Paul Bouchard***, Gerry Guay).

Thirty-five griffons were tested that spring. Pretty impressive.

That fall more griffons were tested all across the country in NAVHDA tests. In California **BOSS VOM WOLFSBERG** did not qualify in Utility due to only a 1 in tracking the wounded duck, yet the year before, at only two years of age he qualified in Utility with nearly all 4's, but a 1 in steady to wing and shot kept him in the Prize III category. **VICTORIA DU BOIS FOLLET** also ran in Utility, but didn't qualify. She came back the following spring and qualified for a Prize III. Like **BOSS**, she fell down in steady to wing and shot, receiving only a 1. Her owner, one of our past presidents, Dick Austin, was determined and brought her back yet a third time in the fall of 1975. It was a beautiful performance and she received a Prize II. Particularly memorable was the track of a duck portion. The duck swam to shore where the gallery was standing. As the duck approached, the gallery backed up. The duck came out, walking on bare dirt up a gradual slope, under a pick-up, out the other side and into some cover. Here came **VICTORIA,** swimming fast, hard on the track in the water, continuing on land, around the pick-up, and into the cover where the duck had gone. She grabbed the duck, came back around the pick-up, entered the water and swam back across to the other side and delivered the duck to hand to Dick.

In the spring of 1976, only 19 griffons were evaluated in Natural Ability, as compared with 35 the previous year. Among the young dogs tested was **LUCAS OF HUNTER'S CREEK**, whom we would use for breeding several times. Another one that we would use for breeding was tested in Quebec with the Griffonniers there—**BENT PINE'S BIFF**.

1976 was a year of turmoil for NAVHDA. A few people who held office in the organization wanted to make drastic changes, which we felt would compromise the quality of the judging. Joe Nadeker, Jack Dallimore, Ed Bailey, Joan Bailey, Bill Jensen, and a few others tried to stop the tide, but we were not successful. Bill Jensen continued his affiliation with NAVHDA and is now vice-president. And that was the end of any formal connection of the WPGCA with NAVHDA.

Above: ***SACKY DES MATINES*** *(See Chapter 28), a male we brought in from France, who went to Gary Whiting in Washington. Here he freezes on an intense point during the Utility Field Test, near Spokane, spring 1974. (Compliments Jim Corbin) Below: In Maryland, a daughter by* ***SACKY***, ***CHRISTIE OASIS***, *demonstrates the same intensity on a point during her Natural Ability Test. (Compliments Ed Bailey)*

*That same weekend near Spokane, in NAT, **PLUMCREEK'S TOBI (Don v.d. Neuburg x Plumcreek's Siri)** did a beautiful job that day of working a covey of wild Hungarian partridge. The covey was moving and **SIRI**, who had been hunted on a lot of wild birds, handled them like a pro, pointing, moving, pointing, moving. After the covey flushed wild, the senior judge brought her up on a planted bird, and that's the point you see here, with less intensity due to a pen raised bird. (Compliments George Adolph). Below: **BENT PINE'S ABERDEEN** and owner Ralph Nodine, in New York, as **DEENY** holds steady on a bird. (Compliments Joan Bailey)*

*Above: Dick Austin sends **VICTORIA DU BOIS FOLLET** into the marsh for the track of a duck work in the UFT.*

*Below: **VICTORIA** completes the retrieve and waits for the command to "give."*

***DOLF VOM GEESTE-MOOR**, Sire: **Arko v.d. Culm (Caro v Waldpark x Gitta v.d. Brech)** Dam: **Bessie v Kastanienhain (Dingo v Teufelstein x Diana v.d. Altenburg)**, at a test in Kansas, overage, therefore entered for evaluation only. Seen here just after he came out of the water. (Compliments Ed Bailey)*

Above: ***BOSS VOM WOLFSBERG****, during a UFT in California, 1975, holding steady while owner Gary Clark moves in to flush the bird. (Compliments Joan Bailey)*
Below: ***VICTORIA DU BOIS FOLLET*** *during a UFT in southern California, 1975, retrieving happily during the field work.*

Above: At a NAVHDA training clinic in Pennsylvania in 1976, clinic leader Ed Bailey demonstrates "whoa" training on the table with ***TONIK DU BOIS FOLLET.*** *(Compliments Joan Bailey)*

Left: ***DON V.D. NEUBURG****, at the test near Spokane, 1975, sitting at edge of water. (Compliments Karen Ralph)*

CHAPTER ELEVEN
GRIFFON CLUB BEGINS OWN TESTING PROGRAM

During 1976 as we were witnessing "the handwriting on the wall" in NAVDHA, the board of directors of the Griffon Club decided to develop what the Europeans call the Herbst-Zucht-Prufung, (fall breeding test). NAVDHA did not have one; they had only Natural Ability and Utility. Yet the fall breeding test is the most important one of all, for it retests the dog's natural abilities, *as well as his ability to take to training (which can be translated to mean his ability to take the pressure of training).*

More times than one would like, and more times than one would expect, a dog does well in natural ability, but because of mental instability, this same dog six or twelve months later, under the pressure of training, will now manifest his instability in a variety of ways. The fall breeding test weeds out this deadly characteristic.

We revised the German test rules to fit the needs of North American hunters and the hunting conditions here.

1976 was an anniversary year for the WPGCA, the 25th year of our existence. We tried, through the GDS, to generate interest for club members to get together during the summer to celebrate. But Griffonniers, not being big on this sort of thing, were not interested. Instead, for the first time in the 25 year history of our club, the board of directors decided to meet. They chose the middle of the country—York, Nebraska, where our president, Roy Speece, lived, and it seemed as good a place as any for us.

In addition to Roy, others attending were vice-president, Harold Baskin; alternate secretary (a position created by Gen. Rogers, but no longer used in our club); Barbara Jensen (with her husband Bill); secretary, Joan Bailey; and Ed Bailey, member of the Breeding Committee.

We spent three days together, over Memorial Day weekend. Here is what we accomplished:

1. The beginning of our own registry, which became the Griffon Registry Book, (GRB, which precedes your dog's registration number).

2. Our Intermediate Hunting Dog Test was gone over carefully, word by word, and some small revisions were made in the text for clarification. Plans were made to hold the first two IHDTs in California and Maine. (After much discussion over several months, we came up with our own name for the fall test, Intermediate Hunting Dog Test. At that time in the history of versatile dogs in the United States, there was a need to use words that would be meaningful to American hunters. We decided IHDT would do it and time has proven us correct.)

3. Discussion of our Breeding Program took a great part of our time, and revisions were made to the Breeder's Agreement. (See Appendix.)

The local newspaper gave us a half page coverage and wrote:

> Happiness to a small band of people meeting a week ago in York is owning a really fine hunting dog. The way to happiness, for these people, is dedication; dedication to the improvement of an already recognized good breed of hunting dog called Wirehaired Pointing Griffon. Our city was fortunate to have been chosen for the meeting.

Roy wrote about this meeting in the August, 1976 GDS:

Yesterday, Today, Tomorrow,
For Us It's Tomorrow That Counts
By Roy A. Speece, President WPGCA

For those of us who know Griffons and believe that they are the best breed yet developed for the heel and toe hunter, this issue of ***The Gun Dog Supreme*** carries a good bit of nostalgia [our 25th anniversary]. However a look at the past, no matter how glowing that record, should bring us face to face with today and today leads on to the realities of tomorrow.

We can all point with pride; bask in the glow of contentment when we look back at history. E.K. Korthals gave us the breed and the breeding. Others that followed Korthals kept the faith. Our American club was founded on the work of those people who believed in the past as we do today, that here is a better hunting dog.

But Korthals is gone. Only his work remains. Others who preserved what Korthals had wrought are also gone. The early importers of Griffons into America and the founder of our Club are gone. Now after twenty-five years of our Club's existence we are suddenly face to face with today.

Sometimes a look at what we are doing today shocks, angers and amazes us. There are those who will try to profit from the good name of our Griffon, all the while allowing soft coats, bad hips, poor temperament or a dozen other congenital faults to be passed on with no attempt at betterment. Sometimes however, we see in the product of a modern breeder an animal of such genuine quality that we know that the genes for true goodness in our hunting Griffons are still alive.

So, with a bit of shame and a bit of pride we must face the future. And that is exactly what we who represent you as officers and advisors did in York, Nebraska on May 29, 30, 31 of this year [1976]. We faced the future.

We know that some of our plans may go awry just as what appears to be a good breeding sometimes does not produce good pups. We know that our plans must be culled, altered or corrected just like the breeding programs of a conscientious breeder. But dedication is the name of the game. With dedication and perseverance our club will succeed.

Our Secretary, Joan Bailey, will tell you on other pages and in other bulletins of our look into the future. I urge you all to join us. I'm sure that E.K. Korthals would approve.

* * * * * * *

Let's now go back to the early 1970s, to the beginning of our Breeding Program.

25TH ANNIVERSARY OF WPGCA, YORK, NEBRASKA, MAY 1976

At our board of directors meeting, Joan Bailey talking, Roy Speece listening, while ***TONIK DU BOIS FOLLET*** *watches dicky birds just outside the window.*

*That fall, in November 1976, we hunted with Roy and his Spinoni, **SPINA,** in southeastern Nebraska. Here **TONIK DU BOIS FOLLET** backs **SPINA**, as Roy and I move in to trap the rooster. (Compliments Ed Bailey)*

CHAPTER TWELVE
GRIFFON BREEDING PROGRAM
1974 - 1982

As was said earlier, during the early 1970s the Griffons that were being tested did not look so good. After the test in Washington state in 1974, where so many Griffons did so poorly, I was very discouraged. But, I'm not one for being down long. Out of that discouragement came the idea for our breeding program.

I spent months writing and rewriting, and finally sent off a draft to our officers, and anyone I could think of who would have positive contributions. There was input from everyone, changes and revisions were made several times, and eventually we came to an agreement on the final version. It was presented to the general membership in the August 1974 GDS with the article, "Let's Stop The Deterioration of the Griffon."

Reading over the articles in the August 1974 GDS 21 years later, I see mistakes, places where sentences could have been better written. But the content stands today, as well as it did 22 years ago. Yes, we've refined the Breeding Program since then. But we've stayed true to its original intent and method. That has not changed. So here is how we started out 22 years ago:

Let's Stop the Deterioration of the Griffon
By Joan Bailey
(Reprinted from the August 1974 G.D.S.)

There has been a noticeable deterioration in our Griffons. Qualification in natural ability tests has become less frequent. More dogs are appearing with poor coats and conformation and with poor nerves. There is only one reason for this and it can be summed up in two words—***indiscriminate breeding.*** The poor breedings arise from three quarters: back yard breeding; puppy factories; and from dogs being shown in the ring exclusively with no test of their hunting abilities.

The danger is so great that this article is the only way left as a last ditch attempt to reverse the disaster. Therefore, with little left to lose, it will be as frank and as honest as possible. It will hurt feelings. It will make people mad. But, if it can help to save our breed, a few hurt feelings and some mad people will be more than worth it.

Therefore, let us get right to the point and people can begin to get mad at the outset. Today in North America we have almost no Griffon breeders. That's right. We have almost no people, who, by their actions, are worthy of the title "breeder."

Korthals was a breeder. He surely earned the title. He waited until he found 8 dogs with characteristics desired. [This was not precisely correct. See earlier chapters and Part Two. According to W. Kantz, in an article, "Origin and History of the Griffon," in the German hunting magazine, ***Das Waidwerk*** from the approximately 600 dogs

Korthals bred up until 1886 with his original stock consisting of the eight patriarchs and their descendants, he considered only 65 worthy of being registered in the GSB.] How many of you, who call yourselves breeders, have culled your litters? How many of you have sold puppies when you had no idea whether or not these puppies would grow into honest hunting dogs? How many of you have started breeding with a bitch and/or dog and found that the bitch, or dog, was not producing good pups, and then culled that bitch or dog, and started over again?

We have had several articles in past issues of the GDS on breeding principles (December 1967; December 1968: February 1969; February 1970; June 1970; August 1971; June 1972; August 1973; June 1974). There is no need, or there should be no need, to repeat these principles. But, the glaring question is: why haven't we followed these principles? No doubt there are numerous answers to the last question—ignorance, money, etc.

Going back to the beginning of this article, let's get two of the factors responsible for the deterioration of the Griffon out of the way: puppy factories, and dog shows. It is a fact that we have some people in North America who are producing so-called Griffon pups for the sole purpose of making financial gain. Some puppy factories are even breeding Griffons to other breeds and registering them as pure bred Griffons. Some are not sure which bitch was bred to which male. It's sad, and it's tragic. There is little anyone can do to stop this. Only one thing can ease this problem slightly—that the demand for Griffon pups be lessened. This means less publicity for our breed. One other thing can hurt the puppy factory. If responsible, honest people don't price their pups too high, they will not force the unknowing buyer to turn to the cheaper priced puppy factory pup.

The second factor affecting our breed is dog shows. What happens when a Griffon is put in the show ring? Some of the people participating in the show, or attending as spectators, learn about the existence of the breed, and become interested in the breed. Why not, they can win ribbons.

Who are these people? Almost exclusively, they are non-hunters, interested in dogs only for pets, and/or showing. If, and they often do, become interested to the point of breeding dogs, they breed for the niceties of the show-fad-of-the-day. Hunting qualities are mostly ignored (this includes poor nerves, manshyness, nose, love of water, desire to hunt, desire to please). Even the hunting conformation of the breed is lost. Show breeders will breed for straight shoulders and elbows in tight. This is just the opposite of what is needed in a hard hunting Griffon. The shoulders must have a good slope and the elbows have to be out enough to allow room for the chest, and for the elbows to make it possible for the front legs to reach out. A dog with too straight shoulders, and elbows in too tight just cannot hunt hard day after day. He can gait in the ring and that's all. These things are happening to Griffons. More show people have gotten involved with our breed in recent years. We will discuss how to deal with this later in the article. For now let us remind you of what has happened to almost every other hunting breed in North America.

In most breeds the hunting qualities were nearly lost. Hunter oriented breeders had to start almost from the beginning to breed back the hunting characteristics into the breed. Many breeds developed, and still maintain today, three strains so different they could almost be called three separate breeds: show strain, field trial strain, and hunting strain.

Dog shows and puppy factories aside, what are we going to do about our third factor, the people who produce most of the Griffon pups, the back yard breeders, or, put another way, our lack of real, dedicated, honest breeders? Will any of you accept the challenge? Will you dedicate the next 10 or 20 years of your life to breeding good, honest, hunting Griffons? If you will, there is still hope left for our breed. We have a FEW good dogs left that could serve as a foundation for us, a starting point. IF we are successful, we still cannot stop the puppy factories. But, we could, in time, make it less easy for them to sell pups. This might, in time, make it so much less profitable for them, that they would quit, at least with our breed.

If we have some people who are willing to take this challenge, how then must we begin? First, on the following pages you will find a tabulation of all young Griffons who have been evaluated in natural ability tests since the [first] test became available to us in 1969. We have a total of 104 dogs that were evaluated. Along with this tabulation you will find pedigrees of every dog tested. And with the above information we shall point out what we consider to be important points for use in future breeding plans.

Secondly for those people willing to dedicate themselves to breeding good Griffons, there must come a program, a real breeder's program that will include the following:

1) Cull the litters. Pups with obvious deformities, weak nerves, or other undesirable traits, MUST BE KILLED. They must not be given away or sold as pets. A very young pup that displays weak nerves (afraid of noises, not playful with littermates, etc. etc.) will lead a miserable life if allowed to live. It might end up biting people out of fear or some equally bad thing. The kindest thing you can do for such a pup is to end it's life. Likewise for a pup with severe, obvious physical deformities.

If you think you are not capable of determining these things then call on other people who have experience in such matters, such as your veterinarian, or other breeders in your area. They don't have to be Griffon breeders. Any good breeder can spot these things in pups of any breed.

2) Be financially able to breed dogs. You must be financially able to not make one cent profit. Indeed, you must be able to sustain a loss. If you can't, for the sake of the breed, leave the breeding to those who can afford to do it, and wait until you are able.

3) Have pups evaluated and also x-rayed for hip dysplasia. Charge an additional $75 for each pup. That $75 will go towards two things: one will be the cost involved in getting the pup x-rayed for hip dysplasia. It should be x-rayed at 12 months of age, and again at 24 months of age (at which time it can be certified by OFA). The reason for having it done twice, is that it will save you, the breeder, an entire year of waiting. If a dog is severely dysplastic it will show up at 12 months of age. [Presently, 1994-95, we only x-ray at 24 months, with the option to do it at 12 months if the Breeding Committee deems it necessary.]

The second item that will come out of this $75 is the fee for having the pup entered in a natural ability test. [Well, that was 20 years ago.] If you are to be a real breeder, you must have your pups evaluated. It is vital to your breeding plans that you have this information. *Do not depend on the owner's personal evaluation of a dog.* An owner rarely can evaluate his own dog objectively [never]. It may be their first hunting dog. It may be their 10th dog. It doesn't matter. Very few people can look at their own dog objectively and see the faults, as well as the good points.

By charging the buyers of your pups this extra $75, and explaining what it is for, your chances of having your pups x-rayed and evaluated increase tenfold. You simply explain that upon receipt of a copy of the report from O.F.A. when the dog is 12 months old, you will send them $25 ($15 for local vet, $10 for O.F.A.). [Again, this was more than twenty years ago.] You explain that when you see the results of the pup's natural ability evaluation published in the G.D.S. you will send them another $25 to pay for the entry fee. At 24 months of age, upon receiving a copy of the report from the O.F.A you will send $25 again. This is their $75. If they want it back, they must comply with your wishes.

4) Register each pup, with your kennel, with you as owner. That's right, you keep the pup registered in your name. Only when the buyer has fulfilled your demands of two x-rays and a natural ability evaluation do you re-register the dog in the buyer's name. Why do this? Only in this way can you positively prevent the buyer from breeding the dog until he has x-rayed it and had it evaluated.

What if the dog is dysplastic? You, as an honest, reputable breeder must offer to replace the dog with another one, or refund at least half the purchase price, less the $75, whichever the buyer chooses. The buyer may choose to keep the dog if it is not severely dysplastic, and has proven to be a good hunting dog and/or family pet, and to have surgery performed if necessary. That's his privilege. If that be the case you must offer him another pup (if you will have one available soon) or you should refund half of the price of the pup, less $75. Whatever the final decision, you keep the registration of the dog, so that it can never be bred.

What if the dog does poorly in its natural ability evaluation? First, if it was a very young dog at the time of the evaluation, you should make every effort to have the buyer have the pup evaluated again when it is a few months older, at your expense. That is, you offer to pay the entry fee....

If, after a second evaluation, the dog does poorly, you must do what you did with the dysplastic dog. You offer to replace the dog with a new pup, if available, or you offer to buy the dog back at the purchase price, less $75. If the dog is going to be kept as a family pet (which you should discourage if possible), refund only half the purchase price, less $75, upon written notice from a veterinarian that the dogs has been made sterile (spayed or vasectomized). If the dog is going to be destroyed, refund the total purchase price, less $75, or replace it.

If the dog does well in its natural ability evaluation, and is certified by O.F.A. as having normal hips at 25 months of age, you make over the registration papers to the buyer, and you relinquish your ownership of the dog.

There will be room for interpretation in such an arrangement. You cannot make it ironclad. There will have to be room for honesty and give and take between breeder and buyer. But, nine times out of ten, any buyer and any breeder who are willing to go along with such a plan are going to be honest people looking for the same solution.... [A long paragraph follows, giving examples of defects in dogs and what to do.]

5) Placing pups in the right hands. This is another extremely important factor. As a reputable, dedicated breeder, you must use all caution and all available information to the best of you ability, in where you place your pups. This is often the most difficult thing a breeder has to do—to get his pups into the right hands. Try to pick good, honest hunting men [and women], who have no qualms about entering into the breeding agreement you set forth for every buyer of your pups. Above all else, DO NOT SELL A PUP TO A NON-HUNTER. This is the fastest way to ruin a hunting breed.

6) Owners of stud dogs. Most of the foregoing is aimed primarily at the owner of the breeding quality bitches. For owners of good males which have been used, or will be used, for breeding, the service of such males should be free. This is how it is done in Germany and so it should be here. If a male dog can help our breed, why should the owner want to make a fast buck from it? It just adds to the expense of the breeder, who has expenses enough without the added cost of a stud fee. Any owner of a male that has the potential to help our breed should be delighted and proud that he is able to help our breed. If he isn't then he cares nothing for our breed, and he is no better than the owner of a puppy factory.

Be discriminating in which bitches you breed to. Only enter into an agreement with owners of bitches who are honestly trying to improve the breed and willing to go along with the principles outlined. Use the stud only with bitches with compatible pedigrees. Outbreedings do not produce homogeneous litters. And homogeneous litters of good pups is what should always be the aim.

To sum up once again, we have a chance to save our breed if we can have some people dedicate themselves to the long, difficult, and financially costly program. In the long run, this should help to some extent in putting the puppy factories out of business, and to curtailing the number of non-hunters who own Griffons. To this end, the Wirehaired Pointing Griffon Club can, and will, do one thing to help. It will no longer run an advertisement for our club and breed in a monthly magazine. Our current ad will run out in October and that will be the end of it. This will create less of a demand for pups. It will curtail to some extent the popularity of the breed (always a downfall to any breed). It will be less easy to sell a Griffon pup, so that the breeders will have to produce only the best in order to sell a pup.

* * * * * * * * * * *

Reading this over 21 years later, I've had several reactions. First, how could I have been so accusing, how could I have come on so strong? Second, couldn't I have done a better job of writing? But, what I said then I would say again today, because of a strong belief in the basic principles. Today I would temper my voice with a more gentle message. That article was followed by 45 pedigrees, accompanied with a detailed interpretation of the pedigrees, then another article, suggesting a plan for carrying out our Breeding Program. A Breeding Committee was suggested. Next was a statement that this would be strictly a voluntary breeding program. And a Breeder's Agreement would be part of the program:

WIREHAIRED POINTING GRIFFON CLUB OF AMERICA
BREEDER'S AGREEMENT

I agree to sell one Griffon pup to................, for the sum of.........., buyer to pay shipping costs.

I further agree to reimburse the buyer $25.00 upon receipt of the report from OFA when the dog is 12 months of age.

I further agree to reimburse the buyer $25.00 upon publication in "The Gun Dog Supreme" of the dog's natural ability evaluation (sanctioned by the North American Versatile Hunting Dog Association).

At 24 months of age, upon receipt of the second report from OFA. I agree to reimburse the buyer $25.00.

If the dog is diagnosed dysplastic by the OFA at 12 months of age, or at 24 months of age, I agree to send the buyer a replacement pup if I have one available. Or, I agree to refund half the purchased price of the dog, less $75.00, if the buyer does not want a replacement pup.

If the dog does not qualify in its first natural ability evaluation I agree to reimburse the buyer $25.00 for a second evaluation if the evaluation is reasonably available.

If the dog qualifies in its first or second natural ability evaluation test, or does well enough to satisfy the members of the Breeding Committee of the WPGCA; is evaluated "fair" or better in conformation and in coat; and is certified by OFA as being free of hip dysplasia at 24 months of age, I agree to re-register the dog in the buyer's name at no charge to the buyer.

If the dog is dysplastic; and/or does not qualify in its first, nor its second, natural ability evaluation for reasons of poor nose, or is evaluated as having poor nerves or being man shy; and/or is evaluated "poor" in either conformation or in coat, I will not re-register the dog in the buyer's name. If the dog is not going to be re-registered in the buyer's name I agree to offer a replacement pup, or a refund of the purchase price less $75.00, whichever the buyer wishes.

If the dog should die by an accident or natural causes before it reaches 12 months of age I agree to refund to the buyer $75.00 of the purchase price

______________ ____________________

Date Breeder's signature

(Signatures of Breeding Committee)

______________ ______________ ____________

This breeding was certified by the Wirehaired Pointing Griffon Club of America.

The present day Breeder's Agreement is refined and revised. (See Appendix.) The original agreement was instantly picked up by other breeders not in the program and copied and/or modified to their individual wishes. And when we started out in 1974 we didn't have an Intermediate Hunting Dog Test (IHDT), so there is no mention of it in the original Breeders Agreement.

The response to the August 1974 GDS was, as I wrote in the October 1974 GDS:

> ...extraordinary! To our knowledge, never before in the history of the publishing of ***The Gun Dog Supreme*** have so many members of the WPGCA written to the Secretary regarding an article in the G.D.S. Even better is the almost one hundred percent endorsement of the new breeding program by those who have sent letters. Some of you who wrote had questions. Some disagreed with some particular item in the program, but agreed with the overall plan. Only one disapproved of the entire plan....

That is not to say that no members of the club disagreed. Many did, and some dropped their membership.

The first Breeding Committee consisted of five people: Roy Speece (club president), Floyd Shikoski (senior judge from NAVHDA), Elmer McIntosh (club member), Ed Bailey (animal behaviorist and senior judge, NAVHDA), and Joan Bailey (judge and secretary). In January 1975, Elmer McIntosh resigned from the Breeding Committee, because he did not agree with decisions being made by the other four members. We then appointed Joe Nadeker to the committee.

As many readers now know, Joe's addition to the committee, his many years of judging our dogs, and his knowledge of dogs have been of such enormous importance to us, it goes beyond naming.

A few years later, we changed from five people on the committee, to the more workable number of three, and that has served us well. The change came about when Floyd Shikoski had to resign, and later, when Roy Speece wished to resign. For many years the committee consisted of Joe Nadeker, Ed Bailey, and Joan Bailey. In the mid 1980's Ed wished to be relieved of this work, and Warren Webster was appointed. To date, the committee remains Nadeker, Webster, and Bailey.

When I helped John Martin (first president of the WPGCA) import a puppy from France in 1970, Madame Frileux had chosen the puppy for us, **TONIK DU BOIS FOLLET**. After seeing **TONIK** at 4 months and again at 12 months, although he had not been hunted nor worked with very much, I did arrange one breeding with him, to **ULLA DE SAINT LANDRY**. This breeding produced **LUCAS OF HUNTER'S CREEK**, who we would use three times in our Breeding Program. In order for this breeding to take place, I had to pay the stud fee out of my own pocket.

The "L" OF HUNTER'S CREEK litter was named by using the French system, because both parents had come from France. A different letter of the alphabet is assigned to each year, as mentioned earlier, so all dogs born in 1975 had to have a name beginning with "L". However, this was the only litter produced by this breeder. The results of the litter were very mixed. **LUCAS** was entered in two NATs and received Prize II in each. A female, **LADY COCO OF HUNTER'S CREEK,** was also entered twice and received Prize III each time. Three others were entered once and none qualified. One due to Water, another due to Tracking, and the third due to Temperament affecting its performance throughout. A sixth dog died before it could be tested. So this turned out to be a very mixed litter. Nonetheless, as in other cases, we used **LUCAS** because we had no other dogs to use, and he did transmit positive qualities to his get (progeny). (See Pedigree in Chapter 28.)

In 1975, after Ed Bailey and I had **TONIK** with us, we discovered he was a delight to own and once we exposed him to wild birds in Nebraska he became a pleasure to hunt over. We did use him for a few more breedings, but unfortunately he died prematurely in his sixth year.

During the spring tests of 1975 we started evaluating dogs who were not entered in the test, but were present at the test grounds, for Conformation, Coat, and Temperament. Shortly thereafter, we gave up on this idea, as it was just not feasible. However, a detailed report follows regarding one dog that was evaluated during the short time we were doing this, because the information gained as a result of the evaluation is important.

The dog was **JUNIPER HEATHER HEN.** Her temperament was described by the judges as "shy of strange people and other dogs." What was not said was that she bit the judge when he tried to look in her mouth. Unfortunately she was bred three times, so this mental instability was passed on to many of her get—and has shown up several generations down the road.

The first litter, sired by **DON V.D. NEUBURG**, tested with a high percentage qualifying in NAT. One dog, **WYOMING'S LUCKY**, was tested in NAT at five months. The scores were low and he did not qualify. But, five months is just too young. He was run again when he was 13 months, in two tests. The first one he did poorly with a 2 in Nose, and a 0 in Tracking. The second test he got a 2 in Tracking, the rest were 4s, and a Prize II. Even in his five months test, he did poorly in Tracking, with only a 1.

A littermate, **SUNNY BRANCHES BEAU BROKK**, received a Prize III in NAT, with a 1 in Tracking, which today would not be a qualifying score. Most importantly, *the entire litter tested poorly in Tracking.*

Often one can trace a temperament weakness in dogs that do poorly in Tracking. Sometimes it's because the dog is uncooperative, sometimes because the dog is too independent (a part of being uncooperative), sometimes the dog is immature, and sometimes it's due to the dog being hyper. It's often a lack of ability to *concentrate*, which can come from being hyper, too independent, too immature, and so on. In this particular case, based on available information, it looks like it traces back to the mental instability of the dam, **JUNIPER HEATHER'S HEN**.

In the second litter out of this dam, sired by **FROSTY'S IMAGE VOM TANA**, only one dog was tested in NAT, at 26 months of age, which is 10 months over the maximum age allowed for qualification. The dog received Nose-3, Search-3, Water-3, Pointing-4, Tracking-2, Desire to Work [Attitude]-3, Cooperation-3. The eyes were ectropic, and temperament was noted as: fear biter. (See appendix.)

The third litter out of this bitch was sired by **DIRK VON MEIRLOH**, and no dogs from the breeding were ever evaluated in any field test.

Two males from the first litter went on to test in Utility. In **WYOMING'S LUCKY's** first attempt he didn't qualify due to a 0 in Retrieve of Dragged Dead Game. In his second attempt, he qualified with a Prize III, due to only a 2 in Search. In his third attempt he did not qualify, due to low scores in several categories. This may have been at the time when the dog acquired a new owner.

SUNNY BRANCHES BEAU BROKK was entered in UFT six times. The first time he was four years old and did not qualify due to a 1 in Tracking the Duck.

PEDIGREE 27
Dirk von Meirloh (A)

- Kentucky von Griff (A)
  - Dago v.d. Neuburg (G)
    - **Arko v.d. Culm (G)**
      - **Caro vom Waldpark (G)**
      - **Gitta v.d. Brech (G)**
    - **Bessie vom Kastanienhain (G)**
      - **Dingo v Teufelstein (G)**
      - **Diana v.d. Altenburg (G)**
  - Anna of Pleasant Hill (A)
    - Tracys Marelu of Cherry Hill (A)
      - Artus vom Kastanienhain (G)
      - Allen's Lacy v Bitterroot (A)
    - Gretal of Cherry Hill (A)
      - **Hansel Zu Den Bergen Gehen (A)**
      - Miss Tempest Nellagram (A)
- Awatobi of Windy Hills (H)
  - Butty (H)
    - Appollo v Batavia-Dodewero (H)
    - Trix (H)
      - Oscar (H)
      - Zalka (H)
  - Freya (H)
    - Tell (H)
      - Berna (H)
      - Trix (H)
    - Cita (H)
      - Oscar (H)
      - Britta v Hermannsberg (G)

PEDIGREE 28
Rico von Malheur (A)

- Frosty's Image Vom Tana (A)
  - Falk vom Waldpark (G)
    - **Ali v.d. Brech (G)**
      - **Alarich vom Mornbach (G)**
      - **Cora v.d. Altenburg (G)**
    - **Brinka vom Waldpark (G)**
      - **Alban v.d. Brech (G)**
      - **Astrid von Malepartus (G)**
  - Tammy's Raggety Ann (A)
    - Alf vom Niddertal (G)
      - **Blucher v.d. Altenburg (G)**
      - **Frigga v.d. rauhen Gracht (G)**
    - Tammy de la Oakes Heuvel (A)
      - Tim Vom Altenburg (A)
      - Gerta Deufer de l'Oakes Heuvel (H)
- Juniper Heather Hen (A)
  - Arapaho of Windy Hills (H)
    - Butty (H)
      - Apollo v Batavia-Dodewero (H)
      - Trix (H)
    - Freya (H)
      - Tell (H)
      - Cita (H)
  - Mickie vom Freidrichtal (A)
    - Graf vom Griff (A)
      - Tracys Marelu of Cherry Hill (A)
      - Gretal of Cherry Hill (A)
    - Auben vom Nellagram (A)
      - Alf vom Niddertal (G)
      - Cora vom Kastanienhain (G)

PEDIGREE 29
Dusty Hills Dandy (A)

Don v.d. Neuburg (G)

Pipo des Vieilles Rouches (F)

Joke des Zizaines

Dacier du Vivier de Cour (F)

Elfie des Zizaines (F)

Kety de la Fontaine St. Germain

Gef (F)

Flora de la Fontaine St Martin (F)

Arda v.d. Neuburg (G)

Ali v.d. Brech (G)

Alarich vom Mornbach (G)

Cora v.d. Altenburg (G)

Doinah v.d. Brech (G)

Ajax vom Waldpark (G)

Arda v.d. Brech (G)

Bent Pine's Alda (A)

Taquin du Bois Follet (F)

Pipo des Vieilles Rouches (F)

Joke des Zizaines

Kety de la Fontaine St. Germain

Ouchka du Bois Follet (F)

Hirsute de Ya Ka Keui (F)

Lorene des Ronciers de Clavieres (F)

Bent Pine's Brigette (A)

Barry v.d. Neuburg (G)

Phebus de Celibuty (F)

Doinah v.d. Brech (G)

Tina de la Reote (A)

Popy de la Reote (F)

Popeline de la Reote (F)

PEDIGREE 30
Anna Ashview Karenina (A)

Boss vom Wolfsberg (G)

Ajax v.d. Culm (G)

Caro vom Waldpark (G)

Blitz vom Bibertal (G)

Brinka vom Waldpark (G)

Gitta v.d. Brech (G)

Alarich vom Mornbach (G)

Cora v.d. Altenburg (G)

Diana v.d. Neuburg (G)

Pipo des Vieilles Rouches (F)

Joke des Zizaines

Kety de la Fontaine St. Germain

Arda v.d. Neuburg (G)

Ali v.d. Brech (G)

Doinah v.d. Brech (G)

Birchwoods Manor's Inga Igiture (A)

Dolf v Geeste-Moor (G)

Arko v.d. Culm (G)

Caro vom Waldpark (G)

Gitta v.d. Brech (G)

Bessie vom Kastanienhain (G)

Dingo v Teufelstein (G)

Diana v.d. Altenburg (G)

Birchwood Manor's Melissa (A)

Alf vom Niddertal (G)

Blucher v.d. Altenburg (G)

Frigga v.d. rauhen Gracht (G)

Geri Vantage Home (A)

Mike von Hessling (A)

Tammy de la Oakes Heuvel (A)

Above: ***JUNIPER HEATHER HEN****, 1975 at the test in Idaho where she was evaluated by Joe Nadeker and other judges. Notice the nervous yawn, typical of any mentally unstable dog in a stressed situation.(Compliments Ed Bailey) Below: From the litter sired by* ***DON, SUNNY BRANCH'S BEAU BROKK****. (Compliments, owner, Kurt Sundquist)*

***WYOMING'S LUCKY**, sitting on his owner,Dale Mackenzie, at the test in Idaho. (Compliments Ed Bailey) Left: **LUCKY** quite a few years later, on point, at a test in Michigan in 1980, when he had a new owner, Edd Rinehart. (Compliments Joan Bailey) Despite all the genetic reasons why **LUCKY** should not have been used for breeding, he was a nice dog and well liked by a number of people, including me.*

A few months later he received a Prize II. In the remaining four UFT he received: age 5, Prize II; age 6, Prize II; age 6, Prize I; and age 8, Prize III. (See Appendix for complete tabulation of test results.)

And in that same spring of 1975 the February GDS published the following from our president, Roy Speece:

People Count Too: Let's Meet the Challenge
By Roy Speece

It takes something in addition to good breeding stock to produce a great line of dogs. No matter how good the breeding stock, no matter how fancy the pedigree, any breed or strain of dog will run down and deteriorate unless we have this extra something. The extra something, the extra ingredient that I am writing about comes from people: good people.

Every breed of dog in existence today has profited greatly, or has its very beginning with a dedicated master breeder or group of dedicated master breeders. The key to any fine strain within a breed or even any fine individual hunting dog is the dedication of the people involved.

To cull undesirable dogs is a must. To establish high standards of excellence is a must. To study pedigrees, to field test, to use those facts of science available and to seek and to use the advice of experts; these things are all a must. The proper use of these tools then is where dedicated people come into the program. People count too whether giving or accepting advice.

Starting about one hundred years ago with master breeder E.K. Korthals, our Wirehaired Pointing Griffons have been blessed by the interest of dedicated people. This writing is not intended as a review of Griffon history nor is it the intent to list all of the dedicated people who have contributed to our breed. But in modern times the Bob Wards and the General Rogers typify the kind of dedication that has kept ours a top notch breed for the shoe leather hunter.

Very recently in the history of our breed we have added a new dimension, a new tool for the use of dedicated breeders large and small. This tool is the available opinion of a group of interested people that our organization has chosen to call the "Breeding Committee."

If I were going to breed a bitch or buy a puppy it just seems reasonable to me to study the advice of other interested people. The Breeding Committee can be another valuable tool; valuable for the breeder, valuable for the buyer and a definite asset to the advancement of the qualities of the breed.

A new idea being explored now is the advisability of our club to establish our own National Griffon Stud Book. Certainly there are distinct advantages in such things as dedication and control in a National Stud Book approach that we have not enjoyed through A.K.C. registration. The idea does have merit and should have the studied consideration of all interested Griffon fanciers. It should only be done if you and I can better serve our chosen breed as dedicated people.

Good dogs? You bet But good dogs don't just happen. Good dogs come from dedicated people. People count too: Let's meet the challenge.

Above: Another littermate to ***LUCKY*** *and* ***BROKK, ALEC VON RIPPOFF****, at the same Idaho test. Below:* ***DIRK VON MEIERLOH****, another dog at that test in 1975. (Compliments Ed Bailey)*

CHAPTER THIRTEEN
FIRST INTERMEDIATE HUNTING DOG TESTS - MAINE and CALIFORNIA

The first test was held in Maine at Merrymeeting Bay near Brunswick, in September 1976. It was very successful and well received by all those participating, though out of the seven dogs entered none qualified. The second test was in October in California, put on by the Sierra Griffon Club, and none of the three dogs entered there qualified either! All of the ten dogs entered in the two tests received a zero in Retrieve of Dragged Dead Game. (This is strictly a retrieving test and requires prior training. Obviously none of us had done our "homework.") And so it goes. But, it was a good beginning for us, a start to see that our dogs would be tested in this critical phase of their development.

It was also the beginning of our own testing program. We followed up in the spring of 1977 with four tests, where we offered both Natural Ability Test (NAT) and Intermediate Hunting Dog Test (IHDT) in California, Nebraska, Michigan, and upstate New York. That was the first year that Joe Nadeker, with the help of members from the Sierra Griffon Club began putting on a test near his home town of Redding, California, each spring.

That year, a month or two before the spring test near Rochester, New York, a man by the name of John Lundberg from New Jersey, wrote me, asking for information on Griffons. I sent him a flyer for the Rochester test. As test weekends go, it was one of the worst in my memory. It rained all weekend and it was cold. On Saturday most of us were wet through by noontime. What saved us—at least saved me—was that someone took all our wet clothing to a nearby laundromat and threw everything into a couple of dryers. It was heaven to put on those warm, dry coats and gloves.

We had with us that weekend, two of our Griffons, **TONIK DU BOIS FOLLET** and a young female about 12 months old, **ADI DE LA COTE**. John and Bonnie Lundberg drove all the way from New Jersey and stayed for the two days. When they returned home, John called and said he wanted a Griffon and would be joining the club. What sold him were our two dogs **TONIK** and **ADI.** That's what he was looking for, he said. Well, as you shall see further on, John eventually ended up as a judge and breeder, and as an outstanding president of our club.

1976 was also the year that John Falk's "***The Complete Guide To Bird Dog Training***," was published, in which John did a great service to Griffons. The book brought a lot of new members to our club (and the newer edition still does today), people who were serious hunters, looking for our kind of dogs.

At the end of 1976 we had an election. The next three-year term—1977 through 1979—would have Roy Speece re-elected as president, and Harold Baskin as vice-president again. Roy had wanted a white dog to be able to see it more easily in the thick Nebraska brush. He couldn't find a white Griffon at the time, though they do exist, so he got the Spinoni and was teased ever after.

Left: At the first IHDT, Merrymeeting Bay, Maine, September 1976, ***ROLF VOM PHILOHELA*** *makes a nice retrieve to owner Lou Taxiarchis. Below: One month earlier, with the Quebec Griffon Club,* ***TAQUIN DU BOIS FOLLET*** *makes his usual impressive water entry, on his way to retrieve a duck from deep water during a UFT. (Compliments Joan Bailey)*

In the spring of 1977 the results of the spring tests in NAT were disappointing, and even worse in intermediate IHDT. The "D" OF DUSTY HILLS litter was particularly disappointing. What went wrong? On paper it looked good at the time. There was line breeding to what we thought were excellent dogs: **PIPO DE VIEILLES ROUCHES** and two littermates **ARDA** and **ALI V.D. BRECH**.

There are several things we know now, that we didn't know then. That **PIPO** had a tendency to throw dogs that were independent, though they had strong desire for game contact. And that too many dogs from the "A" V.D. BRECH litter were used too often for close inbreeding. And although those inbreedings are back many generations, they still exert negative influence today. (See Part Two.) And both males from Germany, **DON V.D. NEUBURG**, and **BARRY V.D. NEUBURG**, though from what appeared to be strong genetic outcrosses, *had not been field tested.* They had been imported as pups by individuals who were not part of our Breeding Program and the dogs simply were not tested. We did get to look at **DON** when he was four years old. He was brought to a test in the Northwest, and one of the judges got to observe him in field work. No faults were seen, but much could have been masked by then.

Given all that, plus the questionable dogs at the bottom of the pedigree, the DE LA REOTE dogs (which were strictly from show stock), in hind-sight, it was a far too risky combination.

Also disappointing was the "A" OF ASHVIEW litter. Looking at that pedigree back in the third and fourth generation, you see the same old thing: line breeding to the "A" V.D. BRECH line through **GITTA V.D. BRECH** (repeat breeding of "A", so same blood)—to what we now know are weaknesses. **BOSS** had tested well, but he was carrying risky stuff (too much close inbreeding of the "A" V.D. BRECH dogs). The Bitch, **INGA IGITURE** had not been field-tested. Her sire, **DOLF V GEESTEMOOR**, had been imported as a pup in 1968 and had not been tested in NAT as a young dog. He was tested later in NAT, for evaluation only, because he was over the age limit and received all 4s except for a 3 in Search. The DUCKPOND "D" litter was not good either. There are similarities in this pedigree to both the "A" OF DUSTY HILLS, and "A" OF ASHVIEW. In this DUCKPOND litter, the dam is a littermate to the DUSTY HILLS dam, so the same problem exists there. And on the sire's side, there is line breeding to **PIPO**, through **TAQUIN DU BOIS FOLLET**, the uncooperative dog we spoke of much earlier.

Those four litters represented the dogs from the Breeding Program for that year. And that spring we also tested 12 dogs in the new IHDT and only 2 qualified.

Once More To Wolferszell

In the fall of 1977, eight years after our first trip to Germany, Ed and I, and Joe and Klara Nadeker made a visit to Wolferszell in Germany, to the German Griffon Club fall test. Following the test, Ed and I went on to France for a visit with Dominique Frileux and her family.

Landing in Frankfurt we met with Joe and Rolf Benseler, both of whom had preceded us by a week or two. They had just returned from attending a special international field test for German Shorthairs. We spent some hours discussing that test. Rolf left for home and a few days later we boarded the train and headed for Donauworth, the home of Dr. Mintscheff and his wife. It was a happy reunion with the Mintscheffs and **HEXE**, now 12 years old.

PEDIGREE 31
Duckpond Dirkael (A)

Dacier du Vivier de Cour (F)
Joke des Zizaines
Elfie des Zizaines (F)
Pipo des Vieilles Rouches (F)
Gef (A)
Kety de la Fontaine St. Germain
Flora de la Fontaine St. Martin (F)
Tonik du Bois Follet (F)
Vickings (F)
Dacier du Vivier de Cour (F)
Uckie du Grand Piquey (F)
Lorene des Ronciers de Clavieres (F)
Atila de la Noi Cado (F)
Cyta de Vrainville (F)
Ardente de Vrainville (F)

Joke des Zizaines
Pipo des Vieilles Rouches (F)
Kety de la Fontaine St. Germain
Taquin du Bois Follet (F)
Hirsute de Ya Ka Keui (F)
Ouchka du Bois Follet (F)
Lorene des Ronciers de Clavieres (F)
Bent Pine's Aberdeen (A)
Phebus de Celibuty (F)
Barry v.d. Neuburg (G)
Doinah v.d. Brech (G)
Bent Pine's Brigette (A)
Popy de la Reote (F)
Tina de la Reote (A)
Popeline de la Reote (F)

PEDIGREE 32
Anka vom Fuchsburg (G)

Nick des Vieilles Rouches (F)
Pyram (F)
Jasmine de l'Ascencion (F)
Eik v.d. Neuburg (G)
Ali v.d. Brech (G)
Arda v.d. Neuburg (G)
Doinah v.d. Brech (G)
Gotz vom Bibertal (G)
Blitz vom Bibertal (G)
Caro vom Waldpark (G)
Brinka vom Waldpark (G)
Kathi v.d. Brech (G)
Claus v.d. Brech (G)
Birga v.d. Culm (G)
Gitta v.d. Brech (G)

Ali von Luda Jane (G)
Cato vom Kochertal (G)
Ella vom Marienheim (G)
Claus vom Wolfsberg (G)
Alarich vom Mornbach (G)
Arda v.d. Brech (G)
Cora v.d. Altenburg (G)
Diana vom Ramsberg (G)
Caro vom Waldpark (G)
Lord v.d. Brech (G)
Birga v.d. Culm (G)
Anka vom Ramsberg (G)
Dago vom Geeste-Moor (G)
Gritta vom Geeste-Moor (G)
Anita (H)

Joke des Zizaines
Pipo des Vieilles Rouches (F)
Kety de la Fontaine St. Germain
Tonik du Bois Follet (F)
Dacier du Vivier de Cour (F)
Lorene des Ronciers de Clavieres (F)
Cyta de Vrainville (F)
Bent Pine's Biff (A)
Phebus de Celibuty (F)
Barry v.d. Neuburg (G)
Doinah v.d. Brech (G)
Bent Pine's Brigette (A)
Popy de la Reote (F)
Tina de la Reote (A)
PEDIGREE 33
Amos van Jagershorst (A)
Popeline de la Reote (F)
Pipo des Vieilles Rouches (F)
Tonik du Bois Follet (F)
Lorene des Ronciers de Clavieres (F)
Lucas of Hunter's Creek (A)
Ripp de la Vieille Oise (F)
Ulla de St Landry (F)
Scarlett de Saint Landry (F)
Desiree de la Cote (A)
Arko v.d. Culm (G)
Dago v.d. Neuburg (G)
Bessie vom Kastanienhain (G)
Happy Hilda Hunter (A)
Jody des Zizaines (F)
Suzy des Zizaines (F)
Ialou (F)

Pipo des Vieilles Rouches (F)
Tonik du Bois Follet (F)
Lorene des Ronciers de Clavieres (F)
Lucas of Hunter's Creek (A)
Ripp de la Vieille Oise (F)
Ulla de St Landry (F)
Scarlett de Saint Landry (F)
Bon Chasseur de la Cote (A)
Joke des Zizaines
Pipo des Vieilles Rouches (F)
Kety de la Fontaine St. Germain
Victoria du Bois Follet (F)
Dacier du Vivier de Cour (F)
Lorene des Ronciers de Clavieres (F)
PEDIGREE 34
Cyta de Vrainville (F)
Mahaska's Merry Susan (A)
Pipo des Vieilles Rouches (F)
Taquin du Bois Follet (F)
Ouchka du Bois Follet (F)
Whiskey du Pironec (FQ)
Hello de Port Giraud (F)
Rana du Sauverain (FQ)
Ketty de Courtil Bissieux (F)
Alice B. Toklias (A)
Pipo des Vieilles Rouches (F)
Taquin de Bois Follet (F)
Ouchka du Bois Follet (F)
Huckle Hill Angela (A)
Barry v.d. Neuburg (G)
Huckle Hill Patty (A)
Tina de la Reote (A)

I'll always remember that afternoon when Dr. Mintscheff took us to see several Griffons in the area. It was then that I met Xavier Friedenberger and his **AXEL VOM ULRICHSQUELL (Urac de St. Landry, x Dia vom Luda Jana)**. We watched **AXEL** do some tracking and retrieving. Every time Mr. Friedenberger went to make a drag track with a piece of dead game, he would leave **AXEL** in the "drop" position—flat, paws stretched out in front, head between the paws—but **AXEL's** tail never stopped wagging! He knew it was a game, pretending and showing off, not serious hunting!

The next day we all traveled in three cars to Wolferszell for the test, where we saw many old friends from 1969: the Kroninger family, Herr Geisel, Herr Willi Fuchsl (breeder of **BOSS VOM WOLFSBERG**), and a number of others. A high point of the test weekend was that Dr. Mintscheff, at the age of 72, ran TWO dogs in the full Utility Field Test. Both dogs qualified, one with a Prize I, the other with a Prize II, and Dr. Mintscheff felt he had been "robbed" on the Prize II! And so it goes the world over.

At the conclusion of the testing weekend it was my observation that the Germans were judging their griffons about one point higher than we would have done at home. Where we would have assigned a dog a 3 in Search, they were giving a 4. Joe Nadeker agreed with me. Later, other club members who visited there came away with the same independent observation.

A few days later we flew to Paris and spent the next five days with our special friend, Dominque Frileux, and her husband, Claude. We had an afternoon of hunting in an area about a two-hour drive south of Paris. We also spent an entire day at a small castle, which had once belonged to Napoleon's gamekeeper (or maybe the gamekeeper of Henry XIV). It was a real castle complete with moat. Its present owners had turned it into what we would call a private hunting preserve. Nearly all the hunting we did that day were driven hunts. There were probably about twenty hunters there all told and we divided into two groups. One group stood just beyond the cover, or stand of trees, with the dogs (all breeds), while the other group walked through the cover, driving the game out into the open where it was shot and then retrieved by the dogs.

The day before we left France we had lunch with the president of the French Griffon Club, M. Yves Droit, and Madame Louiseau, whose kennel name is DU BOIS FOLLET. We had been to her home in 1969 and seen her dogs, including **LORENE DES RONCIERS DE CLAVIERES**. After lunch we got to see **VIKINGS DU BOIS FOLLET** (littermate to Dick Austin's **VICTORIA**) and a few other dogs.

Just prior to this trip, **TONIK DU BOIS FOLLET** had died and we were suddenly down to one very young dog and one very old one. We felt rather desperate with our hunting season beginning as soon as we returned from Europe. So we bought an eight-month-old male from M. Droit, **NUMA DU RUISSEAU DU MASSACRE**. He was shipped to us shortly after we got home. He turned out to be severely dysplastic, and had a soft temperament. We should have known better, because we already had indications of dogs from that bloodline with dysplasia. (See Part Two for pedigree and additional information.) He had an outstanding nose, strong pointing instinct, good searching qualities, and did produce a lot of game, but...

In the spring of 1978 we held three WPGCA field tests and participated in a fourth test sponsored by the Club Drahthaar of Canada in Ontario. The test results were not promising.

Above: 12 year old ***OONA DE ST LANDRY*** *at the Frileux country home. (Compliments Joan Bailey) Below: Hunting Hungarian partridge and pheasant,* ***URAC DE ST LANDRY*** *holds intensely while Dominique moves in to flush the bird. (Compliments Ed Bailey)*

Above: ***VICKINGS DU BOIS FOLLET*** *with owner Mr. Yves Droit, President of the French Griffon Club, now deceased.* ***VICKINGS*** *and* ***VICTORIA*** *were littermates. (Compliments Joan Bailey) Below:* ***LORCKY DE SABLONVILLE****, 10 years at time of photo, was used for breeding several times.*

As far as the Breeding Program goes, in NAT we tested the "A" litter DE LA COTE. Out of six dogs tested, only three qualified. In IHDT, we tested four dogs from the GLENAIRE kennel (**Boss v Wolfsberg x Snow Que Blanc**) and all four qualified, two of them with prize I. From the HUNTER'S CREEK breeding (**Tonik du Bois Follet x Ulla de Saint Landry**) we tested two dogs and neither qualified. From the only litter of DUSTY HILLS, (**Don v.d. Neuburg** x **Bent Pine's Alda**) we tested two dogs and neither qualified. Again we tested two dogs from the "A" ASHVIEW'S breeding and neither qualified.

In 1978 the German Griffon Club celebrated their 90th anniversary. Here are a few Griffons featured in a long article written by the president of the club, Franz Kroninger, which appeared in the *Jagdgebrauchshund* a magazine that covers the news of all versatile breeds in Germany.

At that celebration they held a "breed show," which evaluates dogs' conformation and coat only. Out of the 53 Griffons judged that day, only six met the requirements of "ideal Korthals Griffon type." These dogs were:

ANTSCHY VOM LEANCHHOF (Arco v Labertal x Christa v Wolfsberg).

CORA VOM WOLFSBERG (Ilko v.d. Brech x Diana v.d.Neuburg).

AURA VON GSCHWENDT (Droll v Kastanienhain x Dina v Wolfsberg).

LORCKY DE SABLONVILLE (Taquin du Bois Follet [not our Canadian **Taquin**, this was a mix-up in naming the litter in France] x **Ile de Barre Mer)**.

ARTUS VOM DISTELPOINT (Hannes v Waldspark x Cora v Wolfsberg).

AXEL VOM ULRICHSQUELL (Urac de St. Landry x Dia v Luda Jana).

Even so, the first three dogs listed: **ANTSCHY VOM LENACHHOF, CORA VOM WOLFSBERG,** and **AURA VON GSCHWENDT** all have **BIRGA V.D. CULM** in their bloodlines. (Remember **BIRGA**?) **LORCKY DE SABLONVILLE** was of French blood mostly unknown to us, and some untested dogs. **ARTUS VOM DISTELPOINT** had **BIRGA** in the bloodlines on both the sire and dam side. And **AXEL VOM ULRICHSQUELL** had hip dysplasia and eye defects in his bloodlines, though he himself was a fine dog. **AXEL**'s sire was **URAC DE ST LANDRY**, littermate to dysplastic **ULRICH**.

Some of these defects were back far enough to be relatively safe, others were too close. But, that's over simplifying a very complicated business. (For further discussion see Part Two.)

These six dogs were all fine, excellent specimens of the breed. We could say they are the "phenotype" of the dog we all want. But, the "genotype" is not without serious defects, *which sooner or later*, are manifested in progeny, or descendants of their progeny. Phenotype refers to the desired specimen, i.e., the dog looks and acts exactly like the definition of that breed of dog. Genotype refers to the genes a dog carries. So a dog can *appear* to be exactly what one is striving for, but he or she may not be the *genotype,* which means he or she will not transmit the desired genes necessary to produce the desired product. *Like does not always produce like.*

The test results in the spring of 1979 were not much better, though there seemed to be a slight improvement. The "B" litter DE LA COTE (a repeat of the "A" litter) did well in NAT, but out of six dogs tested in IHDT, only two qualified.

In the fall of 1979 our good friend, Dominique Frileux from France, visited us. Luckily we had a Club Drahthaar test close to home, so we were able to take Dominique to that, as well as to see Niagara Falls.

I called several Griffon owners and asked them to come to the Drahthaar test with their Griffons so that Dominique could see some of our dogs. Club members on hand that weekend were: June and John Accardi, Hugh Stark, Howard and Irene Coutu, John Zawacki, and Matt Crews. Dominique then went on to California and visited with a small gathering of members of the Sierra Griffon Club in the home of Warren and Helen Webster. I still keep in contact with Dominque and she visited me in the summer of 1992. She no longer is as active in the French Griffon Club as she once was, but continues to breed a litter now and then.

***FURST V.D. NEUBURG**, 13 months, Nebraska 1979, NAT. He did not qualify due to pointing. His uncooperative temperament manifested in not pointing. (Compliments Ed Bailey)*

Above and below: ***LUCAS OF HUNTER'S CREEK****, a dog that really left his mark on the breed. We still see him today in many of our Griffons, especially his face, and of course his French charm. (Compliments Rolf Benseler)*

Littermates out of ***VICTORIA*** *by* ***LUCAS****, above:* ***BRIDGETTE DE LA COTE*** *during NAT, intense and solid on the bird. (Compliments Rolf Benseler) Below:* ***BON CHASSEUR DE LA COTE****, demonstrating the same intensity at the same test in California in 1979. (Compliments Warren Webster)* ***BON CHASSEUR*** *was used for breeding twice with the same bitch, and out of those two litters came* ***MAHASKA'S MERRY SUSAN****, whom you will meet soon and learn of her contribution to the breed.*

CHAPTER FOURTEEN
GRIFFON BREEDING PROGRAM
1980 - 1983

First Judges Seminar - Nebraska

In the spring of 1980 we held our first judges seminar in conjunction with our annual spring test in Nebraska. Attending were Ed Bailey, Joe Nadeker, Jack Dallimore, Dick Austin, Harold Baskin, Joan Bailey, Warren Webster, Roy Speece, Tom Whitley, Lee Fulton, Connie Tidwell, Ken Harris, Charles Neeley, and a bunch more. Judges and participates came from: California, Florida, Tennessee, Minnesota, New Mexico, Colorado, Kansas, Iowa, and Canada.

Harold had just begun his three-year term of office as president; Dick Austin, vice president; Connie Tidwell, treasurer; and Joan Bailey, secretary.

At dinner on Saturday evening, 30 of us gathered in the small town of Alexandria, at the uniquely marvelous Four Thieves Steak House. We honored Roy Speece, our outgoing president, and engraved on our gift was:

FOR ROY A. SPEECE
PRESIDENT
WIREHAIRED POINTING GRIFFON CLUB OF AMERICA
1971 - 1979
You led us through the most difficult and most vital years—
the first years of our Breeding Program. You never lost sight
of our goal—to produce honest hunting Griffons. You were a strong president and
you were always here when we needed you. We thank you.

That spring we tested the "C" DE LA COTE litter in NAT, who did well by the standards of those days. In IHDT the "B" DE LA COTE litter did well.

One of our problems, and had been for some years, was that we were not producing *enough dogs* each year. You just can't get anywhere when you are only breeding one, two, or three litters per year. It's just not enough to sustain a gene pool, nor to provide new owners with pups.

For example, in the spring of 1981 we had three approved breedings planned: 1) **BENT PINE'S BIFF x BRISSETTE DE LA COTE.** 2) **BON CHASSEUR DE LA COTE x ALICE B TOKLAS**. 3) **BENT PINE'S BIFF x BRIDGETTE DE LA COTE.** To check the bloodlines of these three breedings look at the pedigrees of **AMOS VAN JAGERSHORST** and **MAHASKA'S MERRY SUSAN.**

Litter One:

Note that **PIPO DES VIEILLES ROUCHES** appears three times in the pedigree. Remember, this is the male from France that was very independent, difficult to train, uncooperative, though he was excellent in searching and use of his nose, and no doubt had a strong desire for game contact. Unknowingly we were breeding to

In Nebraska on Sunday morning, we had taken the judges seminar to the field during the judging of the dogs. We paused for a group photo: From left to right: Warren Webster, Dick Austin, Don Dack and **ALDERSEDGE ATTATURK**, *Tom Whitley, Harold Baskin, Roy Speece, Mary Tidwell, Jack Dallimore, Ed Bailey, Joe Nadeker, Connie Tidwell and* **PECOS GYPSY TAMBOURINE**, *Ted Williams, Lee Fulton and* **CACEI DE LA COTE.** *(Compliments Joan Bailey)*

uncooperative dogs. Also in the fourth generation is **SCARLETT DE ST LANDRY** mentioned earlier, the bitch whose eyes were ectropic, a genetically transmitted disease to progeny. But, these were the only dogs we had at the time.

In NAT, the litter tested fairly well, three out of five qualifying, one with a temperament problem. The following year only two dogs tested in IHDT, and neither qualified. One dog didn't even come close, the other missed only because of the Retrieve from Drag Track (training). The following year, 1984, two dogs tested in IHDT and both qualified. But, by this time they were three years old, and much would have been "masked," meaning through extensive exposure to hunting, many inherited negative traits were probably hidden from our eyes. Nonetheless, both these dogs continued to be good hunting dogs for the rest of their lives.

The important point here is that, as a litter, it was not altogether successful. Not enough dogs from the litter became useful hunting dogs.

Litter Two:

In the second litter you'll note that once again **PIPO** shows up several times, actually *four* times, and again we have **SCARLETT** one time, which could produce eye problems several generations down the road. This litter also tested well in NAT, probably a bit better than the first litter. Out of six dogs tested, four qualified. One dog that did qualify with a Prize III, was judged in temperament as "very hyper; close to being gun sensitive."

In IHDT a year later, only two dogs were entered and neither qualified. Both dogs received only a 1 in Tracking the Duck. This is significant, because the water work often brings out weakness in temperament.

In the meantime, this breeding was repeated—only because we had nothing else to breed. Five dogs from the repeat litter were tested in NAT at the difficult age of seven and eight months. Three qualified, two didn't because of Water.

In 1984, three dogs from the repeat litter were evaluated in IHDT. One qualified with a Prize II and that was **MAHASKA'S MERRY SUSAN**. The other two did not qualify and demonstrated temperament problems. But, there was **"SUZIE."**

Litter Three:

The third litter was **BENT PINE'S BIFF** again, x **BRIDGETTE DE LA COTE**, a littermate to **BRISETTE** above. There were only two pups in the litter. Both dogs qualified in NAT, but both bombed in IHDT. One was killed at an early age, the other came back when he was four years old and qualified in IHDT with a Prize II. This was **ENCORE DE LA COTE** who turned out to be a fine dog—unfortunately, he died of stomach torsion when he was in his prime.

If you look closely at these three pedigrees, you see that they are all pretty much the same blood.

The same year that we tested the "E" DE LA COTE litter in NAT, we also tested the "D" DE LA COTE litter. (See the pedigree for **AMOS VAN JAGERSHORST.**) The "D" litter did not do well in NAT. Out of five dogs, only one qualified. Water was a weakness, which we now all know is a warning for mental instability. Four of the dogs from this litter came back the next year for IHDT, but only one qualified; the others did poorly.

We learned something from this breeding. One of the dogs from this litter, a female, went on to qualify in Utility Field Test, though she had not qualified in either NAT or IHDT. By hard training, and lots of exposure to wild game, her owner managed to qualify her in UFT. Only because of that (because we were so desperate

From litter # 1, above, ***ASTOR VOM MAYERHOF****, NAT, Calfornia 1982, Pr. I. Below: In Michigan,* ***AMOS VAN JAGERSHORST****, IHDT, Pr. II, 21 months. (Both photos compliments Joan Bailey)*

Two Littermates, out of ***SNOW QUE BLANC****, by* ***BOSS VOM WOLFSBERG****. On the left,* ***LADY DAWN OF GLENAIRE****, Warren Webster's first Griffon. On the right is* ***SIEGRICH JAGER OF GLENAIRE****. This was taken at IHDT in California, 1978, where each dog received a Prize I. (Compliments Ed Bailey)*

In Nebraska 1980, NAT, 8 months old ***CACEI DE LA COTE****. This was the tracking portion of the test. We had released a pheasant for the previous dog who was not able to locate the bird after about 10 minutes. We brought* ***CACEI*** *up and gave him a chance, figuring if he couldn't find the bird, we would set out a new bird for him. With utter concentration this handsome young dog put his nose down and let the track pull him. He must have been gone for a long five minutes, then out of the brush he came running with that cock bird and delivered it to Lee.* ***CACEI*** *received all 4's with a 4H in Tracking. (Compliments Warren Webster)*

for dogs) did we give approval to a breeding of this bitch. This was the "A" VAN JAGERSHORST litter. Again we used **BENT PINE'S BIFF** and the bitch was **DESIREE DE LA COTE**. This produced **AMOS VAN JAGERSHORT**. Five pups from the litter were tested in NAT, at the age of nine months. Only one qualified—with a Prize I. This was **AMOS**, owned by Bill Toner. The other four littermates bombed at the water; each getting a zero.

Look at the pedigree of this litter: Notice in the third generation, **DAGO V.D. NEUBURG**. That's a littermate to **DON**, and **DAGO** was not field tested. Nor was his get, **HAPPY HILDA HUNTER**. We took too many risks.

AMOS went on to receive a Prize II in IHDT the next year. Four of his littermates failed in IHDT, all due to water. Even **AMOS** only received a 2 in Tracking the Duck.

If we study this pedigree now, with hindsight, it is easier to see the weaknesses. We should never have bred **DESIREE DE LA COTE**, a dog that could not qualify in either NAT or IHDT. Her dam was not field-tested, nor was the grandmother.

And **AMOS**, good dog that he was, should not have been bred, due to the poor performance of his littermates. No matter how good a dog may "look," (meaning his phenotype), he carries genes similar to his littermates', and often transmits many of the same characteristics as his mates.

It is easy for readers to say to themselves, "How could they have bred dogs like that?" And we would answer, "We had no better dogs to breed. We were breeding the best we could find."

And we looked everywhere, both within the Breeding Program, and outside of it. Occasionally we found dogs outside the program and we used them. But the problems were always the same: We might find one good dog, but none of its littermates had been tested. So genetically, we really didn't know what we were getting. If the dog tested well, did it mean he would pass his positive attributes to his progeny?

There are two more breedings to look at before we look at the next phase. The first was a result of our effort to bring desperately needed new blood into our breed. We looked to Germany and took all the female puppies from the "A" VOM FUCHSBURG litter. (Pedigree in previous chapter, #32.) The four pups, age 12 weeks, arrived in Toronto and went directly to the Bailey farm and then were shipped to their new owners.

When they were tested in NAT in 1981, two out of the four qualified, and one of the qualifying dogs was judged with a slight temperament problem: "slightly skittish at times around people." Of the two that did not qualify, guess what area they were weak in? Yes, water. Two would not swim. And one of those had this evaluation in temperament: "shy of strangers sometimes." Look now at the pedigree: There's our old friend, **BIRGA V.D. CULM**. She is in both sire and dam, so there was loose line breeding to her.

Despite these weaknesses, we went ahead and bred one of the bitches to one of the males from the Breeding Program, because we had no other bitches to use. This was a complete outcross—the male was entirely French blood (**CACEI DE LA COTE**) and the female entirely German (**ANKA VOM FUCHSBERG**). The litter, FREEWIND'S "A," did not test well, with only three out of the seven qualifying in NAT. Three of those that did not qualify had temperament problems: One was " soft, slightly timid," the next was "skittish," and the last one "soft." And that was the

*In Nebraska 1984, **ENCORE DE LA COTE**, completing the retrieve of dragged dead game to owner Brad Meyen in the IHDT, where they received a Prize II. (Compliments Joan Bailey)*

And later that spring, in New Jersey, ***MAHASKA'S MERRY SUSAN*** *during the IHDT retrieving the duck from deep water, and below, completing the tracking of the live pheasant, on a dead run to owner Tom Whitley. (Compliments Joan Bailey)*

only litter we were able to produce in 1983. It was the spring of 1984 when we tested that litter. There was one dog that received all 4's and appeared to have a sound temperament—**FREEWIND'S ALAMANCE**. In 1985 two dogs from this litter tested in IHDT and both qualified with a Prize II. One of those was **ALMANCE**. There were not many acceptable dogs to breed.

And, here is what happened.

*Ed Bailey hunting in Nebraska, 1980, with **ADI DE LA COTE** and **NUMA DU RUISSEAU DU MASSACRE** holding tight on Bobwhite quail, until Ed can flush the birds. (Compliments, Dean Terrill)*

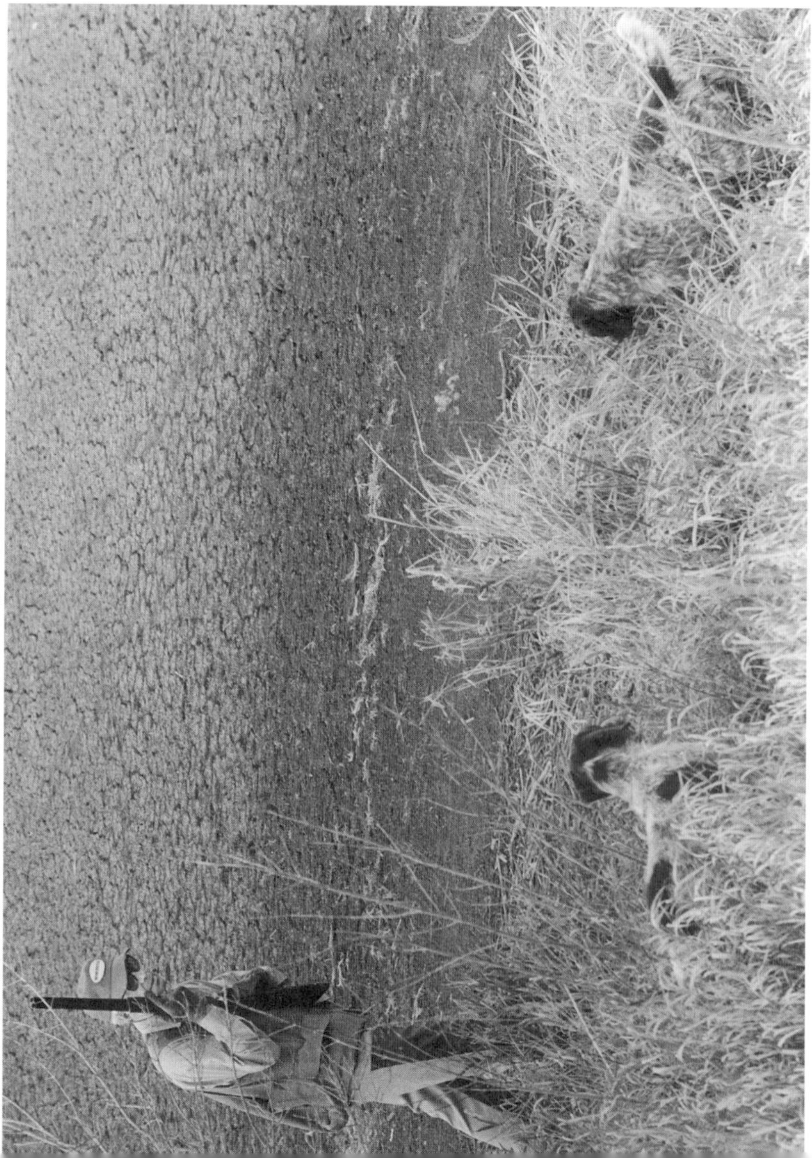

CHAPTER FIFTEEN
RESTORATION OF THE GRIFFON BREED IN NORTH AMERICA 1984

In 1983 we held our annual board of directors meeting in conjunction with the field test in Redding, California. We met in one of the hotel rooms Friday evening. Voting members present were: Harold Baskin, president; Dick Austin, vice-president, Joan Bailey, secretary. Non voting, invited guests were Joe Nadeker (Breeding Committee and senior judge), Rolf Benseler (senior judge), Warren Webster (judge and president Sierra Griffon Club), Jack Dallimore (senior judge) and Bodo Winterhelt (senior judge and past president NAVHDA).

Early in the meeting someone asked, "What females do we have for breeding?" The answer was "Few or none." Soon Bodo Winterhelt spoke and said that the only way we would get out of this hole was to inject "foreign" blood, and he suggested we use German Shorthair. I must say at the time I was shocked, but I stayed open and listened to what everyone else had to say that evening, and reluctantly, I had to agree with Bodo's suggestion, as did everyone else. I remember clearly the look of sadness on everyone's face. Later, when we told Glen Raker, he said, "Well, we have to do what we have to do." Following is a long article detailing the history of the problems within our breed up to 1983, and what the Board of Directors, after extensive research, decided to do to save this breed.

Restoration of the Griffon Breed on the North American Continent
By Joan Bailey
[Condensed version]
(Winner of "Best Article By a Breed Club 1984"
from Dog Writers Association of America,
August 1984 *GUN DOG SUPREME*.)

On March 24, 1983, slightly more than a year ago, the Board of Directors of the Wirehaired Pointing Griffon Club of America held a meeting in Redding, California. During that meeting one of the board members asked, "What females do we have for breeding now?" The answer from the Breeding Committee was, "Very few." Something had to be done if the Griffon was to remain a top hunting breed. The discussion and research that ensued, and the subsequent decisions that were made, and their implementation, will restore the breed. But, in order to look into the future one must first understand the past...[A brief history of the Griffon was included here.]

WPGCA Breeding Program

Ten years ago this program was initiated, using the best Griffons we could find at that time. Nearly all had at least been tested in Natural Ability Tests, though at that time we did not have an Intermediate Hunting Dog Test ("Breeding Test"). Not only did we not have enough adequate dogs, we did not have enough people participating in the program, to build up a large enough genetic pool.

Nevertheless, progress was made. Good hunting Griffons were produced, as well as some that were sub-standard. During the past ten years those of us participating in the program—breeders, owners of the progeny, and the Breeding Committee, and other club members who helped in one way or another—have improved the Griffon in the United States. This is in the records. It is fact. However, because of the limited material that we had to work with (specifically material that had come from a very decimated breed over a long period of time), on a hypothetical scale of 100 we were only able to bring the Griffon from its low point of say 20, up to 40 or 50. We cannot move beyond that point in the scale. We have no where to go. We cannot even maintain this position. This brings us to today. It brings us back to the question posed at the beginning of this article, "What females do we have for breeding now? Very few." Something has to be done or else we might as well forget about the Griffon.

Facing The Truth

It is difficult for most of us to look at our Griffon and believe that the breed is in serious trouble. But, most of us look at our Griffon through rose-colored glasses. This is a perfectly normal thing for us to do. I've done it, we've all done it. Some of you will look at your Griffon and picture him on a beautiful point, you flush the pheasant, and shoot. You tend to forget the rest of the story—your Griffon was not able to follow the track of the wing-tipped, running pheasant, and you lost the bird.

Or, you look at your faithful hunting companion, who has almost never failed you in the field, and you think, "I've got an excellent Griffon, worthy of breeding." You've pushed to the back of your mind that your dog is somewhat "man shy"—he's afraid of strange people. This is a dog with unstable mental behavior, despite his excellence in the field, and should *never* be bred.

Another Griffon owner looks at his Griffon, after he has read this article, and thinks, "That woman is nuts—my Griffon has all the qualities and should be bred." The dog has a marvelously sound temperament, does all he should do in the field and marshes, good nose, desire, conformation, coat and good hips. But, in his pedigree is a line of dogs with bad nerves.

And on and on we could go—all the dogs that are great, but...The truth, the real truth, is that there are almost no Griffons that are all-around good—not outstanding—just good, without serious defect. We all have to take off our rose-colored glasses.

Solving the Problem

At the Board of Directors meeting in Redding, California in March 1983, we faced the problem squarely. We acknowledged that there are only three ways to rejuvenate a failing breed: 1) By using material remaining in the breed; 2) by imports; and 3) by using "foreign blood." It was agreed that we had tried the first two methods over and over without lasting results. We accepted the fact that the only way to save the Griffon was to inject "foreign blood."

Foreign blood means blood from a different breed. This is a shocking concept to most North Americans. Years ago it would have been a shocking concept to me. But, facts are facts. It is a fact that all successful hunting breeds, especially versatile hunting breeds, in order to maintain a sound and strong breed, have had to inject "foreign blood" from time to time.

For example, the Pudelpointer, which is one of the wirehaired breeds, had English Pointer blood injected 3 times after the war (W.W.II), and again in North America since the early 1950s pointer blood was injected three more times.

The German Wirehaired Pointer (called in Germany the Deutsch Drahthaar) was developed by crossing the Pudelpointer and German Shorthaired Pointer. A short time later they used quite a number of Griffon injections. A German pedigree of a Drahthaar always has in one corner a notation telling what line it stems from: GR for a Griffon line, or PP for a Pudelpointer line. An extremely important lesson to be learned from these examples above, of injecting foreign blood, *is that this is never hidden.* It is done honestly and openly. Accurate records are vital in any breeding program.

To our knowledge, aside from some very early experimental breeding by the early Korthals disciples, the Germans never injected foreign blood into the Korthals Griffons. However, do remember that one of the eight patriarchs of the breed was 1/2 shorthaired pointer. France never documented any foreign injection, but it is my belief that some German Shorthair was used secretly from time to time.

About ten years ago one of our club members received a Griffon from France that was absolutely shorthair in appearance. It came from a reputable kennel in France and I am sure the shorthair blood was not injected at the time of that breeding, but back a couple of generations, but hidden—hidden even from the innocent breeder. Or it could have been coming from much further back, or all the way back to one of the patriarchs, **JUNON,** who was 1/2 GSP.

We have cases in the United States where I am sure foreign blood, probably German Wirehair, rather than German Shorthair, was injected secretly.

Where would we be today with hip dysplasia in Griffons if we had hidden this information? On the contrary we have documented both our clear dogs and our dysplastic dogs. By doing this we were able to breed a line of dogs with very good hips. At the same time we made it possible for all breeders to avoid dysplastic lines. [See Part Two.]

Research for Injection of Foreign Blood

Before one tries to solve a problem the problem has to be correctly analyzed. The basic, overriding problems of the Griffons are: 1) *Temperament* (sound nerves, sound mental stability); and 2) *Desire* (this means "passion for the hunt," the intense desire for game contact, the drive to pursue the game under all conditions). Temperament and desire go hand in hand, are very closely intertwined. And, lack of these traits is always associated with a deteriorating breed.

After the decision (March 1983) was made that we would inject foreign blood we tentatively decided to use German Shorthair blood. But, we asked Joe Nadeker to research this for us before any final decisions were made.

This was followed by a report from Joe:

Redding, March 31, 1983

TO: The Board of Directors of the W.P.G.C.A.

Subject: Restoration of the Griffon Breed on the North American Continent.

Following up on the decision to exert our efforts for the rejuvenation of our Griffon population I started immediately to research records dealing with similar situations that occurred in the past within other breeds of hunting dogs and am able to report at the end of the two days study on the first conclusions. Some of the facts are known to you, nevertheless they have to be put forward again with the greatest emphasis, in order for the program of restoration to be honored during it's implementation:

Fact: All the successful breeds of versatile and other working dogs reached their level of excellence through CONTROLLED AND SELECTIVE BREEDING ONLY, mating the best individuals and grading the quality of the parents by their progeny. The tighter the control the faster the results.

Fact: At any time that the centralized authority lost its potency, the breed rapidly deteriorated. This is followed by a decline in popularity and consequently in numbers until there is not a sufficient population base left for regeneration of the breed without influx of "foreign blood."

From the records available to me, a situation closest resembling our plight, existed in Czechoslovakia around the year of 1924, a period "when the bells almost tolled for the Czech Fousek" (Czech moustache pointer, very closely resembling our Griffon and properly called "Cesky Fousek [foe-sick] in Czechoslovakia). The breed club reorganized, introduced one man breed warden with unlimited power in breeding decisions and all possible methods were introduced (few of them were failures) to restore the population. Their success is best measured by the fact that the Cesky Fousek is the most numerous breed in Czechoslovakia today and validly competing with the older established breeds.

Methods of Restoration

1. By using salvaged material from the remaining population. In our case, this is not believed to be possible, judging from the experience of the last few years when the Breeding Committee tried to bring some order in the chaos of the one dog breeding experts. The very few intelligent breeders taking part in the program are below the number to form a minimal genetic pool for continuity of improvement. The results were barely holding up the status quo in quality and that is not enough. That was conceded during the B.O.D. meeting in Redding when we had to admit that the breed as a whole is below the performance level of the standard of the other leading versatile breeds largely due to the fact that the other breeds were able in time of need to boost their population by imports of high quality from Europe.

2. By using imports of the same breed. This has been tried again and again with the Griffons. The results are known to all of you, no need to elaborate. In all fairness to the German Griffon Club, they do not have a surplus of dogs and any substantial drain on their pool would result in problems for Germany.

3. By using related breeds. This was considered at the meeting in Redding, and it still appears to be the primary consideration for the recovery. Carefully selected individuals from German Shorthaired Pointer, German Wirehaired Pointer, and/or Czech Fousek, that is almost identical with the German Stichelhaar Pointer, and have an attraction because of the stable coat, the most stable of the wirehaired breeds [will be used].

* * * * * *

After this report from Joe was received by the members of the Board of Directors we then asked Joe to write to his contacts in Czechoslovakia, inquiring about the possibility to buy three adult, tested German Shorthaired Pointers. Why did we choose Czechoslovakia, rather than some other country? Remember earlier in this article we told you that not all imported dogs are "automatically" great dogs. Breeders do not always send their "best," or what they think is their best. After all, let us be honest with ourselves—would we send our "best" out of the country? No, we wouldn't. This is simply human nature. We want to keep the best for ourselves.

Another factor that determines the quality of the import is *who* you get it from. Just knowing a breeder of dogs is not enough. You must have a strong contact with a very knowledgeable person, and one who has great influence with the breed you are proposing to deal with.

So Joe wrote to the Secretary of the German Shorthaired Pointer Club in Czechoslovakia, a man Joe knows and respects, who has great respect for Joe. Following is the letter Joe received from Dr. Petr Dvorak.

November 30, 1983

Esteemed Mr. Nadeker:

First many thanks for your packet. Also any kind of news from you is received here with delight but particularly this one, dealing with your tentative arrival in Europe. Many thanks for the photos and I am very glad that **TANYA** did acclimatize herself so well to the hunting conditions in the U.S.A., and judging from the pictures and the test reports, produced also good looking and efficient hunting progeny [this was a German Shorthair bitch that Joe imported and bred.] I thank you again for the remaining material enclosed in the letter and rest assured that in the case of my involvement in kynology I will always do the best of my ability and in my power.

...Now I would like to turn to your inquiries. The case as a whole took me unprepared and before I was ready to answer you I consulted with Dr. Dostal, geneticist by profession; a specialist on utility animals and also senior breedwarden of the Cesky-Barbette Club (Czech Fousek). Wirehaired Pointing Griffon does not exist in Czechoslovakia, therefore export to boost your breed cannot take place. What is left then is an infusion (regenerative refreshment) of blood as proposed in your communication.

I did not precisely comprehend from your letter if the purpose of the blood infusion would serve to dilute concentration of undesirable qualities within a small and therefore considerably related population or, if the motivation includes a desire to upgrade the exterior and mainly the working qualities. Your option to utilize GSP [German Shorthair Pointer] blood lets me suspect that the later is the case and your goal is to improve the working skills and desires, perhaps mainly the field work, which would be a valid assumption considering the high and stable level of the continental GSP strains (lines).

The problem here is the completely different type of coat and the problems stemming thereof. During the regeneration of the Cesky Fouseks, GSP blood was also used, and it is only fair to bring your attention that strains of Czech Fousek do exist where short-coated whelps are not a rare exception. This, as I am sure you are well aware of, would create the same problem in view of the recessive character of the short coat. On the other hand, one isolated infusion, followed by use of pure Griffons only, may not carry the hoped for stabilization of the improved working traits in receding generations.

Because of the above mentioned negative reasons allow me to bring to your attention another solution, that is the employment of the Cesky rough haired Fousek for the proposed regeneration. You know me well as a convinced supporter of the GSP. It is necessary however, to state for the sake of objectivity, that the working talents of the present day Cesky Fousek are also on a high level. The dogs are perhaps not as elegant performers in the field [as GSP], but even that cannot be stated "across the board." As you know, Cesky Fousek and other rough haired breeds do not have stabilized coats, but in view of the fact of a quarter century of lineal breeding system, we have now strains with quite uniform coat types.

Of course the coats differ from strain to strain. From almost short-haired type (slight rougher coat with noticeable marks on the nose and eyebrows) [he means what we call "furnishings"] to the "hairy ones" with longer and somewhat finer coats. The latter, in my opinion, correspond completely with Korthals Griffons. This is the reason why I am suggesting this route for your consideration as more passable. The modern Cesky Fousek are very easy to handle, many have outstanding noses, train easily and therefore are very popular with the rank and file hunters. They are versatile but their work in the field is not as elegant [as GSP], for this reason the majority of the top trainers and versatile dog handlers reach for the more temperamental and less manageable (in comparison) GSP, because to the experienced the additional effort will pay back in a more impressive final product.

This is our opinion and it is of course up to you to weigh the conditions and decide which risks are more acceptable for the purpose...Today the game density is on a moderate upswing, consequently the interest in dogs is greater and demand exceeds the supply. I am writing this mainly because it would be necessary to know your decision ahead of the time of your arrival so as to have enough time to find and secure fitting dogs for your purpose.

This is for the time being all in regard to your request. It goes without saying that I will strive to meet the challenge according to your instructions which I will be awaiting. Esteemed Mr. Nadeker, I am looking forward to your planned visit very much. I do believe it will materialize and that you will find time to spend a few hours with me, talking what is new in kynology. Personally, I do sincerely wish you the best results in breeding of the G.S.P. and success in the work you do with other breeds.

With many regards and hope for the next letter I remain with "Hail to the Hunt and Kynology"

Yours,

Petr Dvorak

The Cesky Fousek

After receiving [a copy of] this letter from Dr. Dvorak, the Breeding Committee and other members of the Board were very encouraged and decided to go with the Cesky Fousek for a number of reasons. First, it will be easier and faster because of the stabilized wirehaired coat. By going this route we will avoid the problems with shorthaired coats. Another important reason is the contact we now have with Dr. Dostal, the senior breed warden of the Czech Fousek Club, and not only that, he is a geneticist. We will be getting adult, tested dogs, from tested lines. Because our contacts and connections are of the highest, we will be getting the "best" for our needs.

The Cesky Fousek ... very closely resembles our Griffon, but is one to two inches taller. The modern day Cesky Fousek has been in Czechoslovakia for nearly 100 years, but traces back to the 14th century (See below.). After World War I, like most of the breeds [in Europe], it was decimated. As Joe told us briefly in his report, a program of restoration was begun in 1924. Ironically, they used a lot of Korthals Griffons in the restoration, as well as GWP, GSP, Pudelpointer, and Stichelhaar.

They developed and established 8 lines (strains). One [additional] line is reserved for use as an occasional boost for the other eight lines when such a line becomes low in numbers. Except for these rare boosts, *line breeding and only line breeding* is used. These lines and the restoration program were completed thirty years ago, and the Cesky Fousek is far and away the most popular versatile hunting dog in Czechoslovakia today.

The infusion of Cesky Fousek blood will raise to an acceptable level our Griffon's desire to work, his desire for game contact, his desire to hunt hard for his master. This desire will manifest itself especially in the field, on tracking of wounded game, and in his love for water. With this will come the sound nerves and temperament, the mentally well-balanced dog. All the things our present day Griffons are lacking will be regained by infusion of this new blood.

Opinions About The Origin Of The Cesky Fousek

(From *Monografie Ceskeho Fouska*, by MVDr. Josef Kunn. Published by Cesky Myslivecky Svaz, Klub Chovatelu Ceskych Fousku, circa 1990 Translated by Joe Nadeker, specifically for inclusion in this book.)

Which breed of dog originally participated in the development of the Cesky Fousek is not creditably documented. The Caucasian dog seems to favor its background. Later it was cross bred, according to the

English, with the Griffon of the French type from Belgium and Holland. But it may have happened the other way around. We know without a doubt that the Cesky Fousek had a considerable share in the development of the German Prickly coated Pointer [which later was called Stickelhaar] and therefore the German Wirehair Pointer.

We know that the Germans opted, at one time or other, whole litters out of prominent bitches from Bohemia and Moravia. At one time the rough-coated pointer club (C.F.) for the Bohemia-Moravia Kingdom had to process a purchase of a valued progeny situated in Prague via Berlin (Documented in 1896.). The particular dogs were likely already secured by a German kynologist.

Some of the above and other historical research are very important for the quest of the origin of the Cesky Fousek as they exclude "the handed down opinions that the evolution of the rough-coated pointers was influenced with great probability by two original types of hunting dogs: those being the "hunting Pudel from Spain" and the rough-coated dog, called in old hunting tunes "the Polish Water dog." Even the esteemed Francis Houska (the major power of the rescue of the Cesky Fousek, following the demise of the breed during the first World War) questioned the quoted theory. He wrote in 1945:

According to the reports and paintings, the Pudel still was in the 18th century explicitly a water dog. Even his name, "Aviricus Aquaticus" so indicates. Also the assigned name the English "French Griffon" (documented), as well as the statement of the Frenchman, De Blanchere, all indicate that the Griffon of today is the Barbet of the 16th century, name designated by the French to identify the Pudel. Buffon wrote about Pudels (Barbets), "They search the reeds as long as it takes to find and retrieve the shot bird. They equally hunt otters, wild cats, crows and foxes."

If we accept the origin of the Griffons as fact, we could easily explain their easy disposition, waterlove, willingness to retrieve, trainability and love of petting.

In the 19th century, changes in the practice and style of hunting caused emergence of the rough-coated breeds and the hunting Pudel suffered decline. Popularity shifted to the versatile dogs. The Griffon, tailored and stabilized as a breed by Korthals, left his heritage from the Barbet in other types of rough-coated breed. It resulted in lower stops, more thickset head with shorter snout, the intelligent look of the round eyes and longer coat.

Thus, the disparity in the conformation negates the older considerations in the origin and development of the Cesky Fousek and we have to accept as a dominant the views of the earlier kynologs among them Dr. Karl Finze and Dr. Hans von Kadich [see Chapter One], that the Cesky Fousek is among the rough-coated hunting dogs in reality the basic (oldest, original) breed and therefore exercised influence in shaping all the rough-coated lines. This is supported by the entries reaching back to the 14th century, where references to any other rough-coated breed emerged 200 years later, i.e., Pudels-Griffons). It was the German kynologs who declared publicly the age of the breed and its following influence.

Explanation of the Scarcity of Documents

It is to be accepted that they may have known more about the breed than they let be known. The Kingdom of Bohemia was subject to the Emperor (Kaiser) of the Holy Roman Empire, following the defeat of the Husites Army in 1421 and later to the Austro-Hungarian Rule under the Hapsburgs. Hunting, and therefore dogs, were exclusively limited for the pleasure of rulers and the nobility that was predominantly German. Therefore, the majority of historical literature and entries pertaining to hunting dogs were jealously guarded in the privacy of the castles and manors. The Bohemian-Moravian nobility, and later influential officials moved within the circles of the Germans of the same rank and all communicated in the German language.

One more factor should be known regarding the Czech rough-coated dog: The changing name of the breed. Historian Dr. S.C Augustin Sedlacek (non kynolog) wrote in his book, ***Castles, Palaces and Keeps in Bohemia***, "The first documents about Cesky Fousek date back to 1348 from the times of Charles the I, King of Bohemia and the Holy Roman Emperor as Charles the IV. In the documents found in the castle "Karlstein," among the files marked "Jagermeister Affair," a letter was found that in A.D. 1348 Charles IV gave Ludvig the Markgraf (count) from Brandeburg "performing hunting dogs" named canis Bohemicus for his amusement."

Further entry states that Charles IV raised and hunted Bohemian dogs. This would let us deduce that the dog breed at the castle was fairly numerous and that the canis Bohemicus had to exist prior to the era of Charles' rule.

On the bag entries at the castle "Hluboka Nad Vltavou" in southern Bohemia is a description of a 1648 celebration ending the 30 year war, with a description of the big hunt where hunting dogs were used, among them canis Bohemicus.

The first painting that includes a Czech dog is preserved in an abbey and judged to be from around 1700.

Through all the centuries the Czechs had access only to fragmentary information due to the social structure—minority and in final analysis we have to be satisfied with conjectures. In reality, we do not know the origin, age and the evolution of the Cesky Fousek, as it is with all the breeds with the exception of the Pudelpointer.

It is almost certain that until the beginning of the second half of the 19th century (before the Kynologic era), the breeding practices did not correspond with today's criteria. Even within what at the time were thought to be established breeds, performance was the goal, the conformation type was of secondary importance, as long as the coat was acceptable.

Gradually decentralization of the breeding from the nobility (large kennels) to the broader use of the dogs among the wealthy middle class and the foresters also contributed to the crossing of the types (conformation) and in some cases to specializing in personal preferences to elevate attributes that best served the types of game predominant in the owner's revier. This caused a fragmentation in the previously stabilized breed lines and the rough-coated Fousek suffered most. This later resulted in litters lacking uniformity in exterior and natural ability consistency in performance.

Because the Bohemia-Moravia countries were part of the Austro-Hungarian state, the Cesky Fousek breed was not recognized and in the registries it was entered under "The Prickly Coated Pointer" (Stichelhaar) and mostly with German names.

At home until 1882 the Breed was known as Czech dog. From 1882 to 1896 it was called Czech Pointer.

The Association for Rough-coated Pointers formed in 1896 started to enter the dogs under the name of Cesky Fousek. In 1924 the Association's name was changed to "Club of the Cesky Fousek Breeder" under the umbrella of the Czechoslovak Hunters Union.

* * * * * * *

[This historical information was not included in the original article, because it was not then available. It helps enormously in the understanding of our breed, as well as the other wirehaired breeds of versatile hunting dogs. It also reinforces the correctness of our original decision to use Cesky Fousek.]

Continuing with the "Restoration of the Griffon Breed on the North American Continent" from the August 1984 GDS:

Immediate Plans

Joe has sent additional information to Czechoslovakia and we are now awaiting further word. It was our belief when this project was first conceived that we would be getting three adult bitches. It is possible that they may make other suggestions—males rather than females, or a mixture of sexes, or perhaps three dogs will not be enough. At any rate, we do know that three dogs will be the minimum required.

We should all be very proud, as I am, that three members of our club have stepped forward and offered to be sponsors of these dogs. Each dog will cost approximately $2,000 [I was wrong, some cost as much as $2,500 in 1985.] This will include the initial cost, plus other expenses such as transportation to get the dogs to the U.S. One of the sponsors is John Lundberg of New Jersey. John is the person who organizes our test in New Jersey each year. Another sponsor is Joe Nadeker. And the third sponsor is Dick Austin, our Vice-President.

If all goes as planned, without any problems, we expect to have the adult Cesky Fouseks in the United States by January, and to have the first litters of pups by spring of 1985. [Problems occurred and I was off by one year.]

Implementation of the Restoration Program

The object of this program is to create a sufficient population (genetic pool) of above average Griffons, to establish a foundation upon which to build. **The only way this can be done is by RIGID BREED CONTROL. No breed has ever been developed or rejuvenated, or maintained without rigid control of the breeding.** We will be maintaining this rigid control with the continued use of our Breeder's Agreement (with some changes to strengthen the control), coupled with the use of our own stud book, the Griffon Registry Book.

We will establish three or four geographic cells within the United States, mainly in the areas where our present tests are now held to make testing of the dogs more affordable. California may expand to two cells, possibly the second cell will be in one of the Northwestern states. [It turned out to be Washington/Oregon, the Northwest Griffon Club.]

In order to make this plan work we must have a cadre of knowledgeable and experienced hunters, within our geographical areas, who will purchase puppies from the first breedings. These hunters must be able to expose a young dog properly to hunting conditions, etc. And, they must be willing to submit to the Breeding Control. I am very proud to say that a number of you at each of our tests this spring, after hearing about our plans, came forward and offered to buy a pup from one of the first litters. Not only that, you were all excited about what we are going to do and wanted to be a part of it! That is the spirit we need and that is the spirit we have.

We ask any members who have a serious commitment to this program to submit a letter of application to the Secretary, explaining your hunting experience, as well as the hunting dogs you have owned.

Incidentally, please do not let these geographic areas discourage you from applying. For example if you live in Nevada you are close enough for testing your dog in Northern California. If you live in Wisconsin you are close enough to test your dog in Michigan, and so on.

Now that the spring tests are concluded we are compiling a list of Griffons that will be considered for possible breeding. Selection of dogs will be based on their field performance. Some will be chosen to use with the Cesky Fousek, others will be bred to Griffons. The use of the Cesky Fousek is another tool, to help in our overall Breeding Program. Some of the progeny from the first Griffon x Czech Fousek litters will be bred back to Griffons, and so it will go, re-establishing a genetically strong Griffon breed.

Expected Results

When you are able to breed from an old, genetically purified line, such as the Cesky Fousek, the influence is amazing. The production of good progeny (puppies) really works, provided the correct choice of parents is used. The production is so uniform it is difficult to believe.

We expect the project to be completed in ten years, though we will begin to see the positive results very quickly with the first and second generations. That means in ten years [That was 1984.] we will have stabilized and upgraded the breed, and [will] have established a large enough, sound genetic breeding pool.

In future issues of the GDS we will present in detail the rules to be used for maintaining strict control of the breeding.

We as Griffonniers must feel very grateful for having Joe Nadeker working with us and for us. Without Joe's knowledge and his contacts in Europe our future success would be much more difficult and would take a much longer time.

Conclusion

I feel the same way that many of you do who attended our spring tests and heard about our plans—excited! I find it exciting for several reasons. First, that we have found a way to upgrade our Griffons, the dogs I love so dearly. I hope that I will be fortunate enough to have one of the pups from the first litters. I want to be a part of this. And finally, I find it exciting to think that it will be us, the American Griffonniers, who will save this breed.

During the commemoration of our club's 25th anniversary in 1976, our President, Roy Speece, from York, Nebraska, wrote something for the GDS that I feel is a very fitting way to conclude this article. [See "Roy's "Yesterday, Today, Tomorrow: For Us It's Tomorrow That Counts".]

July 1, 1984

At the judges seminar/clinic in New Jersey in 1984, Joe Nadeker explains something about conformation judging, as we evaluate ***MAHASKA'S MERRY SUSAN****. Tom Whitley with "****SUZIE,****" then Joe, and John Lundberg. This was the same weekend that "****SUZIE****" did her IHDT. Just behind Tom, is Lou Taxiarchis from Maine. (Compliments Joan Bailey)*

ERIK OD JEZERAK's *first day in America, late December 1985, at the Lundberg's in New Jersey.He checks things out, and makes a quick assessment that life will be a lot better here than behind the Iron Curtain.To speed the adjustment to his new home,* ***ERIK*** *slept in the Lundberg bedroom for the first few months. (Compliments Bonnie Lundberg)*

CHAPTER SIXTEEN
THE BEGINNING OF THE SECOND PHASE OF THE WPGCA APPROVED BREEDING PROGRAM-1984

During the remainder of 1983, Joe began the search for our Czech Fouseks, properly called Cesky Fousek. Much was done by mail, some by phone, and Joe flew to Czechoslovakia several times. Because Czechoslovakia was still behind the Iron Curtain, everything was under strict government control, so bribery had to be employed; Joe was slipping money under the table whenever he had to.

In the spring of 1984, as the officers, members of the board of directors, and judges traveled to tests in many parts of the country, we explained the plans, and the need to use the Fouseks. Members were quite shocked at first, but as we talked and explained and answered questions, many members began to agree with us. Many of those who were opposed to the plan were adamant and most dropped their membership in the club. Those who dropped out were hung up on the phrase "purebred." (For a detailed discussion of "purebred," see Chapters 26 and 27 on breeding.) There were also many members who didn't agree with us, but who stayed in the club, and are still with us today.

Wherever we went there was one question that was always asked: How long will it take for this to work, or until we can actually see the results?" Joe always answered, "Because we will be using a stabilized breed, a breed that has been stabilized for about 20 years, and because it is genetically very close to our Griffons, it will take ten years." As it turned out, it took less than 10 years. The first Griffon x Fousek breeding took place in 1986. By the end of 1994 and the spring of 1995, the stabilization and improvement was evident.

After the spring tests in 1984, I began writing the long article on restoring the Griffon. I sent drafts to Joe and perhaps to a few others. I can't remember now. But it was Joe that I depended on most for guidance. Finally Joe and I felt the article was ready and the entire August 1984 GDS was devoted to the article on restoring the breed.

As the end of 1984 approached, we were expecting to have two or three Fouseks here early in 1985. Delays occurred. More delays. In June Joe made plans to go to Czechoslovakia for two months in the fall. The fall came and went. In the December GDS of that year, I wrote:

The End of a Year

The Beginning of a New Decade for our Griffons

> For Griffonniers in North America 1985 has been a year of hope, a year of frustration, and a year of learning. We hoped that the Cesky Fouseks would arrive early enough in 1985 to produce some spring litters of pups. That did not happen, and it has been frustrating for us to miss an entire year in our breeding plans. At the same time, as we have

waited for the dogs to arrive we have used the time to learn and understand more about the principles involved in breeding, and how to evaluate our dogs. So 1985 has had its mixed blessings.

As this was being written the first week of November, the call came that the first Fousek would arrive by the last week of November! This is our Utility tested male, **ERIK**....His credentials are impeccable and he looks very grand....Not only do we look forward to the pups that will be sired by **ERIK,** but we also wish to his new master, John Lundberg, many, many enjoyable days in the field with **ERIK**!

The first Fousek bitch has been secured for us and will be arriving about two weeks after **ERIK.** She will go to Warren Webster in California, and we hope to have a photo of her for the February GDS. She is Intermediate tested with an outstanding performance, and excellent in conformation and coat.

The second bitch has not been secured for us to date, but we expect to have her very soon. This one will go to Dick Austin in California. The search is also on for our second male and hopefully he will come to us within the next few months.

As we wait for the dogs to arrive, and for the first litters to be on the ground, it is a good time to look ahead at the next decade and understand what we should expect.

Realistic Approach to the "Fousek" Injection

You will remember from reading the August 1984 GDS what the expected results will be from the Fousek injection. By using an old, genetically pure line we will quickly establish uniformity, and by the end of the decade we will have stabilized and upgraded the breed and established a large enough, sound genetic breeding pool to ensure the future of the breed.

Along the road during the next ten years it is very important that we all understand that such an endeavor is not without some disappointments. It will not all be a bed of roses. If we were just going to breed pure Cesky Fouseks with pure Czech Fouseks it would be fairly easy. We would simply be breeding dogs from genetically pure strains and could expect a very high percentage of each litter to be very good, sound hunting dogs.

But, that is not our goal. Our goal is to reestablish the Griffon breed on the North American continent. As you all know by now, our breed is decimated. As stated in other issues of the GDS, when a breed declines to such alarming levels it is manifested primarily in the dogs' mental makeup. You begin to see more and more dogs that are mentally unstable.

Given this situation we must all face the fact that not all the pups from the first litters of Griffon x Fousek will be breedable. There will even be some rejects. Why will this happen? The mental instability which has crept like a weed into our Griffons will be transmitted to the first Griffon x Fousek litters. That is unavoidable. I don't think anyone could find a Griffon in the United States today without at least one mentally unstable dog in its pedigree. And many, probably the majority of Griffons today have several mentally unstable dogs in their pedigrees.

Even when we use Griffons for breeding who manifest no mental instability, it will be there somewhere in the bloodline. But, although this will be passed on in the first generation of breedings, the pure, sound Czech Fousek will begin to dilute this major fault.

As we breed each succeeding generation, 1st, 2nd, 3rd, etc. we will always be culling this trait, diluting it further, trying to wipe it out. Eventually this will give us a genetically pure strain again. But along this road we must be prepared for disappointments. Not every pup is going to turn into super dog....

It's best to face this possibility now, remembering that there will be some inferior dogs. This program will work and we will be seeing more and more sound, hunting Griffons. But along the way we must be prepared that some of us will be disappointed. Once we accept that, we can move on with the knowledge that there is always the new pup to start over with. And, if we have been one of the unlucky ones we can know that although the dog did not turn out to be what we had hoped, we have, in our way, helped the breed and the program.

Being realistic should not dampen anyone's enthusiasm for our project, nor for getting a pup. It just makes common sense to face all the possibilities—to go into the venture with our eyes open. It is very exciting to know that within just a few months puppies will be walking around in the United States, and some of them will become one day the foundation from which we build our genetic pool!

For 1986 I wish all Griffonniers everywhere, both here and across the ocean, good health, good dogs, and good hunting. To members of our own Griffon Club my very deep thanks to each and everyone of you for your support throughout the past years and for the years ahead.

* * * * * * *

In writing that article I had hoped to prepare us for disappointments along the way. I'm not sure that it helped. And we did have some disappointments, some bad luck. But, that is how it is when one is brave enough to step out of the mold and try for something better. It's hard, tough work.

That was in 1984. Today, in 1996, as this book heads to press, there is absolutely no doubt in my mind that we have succeeded. In the last two years we have continued to produce litters which have a high percentage of good hunting dogs. That is our goal. To produce sound, easy-to-train dogs, that have all the necessary inherited talent to make good hunting dogs, and good family dogs.

December 1985 - ERIK OD JEZERAK Arrives in America

At long last, in December 1985, our first, and soon to be much loved Cesky Fousek arrived from behind the Iron Curtain.

Being a very sentimental person, and even more so when it comes to our Griffons, I feel the tears behind my eyes, because as I sit here writing today, **ERIK** is 14. The time has gone so swiftly. When he arrived in December 1985, he was four years old, in his prime. His new owners, John and Bonnie Lundberg, met **ERIK** at Kennedy Airport in New York. It had been a very long journey, perhaps 12 hours. **ERIK** simply walked out of his crate, tail up and wagging, with a smile on his face, as if to say, "Hello, here I am!"

John says **ERIK** has been the best dog he has owned in his entire life. His temperament is exactly what we want in our dogs: In addition to having all the natural hunting abilities—he won the versatile test in Czechoslovakia in 1984 for all around best versatile dog of the year (of all breeds) in that country—above all else he wants to please.

If I sound as if I'm getting carried away, I probably am. You have to remember the context, our history. For me, **ERIK** symbolized the chance we had to save this breed. Here, in living flesh, was our beginning.

ERIK did not travel alone. **JISKRA,** the second Fousek, traveled with him. John and Bonnie took **JISKRA** home for an overnight rest, returning the next evening to Kennedy Airport where they met Dick Austin who had flown in from California just to take **JISKRA** on the final lap of her journey back to Warren and Helen Webster.

Jiskra had been chosen for us as a suitable female to breed to **ERIK**. Genetically, they were compatible. Unfortunately, **JISKRA** was killed about a year after she arrived. But for the short time he had her, Warren said she was the best hunting dog he had ever owned.

We didn't waste much time and a couple of weeks later **MAHASKA'S MERRY SUSAN** (one of the last dogs from the first phase of the Breeding Program) was bred to **ERIK.** On March 12, 1986, the first "Fousek x Griffon" litter was whelped. We had our beginning. At the end of April, **FREEWINDS ALAMANCE** was bred to **ERIK**, and the second litter was whelped on July 4th.

These first two litters were not what we would call all together successful, the reason being that a litter is only successful if it produces a high percentage of good hunting dogs. We did not get that high percentage. Today we would not breed either of the above bitches. But in 1986 they were all we had. However, from each litter we got *one* bitch we thought *might* be breedable.

One was **AVAJ OF IAMONIA**, and the other was **AUTUMN OF HOFFMAN MILL**. **AVAJ** had better genes going for her, than did **AUTUMN**, primarily because **AUTUMN** carried in her genetic make-up **BIRGA V.D. CULM**. That is the primary reason why **AVAJ's** litters were more successful than **AUTUMN's**. Each bitch produced a good number of sound hunting dogs, but because of the "cleaner" bloodlines in **AVAJ**, she had more good dogs per litter. Both **AUTUMN** and **AVAJ** have been excellent hunting dogs.

In **AUTUMN's** pedigree, on the dam's side, you will see **ANKA VOM FUCHSBERG**. This was one of the four female pups we got from Germany, and you can see in the fourth generation, the female **KATHI V.D. BRECH**. Behind **KATHI** is **BIRGA**. Also in the fourth generation, the last dog down, **ANKA VOM RAMSBERG**, also has behind her **BIRKA**. No wonder the four female pups from Germany did not turn out well. They were line bred to **BIRGA**.

It's easy to see in **AVAJ**'s pedigree, that there are fewer weaknesses. On the dam's side, **MAHASKA** was slightly soft in temperament. Her dam, **ALICE B. TOKLAS**, was not a dog we would ever consider for breeding today. Even the sire's side of **MAHASKA** was not as genetically strong as one would wish for. But, **BIRGA** was not there.

ERIK's pedigree will serve as a partial illustration for us, to document how the Czech breeding is conducted for the Fouseks. Only on rare occasion will they do a close line breeding. Line breeding is breeding to a mate that has some common blood. An outcross is breeding two dogs that have no common blood. A loose line breeding is where two dogs have one or two or even three dogs in both bloodlines, *back at least three generations.* A close line breeding is when two dogs have com-

Arohn Z Devaterek (CF)
Aris Z Javorové doliny
Borka Štemflík (CF)
Argo z Polední stráně (CF)
Bor z Borové doliny (CF)
Erika Z Želivce (CF)
Dana ze Želivce (CF)
Erik od Jezárek (CF)
Flot z Čelechovic na Hané (CF)
Avar Z Faralce (CF)
Borka z Klasinky (CF)
Asta Od Vejřice (CF)
Aran z Muticka (CF)
PEDIGREE 35
Cora Vejříky (CF)
Avaj of Iamonia
Tonik du Bois Follet (F)
Lucas of Hunter's Creek (A)
Ulla de St Landry (F)
Bon Chasseur de la Cote (A)
Pipo des Vieilles Rouches (F)
Victoria de Bois Follet (F)
Lorene des Ronciers de Clavieres (F)
Mahaska's Merry Susan (A)
Taquin du Bois Follet (F)
Whiskey du Pironec (FQ)
Rana du Sauverain (FQ)
Alice B. Toklias (A)
Taquin du Bois Follet (F)
Huckle Hill Angela (A)
Huckle Hill Patty (A)

Arohn Z Devaterek (CF)
Aris Z Javorové doliny
Borka Štemflík (CF)
Argo z Polední stráně (CF)
Bor z Borové doliny (CF)
Erika Z Želivce (CF)
Dana ze Želivce (CF)
Erik od Jezárek (CF)
Flot z Čelechovic na Hané (CF)
Avar Z Faralce (CF)
Borka z Klasinky (CF)
Asta Od Vejřice (CF)
Aran z Muticka (CF)
Bora Od Teplého vrchu (CF)
PEDIGREE 36
Cora Vejříky (CF)
Autumn of Hoffman Mill (A)
Tonik du Bois Follet (F)
Lucas of Hunter's Creek (A)
Ulla de St Landry (F)
Cacei de la Cote (A)
Pipo des Vieilles Rouches (F)
Victoria du Bois Follet (F)
Lorene des Ronciers de Clavieres (F)
Freewinds Alamance (A)
Eik v.d. Neuburg (G)
Gotz vom Bibertal (G)
Kathi v.d. Brech (G)
Anka vom Fuchsburg (G)
Claus vom Wolfsberg (G)
Diana vom Ramsberg (G)
Anka vom Ramsberg (G)

Horan ze Žampachu (CF)
Arohn Z Devaterek (CF)
Bela Šachovna (CF)
Aris Z Javorove doliny (CF)
Bor od Tloskova (CF)
Borka Štemflík (CF)
Asta z Jedláku (CF)
Argo z Polední stráně (CF)
Blesk of Tloskova (CF)
Bor z Borové doliny (CF)
Blanka z Petřínské osady (CF)
Erika Z Želivce (CF)
Blesk z Mézlova sadu (CF)
Dana ze Želivce (CF)
PEDIGREE 37
Erik od Jezárek (CF)
Ada ze Želivce (CF)
Ajax ze Starého dolu (CF)
Flot z Čelechovic na Hané (CF)
Bojka Ovčáry (CF)
Avar Z Paralce (CF)
Alan od Svidníka (CF)
Borka z Klasinky (CF)
Alma z Klasinky (CF)
Asta Od Vejřice (CF)
Bor od Tloskova (CF)
Aran z Muticka (CF)
Dina z Hlasiva (CF)
Bora Od Teplého vrchu (CF)
Blesk z Mézlova sadu (CF)
Cora Vejříky (CF)
Cela Z Běláku (CF)

Pipo des Vieilles Rouches (F)
Tonik du Bois Follet (F)
Lorene des Ronciers de Clavieres (F)
Bent Pine's Biff (A)
Barry v.d. Neuburg (G)
Bent Pine's Brigette (A)
Tina de la Reote (A)
Amos van Jagershorst (A)
Tonik du Bois Follet (F)
Lucas of Hunter's Creek (A)
Ulla de St Landry (F)
Desiree de la Cote (A)
Dago v.d. Neuburg (G)
Happy Hilda Hunter (A)
PEDIGREE 38
Point's Algernon (A)
Suzy des Zizaines (F)
Tonik du Bois Follet (F)
Lucas of Hunter's Creek (A)
Ulla de St Landry (F)
Bon Chasseur de la Cote (A)
Pipo des Vieilles Rouches (F)
Victoria du Bois Follet (F)
Lorene des Ronciers de Clavieres (F)
Point's Pewter Tip (A)
Taquin du Bois Follet (F)
Whiskey du Pironec (FQ)
Rana du Sauverain (FQ)
Alice B. Toklias (A)
Taquin du Bois Follet (F)
Huckle Hill Angela (A)
Huckle Hill Patty (A)

mon blood in the second generation. Inbreeding is when the common blood occurs in the first generation. (More detailed information on this appears in Part Two, Chapter 26 and 27, on breeding.)

Look in the fourth generation of **ERIK**'s pedigree. Count down from the top to the third dog **BOR OD TLOSKOVA**. Go down two more dogs to **BLESK OD TLOSKOVA**. **BOR** and **BLESK** were littermates. Go to the third generation , second and third dogs down, **BORKA STEMFLIK** and **BOR A BOROVE DOLINY**. Their sires were littermates, so it was almost breeding half brother to half sister. This would be inbreeding, and was rarely done. They must have been trying to "fix" (stabilize, or cement) some positive traits from that "B" litter of TLOSKOVA.

It's interesting to go down the dam's side, in the fourth generation, fourth dog from the bottom, **BOR OD TLOSKOVA** and then look up on the sire's side, third dog from the top. **ERIK** was from a loose line breeding to **BOR OD TLOSKOVA**.

*Below: **MAHASKA'S MERRY SUSAN**, February 8, 1986, and Tom wrote on the back of the picture: "I am enclosing a picture taken while quail hunting. **SUZIE**, being a versatile hunting dog, pointed a rabbit which was shot and retrieved nicely. It is not obvious from the picture, but this is also the first hunt for the Griffon x Fousek litter—getting a little early imprinting." The pups were born 4 weeks later.*

Again in the fourth generation, look at the dog second from the bottom, **BLESK Z MEZLOVA SADU**. Go up to the seventh dog from the top. It's **BLESK Z MEZLOVA SADU**. So, **ERIK** was also loosely line bred to **BLESK**.

This is how much of the Cesky Fousek breeding is done, with the exception of when they need to "fix" a line. (Again, there is more about this in Part Two.) It is also the same system we are trying to hold to in our Griffon Breeding Program. In the beginning of the Fousek injection that was impossible, because breeding ANY of our Griffons to a Fousek was a complete outcross. But, that is where one starts, and is where we were with the first two litters by **ERIK** out of **MAHASKA** and **AUTUMN**.

JISKRA *completing the Track of the Duck and Retrieve to Warren Webster during IHDT, March, 1986, Redding, California. (Compliments, Joan Bailey)*

CHAPTER SEVENTEEN
THE LAST HALF OF THE EIGHTIES

In September 1985 **LUCAS OF HUNTERS CREEK** died of stomach torsion. **VICTORIA DU BOIS FOLLET** had died of stomach torsion a few years earlier. *And* some of their progeny had died of it. No matter what the veterinarians and research people were telling us, we knew there had to be a genetic predisposition to stomach torsion. Yes, environmental factors do play an important role. But sire and dam and several get? So that was more information to feed into our genetic memory bank on our dogs.

As 1986 rolled around, so a did new slate of officers. Dick Austin became our president, and John Lundberg, our vice-president, while Harold Baskin moved from president to treasurer, and I continued as secretary. Here's what Dick had to say to us as he embarked on becoming our president for the next three years (reprinted from the April 1986 GDS):

> Dear Griffonniers: March 10, 1986
>
> It is with a great deal of excitement and anticipation that I look forward to the future of the Griffon Club.
>
> The Breeding Committee's long and diligent efforts to import and breed the first Fousek to one of our better Griffons has at last taken place. The decision to inject new blood into the Griffon breed was the result of many years of discussion and research on the part of our Breeding Committee. Only time and hard work, on the part of our membership, will determine how successful we will be.
>
> The infusion of the five Czech Fouseks in our breed is an important step in re-establishing the "desire to produce game" in our Griffons. However, equally important is the responsibility of every Griffon owner to have their Griffons x-rayed for hip dysplasia and evaluated in a sanctioned Intermediate Hunting Dog Test. We as a club must build our base of breedable Griffons, and we accomplish that task by evaluating as many dogs as possible in the very important Intermediate Hunting Dog Test.
>
> The future of our breed looks very promising, and with your help we can re-establish the fine hunting qualities our breed is known for....

* * * * * * *

As the spring testing season got underway, the first litter from the second phase of the Breeding Program was on the ground in Tallahassee, Florida, with long-time club members Tom and Mahaska Whitley. I was to receive one of those pups and I kept getting exciting reports from Tom—with pictures.

Next page: ***ERIK OD JEZERAK****, at a field test in New Jersey, 4 months after his arrival in America. He holds intensely on Bobwhite quail. It is a continuing joy to see dogs like this one live on in their progeny, for many generations. (Compliments Howard Coutu)*

The first test of the spring was held early in April in Northern California. It was our annual three-day event, with a judges seminar on Friday, followed by two days of testing. John and Bonnie Lundberg flew out from New Jersey with **ERIK**, so that everyone could meet him. And of course, Warren and Helen Webster were there with **JISKRA**. It is difficult to convey what it felt like to observe John and Warren walking out in the field together with **ERIK** and **JISKRA** that Friday morning before the start of the judges seminar. It had been a long wait and now, now we were excited. John and Warren had just met for the first time. **ERIK** and **JISKRA** remembered each other from their short meeting at the Lundbergs and **JISKRA** was ecstatic when she saw **ERIK**. As I watched them move out to the field I wished there could have been a recording made of the conversation between John and Warren—their heads together, obviously comparing notes, as the dogs ranged out in front of them. Remember, these dogs had been trained in Czech, and hence John and Warren gave all their commands in Czech. I won't even tell you what Joe Nadeker said about their accent! But, the dogs, being essentially intelligent and kind, obeyed the commands.

Although **JISKRA** had been field-tested in Czechoslovakia, Warren ran her that weekend in IHDT, and she got a Prize II. This is quite remarkable, because it takes six months to a year for an adult dog coming over, to adjust to a new home, new environment, many new smells, and even some new game birds.

In the fall of 1987, about 18 months after **JISKRA**'s arrival, and a few months before she was killed, Warren ran her in Utility Field Test near Ellensburg, Washington. She received 232 points and a Prize III. They were a good team.

In addition to the California test, we held tests in Oregon, Nebraska, Michigan, and New Jersey. We tested one of the last litters from the first phase of the breeding program, in natural ability (**AMOS VAN JAGERSHORST x POINT'S PEWTER TIP,** Pedigree 38 in previous chapter). A glance at the tabulations of the test results of this litter looks good to the unknowing eye. (See Appendix for complete tabulation of test results.) Seven dogs were tested; six out of seven qualified. If one looks closer, four out of the seven dogs were evaluated as having some defect in temperament: "skittish during conformation examination;" "immature, skittish;" "calm, but exhibits negative behavior in presence of game;" and "apprehensive."

In conformation, five out of the seven had eye defects: "right eye open;" and "eyes open;" and "right eye open;" "both eyes entropic;" and "left eye slightly open." In addition, two out of the seven had short coats, no furnishings. (Furnishings refer to whiskers, eyebrows, and moustaches, as our Griffons have.)

This was not a successful litter, from a breeding standpoint, though most of the pups went on to become adequate hunting dogs once they had lots of exposure. Several of the dogs also overcame temperament problems due to positive exposure, which helped them to become productive hunting dogs.

From the Breeding Committee's point of view, no dogs would have been used for breeding from this litter. Unfortunately the breeder did not adhere to the WPGCA Breeding Rules, and because sire and dam had been registered with AKC, he was able to register the entire litter with AKC, and at least two dogs from the litter were used for breeding (unsuccessfully in my opinion, from the limited test results available), because the breeder did not keep control. He also did not name the pups properly. This could not happen today, because our dogs can only be registered in our own stud book.

When we had discussed the possibility of breeding this bitch, we chose as a stud **BENT PINE'S BIFF** (See Pedigree 33) in Washington state. But the breeder did not want to ship the bitch from Michigan out to Washington. He wanted to use **AMOS** who lived within driving distance. We acquiesced to this.

In hindsight, we should have stuck to our original decision to use **BENT PINE'S BIFF**. If we had, we would have bypassed **DESIREE DE LA COTE** (temperament problems), **LUCAS OF HUNTERS CREEK** (who gave us eye problems coming from **SCARLETT DE ST LANDRY**). Using **BIFF** would have been a much stronger genetic base. (For more on breeding principles see Chapters 26 and 27, Part Two.)

As we waited for the Fouseks to arrive and for puppies to be produced by them, we were running out of even marginal dogs to breed, yet there was a need to keep our testing areas viable. We put out a plea to all club members to help in this endeavor by entering their dogs in Utility tests. In the spring of 1986 that is exactly what seven members did. All qualified but one dog. We thanked them then and I repeat that thanks now.

Earlier in the year, word came that Marg Allen had died. An excerpt from the obituary I wrote for the June 1986 GDS said, "Newer members of the Griffon Club may not know this name, but we old timers surely do, and especially many Griffonniers in the Northwest...Without doubt she was a driving influence in the breed and club for many years and will be remembered by many Griffonniers all across America. Joan Bailey, May 15, 1986."

Marg disagreed with a number of things I was saying and doing, mostly any criticism, or pointing out faults or problems in the breed. It angered her very much that anything negative was being said or written about Griffons. Around 1976 she broke all contact with me, and we were never in touch again.

During 1986 the board of directors, after much discussion and thought, inaugurated fall testing for our club. Selfishly, we had all dragged our feet on this, because no one wanted to give up a weekend during hunting season to participate in a field test. However, we all came to realize the importance of fall testing, and of course the Europeans had been doing it for more than one hundred years.

Ideally a dog is run in the spring in Natural Ability when she is around 12 months old, give or take a few months. Then, with more exposure and training during the next six months, the dog comes back in the fall for Intermediate Hunting Dog Test. Additionally, there are some dogs that are too young to run in Natural Ability in the spring, but need to be tested in the fall. Also, it is the best time for Utility dogs to be tested.

Our first fall test took place in Ellensburg, Washington. Del Peterson, president of the German Longhair Club of America, secured the grounds for us, which had wild Hungarian partridge. Most of the organizational duties fell to the Northwest Griffon Club, primarily with Clay and Cheryl Zumwalt, who had started this regional club earlier in the year with a spring test in Oregon.

We tested four Utility dogs, three Intermediate dogs, and two Natural Ability. Bill Toner flew out from Wisconsin to run his **AMOS VAN JAGERSHORT.** Harold Baskin and I ran our five-and-a-half-month-old **AMOS** and **ALF** (mine) **OF IAMONIA** for evaluation. There was one Pudelpointer, one German Longhair, and one Brittany Spaniel.

At the end of 1986, in the December GDS, we announced that a group of Griffonniers would travel to Germany in 1988 to join in the celebration there, com-

Above: ***BENT PINE'S BIFF****, a male we used several times for breeding. Below:* ***AVAJ OF IAMONIA****, from the first litter of Fousek x Griffon, at 13 months at her natural ability test in Iowa, 1987. She proved to be an outstanding dog for passing on her excellent attributes to her progeny, and thus a very important dog in the history of our breed. (Compliments Larry Mueller)*

memorating the 100th anniversary of the forming of the original Griffon Club by Korthals. The early announcement was to give club members a few years to save and plan.

And on November 8, 1986, long-time and faithful member of the Griffon Club, Glen Raker, died in California. Here's part of what I wrote in the December GDS, "Glen and his most faithful friend, **SNOW QUEUE BLANC**, were making their way to the duck blind early on the morning of November 8th when Glen suffered a massive heart attack and died at the place he loved so much. At the time **SNOW** was 15...." Glen had been with us from the beginning, back in 1973, when we had our first versatile test in California, and had stood by us when we decided to use the Fousek injection.

In the spring of 1987 we tested the first two litters from the Fousek injection. Both were sired by **ERIK**. The litter out of **MAHASKA'S MERRY SUSAN** tested well. (See tabulation in Appendix.) Three dogs received Prize I, three Prize III, and two did not qualify, due to of all things, Pointing, or lack thereof. One of those dogs had been worked on pen-raised birds, but I don't know about the other. However, there were a lot of conformation faults: eyes, bites, some poor coats, though some very good ones.

This litter really demonstrated the importance of the Intermediate Hunting Dog Test (IHDT). Of eight dogs in the litter, six were tested in IHDT. Three dogs qualified, three did not. The three that did not qualify fell down at the water, under pressure, manifesting a defect in temperament. So the litter was very mixed, but most of the dogs went on to be good hunting dogs. (See Pedigree 35 for the "A" OF IAMONIA litter.)

And, there was **AVAJ OF IAMONIA**, who qualified with a Prize I in IHDT, conformation 4, coat 4, temperament sound. She was the one breedable dog, coming from a questionable litter, so we were aware that she might carry the undesirable traits and might pass them on to her get.

The other litter, out of **FREEWINDS ALAMANCE**, did not do as well in Natural Ability. The pups were only 9 and 10 months old when tested, whereas the "A OF IAMONIA were 13 months, which is an optimum age to test NAT. Out of the "A" OF HOFFMAN MILL litter of eight, two received Prize I, the other six did not qualify, *all due to water*. **BIRGA**. Bingo. In IHDT, the two dogs that had received Prize I in NAT, did the same in IHDT. Only two other dogs from the litter were entered in IHDT and both did poorly. One of the two that did so well was chosen to be used for breeding and that was **AUTUMN OF HOFFMAN MILL**. (Pedigree 36) She was run in Utility Field Test (UFT) a few years later, receiving Prize I, and gave one of the finest utility performances any of us had ever seen. (See chapter 19 for photo.)

The Third Fousek Arrives - HELA Z DOBROWSKA

HELA had been bred to a male in Czechoslovakia before she was shipped to Joe Nadeker in California. The litter of eight puppies was whelped in June 1987, and two months later they were placed with various club members from all parts of the country. It was exciting. Dogs from this litter would be our "seed" for the coming years, we thought.

nother dog from the first ousek x Griffon breeding, bove: ***ALF OF AMONIA*** during his atural ability test in regon, April 1987, Prize I. Compliments Tom Whitley) elow: ***AVAJ*** all grown p, November 1990, unting Hungarian artridge in Iowa. By this ime she had qualified in HDT, Prize I, and pro-uced the very successful "A" OF DUTCHMAN'S IOLLOW litter. (Compli-nents John Pitlo)

Below: ***HELA Z DOBROWSKA*** *in April 1988, during the utility field test in Oregon as she brings the dead bird from the drag to Joe Nadeker. (Compliments Joan Bailey)*

***AMBER OF IAMONIA**, September 1987, during her IHDT in Ellensburg, Washington, completing the retrieve to owner Brad Meyen. She received a Prize II, and was a fine hunting dog.*

***Next page: WOLFERZELL, GERMANY**, The beginning of the three day celebration commemorating the 100th anniversary of the Korthals Griffon Club. Friday morning and the traditional playing of the hunting horns signaling the beginning of the hunt. (Compliments Harold Baskin)*

1888
100
Years
1988

CHAPTER EIGHTEEN
1988, THE 100TH ANNIVERSARY OF ORIGINAL KORTHALS GRIFFON CLUB IN GERMANY

During the year of 1988, we used this special heading on every issue of ***The Gun Dog Supreme***, as did the German Griffon Club, with a similar heading in their news bulletin. And we began making plans to have our own celebrations all across America.

In the spring we tested the Fousek litter "B" OF THE CASCADES in NAT, Joe Nadeker assuming the responsibility of breeder as the new owner of **HELA**, though technically the breeder was in Czechoslovakia. The results were mixed. There were some excellent dogs, two culls, and the others were in between. It was not what we had expected. In conformation and coat, they were all good, mostly with 4's and only two received 3's.

100th Celebrations Across America

During the summer many Griffonniers met at picnics which we held on the same day, July 30, 1988, to celebrate the founding of the mother club in Germany on July 29, 1888. We met in IDAHO, MINNESOTA, MAINE, ILLINOIS, OREGON, CALIFORNIA, and WISCONSIN. Here are just a few of the many photos taken from all those places where fun and memories were the order of the day.

One of the celebrations I described in the October 1988 GDS:

The Rocky Mountain Griffon Club

> Yes, another regional chapter of the WPGCA is now in existence, formed July 30, 1988, on the celebration day of the 100th anniversary of the original Griffon Club...
>
> Now to the important part of our day! The fun, the good people and the good dogs! I hated to miss our own Oregon picnic at the Zumwalt homestead in Cottage Grove. However, I also wanted to see my friends in Idaho. So with a difficult decision made, I loaded my car Thursday morning and took the long way, going via the John Day country which was new to me, and very beautiful. I gave myself two days to make the drive and during that time I thought a lot about the people in the past who are no longer with us, and about the contributions they each made in their own unique way, to the Griffon cause here in America. And, I decided that I would talk about these people at our gathering.
>
> And so on Saturday afternoon, after we returned from the ponds where the dogs had great fun chasing ducks, we all sat around under the big shade trees in this lovely park by the Snake River, and we talked [about the past, about dogs present and past]. All the dogs were all off leash and most of them were sleeping after the duck chase. If not sleep-

ing, they were running around, staying within sight, and enjoying themselves. We had about six Griffons, two Fouseks, and one Pudelpointer...

The picnic tables, people sitting around, and the dogs loose and running around, reminded me of the days when we used to go to the field tests up in Quebec with our old French Griffon friends there. The dogs were always loose when we sat at the long picnic tables for our meals, and the dogs begged, got in little "fights" now and then, and in general had a great time...

* * * * *

Late in September 14 members of the Wirehaired Pointing Griffon Club of America left for Germany to take part in the 100th Jubilee there. Below are a few excerpts from the special edition of the December 1988 GDS:

ONCE MORE IN WOLFERSZELL FÜR DEN 100TH MIT DEM MUTTER-KLUB

By Joan Bailey

The haunting lit of the brass horns sounded at the old mill in Wolferszell on Friday morning, September 30, 1988, thus officially beginning the European part of the celebration of the 100th Jubilee of the formation of our original Mother Griffon Club in Germany by Korthals....

The fourteen members of the WPGCA who made the journey to Wolferszell were: Dick and Joanne Austin, California; Harold and Sally Baskin, Oregon; Warren and Helen Webster, California; Brad and Kathleen Meyen, Alaska; Bill and Barbara Jensen, Minnesota; Joe and Wanda Kasmedo, New Jersey; Silke Alberts, California; Joan Bailey, Oregon.

...The club aspect of our trip really began around September 14th when the Websters and Joe and Klara Nadeker met in Frankfurt and traveled together to Czechoslovakia. There Joe and Warren toured the countryside looking at Czech Fouseks and trying to get some more tested dogs for our Breeding Program. On September 23rd they joined part of our group in Prague. The Austins, Jensens, and Brad Meyen arrived that day....

A few days later they all traveled about 100 miles from Prague to Litomysl, to attend the annual Karla Podhajskeho special utility test for the 16 best pointing and versatile dogs of the year from Czechoslovakia. It was at this test in 1984 that our **ERIK** earned best dog of the year, and where **HELA** also won high honors a few years later. Of the 16 dogs in 1988 there were several Fouseks, German Shorthairs, one Irish Setter, one English Pointer, one Pudelpointer, and one Spanish Pointer.

The following photos and captions tell some of the story of the time in Wolferszell. Anyone wishing a copy of the large, special edition GDS, covering this event, can order it from the WPGCA, 4N474 Pin Oaks Ln, Maple Park, Il 60151, for $5.00.

As Dick Austin came to the end of his term as president in 1988, he wrote the following for the December 1988 GDS:

The following photos are samplings of the fun and good cheer that Griffonniers had on July 30, 1988 all across America. Above: The Wisconsin gathering, mostly members of the Heartland Griffon Club, hosted by Bill and Cherrie Toner in Black Earth. Below: The Toner Griffons ready to party! ***AMOS****,* ***BLISS****, and* ***MANDY****.*

Above: Typical of the cakes across America that day, this is the Idaho cake, courtesy Rocky Mountain Griffon Club. (Compliments Joan Bailey) Below: In Idaho, a "look-alike contest" of dog and owner, and the winner, leaving all the competition way behind was "Shining Bill Barrett" and his partner ***BREEZE OF THE CASCADES****. (Compliments Gary Pool)*

Looking Back
By Dick Austin

It has been my pleasure to serve as President of this organization for the past three years. I leave my post with a great deal of pride and appreciation for the work completed by our Board of Directors and dedicated members.

Noteworthy are the accomplishments of our Board. Harold Baskin as Treasurer, has increased our club membership by contacting past members in a "one man" membership drive, resulting in bringing our Treasury into the black again. Harold's friendship and council over the past three years have been invaluable to me. Our vice-president, John Lundberg, has devoted a great deal of time and effort in supporting the club. John is the owner of **ERIK**, the first Fousek to be used in our Griffon/Fousek Breeding program. Also, John has been called upon many times in the past to do a variety of assignments, from organizing field tests in his area, to providing legal opinions. His obvious leadership abilities and dedication to the club will serve him well in his next assignment as club president.

From our club secretary and newsletter editor, we have grown to expect much, and have received more. To say that Joan Bailey is the "backbone" of our club would be an understatement. Rebounding from a most tragic illness, Joan successfully handled **ALF OF IAMONIA** to a perfect Natural Ability Prize I score in Oregon, five days after being discharged from the Rehabilitation Institute of Oregon in Portland. And, as editor of the award winning ***Gun Dog Supreme***, Joan keeps our membership informed with vital information, such as her June 1986 article, *"The First Twelve Months—A Lifetime Investment*," winner of the Dog Writers Association of America's "Best Article" of the year award...

Four new faces were added to the ranks of our judging crew during the past three years: John Pitlo, John Zawacki, Clay Zumwalt, and Del Peterson now join Warren Webster, Phil Swain, Susan Swain, Joe Kasmedo, Jack Dallimore, Joan Bailey, Dr. Rolf Benseler, Ted Williams, and of course, Joseph Nadeker. These fine people give of their time, resources and expertise in making possible the accurate evaluation of our Griffons; a responsibility that is of utmost importance in the improvement of our breed.

Club member Brad Meyen completed the incorporation of the WPGCA in 1987. As an attorney, Brad has given countless hours working for the club on this important assignment.

The 100th anniversary of the founding of the Griffon Club was celebrated in the United States and Germany in 1988. I am extremely pleased and honored to have had the opportunity to participate in the U.S. celebration this July with friends and family. That special occasion was followed by the celebration in Wolferszell, Germany in October, again with family and friends.

Of course, special celebrations, as we have had in the U.S. and Germany don't just happen, they take scores of hours in planning and hard work. Again, our Secretary, Joan Bailey, made it all possible for us. I am sure I speak for all who participated in the events when I thank

Joan for all her hard work in making the U.S. and the Germany celebrations successful.

Our Breeding Committee, made up of Joan Bailey, Joseph Nadeker, and Dr. Ed Bailey (and most recently, Warren Webster replacing Dr. Bailey) is in the third year of a ten year program to improve the temperament and hunting abilities of the breed by selective injection of Czech Fousek Blood into the Griffon...

Also, in an effort to increase the gene pool, the Board of Directors issued an appeal in the June 1987 issue of the G.D.S. to "please help the breed by entering your dog in one of our field tests this fall or next spring." That appeal is still valid today. At this time, in the history of the Griffon, I strongly believe it is the duty of every owner of a Griffon (under the age of four) to have that dog tested in one of the many field tests we have each year. The success of our breed depends on the ability of our Breeding Committee to evaluate and identify the breedable dogs we have in the U.S.

As my tenure comes to an end, I look forward to the future of the Griffon Club, secure in my belief that with the support of our new Board of Directors and dedicated members, we will accomplish our goal to restore the Griffon breed to the expectations of Eduard Korthals.

***JISKRA**, the second Fousek to arrive in America. She is the one who went to Warren Webster, but was killed before we had a chance to breed her. As you can see, she had a very expressive face. (Compliments Warren Webster)*

e Karla Podhajskeho Memorial Field test, held annually in the village of Litomysl, Czechoslovakia, birth place Podhajskeho, a respected kynologist. It is for the 16 best pointing dogs of the year, for all pointing breeds. ove: At the conclusion of the testing on Saturday, all the game is laid out, hunting music is played, honoring game. In the photo are 2 deer, 4 hare, about 6 ducks and 3 foxes. (Compliments Joanne Austin) Below: At end of the testing weekend, Dr. Dostal, Breed Warden of the Cesky Fousek club, says a fond farewell to Joe deker. (Compliments Helen Webster)

Above: This is a special book kept just for this field test. It contains the complete records of every dog ever run in every test. It is filled with beautiful paintings and drawings and all entries are hand written. Below: Joe Nadeker reads from the book to members of our group gathered in the room. (Compliments Warren Webster)

ve: On Sunday morning, in the courtyard of Castle Steinach, the Jaghorn-Blasergruppe from Donauworth performed 'ng the conformation parade of 63 Griffons. (Compliments Warren Webster) Below: Three Griffon Club presidents ew the dogs. Dick Austin, president of the American club; Dr. Claude Rochebeuf, president of the French club; and nz Kroninger, president of the German club. Beside him is Dr. Munker, breed warden, and just behind Munker is Mintscheff with his 15 year old **ARDA**, that he ran in UFT in 1977. (Compliments Joan Bailey)

*In Germany, circa 1978, **ANJA VOM OSTERBACK**, one of Maria Zumbaum's early Griffons, during the end of a blood track, when the dog finds the dead animal, then barks a special bark which summons the handler to the game. Below: She waits intently beside the deer for the handler to arrive. This is called Totverbeller, and is one of the tasks required in a full utility test in Germany. (Compliments Maria Zumbaum)*

BOSS OF THE CASCADES*, another dog that would leave his mark on his progeny and subsequent generations, and therefore important in the history of the Griffon in America. Above: About 3 years old, he shows good intensity, from his tail to his ears, convincing that there is game there. (Compliments Jack Dallimore) Below:* ***BOSS*** *demonstrates not only his love of water, but also his enthusiasm and eagerness to be part of the team, as he joyfully brings in the mallard on a Thanksgiving day hunt in eastern Oregon, 1990. (Compliments Joan Bailey)*

*Two littermates to **BOSS**. Above: **BLADE OF THE CASCADES** on a 1989 hunting trip. He earned a Prize II in IHDT, a month or two earlier. Below: **BLITZEN OF THE CASCADES**, during his IHDT in Iowa, fall 1988, Pr II, and came back a year later to earn a Prize I. (Compliments, Joan Bailey)*

In the fall of 1980 in Alexandria, Nebraska, a bunch of members of the WPGCA board of directors take a break during a hunting trip. Left to right: Harold Baskin, vice-president, with his ***LUCAS OF HUNTER'S CREEK****, Joan Bailey, secretary, with* ***ADI DE LA COTE****, Connie Tidwell, treasurer, with his* ***PECOS GYPSY TAMBOURINE****, Roy Speece, president, with his "****KRAUT****," (a Munsterlander), and Ed Bailey with* ***NUMA DU RUISSEAU DU MASSACRE****. Dick Austin probably took the photo, because he was part of our group on the trip.*

April, 1990, Iowa. ***AMY OF DUTCHMAN'S HOLLOW*** *after the water portion of her NAT, the judges check her coat. Owner Bob Hinckley wonders about all of the checking--he knows the coat is great!* ***AMY*** *got all 4's and 4 and 4 in conformation and coat, and became an important dog in the Breeding Program, as you will discover as you read on. (Compliments Tom Whitley, the breeder.)*

CHAPTER NINETEEN
END OF THE EIGHTIES, BEGINNING OF THE NINETIES

As Dick Austin finished his term of office, John Lundberg took the reins and served as our president from 1989 through 1994. Serving as vice-president with John was Warren Webster. Warren had been president of the Sierra Griffon Club for many years, one of our finest senior judges, and a member of the Breeding Committee. Our regional chapters were growing and developing strength and substance due to the leaders and to the fine people who made up their membership. This was happening because now we were able to consistently supply serious hunters with good hunting dogs. This was the key, but still we did not have enough dogs.

During the last few years of the eighties we had very few litters, because there were so few dogs to meet even minimum standards for breeding. Other Griffon owners may have said, or might say today, that there were plenty of Griffons available for breeding. In fact, a number of people were breeding Griffons—in New England, in the Midwest, and in the Northwest. They were people who did not agree with the WPGCA Breeding Program, a strictly voluntary program, and there were others who simply did not care.

The majority of other Griffons that were being bred were not field-tested, and the very few *entire* litters that were tested, were only tested in NAT, not in IHDT. Sometimes one, or even two dogs from a litter would be tested in NAT, but you can't make informed breeding decisions based on such limited information. (See Part Two.)

In the January 1988 issue of ***Outdoor Life*** magazine, the hunting dogs editor, Larry Mueller, wrote about our breeding program in his article, "How To Improve A Breed." Larry had been a long-time friend of the Griffon Club since he met some of us back in 1972 at the first field test for versatile hunting dogs in Minnesota. Even then he liked what he saw. He came to our first test in Iowa in the spring of 1987. He simply wrote about what we were trying to do. This article helped our endeavor more than Larry could have ever dreamed.

Because Larry is a good writer, an honest writer, he simply told what he had witnessed and learned that weekend in Iowa. He ended the article with:

> ....Obviously, the club's members know what they want, and they go about getting it in a manner that differs radically from that of the usual dog club. They hold tests, not trials. They are cooperative, not competitive. There are no cover-ups of bloodline faults, taboos do not prevent objective publication of breed facts. In 10 years, hip dysplasia was licked and the breed improved by 100 percent. Nothing like that has ever been achieved in such a short time under field-trial competition.
>
> ....With patience and perseverance, there may one day be enough really good Griffons to go around.

Larry's article created an interest and a demand from *serious* hunters. Many people had to wait two, even three years, to get a pup from the program, because we did not have enough breedable dogs, especially bitches. But they waited because they believed in our program. Today, in the mid-1990s, we can produce six, seven, eight litters a year. We can supply nearly every hunter who applies for a pup in the same year, without long waits, while at the same time maintaining a viable gene pool.

These serious hunters have become the backbone of our club. The majority of our leadership positions today—officers, members of the board of directors, new judges, and other appointed positions—are being filled by people who joined our club, waited a couple of years to get a pup, liked what they got, liked the people in the club, and decided to give back a little of what they had received.

So we owe a great deal to Larry Mueller for having seen the possibilities, believed in us, and for having told the hunting public about us.

In the fall of 1988 we tested six of the "B" OF THE CASCADES litter in IHDT. Results were mixed again. Two dogs got Prize II, **BOSS OF THE CASCADES** did not qualify due to a 1 in pointing. His owner, Jack Dallimore, freely admitted that he had worked the dog on pigeons and the dog had stopped pointing. He entered **BOSS** again and he qualified.

Nevertheless, I *did* see **BOSS** sight point a duck (during his first IHDT), so I knew the dog had a strong pointing instinct. ("Freezing" into a point by sight or scent is manifesting pointing instinct.) I was proven correct some time later, after Jack worked with the dog and reconditioned him to "freeze," or point, when his nose encountered a bird. Two months after his first IHDT, he was entered again in California and received a Prize II. And he sired two litters in which all the progeny had strong pointing instinct.

Two dogs of this "B" OF THE CASCADES litter did poorly and were judged to be mentally unstable. Another dog failed because of water.

Four dogs came back in the spring of 1989 and all qualified in IHDT. Three of them had been previously tested in IHDT. In addition to the mixed results of the litter, we were also learning that the Fouseks were slower to mature than some of the other versatile breeds.

There was so much good in the "B OF THE CASCADES" litter that we tried to figure out how we could use some of this blood for breeding. One male, **BREEZE**, had turned up with OCD, a condition of the shoulder that is caused partially by environmental things, such as a young dog jumping down from high places, such as the back of a pick-up, but there also appears to be a genetic predisposition.

We decided to use **BOSS**, whose OFA came back "excellent," and we bred him to two different bitches. Each litter produced two dogs with OCD, so we could not use **BOSS** again. But with one of the bitches, **AVAJ OF IAMONIA**, we got an outstanding litter of dogs (B OF DUTCHMAN'S HOLLOW), despite the OCD. After treatment, both the dogs from the **AVAJ** litter that had OCD went on to become good hunting dogs, as did the two from the other litter.

The other bitch we used with **BOSS** was **AUTUMN OF HOFFMAN MILL**, and as stated earlier, again because of **BIRGA** in her pedigree, this litter was not as good as the litter with **AVAJ**, but did produce some good hunting dogs.

In the fall of 1988, a male dog was run in IHDT at the Oregon test put on by the Northwest Griffon Club. The dog was **BLUE MOUNTAIN BREW**, owned by Jean and Al Norman from Washington. Jean had been a club member for many years and this was not her first Griffon by any means. She called me before the test and asked me about entering the dog, even though he had had no experience. I encouraged her to enter. The rest is history. **BREW** had only been hunted a couple of times on ducks. No upland hunting at all. And he had been allowed to run loose and had learned not to point.

With so little exposure the dog did quite well, except for the training areas—a 0 in Retrieve of Dragged Dead Game, and a 0 in Pointing. But, in all the natural, inherited qualities, except Pointing, he was just fine. He had no conformation faults, except for being oversize, which most Griffons were until we brought the standards up to date, and his coat was a 4, hard, dense. His temperament appeared to be solid. And, he did pass on strong pointing instinct to his progeny.

BREW did not have all the qualifications required by our breeding rules, to be used for a stud. Far from it. But we have a sentence just after these requirements which says, "Exceptions may be made in special cases by the WPGCA Breeding Committee." (See Appendix for entire WPGCA Breeding Rules.)

He was 19 months old at the time of the test, so we waited to hear the OFA results, and then we used **BREW** with **AVAJ OF IAMONIA**. When the first litter turned out so well, we repeated the breeding one more time.

When we considered **BREW** for breeding purposes, we examined his pedigree carefully and realized there were risks involved. But we needed dogs to breed and felt this was worth a try, as long we understood the risks.

Looking at the four-generation pedigree, it is difficult to see the risks unless you know what to look for. In the fourth generation, on the right hand side, starting at the top, go down to the second dog, **KATHI V.D. BRECH**. The dam of that dog is **BIRGA V.D. CULM**. Go to the next dog, the third down, **HANNES VOM WALDPARK**. The dam of that dog was **KITTY V.D. BRECH**, littermate to **KATHI**, so **BIRGA** is there again. This means that they line bred to **BIRGA**.

Going down to the twelfth dog, **KATHI V.D. BRECH** again, which means **BIRGA** again. So the breeding of **GLAC[I]ER COOL DEECEE** to **INGO VOM KASTANIENHAIN** was a line breeding to **BIRGA**.

Going further down the fourth generation to the third dog from the bottom, **GARYS DANDY BRANDY**, his sire was **HARDROCK MONTANA RAFE**. I had a lot of telephone calls from people that had Griffons sired by **RAFE**, telling me their dogs had gone blind.

With all these negatives one can understand that there were risks involved in breeding any dogs from this pedigree. In addition to the risks encountered in the pedigree, there was the factor of test results of some of **BREW's** littermates.

The breeding of **INGO VOM KASTANIENHAIN x GLAC[I]ER COOL DEECEE** was repeated two more times. Out of the three litters, very few dogs were tested. Of those tested, three had a temperament problem. In addition another dog could not qualify in NAT due to lack of Pointing, and in her IHDT didn't qualify because of Water.

One of the dogs that was tested only in IHDT, did not qualify due to a couple of 0's and because the dog appeared to collapse under the pressure of training and was judged mentally unstable. The temperament problems in these dogs were manifested in different ways: at the water, not being able to take the pressure of training, and one was very independent and hard-headed.

BREEZE OF THE CASCADES, a littermate to BOSS. BREEZE is one of the dogs from the litter that developed OCD, went through the treatment, and did well in his NAT and IHDT, became a fine hunting dog, and as this photo demonstrates, has a laid back temperament. This was a sportsman show in Portland, Oregon, and BREEZE and his owner, Bill Barrett, spent the day "telling people about out dogs." Like most Griffons, he was a great hit with the kids. (Compliments Mary Barrett)

Eik v.d. Neuburg (G)
Falk vom Bibertal (G)
Kathi v.d. Brech (G)
Axel vom Baldeneysee (G)
Hannes v Waldpark (G)
Alfa vom Distelpoint (G)
Cora vom Wolfsberg (G)
Ingo vom Kastanienhain (G)
Basko v.d. Neuburg (G)
Droll vom Kastanienhain (G)
Ansel vom Kastanienhain (G)
Aura von Gschwendt (G)
Ilko v.d. Brech (G)
Dina vom Wolfsberg (G)
PEDIGREE 39
Diana v.d. Neuburg (G)
Blue Mountain Brew (A)
Urac de St. Landry (F)
Axel vom Ulrichsquell (G)
Dia von Luda Jana (G)
Furst v.d. Neuburg (G)
Eik v.d. Neuburg (G)
Freya vom Bibertal (G)
Kathi v.d. Brech (G)
Glac[i]er Cool Deecee (A)
Don v.d. Neuburg (G)
Rockymount Happy (A)
Garys Dandy Brandy (A)
Flatheads Jagdhund Gretel (A)
Schnaps (A)
Happy Vantage Home (A)
Geri Vantage Home (A)

Greif vom Marienheim (G)
Alarich vom Mornbach (G)
Citty vom Kochertal (G)
Ali v.d. Brech (G)
Barri vom Tannenberg (G)
Cora v.d. Altenburg (G)
Astrid v.d. Michelherd (G)
Dux vom Waldpark (G)
Alarich vom Mornbach (G)
Alban v.d. Brech (G)
Cora v.d. Altenburg (G)
Brinka vom Waldpark (G)
Bari v.d. Wingertsau (G)
Astrid von Malepartus (G)
PEDIGREE 40
Diva vom Finkenhof (G)
Hannes v Waldpark (G)
Alarich vom Mornach (G)
Blitz vom Bibertal (G)
Geissa vom Marienheim (G)
Caro vom Waldpark (G)
Alban v.d. Brech (G)
Brinka vom Waldpark (G)
Astrid von Malepartus (G)
Kitty v.d. Brech (G)
Cato vom Kochertal (G)
Claus v.d. Brech (G)
Arda v.d. Brech (G)
Birga v.d. Culm (G)
Alarich vom Mornbach (G)
Gitta v.d. Brech (G)
Cora v.d. Altenburg (G)

PEDIGREE 41
Garys Dandy Brandy (A)

Duke v Kirchdorf (A)
Mike von Hessling (A)
Gee Gee Golo (A)
Hardrock Montana Tommy (A)
Tim vom Altenburg (A)
Tammy de la Oakes Heuvel (A)
Gerta Deufer de l'Oakes Heuvel (H)
Hardrock Montana Rafe (A)
Astor vom Teufelstein (G)
Dingo v Teufelstein (G)
Gerda v Marienheim (G)
Cira vom Kastanienhain (G)
Cato vom Kochertal (G)
Diana v.d. Altenburg (G)
Alma v.d. Brech (G)

Tracys Marelu of Cherry Hill (A)
Graff vom Griff (A)
Gretal of Cherry Hill (A)
Graff v Friedrichthal (A)
Alf vom Niddertal (G)
Auben vom Nellagram (A)
Cora vom Kastanienhain (G)
Zuabekunst Tal Dandy Hi Di (A)
Artus vom Kastanienhain (G)
Rob Roy of Rob Roy (A)
Gee Gee Golo (A)
Gretel v Friedrichthal (A)
Mike von Hessling (A)
Candice v Nellagram (A)
Tammy de la Oakes Heuvel (A)

PEDIGREE 42
Brittany of Dutchman's Hollow (A)

Gasto z Vanišovca (CF)
Argo z Vejrova (CF)
Era z Hořické dubiny (CF)
Čagan z Dračína (CF)
Alan od Dítětů (CF)
Cita z Runšova (CF)
Erna od Lačnovské vokle (CF)
Boss of the Cascades (CF)
Brit z Hradu (CF)
Alan od Dítětů
Brita z Hořické dubiny (CF)
Hela Z Dobrovska (CF)
Bojar z Bezděku (CF)
Brita z Bílých skal
Elka ze Skulických luk (CF)

Aris z Javorové doliny
Argo z Polední stráně (CF)
Erika z Želivce (CF)
Erik od Jezárek (CF)
Avar z Faralce (CF)
Asta Od Vejřice (CF)
Bora Od Teplého vrchu (CF)
Avaj of Iamonia (A)
Lucas of Hunter's Creek (A)
Bon Chasseur de la Cote (A)
Victoria du Bois Follet (F)
Mahaska's Merry Susan (A)
Whiskey du Pironec (FQ)
Alice B. Toklias (A)
Huckle Hill Angela (A)

*During his NAT in Iowa, **ARROW OF DUTCHMAN'S HOLLOW** with owner Dean Umphrey, as they wait their turn to do the track of the pheasant. Notice the loose leash, though **ARROW** is intent, he remains calm. He received Prize I, all 4's. (Compliments Tom Whitley)*

Falk vom Bibertal (G)
Axel vom Baldeneysee (G)
Alfa vom Distelpoint (G)
Ingo vom Kastanienhain (G)
Droll vom Kastanienhain (G)
Aura von Gschwendt (G)
Dina vom Wolfsberg (G)
Blue Mountain Brew (A)
Axel vom Ulrichsquell (G)
Furst v.d. Neuburg (G)
Freya vom Bibertal (G)
Glac[i]er Cool Deecee (A)
Rockymount Happy (A)
Flatheads Jagdhund Gretel (A)
Happy Vantage Home (A)

PEDIGREE 42–A
Arrow of Dutchman's Hollow (A)

Aris Z Javorové doliny (CF)
Argo z Polední stráně (CF)
Erika Z Želivce (CF)
Erik od Jezárek (CF)
Avar Z Faralce (CF)
Asta Od Vejřice (CF)
Bora Od Teplého vrchu (CF)
Avaj of Iamonia (A)
Lucas of Hunter's Creek (A)
Bon Chasseur de la Cote (A)
Victoria du Bois Follet (F)
Mahaska's Merry Susan (A)
Whiskey de Pironec (FQ)
Alice B. Toklias (A)
Huckle Hill Angela (A)

The tally from three litters:

Five were tested in NAT, one qualified and went on to receive Prize I in IHDT, and qualified two or three times in UFT.

One that did NOT qualify in NAT was entered in IHDT and did not qualify due to Water.

Three more were entered in IHDT only. One qualified with a Prize II, but had not been run in NAT.

The other two did not qualify—one due to mental instability.

And then there was **BREW**.

So, we use **BREW**, but we use him very carefully. He is a lovely dog with sound temperament, and we've been *lucky* in that his genes have connected well with the genes of the couple of bitches we have used with him. Also, some of the F-2 generation, his off spring, have produced well. Those dogs are: **AMY** and **ARROW OF DUTCHMAN'S HOLLOW**, **CASSIE**, **CALLAJ**, **CHAMPAGNE BLAZE** and **CERA OF DUTCHMAN'S HOLLOW**. Presently we have bred a bitch of different bloodlines to **BREW** and this will provide additional information about **BREW**. At 6 and 7 months the pups looked promising. That's the hard test in breeding, how do the next generations test? If you can't keep reproducing consistently, you have not been successful.

Heartland Griffon Club

Our first test in Iowa was held in the spring of 1987. We had been holding tests in southeastern Nebraska since 1976, but the population of Griffons in Nebraska was dwindling, yet at the same time it was increasing in Iowa. So, we moved to Iowa, where John Pitlo spear-headed the group that would organize the test. His right-hand man was an old hunting buddy, Ken Hurtig, who had come to a couple of Nebraska tests with John, but Ken had yet to own a Griffon.

I put John in touch with long-time club member Don Nicholson and his family in Coralville, Iowa, where the test site was located. With the three families—Pitlos, Hurtigs, and Nicholsons, this became a strong and efficient group, and, in the spring of 1989, we formed the regional club with John, president, Herm Welch, vice-president, Carla Cornick, secretary, Don Nicholson, treasurer, and Ken Hurtig, field test chairperson. Herm dropped out of his slot a couple of years later, and Dean Umphrey now serves as vice-president and Ken Hurtig has moved to the presidency.

The newly formed (1988) Rocky Mountain Griffon Club held their first test in Jerome, Idaho in the spring of 1989, and it was a huge success.

In 1989 we had few dogs to test, so we devoted many of our test weekends primarily to puppies, exposing them, giving them a preliminary evaluation.

In January 1989, the newly formed Klub Deutsch Kurzhaar-USA (KDK-USA) held their first field test on Grizzly Island, near Sacramento, California. This club for German Shorthairs was the first regional club for Shorthairs from the mother club in Germany, ever approved in the United States. It happened due to the efforts of Joe Nadeker, with help from Rolf Benseler. Both men had connections in the German club, and visited Germany frequently.

What did this mean for us, for Griffons in North America? It meant that we now had another testing area for our dogs, because the KDK tests and our tests were interchangeable. We could run our dogs in their tests, with their judges, and they could do the same. The judges were most of the same people who judge for us: Joe

Nadeker, Rolf Beneseler, Joan Bailey, Dennis Carlson, Silke Alberts, Warren Webster, and Phil Swain. All these people are official judges for the WPGCA.

In the spring of 1990 we had four tests: the KDK-USA in California, Northwest Griffon Club in Washington, Rocky Mountain Griffon Club in Idaho, and the Heartland Griffon Club in Iowa.

We tested three litters from the WPGCA Breeding Program that spring.

1. **BREW** x **AVAJ**: All seven pups were tested in NAT. Three received Prize I, three Prize II, and one Prize III. Conformation, Coats, and Temperament were all good.
2. **BOSS** x **AUTUMN**: Out of seven pups tested, two received Prize I; two Prize II; and three did not qualify and had temperament problems. There were some minor conformation faults.
3. **ERIK** x **PATCHES**: Only five out of the eight pups were tested. Two dogs received Prize I (though one was judged to be "soft"). One dog got Prize II. The other two did not qualify, and one of those was judged to have a temperament problem.

The Breeding Committee learned from this third breeding the pitfalls of depending only on a dog's field testing record to make breeding decisions. **PATCHES** had not qualified in NAT, but did receive a Prize II in IHDT when she was 16 months, and a Prize I in IHDT at 21 months (with all 4s, a perfect score), and her temperament was evaluated as: "calm, eager." We talked over the proposed breeding with the owner, pointing out the temperament weaknesses in **PATCHES**'s pedigree.

Few of her ancestors had been field-tested, so there was too much unknown. And in the third generation, second from the top was **JUNIPER HEATHER HEN**, a dog known to us to be mentally unstable, and a fear biter. (See earlier chapter about this bitch.) In the fourth generation there is **KATHI V.D. BRECH** appearing *twice*, which means right behind her is **BIRGA V.D. CULM**. Another dog in the fourth generation, fifth from the bottom, is **SWEET MOLLY MALONE**. This dog was mentally unstable. In hindsight, we should never have bred **PATCHES**.

Study the pedigree of **SWEET MOLLY MALONE**. First, *no dogs* field-tested. Back in the third and fourth generations there was a lot of inbreeding. Notice that the bitch, **TROUBLE GAL,** appears three times. See that **TIM V ALTENBURG** and **SIEGBERT V.D. ALTENBURG** (improperly named) were littermates, coming from **GARCENDA'S VICTORIA** (bad temperament).

Just behind **TROUBLE GAL** is **GIGI GIRL**. Look at her pedigree: She is the product of very close inbreeding. The sire, **RUSTY OF GRAND HAVEN**, was the product of daughter to father. As we already know, **GARCENDA'S VICTORIA** was the product of half brother to half sister. So **RUSTY** got a double whammy, so to speak, of improper inbreeding. Then on the dam's side, **THE HARE**, there is more close inbreeding with **THEIL OF BIEBESHEIM** and **TRIENTJE OF BIEBESHEIM** being half sisters. If you go back far enough, the dogs out beyond what you can see on both sire and dam's side are from the same bloodlines. (For more on inbreeding see Part Two.) Despite all this we went ahead with the breeding.

Also tested that spring of 1990 were three more dogs from the same bloodlines as **BLUE MOUNTAIN BREW**, and one more from the year before. They were from a repeat breeding. None of the four qualified. There was a definite weakness in Water: one dog got 2, two got 1, and one was gun sensitive. A fifth dog was judged to be "very hard-headed, independent."

PEDIGREE 43
Patches von Ripoff (A)

Finnigan von Ripoff (A)	**Alex von Ripoff (A)**	Don v.d. Neuburg (G)	**Pipo des Vieilles Rouches (F)**
			Arda v.d. Neuburg (G)
		Juniper Heather Hen (A)	Arapaho of Windy Hills (H)
			Mickie vom Friedrichtal (A)
	Amanda Sueann Igiture (A)	**Sunwheel Buzz (A)**	Sacha de Saint Landry (F)
			Saga (F)
		Christine Igit. d. Matines (A)	Sackey des Matines (F)
			Birchwood's Manor Inga Ingiture (A)
Peppermint Patty v Carter (A)	Magic Valley's Raffle (A)	Ilk vom Bibertal (G)	**Artus vom Distelpoint (G)**
			Kathi v.d. Brech (G)
		Magic Valley's Dolly (A)	Sacha de Saint Landry (F)
			Sweet Molly Malone (A)
	Glac[i]er Cool Deecee (A)	Furst v.d. Neuburg (G)	**Axel vom Ulrichsquell (G)**
			Freya vom Bibertal (G)
		Flatheads Jagdhund Gretel (A)	Rockymount Happy (A)
			Happy Vantage Home (A)

PEDIGREE 44
Sweet Molly Malone (A)

Boulger Hollow Dan (A)	Husky Tuffy (A)	Show Boat (A)	Jacque d'Argent (A)
			Trouble Gal (A)
		Charlotte Charlie (A)	Show Boat (A)
			Patti v Michelherd (G)
	Staley Smokey Gal (A)	Staley Whiskers (A)	Samson v.d. Altenburg (A)
			Trouble Gal (A)
		Trouble Gal (A)	Siegbert v.d. Altenburg (A)
			Gigi Girl (A)
Effigie du Val de Tonnerre (A)	Samson de l'Oakes Heuvel (A)	Tim vom Altenburg (A)	Zimas d'Argent (A)
			Crissi vom Altenburg (A)
		Gerta Deufer de l'Oakes Heuvel (A)	Golo (H)
			Astrah (H)
	Cache-Cache du Val de Tonnerre (A)	Siegbert v.d. Altenburg (A)	Zimas d'Argent (A)
			Crissi vom Altenburg (A)
		Gigi Girl (A)	Rusty of Grand Haven (A)
			The Hare (A)

PEDIGREE 45

Gigi Girl (A)	Rusty of Grand Haven (A)	Garcenda's Jacque (A)	Bonaparte (A)	Mickey of Warrenville (A)
				Kadine de Gagny (F)
			Milisande (A)	Staunchdown (A)
				Hardrock Montana Birdie (A)
		Garcenda's Victoria (A)	Garcenda's Jacque (A)	Bonaparte (A)
				Milisande (A)
			Garcenda's Collette (A)	Bonaparte (A)
				Nanon d'Argent (A)
	The Hare (A)	Theil of Biebesheim (A)	Stop de Fort Manoir (F)	Haxo de Sagrolle (F)
				Jockasse de Fort Manoir (F)
			Pago of Biebesheim (A)	Stouthearted Rex (A)
				Bernadette de Gagny (F)
		Trientje of Biebesheim (A)	Trouble of Warrenville (A)	Mickey of Warrenville (A)
				Kadine de Gagny (F)
			Pago of Biebesheim (A)	Stouthearted Rex (A)
				Bernadette de Gagny (F)

PEDIGREE 46

Rusty of Grand Haven (A)	Garcenda's Jacque (A)	Bonaparte (A)	Mickey of Warrenville (A)	Stump of Warrenville (A)
				Banko's Judy Merlimont (A)
			Kadine de Gagny (F)	Estoc de Gagny (F)
				Helda de Merlimont (F)
		Milisande (A)	Staunchdown (A)	Hardrock Montana Dan (A)
				Hardrock Montana Birdie (A)
			Hardrock Montana Birdie (A)	Staridge Clive (A)
				Hardrock Montana Queen (A)
	Garcenda's Victoria (A)	Garcenda's Jacque (A)	Bonaparte (A)	Mickey of Warrenville (A)
				Kadine de Gagny (F)
			Milisande (A)	Staunchdown (A)
				Hardrock Montana Birdie (A)
		Garcenda's Collette (A)	Bonaparte (A)	Mickey of Warrenville (A)
				Kadine de Gagny (F)
			Nanon d'Argent (A)	Bonaparte (A)
				Milisande (A)

In the fall we tested six of the "A" OF DUTCHMAN'S HOLLOW litter in IHDT (**BREW** x **AVAJ**), at the age of sixteen months. (See Ped 42-A.) Three dogs qualified well, the others did not because of lack of work on retrieving. The following spring, when they were 23 months and had had one more hunting season, three came back for IHDT. Two qualified well, the third missed qualifying because of lack of work on retrieving again.

For the "A" OF AUGER FALLS litter (**BOSS** X **AUTUMN**), one dog was tested at sixteen months, and qualified with a Prize III. In the spring, when they were 23 months, three more dogs entered. Two qualified, and one did not due to retrieving. (See photo of one of these dogs, **AUGUST OF AUGER FALLS** in this Chapter.).

For the "A" OF WHITE WATER (**ERIK** x **PATCHES**) litter, four dogs entered IHDT in the fall of 1990. One qualified with Prize I, perfect score, but was judged in Temperament "soft." The other three dogs did not qualify, one due to lack of work on retrieving, the other two because of Temperament, which meant that because of their soft temperament they couldn't take the pressure.

In the spring of 1991 we tested a litter of eight dogs from the "B" OF DUTCHMAN'S HOLLOW litter in NAT. This was the second time we used **BOSS**, this time with **AVAJ OF IAMONIA**, again a complete out cross. (See Ped 42.) All eight dogs in the litter qualified, six with a Prize I, the other two with Prize III and each of them were evaluated with temperament problems. Three of the Prize I dogs received 4 and 4 in Conformation and Coat.

In the fall, four of the eight dogs came back for IHDT at the age of 17 months: None qualified, due mostly to lack of work on retrieving. One of these four had been judged with a temperament problem in NAT. The temperament problem was not manifested in the IHDT, so because of exposure and positive experiences, this mental defect had now been masked (covered). Two dogs from this litter turned up with OCD, as stated earlier. Nevertheless, they went on to become fine hunting dogs.

In the spring of 1992, six of the eight dogs came back for IHDT; Three of them had run in the fall and not qualified. Now the dogs were 23 months, had gained more maturity, and had had their second hunting season.

As we began testing more of the Fouseks, and more of the Griffons with Fousek blood, the slow to mature Fouseks became noticeable. Judges were writing on their scorecards, "immature" time and time again in Natural Ability. The same dogs would come back six or ten months later and do just fine. By "immature" we mean that a ten-month-old pup might act more like a seven or eight-month-old pup.

Out of the six dogs in IHDT, two received Prize I; two, Prize II; and the other two just missed qualifying, due to lack of training in Retrieve of Dragged Game. One of those qualifying with Prize III was the one that had been evaluated with temperament deficiency in NAT. As above, this had been masked and the dog had been exposed to plenty of wild birds. The other dog that had been evaluated with a temperament weakness in NAT, did not qualify in this IHDT, but missed only due to a 0 in Retrieve of Dragged Game. This dog, too, had not qualified in the spring.

Because we now knew that **BOSS** was a carrier of OCD, we could no longer use him for breeding. *However*, we could certainly use his get and thus benefit from all the good qualities **BOSS** and his dam, **HELA**, had to give us. You will see in the next chapters that we were able to use 3 of the females for breeding, all with good results.

***AUBIE OF IAMONIA**, another dog from the "A" OF IAMONIA litter, at the NAT in Iowa in 1987, during his field work, demonstrating strong pointing instinct. (Compliments Joan Bailey)*

*Below:One of the dogs sired by **BOSS, AUGUST OF AUGER FALLS** during his IHDT in Iowa. (Compliments Greg Hurtig)*

Above: ***ABSAROKA OF DUTCHMAN'S HOLLOW****, after a successful hunt for blue grouse west of Fort Collins CO. (Compliments, owner, Warren Clark). Below:* ***ASPEN****, during her IHDT in Iowa with owner Ben Niemann. Joe Nadeker is the senior judge. (Compliments John Lundberg)*

Above: ***BUCKINGHAM OF DUTCHMAN'S HOLLOW*** *on a successful goose hunt, 1992. Right:* ***BLUE MOUNTAIN BREW****, 19 months old, at his IHDT in Oregon, fall 1988, taking a lunch break with owner Al Norman. (Compliments Rolf Benseler)*

CHAPTER TWENTY
TURNING THE BEND INTO THE NINETIES

In 1990, again with Joe Nadeker's help, we brought over another Fousek, **AXA OD PASTEJRIKO**, a female who went to Warren and Helen Webster. We now had three Fouseks: **ERIK**, **HELA**, and **AXA**. The fourth, **JISKRA**, had died. **AXA** was bred to **ERIK** soon after her arrival, and the litter was whelped in April.

The **ERIK** x **AXA** litter, "A" DE LOS ALTOS, was somewhat disappointing in NAT, with two out of four qualifying, and soft temperaments showing up in two dogs. However, **AMBROSE DE LOS ALTOS**, was entered in IHDT at 17 months and received a Prize II, all 4s except 2 in Tracking the Duck, and later went on to qualify with very high scores in his second OHDT, and then in UFT, Prize II. One dog from the litter was never tested, and one was a cull. Except for the cull, all the other dogs from this litter (including the non tested dog) turned out to be good hunting dogs, which is the name of our game. (Ped HD33, Part Two.)

March 1991, Two More Fouseks Arrive

We felt we needed still more "new blood" if we were to continue to build a broader gene pool. Once again Joe Nadeker came to our rescue. With his contacts and travels in Czechoslovakia it wasn't much longer before "our" **DAN** arrived to begin his new life with Jim and Arlene Seibel in the mid west. A few weeks later one more female came, **BORKA**. Both were fully tested adult dogs, as were all the previous ones.

Each of these dogs cost several thousand dollars. In the years to come, when all of us are out hunting and enjoying our fine dogs, we must never forget all the people that made this possible. First Joe, then all those who were willing and able to fork over several thousand dollars, then all the people who have worked for years to bring this all together. This includes every person who has tested his dog to provide us with vital information on which to base our breeding decisions. Without all these people and their own unique contributions we would have very little.

DAN arrived March 10, 1991, and in April Jim and Arlene brought him to our spring test in Iowa. It was so exciting to see him. I remember, as Jim and I walked in the field behind **DAN**, it brought back my memories of when **ERIK** had arrived, and when John Lundberg brought **ERIK** to California. Again I was excited for what this one dog would no doubt mean to the saving of a breed. The males always have more influence on a breed than do most females, simply because a male can be used for more breedings than a female. So we tend to get more excited with the possibilities of the males.

*Left: Idaho, March 1990, **AUTUMN OF HOFFMAN MILL**, Prize I, Utility Field Test. Photo shows "**MICKEY**" after she has tracked and caught the duck, beginning her way back to owner Gary Pool. (Compliments John Lundberg Jr)*

Disappointments

Trying to be realistic, we cautioned ourselves to be ready for disappointments, because they always come in an endeavor such as ours. **BORKA** was bred to **DAN**, and the litter, "A" OF DRUMMER'S RIDGE, was a disappointment in NAT. We saw several dogs in the litter that had soft temperaments, and one that was so timid it should have been put down, in my opinion, but the owner opted to keep it as a pet. Only two dogs were tested in IHDT; one qualified, and one did not and was judged "soft."

We bred **BORKA** again, to a different sire, **ABBOT OF DUTCHMAN'S HOLLOW**, and out of eight pups, even before their NAT, we knew about half of the litter had soft temperaments, manifested in different ways, such as shy with strangers, and difficult to house break. Their owners described them as "tentative," "cautious." Two pups were tested in NAT at the age of 12 months in the fall of 1994. Each received Prize I, all 4's. (See Appendix for complete tabulations.) The other six pups were not tested, but we know from their owners description, that most of them had temperament problems.

With these results from two different sires, we have had to drop **BORKA** from the WPGCA Breeding Program. It happens.

In 1991 **AXA** was bred again, this time to **DAN,** shortly after his arrival from Czechoslovakia. A couple of months later, with Warren Webster saying that **AXA** didn't appear to be pregnant, Warren, Helen, and **AXA** took off on a vacation trip, pulling their trailer. In Montana, on the way out of Glacier National Park during a wicked lightening and thunder storm, **AXA** gave birth to the next litter of pups in the back of the pickup with Warren acting as mid-wife while Helen drove the pickup down all the switchbacks. This was the "B" DE LOS ALTOS litter.

The testing of this litter of six pups was interesting. Four of the dogs were tested in NAT at 10 months. None qualified due to Water. They did well in their field work, average in Tracking, but, at the water, all four simply stood in the water and would not swim. The other two dogs were tested in NAT at 15 months and each got all 4's.

About a year later three of the six came back for IHDT. All qualified, though there was a slight weakness in Tracking the Duck. One of these three was the male, **BARTON DE LOS ALTOS**, a unique case, which is discussed in detail in Part Two, Chapter 24, judging. All the dogs have become good hunting dogs.

The "B" OF AUGER FALLS litter was good, producing a high percentage of good hunting dogs, and one breedable bitch, **BREENA OF AUGER FALLS**. In fact, **BREENA** received all 4's in both her NAT and IHDT, and a 4H in Tracking the Duck. (Ped 51)

In studying **DAN's** pedigree, and breedings where we used him, look in the third generation, 7th dog from the top, **BLESK OD JEZAREK**. **BLESK** is from a repeat breeding of **ERIK's** sire and dam, so **ERIK** and **BLESK** are from the same breeding. This is very good for us, because it provides with many opportunities to loose line breed to **ERIK**.

DAN is line bred to **AJAX OD DITETU**, in the 2rd and 3rd generation. **HELA's** sire is a littermate, **ALAN OD DITETU**. I have no proof, but I have a gut feeling that those "A" OD DITETU were strong in water and desire.

In the pedigree of **BREENA OF AUGER FALLS**, we loose line bred to **ERIK** in the 2nd and 3rd generation, and to the "A" and "C" DE LA COTE in the

Right: ***BARTON DE LOS ALTOS****, "at home" in California. (Compliments Irene Webster.) Below:* ***BREENA OF AUGER FALLS****, during her IHDT in Washington. (Compliments Joan Bailey)*

On Grizzly Island, near Sacramento, at a KDK test in January 1991, when Warren ran ***AXA*** *in UFT (Prize II). Below: During part of the water testing,* ***AXA*** *holds steady, waiting for the command to retrieve. These photos were taken 6 months before the adventure in Glacie Park. (Compliments Rolf Benseler)*

AN CERNIKY, *during a UFT in Iowa. (Compliments Greg Hurting) Below: Same place, different scenario, this e is called, "Waiting for Jim and Arlene with friend "Mariah." (Compliments Joan Bailey)*

Alan z Hronovských revírů (CF)
Avar ze Železnice (CF)
Heda od Kopánek (CF)
Avar z Lusku (CF)
Alán z Kněžických hájů (CF)
Alka od Petrovce (CF)
Centa ze Sekanců (CF)
Beno z Nolkopu (CF)
Brit z Hradu (CF)
Ajax od Dítětů (CF)
Brita z Hořické dubiny (CF)
Dina od Krounky (CF)
Cyr z Plinkoutu (CF)
Ira z Tichého revíru (CF)
PEDIGREE 47
Dan Černíky (CF)
Heny z Tichého revíru (CF)
Car Všebořice (CF)
Brit z Hradu (CF)
Chyra z Petřínské osady (CF)
Ajax od Dítětů (CF)
Alan z Braskova (CF)
Brita z Horičké dubiny (CF)
Brita ze Železnice (CF)
Ara Černíky (CF)
Argo z Polední stráně (CF)
Blesk od Jezárek (CF)
Asta od Vejřice (CF)
Asta z Libenské bažantnice (CF)
Borek z Cejpovny (CF)
Farina z Polední stráně (CF)
Erika z Želivce (CF)

Axel vom Baldeneysee (G)
Ingo vom Kastanienhain (G)
Aura von Gschwendt (G)
Blue Mountain Brew (A)
Furst v.d. Neuburg (G)
Glac[i]er Cool DeeCee (A)
Flatheads Jagdhund Gretel (A)
Abbot of Dutchman's Hollow (A)
Argo z Poledni strane (CF)
Erik od Jezarek (CF)
Asta od Vejrice (CF)
Avaj of Iamonia (A)
Bon Chasseur de la Cote (A)
Mahaska's Merry Susan (A)
PEDIGREE 48
Alice B. Toklias (A)
Bart of Drummer's Ridge (A)
Beno z Výverek (CF)
Erno z Doupova (CF)
Minka z Hajdovce (CF)
Bojar z Burdovny (CF)
Chvoj z Bartoně (CF)
Alma ze Všejanské fary (CF)
Ata Juniperus (CF)
Borka z Kolodev (CF)
Chvoj z Bartoně (CF)
Ferro od Hraběcí pěsiny (CF)
Charlotte od Černých Mostů (CF)
Dora Remicova (CF)
Brit z Hradu (CF)
Cita z Podsvětlé (CF)
Blanka z Podsvětlé (CF)

Arohn z Devaterek (CF)
Aris z Javorové doliny
Borka Štemflík (CF)
Argo z Polední stráně (CF)
Bor z Borové doliny (CF)
Erika z Želivce (CF)
Dana ze Želivce (CF)
Erik od Jezárek (CF)
Flot z Čelechovic na Hané (CF)
Avar z Faralce (CF)
Borka z Klasinky (CF)
Asta od Vejřice (CF)
Aran z Muticka (CF)
Bora od Teplého vrchu (CF)
PEDIGREE 49
Cora Vejříky (CF)
Ambrose de los Altos (A)
Beno z Vývěrek (CF)
Erno z Doupova (CF)
Minka z Hajdovce (CF)
Bojar z Burdovny (CF)
Chvoj z Bartoně (CF)
Alma ze Všejanské fary (CF)
Ata Juniperus (CF)
Axa od Pastejříků (CF)
Bart z Palavy (CF)
Egon od Nemilské (CF)
Avara z Údolí hojnosti (CF)
Cila ze Strážného kopce (CF)
Bor z Kravska (CF)
Dora z Poloudělí (CF)
Alma z Poloudělí (CF)

Avar ze Zeleznice (CF)
Avar z Lusku (CF)
Alka od Petrovce (CF)
Beno z Nolkopu (CF)
Ajax od Ditetu (CF)
Dina od Krounky (CF)
Ira z Ticheho reviru (CF)
Dan Cerniky (CF)
Brita z Hradu (CF)
Ajax od Ditetu (CF)
Brita z Horicke dubiny (CF)
Ara Cerniky (CF)
Blesk od Jezarek (CF)
Asta z Libenske bazantnice (CF)
PEDIGREE 50
Farina z Poledni strane (CF)
Barton de los Altos (A)
Beno z Vyverek (CF)
Erno z Doupova (CF)
Minka z Hajdovce (CF)
Bojar z Burdovny (CF)
Chvoj z Bartone (CF)
Alma ze Vsejanske fary (CF)
Ata Juniperus (CF)
Axa od Pastejriku (CF)
Bart z Palavy (CF)
Egon od Nemilske (CF)
Avara z Udoli hojnosti (CF)
Cila ze Strazneho kopce (CF)
Bor z Kravska (CF)
Dora z Poloudeli (CF)
Alma z Poloudeli (CF)

3rd and 4th generation. Knowingly, but cautiously we also line bred in about the 6th generation to **BIRGA V.D. CULM**. It was a *controlled* risk we took that paid off. After the "B" OF THE CASCADES litter, (which was **CAGAN** x **HELA**, **HELA** having been bred in Czechoslovakia before she left for the United States), we bred **HELA** three more times. To avoid some confusion, this requires some explanation. Originally **HELA** had gone to Joe Nadeker in California, so her first litter was whelped there and Joe chose OF THE CASCADES for his kennel name. Later, because we wanted to breed **HELA** to **ERIK**, she was sent to live with John and Bonnie Lundberg who had **ERIK**. So the next three litters out of **HELA** go under the Lundberg kennel name of VOM ERIK.

Over the course of about two years, we bred **HELA** to **ERIK** three times. The first litter produced one pup, second litter three pups, and third litter two pups. **HELA** had developed tetanus after her first litter ("B" OF THE CASCADES) was whelped, and we think her fertility was affected, so she was spayed. The first pup, **ARIKO VOM ERIK,** got Prize I in NAT, the next three pups ("B" VOM ERIK) qualified with two Prize I's and one Prize III. Of the final two pups ("C" VOM ERIK), one got Prize I, all 4's, and the other didn't qualify because of temperament (gun sensitivity), though it had all 4's and 3's.

Of these six dogs five were entered in IHDT. Two received Prize I and two received Prize III. One did not qualify due to a 0 in Drag of Dead Game. This was the dog that had been judged gun sensitive in NAT. In IHDT he exhibited absolutely no sign of gun sensitivity, which leads me to think the gun sensitivity had been caused by improper introduction to the gun. Whatever the cause, by taking the dog through a hunting season the gun sensitivity had been masked or overcome.

The Breeding Committee feels that **ARIKO** is an outstanding dog (prototype), and we want to use him for breeding, hoping that he is also a genotype, that he will be able to pass on all the good genes he carries from his parents. Time will provide the answer.

ove: ***AMBROSE DE LOS ALTOS*** *retrieving for Joe Kasmedo.(Com. Tina Molt) Below:* ***ABBOT OF DUTCHMAN'S*** ***OLLOW*** *holding for owner Ken Hurtig (Com. Warren Webster)*

Axel vom Baldeneysee (G)
Ingo vom Kastanienhain (G)
Aura von Gschwendt (G)
Blue Mountain Brew (A)
Furst v.d. Neuburg (G)
Glac[i]er Cool Deecee (A)
Flatheads Jagdhund Gretel (A)
Arrow of Dutchman's Hollow (A)
Argo z Poledni strane (CF)
Erik od Jezarek (CF)
Asta od Vejrice (CF)
Avaj of Iamonia (A)
Bon Chasseur de la Cote (A)
Mahaska's Merry Susan (A)
Alice B. Toklias (A)

PEDIGREE 51
Breena of Auger Falls (A)

Aris z Javorové doliny
Argo z Polední stráně (CF)
Erika z Želivce (CF)
Erik od Jezárek (CF)
Avar z Faralce (CF)
Asta od Vejřice (CF)
Bora od Teplého vrchu (CF)
Autumn of Hoffman Mill (A)
Lucas of Hunter's Creek (A)
Cacei de la Cote (A)
Victoria du Bois Follet (F)
Freewinds Alamance (A)
Gotz vom Bibertal (G)
Anka vom Fuchsburg (G)
Diana vom Ramsberg (G)

Arohn z Devaterek (CF)
Aris z Javorové doliny
Borka Štemflík (CF)
Argo z Polední stráně (CF)
Bor z Borové doliny (CF)
Erika z Želivce (CF)
Dana ze Želivce (CF)
Erik od Jezárek (CF)
Flot z Čelechovic na Hané (CF)
Avar z Faralce (CF)
Borka z Klasinky (CF)
Asta od Vejřice (CF)
Aran z Muticka (CF)
Bora od Teplého vrchu (CF)
Cora Vejříky (CF)

PEDIGREE 52
Ariko vom Erik (CF) (A)

Car Všebořice (CF)
Brit z Hradu (CF)
Chyra z Petřínské osady (CF)
Alan od Dítětů
Alan z Braskova (CF)
Brita z Hořické dubiny (CF)
Brita ze Železnice (CF)
Hela z Dobrovska (CF)
Alan z Braškova (CF)
Bojar z Bezděku (CF)
Alma z Rezku (CF)
Brita z Bílých skal
Car Všebořice (CF)
Elka ze Skalických luk (CF)
Bora ze Skalických luk (CF)

***ARIKO VOM ERIK**, during his natural ability test in Iowa in 1991, where he received all 4's, Prize I. (Compliments Joan Bailey)*

CHAPTER TWENTY-ONE
HEADING FOR HOME

In 1992, after having served on our board of directors since 1980 (three years as president), having been one of our breeders for many years, and having been a judge (and senior judge) for a long time, Dick Austin stepped down to make room for new blood. Here's what I wrote in the February 1992 GDS:

DICK AUSTIN
Steps Down From the Board of Directors

Dick has decided to step down to make room for "new blood" on our executive Board of Directors. No, we're not injecting "Fousek" blood into our Board! But, with Dick's departure we have the opportunity to bring a younger club member on board, with new ideas, and fresh approaches.

Dick has been a member of the Griffon Club since 1972, and a judge since 1976, flying all over the United States for us, on judging assignments.

When the first phase of our Breeding Program began in 1974, Dick was in the thick of it. He brought over from France a fine bitch, **VICTORIA DU BOIS FOLLET**, who became a foundation dog for the beginning of our program. With his kennel name DE LA COTE, he produced five litters, four with **VICTORIA**.

In 1979 Dick was elected vice-president and served in that job for two terms (six years). In 1986 he was elected President and in 1988 he went to Germany with our American group as our President, to take part in the 100th celebration of the founding of the Griffon Club in Germany by Korthals.

He choose not to run for President the next term, but was appointed to the Board of Directors (1989).

Now that's not all Dick has done for us. No, no, there's been much more. Because his wife, Joanne, has worked for TWA, Dick has been able to fly for practically nothing all these years. In addition to judging assignments, we've asked him to do things for which most people would have told us to just get lost. Not Dick. He almost never said NO. It was always, "Sure. When do I leave?"

Left: In the early spring of 1992, we brought the European tradition of hunting horns to Idaho. The two horn players are John Lundberg Jr., and Glen Johnston (head player), both from Bozeman, Montana. It was a very wonderful treat for us, and we continue it whenever Glen can get to a test. Standing right next to Glen is Joe Nadeker, who said he never expected to hear the horns in the U.S. (Compliments John Lundberg Sr.)

The craziest caper we sent him on was in the late 70s or early 80s, I don't remember the exact year. We had a bitch in our Breeding Program, **BRISSETTE DE LA COTE**, belonging to Ben and Elizabeth Mayer in British Columbia. The male we wanted to breed the bitch to, **BENT PINE'S BIFF**, was in Maine! Of course, what else? So this is what we asked Dick to do: The bitch would be shipped down from B.C. by air to San Francisco. Dick would pick her up and together they would board a flight to Boston (TWA didn't serve Portland, Maine). Have no doubt, it was winter. Dick had left the east coast years ago to escape from snow. Ha! Life has a way of playing tricks on us.

Dick and **BRISSETTE** landed in Boston in a snow storm; Dick picked up a rental car and off they went to Maine. Mission was accomplished, Dick and dog drove back to Boston, flew home to California and dog was shipped back to British Columbia!Two months later the litter "A" VOM MAYERHOF was whelped.

Dick handles our items that we sell for the club. Over the years no doubt many of you, if not all, have sent away to Dick for hat pins and other items. Luckily for us Dick will continue to handle this, and will continue to judge when he can.

So how do you thank someone like Dick? I surely don't know. Just remember that if it were not for people like Dick our club would be much less than what we are. We are an exceptional club with exceptional people, who over long periods of time, over and over again, have given of our time and talent. Know that when you have a good Griffon the efforts of people like Dick, over the years, have a great deal to do with the living proof—your dog. *Our dogs don't just happen like manna from heaven. They happen because of people like Dick Austin.*

In the spring of 1992 I decided to step down as editor of ***The Gun Dog Supreme***. Here's what I wrote:

Joan Bailey Steps Down From Editor of Gun Dog Supreme

Twenty five years is a very long time. It was August 1967 when the first GDS with my name as Editor appeared. Appropriately, at least for me, the cover picture of my first issue showed an 11 month old Montana Griffon, **GERI VANTAGE HOME**, retrieving a mallard from some back water of the Bitterroot River, a few miles south of Missoula. The dog was from Marg Allen's stock, an important person in our history.

While I was living in Missoula I got my first Griffon from Marg, and because Griffons and Montana are both of great importance in my life, you begin to see the historical connections.

If ever there was a job that was a joy, for me it has been putting out the GDS all these years. During this span I can count on the fingers of one hand the times I was at a loss for material to print. For me the problem has nearly always been having to cut material out because of lack of space/money. I'm sure it's been a combination of my need to write, and writing about dogs that I love, and about their owners who have become my friends over the years. For me it's been truly a labor of love.

So why quit something I love doing? There are only so many hours in a day, as we all know and I have some more books to write. The book on Griffons should be out by next fall. *If I am to keep to this schedule something has to give.* [Well, that's one more deadline I missed, off by only two years.] I don't feel I do a good job if I'm stretched in too many directions. Twenty-five years seems long enough.

Not having to meet that deadline any longer will lighten my load considerably. Not only will it give me the time I need to complete the Griffon book and a couple more books after that, but it will also give me time to take care of the duties of the secretary's office which are considerable. A lot of stress will be lifted from my life, because I will know I'm devoting the necessary time to the work of the secretary, as well as important work on our Breeding Committee. And, I will have the best of both worlds, because I will be contributing articles for the G.D.S. Those who know me well know I can't be silenced!

Naturally one does not leave a post like this one after so many years without mixed emotions. Of course I shall miss it, just as I will be joyous in not having to meet that deadline. This decision is not unlike most decisions we make in life: We give up something to gain something else. In my case I'm giving up being editor of the GDS, which I love, to gain time to do other things that I love. It's a trade-off. A good one, I think.

I thank all of you who, over the years, have thanked me for my work as editor. Your words have **ALWAYS** been my reward and encouragement, more than any awards I've been given. I remind you of this especially because I cannot stress enough the importance of encouraging and acknowledging our new editor. He will need our support.

* * * * *

This was followed by a write-up introducing the new editor, Richard Bovard, who served in that appointed position until June 1995, when he resigned due to work pressures. We all enjoyed his fresh voice and humor for the three years of his editorship, and thank him enormously for the time he spent, getting out our GDS. Equally important was his contribution as a breeder, producing two fine litters, the "A" and "B" OF PRAIRIE STORM (repeat breedings). As we said in the June 1995 GDS, "So we say a big thank you to **DICK, JANE and SPOT**. The three of them have provided us with wonderful dogs from two litters, and some of these dogs will be used for breeding, a part of the legacy **DICK, JANE and SPOT** leave to us."

The June 1995 GDS was co-edited by Joan Bailey and John Pitlo. I was to do the August GDS, but we skipped it because I was on overload. Our new editor, **LEE FULTON**, took over beginning with the August/October 1995 GDS. Lee is a long-time club member, just now starting out with his fourth dog from our breeding program. (See Chapter 14 for more about Lee and his first Griffon, **CACEI DE LA COTE**.) Lee is a serious hunter, and works for the U.S. Fish & Wildlife Service, so he has a great background for putting together the GDS.

With these changes in editorship, the board of directors decided to "spread the load," of the GDS, so that in the future the editor will not have to do ALL the work. John Pitlo and I were able to each contribute to make the June 1995 GDS happen, and it was a good issue. So we'll be doing this in the future, to help out the editor.

* * * * *

During the previous year, 1991, we were able to breed four litters:

"C" OF DUTCHMAN'S HOLLOW, (**Blue Mountain Brew x Avaj of Iamonia)** (a repeat of "A").

"B" OF AUGER FALLS (**Arrow of Dutchman's Hollow x Autumn of Hoffman Mill**).

"A" OF OCEAN HOUSE (**Erik od Jezerad x Amy of Dutchman's Hollow**).

"B" DE LOS ALTOS (**Dan Cerniky x Axa of Pastejriko**).

We tested these four litters in the spring and fall in Natural Ability and all litters did well, producing a high percentage of good hunting dogs. The important point for 1992 was that our gene pool was beginning to build, AT LONG LAST.

At the Idaho test (Rocky Mountain Griffon Club), thanks to club members, Glen Johnston and John Lundberg Jr., both of Bozeman, Montana, we were able to bring a European versatile hunting dog tradition to the United States. Hearing the hunting horns early in the morning, echoing off of the Snake River canyon walls produced goose bumps. It had been a well-guarded secret, only a few of us had been in on the planning, so it was a great surprise to nearly everyone.

In the fall of 1992, the old Northeast Griffon Club was resurrected at the test in New Jersey. President was Bob Carlson (New Jersey); vice-president, Bob Hinckley (Maine); Secretary-Treasurer, Betsy Blair (New Jersey). This was the club that had been formed in Maine around 1970. During the fall test in Maine in 1994, Rick Molt was elected president, and appointed Bob Hinckley vice-president; Tina Molt, secretary, and Tom Takesian, treasurer. Testing activity for the Northeast Griffon Club has now shifted from New Jersey to Maine, serving all of New England, and the Atlantic states.

As we approached our spring testing season in 1993, the new editor of ***The Gun Dog Supreme***, Richard Bovard, wrote in the April 1993 GDS: "Waiting For a Puppy?" Here are some excerpts:

> If you have been reading the GDS lately, following the test results, reading the letters to the editor, and studying the questions to the Breeding Committee itself, you have probably been pretty optimistic... and eager...
>
> ...You can see that we have a number of new members. This is another cause for optimism,naturally. But many of them are waiting for puppies. And some of them will be disappointed, because the breedings that the Committee has planned for may not occur. I would urge members to be patient, and I offer my own experience as perspective.
>
> ...Back then [1988], this breeding program was a controversial experiment. Indeed, in many places it still is. I talked with club members, and I attended tests in Iowa. I talked with breeders who did not support the club's program...I studied test scores from the club's tests and from NAVHDA's tests.
>
> I became convinced of two things: one, I could find a very good versatile dog that was not a Griffon (a Shorthair, a Wirehair, a Brittany); and two, this was a confusing situation. But I decided to stay on the list. I liked the idea, I liked the people in the club, and I liked the dogs. Most of all, I liked the idea. After all, I could get another kind of dog; after all, I might find a Griffon from outside the program that was OK. I knew it would be a risk, this program. But I decided to wait. I could change my mind, after all.

...Finally, after two years, my name was coming up. Then, of course, the bitch didn't go into heat. Or, the dogs didn't breed. Or they bred, and the breeding didn't take. Or there was only one puppy in the litter...

I thought that I was seeing some improvement in the dogs. Their scores were better. More dogs were qualifying, even dogs from parents that I was not interested in. People, of course, were optimistic and eager. I felt worse, and I thought of the wait...

Perhaps I waited well. Perhaps.

I could have a puppy from a litter that would be born in a month. It would not be from a breeding that I had selected, of course. It would not have "pure" blood or parents with an impressive, if unpronounceable, background. It would come from the heart of the program itself. It would come from a breeding that I had consistently avoided in my selection process.

I thought about the waiting. I thought that dogs from the same blood lines had done pretty well that weekend. And I said, "OK." I confess that I was neither overly optimistic nor very eager. And (I hesitate to say this in an article meant to encourage and console those who wait) I was getting a little tired of waiting.

I drove to Iowa twice that summer. The second time, I returned with **BRITTANY OF DUTCHMAN'S HOLLOW**. She was not the dog that I had spent so much time worrying about and studying test scores for. She was not the dog my NAVHDA friends said to select. She was not the dog that even some club members themselves had recommended, that is, when they would risk such a recommendation at all. At that time, she was simply a dog that I had waited for.

The rest, as they say, is—another story.You could read about it, and you could study the test scores.You could talk to me at a test in Iowa.I would tell you about study and talk and travel and time and confusion and risk-taking and an "experiment." I would tell you about waiting. And I would tell you about the "pure" luck of getting the dog that I had not even considered getting, that I had not dared to dream of getting.

I would tell you about "Spot." Now, she is the dog that I have waited for. She is a gun dog supreme.

* * * * * *

And indeed "**SPOT**" (**BRITTANY OF DUTCHMAN'S HOLLOW**) is a gun dog supreme: Prize I in NAT; winner of the Laurent Frileux Award for 1991, along with two of her littermates; a Prize III in IHDT; and the dam of two very successful litters, the "A" and "B" OF PRAIRIE STORM litters (1993 and 1994, **Dan x Spot**).

* * * * * *

In the spring of 1993 we tested two litters in NAT from the breeding program—"B" OF OCEAN HOUSE, and "C" OF AUGER FALLS, and a third litter not from the program, "C" OF PERKINS CORNER.

In the OCEAN HOUSE litter, out of the pups (9 months), five received Prize I, one a Prize III, and the seventh missed out because of water. In the fall and following year, these dogs did well in IHDT. Two bitches will be bred in 1996.

The AUGER FALLS litter was not considered successful though three dogs out of seven qualified. There were too many of the other dogs with temperament problems. **BIRGA** again.

Out of the five dogs from the PERKINS CORNER litter that were tested, 3 qualified, but not all of the litter was tested. Checking the four generation pedigree, you will find out beyond the fourth generation **BIRGA V.D. CULM** four times in the fifth generation, and also two dogs in the fourth generation that have eye problems (ectropic or entropic) in their bloodlines: One is **LUCAS OF HUNTER'S CREEK** and the other **AXEL V ULRICHSQUELL,** each tracing back to the same bitch, **SCARLET DE ST LANDRY**.

The Laurent Frileux Award

This award was developed by the WPGCA in 1971 to honor the memory of Laurent, after he died tragically in Quebec in June, 1971. It was to go to the young dog that had the highest score in natural ability for the year. Early in 1991 and again in 1993, his mother, Dominique Frileux, wrote to us expressing her wishes that this award not be given to any dog with Fousek blood. She also wrote to the president of the French Griffon Club and he concurred with her on this.

Though the award is one that *we* developed as *our* tribute to Laurent's memory, we do not in any way wish to cause Dominique any pain surrounding her dear son who was such a joy to so many of us. Therefore the board of directors has decided to discontinue this award, believing that awards for dogs usually don't do the dogs much good anyway.

We will simply go on remembering a wonderful young man whom we met through our Griffons, who died much too soon.

General Rogers Award

In 1969-1970, shortly after General Rogers died, this award was started in his memory. It was to go to the Griffon that receives the highest score in Utility Field Test each year.

It does not mean that the dog that receives this award is "the best Griffon," it simply means the dog that has received the highest score in UFT for that year. Very few dogs are entered in UFT, therefore, to say that the winner is "the best," the question must be asked, "best of what?" For example, the first dog to win this award, **HANSEL**, was the ONLY dog entered in UFT in 1972. He was not an exceptional dog at all. He was my hunting dog, and through lots of exposure to wild birds, he overcame, or masked some of his shortcomings. As said earlier, qualifying one's dog in UFT is a great accomplishment, and then to have the good luck to receive the General Rogers Award, is icing on the cake. But let's keep it in perspective. *Receiv-*

*Next page: Above: In Maine, **AMOS OF OCEAN HOUSE**, retrieving the duck during his IHDT, where he and owner Grov Blair earned a Prize III. (Compliments John Lundberg) Below: In Washington with Northwest Griffon Club, **CHAMPAGNE BLAZE OF DUTCHMAN'S HOLLOW** holds well in IHDT, where she and owner Steve Grieser earned a perfect score, all 4's, Prize I. She whelped her first litter in the spring of 1995, and the pups look promising. The sire was **BARTON DE LOS ALTOS**. (Compliments Joan Bailey)*

ing it has little to do with whether or not the dog should be used for breeding. That information comes primarily from NAT and IHDT, which allows us to see the inherited qualities of the dog before they are masked by much training and exposure.

Receiving the General Rogers award does mean that the handler worked hard to train his dog, and the two of them became a good hunting team, and they deserve a lot of credit for these accomplishments. To qualify your dog *that you have trained yourself* in a utility test is a very special achievement and those of us who have done this deserve to be proud of ourselves and of our dogs.

Following is a list of Griffons that have won this award:

DOG/OWNER

1972 Hansel Zu Den Bergen Gehen, Prize III, Ontario/ Joan Bailey

1974 Heidi von Link, Prize II, California/ Peter Link

1975 Victoria Du Bois Follet, Prize II, California/ Dick Austin

1976 Wyoming's Lucky, Prize III, North Dakota/ Dale MacKenzie

1978 Sunny Branches Beau Brokk, Prize II, North Dakota/Kurt Sundquist

1079 Wingmaster's Trouble Maker, Prize I, Wisconsin/ Rod Lein

1980 Sunny Branches Beau Brokk, Prize I, Wisconsin/ Kurt Sundquist

1982 Duckpond Ebullent Kasy, Prize II, Wisconsin/ Don Dack

1984 Desiree de la Cote, Prize III, Michigan/ Dick DeJager

1985 Quail Queen Barmi's Pepper, Prize II, Minnesota/ Dwight Beavers

1986 Three Oaks Lonka, Prize I, Oregon/ Cheryl Zumwalt

1987 Points Pewter Tip, Prize I, Iowa/ John Picconatto

(Trained and handled by Bob West)

1988 Point's Algernon, Prize II, Maine/ Bob Mularczyk

1989 Tawna's Chelsea Morning, Prize II, Idaho/ Tawna Skinner

1990 Autumn of Hoffman Mill, Prize I, Idaho/ Gary Pool

1991 Aldersedge Fetiche, Prize 1, Canada/ Aime Quintal

1992 Aspen Points Barrel, Prize I, Iowa/ Tom Knudson

1993 Acajou du Feu Follet, Prize I, Minnesota/ Tom Mix

1994 Bailey of Ocean House, Prize II, Maine/ Rick Molt

* * * * * *

WPGCA Board of Directors
Changes Qualification Requirements for General Rogers Award

At the annual board of directors (BOD) meeting in 1995, in Jerome, Idaho, the BOD voted to make an additional requirement for the General Rogers award: "A dog must have qualified in a test recognized by the WPGCA BOD and Breeding Committee, as having sufficient categories of testing to justify it being called a test for versatile hunting dogs. This means that in addition to the usual field work, and retrieving from land and water, there must be at least two tracking categories in the test, one on land and one in water (on live, released game), in order for a dog to be eligible for the General Rogers Award."

* * * * *

Arohn z Devaterek (CF)
Aris z Javorové doliny
Borka Štemflík (CF)
Argo z Polední stráně (CF)
Bor z Borové doliny (CF)
Erika z Želivce (CF)
Dana ze Želivce (CF)
Erik od Jezárek (CF)
Flot z Čelechovic na Hané (CF)
Avar z Faralce (CF)
Borka z Klasinky (CF)
Asta od Vejřice (CF)
Aran z Muticka (CF)
Bora od Teplého vrchu (CF)
PEDIGREE 53
Cora Vejříky (CF)
Amos of Ocean House (A)
Axel vom Baldeneysee (G)
Ingo Vom Kastanienhain (G)
Aura von Gschwendt (G)
Blue Mountain Brew (A)
Furst v.d. Neuburg (G)
Glac[i]er Cool DeeCee (A)
Flatheads Jagdhund Gretel (A)
Amy of Dutchman's Hollow (A)
Argo z Polední stráně (CF)
Erik od Jezárek (CF)
Asta od Vejřice (CF)
Avaj of Iamonia (A)
Bon Chasseur de la Cote (A)
Mahaska's Merry Susan (A)
Alice B. Toklias (A)

Avar ze Železnice (CF)
Avar z Lusku (CF)
Alka od Petrovce (CF)
Beno z Nolkopu (CF)
Ajax od Dítětů (CF)
Dina od Krounky (CF)
Ira z Tichého revíru (CF)
Dan Černíky (CF)
Brit z Hradu (CF)
Ajax od Dítětů (CF)
Brita z Hořické dubiny (CF)
Ara Černíky (CF)
Blesk od Jezárek (CF)
Asta z Libeňské bažantnice (CF)
PEDIGREE 54
Farina z Polední stráně (CF)
Bailey of Ocean House (A)
Axel vom Baldeneysee (G)
Ingo Vom Kastanienhain (G)
Aura von Gschwendt (G)
Blue Mountain Brew (A)
Furst v.d. Neuburg (G)
Glac[i]er Cool DeeCee (A)
Flatheads Jagdhund Gretel (A)
Amy of Dutchman's Hollow (A)
Argo z Poledni strane (CF)
Erik od Jezarek (CF)
Asta od Vejrice (CF)
Avaj of Iamonia (A)
Bon Chasseur de la Cote (A)
Mahaska's Merry Susan (A)
Alice B. Toklias (A)

Avar ze Železnice (CF)
Avar z Lusku (CF)
Alka od Petrovce (CF)
Beno z Nolkopu (CF)
Ajax od Dítětů (CF)
Dina od Krounky (CF)
Ira z Tichého revíru (CF)
Dan Černíky (CF)
Brit z Hradu (CF)
Ajax od Dítětů (CF)
Brita z Hořické dubiny (CF)
Ara Černíky (CF)
Blesk od Jezárek (CF)
Asta z Libeňské bažantnice (CF)
PEDIGREE 55
Countess of Auger Falls (A)
Farina z Polední stráně (CF)
Aris z Javorové doliny
Argo z Polední strane (CF)
Erika z Želivce (CF)
Erik od Jezárek (CF)
Avar z Faralce (CF)
Asta od Vejřice (CF)
Bora od Teplého vrchu (CF)
Autumn of Hoffman Mill (A)
Lucas of Hunter's Creek (A)
Cacei de la Cote (A)
Victoria du Bois Follet (F)
Freewinds Alamance (A)
Gotz vom Bibertal (G)
Anka vom Fuchsburg (G)
Diana vom Ramsberg (G)

Axel v.d. Ulrichsquell (G)
Furst v.d. Neuburg (G)
Freya vom Bibertal (G)
Sharon's Mt John Reggie (A)
Bar-Mi's Ace High (A)
Bar-Mi's Gretchen (A)
Gilead Lady's Lake of Bar-Mi (A)
Aspen Point's Barrel (A)
Lucas of Hunter's Creek (A)
Bon chasseur de la Cote (A)
Victoria du Bois Follet (F)
Point's Pewter Tip (A)
Whiskey du Pironec (FQ)
Alice B. Toklias (A)
PEDIGREE 56
Crissi of Perkins Corner (A)
Huckle Hill Angela (A)
Falk vom Bibertal (G)
Axel vom Baldeneysee (G)
Alfa vom Distelpoint (G)
Ingo Vom Kastanienhain (G)
Droll vom Kastanienhain (G)
Aura von Gschwendt (G)
Dina vom Wolfsberg (G)
Cindy of Perkins Corner (A)
Axel v.d. Ulrichsquell (G)
Furst v.d. Neuburg (G)
Freya vom Bibertal (G)
Glac[i]er Cool DeeCee (A)
Rockymount Happy (A)
Flatheads Jagdhund Gretel (A)
Happy Vantage Home (A)

Shock and sadness for those who knew Don Nicholson came to us in 1994. From the June 1994 GDS:

IN MEMORY: DON NICHOLSON

Don Nicholson died suddenly on April 22. It was a heart-wrenching shock to his family—his wife Elaine, sons Dave and Mike, Dave's wife Amy, and three little grandchildren who thought that their grandfather was someone very special.

All of us in the Griffon Club who knew Don, and all the members of the Heartland Griffon Club, we are also in deep shock. We too thought that Don was very special. He was a fine, giving man. I simply cannot imagine a field test in Iowa without Don there.

Don joined the Griffon Club in 1967, the year that I became secretary. During the late 1960's and the 1970's, Ed Bailey and I, with our three Griffons, would drive from near Toronto, Canada, for a thousand miles to go hunting in Nebraska every November. As we sped along Interstate 80 in Iowa, we always went by the turnoff for Coralville, and I would always say, "A Griffon lives here."

In 1973, I finally got to meet that Griffon and most of the family. Those were the early years of NAVHDA, and we held the first test for versatile dogs in the state of Iowa, near New Sharon. We had a training clinic on Saturday, and ran dogs on Sunday. Elaine Nicholson came with her two young sons, Dave and Mike, who ran their dogs in Natural Ability. Don was working and could not make the trip.

I did not see Elaine and "the boys" again, or meet Don, until the WPGCA held its first test in Iowa in 1987. John Pitlo was the organizer, and I told him to get in touch with the Nicholson family. And that was it. Don took charge of feeding us, and with Elaine's help, they have remained "top in the country" for caring for handlers and judges. A couple of years later, the Heartland Griffon Club was formed and Don was Treasurer. The Nicholson family—Don, Elaine, Dave, and Amy—has been a key in making these tests so successful.

It was not just the lunches, though they were always outstanding, with so many details provided for us, but it was everything else they did, such as arranging the Saturday night dinners, and Dave securing the grounds for us, because he works for the Iowa Fish and Game on those very grounds. We just knew that when we arrived in Iowa that the Nicholsons would take care of us. It has been very special, and Don headed that special team.

We love the Nicholson family, and we will miss Don sorely.

Joan Bailey, April 24, 1994

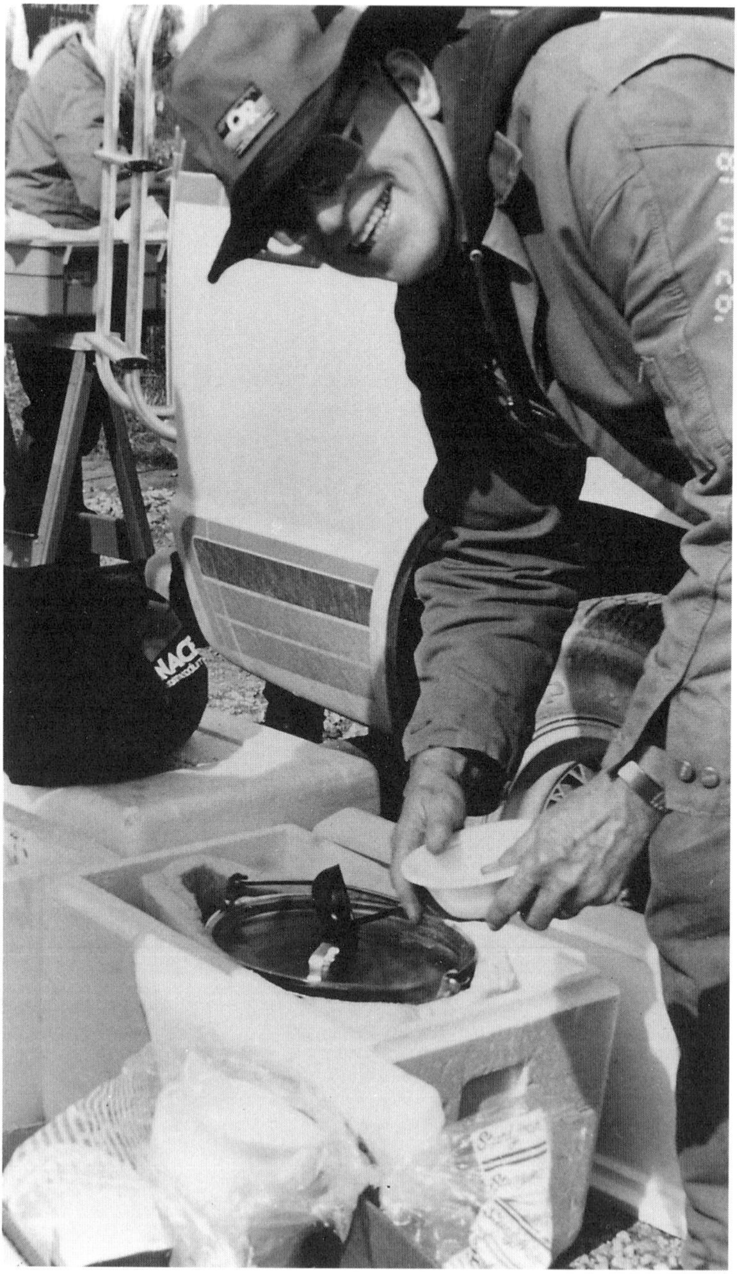

DON NICHOLSON

In Iowa with the Heartland Griffon Club, fall 1992, Don Nicholson doing what he loved to do, cooking for us and feeding us. (Compliments Warren Webster)

Two more of the "C" OF DUTCHMAN HOLLOW litter that have already been used for breeding. Above: ***CASSIE****, during her NAT, where she earned a Prize I, and went on to do the same in IHDT, perfect scores in each test. Her first litter, "D" OF AUGER FALLS, tested very well in the spring of 1995. (See chapter 22.) Below:* ***CERA****, like* ***CASSIE****, produced an outstanding litter, with all 9 pups qualifying in NAT. (See chapter 22). This photo, fall 1995, during a hunting trip in Montana. (Compliments Joan Bailey)*

BAILEY OF OCEAN HOUSE, *October 1994, Maine, in an obviously posed photo—but even if it is a set-up, it sure is pretty. (Compliments Rick or Tina Molt)*

CHAPTER TWENTY-TWO
PAST, PRESENT, FUTURE

You will recall from chapter ten—The Early Years of NAVHDA—that through his son, Henry Tabel, we were able to meet the famous Dr. Carl Tabel in 1973. Word came to us late in 1993 of Dr. Tabel's passing.

DR. CARL TABEL †

(Translated by Silke Alberts from the German magazine ***Der Jagdgebrauchshund,*** October 1993. It was written by the president of the Jagdgebrauchshundverbandes, Versatile Hunting Dog Association, Christoph Frucht.)

A large mourning community said farewell to the retired judge, Dr. Carl Tabel, who was laid to rest at the age of 96 years in Annweiler on Trifels.

His greatest passion, next to his family and his profession, was the hunt with a useful, versatile hunting dog. To them he dedicated his life. Perhaps because of this the following Indian proverb will best describe this event:

"He was called to the eternal hunting grounds."

Dr. Tabel was our unsurpassed advisor, guide and initiator.

He is the idol of many dog trainers, and generations of hunters. His idealism made it possible that for more than half a century there have not been any problems between the two. He lived for this union of generations. For all of us who considered hunting with a useful dog more than a hobby or passing time, he has always been our idol and mentor.

He is the soul of the versatile hunting dog community and with them the soul of our organization. He is almost as old as the JGHV organization [jagdgebrauchshundverbandes]. His tremendous influence on the work of the organization for more than half a century is unmistakable:

Co-founder and revered editor for so many years of our JGHV magazine, cynological editor of several German hunting magazines. He is the author of numerous hunting books. A vast amount of special contributions about hunting dog problems originated with him. His spirit and elan have helped to model the seminars of the organization. His contributions always lead to sold-out seminars of the JGHV. Here he showed his unsurpassed knowledge and unequaled social skills.

I can still remember his recital of Hulverscheidt's poem about the work of the versatile hunting dog, from memory, of course, and that at the age of 84 years.

Even today his spirit gives wings to our seminars, and not only ours, but many other institutions with similar problems.

He is the founder of all ambitious, correct, and above all, as close to real hunting situation dog work. Our tests reflect his spirit and influence.

His books and articles are so clear and user friendly that they were the foundation for proper hunting dog education for generations of dog handlers. The broad German hunting kynology is based upon his experience and knowledge.

He possessed a great magnetism. People who knew him closely, adored him, yes loved him like a father. So one can't be surprised when he was lovingly called master, boss, or even old master. He is and remains the nestor [architect] of the German hunting organization.

His influence reached over many boundaries world wide. Wherever you are in this world it is impossible to talk about hunting dog work without mentioning the name of Dr. Carl Tabel. In this sentiment rarely has a Bundesverdienstkreuz (German medal of merit) been given to a more deserving person.

He formed us, walked with us and led us. On this path we all followed him willingly and we found it to be a blessing that he could be with us for such a long time.

Through his work in the Jagdgebrauchshundverbandes he lives on. We all owe him a great deal. Let us try to continue in his spirit. With great sympathy for the family the JGHV says good bye to this great man with reverence and gratitude.

Christoph Frucht
President of the JGHV

Tribute from the Large Munsterlander Club of North America (Newsletter, Fall/Winter 1994, By Joe Schmutz, President)

[In Joe Schmutz's tribute—which was titled: "A Loss To The Hunting Dog World"—Joe talked about one of Dr. Tabel's books, ***Thirteen Of My Best Dogs,*** in which he included a poem written by his sister on the occasion of his marriage. One of his best dogs was **SAUL**. Joe translated the poem:

Saul's Lament

All is open to days pleasure,
all the hearts are near to burst
and the happy guests they treasure
the new bride with romances thirst.
I alone here lonesome lie,
my sense of worth flees ever faster,
because - oh pain - I do not spy
the familiar sight of Master.
I used to be his first in life.
I was his love, his friend, his dear,
now, he contemplates a wife
to occupy his hearts revier.

Will this trade serve Master well?
to take a wife who's proven little,
are there prizes she has held?
has she shaken foxes brittle?
Will she fetch with natural bent?
Will she refrain from rabbit chase?
Will she tease apart track's scent?
Will obedience match order's pace?
I'm puzzled how my master could
- me, Saul, of triple prizes earned
forego for such plain youthful good
when her performance he's not learned.

Continuing his tribute, Joe wrote, "Dr Tabel was a firm believer in the command `Halt.' [We call this "Drop."] He felt that this command and unwavering obedience to it by the dog is the foundation for all levels of hunting dog training." I agree.

The German hunting magazines, and versatile breed clubs were filled with articles and obituaries about Dr. Tabel. Personally I feel extremely blessed that I met and became friends with his son, Henry, and that when Dr. Tabel came to Canada in 1973, I was able to meet him, to take part in a field test with him, and later to have him visit in my home. It was a great privilege in my life to have had this opportunity, to have read the translation of his book, and to actually have trained my dog, using his methods.

Late in his life he was presented the Meritorious Cross 1st Class by the President of the West German Federal Republic, for all his work and contribution to further hunting and hunting dogs in Germany.

* * * * * * * *

In the July 1993 issue of the German Griffon Club news bulletin, a report appeared on the status of breeding there. One section of the report dealt with "*Zuchtprogramm Korthals-Griffons franzosischer Herkunft*" (Using the French Korthals-Griffon in our Breeding Program).

The gist of the report, written by their Breed Warden, Dr. Klaus-Ulrich Loss, (according to WPGCA club member, Silke Alberts), is that the German Griffon Club says they need to expand their gene pool. They don't want to infuse different blood, i.e. Deutsch Drahthaar, Cesky Fousek, or whatever. Therefore they have decided to ask the French Griffon Club to ask for volunteers to provide at least four bitches and two males, which should be without genetic faults. These dogs would be tested in the German hunting test to see if the dogs have what is needed. If they pass, they would be bred amongst themselves (obviously all candidates should be unrelated) for at least two generations to enable the Germans to watch for genetic faults to crop up. Then and only then would the third generation offspring be bred to German Griffons.

* * * * * *

From the Nederlandse Griffonclub
(Dutch Griffon Club)

In the August, 1994 Dutch Griffon Club news bulletin appeared a long article, "Breeding Problems With Griffons in the U.S.A.," by Partout (This is a pen name used by Mr. Van Dam, a member of the Dutch Griffon Club, whom I met in Germany in 1988. He is past secretary of that club.) The article, translated by John and Vivian Pitlo, follows in its entirety:

> The Wirehaired Pointing Griffon Club of America was organized by Brigadier General T. Rogers in 1951. This American officer was a lover of Griffons during his duty in Germany. He obtained a Griffon "Cisa von der Hohen Linde." This was not the first Griffon to be imported into the United States. More had preceded her, however incidental. After 1951, import of Griffons occurred more regularly and systematically. Griffons with known kennel names from Germany and France were shipped across the ocean. Also out of our land (Netherlands) came several griffons. There are possibly offspring from **FELLOW VON DE MATEN** and **NANCY V.D. KOORUD**—still running around.

In the U.S.A. several regional Griffon clubs were organized which were under the direction of the national club. These regional Griffon clubs were widely separated due to large expanse of land within the continental United States. These regional clubs existed because of membership by enthusiastic hunters. Because the membership was so widespread, it took some time before some insight was gained concerning the quality of the Griffon breed.

Above this were the tests, similar to our K.N.J.V. test and field test, which were unknown at that time. These tests were first used for hunting dogs after 1969 in the United States. These various tests, for both young and older dogs had naturally the purpose of selecting useable dogs for breeding purposes. Also, the various regional Griffon clubs began organizing and holding similar all around tests for young and older Griffons.

With these efforts the American Griffon Club obtained better insight into the quality of the Griffon breed. These tests, which were based on those used in Germany, allowed to be seen how the American Griffon fared, because it was now possible to compare results with other hunting dog breeds evaluated in the same tests. The conclusion was that the quality of the dogs was in sad condition. This was not a sudden or surprising result, but now the problem was in the open and on the table awaiting action. There were too many Griffons with bad coats (too soft, too long, no undercoats), with bad noses, had lost the desire for game contact, and bad temperament. Also bad bites, eye problems (ectropic, entropic) and hip dysplasia (H.D.). The character of too many dogs was not good because they were mentally unstable, were timid or aggressive.

Many breeders were unfamiliar with the breed standards: how should the dog look, what hunting characteristics should they possess, and what the character of a Griffon should be. An important role undoubtedly was the large distances between Griffon lovers in this enormous land, thereby the exchange of experiences and knowledge was not easy.

The Board of Directors of the Griffon Club, having identified the problems with the breed, decided to take action. After detailed internal deliberation, the Board decided in 1974 on a ten-year breeding program. This could only work on the basis of voluntary cooperation of breeders, because forceful regulations are not well accepted in the U.S., nor anymore than in Holland.

The purpose of the breeding program was to use the results of the aforementioned field tests to perpetuate the good qualities of individual Griffons. The breeding committee, which had recently been established, was given responsibility of deciding which dogs could be bred, and which dogs could not. The advice of this committee, composed of three experienced judges, gained a certain status because all of the decisions, such as results of the tests and the reasons some dogs should be bred rather than others, were all regularly published in the club newsletter, "***The Gun Dog Supreme.***"

These tests were held each year in four or five places in the United States. There are three kinds of tests: one "Natural Ability" for young dogs, one "Intermediate Hunting Dog Test" for older dogs, and one "Utility Field Test" for experienced dogs. All aspects of hunting dog work, the same as we know, are part of the test; manner of search, quality and use of nose, point, waterwork, retrieving, desire and temperament, obedience and cooperation. Just as in German tests, the dog is awarded a number for each portion of the test which are then totaled for a final score. A part of these tests include exterior judging for coat and build of the dog. They breed Griffons for practical hunting, not for showing.

A vital part of the breeding program was the "breeding agreement."

This agreement allowed the breeder and the breeding committee to control the registration of each dog to prevent the breeding of dogs that were not qualified. Registration of breeding dogs required two conditions: 1) the dog must have been x-rayed for hip dysplasia and 2) the dog must have had good results in the "Natural Ability Test," as well as the "Intermediate Hunting Dog Test."

This registration carried more weight because since 1981 the Griffon Club has its own stud book and gives out its own pedigrees of four generations of ancestors for a particular dog as well as results of aforementioned tests. Besides that, the club gave detailed directions on all the things breeders needed to do and know, which brought the quality of the breeding program to a higher plateau, primarily because a reasonable number of breeders and club members recognized the need to work closely together to reach club goals. The buyers of the pups from an approved breeding also had positive benefits. Through the breeding agreement, the buyer was guaranteed that a pup with major faults could be returned to the breeders with financial compensation.

This ten year breeding program worked well, especially for the self-discipline, the understanding and cooperation of great numbers of enthusiastic members through the effort of the club leaders and their own group of experienced judges, who traveled regularly across most of the U.S.A.

Evaluation of the breeding program after nearly ten years:

It became apparent that the quality and improvements of the Griffon breed was less than hoped for. There were still too many Griffons with the before mentioned shortcomings. Breedable females that did not possess these shortcomings were still not available. It was recognized in 1983 that the direction of this breeding program had arrived at a dead end. The reason for this was because the gene pool for Griffons was too small in the U.S.A. The breeding program could only keep on going in circles. The only solution to this problem was to bring in new blood, that is to say the application of an out cross. This conclusion was reached after detailed deliberation, both inside and outside the club, and with geneticists and kynologists. The only hunting dog breed that was compatible, in their opinion, was the Cesky Fousek (Tsjechische rewbard).

A club member with ties to Czechoslovakia knew about this breed. The Cesky Fousek has during the years, been the most used hunting dog breed in Czechoslovakia. A number of Fousek lovers began after 1950 to rebuild this breed with new blood from other wirehaired breeds, which included the Griffon. This was no arbitrary choice, because the similarity between the Fousek and the Griffon is great. The present day Cesky Fousek has in the meantime become established with 30 years of stable hunting dog breeding.

After consultation with Czechoslovakian kynologists and geneticists, it was determined to use the Cesky Fousek for necessary improvements of the American Griffon. With the infusion of Cesky Fousek, the beginning of the second ten year breeding program was started in 1984 with the same selection and breeding methods as the first program. During 1985, the first Cesky Fousek, a highly qualified male arrived in the Griffon Club in the U.S.A., later followed by several females. These Fouseks were not only bred to Griffons, but also to build a bloodline of pure Fouseks in America, to allow further injection in later years.

The importing of Fousek blood has after eight years made significant improvements. In 1983 there was no breeder with a pure, stable genetic bloodline. In 1993 we are happy to report that the Griffon club had eight breedable bitches with good genetic backgrounds. It appears they are on the right road.

We hope these efforts of the small American group of enthusiastic and motivated Griffonniers (their club is not as large as ours) will achieve the goals they have set in ten years. It appears they will succeed.

* * * * * * * * *

In the fall of 1993, Glenn and Lyla Lehrer organized and put on a three day test weekend, near Bozeman, Montana, with a half-day seminar on Friday, led by Joe Nadeker. Glen Johnston organized a few of his music students from the music department at the University of Montana at Bozeman, and we were treated to some of the best hunting horn music you will ever hear—in America, or across the ocean.

At that test Glenn's **AMIE OF WHITE WATER** (Ped 37 & 43) qualified for a Prize III in UFT, 10 days after undergoing surgery for stomach torsion. Quite a feat for this team, and a very well deserved qualification.

In the spring of 1994, at the annual field test of the Klub Deutsch Kurzhaar (KDK) in California, **BOSUN OF OCEAN HOUSE** received a Prize I in IHDT. He is admired and coveted by many who have seen him. His only defect is slightly open eyes, so we doubt if we will be able to use him for breeding. But he is one fine dog. Later in the spring, in Iowa, littermate **BUDDY** also got a Prize I in IHDT. The previous fall, littermate **BAILEY OF OCEAN HOUSE** had also earned a Prize I in IHDT, with a perfect score.

And that spring, 1994, we were able to produce six litters. We had four other breedable bitches, but either we didn't have a compatible male, or the owner of the bitch was going to be on vacation. We also had eight breedable males.

In May 1994 Bill Tarrant's flattering article about us in *Field & Stream* brought inquiries from all over the country, and some of those folks ended up with a pup from the 1994 breedings. Most will get a pup from the 1995 breeders and still others will wait for 1996. We thank Bill enormously for writing about us, and letting people know about our fine dogs.

That fall in Iowa, Dean Umphrey qualified his wonderful **ARROW OF DUTCHMAN'S HOLLOW** for a Prize II UFT, and in Maine **BELL OF OCEAN HOUSE** and her owner John Diller earned a solid Prize II in IHDT, while her littermate, **BAILEY**, and owner Rick Molt, received a Prize II in UFT, and with only two points more than **ARROW,** had the highest UFT score for the year, making them the receivers of the General Rogers Award.

*At the Montana test, near the confluence of the Jefferson, Madison and Gallatin rivers, at the lunch break, Glen Johnston and four of his music students gave us a wonderful performance of German hunting music. (Compliments Warren Webster) Below: **AMIE OF WHITE WATER**, happily making the retrieve of the duck to Glenn Lehrer, during a portion of the UFT, where she received a Prize III. (Compliments Joan Bailey)*

*Above, **BAILEY OF OCEAN HOUSE**, Maine, September 1994, during her UFT, completing the retrieve of the duck from the marked fall to owner Rick Molt. They earned a Prize II and the General Rogers Award for that year. (Compliments Alan Russell) Below: Sister, **BELL OF OCEAN HOUSE**, during her OHDT, completing the retrieve of the duck to owner John Diller. They earned a solid Prize II. (Compliments Tina Molt)*

In the fall of 1994, Joe Nadeker went to Czechoslovakia and began the search for another male for us. We will also be investigating the possibility of bringing frozen semen from there in the next few years. Whether this will be feasible remains to be seen. It could cut our costs considerably, but it has its limitations in that you don't get to see in the flesh the dog you will use. But it could turn out to be a great aid for us. Joe's search will continue in March 1996, when he will travel to Czechoslovakia once again on our behalf.

1995

We had seven breedings planned for this year, but three bitches ended up with false pregnancy. Some of these breedings were repeats of successful breedings from last year, others are slightly different combinations. All, of course, are from tested parents. There will be more than enough breedable bitches, and sires for 1996.

The spring test results showed that we are continuing on the right track. Nearly all the dogs tested were from our breeding program. In NAT only 2 dogs did not qualify and each was due to lack of, or improper conditioning. In IHDT, out of all dogs tested, two did not qualify for the same reasons as the two in NAT—lack of conditioning/training, or improper work. Each of the two IHDT dogs that did not qualify are fine dogs and had received all 4's in NAT. One dog fell down in retrieving, the other in pointing due to being worked on a drag track every day for four weeks prior to the test and had stopped pointing. Both dogs came back in the fall for OHDT (Older Hunting Dog Test), and each qualified.

What we learned from the spring tests was that the breedings the Breeding Committee chose for 1993 proved to be good ones, as we saw the results of IHDT from the fall of 1994 and spring and fall 1995. Likewise, the breeding decisions for 1994 proved that the sires and dams used, and the *combinations used, were correct. Only one breeding is questionable, and that bitch will not be used again.*

WPGCA Officers for 1995-1997

Warren Webster, president		Joan Bailey, secretary
Gary Pool, vice-president		Jim Seibel, treasurer

Additional members appointed to the Board of Directors are:

John Lundberg (Outgoing president)	John Pitlo	Glenn Lehrer

Breeding Committee members, appointed by the board of directors are:

Joe Nadeker	Warren Webster	Joan Bailey

Serving as an apprentice on the Breeding Committee will be: Dr. Tom Whitley, D.V.M.

The presidents of our regional clubs are:

Dennis Carlson, Northwest Griffon Club
Bob Matsuoka, Rocky Mountain Griffon Club
Ken Hurtig, Heartland Griffon Club
Rick Molt, Northeast Griffon Club

Registrar, Lyla Lehre — Editor, GDS, Lee Fulton

Judges:

Joe Nadeker (Sr)	Warren Webster (Sr)	John Lundberg
Rolf Benseler (Sr)	Dick Austin (Sr)	John Pitlo (Sr)
Jim Seibel (Sr)	Gary Pool (Sr)	Vic Jaro (Sr)
Ken Hurtig	Bill Toner	Glenn Lehrer
Tawna Skinner	Anita Andrus	Dennis Carlson
Joan Bailey	Steve Grieser (pending UFT)	Dean Umphrey
Rick Molt		

* * * * * * *

John Lundberg

John Lundberg stepped down after serving as our President for six years, years that were extremely crucial to the success of the WPGCA Breeding Program. His wisdom, insight, diplomacy, and, most of all his love and genuine appreciation for these dogs contributed greatly to the successes we have all enjoyed and will continue to enjoy. John's connection as a trustee for the Seeing Eye Dog Program in New Jersey has been a great advantage for us, making it possible for him to bring breeding and genetic information to our program.

There was also great involvement of time, effort, and money in bringing **ERIK** to us, taking care of a number of breedings, going to Philadelphia many times so that **ERIK's** semen could be collected and frozen for future use. And there were many, many unsung efforts by not just John, but also his wife, Bonnie, especially so when they bred three litters for the WPGCA Breeding Program. Presently, John has agreed to serve on the board of directors for one more three-year term. We thank the Lundbergs.

* * * * * *

A Look To The Future

In October 1993, at the judges seminar in Montana, Joe Nadeker outlined a guideline to insure our continued success in the future. He said:

> 1. We have now stabilized the breed. Much of the stabilization was done for us by the people in Czechoslovakia, who spent years stabilizing their breed and then sent us some dogs for us to use to rejuvenate the Griffon.

*Next page: Above: **CALLAJ OF DUTCHMAN'S HOLLOW**, during a pheasant hunt in Iowa, December, 1994. Owner/breeder John Pitlo was able to shoot a fox and got this nice retrieve with **CALLY,** who was only about two years old, and not yet fully trained to carry such a heavy weight. Four bitches from this breeding, including **CALLY**, are being used for breeding. (Compliments John Pitlo) Below: Early September, 1995, a 12 week old pup from **CALLY**, (sired by **DAN**), **DINA OF DUTCHMAN'S HOLLOW**, owned by Rick Molt, demonstrates that she can retrieve fur too, though a gray squire is quite heavy enough, thank you. (Compliments Rick Molt)*

PEDIGREE 57
Prairie Storm's Abby (A)

- **Dan Černíky (CF)**
  - **Beno z Nolkopu (CF)**
    - **Avar z Lusku (CF)**
      - **Avar ze Železnice (CF)**
      - **Alka od Petrovce (CF)**
    - **Dina od Krounky (CF)**
      - **Ajax od Dítětů (CF)**
      - **Ira z Tichého revíru (CF)**
  - **Ara Černíky (CF)**
    - **Ajax od Dítětů (CF)**
      - **Brit z Hradu (CF)**
      - **Brita z Hořické dubiny (CF)**
    - **Asta z Libeňské bažantnice (CF)**
      - **Blesk od Jezárek (CF)**
      - **Farina z Polední stráně (CF)**
- **Brittany of Dutchman's Hollow (A)**
  - **Boss of the Cascades (CF)**
    - **Čagan z Dračína (CF)**
      - **Argo z Vejrova (CF)**
      - **Cita z Runsova (CF)**
    - **Hela z Dobrovska (CF)**
      - **Alan od Dítětů (CF)**
      - **Brita z Bílých skal (CF)**
  - **Avaj of Iamonia (A)**
    - **Erik od Jezárek (CF)**
      - **Argo z Polední stráně (CF)**
      - **Asta od Vejřice (CF)**
    - **Mahaska's Merry Susan (A)**
      - **Bon Chasseur de la Cote (A)**
      - Alice B. Toklias (A)

PEDIGREE 58
Amos of the High Country (A)

- **Barton De Los Altos (CF)**
  - **Dan Černíky (CF)**
    - **Beno z Nolkopu (CF)**
      - **Avar z Lusku (CF)**
      - **Dina od Krounky (CF)**
    - **Ara Černíky (CF)**
      - **Ajax od Dítětů (CF)**
      - **Asta z Libeňské bažantnice (CF)**
  - **Axa od Pastejříku (CF)**
    - **Bojar z Burdovny (CF)**
      - **Erno z Doupova (CF)**
      - **Alma ze Všejanské fary (CF)**
    - **Cila ze Strážného kopce (CF)**
      - **Egon od Nemilské (CF)**
      - **Dora z Poloudelí (CF)**
- **Cera of Dutchman's Hollow (A)**
  - Blue Mountain's Brew (A)
    - Ingo v Kastanienhain (G)
      - **Axel v Baldeneysee (G)**
      - **Aura von Gschwendt (G)**
    - Glacier Cool DeeCee (A)
      - **Furst vd Neuburg (G)**
      - **Flatheads Jaghund Gretel (G)**
  - **Avaj of Iamonia (A)**
    - **Erik od Jezárek (CF)**
      - **Argo z Polední Stráně (CF)**
      - **Asta od Vejřice (CF)**
    - **Mahaska's Merry Susan (A)**
      - **Bon Chasseur De La Cote (A)**
      - Alice B. Toklias (A)

Avar z Lusku (CF)
Beno z Nolkopu (CF)
Dina od Krounky (CF)
Dan Černíky (CF)
Ajax od Dítětů (CF)
Ara Černíky (CF)
Asta z Libeňské bažantnice (CF)
Barton de los Altos (CF)
Erno z Doupova (CF)
Bojar z Burdovny (CF)
Alma ze Všejanské fary (CF)
Axa od Pastejříku (CF)
Egon od Nemilské (CF)
Cila ze Strážného kopce (CF)
PEDIGREE 59
Dora z Poloudělí (CF)
Arney of Whatcom Woods (A)
Ingo v Kastanienhain (G)
Blue Mountain's Brew (A)
Glacier Cool DeeCee (A)
Arrow of Dutchman's Hollow (A)
Erik od Jezárek (CF)
Avaj of Iamonia (A)
Mahaska's Merry Susan (A)
Brenna of Auger Falls (A)
Argo z Polední stráně (CF)
Erik od Jezárek (CF)
Asta od Vejřice (CF)
Autumn of Hoffman Mill (A)
Cacei de la Cote (A)
Freewinds Alamance (A)
Anka vom Fuchsberg (G)

Avar z Lusku (CF)
Beno z Nolkopu (CF)
Dina od Krounky (CF)
Dan Černíky (CF)
Ajax od Dítětů (CF)
Ara Černíky (CF)
Asta z Libeňské bažantnice (CF)
Barton de los Altos (CF)
Erno z Doupova (CF)
Bojar z Burdovny (CF)
Alma ze Všejanské fary (CF)
Axa od Pastejříku (CF)
Egon od Nemilské (CF)
Cila ze Strážného kopce (CF)
PEDIGREE 60
Dora z Poluděli (CF)
Abe of Beci's Paradise (A)
Aris z Javorové doliny (CF)
Argo z Polední stráně (CF)
Erika z Želivce (CF)
Erik od Jezárek (CF)
Avar z Faralce (CF)
Asta od Vejřice (CF)
Bora od Teplého vrchu (CF)
Beci vom Erik (CF)
Brit z Hradu (CF)
Alan od Dítětů (CF)
Brita z Hořické dubiny (CF)
Hela z Dobrovska (CF)
Bojar z Bezděku (CF)
Brita z Bílých Skal (CF)
Elka ze Skalických luk (CF)

Above: ***BRITTANY OF DUTCHMAN'S HOLLOW****, during the 1993 hunting season in North Dakota. You KNOW there's a big old cock bird hungered down in that grass. (Compliments Richard Bovard.) Below:* ***ARIKO VOM ERIK****, typical of what our males should look like, especialy the furnishings, eyes, and expression. Hopefully he will prove to be an important stud in our program. Three bitches will be bred to him in 1996. (Compliments John Lundberg Jr.)*

2. Our current work is to *preserve* this stability, while enlarging our population in order to do more selection.

3. We can decide whether or not we want to breed for dogs that mature earlier. If that is our decision we must use extreme care not to lose the calm, easy-to-train dog that we have.

4. We must always stand strong to our commitment to use CONTROLLED BREEDING ONLY, which means continuing our self discipline in all matters of breeding dogs.

* * * * * *

Now it is time to find out more about how a program worked for us, enabling us to re-establish and stabilize a breed.

*Next page: Three good dogs with three good women. Jane Mckenna and her **PRAIRIE STORM'S ALDER** (littermate to **ABBY**, page XII), Mahaska Whitley with **AMY OF DUTCHMAN'S HOLLOW**, and Tina Hinckley with **DEMI OF AUGER FALLS**, at the spring test in Maine 1995. (Compliments Tina Molt) Below: About 18 months earlier, at Bob Hinckley's hunting camp, a younger **ALDER** thinks it's pretty nice to snuggle up to "aunt" AMY.*

Oh boy, this is great. ***AMY's*** *not so sure about that, but tolerates the youngster. (Compliments Jane McKenna)*

Above: ***PRAIRIE STORM'S AMOS (Dan Cerniky*** *x* ***Brittany of Dutchman's Hollow****), 1994 hunting season in Nebraska. Below:* ***BRIANNA DE LOS ALTOS*** *with owner Rob Morse during their NAT in Iowa, 1992.* ***BRIANNA*** *received a Prize I. (Compliments, Sue Kelsey)*

PART TWO

TESTING, JUDGING, AND BREEDING VERSATILE HUNTING DOGS WITH AN EMPHASIS ON GRIFFONS

'I Just Want A Good Hunting Dog'

Over the past 20 some years we have heard that phrase hundreds of times. Hunters call, asking for information on Griffons, and sooner or later we come to the place in the conversation where commitment to field-testing a dog is explained. The response is often, "I just want a good hunting dog. I'm not interested in field trials."

Field tests are not "field trials"; instead we try to simulate natural hunting conditions. Our dogs are tested, or evaluated, one at a time, not in braces; they are not competing against one another, but are judged against a standard, using three impartial, experienced judges.

The purpose of our club is to produce good hunting dogs that are easy to train, and that make good family dogs. We know that there is only one way to do this—by testing sire, dam, and progeny, and then making sound breeding decisions based on test results, bloodlines, and genetic principles. It sounds so simple when condensed into one sentence. But most of us also know what a complicated business it is to produce "good hunting dogs." It's blood, sweat, and tears. It's costly. It's rewarding. It's heartbreaking. It's hard work. It's dedication.

Why then do we continue to struggle and work so hard, give up hours of our time, face disappointments, and spend a lot of money? Because what each of us wants is "just a good hunting dog." And we want others to have this too. But you don't get this "good hunting dog" by chance. Oh, if you produce a lot of litters, statistically you will produce a good dog now and then. But you will not *consistently* produce entire litters where all or nearly all the dogs turn out to be "just good hunting dogs." That simply doesn't happen by chance. The uniform litters, in which a high percentage of dogs are mentally stable and genetically sound, without transmitted conformation and coat faults—these litters come only from field-tested stock, and from genetically pure lines.

What we are attempting is a very objective endeavor within a very subjective atmosphere. As one of our judges, Jack Dallimore, said, "We love our dogs too much." What Jack meant was, it is very difficult for most of us to look at our own dog and see a fault, or to look at a litter of pups we have produced and see a fault in one of "our babies." We become very emotional and subjective about our own dogs. That is why a real breeder has his dogs objectively tested, and why our judges cannot judge dogs that they have bred.

So the bottom line is, if you *just* want a good hunting dog, get the dog from tested stock. And if you want your son or daughter to be able to get one of these good hunting dogs some years down the road, you had better do your part to help, by being sure that you have *your* dog tested. What goes around does come around.

BUDDY OF OCEAN HOUSE *and friends. This is what having a Griffon is all about—a hunting dog and a family dog.*

CHAPTER TWENTY-THREE
WHY AND HOW WE TEST VERSATILE HUNTING DOGS

Testing versatile hunting dogs in the field, forest and marsh began more than one hundred years ago in Western Europe. At the time these dogs were owned and bred mostly by wealthy people who had the time and the money to indulge themselves in this avocation or hobby. Most of the owners of these hunting dogs were from the newly evolving middle class of professional people such as doctors, lawyers, and merchants.

Some say that field-testing was designed or conceived by Korthals. Two different publications, one from the Dutch (see below), the other written by the Stammbuchfuerien (Registrar) of the German Griffon Club (See Part One.), support the view that Korthals instigated the fall testing. Yet others claim it was Hegewald. (See Part One.)

No doubt each man played an important role in starting formal testing of versatile hunting dogs. What matters for us is the fact that it was started, and that it still stands today, more than 125 years later, as an essential tool for breeding sound dogs.

The purpose of testing is so that objective breeding decisions can be made. It is a given that no owner can judge his or her own dog; judgment becomes too subjective. It is also a given—for the same reason—that no breeder can judge dogs he or she has bred, for that is just an extension of the owner of a dog judging his own dog.

When testing was started around 1870 it began with testing young dogs in the spring. In the fall of 1888, according to ***Toepoel's Honden Encyclopaedie,*** by P.M.C. Toepoel (published by H.J.W. Brecht, Amsterdam, The Netherlands), Korthals initiated the fall testing of dogs, in what became known as the Herbst-Zucht-Prufung (HZP; translated as Fall Breeding Test.) Testing of the fully trained utility dog also began in the fall about that time. It was called in Germany "Verbands-Gebrauchs-Prufung" (VGP; translated as Full Versatile Test).

In a special publication (*100 Jahre Griffon-Club E.V.)* put out by the German Griffon Club in conjunction with the 100th anniversary of the club, there was an article about the first "Preissuche" of the Griffon Club, September 27 and 28, 1888, at a hunting area near Darmstadt, about 60 miles south of Frankfurt. There is no way of telling if this was a versatile test or, more like a field trial, where dogs are only tested in searching and pointing. Some dogs that placed in that trial were:

First prize, **GROUSE MOUSTACHE (Chasseur Moustache x Yanka),** owner, E.K. Korthals.

Second prize was **DONNAR (Marquis x Jessy),** owner, General-Lieutenant x. D. Excellenz von Pannwitz.

Third prize, **PARTOUT (Cavour x Nitouche),** owner, E.K. Korthals.

(*Der Hunde-Sprot, Bd. III. Nr. 40.*

And there were other prizes given that weekend, for other categories. Many of the qualifying Griffons belonged to Prince Albrecht of Solms-Braunfels.

Let's look now at the present day testing for our Griffons and other versatile hunting dogs in the United States. We use the European (German, Austrian, Czechoslovakian) system of three tests: Natural Ability Test (NAT), Intermediate Hunting Dog Test (IHDT), and Utility Field Test (UFT).

Our three tests are based on the 4 point system. Each dog is assigned a number for each category of the test:

Very good	4 points
Good	3 points
Satisfactory	2 points
Poor	1 point
Failure	0 points

Each test category has a minimum score required for each classification, without which a dog may not qualify, despite good scores in every other category of the test. Such a scoring system prevents a dog that may be very weak in a portion of his work from qualifying, and therefore such a deficient dog is prevented from contaminating the gene pool. For example, a dog that got only a 1 in Tracking could not qualify even though he may have had high scores in most other categories. Dogs that are judged as being gunshy or gunsensitive may not qualify for classification. The temperament of every dog entered in a test is evaluated by the judges and this is entered on the scorecard. Dogs are judged by a team of three judges, with one of the three designated senior judge for that day. In NAT, dogs are eligible from six months up to sixteen months.

Scoring Natural Ability Test

Test	**Minimum Points Required For:**		
	Prize I	**Prize II**	**Prize III**
Nose & Use of Nose	4	3	3
Searching	4	3	2
Affinity For Water	3	3	2
Pointing	3	3	2
Tracking Live Game Bird	4	3	2
Attitude Toward Work	3	2	2
Cooperation	3	2	2

The optimum age for testing the natural ability of a young dog is around twelve months. However, judges take into consideration the age of the dog when they assign scores. A seven-month-old pup is not going to search like a fifteen-month old. Usually the judges take three dogs at a time and go off to search, find, and point game. They keep two of the dogs on leash, and these two dogs and their handlers, walk along about 50 yards behind the judges, while the other dog is searching, so as not to distract the working dog.

After about ten minutes the dog is called in, leashed up, and another dog is released. Judges keep changing dogs so that each dog gets about two 10-minute searching periods, or a total of at least 20 minutes.

The dogs are later taken to a fresh field area where they track a wounded pheasant, simulating hunting conditions where a pheasant has been wing-tipped, is down and running, and the dog must find the crippled bird.

The last task usually is to go to the water, where the young dogs are only tested on how they take to water, not on retrieving. In Europe they do not test the NAT dogs in water. We introduced this in North America when we started the versatile hunting dog movement in 1969, because we didn't have an IHDT or breeding test at that time. Also, as a member of the NAVHDA board of directors, I was adamant that we have a water test because we would not see 95 percent of these dogs again, and those we did see would be in UFT, where most defects have been masked by training and extensive exposure. (This was 1969 or 1970—seven or eight years before the Griffon Club began the IHDT.)

We find 25 years later that the water test in NAT is still valid, even though we now have the Intermediate Test. The water test in NAT provides valuable information which is used in making breeding decisions later on.

Throughout the NAT test the dog is judged for his nose, his attitude toward work, and his cooperation.

The IHDT is designed to test the young dog several months or a year after his NAT, but before the dog has been fully trained. The IHDT is a breeding test with several objectives: one, to evaluate the natural abilities of the dog again, when he is more mature; two, to determine how well the dog takes to training; and three, to use these results to determine whether or not the dog should be used for breeding.

It is these two tests, NAT and IHDT, that carry nearly one hundred percent of the information necessary for making sound breeding decisions. The Utility Field Test tells us that a mature dog was able to be trained to do the tasks required of a versatile hunting dog. What it cannot tell us is: Did this dog have some temperament problem (manshy, gunshy, soft, uncooperative) that the handler was able to mask (cover up) with a lot of training and exposure? Did this dog have a 4 nose, or, by lots of exposure and hunting experience, did the dog learn to compensate for any innate deficiencies and "use" his nose so that he now "appears" to have a 4 nose? Did the owner have to have a professional trainer train the dog, because the dog was so independent and uncooperative that the owner, an average hunter, was not able to train the dog himself?

So the UFT is of little use in making breeding decisions, though it can give us a bit of additional information. Primarily the UFT tells us that yes, this dog was trainable. And perhaps it may tell us that the owner of the dog is capable of training a versatile hunting dog. Primarily it is an ego trip for the owner of the dog. But no person should ever be made a judge who cannot train, or has not trained, a dog for utility. A judge needs to know what it feels like to walk in those shoes. It is a very special experience to raise a dog, hunt over her, and train and qualify her in Utility. Qualification in a UFT really says to the hunting world, "My dog and I are a good hunting team." That's what Utility is.

* * * * *

Scoring the Intermediate Hunting Dog Test

Test	Index No.	Max Points Possible	Min Points Required For: Pr I	Pr II	Pr III
WATER					
Tracking Duck in Water	5	20	15(3)**	10(2)	10(2)
Retrieve Duck Deep Water	3	12	9(3)	6(2)	6(2)
***Blind Retrieve, Reeds	4	16	12(3)	8(2)	8(2)
FIELD					
Searching	5	20	20(4)	15(3)	10(2)
Pointing	4	16	16(4)	12(3)	8(2)
Retrieve Dragged Game (pheasant)	3	12	9(3)	6(2)	6(2)
Track Live Game Bird	3	12	9(3)	6(2)	6(2)
***Track Live Rabbit/Hare	3	12	9(3)	6(2)	6(2)
***Retrieve Dragged Game (fur)	3	12	9(3)	6(2)	6(2)
JUDGED THROUGHOUT					
Nose & Use of Nose	6	24	24(4)	18(3)	18(3)
Attitude Toward Work	4	16	16(4)	12(3)	8(2)
Cooperation	3	12	12(4)	9(3)	6(2)
Obedience	3	12	9(3)	9(3)	6(2)
Manner of retrieving	3	12	9(3)	9(3)	6(2)
TOTALS		208	181	132	128

*** Test is optional, not required for qualification.
** figures in parentheses indicate rating needed to score minimum points.
4-H, not shown, is an honorary award.

Our UFT is based on the German Verbands-Gebrauchs-Prufung (VGP), but was modified considerably to accommodate some of the differences of hunting conditions in North America. Our Griffon UFT will be revised and updated in the next year or so.

Around the middle of the 1970s the German Versatile Hunting Dog Association, after several years of intense debate and great controversy, changed the NAT and IHDT judging/scoring system from a 4-point system to a 12-point one. As I understand it, the initiative for the change came from the Verein Deutsch Drahthaar (VDD). The Deutsch Drahthaar translates to German Wirehair (or rough hair).

The new scoring system, of either pass or fail, with no prize categories, allows dogs to qualify that would have not qualified under the 4-point system.

Because the VDD has, by far, the largest population of versatile dogs, they were able to push the 12 point system through by sheer numbers. The Utility Field Test, their VGP, still remains today on the 4-point system.

At a summer work/exposure day with the Northwest Griffon Club, 3 month old ***ARCHIE OF THE HIGH COUNTRY (Barton de Los Altos** x **Cera of Dutchman's Hollow)** has just tracked and caught a winged pheasant and is bringing it to his owner, Kevin Kennedy. (Compliments, Joan Bailey)*

Scoring the Utility Field Test

Test	Index No.	Max. Points Possible	Min. Points Required For: Pr I	Pr II	Pr III
WATER					
Tracking Duck	5	20	20(4)**	15(3)	10(2)
Search w/o Duck	3	12	9(3)	6(2)	3(1)
Blind Retrieve	3	12	9(3)	6(2)	6(2)
Steadiness at Blind	2	8	6(3)	4(2)	2(1)
Ret. Marked Fall	3	12	9(3)	6(2)	6(2)
FIELD					
Searching	5	20	20(4)	15(3)	10(2)
Pointing	4	16	16(4)	12(3)	8(2)
Steady Wing/Shot	3	12	9(3)	6(2)	3(1)
Ret. Shot Bird	3	12	9(3)	6(2)	3(1)
Whoa or Down	3	12	9(3)	6(2)	3(1)
Track Live Bird	4	16	16(4)	12(3)	8(2)
WOODS					
Search in Woods	4	16	16(4)	12(3)	8(2)
Walk At Heel	2	8	6(3)	4(2)	2(1)
Ret.Dragged Game	3	12	9(3)	6(2)	6(2)
***Ret.Dead Game	3	12	9(3)	6(2)	3(1)
***Blood Track	4	16	16(4)	12(3)	8(2)
JUDGED THROUGHOUT					
Nose/Use of Nose	6	24	24(4)	18(3)	18(3)
Attitude To Work	4	16	16(4)	12(3)	8(2)
Cooperation	4	16	16(4)	12(3)	8(2)
Obedience	3	12	9(3)	9(3)	6(2)
TOTAL		**284**	**253**	**185**	**129**

***Test is optional, not required for qualification.

**Figures in brackets indicate rating needed to score minimum points.

H is for "Honorary," for an exceptional performance (not shown).

CHAPTER TWENTY-FOUR
JUDGING

A testing system is only as good as its judges. Breeding decisions are based primarily on what the judges have written on their scorecards. But, someone will say, I thought the dog's bloodlines (pedigree) is part of the decision-making. Yes, it is. But the piece of paper that has a four-generation pedigree on it, containing the names of 30 dogs is only as good as the judgment of each of those 30 dogs by the people who judged them in the field. What the judges write down that day stays on the dog's record forever. If the dog is judged incorrectly, it can mean a fine dog could be eliminated from breeding. Or, a dog with a negative trait could be bred, causing great harm to the breed.

So the responsibility that judges take on carries enormous weight. Their decisions are primarily what breeders, breed wardens, and breeding committees use to make final breeding decisions. Their assignments must never be taken lightly because their decisions affect the outcome of the breed for decades.

Requirements for Judges

There are a number of attributes that a person must have in order to be a judge of versatile hunting dogs. The first one is a knowledge of nature that was acquired by experience. This means being *in nature,* and really seeing it.

A judge must be an experienced hunter and his or her hunting experiences will have taken him or her into nature. You cannot hunt without partaking of nature. A judge's years of hunting over several different dogs will provide the backbone of knowledge he will carry with him when he evaluates each dog in a test.

My definition of a hunter came from Joe Nadeker in our judges seminar in Iowa in 1991: "A man or woman knowledgeable in the behavior and habitat of game, actively participating in the protection of the wild population levels and deeply motivated to prevent any waste or loss of all animals subjected to his control."

During the time a judge is observing a dog in a test, he is unconsciously probing his memory bank for a similar experience he remembers from a particular day when he was hunting with a dog under similar conditions. Or, he might be remembering a dog that he judged five years ago. Those experiences are much of what provides the judge with his ability to evaluate. That, and the apprentice judging.

If a person has not had much hunting experience it is unlikely he will make a good judge, because he will not have that memory bank to call on. But, beyond hunting experience—which is bound and connected to nature—there must also be a *talent to see and interpret the behavior of animals.* Many people have hunted for a lifetime, but they lack talent for observing and *interpreting* what they see. That is really what judging is, observing and interpreting. And this takes some training.

Apprentice judging offers an opportunity to learn to observe and to interpret. Because each of us is an individual, it takes some of us longer than others to learn this skill. How long it takes is of no concern. That we have the ability to learn is what counts.

A great deal of knowledge about dogs is also gained from reading, from study, from seminars, from talking to judges, talking to dog owners, talking to breeders, and from being a breeder. Knowledge comes from many different avenues. Above all, a judge must understand how little he or she knows and always remain open for new knowledge.

The reason we have judges is so that we can objectively evaluate our dogs in order to make informed breeding decisions. Just being able to interpret what a dog is doing out in the field is not enough. Judges must have a basic knowledge of breeding principles, of genetics, of hunting, and of the game we hunt, and he or she must also be an amateur animal behaviorist.

A judge accepts a tremendous amount of responsibility when he agrees to judge a dog. As said earlier, what the three judges say about a dog on a particular day is in the record forever.

Judging hunting dogs is not an exact science. Each dog is an individual, each testing day the weather and terrain is different from that of the next day, or the previous day. Each handler is different. Each dog has had a different exposure to life. For the judge, each dog is a new and fascinating challenge.

Starting out on the morning of a test with three young Natural Ability dogs, two on leash, the other released to begin searching, a judge might think, "This 10-month-old-dog is hanging kind of close to the handler. What's going on here?" The group keeps moving forward through the field. He watches intently. The dog improves slightly, beginning to move away from the handler more. After 10 minutes that dog is leashed up and another one released.

After all three dogs have had a chance to search for 10 minutes or so, the judges start again with the first dog, the one that was working a bit close, exhibiting dependency, we might say. Now they come into an area where a few birds have been released. The 10-month-old-pup gets a whiff of a bird, and the judges observe as the dog lets the scent pull him toward the bird. All of a sudden the dog freezes. The nervous and inexperienced handler also freezes. In fact, he is just about paralyzed. The senior judge tells him, "Move up and flush the bird." The handler starts creeping up, from *behind* the dog, so the dog can't see him.

At this point, in order to help the dog, the judge has to intervene and give the handler some help and advice. The judge says quietly, "Bill, walk in boldly and flush the bird." Bill starts walking instead of creeping. The judge says, "Walk faster, Bill. What would you be doing if this was a hunting situation?" That breaks part of the handler's terror and he walks faster, approaching his dog at a brisker pace. He gets to the dog and starts kicking the grass in front of the dog, NOT LOOKING AT THE DOG, NOT SEEING IN WHAT DIRECTION THE DOG'S INTENSITY IS AIMED. He fumbles around, kicking the grass, and if we are extremely lucky at this point, the bird flushes and flies away. The dog starts chasing the bird full tilt.

As the handler starts to put his whistle in his mouth, the senior judge says, "Let the dog chase." When the dog stops and makes a turn back, the judge says, "Okay, turn and go in the other direction." All the judges watch as the dog comes running back, goes past the handle, and begins a much more aggressive search than he had exhibited earlier. Now the dog is really out there working and you get the feeling that if there are any more birds in the field, they will not be missed by this dog.

The field work is completed for this dog and the three judges and their apprentice judges stop and write down their observations on their scorecards. Then, beginning with the apprentice judges, each gives their score. The apprentice judges often would give this dog a 3 in search. But in this particular scenario, the dog will receive a 4 for search. How can he get a 4 if he didn't search so well during the first 10 minutes?

Because in Natural Ability, and to a slightly lesser extent in Intermediate, we are judging *potential.* This 10-month-old-dog demonstrated to the judges during his second time in the field that once he understood there were birds to find out there, he turned on his hunting machine mentality and left no game. Judges interpret that to mean the dog has a very good (4) natural ability to search and has the potential to become a dog that will put a lot of game in the bag, especially after he gets a lot of exposure to wild game.

Judging the potential of young dogs is not an easy task. If a person is not truly qualified in all the ramifications of judging, he or she is not capable of judging the potential of young dogs.

Some disagree about judging potential. They say it can't be done. It *can* be done if a judge has the qualifications and the experience. And potential is really what Natural Ability tests are all about.

That fictional 10-month-old-dog will come back 6 or 12 months later for IHDT, and he will search for 30 minutes beautifully, covering all likely places where game might be. He will find and point several birds. And the dog may have had his first full hunting season, depending if it is fall or the following spring. His potential will have been tapped.

In Europe field-testing conditions have been such, up to now, that during the test the judges are able to work the dogs only on wild game, not on pen-raised birds. A judging group of three judges takes no more than six NAT dogs and goes off for the day to a hunting area (called in German a "revier"). One dog is released, while the others stay leashed, walking together far enough behind the judges so as not to interfere with the working dog. Each handler does his own shooting. There is no gunner. They hunt until the first dog finds game, points, the bird is flushed and shot (if it is fall hunting season), and the dog makes the retrieve. Then the next dog is released and so on, until all dogs make game contact. Each dog gets at least two chances to hunt. Tracking, mostly on rabbits and hares, is observed by the judges throughout the day while the dog is searching.

Though we have to use pen-raised birds in North America, our system is based on the example above, which is the reason that we give NAT and IHDT dogs two opportunities to search. This is quite important, because nearly always a young dog improves during a second search. Probably the dog now has a better idea of why he's there, and has gained a little more confidence. Over the years we have found that having two searches, *especially in NAT,* is critical is obtaining a more valid evaluation of a young dog's potential as a hunting dog.

In this little vignette, our fictional dog also demonstrates why we, as judges, can't put dogs into "slots." We have to be ever vigilant about remembering that each dog is an individual, no matter how many young dogs you judge over the years, each one comes to us as a fresh entity. Not only is each dog an individual, each dog has had different *environmental* (i.e., exposure, conditioning) influences since the day he was born. If a young dog arrives at a NAT and has had very limited exposure to game and field conditions, it is the judges' duty to expose the dog then and there, in order to bring out the natural abilities and potential enough, so that the judges can make a valid evaluation.

Some people would like to design judges' scorecards with "helpful" boxes; for example, five boxes, each with a different description of a dog's pointing ability. If you are reduced to this kind of judging, how do you score the dog that doesn't fit into one of those boxes?

The most important part of a judge's scorecard is his written comments, not the numbers he puts down. It is the *individual* comments that feed us the rich knowledge and observations made by a talented, well-trained judge. Numbers are useful, of course, and we do depend on them. But in matters of difficult decisions, or when someone doesn't understand why we want to use a particular dog for breeding even though he only got a 2 in tracking the duck in the IHDT, we have to be able to go back (sometimes several years) and look up the judges' handwritten scorecard.

There we will find exactly what happened at the water that day with that dog. Why did the dog get a 2 in tracking the duck? Oh, this dog was given no exposure to ducks before coming to the test. So the senior judge took an extra 15 minutes and exposed the dog to a live duck, letting the dog chase for a few minutes. Then a fresh duck was released while the dog was hidden and could not see. The dog was brought up and put on the track. He earned a solid 2 in tracking the duck, a 4 in retrieve of the duck from deep water, and a 4 in the blind retrieve.

This is a true story. The dog was **BARTON DE LOS ALTOS.** After the IHDT in January, 1993, the dog was hunted extensively during the remainder of that hunting season, and again the following fall. He became an excellent duck dog, as well as a good upland dog. We used him for breeding with two different bitches in the early spring of 1994. In the early fall nearly all the young dogs from both litters came to fall tests, not to be tested, because they were too young, but to be exposed to the test weekend situation, and given a chance to track a pheasant and chase a duck. Based on what all our judges saw, we knew **BARTON** had been a wise choice. In the spring of 1995 these two litters did very well in NAT, as stated in Part One.

What the judges had seen that January day was an 18-month-old-dog getting his first exposure to ducks, and then they watched the dog build on that exposure, earning a 2. The Breeding Committee could then project the *potential* of that dog, once he was given a chance to work on live game.

Again and again we come back to reminding ourselves that EACH DOG IS AN INDIVIDUAL. We can use the judging of a dog's nose as another example. Nose can be divided into two parts: 1. Sensory is the physical part, which filters all the scents reaching a dog. This is somewhat uniform in dogs; there is very little difference among dogs in their sensory equipment. 2. The other part is the dog's *interpretation of* and *reaction* to the scents. *How* the dog interprets and reacts to the bird or the rabbit is of utmost importance. But each dog has its own unique combination of genes, *and* each dog has had completely different environmental influences throughout his life.

Sometimes a dog has the usual good physical equipment, that is, the sensory equipment for smell, but due to a fault somewhere, possibly a mutation, the dog does not receive the scent properly.

And, if a person is not a hunter, he won't *see* the dog's reaction to the scent. This is just one example out of hundreds of why a judge must be an experienced hunter and why each dog must be approached as an individual.

Another example of scenting and how it relates to judging dogs, especially versatile dogs, is in pointing. In most field tests we are forced to use pen-raised birds.

Occasionally we are lucky to have tests in areas where there are wild birds, but that is rare. Versatile hunting dogs usually do not have as strong a pointing instinct as the specialist pointer, because they are bred to do many different tasks (the Jack of all trades). With versatile dogs that have good scenting ability, we often have a problem with pointing during the test. This is especially likely if the dog has been worked and hunted on wild birds. What happens is that the dog gets a whiff of the pen-raised bird, moves closer, and then *correctly* interprets this to be a wounded bird. Because the bird has been in a cage with other birds, it may be wounded, it may be dirty from excrement. It is also traumatized. All of this changes the odor that the bird gives off and the dog "smells" a wounded bird. The dog then does what any good dog would do, he moves in and picks up the dizzied bird and retrieves it to his handler.

When this happens we have to rig things so that the dogs gets a chance to point. Sometimes we can just use a fresh bird. More often we have to let a bird fly, so it gets air-washed, then work the dog into the bird. Or, we may have to truss a pheasant and put it up in a bush, raising it off the ground so there is more chance for scent to be blown toward the dog and give him an earlier whiff. With this wind-swept-drift, we hope the dog will "freeze." These tactics usually work.

Another strategy is to wait and see what happens when the dog tracks the wounded pheasant. Sometimes the young dog will point when it gets close to the bird.

The object in judging a dog's pointing instinct in NAT and IHDT is to assess just that, pointing *instinct*. It has nothing to do with the dog's scenting ability. That is not what is being judged, only the pointing instinct. The scenting ability is being judged in other ways, such as how the dog winds and locates the bird and so on.

It's a real pleasure for experienced judges to go into the field and be challenged once again. We know we can never know everything. The dogs teach us that. Occasionally during a test something happens for which we can find no explanation. Why didn't the dog track the live pheasant? Why didn't the dog follow the scent left by a piece of dragged dead game? What is happening here? Then detective work begins. And we stay at it and at it some more until we feel we have solved the mystery to the best of our abilities.

Sometimes an entire group of young dogs appears to be unable to track a wounded pheasant. So the senior judge says, "I don't know what's going on here. Maybe there's something wrong with the scenting conditions here. Let's move to that field over there and start over." Everyone moves to the new field, fresh birds are brought up, and we start again. Now the dogs track. It may have taken an extra hour or two, but we got a valid judgment of the dogs. And that is our job.

Judges are not only physically exhausted at the end of a test weekend, they are mentally exhausted as well. A tremendous amount of intense focus is required of good judges for the eight or ten hours they are in the field each day. Their eyes bore into the dog working in front of them, or the dog that is pursuing the scent of a duck on the pond.

A good judge has an intense love of hunting, and of the hunter's companion, the other piece of the team. It is an unpaid job that a good judge takes very seriously. It's a personal commitment. It's like no other thing in the world. It's part of a tradition, which involves respect for the game we hunt, and we care passionately about recovering any wounded game.

Apprentice Judging

Unlike many other field-testing organizations for versatile dogs, there is no long list of requirements to become a judge for the Griffon Club. We simply have an apprentice judge program whereby people who are truly interested in becoming judges apprentice in tests with the official judges, *once they have run a dog in NAT and IHDT.*

We discourage anyone who is not intensely interested in the study of dogs, and in their breeding (kynology). There must be a strong commitment to the entire concept: testing, judging, controlled breeding.

There is no set number of times an apprentice judge must judge. Over the years I've seen some people apprentice only a few times and demonstrate an ability to move into official judge status. I've seen others, in fact most others, including myself, who apprenticed for several years before we were qualified to move into official status.

Apprentice judges are encouraged to attend our judges seminars as often as they can. One seminar is not enough. Two is not enough. There is much to learn.

About the only specific qualification we require is that a potential judge demonstrate that he or she can train a dog for a Utility test, and run the dog successfully in such a test. Since the beginning of versatile testing, over one hundred years ago, this has been a requirement. A judge must have walked the walk.

We spend a lot of time in the field with our apprentice judges, which makes for boring times for the gallery. There's a lot of standing-around time for spectators and other handlers. There's no way around it. The apprentice judges are our future. Ideally we should have only two apprentices per judging group. Realistically, we often end up with more. We hate to turn someone away. The opportunities to judge are not all that many. Often we end up with three or four apprentice judges plus the three official judges. It's unavoidable.

From our years of experience we figure it takes one hour to run one NAT dog, two hours to run one IHDT dog, and three hours to run one UFT dog. That means we can't run a whole bunch of dogs in one day, or two days, with one judging group. So not only are our tests long, they are also expensive to put on because we can only run a limited number of dogs per test. We won't sacrifice quality of judging in order to have a few more entry fees.

Judging Teams

First, why "three?" What is so magical about that number? When testing began over a hundred years ago, three judges were used. I don't know why they did it then, or how it became three. But, we know today that three is right. One person alone in the field cannot possibly observe everything. There is so much to observe: the dog, the handler, the environment. If you look away from the dog for an instant—literally one or two seconds—you can miss something. We know from experience that one judge cannot see everything. Why not take two then? I don't know. But I know that three works, three is comfortable, three breaks a tie. I know that on rare occasions when we only had two judges, it didn't feel comfortable.

The three people who make up any judging team cannot just be grabbed from the list of official judges. In many organizations they are chosen that way, or in a similar manner, but not in the Griffon Club. Like dogs and people, judges are not all the same. Each is an individual. Of absolutely vital importance in a solid testing organization is the need for a person, or small group of people, qualified to put judging teams together. If you just grab out of a bag, you can easily end up with a poor combination, which will result in weak, invalid judgments of the dogs, despite the fact that each of the three is an official judge.

In our club the members of the Breeding Committee (who are all judges), perform this function. In consultation with chapters sponsoring the test, the Breeding Committee assigns the judges to each test, designates who will be senior judge for the test. Things to be considered are: qualifications of each judge, geographical locations, finances. Because we are such a small club, finances are always a major problem. If we did not have a number of judges who pay their own way, or use their frequent flyer tickets, we just couldn't make it. That's reality for us.

Most other testing organizations for versatile dogs (including those in Europe) are not this restrictive in assigning judges. But this is how we operate, feeling it provides us with the most objective evaluation of our dogs that's possible within a very subjective endeavor.

Judges Seminars

Years ago, when the versatile hunting dog movement was first underway, we began holding what we called "Judges Clinics." Sometimes they were one-day affairs with judges and would-be judges working outside in the field with several dogs. This was a hands-on approach, like apprentice judging, learning how to read and judge the dogs. Later these events filled an entire weekend, the first day inside with lecture and questions.

The Griffon Club began their own judges seminars in 1980 in Nebraska, in conjunction with the annual spring test there. (See Chapter 14.) That year Dr. Ed Bailey (senior judge and animal behaviorist, University of Guelph) led the seminar on Friday. Then we simply extended the seminar on Saturday and Sunday as we all took to the fields to test dogs.

At that first seminar, Joe Nadeker said the following:

> "The primary mission of this [seminar] is to motivate the participants to broaden their horizons, with more knowledge of kynology with a special focus on versatile dogs. I regard the members of the founding group that are present, and some of the later entries, as among the most knowledgeable and what is of utmost importance, devoid of political ambition and breed barriers. For myself, I can say that it is a good feeling to move in such company. If we move forward and keep up with the times, we will keep the right to the contacts so stimulating to our lives. If we allow ourselves to stagnate we will quickly become pompous has beens."

Since that time in Alexandria, Nebraska, up until the present, we continue to offer one judges seminar each spring in conjunction with one of our tests. We try to alternate location, but at the same time we try to go where the most people will be, which is wherever the most dogs are to be tested.

Our seminars are pretty much a dialogue among ourselves, a sharing of knowledge, because each of us knows something about the dogs that no one else in the room knows.

And, as Joe Nadeker often says, "We knew quite a bit more when we first started out than we know now."

We usually have a theme for each seminar, but mostly our discussions just evolve. We all learn. It's important for judges to keep coming to seminars year after year, because there is always more to learn. When we talk and dialogue, we learn.

Dogs Are a Combination of Their Genetic Predisposition and Their Environment

A dog's behavior does not just happen because of his genes. He doesn't point or not point because of a certain number of genes, or a combination of specific genes. It's much more complicated than that, and we've given a few examples in the past few pages.

However, the purpose of testing dogs is to have a genetic record to help us make breeding decisions. During the short time he observes the dog, the judge must sift out what is genetic and what is environmental in order to arrive at the proper score. If the young dog comes to NAT and makes absolutely no attempt to point a bird, but instead moves in on the bird the moment he scents it, then the judges know something is wrong, because it is quite rare that a pup from any pointing breed is born with no pointing instinct. If the dog doesn't point, there are several possible explanations. As a very young dog it may have been hunted on grouse during the early part of the season. The owner may have shot grouse over the young, inexperienced dog, after the dog bumped the bird. It only takes a few times before the dog has *learned* not to point. Or, as mentioned earlier, the dog may decipher the bird as being wounded, and then move in to retrieve.

There are other scenarios, but you get the picture. The judge has to remember always that the final product is a combination of the dog's genetic predisposition and his environmental influences. To arrive at the right score, the judge must use his powers of interpretation, and also remain flexible and able to improvise.

CHAPTER TWENTY-FIVE
GRIFFON REGISTRY BOOK (GRB)

As explained earlier in Part One, we proposed the idea of our own registry in conjunction with the 25th anniversary of our club in 1976, during our board of directors meeting in Nebraska. However, it was a number of years before we actually got it going. For a few years I took on this job, but eventually I found I didn't have the time to do it justice.

In 1991 I asked Lyla Lehrer of Bozeman, Montana, if she would take over the registry from me. She agreed and became our first Registrar. She does a wonderful job and she accepted additional chores that go with the Registry—Breeders Agreements and related matters. She uses the old world method. She purchased several handsomely bound books and makes all her entries by hand. She does the four generation pedigrees on her electric typewriter. Each purchaser of a pup from our program gets one of these impressive pedigrees, stamped with the club seal.

Why the Need for a Breed Club Registry?

Why have our own registry? Why not just use AKC and FDSB (Field Dog Stud Book, for American Field, a field trial organization for pointing breeds, not for versatile hunting dogs)? Because those types of registries do not allow the breeder—or the breed club—to keep any control over the breeding of the dog. Once you have registration papers from AKC or FDSB you can breed that pup to any dog that comes down the pike, field-tested or not.

No breeding program for hunting dogs has ever been successful that did not exert control over breeding by having its own registry. In rare cases a breeder has been able to discipline himself and to develop a sound breeding program over time, producing sound hunting dogs. One example is, of course, Korthals. A modern example in our time is Robert Wehle, who produces sound English Pointers. What usually happens with a successful one-person breeding program is that sooner or later the breeder dies, or retires. Without control, the breeder's work gradually is diluted with inferior specimens and the breed, or strain, goes downhill.

In Germany and several other European countries, each breed club has its own registry and issues its own certified pedigree. Without that pedigree, plus certification of qualification in a breeding test, the dog cannot be bred.

American Kennel Club and Other Mass Registration Bodies

Registration of dogs eventually brings us to that familiar name in the United States, American Kennel Club (better known as AKC). AKC registers any recognized breed (recognized by AKC, that is) that can produce a four-generation pedigree. So you can get a Griffon puppy from Germany or France or Holland, and with the pup will come his certified pedigree from the breed club there. In Germany you could not breed this dog, even though you have the pedigree, until the dog qualified in the breeding test. But here, you fill out the application for registration and send it along with the German pedigree to AKC. After the appropriate time has passed you will receive AKC registration. Then you can breed your dog to any AKC-registered Griffon in the United States or Canada. Or even easier than that, buy a Griffon pup from most anyone in this country and you will automatically receive AKC or FDSB registration papers, or both. (In Canada it's the Canadian Kennel Club, CKC) Now you can breed that dog to any other registered dog. It's that easy.

A few breeders will have some restrictions for breeding, and fewer will have fashioned their own breeder's agreement. But, for the most part, there is no control of breeding in the general population of Griffons in North America, except for the WPGCA Approved Breeding Program.

Over the years, a few club members have said that putting Griffons into the show ring does not destroy the Griffon's hunting ability, that showing does not destroy a breed. They say that showing Griffons enables people (non-hunters) to get to know and appreciate their fine qualities, especially in obedience.

My response is that, of course, it does not hurt a particular dog to put it in the show ring, but putting Griffons in the show ring will most certainly harm the breed over time.

Of all the people who attend and participate in dog shows few are hunters. Despite what one may say about the Griffon not being beautiful enough to attract attention from people at dog shows, the Griffon *does* appeal to dog show people. Some find the breed appealing because the Griffon looks "cute" to them. Others find the breed "handsome."

By far the worst situation is when a show person finds the Griffon both "cute" and a *rare* breed. With few dogs to compete against in the ring Griffons are almost assured of collecting a large number of ribbons. Taking this further, when a show person decides to get a Griffon and start breeding, he most likely will breed for conformation only, and in a few generations the hunting qualities of the breed will have deteriorated greatly.

The detrimental effects of breeding only for conformation—in any breed—has been demonstrated over and over again, especially in hunting breeds. Some hunting breeds produce successful show dogs as well as successful hunting dogs. These dogs are owned by people who participate in both activities, and who breed with both conformation and hunting abilities in mind. Yet, if you make a breed known to the general dog show public, in a short time you will have a lot of people breeding who have little or no interest in or knowledge of the hunting abilities of the breed, and these abilities will be lost in a few generations of breeding. What you end up with is a pretty dog that is useless in the field. This dog nearly always exhibits mental instability, manifested in a variety of ways such as "soft," "manshy," "spooky," "fear biter," etc.

It has happened with the Griffon. Not often, but it happened back in the 1960s. (See Part One.) And in the 1980s a new Griffon club (American Griffon Club) was formed by show oriented people. Shortly thereafter AKC recognized it as the official (official for AKC) Griffon club simply because the dogs in this club are "pure," but equally as important (for AKC), they are in AKC shows. There is no assurance of breed purity except breeders' say-so; AKC seldom checks anything. These dogs may not be able to hunt, and some may have weak temperaments, but they are "pure." In another decade the Griffon will have achieved strong popularity among the show fancy and there will be show Griffons and field Griffons, just like so many other hunting breeds. A few dogs from these bloodlines were field tested in NAVHDA Natural Ability Tests, and even fewer in the WPGCA tests. (See the Appendix for test results.) The numbers are pretty grim. And usually only one, two, occasionally three dogs from a litter, are tested. And they are advertised as "NAVHDA tested," implying that they qualified, when, in fact, most received poor scores and did not qualify, and some were judged gun shy or gun sensitive.

Dr. Michael Fox, animal behaviorist and president of the American Humane Society, said in his book, ***Superdog: How To Raise The Perfect Canine Companion (1990):***

> Remember, the more popular the breed (reflected by the numbers of each breed registered by the AKC), the greater is the incidence of genetic defects. This is due to excessive inbreeding and also to what I term "overbreeding," which means the production of lots of purebred pups without any careful selection or quality control both of parents and offspring...Most of these breeds are afflicted by a variety of heritable diseases *which aren't usually apparent when dogs are young.* [Emphasis added.]

In March 1990 the prestigious magazine ***The Atlantic Monthly*** published a feature article "The Politics Of Dogs," By Mark Derr. The entire 6,000-word article denounced the AKC as an organization doing nothing to protect dogs, and, in fact, accused it of being greatly responsible for the sad state of most breeds of dogs today in the United States. Derr pointed out that the criticisms against the AKC come primarily from three related interest groups: veterinarians, breeders and trainers, and animal-rights advocates. Mostly they focus on three areas, said Derr:

1. That AKC gives little attention to health, temperament, and the work of the breed,
2. "...because it benefits financially from the registration of dogs produced and sold commercially, the AKC has failed to take a stand against the puppy mills and pet stores that exploit purebred dogs."
3. "...the AKC and its member clubs define *purity in a breed according to an out-moded notion that is destructive of the health of dogs."* [Emphasis added.]

Derr continued:

> The AKC relies on its certificate of pedigree, or papers, to guarantee that the bloodlines of, say, a Chesapeake Bay retriever are pure for at least three generations....The standards do not demand that a dog be able to per*form its traditional function—that the Chesapeake be able to swim and fetch, for example.*

What the AKC means by "pure," is that the three generations of Chesapeakes be from dogs registered as Chesapeakes with AKC.

In another section of Derr's article he quotes Dr. Donald Patterson, chief of medical genetics at the University of Pennsylvania School of Veterinary Medicine. Dr. Patterson has also been actively involved with the Seeing Eye Dogs of Morristown, New Jersey. "While the differences between breeds are genetic," said Dr. Patterson, "the determination of when a breed becomes a breed is a human one."

Derr gave abundant examples throughout history of people outcrossing their dogs in order to improve their function. One example was with the ancient Greeks, who tied their bitches outside, hoping a wild wolf would mate with them, to add vigor to their domestic dogs. He said that Native Americans sought the coyote occasionally, hoping for an injection of intelligence to strengthen their dogs.

One of the most depressing statements made by Derr was, "...By the AKC's own estimates, a majority of newcomers to the sport, obsessed with championships and ribbons, stick with it an average of five years. When they give up or move on to a new hobby, they leave behind a trail of damaged bloodlines..."

Dr. Patterson, according to Derr, acknowledges the huge increase in hereditary diseases in dogs, with about 10 new ones discovered every year. "Many of those," said Patterson, "are associated with recessive genes, which can become expressed during inbreeding for desirable characteristics."

Derr used information from Robert Baker, an investigator for the Humane Society, who experimented with the reliability of AKC's registration of purebred dogs. Derr explained how Baker, "...to prove how easy it was to cheat,...registered nonexistent Labrador retrievers."

Derr ended his outstanding, well-researched article with this recommendation: "The necessary course ahead...involves the acceptance of a more expansive and traditional definition of purebred dogs, which recognizes their essential characteristics as herders, hunters, and companions, as intelligent and uniquely talented creatures, not as objects of beauty alone."

In the December 12, 1994 issue of ***Time*** magazine, "A Terrible Beauty," a feature article by Michael D. Lemonick, the magazine cover showed the face of a bulldog—very similar to the cover used in ***The Atlantic Monthly***. Lemonick quoted the Derr article, and pointed out the "appalling truth...that as many as 25 percent of the 20 million purebred dogs in America—1 in 4 animals—are afflicted with a serious genetic problem...Labrador retrievers are prone to dwarfing...At least 70 percent of collies suffer from genetic eye trouble...dalmatians are often deaf. Cocker spaniels tend to have bad tempers. Great Danes have weak hearts..."

Other quotes read:

> The stress on winning looks has created purebreeds that are attractive but unhealthy....Americans spend more than $8 billion a year on their dogs, not counting the initial purchase. The AKC alone raked in $29 million last year, about three-fourths of it from the $25 or more it charges to register each pedigreed pup and provide a copy of its family tree.

Lemonick said, "All it takes to get AKC certification is proof of pedigreed parentage..." Quoting Dr. Fox of the American Humane Society, Lemonick wrote:

> The best use of [AKC] pedigree papers is for housebreaking your dog. They don't mean a damn thing. You can have an immune-deficient puppy that is about to go blind and has epilepsy, hip dysplasia, hemophilia and one testicle, and the AKC will register it....They [AKC] simply want to gain as many registrations as possible because money is power.

In the summer of 1994, ABC Television's "20/20" had a 15-minute segment on this very subject—AKC—with a viewpoint similar to the articles in ***Time*** and ***The Atlantic Monthly.***

A breed club registry is essential for a breeding program, especially for any working breed, such as ours. Without it there is no control, and without control one cannot maintain a hunting breed.

CHAPTER TWENTY-SIX
BREEDING PART ONE

Kynology

Kynology comes from the Greek word "kynos," meaning dog. It is the study of breeding dogs. And to be a judge or a breeder you must study, learn, and become a kynolog. There are many books to help you on your way (see Bibliography). One of the most important is the translation from German of Eberhard Trummler's, ***Your Dog And You***. It will tell you more about dog behavior than any other book. Along with Scott and Fuller, and Konrad Lorenz (See Bibliography.), it relies heavily on the behavior of wolves. It's interesting to know that domestic dogs and wolves have the same number of chromosomes, but foxes and coyotes have four chromosome fewer than dogs and wolves. Trummler's book is good for anyone interested in dogs, be you a one-dog owner, breeder or judge. It will help you to understand dogs. It will help you to train your dogs. It will help you to judge them and to breed them. If you love dogs, it will fascinate you.

* * * * * * *

Breeding uniform, capable, sound hunting dogs is a complicated business. Breeding versatile hunting dogs is a tough, expensive, complex endeavor. It takes dedication to the breed, respect for the game we hunt, and most difficult of all—the ability to discipline ourselves.

The WPGCA Approved Breeding Program (which I will refer to as the Griffon Club Breeding Program) is based on the following principles, which have been followed by versatile breed clubs in Europe for more than one hundred years:

1. Dogs used for breeding must be successfully field-tested (NAT and IHDT) and demonstrate sound temperament, which includes the strong desire for game contact, with a well balanced strong desire to please, which makes the dog easy to train.

2. Lineage (pedigrees, bloodlines) *must* be taken into account.

3. Test results of littermates (siblings) are of utmost importance, as well as the test results of the parents, grandparents, and great-grandparents.

4. Absolute control.

Control is perhaps the most difficult of all, at least for many people. This is especially so for Americans, who pride themselves on being independent. It is grounded in our democratic heritage. The Oxford American Dictionary defines democracy: "1. government by the whole people of a country, especially through representatives whom they elect...." Roget's Thesaurus gives the following synonyms: friendly, informal, free and easy (sociality); self-government, free, republican..." This all certainly sounds like us Yanks, and also our Canadian friends to the North.

Allowing ourselves to be under the control of others in the breeding of our dogs, feels foreign, uncomfortable, very unusual. It surely isn't democratic. It isn't the "American" way. That's what makes it difficult for us. But, it's not impossible. We've proven that in the Griffon Club. And, by disciplining ourselves, we wind up working together. When one person, working alone, makes the decisions there is far more statistical probability for making a mistake. There is more risk involved. With a group of talented people there is the advantage of available knowledge from more people. It is a pooling of our knowledge, putting it on the table, studying it, and then making an unemotional decision. There is a built in automatic checking system. The odds of making good decisions are much increased.

Genetics

We don't have a specific category for genetics in the philosophy and principles listed above, but bloodlines, or lineage of course, implies genetics. Judges and breeders must know the basics of genetics. It's a tough study. The best book I ever came across for the lay person is ***Genetics For Dog Breeders***, by Dr. Frederick B. Hutt, D.V.M., 1979. It has been out of print for quite some years. If you can't find it in your library, or through your inter-library service, try a good book store; they can do a search for you.

The book presents the basic information in a manner that a lay person can grasp. Still, it is not easy material. But if you want to get into breeding and judging (kynology) in a serious manner, you've got to have a basic understanding of genetics. Over the years I've found that Hutt offers an excellent, workable solution.

For dog breeding, one of the basics is getting over the false idea that dog inheritance is strictly Mendelian: that there's a particular gene for pointing, and if I breed a male and a female that both point, all the puppies from the litter will point. Nearly all dog inheritance is polygenic, meaning traits are transmitted through a complex *combination* of genes. And it is that fact that makes the genetics of dogs and consequently the breeding of dogs so difficult.

Another basic piece of knowledge, according to Hutt, "...contrary to the old adage—like does not always beget like, particularly when quantitative characters are concerned. As the geneticist would put it, the phenotype does not always reveal the genotype; the progeny tell more." Phenotype refers to what the dog looks like and acts like (meaning all his behavior, in the field and at home). Genotype refers to the genetic make-up of the dog, the genes he or she carries and more importantly, the ability or lack of ability to pass his genetic composition on to his or her progeny. The genotype is hidden from us; we cannot *see* it. A dog that is able to pass on positive or negative characteristics to its offspring is called prepotent. It applies to both male and female.

Of great importance when trying to eliminate a negative trait in a breed is "*...not to breed from affected dogs, their litter-mates, their parents, or (if there are any) their offspring.*" Much damage to dog breeds could be avoided if this one piece of advice from Hutt's book was followed faithfully by all breeders. He points out that there are only two kinds of selected breeding :

1. **Mass Selection.** Almost all dogs have been bred using this method. It is selection based on the *phenotype* and on the old saying that like begets like. But, champions do not always beget champions. In the wild, what we think of as natural selection, is really *mass selection* on a *grand scale*—and it is very efficient, *in that setting.*

2. **Progeny Testing.** "Whereas mass selection evaluates prospective breeding stock by the phenotype, progeny-testing does so from es-

> timates of the genotype. Those can be made only by inspecting [testing] the progeny....Hutt continues, "Even though most dog breeders will have to continue using mass selection in their own kennels, by cooperative efforts of its members, a breed society could initiate progeny tests and use them to reduce the incidence of whatever polygenic defects are recognized as being sufficiently prevalent in the breed to warrant concerted attempts at control."

This sounds familiar, doesn't it? Hutt confirms our belief in the importance of lineage (pedigrees, bloodlines) when making breeding decisions, and agrees on "...the importance of excluding from reproduction the parents and litter-mates of the defective dogs."

Mutants

One more tangle in the maze of genetics as it relates to breeding dogs is a mutant. A mutant is produced when, for no apparent reason, the complex makeup of a gene changes. There are millions and millions of variations of mutant genes. A mutation appears to be a more or less random act, though it is not that simple. But, we can think of it as a random act, cause unknown.

Let's use an example of a mutant occurring when dog A is bred to dog B and the pups in the resulting litter end up with 47 chromosomes instead of 46. When this happens in humans we call it Down syndrome. This is only one example out of millions.

With wild canines such as wolves there is a built-in natural selection. There is a dominant male with the best, strongest, most useful physique, combined with a built-in survival mechanism. If a mutant occurs in an individual wolf that wolf has NO chance of reproducing. He or she will be excluded from breeding by the dominant males and females.

People who breed dogs must always be on the lookout for mutants and CULL THEM RUTHLESSLY. They must never be allowed to breed.

Inbreeding And Line Breeding

Inbreeding is breeding to a close relative, for example breeding a daughter to a father, or a half-brother to a half-sister, or brother to sister. Line breeding is breeding to related animals, but not as closely as with inbreeding. Even so, some line breeding can be pretty close, such as grandfather to granddaughter. Anything closer would be considered inbreeding. Some might call grandfather to granddaughter inbreeding, but I don't. The purpose of both line breeding and inbreeding is best explained by Lloyd Brackett in his booklet ***Planned Breeding:***

> The purpose of both line breeding and inbreeding is to bring about breed improvement—to get the best that is possible out of one's matings and to upgrade his stock. Experience has shown that if more than mere multiplication is to be had, and any real and lasting results toward breed improvement are to be obtained, a breeder must use a system of line breeding, which not only combines animals very similar in their characteristics [phenotypes] but narrows the pedigree to a few closely related lines of descent [genotypes]. This "purifies" the pedigree rapidly and enables a breeder to control, to some degree, all characteristics. It discourages variability and reduces it to a minimum.

Inbreeding is not bad in itself. In fact, most breeds and strains would not have been developed if inbreeding had not been used. It brings to light negative attributes. For example, if there are temperament defects, they will usually show up immediately in the progeny resulting from inbreeding (parent to offspring, brother to sister). So, if serious breeders want to find *where* any defects may be, they can do so much faster by inbreeding. But, it must be done with absolute control, because, as Larry Mueller says: "Inbreeding has a second face, a good news/bad news situation. Dogs that have inherited desired traits can also inherit negative ones. In the hands of inept, careless, or greedy breeders (who sell rather than cull defective animals), the defects can spread rapidly through a breed."

The results of brother-to-sister inbreeding is different from parent-to-offspring, because mathematically parent-to-offspring inbreeding intensifies the parent's influence, meaning there will be more of the parent's genes emphasized. But brother-to-sister is of equal intensity, and nearly always brings negative traits to light more quickly than parent-to-offspring.

Line breeding is, in a sense, inbreeding with less intensity. We did a modified form of line breeding in 1991 (tested in 1992-93 "A" OF OCEAN HOUSE, Pedigree in Part One) when we bred **AMY OF DUTCHMAN'S HOLLOW** to her grandfather, **ERIK OD JEZERAK.** We did this with our eyes open, knowing the risks. As Joe Nadeker said at the time of the decision, "We'll find out right away if there is any trouble." And we did. In the resulting litter we got two or three dogs with soft temperament. However, except for one dog, all the rest went on to be good hunting dogs. (See Appendix for tabulations.) BUT, NO DOGS FROM THE LITTER WERE EVER USED FOR BREEDING.

What did we gain? What did we find out? Far back in **AMY's** bloodlines is soft temperament (tracing back through her grandmother, **MAHASKA'S MERRY SUSAN**). But we were not inbreeding or line breeding to that side of the pedigree, we were close line breeding to **ERIK.**

Remember that many versatile dogs from Europe are bred to be "sensitive"—sensitive to us, so that one of their strongest desires is to please us. This desire is what makes these dogs cooperative and easy to train. But, if you go "over the line" so to speak, as in close inbreeding, you stand the chance of going beyond sensitivity to softness. We found that we must be careful not to breed too close to **ERIK.** We can loose line breed to him with great success, but we can't do close line breeding (grandfather to granddaughter). For a more in depth explanation of this subject (sensitivity as a positive attribute) see ***How to Help Gun Dogs Train Themselves.***

Inbreeding takes place in nature all the time and it works there because nature culls the weak. Only the best are allowed to breed, thus keeping the population both strong and pure.

How Korthals Used Inbreeding and Line Breeding with the Eight Patriarchs to Fix and Stabilize the Breed

Korthals began his serious breeding program of Griffons around 1870. But not until he felt he had stabilized the breed did he form the Griffon Club in 1888.

On the following pages are photographs of some of the Korthals dogs, or their direct descendants, along with pedigrees to illustrate exactly how Korthals did his work. Each dog was an excellent specimen, most winning many field prizes and expositions as well. These were dogs that could hunt all day on a variety of game, both fur and feather, on land or water.

As we look at his work it is apparent that success did not come overnight. It took him many years. Out of 600 dogs, he registered only 65. This means he culled a lot of dogs. In those days there was no town veterinarian to put the dogs to sleep with a painless injection. No doubt the culled dogs were shot.

After Korthals' death in 1896, Gingins continued breeding Griffons for a short time, but, unfortunately, he died in 1911. In 1916 Mr Leiman died, and the first World War began and breeding activity was curtailed. Most hunting breeds in Europe were hurt badly. It was after the war that Dr. Ilyus and Mr. Thebaud began bringing Griffons to the United States, and that was followed by breeding activity in the Northwest with Kirk Kirkilee and Bob Ward, which included **KADINE DE GAGNY.**

If you are a history buff and you have a Griffon that you can trace back to: **ELFIN D'ARGENT, SILVER FIZZ, MIKE VON HESSLING, DUKE VON KIRCHDORF, CAPTAIN HARP GRADY, JUNIOR OF WARRENSVILLE, LA BELLE CHERRIE, BEAUCOUP D'ARGENT, JOHN'S NEVADA GEORGE, MILSHIRE ORRIS, CIAN'S BYOU BON BON, BRUCE'S RIPSNORTER, CHUKAR LADY REEVA, LEE'S IDAHO LADY, BOB'S NEVADA DON JUAN, MUFFET D'ARGENT, MOLLY OF JUNIPER HILL, BONAPARTE,** or **MILISANDE** your Griffon is a direct descendent of **KADINE DE GAGNY,** and therefore traces back to one or more of the eight patriarchs. Using other dogs from Europe, you could also trace back to the eight patriarchs.

One of my first Griffons, **HANSEL**, traced back via **BONAPARTE** and **MILISANDE**. What did that mean to me? JUST THAT, NOTHING MORE. It had nothing to do with his inherent qualities. In reality, he was not a great dog. He had some major defects, the worst being temperament. But, he was "pure Korthals Griffon."

How Korthals Did It

Following are several pages of pedigrees of dogs bred by Korthals, accompanied by photos. You can see in the beginning how he used inbreeding to *fix* his strain of Griffons.

NOTE: Wherever you see an asterisk (*) in front of a dog's name it signifies that the dog was one of the eight patriarchs.

- KATE BELLA
  - Partout
    - Cavour
      - Marquis
        - Moustache II
          - Moustache I
          - Zampa
        - Lina
          - *Banco
          - Trouvee
            - Huzaar
            - *Junon
      - Diane
        - Moustache II
          - Moustache I
            - *Banco
            - Trouvee
          - Zampa
            - *Satan
            - Madame Angot
        - Clairette
          - Moustache I
          - *Donna
    - Nitouche
      - Tambour
        - Chasseur Moustache
          - Moustache I
          - Clairette
        - Yanka
          - Moustache I
          - Querida
            - *Banco
            - Trouvee
      - Mascotte
        - Moustache II
          - Moustache I
          - Zampa
        - Angot
          - Moustache I
          - *Donna
  - Caille
    - Tambour
      - Chasseur Moustache
        - Moustache II
        - Clairette
      - Clairette
        - Moustache I
          - *Banco
          - Trouvee
        - *Donna
    - Becasse
      - Marquis
        - Moustache II
          - Moustache I
          - Zampa
            - *Satan
            - Madame Angot
        - Lina
          - *Banco
          - Moustache I
      - Zampa
        - *Satan
        - Madame Angot
          - *Hector
          - *Mouche

PASSEPARTOUT

- Partout
  - Cavour
    - Marguis
      - Moustache II
        - Moustaches I
        - Zampa
          - *Satan
          - Madame Angot
            - *Hector
            - *Mouche
      - Lina
        - *Banco
        - Trouvee
          - Huzaar
          - *Junon
    - Diane
      - Moustache II
        - Moustaches I
          - *Banco
          - Trouvee
            - Huzaar
              - *Janus
              - *Mouche
            - *Junon
        - Zampa
      - Clairette
        - Moustache I
          - *Banco
          - Trouvee
        - *Donna
  - Nitouche
    - Tambour
      - Chasseur Moustache
        - Moustache II
          - Moustaches I
          - Zampa
        - Clairette
          - Moustache I
          - *Donna
      - Yanka
        - Moustache I
        - Querida
          - *Banco
          - Trouvee
    - Mascotte
      - Moustache II
        - Moustache I
        - Zampa
          - *Satan
          - Madame Angot
      - Angot
        - Moustache I
        - *Donna
- Rita
  - Tammo
    - Murzuk
      - Moustache II
        - Moustache I
          - *Banco
          - Trouvee
        - Zampa
      - Angot
        - Moustache I
          - *Banco
          - Trouvee
        - *Donna
    - Madame II
      - Moustache II
        - Moustache I
          - *Banco
          - Trouvee
        - Zampa
          - *Satan
          - Madame Angot
      - Madame I
        - Moustache I
        - Zampa
          - *Satan
          - Madame Angot
  - Clairette
    - Moustache I
      - *Banco
      - Trouvee
        - Huzaar
          - *Janus
          - *Mouche
        - *Junon
    - *Donna

Left: ***KATE BELLA****, whelped in 1890, bred by Korthals, owned by Gingins. Below:* ***BADINE****, whelped in 1893, bred by Gingins. Sire:* ***PASSEPARTOUT****. Dam:* ***ELLA-NASSAU.***

- ELLA-NASSAU
  - Murzuk
    - Moustache II
      - Moustache I
        - *Banco
        - Trouvee
          - Huzaar
            - *Janus
            - *Mouche
          - *Junon
      - Zampa
        - *Satan
        - Madame Angot
          - *Hector
          - *Mouche
    - Angot
      - Moustache I
        - *Banco
        - Trouvee
          - Huzaar
            - *Janus
            - *Mouche
          - *Junon
      - *Donna
  - Thyra
    - Marquis
      - Moustache II
        - Moustache I
          - *Banco
          - Trouvee
            - Huzaar
            - *Junon
        - Zampa
          - *Satan
          - Madame Angot
            - *Hector
            - *Mouche
      - Lina
        - *Banco
        - Moustache I
          - *Banco
          - Trouvee
            - Huzaar
            - *Junon
    - Caille
      - Tambour
        - Chasseur Moustache
          - Moustache II
          - Clairette
        - Clairette
          - Moustache I
            - *Banco
            - Trouvee
          - *Donna
      - Becasse
        - Marquis
          - Moustache II
            - Moustache I
            - Zampa
          - Lina
            - *Banco
            - Moustache I
        - Zampa
          - *Satan
          - Madame Angot
            - *Hector
            - *Mouche

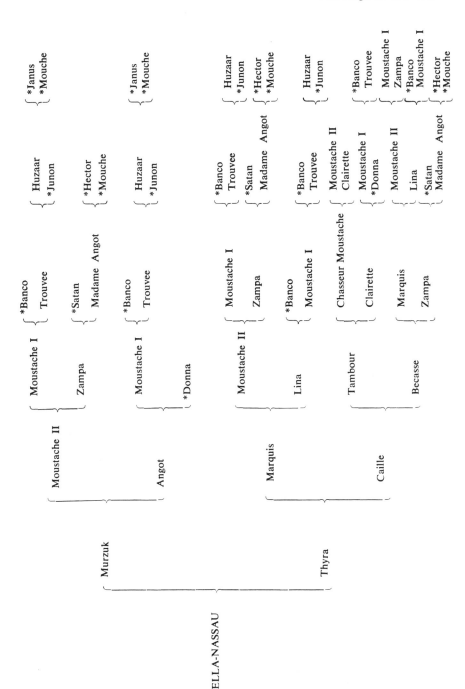

- MIRALDA
  - Robin Moustache
    - Partout
      - Cavour
        - Marquis
          - Moustache II
            - Moustache I
            - Zampa
          - Lina
            - *Banco
            - Trouvee
        - Diane
          - Moustache II
            - Moustache I
            - Zampa
          - Clairette
            - Moustache I
            - *Donna
      - Nitouche
        - Tambour
          - Chasseur Moustache
            - Moustache II
            - Clairette
          - Clairette
            - Moustache I
            - *Donna
        - Mascotte
          - Moustache II
            - Moustache I
            - Zampa
          - Angot
            - Moustache I
            - *Donna
    - Comtesse de Corneville
      - Cavour
        - Marquis
          - Moustache II
            - Moustache I
            - Zampa
          - Lina
            - *Banco
            - Moustache I
        - Diane
          - Moustache II
            - Moustache I
            - Zampa
          - Clairette
            - Moustache I
            - *Donna
      - Reine Ratio
        - Tambour
          - Chasseur Moustache
          - Clairette
        - Cavour
          - Marquis
            - Moustache II
            - Lina
          - Diane
            - Moustache II
            - Clairette
  - Wachtel
    - Tasso
      - Cavour
        - Marquis
          - Moustache II
          - Lina
        - Diane
          - Moustache II
          - Clairette
      - Flora
        - Tambour
          - Chasseur Moustache
          - Clairette
        - *Vesta
    - Jessy
      - Chasseur Moustache
        - Moustache II
          - Moustache I
          - Zampa
        - Clairette
          - Moustache I
          - *Donna
      - Clairette
        - Moustache I
          - *Banco
          - Trouvee
        - *Donna

(See Chapter 3 for photo.)

LE CAPITAINE FRACASSE	Arlequin	Passepartout	Partout	Cavour	Marquis Diane
				Nitouche	Tambour Mascotte
			Rita	Tammo	Murzuk Madame II
				Clairette	Moustache I *Donna
		Miralda	Robin Moustache	Partout	Cavour Nitouche
				Comtesse de Corneville	Cavour Reine Ratio
			Wachtel	Tasso	Cavour Flora
				Jessy	Chasseur Moustache Clairette
	Riposte	Passepartout	Partout	Cavour	Marquis Diane
				Nitouche	Tambour Mascotte
			Rita	Tammo	Murzuk Madame II
				Clairette	Moustache I *Donna
		Kate Bella	Partout	Cavour	Marquis Diane
				Nitouche	Tambour Mascotte
			Caille	Tambour	Chasseur Moustache Clairette
				Becasse	Marquis Zampa

CRACK DE MERLIMONT	Cavour de Merlimont	Loth	Cap de Merlimont	Passepartout
				Miss Aurore
			Becasse de Merlimont	Black
				Dunette
		Broussaille	Cap de Merlimont	Passepartout
				Miss Aurore
			Cigale de Merlimont	Cachou
				Trompette
	Coquette II de Merlimont	Nougat	Passepartout	Partout
				Rita
			Ella-Nassau	Murzuk
				Thyra
		Cora de Merlimont	Cap de Merlimont	Passepartout
				Miss Aurore
			Cigale de Merlimont	Cachou
				Trompette

Above: ***CRACK DE MERLIMONT****, whelped in 1903, bred by Mr. Cuvelier of France. Below:* ***CRICK DE MERLIMONT****, whelped in 1904, son of* ***CRACK****, out of* ***CIGARETTE DE MERLIMONT****, a sister to* ***COQUETTE II DE MERLIMONT****, the dam of* ***CRACK DE MERLIMONT****.*

(See Chapter 6 for photo.)

KADINE DE GAGNY

- Estoc de Gagny
  - Alto de la Dernade
    - Baschus de Menu Bois
      - Ximo d'Amely
        - Maro
        - Galouche
      - Mine du lo Hant
        - Cadet de Beaumont
        - Tango Castagnette
    - Yece du Warnier
      - Calin de Montignies
        - Fifre d'Isledoux
        - Rita de Montignies
      - Touquette de Merlimont
        - Stop d'Orville
        - Sap de Merlimont
  - Babette de Gagny
    - Ardent de Gagny
      - Caillou de Diss
        - Unico de la Mare
        - Pax des Pins
      - Tulipe de Gagny
        - Bab de Merlimont
        - Raquette d'Avrainville
    - Yanne de Gagny
      - Up de Merlimont
        - Stick de Merlimont
        - Sibelle de Merlimont
      - Tulipe de Gagny
        - Bab de Merlimont
        - Raquette d'Avrainville
- Helen de Merlimont
  - Ardent de Gagny
    - Caillou des Diss
      - Unico de la Mare
        - Piff de Merlimont
        - Ghetty
      - Pax des Pins
        - Luron dArgent
        - Lady de Merlimont
    - Tulipe de Gagny
      - Bab de Merlimont
        - Moustache de Moulignon
        - Manon de Merlimont
      - Raquette d'Avrainville
        - Kodack de Ressons
        - Mascotte d'Avrainville
  - Dune de Marguentaire
    - Yack de Merlimont
      - Stick de Merlimont
        - Moustache de Moulignon
        - Nell de Merlimont
      - Utah de Rinxent
        - Stop de Rinxent
        - Yvette d'Orville
    - Girouette de Fimes
      - Fifre d'Isledoux
        - Anno des Pres a Vivres
        - Basse d'Isledoux
      - Draga de Fimes
        - Clown de Fimes
        - Mirabelle de Fimes

(See Chapter 5 for photo.)

STICK DE MERLIMONT

- Moustache de Merlimont
  - Halo
    - Le Capitaine Fracasse
      - Arlequin
        - Passepartout
        - Miralda
      - Riposte
        - Passepartout
        - Kate Bella
    - Claudine
  - Helas de Moulignon
    - Dick de Vic
      - Cadeau de Beuville
        - Bato
        - Chatelaine
      - Yvette
    - Mabel Urian
      - Le Capitaine Fracasse
        - Arlequin
        - Riposte
      - Gin-Urian
        - Faust de Baccara
        - Ironie
- Nell de Merlimont
  - Marquis de Merlimont
    - Ivan de Moulignon
    - Kame de Merlimont
      - Cob
      - Jonquille de Merlimont
        - Crack de Merlimont
        - Phane de Merlimont
  - Kata de Merlimont
    - Igor de Merlimont
    - Bella Villeroux

PRINCESSE NADINE (GSB 1655), *bred by gingins, whelped July 31, 1889,* ***(Passe Partout x Miralda).*** *She earned many field prizes and was closely related to the other dogs in this chapter.*

CHAPTER TWENTY-SEVEN
BREEDING PART TWO

A Further Look at Inbreeding

In Part One, Chapter Six, in the section about the 1969 visit to Germany, there is a brief mention of a bitch, **BIRGA V.D. CULM**, who had to be forced into the water with the use of ropes and a pulley, and her subsequent qualification in the fall breeding test, her use in breeding, and the negative attributes passed on to so many of her descendants. Let's dissect this as best we can, in order to learn and to avoid such mistakes in the future.

Look at the fourth generation of **BIRGA's** pedigree (Ped 61). At the top is the famous **SIEGFRIED V.D. KREUZEICHE**, owned by Dr. Mintscheff. **SIEGFRIED** won many field test prizes. Go down two dogs and you find **SIEGFRIED** again. So **CATO VOM KOCHERTAL**, in the second generation, is a product of a breeding of half-sister (**ELLA V MARIENHEIM**) to half-brother (**ALI V LUDA JANA**). (**ALI**, incidentally, was owned and bred by Dr. Mintscheff; VON LUDA JANA is his kennel name.)

Then look in the fourth generation again, down to the sixth dog, **CITTY VOM KOCHERTAL. CITTY** is a littermate to **CATO**. In the third generation go down to the sixth dog and you find **CITTY** again.

In the second generation, the second dog from the top, is **ARDA V.D. BRECH**. Her dam, **CORA V.D. ALTENBURG** was an outstanding dog, from all reports. In the first generation the second dog, **GITTA V.D. BRECH,** is from a repeat breeding of the "A" V.D. BRECH. So breeding **GITTA** to **CLAUS V.D. BRECH** was almost like breeding **GITTA** to her half-brother.

The "B" V.D. CULM litter was not outstanding in NAT, in Germany (Remember, no test for water in NAT in Germany). Out of a litter of 6, one Prize I, one Prize II, 3 Prize III, and one did not qualify. The Prize II dog was run again and got a I. In IHDT the litter did worse, especially in the water work. Only three dogs were entered. Only one dog of the three did well—**BIRGA,** and we know *why* she qualified in IHDT. One dog got a Prize III, due to a 2 in tracking the duck. Another failed because of a zero in tracking the duck. So it was risky to have bred any dog from this litter, unless there were no other dogs available that year.

This is too much close inbreeding in one pedigree to be *safe*. Or, too close unless you are going to monitor the get ruthlessly. The breeding of the "D" VON LUDA JANA is also fraught with risks from so much close inbreeding. See how many times "A" V.D. BRECH dogs appear in the pedigree? And this was not monitored. One dog, **DAVY**, was sent as a pup to the United States, never tested, and used for breeding several times.

It is my opinion that **SIEGFRIED V.D. KREUZEICHE** and **CORA V.D. ALTENBURG**, though excellent dogs, were used for too much close inbreeding, too many times, *without culling any defective offspring,* thus weakening a large population of Griffons.

Siegfried v.d. Kruezeiche (G)
Ali von Luda Jane (G)
Uta v.d. Kruezeiche (G)
Cato vom Kochertal (G)
Siegfried v.d. Kruezeiche (G)
Ella vom Marienheim (G)
Dolde vom Karental (G)
Claus v.d. Brech (G)
Greif vom Marienheim (G)
Alarich vom Mornbach (G)
Citty vom Kochertal (G)
Arda v.d. Brech (G)
Barri vom Tannenberg (G)
Cora v.d. Altenburg (G)
PEDIGREE 61
Birga v.d. Culm (G)
Astrid v.d. Michelherd (G)
Aras of Gerbert (B)
Greif vom Marienheim (G)
Afra vom Kochertal (G)
Alarich vom Mornbach (G)
Ali von Luda Jane (G)
Citty vom Kochertal (G)
Ella vom Marienheim (G)
Gitta v.d. Brech (G)
Argus vom Kynast (G)
Barri vom Tannenberg (G)
Cara v.d. Hohen Linde (G)
Cora v.d. Altenburg (G)
Argus vom Kynast (G)
Astrid v.d. Michelherd (G)
Brinka v.d. Hohen Linde (G)

Greif vom Marienheim (G)
Alarich vom Mornbach (G)
Citty vom Kochertal (G)
Ali v.d. Brech (G)
Barri vom Tannenberg (G)
Cora v.d. Altenburg (G)
Astrid v.d. Michelherd (G)
Artus v.d. Neuburg (G)
Astor vom Teufelstein (G)
Ajax vom Waldpark (G)
Astrid von Malepartus (G)
Doinah v.d. Brech (G)
Alarich vom Mornbach (G)
Arda v.d. Brech (G)
PEDIGREE 62
Cora v.d. Altenburg (G)
Davy von Luda Jana (G)
Alarich vom Mornbach (G)
Blitz vom Bibertal (G)
Geissa vom Marienheim (G)
Caro vom Waldpark (G)
Alban v.d. Brech (G)
Brinka vom Waldpark (G)
Astrid von Malepartus (G)
Hexe v.d. Altenburg (G)
Greif vom Marienheim (G)
Alarich vom Mornbach (G)
Citty vom Kochertal (G)
Alma v.d. Brech (G)
Barri vom Tannenberg (G)
Cora v.d. Altenburg (G)
Astrid v.d. Michelherd (G)

Again, inbreeding can be used for positive results, as proven by Korthals and a few others, but used without 100 percent strict control, it can be disastrous.

Dogs that Don't Qualify for Breeding Are Not *Bad* Dogs

There are many, many dogs that don't qualify for breeding, but are very fine hunting dogs. Many are not just fine, but also qualify in all three tests: NAT, IHDT, and UFT. And, they are good family dogs as well. Why then, many ask, shouldn't a dog described like that be bred? There might be one reason, or several.

It could be that the hip x-ray comes back "fair," "borderline," or "mild dysplasia." Only under extremely desperate conditions should such a dog be bred. It's almost like being "slightly pregnant." If there is mild dysplasia, the dog is dysplastic and is going to carry the genes. Or, there might be strong negative blood somewhere in the pedigree. For example, when we see a dog with **BIRGA V.D. CULM** in the pedigree, that's a red alert, and the dog is used ONLY if nothing else is available, and then with 100 percent control.

Weak temperament of any kind should never be bred. For example, I know of two Griffons, littermates, each with soft temperament, who have qualified in both NAT and UFT. One of them even qualified in IHDT with a Prize I. The reason they qualified is that each belongs to a serious hunter who exposed the dog extensively to wild game, shot a lot of birds over the dog, and used great patience in training it. As a matter of fact, these two Griffons are great examples of good hunting dogs that shouldn't be bred. The dogs are **ALYA** and **AMIE OF WHITE WATER. AMIE** bombed out in IHDT, due to water (temperament), but the owner worked with her and brought her along through UFT just fine. She's a lovely dog to hunt over. (See Chapter 22, for her 1993 UFT, and below for **ALYA's** UFT.) I have hunted over both **AMIE** and **ALYA.** I've watched each of these dogs track wing-tipped pheasants that have gone long distances, birds that would have otherwise been lost if we hadn't had the dog. Yet both are spayed, because they should not be used for breeding.

It will help us to look at a more complicated example. Let's turn to Germany. We've talked in previous chapters of our attempts to bring new blood from Griffons in Germany, but the pitfalls resulting from those attempts made us ultimately turn to Czechoslovakia, to the Fousek.

While in Germany for the 100th anniversary of the German Griffon Club everyone in our group met a special person, Maria Zumbaum, whose kennel name is VOM KEMPTER WALD. She is a protege of Dr. Mintscheff, and, like Dr. Mintscheff, she is what I call a "gifted dog person." Such people spend a lot of time with their dogs, much more time than most of us do here, or do even in Germany, for that matter. Gifted dog people who spend a lot of time with their dogs, get more out of them than you or I.

In the summer of 1992 one of our judges, also a member of the board of directors, John Pitlo, and his wife, Vivian, decided to go to Europe. John was born in Holland and came to the United States when he was very young. So I gave John names of members of the Dutch Griffon Club, and I gave him Maria Zumbaum's name and address in Germany. Maria being the lovely, kind, gracious person she is, invited John and Vivian to stay with her at her home. They did, and spent three wonderful days with just Maria and her dogs.

Maria had five Griffons at the time, of varying ages. One was very old. The youngest, **LARA VOM KEMPTER WALD,** born the year before, was already tested in NAT. Maria also had **HILKA VOM KEMPTER WALD**, who I had seen

At a UFT test in Washington with the Northwest Griffon Club, ***ALYA OF WHITE WATER*** *holds steady while owner Dennis Carlson moves in to the flush the bird. This fine team earned a Prize II.*

in Wolferszell in 1988, along with some littermates being tested in IHDT, where all did well. Maria had already repeated the breeding of **LARA,** which was her "M" litter, but it had not yet been tested, and the "L" would be tested in IHDT that fall. Confident that this was a very successful breeding, and wanting to help our club get a pup or two from such a breeding. Maria offered to try to get permission from the breed warden to repeat the breeding a third time. Their rules usually allow a breeding only to be repeated once, so that the breed is not overly saturated with the same blood.

John came back from his trip very impressed with Maria's dogs and told us about the offer. I researched it, and the proposal was discussed both at our judges seminar in Iowa in the spring of 1993, and at our board of directors meeting that same weekend. We decided the only way to pursue the offer would be to take the entire litter, so that we could test each dog and then breed only the best ones.

Here's what the research turned up on the pedigree of the "L" litter. Nearly all dogs for four generations were field tested and qualified, except for four from France. But, in the fifth and sixth generations, **BIRGA V.D. CULM** appears at least four times. And the French dog, **TIBO DE LA BASTIERE,** had been x-rayed for hip dysplasia and diagnosed as "grenzfal" which in English means "borderline" result. Notice that one of his grandfathers, **UCKY DU RUISSEAU DU MASSACRE** is from a dysplastic line. (See Chapter 28 on hip dysplasia.) So that was another risk. And, all of us who had been to Germany in 1988, had observed **TIBO**'s overly aggressive attitude toward other dogs during the conformation judging. He wanted to kill every male there. This was not what we were looking for.

Another point to consider was cost. Including shipping from Germany, each pup would cost close to $1,000. What if some pups didn't turn out well? What recourse would we have? We could end up with several very unhappy people, and would have burdened some excellent owners who wouldn't be interested in trying again.

With all these negatives going for us, we still stayed open, awaiting the outcome of further testing of the "L" and "M" litters. The outcome was that not all dogs from each litter were tested. For those that were, some failed because they wouldn't enter water. There were other areas where some did not do well. Further, there were one or two cases of hip dysplasia from each litter. That was it. As much as we wanted some new blood, we scrapped this idea. And actually, when you look at the pedigree, it really isn't new blood at all, just a slightly different mixture of old blood.

Although we dropped the idea of getting that litter of pups, we came up with an alternative that would carry far fewer risks. A few years before, a male pup from Germany had been sent to someone in Alaska. The dog, **ALF VOM SUDERMERBERG**, and his owner, Ann Marie Acord, flew down to the Northwest Griffon Club's test in Washington and Ann Marie ran **ALF** in IHDT. He did very well, a bold dog with great desire for game, a dog that could take pressure. His pedigree was very similar to the "L" and "M" VOM KEMPTER WALD dogs. So we waited for hip x-ray results. One or two littermates in Germany were diagnosed with mild or light dysplasia. Then **ALF**'s x-ray report came back from OFA—"fair." That was the end of that alternative. Again it was too risky. But here, once more, was a good dog, a very good dog, but not one that we felt should be used for breeding.

Another piece of the puzzle was a dog from the "K" VOM KEMPTER WALD litter (similar bloodlines to the "L" and "M" litters), **KARLO VOM KEMPTER WALD** (See Pedigree 64.) This male had been sold to someone in Texas. The dog's hips were cleared by OFA. The dog was tested in NAT in NAVHDA at the age of thirteen months. Results were: Nose-4, Search-3, Water-2, Pointing-4, Tracking-1, Desire(Attitude)-3, Cooperation-3. Prize III. Temperament: sensitive, dog growled during examination [conformation]. Jaw misaligned. (See Appendix for complete tabulation.) **KARLO** has been used in an advertisement in ***Gun Dog*** magazine, for puppies he sired, as "Ultimate German Stud...produce natural pointing, backing, waterloving pups...Navhda, OFA'D, and AKC registered." (***Gun Dog***, August/September 1994, page 94.)

Because we receive the test results from the German Griffon Club, we know that many of **KARLO**'s littermates did well in their tests. We also know that **BIRGA V.D. CULM** is in the fifth and sixth generations at least four times. And I know the same risks for hip dysplasia exist for the "K" litter as for the "L" and "M" litters.

It's difficult to write negative things about the dogs from Germany. But, we have to write the truth as we see it, and present as much information as possible for the reader.

The dogs from Holland are from Dutch blood, Belgian blood, German blood, and French blood. It isn't anything very different, just slightly different variations on the same blood, though in Holland they probably have far less **BIRGA V.D. CULM** blood. And probably they have less temperament problems as a result. In the future we might be able to get some Griffons from Holland (free of **BIRGA**) that could help us. This has to be investigated and researched.

Again, inbreeding is not bad in itself. But, if it is not monitored and ruthlessly controlled, it almost always produces disastrous results, that often last for generations. Used correctly, it is an absolute must for developing a breed, and for upgrading a breed from time to time.

Control of Breeding in Germany

In Germany, and in most other European countries that have versatile hunting dogs, there are strict breeding rules, much like those of the WPGCA, which were fashioned after the German Griffon Club rules. However, there is one very major difference between our breeding rules and those of European clubs. In Europe, as long as the dog has qualified in the tests and fulfilled all the obligations of the breeding rules, it may be bred. The owner of the bitch is required to get counsel from the breed warden. Even if the breed warden is against the use of a particular stud, or feels that the bitch should not be bred, as long as the bitch and the stud have qualified in the tests and fulfilled all requirements, i.e., test qualifications, conformation, hip x-rays, etc., the dogs can be bred.

In our Griffon Club, each *breeding* must be approved by a three-member Breeding Committee. This is a significant difference.

How to "Read" a Pedigree

In studying and interpreting pedigrees one must be cautious not to be enticed or seduced when a particular kennel name begins to show up over and over again. Often our reaction to this is to *assume* that dogs with this kennel name are good or excellent dogs. It's very similar to advertising or marketing—if we hear or read the same message enough times we begin to believe it. *Not every kennel that appears often in pedigrees produce a high percentage of sound hunting dogs.*

Occasionally someone who calls himself a breeder produces a lot of dogs—several litters per year—year after year. When someone produces that many dogs, say 16 dogs per year (or twice that if they have two bitches), over a short period of time that kennel name will be seen and heard more than the name of many other kennels that produce dogs far superior to those coming from a mass producer. Someone uninitiated in the world of dog breeding who sees the kennel name of the mass producer over and over, will assume wrongly that the dogs from that kennel are good.

A Short Resumé of Cesky Fousek Breeding History

Around 1924 the Fousek, like most other breeds, was in weak shape as a result of World War I, and needed boosting. First breeders tried using Pointer, Pudelpointer and German Shorthair, but this new blood did not work. Then they tried Korthals Griffon, Stickelhaar, and Deutsch Drahthaar (German Wirehair), and these worked. This is when the Fousek Club developed the eight lines, seven of which were founded on a dog that was NOT a Fousek. Each line was pretty much founded on one dog. The Fouseks in our program all come from line four. Our Fouseks are closer to the Griffon attributes within the eight lines than are the more short-coated ones.

Apparently, when a gene pool of a breed becomes large, breeders are forced to line breed and create separate lines, usually ending with about 50 dogs in a line. Then they divide and select founding parents that are *very* compatible in genotype and phenotype.

Urac de St. Landry (F)
Axel vom Ulrichsquell (G)
Dia von Luda Jana (G)
Alf v.d. Hochzeitslinde (G)
Eik v.d. Neuburg (G)
Fuchsi vom Bibertal (G)
Kathi v.d. Brech (G)
Bazi vom Rhonblick (G)
Dago vom Geeste-Moor (G)
Artus vom Rohrfeld (G)
Cyra vom Eichhorst (G)
Afra vom Kempter Wald (G)
Claus vom Wolfsberg (G)
Anja vom Osterbach (G)
PEDIGREE 63
Fella vom Bibertal (G)
ara vom Kempter Wald (G)
Toscar de la Reote (F)
Orin de Barre Mer (F)
Taloche de Barre Mer (F)
Tibo de la Bastiere (F)
Ucky du Ruisseau du Massacre (F)
Lambda de la Bastiere (F)
Sido de la Vieille Oise (F)
Hilka vom Kempter Wald (G)
Axel vom Baldeneysee (G)
Hasso vom Kastanienhain (G)
Aura von Gschwendt (G)
Ela tuk vom Kempter Wald (G)
Claus vom Wolfsberg (G)
Anja vom Osterbach (G)
Fella vom Bibertal (G)

Dago vom Geeste-Moor (G)
Artus vom Rohrfeld (G)
Cyra vom Eichhorst (G)
Aquila vom Kempter Wald (G)
Claus vom Wolfsberg (G)
Anja vom Osterbach (G)
Fella vom Bibertal (G)
Ex vom Ulrichsquell (G)
Urac de St. Landry (F)
Axel vom Ulrichsquell (G)
Dia von Luda Jana (G)
Cylla v.d. Hochzeitslinde (G)
Lord v.d. Brech (G)
Freia v Wolfsberg (G)
PEDIGREE 64
Diana v.d. Neuburg (G)
Karlo vom Kempter Wald (G)
Toscar de la Reote (F)
Orin de Barre Mer (F)
Taloche de Barre Mer (F)
Tibo de la Bastiere (F)
Ucky du Ruisseau du Massacre (F)
Lambda de la Bastiere (F)
Sido de la Vieille Oise (F)
Hilka vom Kempter Wald (G)
Axel vom Baldeneysee (G)
Hasso vom Kastanienhain (G)
Aura von Gschwendt (G)
Ela tuk vom Kempter Wald (G)
Claus vom Wolfsberg (G)
Anja vom Osterbach (G)
Fella vom Bibertal (G)

Developing a Line
by Joe Nadeker

The accepted definition of a line: A group of individuals of a specie with an upgraded potential to reproduce certain attributes [traits] with more than normal frequency.

Since we will deal with line breeding in dogs, it is necessary to point out that we are dealing with animals among the most intelligent in existence, which means that the genetic structure in control of all the attributes [traits], morphological (physical) as well as physiological (behavioral), it becomes very complicated. Although many traits, mainly the physical are safely stabilized from millennia, by the screening of survival of the fittest, the manifestation of behavioral attributes [traits] are predisposed by complicated gene structure and finalized by environmental influences in the phenotype.

The inherent pecking order in dogs and the evident flexibility of combining various traits allow us (with some help from mutation) to form by selective pairing of individuals to approach stabilization to the described prototype. The creation of an aggressive hunter that displays text book cooperation to the handler is perhaps the ultimate achievement in selective dog breeding, because it is contradictory to the evolutionary behavior where the strong keeps the pray. [The previous sentence refers to the dog giving up the game to us, which in the wild he would not do, and which is against his normal behavior necessary for survival.]

It is generally accepted by kynologists/geneticists that the most successful formula to start a line within a breed is with an individual dog displaying high quality of behavior in all or most of the desired traits, who transmits these traits to the progeny in a high percentage with most of the mating partners.

Applying a Mendelian approach, we can assume that such a dog is genetically clean in the majority of the preferred attributes [traits]. As we deal with polygenic structure, it is highly probable that the genetic combination of all the genes on different loci [Loci is plural for parts of a gene.] involved in the formation of the genotype for most or all of the needed attributes [traits], are dominantly predisposed, and withstand even strong negative environmental pressures. [Different owners, different hunting conditions put different influences on each dog from the litter.] Such a dog is labeled "prepotent." Once such a dog is identified, the effort to preserve the qualities will dictate kinship breeding to check the validity of the evaluation and perhaps further purify the beginning of the new line, usually with son to dam or father to daughter, which is the closest inbreeding possible. The resulting litter must be under the following structure:

Preconditions for Establishing Controlled Breeding
and Breed Lines:

1. A club with disciplined membership, all willing to follow an accepted breeding program.

2. Population of dogs with sufficient number to form a pool that contains all the desired genetic combinations and without faults that

permeated the whole population, and were hidden, in genotype. If certain desired traits are missing, they have to be inbred through carefully selected dogs, in some cases from other breeds.

3. The breeding selections and other breeding decisions have to be fully entrusted to a breed warden, or some other central control, such as a committee.

4. Experienced judges capable of uniform evaluation of all tested dogs to supply valid information upon which the dogs can be selected for breeding.

5. Entire litters must be judged (tested).

6. A method of enforcing the above through conditional registration.

Providing that the preconditions are set and able to function, the upgrading of the quality of the breed will follow as proven and documented over and over in the past.

A regeneration of a breed, as was the case of the Griffon, is traditionally more difficult than formation of a new breed (such as the Pudelpointer), because one must save the general character and form of the breed, scattered throughout the remaining population, and replace the faults that caused the decline by attributes from outside. A new breed can be started with carefully selected individuals with proven ability to transmit to the progeny these traits that are expected to be stabilized in the new format.

In regeneration, the selection of the "blood" to be infused into the ailing breed can also be difficult to decide upon, if the desired prototype deviates harshly in the form (conformation) with any of the available stabilized breeds.

In the case of the WPGCA we had the advantage to be able to tap the resources of the Cesky Fousek Club, from a solidly stabilized line, that with the exception of size, corresponds to the image of a well-performing wirehaired pointing griffon (WPG), and what is invaluable, we got the quality of performing attributes that had been stabilized by 50 years of selective matings directed by the best available kynologs in the nation. (Cesky Fousek is the dominant breed in the Czech Republic.)

The litters whelped since the importation of the Cesky Fousek, greatly elevated the reputation of the WPGCA, and allowed broadening the gene pool to the extent where it is no longer necessary to allow questionable matings that carry a possibility of liability to the club's reputation.

The gained awareness of the members of the WPGCA to the scientifically directed approach to a "re-formation" of a utility dog is an additional bonus to the club's activity.

How to Start and Maintain a Line Within a Breed
By Joe Nadeker

Starting a line within a breed begins usually with an outstanding dog in conformation and behavior (temperament and hunting abilities) which is as close to the ideal prototype desired as possible. This indicates that the necessary genes expressing these qualities are present.

What it does not guarantee is whether the polygenic structural combinations manifesting the phenotype are "clean," meaning that the great majority of the individual genes in the complex that predisposes the expression of the desired behavior are "friendly" which would make them resistant to easy pollution to the undesired influences entering upon the fertilization by a mate dog.

Part of the information can be deduced from progeny of the candidate. If the litters show overwhelming transmission of the qualities than the dog may be labeled "prepotent." It is easier to make judgment about males for obvious reasons. One could stop right here and use such a dog broadly in breeding.

But, if more information is desired, mating of the primary dog with selected son or daughter is provided to corroborate the value of his or her genotype. The progeny from this inbreeding will indicate, apart from the positive, the possible negative influences that "doubling up" will show in the phenotype. Now depending on various factors, the observed fault may disqualify the dog from further breeding or, consider breeding it to selected partners or, if the defect is insignificant disregard the occurrence. *Since all dogs have some faults, breeding committees have to deal with them all the time.* It has often happened, that if the F1 generation of the inbred litter is a success, it may produce a male where the genetic structure is "cleaner" than the one of the primary individual and he can become the founder of a line.

Once a successful line is established, dogs are produced frequently with superior value and ability to transmit it further. Half sister to half brother of superior parents can produce a founder of a line. The purpose of the inbreeding is to analyze the desired qualities and to concentrate these so they could dominate the form and behavior of most of the progeny.

The cases sketched above are examples of the approaches to achieve a family of dogs that truly reproduce "like-to-like." For example, the case of the Cesky Fousek sire, **BOJAR Z JEDLOVEHO VRCHU**, is a product of inbreeding. At the national exposition in 1952 in Prague, from the 14 dogs judged excellent out of the numerous participants, 13 were direct descendants, or F2 generation, of **BOJAR**.

As the numbers in the population of the breed grows, the line breeding system can reach a status, that because of the continuous select breeding for the same attributes, all the dogs are genetically related and the line, or later the breed is "pure bred," or, "thorough bred," and mass selection in pairing is proper. However, selective breeding is the only defense against degeneration as we all well know.

* * * * * * * * * * *

At the time of the Communist take-over of Czechoslovakia in 1954, like everything else, the breeding of hunting dogs became controlled by the government. Although people suffered in many respects under this total Communist control, the dogs did not. Absolute control in breeding benefitted hunting dogs. At this time the Cesky Fousek Association decided to maintain these eight lines, which were already formed and were consistently producing uniform, sound, easy-to-train wirehaired dogs.

To maintain these lines they have used loose line breeding—to the third or fourth generation, and only with few exceptions do they inbreed, as described on previous pages.

The association for the seeing eye dogs for the blind never breed closer than the third generation. In our Griffon Breeding Program we have tried to follow this guideline, and have done so with only one or two exceptions. Third and fourth generations is what we look for. This works once a breed has been stabilized.

The breeders of the Fouseks kept an eight line to use only when one of the other seven lines needed a boost, a refreshment (gene pool becomes insufficient). Then they could outcross to the eight line. Perhaps this is not technically an outcross. If one goes back enough generations he would find common blood, but it would be so diluted as to have very little influence, except in a stabilizing way.

How a Dog Becomes a Foundation Male or a Foundation Female of a Line
By Joe Nadeker

A foundation dog is not created, it just happens. However, the chances of finding a dog with outstanding prepotency to pass desirable genotype structure on to progeny, with different mates, are more likely to occur within selectively bred programs, because those dogs, and their ancestors, have been subjected to filtering out of faults by selective breeding.

The tremendous complexity of the genetic maps which form the attributes are awesome. That is the reason why dogs are individually different; why each dog is different from even his littermate. *But in the case of a foundation dog, we are looking at a dog with the least individuality expressed in the progeny which is further transferable to the F2 and F3 generations, displaying very dominantly ideal attributes.* This is a tall order, yet occasionally a dog is discovered that performs with minimal guidance all that is expected from a cooperative, talented hunting dog, and also had the potency to pass all the talents to the progeny with little deviation.

The dog becomes a valuable asset to the breeding program and the "purity" of the genotype would influence his or her line positively for many generations, as long as line breeding is practiced, producing a high percentage of breedable dogs, thus allowing for stricter criteria in selecting dogs for breeding. Obviously that will result in the elevation of the quality in the entire population.

Such a dog stands on the top of the pyramid and becomes a founder of a line, a foundation dog. So it was with the Korthals breeding, the eight patriarchs only became patriarchs much later, *after* their influence was realized.

No Mathematical Formula for Breeding Dogs

When you think you have found a "formula" for breeding hunting dogs, you are in trouble. There are principles, but principles are just guidelines, not a formula. The reason you cannot be attached to a rigid formula is twofold:

1. EACH DOG IS AN INDIVIDUAL. Serious kynologists, judges, and breeders must come back to this again and again. Every bitch you set

out to breed is different from every other—even if the bitch is a littermate to a bitch that has already been bred. Their genetic composition is not exactly the same. The sire that may work well for the first bitch may not work well for the second bitch.

2. THERE IS NOT JUST ONE GENE FOR AN ATTRIBUTE. It's not that simple. Remember nearly all dog inheritance is polygenic, an intricate combination of multi genes.

Progeny Testing

Earlier I mentioned the importance of progeny testing, and said that it is one of two methods of breeding, the other being mass selection. One of the most important reasons that we have been so successful in our Griffon Breeding Program over the years is that we simply refuse to sell pups to people who do not make the commitment to test. Sure, sometimes we make a mistake, but not often. For Natural Ability we have a 95% rate of the litter being tested. In Intermediate, it drops to around 75 percent. These rates for percentage of litters tested are higher than for most other breed clubs that we know about, both here and in Europe.

How do we accomplish 95% of our dogs tested in NAT and 75% in IHDT?

1. By using our Breeding Rules.

2. By having our own registry.

3. By using our Breeder's Agreement.

4. By placing our dogs only with serious hunters who are prepared to make the commitment to hunting and testing the dog.

What About Griffon Breeders Outside of the Breeding Program?

Among Griffon breeders in the United States (today and over the past 20 years), only one or two breeders who are not a part of our Breeding Program, test a high percentage of their dogs in NAT and IHDT.

In our Griffon world we would not be doing history justice if we did not mention the efforts of Bill and Barbara Jensen, in Minnesota, whose kennel name is ALDERSEDGE. Over the years (through 1994) they have bred 10 or 11 litters. They have their own breeder's agreement, fashioned after our club agreement, which was designed at the beginning of our program in 1974 (See Appendix). About 9O-95 percent of the Jensen pups get tested in NAT in NAVHDA tests. But almost none go beyond that, to Intermediate or even to Utility. And the qualifying requirements in NAVHDA in NAT are slightly less than in WPGCA. (See Appendix for tabulation of test results of the ALDERSEDGE dogs in NAVHDA NAT tests.)

Another name in our history is DUCKPOND, the kennel name of Ralph and Dorothy Nodine, in Maine. They have bred approximately 16 litters over the years, through 1994. The percentage of DUCKPOND Griffons tested in Natural Ability and Intermediate is low, though more DUCKPOND dogs have tested in IHDT than have the ALDERSEDGE dogs. The Jensens are the *only* breeders outside the WPGCA Breeding Program who test entire litters in NAT.

In my opinion, there is no one else producing Griffons in the United States who would be in the same category as the Jensens and Nodines. If you decide that getting a pup from our WPGCA Breeding Program isn't for you, try either the Jensens or Nodines. They are good, honest people who happen to disagree with our Breeding Program, especially the injection of Fousek blood. Everyone is entitled to their own opinion. They will treat you well, of that I am sure.

Dorothy Nodine and I have worked together for years with OFA results, and both Ralph and Dorothy have helped me out with other chores over the years. They helped me with the enormous job of organizing an index for all the issues of the **GDS** so that I could find articles when I need them.

And Barbara Jensen was alternate secretary of the WPGCA for a few years when we still had that position. Bill and Barbara dropped their club membership around 1992, but they continue to be very active in NAVHDA, and breed about one litter of Griffons a year.

What about breeders who say that they know they are producing good dogs, because none of the people who buy their pups complain or want their money back? Dog owners in the United States can no more fault their dog, than they can fault their child. A dog has to be really terrible before an owner will ask for a refund, ask to return the dog, or put the dog to sleep and get another one. Hundreds of times I've heard dog owners—of *all breeds*—say, "Rover is so hyper, he drives us crazy, BUT HE'S A GREAT DOG." Conversing with dog owners on planes, as I fly to and from field tests, I also hear, "Oh, we have a dog (could be any breed, doesn't matter) and he's the smartest dog." That's the way we are, each of us owns the smartest dog in the world.

Proposed Revision for the Breed Standard for Wirehaired Pointing Griffon

(This is a working document prepared by Joe Nadeker in 1995 and is being studied by the board of directors. The original old standards from the German, French, and American Griffon clubs appear in the appendix.)

The standard is a totality of exterior as well as interior traits. It could be closely projected in prototype, but it still will remain the concept of impression. It must be sufficiently pliable and in constant advancement, so as not to allow it to remain rigidly conservative. Why? Because in changing demands in various time eras of usage the breeding must be adapted to best serve the contemporary needs of hunting (or in the case of non-hunting dogs the current demands).

A breed has to adapt to the changing conditions to be able to hold its own with the current quality of the competition—therefore the standard has to be aligned from time to time to keep pace with progressive demands without change in the basic traits upon which the breed was created and which characterizes its capabilities to perform certain desired tasks, and also maintain the basic form inherent to the breed.

Basically, the Wirehaired Pointing Griffon, according to the original standard (see appendix), differed from the other versatile wire and short-haired breeds in the height at the withers by 5 to 6 cm. The older type, with rounded and at times somewhat cumbersome head is being slowly replaced by flatter, longer nose and jaws, stronger skeleton and the soft coat, which for hunting was unsuitable is being replaced by a serviceable, protective wire coat. The soft coat is a liability in all hunting situations, therefore unacceptable. As to working talents, requirements are an early development, innate behavior after the shot, track, water and forest (brush). All these talents have to become solidly anchored in the genetic makeup and must be transmitted on to the progeny. In the end it is this all-around utilization "all gebrauch" that is the goal of the club's efforts.

Slight deviations from the ideal should not play a deciding role. In reality the breed is an end result of various breeds participating to finalize the breed and from time to time throwbacks will occur to one of the ancestors that was used in the process of developing the standard. In fact all the dogs differ from each other more or less. For that fact it requires someone who will direct the minor deviations and direct them to suppression or enhancement, for the future of the breed.

This is possible only by a breed club for each special breed. Various breeds require various ways and methods, some with more lenient decision than others. Clubs are composed of people, each an individual. Voluntary subordination of all the breeders to the common goal is an absolute requirement to success. It is also the only system documented to produce. All others have been tried and forgotten.

What To Demand?
or
A proposed standard for the Griffon of the twenty-first century

A medium strong and tall dog. Height at the top point of the withers for males should be 24 to 26 inches, ideally 25 inches; for females it should be 23 1/5 inches to 24 4/5 inches. The dogs display a distinct male character through a certain "hardiness" (masculine) display of bodily characteristics and movement attitude.

In bitches a certain elegance in total presentation is welcomed, also a more delicate (feminine) build of the body and skeleton and somewhat more supple behavior.

Complete lack of any trace of fear is absolute. Hard, overaggressive behavior, biting, attacking are also indications of nervous overreaction that is unacceptable. Analysis should be made as to where it originated.

The proper mechanics of movement, cross walk and cross trot, maintaining the back in the same line lend to the dog's progress a certain impression of harmony and feeling of endurance (stamina).

Proportion of height to length should be square. The bitches can be 9:10.

Following is the standard on whose basis was the Cesky Fousek (CF) accepted as a national breed by the Federal International Canine Association (FCI). Our proposal is to modify, or use as is, the CF standard for Wirehaired Pointing Griffon:

1. **HEAD.** Head as long as possible, medium wide, somewhat squarish, but not too fine, not even in bitches. The muzzle should be long and softly arched. A concave bridge is not acceptable. The sufficiently wide muzzle ends with a blunt nose with large nasal openings. The color of the snout should be dark or light brown matching the basic color of the body. A pointed nose, ending with a sharp snout with small nasal openings is not desirable. The mouth must be completely closed, with the flews (top lips) softly overlapping the bottom lips. The linear transition from the muzzle into the forehead and head is gradual and softly elevating. The vertical stop is out of standard and one that is too flat is undesirable, mainly because it is ugly. The bows over the eye sockets are noticeable, more so in the males. (Sex trait.) The top of the head is flat, only lightly arched and ends with a not too pronounced occiput. A complete set of teeth is required, properly positioned and healthy. A scissor bite is ideal.

2. **EARS.** The ears are middle long, covering approximately two-thirds of the cheek. They are not too wide at the top, evenly and fully hanging. The lobes are round at the tips. The ears do hang close to the head without unnecessary bends. The muscles at the root of the ears must be well developed to allow control of the ears on both sides. Sharp tips or too long ears are undesirable.

3. **EYES.** The eyes are lengthwise, oval, bright, and sincere, rather smaller than bulging, with almond-like eyelids tight to the eye. The demand is for as dark

brown as possible. Lighter brown is acceptable on dogs having a basic white color, but "fisheye," almost without pigment is out of standard. Entropium and ectropium is a hereditary fault and disqualifies the dog from breeding at all.

4. **NECK.** The neck should be longer than short, muscular and full "dry" (taut skin). Folds under the throat or unnecessary skinfolds are not allowed. The top portion is slightly bent (so called rooster neck) and slowly reaches the head without noticeable transition (elevated occiput). This causes the head to be set up high. The lower portion of the neck transfers slowly into the withers, and smoothly elsewhere.

5. **CHEST AND RIBS.** In front, the chest is wide (the shoulder point noticeably shifted forward) with well-developed muscular shoulders. It should form the shape of a lyre. The lowest depth of the chest from the side should reach to the elbow. The ribs are proportionally (medium) arched, the vault starting right from the vertebrae. They are not evolved to form a flat chest as is overdeveloped by the Irish Setters, where the ribs start falling down right next to the vertebrae. A barrel chest is not allowed. The thoracic portion of the back stretches from the high point (withers) along one-half to two-thirds of the vertebrae and should be standing out. It is high, broad and well enveloped with muscles. The height of a dog will be measured from the highest notch.

6. **UPPER LINE.** The upper line includes the neck, back, loins and croup (above the hind legs) including the setting of the tail. The whole top line from the back to the other parts should be smooth. The back and loins should be straight and broad, enclosed in well-developed muscles. The croup should be slightly falling with broad and long pelvis. This should stand out mainly in bitches. The flanks and abdomen are tightly enclosed and drawn up.

7. **TAIL.** The tail is medium in substance, and always straight. The root of the tail is always stronger and narrows gradually to the tip. It should not be set too high on the back bone. It is shortened to one-third of its length on dogs, and two-fifths on bitches. A somewhat longer tail does not interfere with conformation as it can be surgically shortened at any time.

8. **SHOULDERS.** The width of the front conforms with the width of the chest. The shoulders are long and as oblique as possible. Small deviations should not be judged to severely. The elbow must be positioned tightly to the chest whether the dog stands or moves. The forearms are straight, sufficiently strong, equipped with obviously dry (tight) and strong muscles. The forearm must be upright (vertical) from the front and the side.

9. **FEET.** Digits are tightly closed and obviously arched, to form round paws. The soles should be hard but elastic. The claws should be medium strong, sufficiently bent and darkly pigmented. The build of the rear feet is the same as in the front.

10. **BACK and HIND LEGS.** The back haunch slopes into the thighs without haunch bumps that are too obvious. The thighs have particularly strongly developed muscles. The shin bone should be as long as possible and should not form too open an angle with the femur (straight stifles). The rear pastern (metatarsus) should be very short and almost vertical. The whole skeleton is strong.

11. **COAT.** The coat in comparison with all the other wire haired dogs is threefold: undercoat, outer coat and guard coat. The undercoat is short—2/5 to 3/5 inch (1 to 1.5 cm), soft and fine and without pith. It is very thick in winter, and in summer sheds completely or stays very sparse in some cases. It covers the whole trunk and the neck. The direction of growth is not directed and usually follows the direction of the outer coat.

The outer coat is 1 1/5 to 1 3/5 inches in length (3-4 cm), straight, very harsh, and when displaced out of normal position it will automatically return to the original set up. It still contains considerable remnants of pith. It covers the rump and neck where it is uniformly long. It is slightly shorter on the sides and inner portions of the thighs and on the legs. In the direction of the paws it is again shorter but equally harsh. The pasterns are covered with a very short coat. The outer coat must fit tightly to the body, running from the head in the direction of the back and on the lines from the top down. It is completely straight and has a rough, coarse feel.

The guard hair is the longest, hardest and lies very close to the body. The length is 2 to 2 4/5 inches (5-7 cm). It has fully developed pith. The rump is covered sparsely, but on the central line of the chest, on the brisket, in the back of the front legs—from the elbow to the carpus and on the back of the hind legs to the hocks is denser and forms a fringe, mainly with the winter coat.

The distribution of the coat (hair): On the upper and lower lips the hair is somewhat longer and softer and forms a typical beard. Also the eyebrow hairs are denser and point over the total lengths of the bow forward and up. On the snout the coat is short and rough and gets even shorter on the forehead and top of the head. The hair cover is shortest on the temples and earlobes, where the cover is only slightly rougher than the shorthaired breeds. Overhanging or even silky hair on the head is not desirable. On the fore and hind members the coat lies dense, becoming shorter closer to the paws where it is very short but rough. Only on the front of the hind legs from the stifle to the metatarsus is the hair longer, forming a "brush." The tail is covered the same as the body with the same quality and without forming a "flag" on the underside of the tail tip.

***FANNE DORA NIMRODSKA**, the female Griffon, imported from Yugoslavia in the 1950's. See Part One.*

CHAPTER TWENTY-EIGHT
HIP DYSPLASIA AND ITS RELATIONSHIP IN BREEDING GRIFFONS

What is it and How Does it Affect Griffons?

Much of the first part of this chapter is taken from an article "Hip Dysplasia in Today's Dogs," ***DOGS*** magazine, September and November issues, 1973, by Dr. S.W.J. Seager, who was then affiliated with the University of Oregon Medical School. Dr. Seager defined the condition thus:

> ...it is a pathological congenital condition in which malformation occurs at the ball, or head, of the femur (thighbone) which articulates in the socket, or acetabulum, of the pelvis. It is the malformation of this joint and the subsequent changes to the head and neck of the femur, related joint capsules, tendons, and muscles that brings about the whole syndrome of hip dysplasia.
>
> The word "dysplasia" is derived from dys' (which means bad) and "plasia" (which means from), hence, a badly formed hip joint.
>
> At birth the hip joints appear normal. The disease, when present, begins shortly thereafter while the bones of the young dog are still relatively soft and cartilagineous. The shape and form of the femoral head and the socket (acetabulum) are changed when there is any degree of looseness, laxity, or play in the joint. There is instability or joint looseness when the supporting tissues that surround the ball and socket joint (made up of muscles, tendons, ligaments, and joint capsules) are stretched. There are various degrees of displacement between the femoral head and the socket; they are known as subluxation if the displacement is slight, and as luxation if the femur is entirely out of the socket. As the dog grows older, further changes take place to the head and neck of the femur as a result of this unstable joint. These changes are known as osteoarthritis or exostosis. The maintenance of good head and socket articulation into adult life are dependent upon a good fit of the joint itself. Looseness of the joint space between femoral head and the acetabulum is the key criterion to hip dysplasia.

Dr. Seager explained that the most accurate way to diagnose hip dysplasia is by radiograph:

> ...radiographs of the tranquilized or anesthetized animal lying on his back with his legs extended, the femurs parallel and turned slightly inward so that the patella (kneecap) lies along the top of the femur at its posterior end...Methods of diagnosis require training, expensive equipment, and much experience in the interpretation of the results...
>
> ...While there is some evidence that diet influences the degree of dysplasia to a small extent, it is certainly not the only consideration, and much more research needs to be done in this area.
>
> ...If radiographs show your dog to be dysplastic, what can you do about this condition? Although hip dysplasia cannot be cured, it can be ameliorated. If in your veterinarian's opinion the condition is in stage two, which means the head of the femur (thighbone) is not completely out of the socket of the pelvis, you may or may not decide to do something about it, depending on the age of your dog. But if hip dysplasia is found to be in stage three or four [severe

> stages] and the secondary bone changes have taken place by six or seven months of age, I strongly advise a pectineus muscular resection. In this operation the dog is anesthetized and a section of pectineus muscle is removed on both sides. This muscle, attached to the pelvis and femur, moves the thigh and helps maintain location of the femoral head in the socket of the hip joint.
>
> Humans have pectineus muscle. The next time you do your exercises, lie flat on your back, put the soles of your feet together, pull your legs up and try to touch your knees to the floor on both sides. Ballerinas may be able to do this exercise but most people cannot.
>
> When the pectineus muscle is cut, it allows the knees to drop. This relieves tension in the hip joint, allows more freedom of movement, lessens restriction in the hip area and relieves the pain of hip dysplasia. The pain of dysplasia is easily recognizable [dog limping, etc.]. When the operation is done, the pain may disappear; the dog has full freedom of movement and feels much better. However, while the pain may be gone, the dysplasia remains, and the dog can pass on the affliction to future generations. Therefore, when this operation is done, the dog, whether male or female, should also be rendered incapable of breeding.
>
> Are there any medicines available to cure hip dysplasia? None. Medicine may curtail to some degree the pain of hip dysplasia. High doses of corticosteroid or Butzzolidin are useful for temporary relief, but are not recommended under normal circumstance for long-term therapy. Some of the procedures used in humans—such as femoral head prothesis and the use of splints and casts—have little application in dogs....

In a 1983 publication by the Orthopedic Foundation for Animals (OFA), Dr. Al Corley, head of OFA said:

> The current concept is: hip dysplasia is a polygenic trait. That is, many genes affect the trait of dysplasia. This concept was presented in the late 1960's and has been supported by independent research efforts throughout the 1970s. One report in 1974, refined the concept to suggest that at least one pair of the genes is recessive and the remaining genes serve to modify the effect. Further refinements and different ideas can be expected as new knowledge becomes available though basic research.
>
> *Regardless of changes in the concepts of the mode of inheritance, or how the genes exert their influence, scientists have repeatedly demonstrated that hip dysplasia is only controllable by selective breeding.*

Why Should I X-Ray My Dog's Hips if I Don't Intend to Breed?

The more dogs that are x-rayed from each litter, the more we will know about the entire breed. If one dog from a litter turns out to be dysplastic, it really doesn't tell us much about the rest of the litter. We need all dogs from every litter x-rayed and checked through OFA, which standardizes the entire program.

The following article, revised and updated from the October 1983 ***The Gun Dog Supreme,*** was prompted in 1983 by a request from Mr. Jacques Carpentier, secretaire general of Club Francais du Griffon d'Arret a Poil Dur Korthals (French Griffon Club). Mr. Carpentier wrote to me, requesting any information we had acquired on the bloodlines of Griffons with hip dysplasia. I proceeded to research and write this article:

Hip Dysplasia in Griffons
(Revised 1994)
Part I

On the following pages are listed all the known dysplastic Griffons in North America, along with their pedigrees. To date we have approximately 45 *known* dysplastic dogs. We estimate that this number could be doubled. This would account for those diagnosed dysplastic Griffons that go unreported to the club, as well as those dogs who are dysplastic, but have not been diagnosed. To date (December 1994) we have 622 Griffons certified by OFA as being free of hip dysplasia. Again, as with the dysplastic dogs, there must be many Griffons free of hip dysplasia that have never been x-rayed.

With the information available, primarily from OFA, we can safely estimate that about 11% [7.2% as of 12/31/94 see below] of the population of Griffons in North America is dysplastic. This is a low percentage. Some of the other versatile breeds have a much higher rate of HD. The Pudelpointers have been plagued with HD since around 1970, about two years after the Griffon Club began x-raying. They discovered it quite by accident and began to x-ray their dogs and found too many dogs with it. They've gotten a handle on it and are doing much better today, but it is still a problem for them. German Wirehairs and German Shorthairs have about the same percentage of dysplastic dogs as have the Griffons, according to OFA reports. But, those breeds have a much lower *percentage* of their dogs x-rayed than do our Griffons. So who knows what is the real percentage.

Of much more interest to us however, are not numbers and percentages, but rather where hip dysplasia comes from in our Griffons? We know it is an inherited disease. Some dogs are born with the genetic tendency to develop hip dysplasia. It is not transmitted by the simple Mendelian mode of inheritance, which we learned in high school biology, but rather by a polygenic mode of inheritance, which makes detective work difficult.

The WPGCA probably has more information on hip dysplasia in its breed than nearly any other versatile breed club in North America, not to mention most other hunting breeds. We have been publishing the names of dysplastic dogs, as well as clear dogs, since 1968. We have in-depth pedigrees on all dysplastic dogs, as well as dogs certified by OFA. Yet, because of the polygenic mode of inheritance, it is not always easy to know with certainty where the HD is coming from.

In some cases we can easily say, "Of course, these particular dysplastic dogs are coming from so and so because Rover, the sire, was dysplastic." But in other cases we can only say that a particular dysplastic dog comes from a certain bloodline, but we cannot pinpoint a single dog as being the transmitter. In some cases dysplastic dogs come from a sire and dam who are both free of hip dysplasia, but carry recessive genes.

We have several cases where one parent produces dysplastic dogs when bred with a particular mate, but this same parent produced dogs free of HD when bred with a different mate. Such cases would indicate strongly that it is that particular combination of genes that produce HD, rather than a single dog. In the end it is the unique combination of genes in each dog within a litter that determines the outcome.

* * * * *

The following pedigrees of the dysplastic Griffons are numbered for ease in identification. They are listed in chronological order beginning in 1962 with number HD1, so as not to confuse them with the pedigree numbers in other parts of this book. For identifying in which country the dog was bred we've used the same key as in Part I, after the dog's name: (A) U.S., (B) Belgium, (F) France, (FQ) Quebec (French blood), (G) Germany, (H) Holland, and (CF) Czechoslovakia. Every dog that has been certified by OFA as being free of HD has OFA underneath their name. An asterisk (*) before a name indicates a dysplastic dog.

HD1 GARCENDA'S VICTORIA–1962	Garcenda's Jacque (A)	Bonaparte (A)	Mickey of Warrenville
			Kadine de Gagny (F)
		Milisande (A)	Staunchdown (A)
			Hardrock Montana Birdie (A)
	Garcenda's Collette (A)	Bonaparte (A)	Mickey of Warrenville (A)
			Kadine de Gagny (F)
		Nanon Ardent (A)	Bonaparte (A)
			Milisande (A)

HD2 DUTCH MASTERS GENERAL DUCHESS VON HEDEL–1968	Artus vom Kastanienhain (G)	**Dingo v Teufelstein (G)**	**Astor v Teufelstein (G)**
			Gerda v Marienheim (G)
		Diana v.d. Altenburg (G)	**Cato v Kochertal (G)**
			Alma v.d. Brech (G)
	Gee Gee Golo (A)	Golo (H)	**Houdoe v Welleseind (H)**
			Cadi of Gerbert (H)
		Astrah (H)	**Houdoe v Welleseind (H)**
			Itanja v Wiesenheim (H)

HD3 GEE GEE GOLO (A)–1968	Golo (H)	**Houdoe v Welleseind (H)**	**Wisky du Madarin (H)**
			Guuka v Welleseind (H)
		Cadi of Gerbert (H)	**Aras of Gerbert (B)**
			Adickie of Gerbert (B)
	Astrah (H)	**Houdoe v Welleseind (H)**	**Wisky du Mandarin (H)**
			Guuka v Welleseind (H)
		Itanja v Wiesenheim (H)	**Wisky du Mandarin (H)**
			Attie (H)

		Dingo v Teufelstein (G)
	Artus v Kastanienhain (G)	
		Diana v.d. Altenburg (G)
Hauptling Laufendes Pferd (A)		
		Bob's Nevada Don Juan (A)
	Viking Girl (A)	
HD4 ATTILA D'ARGENT (A)–1968		Muffet d'Argent (A)
		Blucher v.d. Altenburg (G)
	Alf v Niddertal (G)	
		Frigga v.d. rauhen Gracht (G)
Jauntie d'Argent (A) OFA		Tim v Altenburg (A)
	Tammy de la Oakes Heuvel (A) OFA	
		Gerta Deufer de la Oakes Heuvel (H)

		Zimas d'Argent (A)
	Tim v Altenburg (A)	
		Crissi v Altenburg (A)
Samson de la Oakes Heuvel (A) OFA		Golo (H)
	Gerta Deufer de la Oakes Heuvel (H)	
HD5 DRAPEAU DU VAL DE TONNERRE–1968 DJINN DU VAL DE TONNERRE		Astra (H)
		De Jon d'Argent (A)
	Shag (A)	
		Garcenda's Victoria (A)
Argile du Val de Tonnerre (A)		
		Sigbert v.d. Altenburg (A)
	Cache-Cache du Val de Tonnerre (A)	
		Gigi Girl (A)

		Dingo v Teufelstein (G)
	Artus v Kastanienhain (G)	
		Diana v.d. Altenburg (G)
Samson v.d. Altenburg (G) OFA		
		Alf vom Niddertal (G)
	Allen's Lacy v Bitterroot (A)	
HD6 2 LITTERMATES–1971		Tammy de la Oakes Heuvel (A)
		De Jon d'Argent (A)
	Cedarview Garcenda's Mickey (A)	
		Garcenda's Victoria (A)
Bonanza's Honeybear (A) OFA		Garcenda's Mickey (A)
	Bonanza's First Lady Lisa (A)	
		April Lady (A)

		Milshire Gorty (A)
	Milshire Sandy (A)	
		Milshire Ruby (A)
Milshire Tex (A)		
		Zimas d'Argent (A)
	Milshire Amber (A)	
HD7 WHITE IPE VOM HOHEN WIND (A)–1971		Crissi v Altenburg (A)
		Siegbert v.d. Altenburg (A)
	Chasseur du Val de Tonnerre (A)	
		Gigi Girl (A)
Pearl du Val (A)		
		Cedarview Chief (A)
	Donner of Windy Hills (H)	
		Astrah (H)

	Hello de Port Giraud	Wicky des Aubiers
Quick du Kiamika (FQ)		Ella de la Villais
	Noisette de Zizaines (F) OFA	Kodack de Ya Ka Keui (F)
HD8 SHEILA DU NOREBIB (FQ)–1971		Jennie de Zizaines (F)
	Luqo de Nadaillac (F)	Estoc de Zizaines (F)
Polka du Haut Leon (F)		Kadi du Courtil Bissieux (F)
	Monig du Moulin du Chatel (F)	Klac des Ellots (F)
		Kenavo du Moulin du Chatel (F)

	Hello de Port Giraud (F)	Wicky des Zubiers (F)
Quick du Kiamika (FQ)		Ella de la Villais (F)
	Noisette de Zizaines (F) OFA	Kodack de Ya Ka Keui (F)
HD9 DHUB SGEIR–1972		Jennie de Zizaines (F)
	Show Boat (A)	Jaque d'Argent (A)
Natalie Bumpo (A)		Trouble Gal (A)
	Tammy's Raggety Ann (A)	Alf v Niddertal (G)
		Tammy de la Oakes Heuvel (A) OFA

	Artus v Kastanienhain (G)	**Dingo v Teufelstein (G)**
Baron von Dunkel (A)		**Diana v.d. Altenburg (G)**
	Gee Gee Golo (A)	Golo (H)
HD10 HEIDI VON LINK (A)–1972		Astrah (H)
	Artus v Kastanienhain (G)	**Dingo v Teufelstein (G)**
Crissi von Bitterroot (A)		**Diana v.d. Altenburg (G)**
	Allen's Lacy von Bitterroot (A)	Alf v Niddertal (G)
		Tammy de la Oakes Heuvel (A) OFA

	Gef (F)	Yo (F)
Oscar des Vieux Grisards (F)		Bobette (F)
	Huc des Vieux Grisards (F)	Caporal du Roselier (F)
HD11 ULRICH DE ST. LANDRY (F)–1973		Etna du Val de Creuse (F)
	Mick de Burly (F)	Hubert des Zizaines (F)
Quinche de St. Landry (F)		Hagala de Villais (F)
	Lydie du Lingond (F)	Iso du Lingond (F)
		Jolie du Lingond (F)

Jarnac des Rossays (F)

Nick des Vieilles Rouches (F)

Kety de la Fontaine St. Germain (F)

Pyram (F)

Grisby de la Cambe (F)

Jasmine de l'Ascension (F)

HD12
URIANE-LAURY DES CHEVECHES (F)–1973

Gina de l'Ascension (F)

Flirt du Vivier de Cour (F)

Micky (F)

Idee de la Beauce (F)

Poupee de Pailloux (F)

Fly de la Fontaine St. Martin (F)

Lady de Pailloux (F)

Josie des Ellots (F)

Duke v Kirchdorf (A)

Mike v Hessling (A)
OFA

Gee Gee Golo (A)

Beau du Burbon (A)
OFA

Tim v Altenburg (A)

Tammy de la Oakes Heuvel (A)
OFA

HD13
FIRST FROST VICTOR (A)–1973

Gerta Deufer de la Oakes Heuvel (H)

Three Acres Bobo J (A)

Binifi Zuber Filde (A)
OFA

Gerta v Nellagram (A)
OFA

First Frost Greta O Vantage (A)
OFA

Mike v Hessling (A)
OFA

Geri Vantage Home (A)
OFA

Tammy de la Oakes Heuvel (A)
OFA

Jarnac des Rossays

Nick des Vieille Rouches (F)

Kety de la Fontaine St. Germain (F)

Pyram (F)

Grisby de la Cambe

Jasmine de l'Ascension (F)

Gina de l'Ascension

Sacky des Matines (F)
OFA

Dacier du Vivier de Cour (F)

Joke des Zizaines (F)

Elfie des Zizaines (F)

HD14
SHAD D'OASIS
GRETA OF MELBOURNE
GHOST'S PROUD LADY D'OASIS
KING D'OASIS–1973
PIERRE LAFFIT DE OASIS
AMANDA VON DITCHHOPPER
DUSTY D'OASIS
BUNO

Patty des Vieilles Rouches (F)

Gef (F)

Kety de la Fontaine St. Germain (F)

Flora de la Fontaine St. Martin (F)

Blucher v.d. Altenburg (G)

Alf v Niddertal (G)

Frigga v.d. rauhen Gracht (G)

Three Acres Bobo Jr. (A)

Bruce's Ripsnorter (A)

Three Acres Nevada Jeep (A)

Chukar Lady Reeva (A)

Miska vom Schlemm Kreide (A)
OFA

Blucher v.d. Altenburg (G)

Alf v Niddertal (G)

Frigga v.d. rauhen Gracht (G)

Gerta v Nellagram (A)
OFA

Tim v Altenburg (A)

Tammy de la Oakes Heuvel (A)
OFA

Gerta Deufer de la Oakes Heuvel (H)

HD15
DE JAGER VON SCHMIDTS-HAUSEN (A)–1973

HD15	Al's Ledaren v Bitterroot (A) OFA	Alf v Niddertal (G)	**Blucher v.d. Altenburg (G)**
			Frigga v.d. rauhen Gracht (G)
		Tammy de la Oakes Heuvel (A) OFA	Tim v Altenburg (A)
			Gerta Deufer de la Oakes Heuvel (H)
	Auben vom Nellagram (A) OFA	Alf v Niddertal (G)	**Blucher v.d. Altenburg (G)**
			Frigga v.d. rauhen Gracht (G)
		Cora v Kastanienhain (G) OFA	**Dingo v Teufelstein (G)**
			Diana v.d. Altenburg (G)

HD16
ROLF VON PHILOHELA–1973

HD16	Barry v.d. Neuburg (G) OFA	Phebus de Celibuty (F)	Oncor de la Font Goirand (F)
			Manon des Grands Marais (F)
		Doinah v.d. Brech (G)	**Ajax vom Waldpark (G)**
			Arda v.d. Brech (G)
	Gretel v Altenburg (A) OFA	Tim v Altenburg (A)	Zimas d'Argent (A)
			Crissis v Altenburg (A)
		Bonanza's Other Heidi (A)	Cedarview Garcenda's Mickey (A)
			Bonanza's First Lady Lisa (A)

HD17
KIRK D'OASIS (A)–1973

HD17	Bonzo of Copper Valley (A) OFA	Bob's Nevada Don Juan (A)	John's Nevada George (A)
			Lee's Idaho Lady (A)
		Muffet d'Argent (A)	Beaucoup d'Argent (A)
			Lady Chukar Dame (A)
	Miska v Schlemm Kreide (A) OFA	Three Acres Bobo Jr. (A)	Alf v Niddertal (G)
			Three Acres Nevada Jeep (A)
		Gerta v Nellagram (A) OFA	Alf v Niddertal (G)
			Tammy de la Oakes Heuvel (A) OFA

HD18
BRISE–1975

HD18	**Taquin du Bois Follet (F)** OFA	Pipo des Vieilles Rouches (F)	**Joke des Zizaines (F)**
			Kety de la Fontaine St. Germain (F)
		Ouchka du Bois Follet (F)	Hirsute de Ya Ka Keui (F)
			Lorene des Ronciers de Clavieres (F)
	Huckle Hill Patty (A) OFA	Barry v.d. Neuburg (G) OFA	Phebus de Celibuty (F)
			Doinah v.d. Brech (G)
		Tina de la Reote (A)	Popy de la Reote (F)
			Popeline de la Reote (F)

Dog	Parents	Grandparents	Great-grandparents
HD19 RAPSCALLION (A)–1976	Pleasant Valley Ozark (A)	Ozark Rustic Rock (A)	Hardrock Montana Rafe (A)
			Zuabekunst Tal Fresca (A)
		Tammy of Dutchland (A)	Husky Tuffy (A)
			Staley Smokey Gal (A)
	Breta d'Oasis (A) OFA	Sacky des Matines (F) OFA	**Pyram (F)**
			Patty des Vieilles Rouches (F)
		Miska v Schlemm Kreide (A) OFA	Three Acres Bobo Jr. (A)
			Gerta v Nellagram (A) OFA

Dog	Parents	Grandparents	Great-grandparents
HD20 J VON OBERJAGER (A)–1977	Hardrock Montana King (A) OFA	Hardrock Montana Tommy (A) OFA	Mike v Hessling (A) OFA
			Tammy de la Oakes Heuvel (A) OFA
		Cira v Kastanienhain (G) OFA	**Dingo v Teufelstein (G)**
			Diana v.d. Altenburg (G)
	Schon von Oberjager (A) OFA	Three Acres Bobo Jr. (A)	Alf v Niddertal (G)
			Three Acres Nevada Jeep (A)
		Allure d'Argent (A) OFA	Hauptling Laufendes (A)
			Jauntie d'Argent (A) OFA

Dog	Parents	Grandparents	Great-grandparents
HD21 MISS MOLLY OF OAK RIDGE (A)–1977	Mr. Griffon of Vantage Home (A)	Mike v Hessling (A) OFA	Duke v Kirchdorf (A)
			Gee Gee Golo (A)
		Geri Vantage Home (A) OFA	Mike v Hessling (A) OFA
			Tammy de la Oakes Heuvel (A) OFA
	Maedchen Heidi (A)	Frosty's Image v Tana (A) OFA	Falk vom Waldpark (G)
			Tammy's Raggety Ann (A)
		Hardrock Montana Royal Belle (A) OFA	Hardrock Montana Tommy (A) OFA
			Cira v Kastanienhain (G) OFA

Dog	Parents	Grandparents	Great-grandparents
HD22 LAURIE OF HUNTER'S CREEK LUNA OF HUNTER'S CREEK	**Tonik du Bois Follet (F)** OFA	**Pipo des Vieilles Rouches (F)**	**Joke des Zizaines (F)**
			Kety de la Fontaine St. Germain (F)
		Lorene des Ronciers de Clavieres (F)	**Dacier du Vivier de Cour**
			Cyta de Vrainville
	Ulla de St. Landry (F) OFA	Ripp de la Vieille Oise (F)	Najac de la Vieille Oise (F)
			Osee de la Casa d'Ardillos (F)
		Scarlett de St. Landry (F)	Olaf du Bois Follet (F)
			Oona de St. Landry (F)

Nick des Vieilles Rouches (F)
Pyram (F)
Jasmine de l'Ascension (F)
Ulmer des Cheveches (F)
Micky (F)
Poupee de Pailloux (F)
Lady de Pailloux (F)
HD23
NUMA DU RUISSEAU DE MASSACRE (F)–1978
Jokes des Zizaines (F)
Pipo des Vieilles Rouches (F)
Kety de la Fontaine St. Germain (F)
Ultra de Ruisseau du Massacre (F)
Laurier du Val Noir (F)
Parkie du Tedlou (F)
Mira de la Toque (F)

Appollo v Batavia-Dodewero (H)
Butty (H)
Trix (H)
Arapho of Windy Hills (H)
Tell (H)
Freya (H)
Cita (H)
HD24
MAR ED'S GRIFF–1976
Al's Ledaren v Bitterroot (A)
Casey von Sturgil (A)
Kelly v Kastanienhain (A)
OFA
Miss Queen of Kimberly (A)
Hardrock Montana Rafe (A)
Sherry's Follie Dixie (A)
Zuabekunst Tal Fresca (F)

Pipo des Vieilles Rouches (F)
Taquin du Bois Follet (F)
OFA
Ouchka du Bois Follet (F)
Whiskey du Pironec (FQ)
OFA
Hello de Port Giraud (F)
Rana du Sauverain (FQ)
Ketty du Courtil Bissieux (F)
HD25
HUCKLE HILL BOOMER–1978
Pipo des Vieilles Rouches (F)
Taquin du Bois Follet (F)
OFA
Ouchka du Bois Follet (F)
Huckle Hill Angela (A)
OFA
Barry v.d. Neuburg (G)
OFA
Huckle Hill Patty (A)
OFA
Tina de la Reote (A)

Ali v.d Brech (G)
Falk vom Waldpark (G)
Brinka v Waldpark (G)
Jackaroo Battue (A)
Graf v Friedrichtal (A)
J and L's Dusti Dee Dee (A)
Gretel v Friedrichtal (A)
HD26
WELCH'S SIR MICHAEL (A)–1977
Gustave v Nellagram (A)
OFA
Roco v Nellagram (A)
Cora v Kastanienhain (G)
OFA
Scherer's Shikari (A)
Frosty's Image v Tana (A)
OFA
Anni v Hexenstein (A)
Allure d'Argent (A)
OFA

HD27
GILEAD'S LAKE'S SAM–1981

Gilead Lake's Dutch Treat (A)	Arapaho of Windy Hills (H)	Butty (H)
		Freya (H)
	Hardrock Montana Bingo (A)	Hardrock Montana Micky (A) OFA
		Camas McDuck (A)
Gretchen von Keefer (A)	Daktarie Rie (A)	**Hansel zu den Bergen Gehen (A)** OFA
		Cannelle du Val de Tonnerre (A)
	Gilead Lake's Meri-Meri (A)	Hardrock Montana Jerry (A)
		Camas McDuck (A)

HD28
ABBEY DE FEU FOLLET–1982

Taquin du Bois Follet (F) OFA	**Pipo des Vieilles Rouches (F)**	**Joke des Zizaines (F)**
		Kety de la Fontaine St. Germain (F)
	Ouchka du Bois Follet (F)	**Hirsute de Ya Ka Keui (F)**
		Lorene des Ronciers de Clavieres (F)
Zest du Montmagny (FQ) OFA	Ygor du Haut Blainville (FQ) OFA	Tarc de la Vieille Oise (F)
		Tanya du Nemtaye (FQ)
	Du Pirdnec (FQ) OFA	**Taquin du Bois Follet (F)** OFA
		Rana du Sauverain (FQ)

HD29
HARDROCK MONTANA JAKE II (A)–1984

Hardrock Montana Talus (A)	Hardrock Montana Jerry (A)	Hardrock Montana Tommy (A) OFA
		Cira vom Kastanienhain (G) OFA
	Camas McDuck (A)	Hardrock Montana King (A) OFA
		Gerta v Nellagram (A) OFA
Spokane Princess (A)	Billy vom Tana (A) OFA	Sacha de Saint Landry (F) OFA
		Saga (F) OFA
	Miss Penny Lane (A)	Casey von Sturgil (A)
		Sherry's Follie Dixie (A)

HD30
ROSA DIT PUPPY (F)–1985

Nec des Landes de Kerkhune (F)	Jim des Landes de Kerkhune (F)	Ugo du Fil du Cher (F)
		Themis de la Vieille Oise (F)
	Lixie des Landes de Kerkhune (F)	**Under du Ruisseau du Massacre (F)**
		Vodka (F)
Nada des Hauts de Gouderlou (F)	**Up du Ruisseau du Massacre (F)**	**Pipo des Vieilles Rouches (F)**
		Parkie Du Tedelou (F)
	Vara de L'Orsuya (F)	Urf (F)
		Rita de la Haute Chalosse (F)

		Billy vom Tana (A) OFA	Sacha de Saint Landry (F) OFA
	Brownie of Walden (A)		Saga OFA
		Breta D'Oasis (A) OFA	Sacky des Matines (F) OFA
HD31 LA RUE'S JENNIFER (A)–1986			Miska v Schlemm Kreide (A) OFA
		Hans von Steinhoff Colbert (A)	Billy vom Tana (A) OFA
	Sugar Baby (A)		Zuabekunst Tel Pepper (A)
		Magic Valleys Daisy Dandy (A)	

		Axel vom Ulrichsquell (G)	**Urac de St. Landry (F)**
	Furst v.d. Neuburg (G) OFA		**Dia von Luda Jana (G)**
		Freya vom Bibertal (G)	**Eik v.d. Neuburg (G)**
HD32 MAGNUM VOGELHUND (A)–1990			**Kathi v.d. Brech (G)**
		Plumcreek's Stitch (A)	Rockymount Happy (A)
	Two Dot (A) OFA		Plumcreek's Siri (A) OFA
		Stony Brook of Vantage Home (A)	Ruff vom Tana II (A) OFA
			Ginger von Vantage Home (A)

		Argo z Poledni Strane (CF)	**Aris z Javorove Doliny**
	Erik od Jezarek (CF) OFA		**Erika z Aelivce (CF)**
		Asta od Vejrice (CF)	**Avar z Paralce (CF)**
HD33 **August de los Altos (CF)–1992**			**Bora od Tepleho Vrchu (CF)**
		Bojar z Burdovny (CF) OFA	**Erno z Doupova (CF)**
	Axa od Pastejriku (CF) OFA		**Alma ze Vsejanske fary (CF)**
		Cila ze Strazneho kopec (CF)	**Egon od Nemilske (CF)**
			Dora z Poludeli (CF)

Hip Dysplasia in Griffons, Part II

Back in the early years—1969, shortly after any of us had become aware of hip dysplasia, it was reported to me that **ARTUS VOM KASTANIENHAIN,** a male imported from Germany, was dysplastic. I do not have any official verification of this, but it turned out **ARTUS** sired a number of dysplastic dogs. So it appears he was at least carrying the genes for hip dyplasia.

We also do not have verifiable evidence that **[CEDARVIEW'S] GARCENDA'S VICTORIA (HD1)** was dysplastic, but this was confirmed to me in writing by General Tom Rogers when he was President of the WPGCA. So I also take that to be fact. (Remember in those days they used the term "faulty hip sockets," or "loose hip sockets.") In this pedigree **(HD1)** notice the amount of close inbreeding. They bred **GARCENDA'S JACQUE** to **GARCENDA'S COLLETTE,** half-brother to half-sister. And, it was doubled up once more by **BONAPARTE** in the third generation. So **GARCENDA'S COLLETTE** was already a product of close line-breeding, and then bred close again.

In Pedigree **HD2,** the dam, **GEE GEE GOLO (HD3),** was dysplastic, and the sire was **ARTUS**, also dysplastic. That's straightforward and easy to figure out. From where either one inherited the right combination for HD can only be speculation. On **GEE GEE GOLO's** side my guess is the close inbreeding of **HOUDOE V WELLESEIND.** It's really almost a carbon copy of what went on in the breeding of **GARCENDA'S VICTORIA.** Half-brother to half-sister.

For the fourth dog, **ATTILA D'ARGENT (HD4)**, we see that **ARTUS** was a grandfather. Then on the dam's side, back in the fourth generation we see **ZIMAS** and **CRISSI,** and behind them is **GARCENDA'S VICTORIA.** Then down below are **GOLO** and **ASTRAH,** the parents of **GEE GEE GOLO.**

In **DRAPEAU DU VAL DE TONNERRE (HD5)** we see a very similar pattern: In the fourth generation **GARCENDA'S VICTORIA** twice, and again in the fifth generation behind **ZIMAS** and **CRISSI.** We also find **GOLO** and **ASTRAH,** parents of **GEE GEE GOLO** again in the third generation.

In **BONANZA'S** pup **(HD6), GARCENDA'S VICTORIA,** twice, and in the fourth generation **GERTA DEUFER DE L'OAKES HEUVEL** has **GOLO** and **ASTRAH** for parents.

For **WHITE IPE V HOHEN WIND (HD7)** in the fourth generation **GARCENDA'S VICTORIA** appears three times, and once in the fifth generation behind **CRISSI**. Also in the fourth generation at the very bottom, **ASTRAH,** the dam of **GEE GEE GOLO**.

SHEILA DE NOREBIB (HD8) is not so easy. It is from French blood mostly unknown to us, except for the sire **QUICK.** Look at the next dog—the same sire.

DHUB SQEIR (HD9) was also sired by **QUICK.** And on the dam's side, beyond the fourth generation **GARCENDA'S VICTORIA** appears twice. **HEIDI VON LINK (HD10)** has three out of her four grandparents dysplastic: **ARTUS** twice and **GEE GEE GOLO** once.

With the 11th dog, **ULRICH DE ST LANDRY (HD11)**, I would be suspicious of **GEF** (second generation) and **GRACE** (fourth generation and closely inbred). They are littermates. It's a long shot. It's mostly an unknown.

The next one, **URIANE-LAURY DES CHEVECHES (HD12)**, has more clues. **PYRAM** appears a number of times in the pedigrees of other dysplastic dogs. So does the dam, **POUPEE.**

With **FIRST FROST VICTOR (HD13),** we find **GEE GEE GOLO** on both the sire and dam sides, plus **GERTA DEUFER DE L'OAKES HEUVEL (Golo x Astrah).**

GHOST'S PROUD LADY D'OASIS (HD14) illustrates a very sad episode for many of us. The dysplastic dogs you see listed from this breeding represent two litters—the second being a repeat breeding. The first litter was whelped in 1971, the second in 1972, both in the days before the start of our breeding program. Today we know that all dogs from a litter must be x-rayed before repeating a breeding. But, we did not know that then, and we paid dearly for that lack of knowledge. [Today, 1995, there is so little HD in the Griffons from the Breeding Program, we do not have to be quite that cautious.]

PYRAM and his line would be where one would look first. But look also to the dam's side, the **THREE ACRES BOBO J** line. That line traces back to very close inbreeding [See pedigrees in Part I. Also see **HD17** here.] There's also the possibility of **GERTA DEUFER DE L'OAKES HEUVEL** in the fourth generation at the bottom. Behind her are **GOLO** and **ASTRAH,** parents of dysplastic **GEE GEE GOLO**.

DE JAGER V SCHMITZ-HAUSEN (HD15) shows us the same old names: **GARCENDA'S VICTORIA** twice in the fifth generation; **CORA VOM KASTANIENHAIN** same parents as dysplastic **ARTUS**; and **ALF VOM NIDDERTAL** appearing twice in a close linebreeding. **ALF** was never x-rayed.

In the 16th pedigree, **ROLF V PHILOHELA (HD16),** there were two more dogs from the litter reported dysplastic, but I only received paper on **ROLF. GARCENDA'S VICTORIA** appears three times in the fourth generation on the dam's side, and once more in the fifth generation.

Pedigree **HD17** has the same dam as in number **HD14**, **MISKA.** I'm suspicious of the same dogs behind her. Above on the sire's side we see the same lines showing up again, through **MUFFET D'ARGENT** and **BOB'S NEVADA DON JUAN.** So much of that traces back to extremely close inbreeding, done without any control. [See part One for more pedigrees of similar bloodlines.]

In **HD18** it's difficult to discern where it might come from. **TAQUIN** via **PIPO**? On the dam's side in the third generation, the **DE LA REOTE** lines are inbred, and primarily from show stock.

In **HD19**, the dam, **BRETA D'OASIS,** was certified by OFA, despite the fact that she came from that disastrous breeding of **HD14.** We had issued an urgent appeal in the G.D.S. to owners of dogs from both these litters not to breed their dogs, because of the high probability that they were all carriers, even if they x-rayed clear. Someone didn't listen.

In the 20th and 21st pedigrees we find familiar names: **GEE GEE GOLO, CIRA VOM KASTANIENHAIN, THREE ACRES NEVADA JEEP, ARTUS VOM KASTANIENHAIN,** and so on.

In Part One, Chapter 12, we talked briefly about this litter, pedigree **HD22.** The hips ranged all the way from excellent, good, fair, borderline, to dysplastic. Where the HD comes from is difficult to determine. The sire, **TONIK,** when bred to a different bitch, **BENT PINE'S ABERDEEN,** did not produce any dysplastic dogs. The dam, **ULLA,** was never used for breeding again. And one of the progeny, **LUCAS OF HUNTER'S CREEK,** sired about four litters and none of the progeny was dysplastic. This particular litter, **HD22**, was again an example of the unique combination of genes producing a high incidence of HD.

Number **HD23** would have seemed destined to produce dysplastic dogs. The dam, **ULMER**, was a littermate to dysplastic dog **URIANE-LAURY DES CHEVECHES (HD12)**. The sire is also suspicious because a littermate, **UP,** is in the pedigree of dysplastic dog number **HD30**.

In number **HD24** the dysplasia may come from the dam's side in the fourth generation, **ARTUS VOM KASTANIENHAIN** and **CIRA VOM KASTANIENHAIN.** In Pedigree **HD29 MISS PENNY LANE** is a littermate to **MISS QUEEN OF KIMBERLY,** which is in this **HD24.**

I suspected **HUCKLE HILL BOOMER (HD25)** was dysplastic when I judged this dog in Natural Ability in Michigan in the early 1970s, and recommended that the owner x-ray as soon as possible. He did and the dog was indeed dysplastic. What alerted me was the unnatural way the dog carried his tail when running in the field. Line breeding to **TAQUIN DU BOIS FOLLET?** Also **RANA DU SAUVERAIN**, a fine dog in the field, who I judged in Quebec in 1969 and 1970, appeared to produce dysplastic dogs. Was it **HELLO DE PORT GIRAUD,** sire of **QUICK DU KIAMIA,** who produced a few dysplastic dogs?

In Pedigree **HD26 ARTUS** is in the sixth generation on the sire's side, and **CORA VOM KASTANIENAIN** (same breeding as **ARTUS**, a repeat breeding) is in the fifth generation. On the dam's side, you see **CORA** in the third generation, and out behind **HAUPTLING LAUFENDES PFERD** is **ARTUS.**

With **GILEAD LAKE'S SAM (HD27)**, there are many clues beginning in the fourth generation with **HARDROCK MONTANA TOMMY**, because behind **TOMMY** is **CIRA** from the same breeding as dysplastic **ARTUS.** Going down to the next dog is **CIRA** again. Then behind **HARDROCK MONTANA KING** is **CIRA.** On the dam's side, unseen in the fifth generation is **GARCENDA'S VICTORIA** three times. **CIRA** is there again in the fourth, and unseen again in the 5th. Perhaps one could call this a loose linebreeding to dysplastic dogs.

Nothing new in Pedigree **HD28**, but there is **TAQUIN** again, appearing twice in the pedigree, and the second time it is the same pairing with **RANA DU SAUVERAIN** as in **HD25**.

Pedigree **HD29** has much the same that we've been seeing. On the sire's side, third generation is **CIRA,** and again in the fourth. In about the sixth generation is **GEE GEE GOLO**. On the dam's side is the similarity to Pedigree **HD24** through **MISS PENNY LANE** who traces back to **GEE GEE GOLO, ARTUS,** and **CIRA.**

Pedigree **HD30** is extremely interesting to me. When I first wrote about it I had only a two-generation pedigree. In the first and second generation there was only one clue, **UP DU RUISSEAU DU MASSACRE**, littermate to dogs that produced other dysplastic dogs (Pedigree **HD23**). Then I came across the three-generation pedigree from Societe Centrale Canine and L.O.F. (Livre des Origines Francaise, French equivalent to AKC). What a difference it makes to have that third generation. The litter that **ROSA DIT PUPPY** came from was line-bred to littermates **UNDER** and **UP DU RUISSEAU DU MASSACRE**, a line that has given us a number of dysplastic dogs in the United States.

What is even more interesting, and perplexing is that the sire of these **"U"** dogs was **PIPO DES VIEILLES ROUCHES**, a male with many field trial wins, a dog who was considered quite exceptional in his day, and who was used for breeding many times. [If you are interested in breeding, check back in Part One, and earlier in this chapter, for more about **PIPO.**] He was also the sire of **TAQUIN DU BOIS FOLLET**, who produced some dysplastic dogs, *as well as many dogs with clear hips.* See how complicated this business is, and how important it is to have in-depth knowledge of bloodlines.

There are two known dysplastic dogs from Pedigree **HD31**, both severely dysplastic. On the dam's side in the second generation is **BRETA D'OASIS,** from the disastrous Pedigree **HD14** breeding.

In Pedigree **HD32** on the sire's side, third generation is **URAC DE ST LANDRY.** Littermate **ULRICH** was dysplastic (Pedigree **HD11**). Also in the fourth generation is **PYRAM** who appears so often in dysplastic dogs. On the dam's side, however, the pedigree is loaded with known dysplastic dogs, and suspected carriers: **GEE GEE GOLO** is there at least six times and **CIRA** and **CORA** are both there.

Pedigree **HD33** is a complete unknown to us. It was the only dysplastic dog in the litter. All others x-rayed clear. Sire and dam came from Czechoslovakia. This is the only dysplastic dog the sire has produced and he's been used with three other bitches. The dam has been bred to one other male and there were no dysplastic dogs. Probably it was the particular combination of genes of sire and dam, or a mutant.

Summary

One could jump to the conclusion that only a very few Griffons have been responsible for most of our dysplastic dogs. But we have to remember that our breeding pool has always been small. The first imports from Europe came in the 1920s when the Griffon breed was quite strong. The breed was still enjoying the fruits of Korthals' labor. The quality of the dogs had not been dissipated greatly, although like all breeds, the Griffon had been adversely affected by World War I.

By the late 1940s and early 1950s when Griffons were once more being imported into the United States, the breed had been decimated in Europe by World War II. And 30 years had passed since the peak years. Thirty years of much less precise breeding in the United States. Thirty years of no controlled breeding gave us a much weakened breed.

Given a less than superior dog, given an extremely small breeding pool in the United States, all we needed were one or two dysplastic dogs and we would find these same few dysplastic dogs in the pedigrees of nearly all of our dysplastic Griffons, *as well as in many of our clear dogs.*

One of the most important points to be gained from this study of hip dysplasia in Griffons is the absolute need for in-depth knowledge of pedigrees. In this respect Griffonniers in North America, especially in the United States, are far ahead of their colleagues in Europe. Only in the past 10 to 15 years have the Griffon clubs there begun to address this disease. Only a few dogs are x-rayed and they do not have a central clearing house such as our OFA.

When you import a dog from Europe there will be a lot of information in the pedigree about the field work of the ancestors and siblings. But there will be little information about the presence or absence of hip dysplasia in his background, nor much about HD in his siblings, because it is not available.

Hip dysplasia is only one of many factors that must be studied when one is contemplating a particular breeding. As with any trait, be it hip dysplasia, temperament, quality of nose, etc., in-depth knowledge of the bloodline is essential. Without such knowledge the results can be, and often are, disastrous.

Most, though not all hip dysplasia can be avoided in Griffons by using knowledge and care when selecting mates for breeding. Since we began x-raying our dogs, and making the results available to the public via ***The Gun Dog Supreme***, we have had very few dogs diagnosed with HD. And within our WPGCA Approved Breeding Program we have an even lower rate of HD than the overall average for the breed, because nearly 100 percent of dogs from the program are x-rayed compared to less than about 50 percent for all other Griffons.

Since O.F.A. began a testing program in the late 1960s, to date there have only been 620 Griffons certified by OFA. Out of those, approximately two-thirds are from dogs bred in the WPGCA Breeding Program. The majority of the other one-third were bred by either the Jensens or the Nodines. So the percentage of other Griffons that have been x-rayed over the years is quite low.

Above: ***TRISTAN****, 12 months old, littermate to* ***GEE GEE GOLO****.*
Below: ***ROB ROY OF ROB ROY*** *(Artus v Kastanienhain x Gee Gee Golo)*

CHAPTER TWENTY-NINE
REDUCING HIP DYSPLASIA AND HOW IT RELATES TO WPGCA APPROVED BREEDING PROGRAM

More information on hip dysplasia comes from a booklet, ***Hip Dysplasia: A Monograph for Dog Breeders and Owners,*** published by the Orthopedic Foundation for Animals in 1983. The author was Dr. E. A. Corley, head of O.F.A. The following is reprinted from this booklet:

Rationale for Selective Breeding

Most of the inherited traits in animals are polygenic. Some examples, other than hip dysplasia, are: conformation, type, size, longevity, disease resistance, temperament, elbow dysplasia, speed, milk and egg production, growth rate, maturation rate and sexual maturity rate.

Intuitively it is recognized that these traits do not follow patterns based on the genetics presented in general biology classes. These introductory courses usually use one pair of genes to explain basic genetics. For example, assume that 1.) the color black is dominant to brown 2.) the black gene is represented by B and the brown gene bb, and 3.) we mate a pure black (BB), or homozygous, with brown (bb). All the offspring are expected to be 3 blacks (1BB and 2Bb) and 1 brown (bb). The ratio of 1:2:1 for the genotypes is based on probability. If only a small number of offspring are available, from this type of mating, they may all be of the same genotype, but larger numbers [populations] will give the expected ratio.

Polygenic traits are affected by many genes. An oversimplified example is two genes affecting the same trait. Assume the mating of two dogs with genotypes, for a trait, of AaBb. The expected genotypic outcome is 9 different genotypes with the following frequencies:

Genotypes	AABB	AABb	AAbb	AaBB	AaBb	Aabb	aaBB	aaBb	aabb
Frequency	1/16	2/16	1/16	2/16	4/16	2/16	1/16	2/16	1/16

As the number of involved genes are increased the possibilities soar. The problem is further magnified if each gene pair exerts a different degree of influence on a trait. The number of genes affecting hip dysplasia, or any other polygenic trait, is unknown. Predictions of a specific outcome from a *particular* mating, involving polygenic traits, is impossible.

Animal geneticists have developed breeding programs to improve milk production in cows, egg production in hens, speed in horses, growth rate in food animals, etc. They used basic genetic principles that have been demonstrated effective in the dog. Some of the following aspects of polygenic traits considered in arriving at these principles include:

1. Polygenic traits have a range of findings from the most desirable to the least desirable characteristic being considered.

For example, mating two dogs of ideal conformation can be expected to result in a larger number of offspring with ideal conformation when compared with offspring of a mating where one or both parents have less than ideal conformation. However, both litters will present a range of conformation findings.

Hip dysplasia follows the same pattern. Normals mated with normals produce more [normal] animals than matings of two dysplastic or a normal with a dysplastic. The appearance (phenotype) of the hips ranges from excellent to severely dysplastic with all degrees between the extremes.

2) Polygenic traits are influenced by the environment. Environmental factors may minimize or maximize genetic potentials.

For example, a horse with respiratory infection will not be able to achieve it's speed capability, or a cow on a starvation diet will not produce milk to it's full potential.

The manifestation of hip dysplasia follows the same pattern. The most studied environmental influence is caloric intake. A higher than needed caloric intake has been shown to result in earlier and more severe dysplastic changes *when the genetic potential for dysplasia is present.* A lower than normal caloric intake may hide the evidence of dysplasia in the same dog, but does not change the genotype.

3. Hereditability estimates are generally offered on polygenic traits to infer the degree of genetic influence versus environment. These estimates are purported to be a statistical measure of the genetic difference between two or more groups under similar environmental conditions.

The estimate is reported on a scale of 0.0 to 1.0 with 1.0 being totally controlled by genetics. Estimates up to .025 (2.5%) are considered as low hereditability, 0.25 to 0.5 (25 to 50%) as moderate and above 0.5 (50%) as high. They are useful only if accurate measures can be made—number of eggs produced, weight gain, etc. Many geneticists find these calculations to be exercises in futility when attempting to measure traits such as conformation, hip dysplasia, etc.

This is supported by reports of hereditability of hip dysplasia ranging from 25% to 80%. There are as many reports above 50% as below 50%. The latest report, in 1979, gave an estimate of between 40% and 50%. Why these figures are of interest to the breeders is unknown. It is already known and accepted that control of dysplasia is difficult, requires commitment and results are slow in being recognized.

4. Polygenic traits are improved by breeding programs based on mass selection but only to a limited degree. Mass selection means that the breeding animals are chosen for their individual characteristics *without regard for the status of their sibs or parents.* [Emphasis added.]

This [mass selection] is the most widely used technique to control hip dysplasia. It focuses on breeding normals to normals. Results have shown an overall reduction in progeny with dysplasia. However, most breeds have the potential for progressing beyond this technique. Other programs, starting with mass selection, are available that will reduce the incidence of dysplasia to even lower levels and do it in an even shorter period of time.

Used for an extended period on large numbers, mass selection identifies family lines and individual animals that produce larger percentages of normals than the breed average. These lines and individuals thus are identified as "superior" to the breed average. They have "fixed" more of the desirable genes.

Identification of "superior" sires becomes accurate when evaluations of all progeny are available. This rarely if ever happens: however, a reasonably accurate determination can be made with at least 30 random evaluations of progeny from 5-10 litters. Identification of "superior" bitches can be done in the same manner but will require an impractical time span.

5. Polygenic traits are more rapidly changed when the breeding animals have pedigree depth for the desired characteristic. For example, the probability of producing dogs with ideal qualities is increased when ideals are mated with ideals and both are out of ideals, etc.

This [pedigree depth] has been shown effective in controlling hip dysplasia. The probability of producing progeny with normal hips is increased by mating normal dogs out of normal dogs, etc. Further increase in the probability of producing normal progeny is noted when the parents have normal sibs and normality extends several generations back in the pedigree.

A Recommended Breeding Program

Sufficient information is available for most breeds to go beyond mass selection. Much of the information has been taken from OFA data. The OFA reports information to affiliated national breed clubs on all dogs receiving normal hip evaluations. The clubs, in turn, publish the information for their membership.

The rare breeds, and kennels choosing to operate in isolation regardless of the breed, are limited to using mass selection until larger numbers of normal dogs are available. In both incidences, the breeders should be aware that breeding normals to dysplastics (even mild dysplasia) has been shown to result in a significantly higher frequency of dysplastic offspring when compared to matings of normal with normals. This report, in 1979, corrects a prior report from the same source that inferred breeding normals to dysplastics demonstrated no statistically significant difference. This is one example of the progress that has been made by research.

The following breeding program has been shown to be effective [in lowering HD in dogs]. The degree of success requires cooperation, honesty and openness between several breeders.

1. Breed only normal to normal.

2. Avoid using: a) normal dogs from litters with a high incidence of dysplasia.

3. Choose sires with pedigree depth for normality and shown to have produced few or nor dysplastic offspring.

4. Cooperate with several breeders to progeny test and identify "superior" sires.

5. Choose replacement bitches that exceed the phenotype of their parents and breed average.

6. As the frequency of dysplasia is lowered, raise the standards for selecting "superior" sires and bitches.

How Doctor Corley's Breeding Program Applies to WPGCA Breeding Program

After reading Dr. Corley's booklet on selective breeding to reduce hip dysplasia, it's apparent that we have been using the same system in our WPGCA Approved Breeding Program as a method of overall improvement in our breed. We used it not only to reduce hip dysplasia, but to reduce mental instability, to improve desire for game contact, and to produce cooperative dogs that are easy to train. His suggestions are all things we have incorporated to improve our breed, including his final piece of advice, *"The degree of success requires cooperation, honesty and openness between several breeders."* That is exactly what we have done, beginning in 1974, and it is what Larry Mueller wrote about in the January, 1988 ***Outdoor Life***: "The Wirehaired Pointing Griffon Club of America is *different*. Its members are doing exactly what I've been told over and over couldn't happen in this country. It has always been my opinion that a few dedicated, cooperating people could accomplish more breed improvement in a few years than field-trial breeders have achieved during their entire history."

Not only have we followed Dr. Corley's recommendations for breeding, we have also paralleled closely the breeding program for the Seeing Eye Dog in New Jersey (See Chapter 30, "Are We on the Right Track?").

I would add one more ingredient for successful breeding that neither Dr. Corley nor Larry mentioned, and that is self-discipline. This is one of the most difficult ingredients to maintain in a breeding program. For example, it's really hard if you are an experienced gun dog person, perhaps a judge, and a breeder, and a decision is made by the breeding committee, or a breed warden, to breed your fine bitch to stud A, but you think stud B will be better. Discussion takes place. The breeding committee weighs the evidence and sticks to its original decision. To accept that call is true discipline.

In my personal experience of working on our Breeding Committee for over 20 years, there is almost always a good, healthy dialogue that takes place between each breeder and the Breeding Committee. The decision of which stud to use is almost always a mutual decision (consensus decision making) between the committee and the breeder, reached after lots of discussion and input from both sides.

An Update on Research About Diagnosing Hip Dysplasia

Early in 1994, results of research begun 11 years ago by Dr. Gail Smith at the University of Pennsylvania School of Veterinary Medicine became available to the public through mailings by the university to organizations such as our club. A program was started at the university based on Dr. Smith's work, called Pennsylvania Hip Improvement Program (PennHIP). It's a new way to diagnose HD.

One of the most important benefits of this new program is that dogs can be evaluated as early as sixteen weeks of age. This could be very important for breeders to have this information at such an early age.

For further information contact PennHIP at 1-800-248-8099. In addition to general information the staff will give you names of veterinarians in your area who have been trained and certified to perform the procedure.

OFA Responds to the PennHIP Announcement

In February, 1994, OFA issued a statement written by Dr. Corley, responding to PennHIP's recent announcement about its research. Not surprisingly, Dr. Corley does not agree that this new method is as valid in detecting HD as the 24-month radiograph. Nearly one year later, in his annual report to breed clubs, dated January 9, 1995, Dr. Corley had more to say about PennHIP:

> The PennHIP method is predicated on forcing the head of the femur from the acetabulum by use of leverage. This technique is not standardized as the pressure applied varies from study to study and investigator to investigator. A 1989 article in the Journal of Bone and Joint Surgery titled "Examining Infants Hips—Can It Do Harm?" raises the question that the examination procedure in the infant may actually cause a stable hip to become unstable. If this is true, then there is a possibility that some dogs examined by stress radiography may actually develop unstable hips and degenerative joint disease as the result of the procedure—not hip dysplasia. These are just a few of the questions that need further investigation. The scientists are encouraged to continue their research, but the public should be cautioned against use of stress radiography until the safety and accuracy has been established. Unfortunately, the premature commercialization of the technique has removed the debate from the scientific arena to the popular press.

WPGCA Board of Directors Responds

The board of directors of the WPGCA intends to stand tight with a wait and see approach while continuing our program with OFA. If the PennHIP program should prove successful we will certainly utilize it. But for now the WPGCA will continue with OFA.

We do question the risk involved in putting young dogs (four months) under anesthesia.

Latest Data From OFA on HD in Griffons

In Dr. Corley's Year End Data Update (1994) to breed clubs from OFA, came the news that we are lowering the rate of HD in Griffons even more than in earlier years:

1. Up to 1980, 218 Griffons had been screened by OFA, and 12% were dysplastic.

2. At the end of 1994 approximately 617 Griffons had been screened by OFA, and the rate of HD had dropped to 7.2%. Nearly 20% of all dogs cleared were rated "excellent."

3. In a different statistical breakdown, among 71 breeds with 500 or more submissions, 6 breeds reduced the frequency of HD by more than 70%. They were: Borzoi, Rhodesian Ridgeback, Siberian Husky, Soft Coated Wheaten Terrier, Welsh Springer Spaniel, and *Wirehaired Pointing Griffon*.

The next best category, was 60-70%, followed by additional breakdowns of: 50-60%, 40-50%, 30-40%, 20-30%, 10-20%.

For the versatile breeds, from 1974 through 1994, the percentage of dogs screened by OFA had the following rate of HD:

German Shorthaired Pointer	6.3 %
Wirehaired Pointing Griffon	7.2
Vizsla	8.5
German Wirehaired Pointer	9.3
Weimaraner	10.2
Pudelpointer	15.8
Brittany Spaniel	17.7

Remember, this study covers between 1974 and 1994. We began screening dogs in 1968. This study only includes breeds which had 100 or more dogs screened during the 20 year period.

*Below: "The Old Griffon" - **CANDICE VOM NELLAGRAM (Mike** v **Hessling x Tammy de L'Oakes Heuvel)**, circa 1965.*

Above: "The New Griffon" - ***AVIAN OF DUTCHMAN'S HOLLOW****, 1990, Iowa, during the water test in NAT, where the dog received Prize I.*

Below: Littermate ***ABBOT OF DUTCHMAN'S HOLLOW****, during his NAT in Iowa. Compliments John Zawacki)*

Above: ***BRISETTE DE LA COTE****, littermate of* ***BON CHASSEUR****, during her IHDT at Redding, California 1979.*

"SUZIE" - ***MAHASKA'S MERRY SUSZN*** *- 8 months, at her natural ability test in Michigan, April 1983, where she got a Prize II, all 4's except for a 3 in tracking, 4 and 4 in conformation and coat. She is the mother of* ***AVAJ OF IAMONIA****, grandmother of all the "A" "B" and "C" dogs of DUTCHMAN'S HOLLOW. Her sire was* ***BON CHASSEUR DE LA COTE****, her grandfather* ***LUCAS OF HUNTER'S CREEK,*** *her grandmother* ***VICTORIA DU BOIS FOLLET****, her great grandfather* ***TONIK DU BOIS FOLLET****. "****Suzie****" is from the first phase of the WPGCA Breeding Program. And, she left her mark on today's Griffons. She has lived all her life with Tom and Mahaska Whitley in Tallahassee, Florida. (Compliments Joan Bailey)*

CHAPTER THIRTY
THE FUTURE

When we began the WPGCA Breeding Program in 1974, we laid down on paper the beginning of a plan. It was the foundation from which we built over the next 20 years. There were revisions along the way, whenever we found something needed changing, or we needed to add new ideas. But the foundation has stayed in place. I believe the foundation was so solid, that once it was in place we could not fail, as long as we stuck to the basic philosophy.

The future of this breed will depend on those who follow to stay firmly attached to the foundation, which is simple, but is hard, tough work to implement. This foundation requires:

1. Absolute control in the hands of a few of the most qualified people.
2. No sales of dogs to non-hunters.
3. Testing entire litters in NAT and IHDT.
4. Refusal to place dogs with people who won't test them. Learn how to filter out those people so that they don't get dogs from the program.
5. Absolute certainty that judges are qualified.
6. Make breeding decisions based on objective information, not on emotional attachments.
7. Use all tools and information available from pedigrees and test results to help make decisions.

Just as our breed has now been stabilized, so has the human part of this endeavor been stabilized. The caliber of people owning dogs from our Breeding Program is of the highest. We are much different from who we were in 1974. We are much better educated in kynology, and we are ALL serious hunters.

So there is one more vital element that doesn't fit exactly into any slot, or on a list. It's the *people* you choose to put in key positions in your club or program. One needs to assess carefully, *over time*, apprentice judges, people for governing positions, people who will serve on a breeding committee. In addition to being experienced and knowledgeable, their primary interest *must* be in the *breed*, not in personal gain or in an ego trip. Most breeding decisions in this country are made for emotional reasons, ego enhancement, and personal gain, without regard for the breed. Look instead for experienced people with a genuine interest in the breed, who are open to learning. Take your time, do not be rushed, because it takes several years to get to know someone well.

We can write all the rules in the world, but they aren't worth much unless the people taking part in the program—from breeding committees and boards of directors, to each dog owner—have a cooperative spirit, trust each other, are ready to work together, and to *really listen* to each other.

In our experience—the Griffon experience—we are up front in saying that we are not democratic; we exert complete control over the breeding. Having said that, we also know that we are cooperative and respect one another, and work together. Over the years a few people have fallen by the wayside—dropped out of the program and the club. Expect that, it will happen. It's called attrition. Some people find that this work is not their cup of tea, and that's okay. Accept this graciously and keep moving forward.

This is not a glamorous endeavor, there are no prizes to hang on one's wall. But if you love a breed passionately, or put hunting dogs and hunting high on your priority list in your life, then you will reap rewards over time. Those rewards are seeing sound, uniform hunting dogs produced with high consistency. Receiving high prizes—say a Prize I UFT—is a tremendous achievement for the handler and dog, and it feels just plain good when it happens to you. In fact, more than good. But, in my opinion, a much more important achievement, for which there is no *prize*, is when entire litters are tested in NAT and in IHDT. That, above all else, is an achievement. No medals, no formal recognition, but it's the most important job of all, and it takes breeders, owners, and a group that promotes these endeavors.

The emphasis in this book, from the period covering 1974 to the present, has been mostly about dogs from the WPGCA Breeding Program. Primarily this is so because nearly all dogs from the program are tested, but very few from outside of the program are entered in tests. There isn't much to say about a dog you've never seen and that hasn't been tested. This doesn't mean it's a "bad" dog, just that we don't know anything about it.

Keeping the Korthals Griffon "Pure"

Yes, some people are fiercely opposed to the WPGCA's injection of the Fousek. We've been accused of ruining the Griffon, of bastardizing the Griffon, of dirtying the Griffon with "impure" blood. Early in the 1980s when we first announced our intention and when the first Fouseks arrived from behind the Iron Curtain we were even accused of bringing "communist" and "red" dogs into the country. Perhaps we were not politically correct.

We do believe that today the genetic bridge to Korthals Griffons is barely a tiny thread, no more than four legs, two ears, and a head. So we've had to rebuild, reconstruct the Griffon, in order for the breed to serve the requirements of the American hunter.

We knew the Fousek decision would not be popular with a lot of people. But, we believed, and the test scores proved, that the Griffons here in North America were beyond repair. So we did what we believed in, knowing that we would make enemies. It does get hot in the kitchen sometimes, especially when you get the pots to full boil on the stove. But we've stayed in the kitchen, stirring the pots, sweating a little with the heat from time to time. Always, we wiped our brows and continued, adhering to what we believed could be done. Now we are enjoying the fruits of our labor from that metaphorical "kitchen"—these grand, solid hunting dogs.

For the June 1993 GDS I wrote the following article. This is a condensed, updated version:

Are We on the Right Track?
Pure Griffons, Pure German Wirehairs, Pure Pudelpointers, Pure Spinoni, Pure Stichelhaars.
What Is "Pure?" Who Is On First?

All these breeds were developed from more than one so-called "pure" breed. Evidently, a breed is considered "pure" when it can consistently reproduce itself. That means that litters have a high percentage of uniformity among the dogs in a litter. Of course, we can use the same definition for an individual "strain" or "line" of dogs within a breed. (See Chapter 27 for how to develop lines within a breed.)

In talking about a gene—one gene, some biologists say that it takes anywhere from 200 to 2,000 nucleotides (that is the individual portion of it) for expressing one attribute. There are functions that we do not even know about. The previous statements are only two examples which demonstrate how complicated genetics is and how very little any of us know.

The question is: Is a dog that has ancestors from American Griffons (which are products of Griffons from several countries—Germany, France, Belgium, Holland, Italy)—a "pure" Griffon, even if he has a coat that is seven inches long, a weak desire to search for game, and a littermate with a coat that is one inch long and also a weak desire for game contact?

Or, is a dog that has "American Griffon blood" and some "Cesky Fousek blood," with a proper two-inch, hard, protective coat and a strong desire to search for game, whose littermates also have proper "Griffon" coats and all have the basic attributes necessary to make a sound hunting dog, "purebred"?

Perhaps more important than anything, as a breed club, we must ask: Is the dog that we are producing really what we want to own? If the dog works the way we say a Griffon should work, if the dog looks like the standard for a Griffon, if the dog has the sound temperament that we say a Griffon should have, is this a Griffon? Is this the dog that hunters want to own? If we say yes, then we must get past our hang-up with "purebred."

We have so many more satisfied hunters today owning dogs from our club than ever before. This must be telling us something. It tells us that we are producing wirehaired dogs that look like Griffons and act like Griffons. These are dogs that serious hunters are interested in owning. These hunters are willing to wait for them; they are willing to do their part by testing the dogs that they get. They understand that in order to keep these good dogs going, each owner must do his or her part.

There has been a significant change in our membership since the second phase of our club's Breeding Program. Presently, the *percentage* of club members who own dogs from the WPGCA Breeding Program has steadily grown over the past 11 years (since 1984) to 64 percent of our membership. Two years ago, 1993, it was 45 percent, so we've had a significant increase in the past two years, due in large part to the increased number of litters each year. Some of these members had dogs from the first phase of our program and came back again for their next dog. A few are even starting with their third dog from the program. In a few cases, we have second generation members who are just starting out with their first hunting dog.

The following remarks about the WPGCA Breeding Program and a breeding program used by The Seeing Eye Program in Morristown, New Jersey, were presented by John Lundberg at our 1993 Judges Seminar in Iowa. John is a trustee for the Seeing Eye Program:

"...This is a national organization that provides guide dogs for blind people [as does the Guide Dogs for the Blind Program in San Rafael, California]. The organization has had a breeding program for a number of years. We have hundreds of dogs in our statistical database. Our Breeding program was designed by a geneticist at the University of Pennsylvania, named Dr. Elmer Leighton. It is based really on the same principles as this [WPGCA] club's Breeding Program. That is to say, the proposition is that the only way you can improve a breed is through *objective testing of progeny.*

"[It is] not evaluation by the breeder, because that is subjective to a high degree, but objective evaluation by the instructors and trainers of these dogs, who have no emotional stake in a particular breeding. They are objectively evaluating the quality of our dogs in many of the same respects as we do in our dogs [in the Griffon Club]. Temperament is of prime importance, as well as hip dysplasia—because it shortens the useful life of that dog for the blind person, and a host of other things as well, general health being of prime importance.

"What they have found, over the years, is that the kind of approach we take here [in the Griffon Club] works. They have the advantage of having far more dogs to use and experiment and cull, and eventually they build on that database and selected breedings take place. They have established a numerical grading system for every dog, which they call "estimate breeding value" of an individual dog.

"They do it by assigning a numerical score of 10 or weighting it to a 10 for the most important quality they are looking for. From all those ratings and objective evaluations, they write down an estimated breeding rating for every dog. And that's what our [Griffon Club] Breeding Committee does here, but not with nearly the statistical rigor because we do not have a computer program we can afford, nor the huge samples that the Seeing Eye program has.

"Instead, we rely on what information we do have, much of which is in people' heads [editor's note: we have test results which the committee relies heavily on], i.e. "I remember this litter, a lot of stomach torsion there."

"But in their [Seeing Eye] breeding, there is an estimated breeding value calculated for every dog, and only those with the highest values are used for breeding. What I am here to tell you is that a system like this works. The Seeing Eye has proven it., And what I am also here to tell you is that our [Griffon Club] approach is necessarily not as rigorous mathematically, because we do not have the resources (number of dogs, a computer program) to make it that way. But the principle is clear to me, based on this background, that we are on the right track. And it is clear to me that there is the most conscientious effort toward objectivity here [WPGCA Breeding Program], as well as in the Seeing Eye.

"And it is also clear to me that in both places you make mistakes. Because human beings are evaluating things, and often times some answers are not clear, particularly in tests. We all have judged dogs where we say a year later, "Oops, we made a mistake on that score last year." That happens. But I think we need to appreciate as a club that nobody is in this for some sort of monetary or political gain., Our objective is to improve the breed. We are following the principles that give us the best chance of doing that. And it seems to me that ought to be enough to satisfy the focal question today, as well as the question, are we on the right track?

"That does not mean we cannot improve the way we do things. I would like to have us start thinking about becoming more numerical, about prioritizing various qualities and arriving at numerical estimated breeding values. I think that would bring a higher degree of rigor to the whole process and would lay to rest some of the concerns people have that these are arbitrary decisions." (John's talk ended here.)

* * * * * *

For me, who at one time was more hung up on the words "pure Korthals Griffon" than anyone else could ever be, I can only say that today I would much rather have a dog from our program with "foreign blood," if you will, than one of the "pure Korthals Griffons" with wooly coat and unstable temperament that I started out with 30 years ago.

Our dogs today, 30 years later, are vastly improved and more pleasurable to work with, to hunt with, and to live with. For me, the dogs we are producing today are genetically closer to what Korthals was producing over a hundred years ago than the "pure" Griffon that wins Best of Breed at the annual Westminster Dog Show in New York City....

Today we are at the point where we are producing a high degree of uniformity in our litters, and where nearly every dog in the litter makes a good hunting dog. Not many breeding programs can *honestly* say that. (They may say it, but can they back it up with test scores of entire litters?) In addition to disciplining ourselves, our judges and our officers and leaders stay open to new ideas and open to learning. All we have to do is to help each other get over our sentimental hang-up with "pure Korthals Griffons," and then to "stay on the right track," which means subjecting ourselves to strict discipline. If we do this, we will continue to enjoy the Griffons that we love so much.

Perhaps our newer club members, those serious hunters who like the dogs that we are producing, will inadvertently help us to get past our sentimental hang-up about the "pure Korthals Griffon." These newer members do not have a history of former "pure" Griffons, no memories of "pure" Griffons from the past, as the rest of us do. What they *do* have is great pleasure in owning these Griffons that we are producing. Their letters and phone calls to me attest to how pleased they are with their new gun dogs.

And remembering the question asked at the board of directors meeting in 1983, as to how many bitches we had to breed (the answer was none), today—in the 1990s—we have six to eight fine bitches to breed each spring. Are we on the right track or what?

* * * * * * * *

Dogs That Have Qualified in IHDT That May Be Used For Breeding in 1996 & 1997

As this book goes to press in January 1996, the following dogs have been tested through IHDT, discussed and approved for breeding in the next two or three years. Other dogs will be added to this list as results of testing become available to us, and some dogs may be dropped if their progeny testing shows us they are not producing the kind of hunting dogs which satisfy our goals. Or, we may decide not to use a dog on the list, if another dog becomes available which we feel will have better potential:

MALES	FEMALES
Ariko vom Erik	**Bailey of Ocean House**
Arrow of Dutchman's Hollow	**Bell of Ocean House**
Abbot of Dutchman's Hollow	**Brandy of Dutchman's Hollow**
****Blue Mountain Brew**	**Birkley Bell of Dutchman's Hollow**
Barton de los Altos	**Champagne Blaze of Dutchman's Hollow**
Chipper de los Altos	**Cera of Dutchman's Hollow**
Prairie Storm's Amos	**Cassie of Dutchman's Hollow**
Dan Cerniky	**Callaj of Dutchman's Hollow**
Archie of the High Country	**Prairie Storm's Alder**
Amos of the High Country	**Prairie Storm's Abby**
Alder of the High Country	**Prairie Storm's Bailey**
***Erik od Jezerek**	**Bryanna de los Altos**

***Frozen semen**
**Brew did not qualify in IHDT, but reasons for using him for breeding are documented in the text in Part One.

Results of Spring Field Tests 1995

Full tabulation of these results may be found in the June 1995 ***Gun Dog Supreme.*** A brief summary follows: In NAT the " A" OF THE HIGH COUNTRY litter of 9 pups, all qualified with 7 out of the 9 receiving prize I. Out of the "A" OF WHATCOM WOODS litter of six pups, 5 qualified, 3 with Prize I, and 2 with Prize III. In the "D" OF AUGER FALLS with 7 out of the 8 pups being tested (The 8th will test in the fall), 6 received Prize I, one didn't qualify. The "B" OF BIRKSHIRE POND, a litter of 7, four were tested, 3 received Prize I, and one didn't qualify. The "B" OF PRAIRIE STORM litter of 3 pups, 2 were tested and each received Prize I, the third dog will be tested in the fall. The "A" OF BECI'S PARADISE, litter of 3, one got Prize I, the other two, Prize III.

In litters not part of the WPGCA Breeding Program, the SHINGOBEE LAKE litter tested three dogs from one litter: one Prize I, one Prize II, and one Prize III. In the "D" WAYFARER'S litter, 3 dogs out of the litter were tested: one received Prize I, two received Prize II. Two other dogs, each from a different breeding, received Prize I.

In IHDT, the "A" OF PRAIRIE STORM litter tested 6 out of the 7 dogs in the litter: 1 Prize I, 2 Prize II, 1 Prize III, 2 did not qualify. In the "C" DE LOS ALTOS litter, (including 1 dog from the fall of 1994), out of 5 dogs in the litter, 4 were tested: 1 Prize II, 1 Prize III, 2 did not qualify (one of these tested again in the fall in OHDT and received Prize II).

* * * * *

In the early spring of 1995, at our annual game dinner during the testing weekend in Idaho, Rolf Benseler, one of our fine senior judges and long-time member of our club, shared with us something that I want to share with you to bring this book to a close. Traveling through a small town in northern California, on his way to Idaho, Rolf passed a small Baptist church which had a lighted sign out front, on which was displayed:

God, Please Help Me To Be the Kind of Person My Dog Thinks I am.

* * * * *

Dr. Thomas Mintscheff †

Early in the fall of 1995, the call came to me from Dr. Mintscheff's son, Tom, a surgeon, practicing in South Carolina, to tell me that his father had died in his 90th year. Tom and I talked a while and I was very touched by some of his words. He told me that he missed his father very much, because he had been more than a father, he had been a very good friend. A father could not ask for more than that from a son.

Dr. Mintscheff—Thomas, to his friends, was one of those special dog people. As I said earlier, he was a very gifted dog person, the rare person who seems to be born with a knack for understanding dogs. And what's more, dogs knew that.

Though he had well trained dogs, and loved to spend time working with his dogs, he also had a sense of humor about it, so that if a dog broke on the shot, or the dog didn't stop on the "down," he would only smile, as if almost saying, "It's no big deal, we'll all having fun here."

He taught quite a number of people how to work with dogs. I don't say train, because what he did was much more than training. He worked with dogs, and that is different. Like most gifted dog people, the dogs always wanted to do what Thomas told them, because they would rather please him than anything else.

Dr. Mintscheff became ill with cancer about two years ago, and Tom finally persuaded him to come and live with him and his family in South Carolina. So he had Tom, his daughter-in-law, and two beloved grandsons with him for the last year of his life. And he died in America, a country he liked, and where he had lived when Tom was just a youngster growing up. He always had a special place in his heart for the American Griffonniers, going back to the 1950s.

He was loved by so many Griffonniers in Germany, a few in France, and by at least a dozen American Griffonniers who knew him. He will be very much missed in the Griffon world. I will miss him.

Joan Bailey
November, 1995

*"**THE OLD GUARD PASSES**." 1988 in the courtyard of Castle Steinach, near Wolferszell, on Sunday morning during the parade of Griffons as part of the 100th celebration for the founding of the mother Griffon Club, dogs over eight begin the parade. In the center of the photo, leading the pack, is Dr. Mintscheff and his 14 year old **ARDA**, whom he qualified in UFT in 1977. At the extreme left of the photo can be seen several members of a visiting hunting horn band. (Compliments Joan Bailey)*

EPILOGUES

The Oxford American Dictionary defines "epilogue" as "a short concluding section in a literary work." The epilogues here are not short. But then, I, like the Griffon Club, have seldom done things "by the book."

JOE NADEKER

The phone rings. The caller asks, "How's Joe?" Or, "Is Joe coming to the test?" Or, "What does Joe think about such and such?" There is no need to ask "Joe who?" because in our world—the world of Griffons and versatile dogs—there is only one Joe. Our Joe has no comprehension of the high esteem, genuine affection, and abiding respect that so many people throughout the United States and Canada hold for him.

Born in 1920 in Czechoslovakia to a hunting family, he grew up among hunters and hunting dogs of all kinds. Hunting, and the dogs, became his passion at an early age.

For several years I had been talking about Joe to Larry Mueller, hunting dogs editor of ***Outdoor Life***. Finally Larry's interest was whetted and he made contact with Joe, spending two days with him near and at Joe's home in Redding, California, in 1991. When Larry's column about Joe appeared in ***Outdoor Life*** (June 1992), though I had known Joe since 1973, I learned things about him I'd never known, due to Larry's expertise and experience in interviewing people. Here's a portion of what Larry wrote:

> ...He has keen perception and a quick intellect. In fact, had he not always been a quick study, Nadeker would have been a Czech convict instead of an American businessman and sportsman.
>
> Nadeker told the story as we drove. He was 28, politically active and vocally anti-communist at the end of World War II when his native Czechoslovakia was about to hold elections. Four days before the elections, realizing that they would be badly beaten at the polls, communist forces swept the country and rounded up what they called dissidents and counter revolutionaries.
>
> An outdoorsman and hunter from boyhood, Nadeker grabbed his skis and jumped on a train, intending to escape via the Bohemian Forest into Bavaria. The end station was overrun by police with dogs, so Nadeker didn't even get off the train. The next night, despite snow and sub-zero temperatures, Nadeker dressed himself in light underwear and a suit coat to appear like someone going on a quick errand. Without a map, food or water—knowing that these also would give him away, if he was stopped—Nadeker took off into the night on foot toward the very tip of western Bohemia. He crossed into Russian-occupied East Germany and found railroad tracks to follow south into the American zone.
>
> With the sky clouded over, Nadeker misjudged direction, and the second night was wasted. The third night he crossed into East Germany with no interference, and then found few guards at the West German border. Nadeker had grasped the situation well ahead of those who would later find escape almost impossible, if not fatal. (Those dissidents who didn't escape were jailed for 15 years.)...

You read on previous pages of some of Joe's contributions to the Griffons, i.e., bringing in the Cesky Fousek. Equally as important to the Griffon club Breeding Program, and to other versatile dog owners with similar interests, has been his guiding force in teaching us how to be good judges. This he accomplishes through our seminars, and equally important his work with apprentice judges. Lucky is the apprentice judge who gets to spend a precious day or two in the field with Joe.

Joe is a humble and a private person. He is the first to tell you that "no man knows it all," meaning that we must all learn from each other. Each of us has something to contribute that the other may not know. Over the years his interest in kynology has deepened greatly. Shortly after we began the WPGCA Breeding Program in 1974 he got many books on genetics and plowed through them, and thus was able to educate some of us at our annual judges seminars. His father had a library of books about hunting and hunting dogs, and Joe's nephew saved the books and gave them to Joe.

Personally, I have been privileged to be able to pick up the phone and call Joe untold number of times throughout the past 23 years, to ask questions, discuss, dialogue. What that has meant for me cannot be put into words. As I began in earnest to write this book, I would send Joe a chapter, then the next chapter, and the one after that. All very rough drafts. His support and understanding of the subject matter cannot be over-emphasized. That was the best part of writing this book—the dialogues, the comprehension, the sharing, the discovering. Many days, as I wrote, I'm not sure whose voice came out onto the page. Was it Joe? Was it Joan? Was it a combination? I like to think it was a combination.

Not only has Joe been a mentor for me, he has been a mentor for untold numbers of hunters who have a passion for the hunting dog as well as for the pursuit of game.

Yes, his accent is unique—part Czech, part German. He told me once that he didn't think he had much of an accent until he listened to a tape recording of himself, and couldn't believe it was himself. But to us, his accent is part of his gracious charm, and goes with his sense of humor, and his ability to laugh at himself.

Joe has brought to us his vast knowledge, acquired through years of hunting experience, combined with his unique perception of dogs. He is the first to tell you how little he knew when we all started out in the versatile hunting dog movement. And he will tell you that "we knew a lot more then than we do today."

What he cannot tell you, because he does not know, is how loved and respected he is, by hunting dog owners throughout this land. He has taught us well.

* * * * * *

Wintering Quail
By Roy Speece, President WPGCA 1971 - 1979

(This first appeared in ***Hunting Dog***, (April 1970), and was reprinted with Roy's permission in (December 1971) ***The Gun Dog Supreme.*** Because of space limitations, some parts explaining how and why Roy trains his dogs to sight point have been omitted.)

> To discover something really new is quite a thrill. At least it is a thrill to me when I learn something that I did not know before, and find that others didn't know it either. This is especially true when I learn the thing as a result

of my own effort and initiative and some great work by my dog rather than by sheer luck. Such a discovery of something really new concerning wildlife has happened to me only rarely, in a lifetime of outdoor activities. Usually I find that what I thought was a new and original discovery, is indeed a documented and established fact and that others have known it for many years.

I am going to risk and share my discovery for two reasons: First, if what I stumbled upon is known by others, I have been unable to find it in print and I possess what I think is a rather extensive library on the subject. Second, I believe the yarn is worth telling because of its interest to dog men, even though my discovery turns out to be "old hat" to wildlife people.

...I have worked with quite a few dogs in my day although I am not what you would call a professional. Of the several dogs of my own and my friends that I have been around I have trained two dogs that I believe would be "big league" gun dogs in anybody's hunting field.

I want the reader to take note that I use the terms "gun dog" and "hunting field." I avoid bench show stock like the plague and field trialing is just not my cup of tea. Field trialing is another sport and no doubt a great one. I am not knocking field trialing. I simply do not choose to run my dogs in field trials. [Roy did, and does, however, endorse the field testing of versatile dogs, which is not field trialing as he meant it here.] I will however put my dogs down for you, with you, or against you, on wild birds in their native fields. You see I am strictly a hunter and my dogs are trained strictly for the gun.

The dog involved in this story is "big league" and perhaps a star to boot. **The General (DUTCHMASTER'S GENERAL)** is a great grizzled, gray Griffon. He is the most willing, hardest working gun dog of my lifetime association with better than average dogs of several breeds. He will do about anything that I can make him understand and he will do it willingly and with gusto. Yes, **The General** is definitely "major league."

The General was broken and staunched as a puppy on a pheasant wing flipped by a fly rod. He will still sight point as long as he can see his bird. I have never felt that this trait detracted in any way from his intense and beautiful scent points. I do, in fact, believe that sight pointing is a great asset in teaching puppies not to chase flying birds as mature dogs.

But then, what is one man's meat may be another man's poison and what works for me is not necessarily the best way for the other fellow. Anyway, the point I wish to make for this story, is that **The General** will sight point—and hold a sight point.

Now for the way that my wildlife discovery came about. I set **The General** down that Sunday afternoon in a ring-tailed dandy of a Nebraska blizzard. Believe me, Nebraska has a well-earned reputation for having first class blizzards. The thermometer said it was ten above zero. The wind gauge said we had twenty to thirty mile an hour winds. It was snowing intermittently and the man on the radio from the dash board of my warm car said that the "wind chill index" was about thirty below zero.

I'm not much of a T.V. buff and so even in this weather I had chosen to try for a cock pheasant or two instead of lolling at home this Sunday afternoon.

My area of Nebraska is an excellent area for pheasants. It is also a rather good area for Bob White quail. Often our bag of birds is mixed between the two although we hunt somewhat different cover when seeking pheasant than we do when we are strictly quail hunting. The habitat preferences of the two birds somewhat overlap. The hunter is apt to flush a pheasant when on a quail hunt and he is also apt to find quail, in pheasant country.

Because Nebraska is on the north edge of the decent quail area of America, we Nebraskans must perhaps observe conservation practices that the southern hunter would not have to consider. It is our weather, particularly our blizzards that causes much concern for Bob White quail and their survival. The game laws of Nebraska and the knowledgeable sportsmen of Nebraska take note of the fact that a covey of quail should not be broken up late in the day nor during periods of severe weather. A broken covey of quail will most certainly lose some of its number by freezing, while a strong covey of birds, tightly bunched, seem to survive our treacherous storms.

It was for this reason that I did not want to scatter quail on a day such as this Sunday that I set **The General** down in prime pheasant country. I purposely tried to avoid quail cover on this hunt. It would not be my intention to help mother nature destroy these quail that I so dearly love to hunt. This day was far too cold and too bitter to spread a covey of quail.

I may have bagged a pheasant or two. I cannot say for sure. I have hunted birds for many years and although I do remember many specific kills, I do not recall any birds being shot on this particular hunt.

I do recall one hen pheasant that breasted into that "blue norther" wind and was literally turned over in a backward roll. Her action would be called an inside loop if it were performed by an airplane. Luckily and by the shearest margins did this hen pheasant avoid actually crashing her body into the ground as the wind caught her and flipped her over.

I was perhaps only one-half mile from my car when suddenly in a swirl of finely driven snow I was lost from my dog. I wasn't really lost, I knew full well where I was. Nor was my dog lost. **The General** had far too much savvy to get lost on a hunt. But the storm had worsened and parted we were and find him I could not.

The tiny bell that I had clipped to his collar this day because of the poor visibility had long since ceased to tinkle. It was jammed tightly with packed snow.

I had seen him only seconds before as he struck to my right for some uncut rows of sorghum milo, along the weedy border of the harvested field. **The General** definitely hunts with you and for you although he tends not to hunt in your path. He ranges to the side and ahead seeking the spots of best cover or he quarters your path as each field dictates. On a day such as this the dog was often temporarily obscured from my sight by the driven snow.

Several minutes slipped by and I returned to the uncut margin of brown headed grain made white by the snow. Still no dog. The wind only howled back in my face as I attempted to call him in.

It's colder I'll tell you when you are lost from your dog. It's windier too and the sky is darker and the snow is suddenly deeper. There was really no place to hunt for my dog as all was whiteness, all was sameness, all was driven snow. But hunt for him I must. **The General** had never quit me. Even as a pup on the New Mexico desert when he ran a mesquite thorn nearly through a front pad, where it remained unknown to me for two days, he never quit me. Nor did he quit in the Utah mountains when he tangled with a porcupine. He has never quit me and I couldn't think of quitting him in this blizzard.

Ten minutes is a long time under these conditions; it seemed like an hour. But ten minutes is probably about the length of time that **The General** was lost from me. Visibility was only a few feet but the mind can wander a million miles: a steel trap; hung in a fence by that damned bell; a cyanide bomb; a thousand thoughts raced through my mind. I was about to panic as I swung larger and larger circles around the spot of last seeing him.

At once and from nowhere, there stood a great ghost of a dog, solidly locked on point. Facing straight down wind was **The General,** his wire-like hair so coated with snow as to make him almost unrecognizable. His coarse and grizzled coat held snow but it also held warmth. I doubt that he was chilled in the least. The amazing thing however was that a few feet off the end of his nose was a seething mass of quail.

This then is my discovery. Did you know that under extreme blizzard conditions a tight covey of quail literally boil with movement? The birds as I viewed them and as **The General** had for some minutes sight pointed them were a constantly moving mass of bodies. Unaware of either the dog or me, these quail caught in the semi-open of this milo stubble in this wicked weather were simply practicing an age-old instinct for survival.

The outside birds of the tightly grouped covey would climb on top of the others, work their way toward the center and slip to the ground in a new and warmer position. This would of course force a new circle of quail to the outside edge of the covey. Again, the outside birds, chilled by the bitter weather, would work their way atop and to the center. Almost continuous was the movement, almost orderly. The cold outside bird would climb on and over his covey mates, slip to the ground near the center and await his turn to be forced to the outside and the cold again.

Ever moving was the mass of birds. Amazing to me but indeed elementary and simple in the light of preservation of life. The idea had never occurred to me that things like this would happen nor that there would be such a need, even in a Nebraska blizzard. Certainly however a covey of birds would freeze to death, from the outside inwardly if they sat still. The movement obviously served two purposes: to let each bird warm itself in the center of the group from time to time and keep the blood of each bird circulating from the activity involved. If the snow became deep no doubt a third purpose would be served; to pack the snow and keep on top of it rather than smother under a deep drift.

That it was a sight point I have no doubt. The dog was facing directly down wind and the wind was a gale. That **The General** had held it for many minutes I have no doubt. I found him within a few yards of where I had last seen him. I cannot guess as to why these quail were in the semi-open in a storm such as this. Perhaps the covey had been broken earlier that day by a fox or coyote patrolling the sparse hedge-row some forty rods away.

I have told of my discovery and be it a new discovery or only new to me really doesn't matter now. It is an important event in my life whether it is new or old. It is important to me because it marks one of the great moments in a lifetime of hunting. It marks the day that I saw the greatest single point that any dog of mine has ever made. Perhaps, just perhaps this was one of the great points of all time.

I was relieved at finding my dog. I had no intention of breaking that covey and I had no intention of embarrassing my dog. I took my large fur-trimmed cap, put it full over **The General**'s face and carried that great mass of muscle toward my car.

There was snow in my hair, joy in my heart, wind in my face and a tear in my eye as I nestled that great gray ghost in my arms...

* * * * *

A Word About "Warmbloods" from John Lundberg

Early in December 1995, in a telephone conversation John told me about the "warmbloods." It sparked my memory of these horses, for I had learned about them twenty odd years ago when I was riding in eastern Canada. John found the history of these horses analogous to our Breeding Program, so I asked him if he would write a few words to include in this book:

> A breed category known as "Warmbloods" has evolved in Europe over several centuries. These warmbloods resulted from blending native stock in various parts of Northern Europe and Scandinavia with the so-called fullbloods, Thoroughbred or Arabian. There are numerous warmblood breeds, perhaps the most prominent being Hannoverian, Holsteiner, Trakhener, Westfalen, Dutch Warmblood and Selle Francais.

The warmblood, like the fullblood, is bred for a purpose—the purpose (today) of sport rather than galloping at speed. The warmblood adds style, temperament, and durability to the speed and stamina it has inherited from its fullblood ancestors.

"Today warmbloods produce almost all the performers who win Olympic medals and national, European and World Championships. They dominate world-class competition in three of the four disciplines." [jumping, dressage, driving and combined training] pp. 11, 12, ***The Warmblood Guidebook***, Charlene Strickland, Half Halt Press 1992.

To continually improve sport horse qualities, the vast majority of European breeders combine pedigree study, third-party evaluations and meticulous record-keeping *with open studbooks.* Their goal has been "excellence of performance rather than purity of blood." Stickland, p. 15.

***ERIK OD JEZERAK**, California, March 1986, 3 months after his arrival in America. He and John Lundberg giving a demonstration at the water, during a break in the testing. (Compliments Joan Bailey)*

APPENDIX A

FIELD TEST RESULTS OF GRIFFONS AND CESKY FOUSEKS 1971 THROUGH 1994

(Only those Fouseks imported by the WPGCA Breeding Program, or bred in the U.S. by WPGCA are included.)

STATISTICS

What Do They Mean? How Do We Read Them?

The Oxford American Dictionary defines "statistics" as "The science of collecting, classifying, and interpreting information based on the numbers of things." The tabulations here are statistics of field tests of Griffons. To understand these statistics, we must ask several questions:

Are the statistics here a true sample of the breed? No, I don't think so. As the years go by, the results of the WPGCA field tests reflect mostly dogs from the WPGCA Breeding Program. Roughly 80 to 90 percent are from the program. In the early years--1969 to 1976--I think our statistics were pretty much a sample of the breed in the United States. Once the Griffon Club split away from NAVHDA testing in 1976-1977, the statistics divided into two parts: dogs that tested in NAVHDA, and those tested in WPGCA.

And then there are those Griffons that are not tested at all. My guess is that there are at least twice as many Griffons that are NOT tested, as those (both WPGCA and NAVHDA) that are.

Accepting that premise, there are clues to help you interpret these statistics. When you look at the test results of one dog, you must ask, "How did the rest of the litter do?" Using an average of 8 pups in a litter, the test results of one dog out of eight has very little significance. When you study the test results of an entire litter, check to see how all the dogs did in Tracking, and again in Water. In NAT, the results of Water, and Tracking, are almost always significant. If there is a weakness in the breeding (which translates to a weakness in the parents), it will almost always show up in Water and/or Tracking.

Also, check the ages of the dogs at the time they were tested. Anything under 8 months is questionable, because the dog is still so young compared to a dog between 12 and 16 months. If an entire litter is tested at 8, 9 or even 10 months, we don't have an entire picture. Those ages are almost what you might call one of the "awkward ages." Around 12 months is an ideal age. If a dog is 16 months at the time of the NAT it should really get all 4's. There is no excuse for a 16 month old dog not to be able to do everything well in a NAT.

In IHDT, watch for the same things as in NAT. Check the water work, and the tracking. And check the age at the time the dog was tested. They usually do a lot better after they have had TWO hunting seasons. However, we do encourage Griffon owners to test in IHDT 6 months after their NAT, which puts the average dog at about 18 or 19 months at the time of the test. Testing at that age gives us added information to help in breeding decisions. If the dog doesn't do well at 18 months, he/she can come back again the following spring at 24 months.

NAVHDA judges, who are also breeders or owners of the stud dog, are allowed to judge dogs they have bred, whereas no judges in the WPGCA may judge dogs they have bred, nor can judges in Europe.

In UFT, check how many times a dog had to be run before it was able to qualify. Some dogs were entered 5 and 6 times. This could be due to lack of talent of the dog, or, lack of training talent by the handler. Sometimes a dog is entered 5 or 6 times in UFT simply because the owner enjoys doing it, or likes to get prizes.

If a litter does well in NAT, always check to see how it did in IHDT. Any litter that only goes as far as NAT does not provide the entire information about that breeding.

RESULTS OF GRIFFONS IN NATURAL ABILITY TESTS SPONSORED BY NAVHDA AND SANCTIONED BY THE WPGCA 1969-1976

All tabulations and test results are listed in chronological order, beginning in 1971, by litter. No Griffons were tested in NAT until 1971.)

(These test results were originally published in issues of the NAVHDA newsletter, and in ***The Gun Dog Supreme***.)

In order for the reader to look up bloodlines, names of sires and dams are provided. Most pedigrees can be found in this book. For those not included, the reader can contact the Registrar of the WPGCA (Lyla Lehrer, 8636 Panorama E,

Bozeman, MT 59715, 406-586-0015) and receive that information for $5.00 per dog.

Pedigree numbers in the appendix refer to the pedigree numbers assigned each litter and listed in back issues of ***The Gun Dog Supreme*** (GDS), beginning in August 1974, i.e. if you find Pedigree 10 here, that litter will be number 10 in the GDS as well. Chronological order has been used so that the reader can go back to the text and easily find something more about nearly every litter. The pedigree numbers used in this book DO NOT correspond to the numbers here in the Appendix, nor in the GDS.

There is an exception to the pedigree numbering system. In Part Two, in a section about hip dysplasia, there are 33 pedigrees which have been given "HD" numbers from 1 to 33.

KEY TO TABULATIONS/HEADINGS

A-Age in Months
N-Nose
S-Search
W-Affinity for Water
P-Pointing
T-Tracking Live Game Bird
A-Attitude Toward Work
C-Cooperation,
TO-Total Points
P-Prize I, II, or III
C-Coat
CO-Conformation
T-Temperament

*** This symbol indicates a temperament problem (dog is manifesting some form of mental instability, such as: gunshy, or gun sensitive, shy, spooky, hyper, fear biter, etc.**

o Means dog's temperament is "ok" and that no defects of mental instability were observed during the test.

**** Dog is dysplastic.**

***** That portion of the test is optional (n/a NAT).**

\+ **Dog is from a litter that is part of the WPGCA Breeding Program.**

++ Dog is over or under age, and is being tested for evaluation only, and is not eligible for qualification.

NOTE: Temperament was not listed on most score cards until 1974. Sometimes notes were made regarding temperament, especially if there was indication of unsound temperament. For most dogs tested before 1974, the space for temperament is left blank unless it was included on a scorecard.

	Age (A)	Nose (N)	Search (S)	Affinity for Water (W)	Pointing (P)	TRacking (T)	Attitude Toward Work (A	Cooperation (C)	Total Points (TO)	Prize (P)	Coat (C)	Conformation (CO)	Temperament (T)
Ped 1 (1971) (Barry v.d. Neuburg x Gretel v Altenburg) (2 litters)													
GHOST'S SHADOW	11	4	4	4	4	4	4	3	102	I	4	4	
GHOST'S SHADOW	11	4	3	4	4	2	4	4	95	II	4	4	
GHOST'S SHADOW	15	4	4	3	4	4	4	3	97	I	-	-	
**ROLF V PHILOHELA	11	4	4	3	4	4	4	4	99	I	3	3	
**ROLF V PHILOHELA	15	4	4h	3	4	3	4	3	95	I	3	3	
BRIGHTON DUKE	11	4	4	4	3	1	3	3	90	III	3	3	
TRINA V ALTENBURG	11	3	2	3	2	1	2	1	59	III	3	2	
*DEBBIE	11	4	4	2	2	4	4	3	86	III	2	3	
BARON V ALTENBURG	11	2	3	3	1	3	3	2	64		2	3	
M.GRETCHEN VON WIBE	11	3	0	3	0	4	2	2	51		2	2	
MAX V TANNENWALD	8	3	3	4	3	2	2	4	80	III	4	2	
MAX V TANNENWALD	12	4	3	4	3	2	4	4	92	II	4	2	
DEREK VD MOORE	8	2	3	4	0	2	3	3	66		3	2	
Ped 2 (1972-73) (Barry v.d. Neuburg x Tina de la Reote)													
BENT PINE'S BRIGETTE	5	4	3	3	3	2	4	3	85	II	3	3	
BENT PINE'S BRIGETTE	14	4	4	4	3	4	4	4	101	II	2	2	
DUCKPOND BRUNEHILDE	14	4	4h	4	4	4	4	4	104	I	3	2	
HUNTER	9	3	2	4	3	0	4	1	71		4	2	
HUCKLE HILL PATTI	9	1	3	3	1	1	4	4	61		3	2	
LOUISE	9	2	2	0	1	0	2	2	35		3	1	
TREUE FREUDIN HEIDI	5	2	1	2	0	2	2	3	43		3	3	
Ped 3 (1973) (Basko v.d. Neuburg x Amsel v Kastanienhain)													
EDDA V KASTANIENHAIN	12	2	2	4	0	2	2	4	62		3	2	

	A	N	S	W	P	T	A	C	TO	P	C	CO	T
Ped 4 (1973) (Ajax v.d. Culm x Diana v.d. Neuburg)													
BOSS V WOLFSBERG	12	4	4	4	4	4	4	4	112	I	4	2	

(Note: You'll notice that BOSS and DUCKPOND BRUNEHILDE each had all 4's, yet they have different total points. This was due to a change in the indexes which are not shown here.)

	A	N	S	W	P	T	A	C	TO	P	C	CO	T
Ped 5 (1973) (Don v.d. Neuburg x Plumcreek's Siri)													
PLUMCREEK'S TOBI	13	4	4	3	3	2	4	4	99	II	3	3	
Ped 6 (1973) (Pipo des Vieilles Rouches x Ouchka du Bois Follet)													
TAQUIN DU BOIS FOLLET	16	4	4	4	3	3	4	2	95	II	-	-	
Ped 7 (1973) (Pipo des Vieilles Rouches x Lorene de Ronciers de Clavieres) (2 litters)													
+++TONIK DU BOIS FOLLET	10	4	2	2	4	4	2	4	78	III	4	4	
VICTORIA DU BOIS FOLLET	13	3	4	4	4	1	4	4	95	III	4	2	

+++-In 1974, after this test, it was declared unofficial (not sanctioned) due to improper selection of judges. But it is listed in the NAVHDA test results as official.

	A	N	S	W	P	T	A	C	TO	P	C	CO	T
Ped 8 (1973, 74, 76) (Taquin du Bois Follet x Huckle Hill Patty) (3 litters)													
BRISE	5	3	2	3	4	3	3	3	83	III	4	4	
HUCKLE HILL ANGELA	12	3	2	4	4	3	3	3	88	III	3	3	
AMITY'S BOUNCING BARNIE	12	2	3	4	3	2	3	3	81		2	3	
++AMITY'S BOUNCING BARNIE	17	3	4	4	4	3	4	3	102		3	4	
KORTNEY V MEIERLOH	11	3	2	1	2	2	2	3	59		4	3	
++KORTNEY V MEIERLOH	24	4	4	2	4	4	3	3	96		4	4	*
Sensitive, butt bite													
BAYWATER SHAG	9	3	3	4	4	0	3	3	87		3	2	
BAYWATER SHAG	14	3	3	4	3	2	4	4	97	II	4	2	
HUCKLE HILL MISTY	9	3	2	2	4	3	2	3	74	III	4	4	
HUCKLE HILL MISTY	14	3	3	4	4	2	4	3	95	II	4	4	
HUCKLE HILL MIKE	8	1	1	0	0	0	1	2	19		3	2	*
HUCKLE HILL GRIFF	9	2	2	0	3	0	2	2	46		4	4	
GRIFFIE OF JOHHSON	10	2	1	2	3	1	2	2	53		2	1	
WINGMASTER'S TROUBLE MAKER	10	3	3	4	4	0	3	4	89		3	3	
WINGMASTER'S TROUBLE MAKER	15	2	2	4	0	1	3	3	62		3	3	
HUCKLE HILL SCKYLER	11	2	2	0	4	2	2	2	14		2	2	*

(Four more dogs from this breeding were tested in 1977 in NAT. in NAVHDA .

	A	N	S	W	P	T	A	C	TO	P	C	CO	T
Ped 9 (1974) (Taquin du Bois Follet x Bent Pine's Brigette)													
BENT PINE'S ASTRID	8	1	1	1	0	0	2	2	28		3	3	
BENT PINE'S ASTRID	14	1	2	4	4	0	2	3	66		3	3	
BENT PINE'S ALDA	9	3	4	4	3	3	4	4	100	II	3	4	
BENT PINE'S ALDA	10	3	4	4	4	1	4	4	100	III	2	3	
BENT PINE'S ALDA	15	4	4	4	4	4	4	4	112	I	3	4	
BENT PINE'S ANNA	8	1	2	4	2	0	3	2	60		3	3	
BENT PINE'S ABERDEEN	9	4	4	4	4	1	4	4	106	III	3	4	
BENT PINE'S ABERDEEN	14	4	4	4	4	2	4	4	100	II	4	4	
BENT PINE'S ALPHA	9	2	2	3	0	0	2	2	49		4	3	
BENT PINE'S ALPHA	15	3	4	4	4	0	3	3	92		2	2	
BENT PINE'S ANGUS	10	4	4	4	4	2	4	4	108	II	3	4	

	A	N	S	W	P	T	A	C	TO	P	C	CO	T
Ped 9 (Continued)													
BENT PINE'S ANGUS	14	3	4	4	4	2	4	3	100	II	4	4	
Ped 10 (1974) (Taquin du Bois Follet x First Frost Unipac)													
FIRST FROST TROUPER	5	2	1	4	2	1	1	1	53		-	-	
FIRST FROST TROUPER	11	2	0	4	0	4	2	1	50		3	2	
FIRST FROST WINNIE	5	3	3	1	4	0	3	4	74		3	1	
FIRST FROST WINNIE	11	2	2	2	4	1	2	2	62		4	2	
FRIEDRICH "O" FIRST FROST	5	3	3	1	4	1	2	4	72		4	3	
+FRIEDRICH "O" FIRST FROST	18	3	4	4	4	2	3	4	98		2	2	
FIRST FROST WILMA	11	2	2	2	2	2	3	2	60		3	2	
Ped 11 (1974) (Taquin du Bois Follet x Ricky de Norebib)													
VERA DE L'ALVERNE	8	4	3	4	4	3	3	3	99	II	-	-	
VIRGULE DE L'ALVERNE	8	4	3	0	2	3	3	1	67		-	-	
Ped 12 (1974) (Kentucky von Griff x Awatobi of Windy Hills)													
DIRK VON MEIRLOH	10	4	4	2	4	4	3	3	96	III	4	3	
Ped 13 (1974) (Sacha de St Landry x Saga)													
PUCCI	6	4	3	3	4	3	3	3	87	II	3	3	
TRACY A'MOUSTACHES	10	3	4	2	3	1	4	4	79	III	4	4	
BUZZ	10	4	2	3	4	4	2	4	89	III	4	4	
Ped 14 (1974) (Sacha de St Landry x Agate d'Argent)													
FANCY QUEUE BLANC	12	**Tested in Germany, qualified in NAT**											
Ped 15 (1974) (Sacha de St Landry x Barrie v Nellagram)													
RINGO V BARRIE	11	3	4	3	4	0	3	3	87		-	1	
GUS T WINDS	11	3	2	4	0	0	1	2	56		-	1	
BILL	11	3	4	4	4	0	3	3	92		2	2	
Ped 16 (1974) (Sacha de St Landry x Riki v Tana)													
J'COBIE DU MONT BRUMEUX	12	3	2	2	4	0	2	2	66		3	2	
HAFFY V TASSO	12	2	2	0	3	0	2	1	44		-	-	
MARGUERITE DU MARECAGE	13	3	3	4	4	3	4	4	99	II	3	2	
Ped 17 (1972-1975) (Sacky des Matines x Miska vom Schlemmkreide) (3 litters)													
RAGS D'OASIS	14	3	3	4	4	1	3	3	89	III	3	2	
**SHAD D'OASIS	13	4	3	4	4	4	4	4	99	II	4	4	
DAX D'OASIS	12	2	2	4	3	2	2	3	72		3	3	
**GHOST'S PROUD LADY D'OASIS	14	3	2	3	4	3	2	2	77	III	3	2	
CHRISTIE D'OASIS	12	4	2	3	4	3	3	3	89	III	3	1	
RAKEL D'OASIS	12	3	4	2	2	1	4	4	82	III	3	2	
SACKY'S GERTA D'OASIS	7	1	2	1	0	1	1	2	30		3	3	

	A	N	S	W	P	T	A	C	TO	P	C	CO	T
Ped 18 (1972-1975) (Sacky des Matines x Birchwood Manor's Inga Igiture) (2 litters)													
BOUCHES DU RHONE	8	3	2	4	3	2	3	3	76	III	3	1	
PIERRE DE FRENEVUE	9	4	3	2	4	2	4	2	81	II	3	2	
HECTOR DAN OF ASHVIEW	7	1	1	0	4	1	1	3	39		2	1	
OPA NEBRASKA FREUND	7	1	1	0	4	0	1	2	35		3	2	
ASHVIEW'S JOSHUA	12	1	2	4	0	1	2	2	50		4	2	
ANGEL'S LULU OF ASHVIEW	6	2	2	0	4	0	2	4	54		-	-	
ANGEL'S LULU OF ASHVIEW	12	4	4	4	4	4	4	4	112	I	4	2	
++RUFFEL OF ASHVIEW	23	3	4	4	3	2	4	3	96		3	2	
Ped 19 (1971) (Bonzo of Copper Valley x Miska v Schlemmkreide)													
**KIRK D'OASIS	16	4	4	3	4	2	4	3	93	II	2	2	
Ped 20 (1972) (Oscar des Vieux Grisards x Quinche de St Landry)													
**ULRICH DE ST LANDRY	9	4	3	2	4	3	3	1	78	II	3	3	
**ULRICH DE ST LANDRY	9	4	4	1	3	3	3	2	77	III	3	3	
Ped 21 (1972) (Pyram x Poupee de Pailloux)													
**URAINE-LAURY DES CHEVECHES	12	4	3	4	3	4	4	4	96	II	3	2	
Ped 22 (1974) (Oscar des Vieux Grisards x Poupee de Pailloux)													
VOYOU DES CHEVECHES	11	1	1	2	0	0	1	1	27		2	1	
Ped 23 (1973) (Stop x Sibyl de St Landry)													
IAN DE ST LANDRY	13	2	2	1	4	0	2	3	57		1	1	
Ped 24 (1972) (Husky Tuffy x Staley Smokey Gal)													
HUCKY MIKE	14	3	2	2	3	2	2	2	61	III	2	1	
Ped 25 (1973) (Mitchells's Azor x Mishka der Jaeger)													
THE KID	10	4	3	3	3	4	3	3	92	II	2	2	
Ped 26 (1973) (Mitchell's Azor x Boulger Hollow Lisa)													
IOWA'S SALT & PEPPER	13	1	1	4	0	1	2	2	45		2	2	
Ped 27 (1973) (Boulger Hollow Dan x Effigie du Val de Tonnerre)													
AUGUST OF LAINELAINE	15	3	3	4	3	2	3	3	87	II	2	2	
ANDRE OF LAINELAINE	15	1	2	4	1	2	2	3	58		2	2	
Ped 28 (1973) (Grand-Duc du Val de Tonnerre x La Brande du Val de Tonnerre)													
**KORRIGANE DU VAL DE TONNERRE	14	3	3	2	3	3	3	4	81	III	2	1	
Ped 29 (1971) (Frosty's Image vom Tana x Sparkle Vantage Home)													
PETER OF SQUANNACOOK	15	4	3	3	3	4	3	3	86	II	3	3	
Ped 30 (1973) (Frostys Image vom Tana x Hardrock Montana Royal Belle)													
HARDROCK MONTANA SUZIE	19	2	3	0	0	2	2	3	43		3	2	

	A	N	S	W	P	T	A	C	TO	P	C	CO	T
Ped 31 (1972) (Mr Griffon of Vantage Home x Zip)													
HEIDI	14	2	2	3	1	3	2	3	58		1	2	
HEIDI	15	3	3	3	3	0	3	3	72		1	2	
BILL'S CHIP ALONG	15	3	3	4	3	1	4	3	82	III	2	2	
Ped 32 (1973) (Mr Griffon of Vantage Home x Maedchen Heidi)													
MISS MOLLY OF OAK RIDGE	16	2	2	4	0	3	2	2	60		3	3	
Ped 33 (1973) (Hardrock Montana Gus II x Juniper Heidi)													
HARDROCK MONTANA RIP	16	3	3	4	4	2	4	3	95	II	2	2	
Ped 34 (1974) (Hardrock Montana Rip x Koko)													
TAWZE ZEERAC	8	1	2	1	0	0	2	1	31		1	1	
LARUE ROGUE	8	2	3	4	4	0	2	3	77		2	2	
LARUE ROGUE	8	1	4	4	0	1	3	3	66		2	2	
LARUE ROGUE	12	4	4	4	3	2	4	4	104	II	3	1	
ORION	8	2	1	3	0	1	1	2	42		3	3	
ORION	8	3	3	4	4	1	3	4	91	III	2	3	
MEYEN'S MOUNTAIN MAN	12	3	2	4	3	0	2	2	72		4	4	*
Ped 35 (1973) (Hardrock Montana King x Schon Von Oberjager)													
HEIDI V OBERJAEGER	11	4	4	2	0	4	3	3	80		2	-	
FAITH V OBERJAEGER	11	3	2	1	2	2	2	3	59		3	2	
DUKE V OBERJAEGER	11	-	-	4	-	-	-	-			-	1	
FROSTY VON OBERJAEGER	11	-	-	0	-	-	-	-			-	1	
Ped 36 (1973) (Lee's Nobleman Flex x Rising's Glengarry Heidi)													
JOBIL'S WHISKERS MCGEE	11	3	3	1	4	2	3	3	76		3	3	
MOCHA	11	2	1	1	2	0	2	2	42		2	2	
Ped 37 (1973) (Hardrock Montana Rafe x Zuabekunst Tal Brigette)													
MARIO'S JUBILANT BELLE	10	1	0	3	0	3	1	2	35		1	2	
HARDROCK NEVADA RUBY	9	2	4	4	3	1	4	4	90		2	1	
++VICTOR TAL ZUABEKUNST	4 YR	3	4	4	3	2	3	3	92		3	3	
Ped 38 (1973) (Hardrock Montana Rafe x Zuabekunst Tal Dandy Hi-D)													
HEIDI	9	3	4	4	4	0	3	4	94		3	3	
Ped 39 (1973) (Carson's City Silver Dollar x Bisera Eskalduna)													
ERRAMUN DE ESKALDUNA	12	4	4	4	4	3	4	4	110	I	3	2	
Ped 40 (1972)(Barkers Bristled Rambo x Whip-A-Roo)													
BURNETTS BRILLO	8	1	2	4	0	0	2	3	50		2	2	
Ped 41 (1973) (Ohio du Sarrot x Pythie du Grand Dormen)													
URICK DU NEMTAYE	13	2	2	3	3	2	2	1	58		2	3	

	A	N	S	W	P	T	A	C	TO	P	C	CO	T
Ped 42 (1972) (Pyro du Grand Dormen x Quinoa du Grand Kiamika)													
THAIS DU CLAIR MATIN	10	3	3	3	1	1	3	4	70		-	-	
THAIS DU CLAIR MATIN	12	3	4	3	0	2	3	4	69		3	4	
Ped 43 (1972) (Nipper x Marinette)													
TWIGY	11	1	1	3	1	2	1	2	40		3	3	
TICK	11	0	1	3	0	0	1	1	25		4	4	
POLLY	15	2	3	4	4	0	3	4	76		3	2	
Ped 44 (1973) (Arko v.d. Culm x Bessie v Kastanienhain)													
++DOLF V GEESTEMOOR	7 YR	4	3	4	4	4	4	4	107		4	3	
Ped 45 was for a German dog not tested in the U.S. or Canada, n/a.													
Ped 46 (1974) (Boss v Wolfsberg x Snow Queue Blanc)													
LADY DAWN OF GLENAIRE	9	4	3	4	3	2	4	4	99	II	4	3	o
LADY DAWN OF GLENAIRE	13	4	4	4	2	3	4	4	102	III	4	3	o
SIEGREICH JAGER	13	3	3	4	3	1	3	3	85	III	4	3	o
GLENAIRE'S DAK	9	3	3	4	4	3	3	3	93	II	4	2	o
GLENAIRE'S DAK	13	3	3	2	4	3	3	2	81	III	4	2	o
GYPSY	9	3	2	4	4	2	4	4	92	III	3	1	o
GLENAIR'S PECOS GYPSY	13	4	4	4	4	3	4	4	110	I	4	2	o
GLENAIRE'S ZSAK	9	2	3	4	4	1	3	3	83		3	2	o
GLENAIRE'S ZSAK	13	2	2	4	2	2	2	1	64		2	2	o
ZBELBLU GUM	8	2	2	4	3	2	2	3	82		4	1	o
REGEN TROPFEN OF GLENAIRE	9	2	3	1	3	2	2	3	62		4	1	o
Ped 47 (1974) (Don v.d. Neuburg x Juniper Heather Hen)													
JUNIPERS ANNIE GETCHURGUN	6	2	3	4	4	2	3	3	85		4	2	o
JUNIPERS ANNIE GETCHURGUN	13	4	4	4	4	3	4	4	110	I	3	3	o
WYOMING'S LUCKY	13	4	4	4	4	2	4	4	108	II	2	3	o
WYOMING'S LUCKY	13	2	3	4	4	0	2	3	77		2	3	o
KELLY OF SUTTERS BUTTE	13	3	4	4	4	3	4	3	102	II	4	3	o
SUNNY BRANCH'S BEAU BROKK	5	2	2	4	2	1	2	3	66		4	4	o
SUNNY BRANCH'S BEAU BROKK	13	3	4	4	3	1	4	4	96	III	3	3	o
ALEC V RIPPOFF	13	3	3	4	4	2	2	3	87	III	2	2	o
Ped 48 (1974) (Mitchell's Bobo x Mishka Der Jaeger)													
RAPPAREE'S BRULE RIVER GRIFF	6	2	2	3	2	0	2	3	59		4	1	o
Ped 49 See Utility Field Test Results.													
Ped 50 (1975) (Taquin du Bois Follet x Huckle Hill Barbi)													
ANNIE OF HECHT	9	3	3	1	4	2	3	3	76		4	4	*
ANNIE OF HECHT	14	2	2	4	1	2	4	3	72		3	3	o
(Fine-boned, lacks substance, shallow in chest.)													
HUCKLEBERRY FINN	9	3	2	1	4	1	2	2	63		2	3	o

	A	N	S	W	P	T	A	C	TO	P	C	CO	T
Ped 51 (1975) (Frosty's Image vom Tana x Juniper Heather Hen)													
++RICO V MALHEUR	21	3	4	3	4	2	3	4	93		3	1	o
Ped 52 (1975) (Orion x Koko)													
GENERAL GRANT	7	3	2	1	4	0	2	2	61		3	2	o
Ped 53 (1975) (Ozark Rustic Rock x Tammy of Dutchland)													
MOSES DU LOGRES	10	3	4	2	3	1	3	3	80	III	3	4	o
Ped 54 (1975) (Hardrock Montana Rafe x Zuabekunst Tal Bichat)													
RAND K HIEDE	13	4	3	4	2	4	4	1	93	III	3	2	o
Ped 55 (1975) (Hardrock Montana Rafe x Dandy Patti)													
HARDROCK MONTANA GIBRALTER	8	1	2	4	0	1	2	3	52		2	2	o
Ped 56 (1975) (Hardrock Montana Rafe x Zuabekunst Tal Pee Wee)													
DIXIE ROSE LEIGH	12	2	1	2	0	2	2	2	43		3	1	o
Ped 57 (1975) (Sacha de St Landry x Sweet Molly Malone)													
ALICIA OF MISTY MEADOW	11	3	3	1	4	3	3	3	78		4	3	o
Ped 58 (1975-76) (Trottenfox Great Gusto x Trottenfox Jaunty Alouette)													
DOGWOOD ACRES FROSTED LADY	10	2	1	0	0	3	1	1	29		2	1	o
	(severe undershot)												
++BARON V BUDD	21	3	2	1	4	2	1	2	61		2	1	*
Ped 59 (1975) (Davy v Luda Jana x Mitchell's Daisy)													
++GRIFFA OF SHERMAN	27	3	2	3	4	1	3	4	81		4	2	o
+Ped 60 (1975-76) (Tonik du Bois Follet x Ulla de St Landry)													
LUCAS OF HUNTER'S CREEK	10	4	3	4	4	3	4	3	103	II	4	4	o
LUCAS OF HUNTER'S CREEK	13	4	3	4	4	3	3	3	99	II	4	4	o
LADY SUNWHEEL COCO OF HUNTER'S CREEK	10	4	3	4	2	2	3	3	89	III	4	3	o
LADY SUNWHEEL COCO OF HUNTER'S CREEK	14	3	3	4	2	2	3	3	83	III	-	-	o
**LUNA OF HUNTER'S CREEK	14	3	2	1	4	0	2	3	63		-	-	*
**LINUS OF HUNTER'S CREEK	15	2	3	4	4	0	2	2	75		4	4	o
LAURIE OF HUNTER'S CREEK	10	3	2	0	4	2	2	2	60		4	1	o
Ped 61 (1975) (Not field tested, evaluated for conformation, coat and temperament only.)													
Ped 62 (1975) (Tonik du Bois Follet x Kattie des Montagnes Vertes)													
FIRST FROST YETTA	6	4	4	3	4	4	4	3	105	I	3	4	o

	A	N	S	W	P	T	A	C	TO	P	C	CO	T
+Ped 63 (1975-76) (Tonik du Bois Follet x Bent Pine's Brigette)													
BENT PINE'S BRANDY	5	3	3	2	4	2	3	3	81	III	-	-	*
BENT PINE'S BLAZE	7	2	2	1	3	0	1	1	45		4	3	o
BENT PINE'S BLAZE	14	3	4	2	4	1	3	4	86	III	-	-	o
BENT PINE'S BIFF	13	3	3	4	4	2	3	3	91	II	3	3	o
BENT PINE'S BLITZ	12	4	4	4	2	3	4	4	102	III	3	3	o
BENT PINE'S BEN	12	2	3	4	2	3	3	4	81		-	-	o
BENT PINE'S BEN	14	4	4	4	3	4	4	4	108	I	-	-	o
BENT PINE'S BAYARD	14	2	1	1	1	1	2	1	38		-	-	o
Ped 65 (1975) (Max v Tannenwald x Edda v Kastanienhain)													
AJAX V TANNENWALD	10	4	3	4	4	3	4	3	103	II	4	2	o
+Ped 66 (1976-77) (Don v.d. Neuburg x Bent Pine's Alda)													
DUSTY HILLS DANDY	6	1	4	2	3	1	4	4	74		-	-	o
DUSTY HILLS DANDY	11	4	3	4	4	4	4	3	105	II	2	2	o
MR DYNOMITE OF DUSTY HILLS	11	3	3	4	4	1	2	2	85	III	3	3	o
MR DYNOMITE OF DUSTY HILLS	11	3	3	4	4	2	3	3	91	II	3	3	*
DIESEL OF DUSTY HILLS	11	4	4	4	4	3	4	3	108	I	3	3	o

In 1976 when the WPGCA began its own testing program, we revised our Natural Ability Test rules. We discontinued using an index for calculating total scores. The much lower TOTAL POINTS reflects this change--where now the highest total points a dog could receive in NAT is 28, rather than 112. Another change was to require a "2", rather than a "1" in Tracking, and a "2" in Affinity for Water, in order to qualify. This change meant that now a dog had to do better than before in order to qualify. See scoring systems in Part Two, for details.
Therefore some dogs from "D" OF DUSTY HILLS were judged under the old NAT rules, and others under the new rules.

++DUSTY HILLS DEMON	17	1	3	0	2	0	2	2	10		3	2	o
++DUSTY HILLS DELIGHT	17	3	4	3	4	2	3	2	21		3	2	o
++DUSTY HILLS DIAMOND	18	3	3	3	4	2	3	2	20		2	2	*

The following dogs tested in NAT in 1976 were still tested under NAVHDA rules in NAVHDA sponsored tests, sanctioned by WPGCA.

Ped 67 (1976) (Don v.d. Neuburg x Gary's Dandy Brandy)													
HAWKS S.O. BOOMER	13	2	3	2	4	1	3	2	72		3	3	o
ALLVIEW'S MANDY	12	2	4	4	0	2	3	2	72		-	-	o
Ped 68 (1976) (Zuabekunst Tal Victor x Dandy Patti)													
CALIBAN ZIYEAR	11	3	3	4	2	1	3	2	79	III	3	2	o
Ped 69 (1976) (Hardrock Montana Rafe x Slange Fluse Gina)													
++EMMIE	17	3	4	4	3	2	3	3	92		3	3	*
Ped 70 (1976) (Billy v Tana x Miss Penny Lane)													
BOBI MCGEE	11	3	3	4	3	4	3	3	91	II	-	-	o

	A	N	S	W	P	T	A	C	TO	P	C	CO	T
Ped 71 (1976) (Roco v Nellagram x Anni Hexenstein)													
GRIFF V NELLAGRAM	10	3	2	2	3	1	2	2	64	III	1	1	o
GRIFF V NELLAGRAM	16	2	3	2	0	3	3	2	59		-	-	o
++FROSTY TARA V LIEBENFIEL	39	3	3	4	4	2	3	3	91		3	3	o
Ped 72 (1976) (Quick du Grand Kiamika x Natalie Bumpo)													
++EMERSON'S RHODORA	7 YR	4	1	4	0	4	3	3	75		3	2	o
Ped 73 was not used.													
Ped 74 (1976) (Griff v Liebschein x Bonne's Windy)													
++BONNE'S SUCHEN	18	3	3	3	3	4	3	3	86		3	3	o
Ped 75 (1976) (Billy vom Tana x Clear Lakes Tiff)													
REINHART DE BONES	14	3	3	2	3	3	3	3	79	III	-	-	o
Ped 76 (1976) (Glenaire's Dak x Glenaire's Diana)													
PRINCESS JADE OF GLENAIR	15	2	2	4	4	1	2	2	72		2	2	o
Ped 77 (1976) (Dirk v Meierloh x Kortney v Meierloh)													
PUNKIN OF SMITH	8	3	4	4	4	2	3	4	98	II	2	3	*
Ped 78 (1976) (Ulrich ("Ulysse") de St Landry x Valy de L'Alverne)													
MOUSTIQUE DE LA POINTE	6	4	2	4	4	4	3	4	98	III	3	3	o
MOUSTIQUE DE LA POINTE	13	4	3	4	4	4	4	3	26	II	4	2	o
Ped 79 (1976) (Igor Du Haut Blainville x Du Pirdnec)													
ZEST DU MONTMAGNY	6	3	3	4	2	1	4	4	87	III	3	2	o

In the fall of 1976, along with having our first IHDT, we began having our own NAT, and UFT, and continued on into the spring of 1977. The following NAT test results are of those sponsored by the WPGCA from the fall of 1977 through 1994. NAVHDA NAT results of Griffons from 1977 through nearly all of 1994, follow immediately after the WPGCA NAT test results.

	AGE IN MONTHS (A)	NOSE & USE OF NOSE (N)	SEARCHING (S)	AFFINITY FOR WATER (W.	POINTING (P)	TRACKING BIRD (T)	ATTITUDE (A)	COOPERATION (C)	TOTAL POINTS (TP)	PRIZE CLASSIFICATION (PR)	CONFORMATION (C)	COAT (C)	TEMPERAMENT (T)
Ped 80 (1977) (Freidrich "O" First Frost x First Frost Unipac)													
ZIPARAK O FIRST FROST	6	1	1	0	0	0	1	1	4		2	2	*
Ped 81 (1977) (Bent Pine's Angus x Meri Belle Lee)													
ROYAL HUNTS LIBERTY	12	4	4	2	4	4	3	4	25	III	4	3	o
+Ped 82 (1977) (Boss v Wolfsberg x Birchwood Manor's Inga Igiture)(2 litters)													
SKEETER'S ASHVIEW V KRIEGHOFF	11	3	3	3	4	3	3	3	22	II	3	2	*
ASHVIEW'S AUGIE D	11	4	4	4	4	4	4	4	28	I	2	1	o
ASHVIEW'S K.C. GEISTESBLITZ	11	3	3	3	4	3	3	3	22	II	2	3	o
ASHVIEWS KATCHA DU FROLICH FREUND	11	3	2	4	2	2	2	2	17	III	3	2	o
JOHANNA V FUN FARM	11	2	1	4	4	2	2	2	17		3	1	*
ASHVIEW AMBERWOOD BUD	11	3	4	4	4	1	3	3	22		3	3	*
ASHVIEWS DUTCH	11	3	3	4	3	4	3	4	24	II	2	2	o
ALEXANDRA BELLE OF ASHVIEW	11	4	4	4	4	4	4	3	27	I	2	2	o
+Ped 83 (1977) (Tonik du Bois Follet x Bent Pine's Aberdeen)													
DUCKPOND DERAFIN	10	2	1	4	3	0	2	2	14		2	4	*
DUCKPOND DONNAMARIA	10	3	4	4	4	1	3	3	22		4	3	o
DUCKPOND DERNHELM	10	4	2	3	1	4	2	3	19		3	4	o
DUCKPOND DIRKAEL	9	4	4	1	3	4	3	3	22		2	3	o
DUCKPOND DE POCO	9	2	3	4	4	0	2	3	18		3	3	o
+Ped 84 (1978, 79, 80) (Lucas of Hunter's Creek x Victoria du Bois Follet)(3 litters)													
ASTRA DE LA COTE	16	4	4	3	4	3	4	4	25	II	3	2	o
ARRAS DE LA COTE	15	3	3	4	4	4	4	3	25	II	3	2	o
ALISE DE LA COTE	15	4	3	4	2	4	3	3	23	III	3	2	o
AVATAR DE LA COTE	16	4	3	1	4	3	3	3	21		3	3	o
ADI DE LA COTE	16	4	3	0	4	4	3	3	21		3	3	o

	A	N	S	W	P	T	A	C	TP	PR	C	C	T
+Ped 84 (1978, 79, 80)(CONTINUED)													
ADI DE LA COTE	16	2	4	1	4	1	2	2	16		-	-	o
AJAX DE LA COTE	15	2	3	2	2	1	2	2	14		2	2	*
		gunshy											
BRIDGETTE DE LA COTE	16	4	4	4	4	4	4	4	28	I	4	4	o
BRIGID DE LA COTE	16	3	3	4	4	3	3	4	24	II	4	3	o
BRISETTE DE LA COTE	16	3	2	4	4	4	3	3	23	III	4	3	o
BON CHASSEUR DE LA COTE	16	3	4	1	4	1	3	3	19		4	4	o
+BEAU JANGLES DE LA COTE	17	4	4	4	4	4	4	4	28		3	2	o
+BELLE LE ENFANT DE LA COTE	17	2	2	1	1	0	1	2	10		3	3	*
CZAR DE LA COTE	8	4	3	4	4	3	3	3	24	II	4	3	o
CACEI DE LA COTE	8	4	4h	4	4	4	4	4	28	I	3	2	o
CAROLINA DE LA COTE	8	4	4	4	4	4	4	4	28	I	4	3	o
CORDILEA DE LA COTE	8	2	3	4	3	1	2	2	17		4	4	o
+CORDILEA DE LA COTE	20	3	4	3	4	1	2	3	20		4	4	o
CHARLES DE LA COTE	9	4	3	1	4	4	3	3	22		2	2	o
+CHARLES DE LA COTE	22	3	2	2	4	1	2	2	16		2	2	o
Ped 85 (1978) (Bent Pine's Angus x First Frost Unipac)													
AMANTE DE COEUR FIRST FROST	11	3	2	4	4	3	2	3	21	III	2	2	o
FIRST FROST AXELSMAX	11	3	3	3	4	4	3	4	24	II	2	3	o
Ped 86 (1978) (Whiskey Du Pironec x Huckle Hill Angela)													
**HUCKLE HILL BOOMER	12	4	4	4	4	4	4	4	28	I	2	3	o
Ped 87 (1978) (Ulmer des Cheveches x Ultra du Ruisseau du Massacre)													
**NUMA DU RUISSEAU DU MASSACRE	14	3	4	3	4	3	3	3	23	II	3	2	o
**NUMA DU RUISSEAU DU MASSACRE	14	4	3	4	4	4	4	4	27	II	-	-	o
Ped 88 (1978) (Peter of Squannacook x Kattie des Montagnes Vertes)													
++BAYWATER PEPPER	21	4	4	0	4	4	3	3	22		2	3	*
Ped 89 (1978) (Billy vom Tana x Montana's Mistress Tara)													
MONTANA'S MISTRESS PRIDE	11	4	4	4	4	4	4	4	28	I	2	2	*
+Ped 90 (1978) (Dolf v Geeste-Moor x Angel's Lulu of Ashview)													
++ANNA CHEN ANGELA FIRS	22	2	3	0	1	2	2	2	12		2	2	*
Ped 91 (1979) (Boss v Wolfsberg x Duckpond de Poco)													
DIABLO'S TESON	10	3	3	2	3	2	2	2	17	III	3	2	*
DIABLO'S TOSCA	10	3	2	0	3	3	3	3	17		3	2	o
DIABLO'S TRUCO	10	2	3	2	4	1	2	2	16		3	3	o
DIABLO'S TIZON	10	1	1	0	4	1	1	1	9		3	2	*
+Ped 92 (1979) (Linus of Hunter's Creek x Baywater Pepper)													
MINDY OF ST MARY'S	9	4	3	4	4	4	4	4	27	II	4	4	o
GREEN BRIAR BUDDY	10	1	1	-	0	1	2	2	7		3	1	o

(This dog had just recovered from distemper and appeared to have lost all scenting ability.)

	A	N	S	W	P	T	A	C	TP	PR	C	C	T
Ped 93 (1979) (Dago v.d. Neuburg x Suzy des Zizaines)													
++MONIQUE LA BONHEUR	5 YR	3	2	1	4	2	2	2	16		4	3	*
Ped 94 (1979) (Rockymount Happy x Plumcreek's Siri)													
WELKIN'S GINGER GUNNER	13	2	3	1	0	1	2	2	11		3	2	o
Ped 95 (1979) (Sacky des Matines x Bent Pine's Anna)													
AMBERWOOD HAPPY TIMES	16	4	4	1	4	4	3	3	23		3	2	*
Ped 96 (1979) (Gilead Lake's Boomer x Gretchen von Keefer)													
GITANA OF ZAMORA	12	3	2	1	4	4	3	3	20		2	3	o
Ped 97 (1979) (Axel v Ulrichsquell x Freya v Bibertal)													
FURST V.D. NEUBURG	13	4	3	4	1	4	3	2	21		3	3	o
Ped 98 (1979) (Ruff vom Tana II x Ginger vom Vantage Home)													
BIRCHWOOD MANOR'S MISTY	11	3	2	4	4	4	3	2	22	III	2	2	o
Ped 99 (1979) (Scrapper x Dutches van Der)													
CASANDRA	14	3	2	1	4	4	3	3	20		3	1	o
+Ped 103 (1980) (Sunwheel Buzz x Glenaire's Pecos Gypsy)													
PECOS GYPSY WAGONMASTER	12	4	3	4	4	4	3	3	25	II	2	3	*
PECOS GYPSY TAMBOURINE	12	3	2	4	3	2	2	2	18	III	3	3	*
PECOS GYPSY CASTANET	13	3	2	3	3	4	3	3	21		3	4	*
++PECOS GYPSY BUZZIN' AROUND	24	4	4	0	4	3	3	3	21		2	2	*
Ped 104 (1980) (Sunny Branches Beau Brokk x Huckle Hill Calliope)													
ALDERS EDGE ATTATURK	7	2	2	4	4	2	2	2	18		2	2	*
Ped 105 (1980) (Alex v Ripoff x Kristine Igiture des Matines)													
ARTHUR LURCHER	13	3	2	1	4	4	3	2	19		2	2	*
Ped 106 (1980) (Gilead Lake's Dutch Treat x Gretchen von Keefer)													
TIMBERLAKE KIP	7	3	4	4	4	2	3	4	24	III	3	3	o
Ped 107 (1980) (Wyoming's Lucky x Arrowhead Montana Teaq)													
ALDA OF ARROWHEAD SHORES	10	3	2	3	2	2	2	3	17	III	2	2	*
BOSCOE OF ARROWHEAD SHORES	10	4	3	4	3	4	4	4	26	II	2	3	o
TYMBRE OF ARROWHEAD SHORES	10	3	2	4	3	2	3	2	19	III	2	2	o
Ped 108 (1980) (Barry v.d. Neuburg x Bent Pine's Aberdeen)													
DUCKPOND FREDA	9	3	3	4	4	2	3	3	22	III	3	2	o
++DUCKPOND FROELICH	22	3	4	4	3	3	4	3	24		3	3	o
Ped 109 (1980) (Smoke Creek Bisko x Duckpond de Poco)													
DIABLO RIDGE SECO	7	2	3	2	2	1	2	2	14		4	3	*
DIABLO RIDGE SENA	7	3	3	4	3	1	3	2	19		2	2	o
DIABLO RIDGE SERGENTO	7	3	2	3	2	3	3	3	19	III	2	2	o

	A	N	S	W	P	T	A	C	TP	PR	C	C	T
Ped 110 (1980) (First Frost Axel-Smax x Adrienne)													
MISS SEAWOOD'S VON TUBBS	10	3	3	2	2	1	2	2	15		3	3	*
+Ped 111 (1981) (Lucas of Hunter's Creek x Happy Hilda Hunter)													
DAUPHINE DE LA COTE	13	4	3	4	4	4	3	3	25	II	4	4	o
DESIREE DE LA COTE	14	4	4	1	4	4	3	3	23		4	3	o
DRYADES DE LA COTE	14	4	3	2	1	4	3	3	20		3	4	o
DELIVERANCE DE LA COTE	13	3	3	3	0	2	3	3	17		3	4	o
DUKE DE LA COTE	13	3	4	2	0	1	3	2	15		3	3	o
+Ped 112 (1981) (Bent Pine's Biff x Bridgette de la Cote)													
EMBER DE LA COTE	9	4	3	3	4	3	3	4	24	II	3	2	o
ENCORE DE LA COTE	10	3	3	4	4	3	3	2	22	II	3	3	o
Ped 113 (1981) (Taquin du Bois Follet x Zest Du Montmagny)													
ABBEY DU FEU FOLLET	15	4	4	4	4	4	4	4	28	I	2	2	o
AIMEE DU FEU FOLLET	15	3	3	4	4	2	3	3	22	III	2	2	o
Ped 114 (1981) (Gotz vom Bibertal x Diana vom Ramsberg)													
AMARA V FUCHSBERG	11	4	4	3	4	4	3	3	25	I	3	2	*
ABBA V FUCHSBERG	10	4	4	4	4	3	3	3	25	II	3	2	o
ARDA V FUCHSBERG	11	4	4	1	4	4	3	3	23		3	2	*
ANKA V FUCHSBERG	11	3	4	1	4	2	3	2	19		3	2	o
++ANKA V FUCHSBERG	23	3	4	1	3	1	3	2	17		3	2	o
Ped 115 (1981) (Diablo Ridge Truco x Heide von Debbie)													
SYSLO'S BROOK V HAMANDEL	11	4	3	2	4	4	3	3	23	III	2	2	*
Ped 116 (1981) (Bar-Mi's Elmo At Rocin x Little Mo's Ginger)													
QUAIL QUEEN BARMI'S GINGER	11	4	3	4	4	4	3	4	26	II	2	2	o
+Ped 120 (1982) (Bent Pine's Biff x Brisette de la Cote)													
ASTOR V MAYERHOF	12	4	4	4	4	4	4	4	28	I	3	2	o
AJAX V MAYERHOF	13	3	4	4	4	2	3	3	23	III	4	4	o
ANNETTE V MAYERHOF	12	3	4	2	3	3	3	3	21	III	4	3	o
ANJA V MAYERHOF	13	3	2	3	4	1	2	3	18		4	4	o
ANKA V MAYERHOF	13	2	3	4	2	2	3	3	19		4	2	*
+Ped 121 (1982-83) (Bon Chasseur de la cote x Alice B Toklias) (2 litters)													
MOLLY B TOKLIAS	12	4	4	4	4	3	4	4	27	II	2	2	o
EIGHT BALL TOKLIAS	12	4	4	4	4	2	4	3	25	III	4	4	o
CHASSIS V LANDKIRK	12	3	3	4	3	2	3	3	22	III	3	3	*
BELLA STELLA DE LA SIERRA	12	3	3	4	4	2	3	3	22	III	3	1	o
POINT'S PEWTER TIP	13	3	4	4	4	1	3	3	22		4	4	o
AMBROSE	12	2	2	3	4	3	2	3	19		3	4	o
BON CHASSEUR DE LA CHAMP	7	4	4	4	4	4	4	4	28	I	4	3	o
MAHASKA'S MERRY SUSAN	8	4	4	4	4	3	4	4	27	II	4	4	o
MISSEY OF OAK RIDGE	8	3	4	2	3	4	3	2	21	III	3	3	o
STREAKER	7	3	3	0	4	2	1	2	15		4	4	o

	A	N	S	W	P	T	A	C	TP	PR	C	C	T
+Ped 121 (1982-83)(Continued)													
WHITE SIDES B TOKLIAS	7	2	3	0	3	2	2	2	14		3	-	*
Ped 122 (1982) (Tracy A'Moustaches x Huckle Hill Angela)													
HUCKLE HILL ALFALFA	11	3	4	4	4	2	4	3	24	III	3	4	o
Ped 123 (1982) (Loys Du Tedelou x Larra des Etangs du Born)													
SINKI DU BOSQUET DU POUILLON	11	3	3	4	3	4	3	3	23	II	3	1	o
Ped 124 (1982) (Nec des Landes de Kerkhune x Nada des Hauts de Gouderlou)													
++ROSA DIT PUPPY	24	3	4	4	4	3	3	3	24		3	2	o
Ped 125 (1982) (Hardrock Montana Jeep x Bisquit McDuck)													
ROCKY MONTANA KNUT	10	3	3	4	3	3	3	3	22	II	4	2	o
Ped 126 (1982) (Ilk v Bibertal x Flatheads Jagdhund Gretel)													
SUZIE V HUNTER	7	3	3	4	4	2	3	3	22	II	4	3	o
Ped 127 (1982) (Ilk v Bibertal x Schatzie v Snake River)													
JOSIE V SNAKE RIVER	13	3	3	4	4	2	3	4	23	III	2	2	*
Ped 128 (1982) (Ilk v Bibertal x Heidi v Debbie)													
JAIK	10	3	2	0	4	1	2	2	14		2	2	*
Ped 129 (1982) (Bar-Mi's Elmo at Rocin x J V's Gilda Griffon)													
QUAIL QUEEN BARMI'S PEPPER	13	3	3	3	4	4	2	2	21	II	3	3	o
LA VITT	13	2	2	4	4	2	3	3	20		2	2	*
Ped 130 (1982) (Bar-Mi Alf v Hamandel x Roci's Nellie Belle)													
++ISLAND CREEK BRIGET V BAR MI	17	2	3	4	3	2	3	3	20		3	2	*
Ped 131 (1982) (Winterwind's Mr. Griffiths x Winterwind's Waldschloss Suzy)													
WINTERWIND'S FEATHER FINDER	9	2	3	4	4	1	3	3	20		3	2	*
+Ped 132 (1983) (Bent Pine's Biff x Desiree de la Cote)													
AMOS V JAGERSHORST	9	4	4	4	4	4	4	4	28	I	3	3	o
ACKER V JAGERSHORST	9	4	4	0	4	2	3	3	20		4	3	o
ADI V D JAGERSHORST	9	4	3	0	3	4	3	3	20		4	2	o
ASTRA V JAGERHORST	9	3	4	0	4	2	2	2	17		3	3	o
AMBER V JAGERSHORST	9	2	2	0	0	1	2	2	9		3	2	o
Ped 133 (1983) (Bent Pine's Blitz x First Frost Yetta)													
SMOKE CREEK MATTHEW	14	3	3	3	4	4	3	3	23	II	3	1	*
Ped 134 (1983) (Sunny Branch's Beau Brokk x Bent Pine's Aberdeen)													
DUCKPOND TRAVELIN' GERTY	11	4	3	4	3	3	3	3	23	II	3	3	o
Ped 135 (1983) (Arn V Hammandel x Diablo Ridge Salina)													
++SMOKEN JOE	16+	4	4	4	4	2	3	3	24		2	1	o

	A	N	S	W	P	T	A	C	TP	PR	C	C	T
Ped 136 (1983-84) (Ilk v Bibertal x Diablo Ridge Tizon) (2 litters)													
TIEGS	8	4	3	3	4	4	3	3	24	II	3	2	o
DIABLO RIDGE GRENA	8	1	1	0	2	0	1	1	6		2	1	o
DIABLO RIDGE SAM	8	1	1	0	0	0	1	1	4		-	-	*
++DIABLO RIDGE GITANO	20	4	4	3	4	4	4	4	26		3	2	o
Ped 137 (1983) (Ilk v Bibertal x Duckpond Frieda)													
OWYHEE CANYON ACE	9	3	3	0	4	2	2	2	16		3	2	o
Ped 138 (1983) (Furst v.d. Neuburg x Ruffs Rye Wiskey)													
HALBSPUR DER BACLEMBARTIG	12	3	2	4	3	3	3	3	21	III	3	3	o
Ped 139 (1983) (Magic Valley's Griff x Magic Valley's Beni)													
SWEET COCOA	11	4	3	3	4	4	3	3	24	II	4	3	o
+Ped 142 (1984) (Cacei de la Cote x Anka v Fuchsberg)													
FREEWINDS ALAMANCE	15	4	4	4	4	4	4	4	28	I	3	1	o
FREEWINDS ASHLEY	15	4	4	4	4	3	4	4	27	II	2	1	o
FREEWINDS ABBRECOT	14	3	4	4	4	2	4	4	25	III	3	2	o
FREEWINDS ANGEL	15	2	3	4	4	1	3	3	20		4	2	*
FREEWINDS ALBERTA	15	3	4	0	4	3	3	3	20		3	2	o
FREEWINDS ALDERBROOK	15	2	3	4	3	2	3	3	20		2	2	*
FREEWINDS ALTA	14	3	2	0	4	3	2	2	16		3	2	*
+Ped 143 (1984) (Boss v Wolfsberg x Ember de la Cote)													
ATHENA PUE DE ELUE	15	4	4	4	4	4	3	3	26	I	4	3	o
ACCOMACK'S PEU DE ELUE	15	3	4	4	4	2	4	4	25	III	3	2	o
ALPHONSO PUE DE ELUE	15	3	3	0	4	3	2	2	17		3	3	*
ALFE PEU DE ELUE	15	2	2	0	0	1	1	1	7		2	1	*
Ped 144 (1984) (Furst v.d. Neuburg x Flatheads Jagdhund Gretel) (2 litters)													
HAMPTON'S FUSILCHEIN DARNE	8	1	2	3	0	0	1	1	8		3	3	*
TIDEWATER ACCENT'S ASA	9	3	4	4	0	2	3	3	19		3	3	o
Ped 145 (1984) (Magic Valley Rafe x Magic Valley Heidi)													
GREEN MOUNTAINS GRIFF	10	3	3	4	4	4	3	3	24	II	3	2	o
Ped 146 (1984) (Huckle Hill Brandy x Duckpond Froelich)													
WEE WINNIE WINKLE	9	2	1	3	3	-	2	2	8		-	-	*
Ped 147 (1984) (Wild Mountain Luke x Wild Mountain Kate)													
WALTON'S MOUNTAIN ZACK	10	4	4	4	4	3	4	4	27	II	3	2	o
Ped 148 (1984) (Gilead Lake's Dutch Treat x Kekinga Katrina of Gilead)													
THORNAPPLES HILLS BIDABLE BEAU	12	1	3	0	0	0	1	2	7		3	1	*
+Ped 150 (1985) (Lucas of Hunter's Creek x Abba v Fuchsberg)													
BON MERCEDES VOM MAYERHOF	11	4	4	1	4	4	3	3	23		3	3	*
BON MERCEDES VOM MAYERHOF	11	4	4	3	4	4	3	3	25	I	3	3	*

	A	N	S	W	P	T	A	C	TP	PR	C	C	T
Ped 151 (1985) (Alders Edge Amundsen x Koele's Meggen)													
DILLON LORD OF AMUNDSON	13	3	3	3	4	4	3	3	23	II	3	3	*
ANDY	13	3	2	3	4	3	2	3	22	III	3	2	*
AMOS	13	2	3	4	4	2	3	3	21		4	2	o
Ped 152 (1982) (Fritz v Becker x Duchess v.d. Umpqua Park)													
BARON V HARRENHAUSEN	8	2	2	4	4	3	3	3	21		3	2	o
Ped 153 (1982, 1987) (Furst v.d. Neuburg x Bar-Mi's Gretchen) (2 litters)													
SHARON'S MT JOHN REGGIE	12	4	3	4	4	4	4	4	27	II	4	3	o
BECKER'S GRAY GRIFFON	11	3	4	4	4	2	3	3	23	III	3	2	o
Ped 154 (1985) (Brownie of Walden x Sugar Baby)													
**LA RUE'S JENNIFER	15	3	3	4	4	4	4	4	26	II	2	1	o
+Ped 156 (1986) (Amos Van Jagershorst x Point's Pewter Tip)													
TROY BOY'S SAGE	12	4	4	4	4	3	4	4	27	II	3	3	o
POINT'S AMANDA	12	3	4	4	4	3	4	4	26	II	2	-	o
ISSAC	12	3	4	4	4	3	3	3	24	II	3	3	*
MAX-A-MILLION	12	3	3	4	4	4	3	3	24	II	3	-	o
DACOTA'S PICC OF THE TIP	12	3	3	4	4	3	2	2	21	II	3	3	*
POINT'S SHOT	12	4	4	4	4	4	1	2	23	III	2	-	*
POINT'S ALGERNON BIFF	12	3	4	1	4	2	3	3	20		3	3	*

NOTE: In addition to four dogs in this litter (Ped 156) having temperament problems, five dogs had "open eyes", or were entropic. (The same genetic influence is present for open eyes, entropia, or ectropia, for turned in eyes.) And two dogs had short coats, no furnishings. This reflects the low evaluations in conformation, coat and temperament in this breeding.

Ped 157 (1986-1988) (Duckpond Eager Baron x Duckpond Ginger) (2 litters)													
MAJESTIC COCO WINFIELD	10	4	4	4	4	3	4	3	26	II	3	3	o
DUCKPOND SWEET SUZETTE	9	2	4	4	1	2	3	2	18		3	2	o
DUCKPOND DUSTIN	14	4	4	3	4	3	4	4	26	II	3	4	o
LADY GINGER OF MEDOMAK VALLEY	14	2	2	1	4	2	2	2	15		2	4	*
Ped 158 (1986) (Ranger des Chaumes de L'Aure D'or x Urfe de la Valle Bertier)													
AXEL DE ST LANDRY	8	3	4	4	4	3	3	4	25	II	3	2	o
Ped 159++++ (1986) (Basto v.d. Hornerhoeve x Gipsy van de Maten)													
GRIFF	10	2	2	1	0	2	1	1	9		3	2	*
Ped 160++++ (1986) (Fellow van de Maten x Erna)													
FON	10	1	1	1	1	0	1	1	6		3	2	*

++++ In all fairness to GRIFF and FON, both from Holland, they were never exposed properly, and what "exposure" they had was mostly negative. These test results are really inconclusive.

Ped 161 (1986) (Pastis de la Reote x Posee de la Reote)													
++TANIA DES BORDS DE LA TAUTE	4 YRS	4	2	2	3	1	2	3	17		3	3	o

	A	N	S	W	P	T	A	C	TP	PR	C	C	T
+Ped 165 (1987) (Erik od Jezarek(CF) x Mahaska's Merry Susan)													
++ALF OF IAMONIA	5	4	4	4	4	4	4	4	28		-	-	o
ALF OF IAMONIA	13	4	4	4	4	4	4	4	28	I	3	2	o
++AMADEUS OF IAMONIA	5	4	4	4	4	4	4	4	28		-	-	o
AMADEUS OF IAMONIA	13	4	4	4	0	4	3	2	21		2	2	o
AUBIE OF IAMONIA	13	4	4	4	4	4	4	3	27	I	3	4	o
AMBER OF IAMONIA	13	4	4	4	3	4	4	4	27	I	3	3	o
AVIANA KATRINA OF IAMONIA	13	4	4	4	2	4	4	3	25	III	4	4	o
AVAJ OF IAMONIA	13	4	4	4	4	2	4	3	24	III	4	4	o
AU NATURAL OFIAMONIA	13	4	4	2	4	4	3	3	24	III	4	4	o
IAMONIA'S AMANDA DU MARECAGE	13	3	2	4	1	4	3	2	19		2	2	o
+Ped 166 (1987) (Erik od Jezarek(CF) x Freewinds Alamance)													
AKRISTIFF OF HUFFMAN MILL	9	4	4	4	4	4	4	4	28	I	3	2	o
AUTUMN OF HUFFMAN MILL	9	4	4	4	4	4	4	4	28	I	3	2	o
ANYA OF HUFFMAN MILL	9	4	4	1	4	4	3	3	23		3	2	o
AMADEUS OF HUFFMAN MILL	9	4	4	1	4	4	3	3	23		3	2	o
AMADEUS OF HUFFMAN MILL	15	3	3	4	4	4	3	3	24	II	2	1	o
ANADRAMOUS RIVER ROGUE OF HUFFMAN MILL	9	4	4	0	4	4	3	3	22		3	2	o
AMBRA OF HUFFMAN MILL	10	4	4	0	4	3	3	3	21		3	1	o
ALIF OF HUFFMAN MILL	10	3	3	1	4	4	3	3	20		2	2	o
HUFFMAN MILL'S ALAMURPHIE	9	3	3	0	4	4	3	3	21		2	1	o
Ped 167 (1987-88) (Jaik x Theresa Mantua v Hasenhof) (2 litters)													
RHINEBERG'S HEIDE	14	2	1	4	2	3	2	2	16		2	3	o
USCHI	14	3	3	4	4	4	3	3	24	II	3	2	o
Ped 168 (1987) (Excaliber Jebadiah x Vancouver Anastasia)													
SIR DONZIE MONOHULL	12	4	4	4	4	4	4	4	28	I	3	3	o
THERESA ALEXANDER	12	1	3	0	0	1	1	1	9		4	2	o
Ped 169 (1987) (Adolph v Duffer x Cora v Glantz)													
CHELSE GENNER SIMONS	8	2	3	2	4	1	2	3	17		3	3	o
Ped 170 (1987) (Finnigan v Ripoff x Peppermint Patty v Carter)													
PATCHES VON RIPOFF	10	4	4	4	1	4	4	3	24		4	4	*
		gun sensitive											
Ped 171 (1987) (Alders Edge Blaze x Quail Queen Barmi's Pepper)													
BLITZ LADY OF VALHALLA	9	4	4	2	4	2	3	4	23	III	3	1	o
Ped 172 (Dog tested in UFT only, see UFT section.)													
Ped 173 (1988) (Magic Valley's Griff x Magic Valleys Kimberly)													
DAKOTA MOLLY D'ARGENT	8	3	3	3	4	4	3	3	23	II	3	4	*
DAKOTA KAMAREE D'ARGENT	8	2	2	0	4	1	1	2	12			**atypical**	o

	A	N	S	W	P	T	A	C	TP	PR	C	C	T
+Ped 174 (1988) (Cagan Z Dracina x Hela Z Dobrovska) (CF)													
BREEZE OF THE CASCADES	9	4	4	4	4	4	4	4	28	I	4	4	o
BLISS OF THE CASCADES	10	4	4	4	4	4	4	4	28	I	4	3	o
BOSS OF THE CASCADES	9	3	3	4	3	3	3	3	22	II	4	4	o
BOSS OF THE CASCADES	9	4	4	4	1	4	4	3	24		4	4	o
BRIDGET OF THE CASCADES	9	4	3	2	4	4	3	3	23	III	4	4	o
BLITZEN OF THE CASCADES	10	3	4	4	4	1	4	4	24		4	4	o
BESSIE OF THE CASCADES	9	4	4	1	4	4	3	3	23		4	3	o
BREEZY OF THE CASCADES	10	3	3	1	4	3	3	3	20		4	4	o
BLADE OF THE CASCADES	10	2	3	4	2	1	3	3	18		4	4	o
Ped 175 & 176 (Dogs tested in UFT only.)													
Ped 177 (1988) (Loys du Tedelou x Alders Edge Dancer)													
ALDERS EDGE GUSTO	7	3	3	4	4	1	3	3	21		3	2	o
ALDERS EDGE GUSTO	13	4	3	4	4	4	3	3	25	II	3	1	o
Ped 178 (1988) (Baron v Herrenhausen x Greta v Herrenhausen) (2 litters)													
AUTUMN V HERRENHAUSEN	14	4	4	4	4	4	4	4	28	I	3	2	o
ANGEL V HERRENHAUSEN	14	3	3	3	4	4	3	4	24	II	3	2	*
BONNIE V HERRENHAUSEN	6	4	4	2	4	4	3	3	24	III	-	-	o
BELLE V HERRENHAUSEN	11	4	4	4	4	3	3	3	25	II	3	1	o
Ped 179 (1988, 89, 90) (Ingo v Kastanienhain x Glac[i]er Cool Deecee) (3 litters)													
KALISPELL INGO VOM GLACIER	13	3	3	4	4	4	3	4	25	II	4	4	o
TINA OF PERKINS CORNER	12	4	4	2	0	4	3	2	19		3	4	o
LOGAN	11	4	3	1	4	3	2	2	19		3	3	o
DRYFUS	11	3	4	1	4	1	2	1	16		3	3	*
+FIRESIDES'S ANIMATION	17	3	4	4	4	2	3	4	24		4	2	o
INGO'S IMAGE VOM GLACIER	16	4	4	4	4	4	4	4	28	I	4	4	o
GOOSE CREEKS REWARD	11	3	3	4	4	2	2	3	21	III	3	4	*
(gun sensitive)													
Ped 180 (1988, 1990) (Bevs Beau Davis Boy x Davids Tiffney Girl Davis) (2 litters)													
SILLE GRAVEL GERTTI	16	2	2	1	0	2	2	2	11		3	4	*
GRETCHEN FELICIA TERA KYA	15	4	4	4	4	4	4	4	28	I	3	1	o
Ped 181 and 182 (Dogs tested in IHDT or UFT.)													
Ped 183 (1989) (Baron v Herrenhausen x Rhineberg's Heidi)													
++WAYLON	5	2	2	1	4	2	2	3	16		2	2	o
Ped 184 (1989) (Malaki von Glantz x Princess Cities Grete)													
GENERAL GRANT	6	2	1	4	4	1	2	2	16		-	-	*
Ped 185 (1989) (Royal Hunts Reward x Grays Duckpond Snowball)													
MEDOMAK VALLEY VANILA	7	4	2	0	4	4	2	2	18		2	2	o

	A	N	S	W	P	T	A	C	TP	PR	C	C	T
+Ped 186 (1990) (Boss of the Cascades(CF) x Autumn of Hoffman Mill)													
ACOOTER'S NIECE OF AUGER FALLS	10	4	4	4	4	4	4	4	28	I	3	3	o
AUGUST OF AUGER FALLS	10	4	4	4	4	4	4	4	28	I	3	4	o
ALPHA OF AUGER FALLS	10	4	3	4	4	4	4	3	26	II	4	3	o
ALEXANDRIA OF AUGER FALLS	10	4	4	4	4	3	3	3	25	II	3	2	o
AUSTIN OF AUGER FALLS	10	2	2	3	1	2	2	2	14		3	3	*
AMIABLE FRIEND OF AUGER FALLS	10	2	2	0	1	0	1	1	7		3	3	*
ASTERICK OF AUGER FALLS	15	4	2	2	4	4	3	1	20		4	2	o
+Ped 187 (1990, 92) (Blue Mountain Brew x Avaj of Iamonia) (2 litters)													
AMY OF DUTCHMAN'S HOLLOW	11	4	4	4	4	4	4	4	28	I	4	4	o
ARROW OF DUTCHMAN'S HOLLOW	11	4	4	4	4	4	4	4	28	I	4	4	o
AVIAN OF DUTCHMAN'S HOLLOW	11	4	4	4	4	4	4	4	28	I	3	4	o
ASPEN OF DUTCHMANS'S HOLLOW	11	4	4	4	4	3	4	4	26	II	4	4	o
ABBOT OF DUTCHMAN'S HOLLOW	11	3	3	4	4	3	3	3	23	II	4	4	o
ASAHEL OF DUTCHMAN'S HOLLOW	11	4	3	3	4	4	2	3	23	II	3	2	o
ABSAROKA OF DUTCHMAN'S HOLLOW	10	3	4	4	4	2	4	3	24	II	4	4	o
CASSIE OF DUTCHMAN'S HOLLOW	11	4	4	4	4	4	4	4	28	I	4	4	o
CERA OF DUTCHMAN'S HOLLOW	11	4	4	4	4	4	4	4	28	I	4	4	o
CHAMPAGNE BLAZE OF DUTCHMAN'S HOLLOW	11	4	4	4	4	4	4	4	28	I	3	3	o
CALLAJ OF DUTCHMAN'S HOLLOW	11	4	4	4	4	4	4	4	28	I	3	3	o
CASIMIR LORING OF DUTCHMAN'S HOLLOW	11	4	4	3	4	4	4	4	27	I	3	3	o
CURSE OF DUTCHMAN'S HOLLOW	11	4	4	4	4	4	4	3	27	I	3	4	o
CHEWBACCA OF DUTCHMAN'S HOLLOW	11	4	3	4	4	3	3	3	24	II	3	3	o
CODY OF DUTCHMAN'S HOLLOW	11	4	4	1	4	4	3	3	23		3	4	o
+Ped 188 (1990) (Erik od Jezarek(CF) x Patches v Rippoff)													
AYLA OF WHITE WATER	12	4	4	4	4	4	4	4	28	I	4	3	*
AMIE OF WHITE WATER	12	4	4	4	4	4	4	4	28	I	3	3	o
ARO OF WHITE WATER	12	4	4	4	4	3	3	3	25	II	3	1	o
AXEL OF WHITE WATER	12	4	4	4	1	4	3	3	23		3	2	o
ANKA OF WHITE WATER	12	3	2	0	0	4	2	2	13		4	3	*
Ped 189 (1990) (Ingo v Kastanienhain x Flatheads Georgia)													
SYSLOS SLYCK MONTANA SURPRYZ	8	3	3	4	4	2	2	3	21	III	3	4	o
Ped 190 (1990) (Duckpond Dustin x Duckpond Joyeux)													
DUCKPOND GABRIELLE LARRABÈE	10	4	4	4	4	4	4	4	28	I	4	3	o
Ped 191 (1990) (Sampson v Herrenhausen x Greta v Herrenhausen)													
DUCHESS V HERRENHAUSEN	9	4	4	2	4	3	3	3	23	III	3	3	o
DIANA V HERRENHAUSEN	14	4	3	4	4	3	2	3	23	III	3	3	o

	A	N	S	W	P	T	A	C	TP	PR	C	C	T
Ped 192 (1990) (Baron v Herrenhausen x Rooster's Copper Penny)													
BARON FRATZKES CHUKAR MAGIC	8	3	2	4	4	4	3	3	23	III	2	2	o
BARON FRATZKES CHUKAR MAGIC	15	3	3	4	4	4	3	3	25	II	3	3	o
WEONA GRIFFCAMPBELL	8	4	3	4	4	4	4	3	26	II	3	1	o
WING MASTERS TURK	8	3	2	4	4	3	2	3	21	III	3	4	o
Ped 193 (1990) (Baron v Herrenhausen x Miss Amanda v Bleck)													
GINA V HERRENHAUSEN	9	3	2	4	3	4	3	3	22	III	4	4	o
Ped 194 (1990) (Sharon's Mt John Reggie x Point's Pewter Tip)													
ASPEN POINT'S BARREL	8	4	4	4	4	4	4	4	28	I	4	4	o
Ped 195 (1990) (Buckshot Buckaroo v Braun x Countess Maddie Larouge)													
COUNTESS ELSA VON BRAUN	10	3	3	4	4	1	3	3	21		3	3	o
Ped 196 (Dog tested in IHDT.)													
Ped 197 (1990) (Duckpond Dustin x Medomak Valley's Vanilla)													
MEDOMAK VALLEY'S WIESER	6	4	4	2	4	4	3	3	24		4	4	o
Ped 198 (1990) (Viking Di San Germano x Astrid de St Landry)													
ELSY DE ST LANDRY	15	4	4	4	4	4	4	4	28	I	4	2	o
+Ped 199 (1990, 91, 92) (Erik od Jezarek x Hela Z Dobrovaka) (CF) (3 litters, total 6 pups)													
ARIKO VOM ERIK	12	4	4	4	4	4	4	4	28	I	4	2	o
BECI VOM ERIK	12	4	4	4	4	4	4	4	28	I	4	4	o
BLUMELEIN V ERIK	12	4	4	3	4	4	4	4	27	I	4	2	o
BEAU VOM ERIK	12	4	4	2	4	4	3	4	25	III	2	3	o
CHANNEL V. ERIK	10	4	4	4	4	4	4	4	28	I	4	2	o
COMMANDER V ERIK	11	4	3	3	4	4	3	3	24		4	1	*
	gun sensitive												
+Ped 201 (1991) (Boss of the Cascades(CF) x Avaj of Iamonia)													
BUCKINGHAM OF DUTCHMANS HOLLOW	11	4	4	4	4	4	4	4	28	I	4	3	o
BIRKLEY BELL OF DUTCHMAN'S HOLLOW	11	4	4	4	4	4	4	4	28	I	4	4	o
BRITTANY OF DUTCHMAN'S HOLLOW	11	4	4	4	4	4	4	4	28	I	4	4	o
BRANDY OF DUTCHMAN'S HOLLOW	11	4	4	4	4	4	4	4	28	I	4	4	o
RU BEA OF DUTCHMAN'S HOLLOW	11	4	4	4	4	4	4	4	28	I	2	3	o
BROOK OF DUTCHMAN'S HOLLOW	11	4	4	3	4	4	4	3	26	I	4	4	o
BUCKEYE OF DUTCHMAN'S HOLLOW	11	3	4	4	3	2	3	3	22	III	3	3	*
BABETTE OF DUTCHMAN'S HOLLOW	11	3	4	4	4	2	2	2	21	III	3	3	*
Ped 202 (1991) (Von Baxter Jakes Gunner x Von Bailey's Axel Gunner)													
JAKE WILHELM VON BRAUN	14	4	4	4	4	4	4	4	28	I	3	3	o

	A	N	S	W	P	T	A	C	TP	PR	C	C	T
Ped 203 (1991) (Dino De L'Etang x Alders Edge Feu Follet)													
AMBERGRIS DU FEU FOLLET	11	4	4	4	4	4	4	4	28	I	2	4	o
Ped 204 (1991) (Sampson v Herrenhausen x Kalispell Ingo v Glacier)													
FRAULEIN V HERRENHAUSEN	14	4	3	4	4	3	3	3	24		3	4	*
FINA V HERRENHAUSEN	14	4	4	4	4	4	4	4	28	I	4	2	o
Ped 205 (1991) (Duke v Herrenhausen x Sophia v Herrenhausen)													
EDEL TRAUT VON HERRENHAUSEN	16	4	4	4	4	4	4	4	28	I	4	2	o
Ped 206 (1991) (Arnie von Beorn x Josephine Queen McDuck)													
SADIE SAGEBRUSH	15	4	4	4	4	3	4	3	26	II	2	1	o
Ped 207 (1991) (Ingo v Kastanienhain x Elk Park Boots)													
BROKEN BOW BABE	12	4	3	4	4	3	3	3	24	II	3	3	o
+Ped 208 (1991) (Erik OD Jezerak(CF) x Axa OD Pastejriko) (CF)													
AUGUST DE LOS ALTOS	12	4	4	4	4	4	4	4	28	I	4	3	o
ANJA DE LOS ALTOS	12	3	4	1	2	2	3	3	17		3	3	*
ANDE DE LOS ALTOS	12	3	3	0	0	2	2	2	12		4	3	*
Ped 209, 210 (Dogs tested in IHDT or UFT.)													
Ped 211 (1991) (Duckpond Dustin x Duckpond Ginger)													
BO	15	2	2	4	4	2	2	3	19		2	3	*
Ped 212 (1991-92) (Andy of Perkins Corner x Cindy of Perkins Corner) (2 litters)													
BREO OF PERKINS CORNER	7	3	4	4	4	3	4	4	26	II	4	4	o
BARNEY OF PERKINS CORNER	13	4	4	4	4	3	4	3	26	II	3	3	o
Ped 213 (1991-92) (Alders Edge Ingos Cool Alpha x Alders Edge Griselda)													
ALDERS EDGE HAGAR	7	4	3	4	4	4	4	3	26	II	3	4	o
ALDERS EDGE HO'OKOA	11	3	4	2	4	1	2	2	18		-	3	o
Ped 214 (1991) (Fritz v Herrenhausen x Roxys Foxs Rooster)													
ROOSTER'S GOOD TIME TALLY HO	12	4	4	4	4	4	4	4	28	I	4	2	o
Ped 215, 216, 217 (Dogs tested in IHDT or UFT.)													
+Ped 218 (1992) (Arrow of Dutchman's Hollow x Autumn of Hoffman Mill)													
BRENNA OF AUGER FALLS	10	4	4	4	4	4	4	4	28	I	4	3	o
BRANDISH OF AUGER FALLS	10	4	4	4	4	4	4	4	28	I	3	3	o
BENJAMIN OF AUGER FALLS	10	4	4	4	3	4	4	4	27	I	3	4	o
BOBETT'S MEGGAN OF AUGER FALLS	10	4	4	4	4	4	3	4	27	I	2	4	o
BRIE OF AUGER FALLS	10	4	4	2	4	4	3	3	24	III	4	4	o
BUCK OF AUGER FALLS	10	4	4	0	4	4	3	3	26		4	3	o
BRANDI OF AUGER FALLS	10	4	4	4	0	4	3	3	22		3	2	o
BLAZIN WHISKEY OF AUGER FALLS	10	2	3	4	4	1	2	2	18		4	3	o
+BIENE OF AUGER FALLS	16+	4	4	3	3	4	3	3	24		3	3	o

	A	N	S	W	P	T	A	C	TP	PR	C	C	T
+Ped 219 (1992) (Erik OD Jezarek(CF) x Amy of Dutchman's Hollow)													
AMOS OF OCEAN HOUSE	9	4	4	4	4	4	4	4	28	I	3	3	o
ANNIE OF OCEAN HOUSE	9	4	3	2	4	4	3	4	24	III	3	3	o
AJAX OF OCEAN HOUSE	15	4	4	4	4	4	4	4	28	I	3	4	o
ALEX OF OCEAN HOUSE	15	4	4	4	4	4	4	4	28	I	3	3	o
AUGUSTUS OF OCEAN HOUSE	15	3	4	4	4	2	3	3	23	III	3	2	o
ANGUS OF OCEAN HOUSE	15	2	3	2	4	2	2	3	18		3	1	*
Ped 220 (1992) (Duckpond Dustin x Duckpond Kossuth)													
DUCKPOND MATINICUS	12	4	4	4	2	4	4	3	25	III	4	4	o
Ped 221 (1992) (Grif von Pointer x Tucker's Spooky Hollow)													
WAYFARER'S NEWLINE	9	3	3	4	4	3	2	3	22	II	4	2	o
+Ped 222 (1992) (Dan Cerniky x Axa od Pastejriko) (CF)													
BRYANNA DE LOS ALTOS	10	4	4	1	4	4	3	3	23		4	3	o
B'LOU DE LOS ALTOS	10	4	4	1	4	3	2	2	20		3	3	*
BARTON DE LOS ALTOS	10	4	4	1	4	2	2	2	19		4	4	o
BARRIUS DE LOS ALTOS	10	3	3	1	4	1	2	2	16		4	4	o
BRIANNA DE LOS ALTOS	15	4	4	4	4	4	4	4	28	I	4	3	o
BURGHLEY DE LOS ALTOS	15	4	4	4	4	4	4	4	28	I	4	3	o
Ped 223 (1991-92) (Korky v Herrenhausen x Patches von Ripoff)													
++EMMYLOU OF WHITE WATER	5	4	4	3	2	4	3	3	23		4	4	o
++EMMYLOU OF WHITE WATER	17	4	3	4	4	4	4	4	27		3	3	o
++LADY OF WHITE WATER	17	3	3	4	4	3	3	3	23		-	-	*
++SAM OF WHITE WATER	17	2	2	3	1	4	2	2	16		3	3	*
+Ped 224 (1992) (Dan Cerniky x Borka z Kolodev) (CF)													
ARCHIBALD OF DRUMMER'S RIDGE	8	4	4	4	4	4	4	4	28	I	4	4	o
ALLIE OF DRUMMER'S RIDGE	15	4	4	4	4	4	4	4	28	I	4	4	o
ADI OF DRUMMER'S RIDGE	8	4	4	1	4	4	3	3	23		4	4	o
ANGEL'S ALIBE OF DRUMMER'S RIDGE	8	4	2	1	4	4	2	2	19		3	2	*
ANNA KATE OF DRUMMER'S RIDGE	8	0	0	1	1	0	0	1	3		4	4	*
ARCHDUKE OF DRUMMER'S RIDGE	8	3	3	1	3	1	2	2	15		3	3	o
Ped 225 (Dogs tested in IHDT or UFT.)													
+Ped 226 (1993) (Dan Cerniky(CF) x Amy of Dutchman's Hollow)													
BOSUN OF OCEAN HOUSE	9	4	4	4	4	4	4	4	28	I	4	4	o
BAILEY OF OCEAN HOUSE	14	4	4	4	4	4	4	4	28	I	4	4	o
BUDDY OF OCEAN HOUSE	13	4	4	4	4	4	4	4	28	I	3	4	o
BEACON OF OCEAN HOUSE	13	4	4	4	4	4	4	4	28	I	3	3	o
BELL OF OCEAN HOUSE	14	4	4	4	3	4	4	4	27	I	3	4	o
BOLINE OF OCEAN HOUSE	13	4	4	2	4	4	3	3	24	III	4	3	o
BARNACLE OF OCEAN HOUSE	9	4	4	1	4	4	3	3	23		3	2	o

	A	N	S	W	P	T	A	C	TP	PR	C	C	T
+Ped 227 (1993) (Dan Cerniky(CF) x Autumn of Huffman Mill)													
CHASE OF AUGER FALLS	11	4	4	4	4	4	4	4	28	I	2	3	o
COUNTESS OF AUGER FALLS	11	4	4	4	4	4	4	4	28	I	3	3	o
CLEO OF AUGER FALLS	11	4	4	3	4	3	3	3	24	II	3	3	o
COVEY OF AUGER FALLS	11	4	4	1	4	4	3	3	23		4	2	*
CHARLEY OF AUGER FALLS	11	4	4	1	0	3	3	2	17		4	3	o
CALLY OF AUGER FALLS	11	3	4	0	4	2	2	2	17		-	-	*
CZECHS OF AUGER FALLS	11	3	3	0	4	2	2	2	16		3	2	*
Ped 228 (1993) (Aspen Point's Barrel x Cindy of Perkins Corner)													
CHINA DOLL OF PERKINS CORNER	12	4	4	4	4	4	4	4	28	I	3	3	o
CRISSI OF PERKINS CORNER	12	4	3	4	4	4	3	3	25	II	3	3	o
COJACK OF PERKINS CORNER	12	3	4	4	4	2	3	3	23	III	3	3	o
CIRA OF PERKINS CORNER	12	2	2	4	4	2	3	3	20		3	3	o
CADILLAC STYLE OF PERKINS CORNER	12	2	3	4	4	1	2	3	19		3	3	o
Ped 229 (1993) (Welch's Sir Timothy x Mac's Maggie)													
WELCH'S LADY CASSIDY	11	4	4	4	4	4	4	4	28	I	3	3	o
SHINGOBEE LAKE'S ELEGANCE	11	4	4	4	4	3	4	3	26	II	3	3	o
SHINGOBEE LAKE'S ABIGAIL	11	4	4	4	1	3	3	2	21		3	3	o
Ped 230 (1993) (Welch's Sir Timothy x Beaver Dams Massie May)													
WELCH'S SIR BENJY	15	4	4	4	4	4	4	4	28	I	3	3	o
Ped 231 (1993) (Cesear v Erlenbruch x Aspen Point's Buttstock)													
UPLAND'S TANGLES	15	3	3	4	4	2	3	3	22	III	2	1	*
Ped 232 (1993) (Grif von Pointer x Camas Hot Springs Suzie)													
NORTH LIGHT'S KACHINA DOLL	12	3	4	4	4	2	3	3	23	III	3	3	o
Ped 233 (1993) (Good Time Furst Griff x Flaheads Magic Dolly)													
TRINA	14	4	4	3	2	4	3	2	22	III	3	4	o
Ped 234 (1993) (D. Frog Pond McNute x Medomak Valley Katarina)													
MEADOWWOOD DRAKE	12	4	3	1	4	2	2	2	18		4	4	*
Ped 235 (1993) (Falcon v Herrenhausen x Gina v Herrenhausen)													
PANDORA V HERRENHAUSEN	15	3	3	4	4	3	3	3	23	II	4	4	*
Ped 236 (1993) (Friedrich v Trendelburg x Fraulein v Herrenhausen)													
WAYFARER'S BRISTLE FACE	13	4	4	4	4	4	4	4	28	I	3	3	o
WAYFARER'S BRETA	13	4	4	4	4	4	4	4	28	I	3	3	o
Ped 237 (1993) (Echo de St Landry x Diana v Herrenhausen)													
FIRESIDES'S ECHO OF ECOLOGY	6	4	3	3	4	4	3	3	24	II	2	2	o

Ped 238 (Dogs tested in IHDT or UFT.)

	A	N	S	W	P	T	A	C	TP	PR	C	C	T
+Ped 239 (1994) (Dan Cerniky(CF) x Brittany of Dutchman's Hollow)													
PRAIRIE STORM'S ABBY	10	4	4	4	4	4	4	4	28	I	4	4	o
PRAIRIE STORM'S ARLEY	10	4	4	4	4	4	4	4	28	I	4	4	o
PRAIRIE STORM'S AMOS	10	4	4	4	4	4	4	4	28	I	4	3	o
PRAIRIE STORM'S AGALE	10	4	4	2	4	4	4	3	25	III	4	3	o
PRAIRIE STORM'S AGALE	15	4	4	4	4	4	4	4	28	I	4	3	o
PRAIRIE STORM'S ALDER	15	4	4	4	4	4	4	4	28	I	4	4	o
PRAIRIE STORM'S AGGOES QUAKEN	9	4	4	2	4	4	4	3	25	III	4	4	o
PRAIRIE STORM'S ASTARR	10	3	3	0	4	2	2	2	16		4	3	*
+Ped 240 (1994) (Dan Cerniky x Axa od Pastejriko) (CF)													
CUCARACHA BONITA DE LOS ALTOS	13	4	4	4	4	4	4	4	28	I	4	4	o
CHUKAR DE LOS ALTOS	13	4	4	3	4	4	3	2	24	II	-	-	*
CHANCE DE LOS ALTOS	10	4	4	2	4	4	3	3	24	III	3	4	o
COLFA DE LOS ALTOS	13	4	4	1	4	4	3	3	23		3	4	o
++CHIPPER DE LOS ALTOS	18	4	4	4	4	4	4	4	28		4	4	o
Ped 241 (1994) (Her Zech von Breicht x Edeltraut von Herrenhausen)													
L'ETOILE DE VIVE	12	3	3	4	3	3	3	3	22	II	4	2	*
DIGGER DINKUM VON HAMPTON	12	3	2	4	2	4	2	2	19	III	4	3	*
SCHATZE FAIR DINKUM	12	4	3	4	1	4	2	2	20		4	2	*
+Ped 242 (1993) (Blue Mountain Brew x Birkley Belle of Dutchman's Hollow) (1 pup in litter)													
AMOS OF BERKSHIRE POND	14	4	3	4	1	4	3	3	22		3	3	o
Ped 243 (Dogs tested in IHDT or UFT.)													
+Ped 244 (1994) (Abbot of Dutchman's Hollow x Borka Z Kolodev(CF))													
BART OF DRUMMER'S RIDGE	12	4	4	4	4	4	4	4	28	I	4	4	o
BADGER OF DRUMMER'S RIDGE	13	4	4	4	4	4	4	4	28	I	4	3	o

(Not all dogs from this litter were tested. Two had temperament problems, were neutured and placed in pet homes where they would be hunted.)

NAVHDA NATURAL ABILITY TEST RESULTS (GRIFFONS) 1976 THROUGH 1994 (LISTED CHRONOLOGICALLY)

Remember that beginning in 1977 NAVHDA REQUIREMENTS FOR QUALIFICATION ARE DIFFERENT FROM THE WPGCA REQUIREMENTS: 1) A dog may qualify in NAVHDA with a "1" in Cooperation, whereas in the WPGCA test a dog must receive a minimum of "2" in Cooperation. 2) The same applies in Tracking and in Water, NAVHDA a "1", WPGCA a "2." And NAVHDA still uses an index, making a maximum total number of points possible of 112, whereas WPGCA maximum points possible are 28.

In 1994, NAVHDA upgraded their NAT minimum requirements for Water from a "1" to "2."

For clarification, Griffons tested in NAVHDA have been given a pedigree number of NAV-: Example, NAV-1, whereas the WPGCA tested dogs have been given a pedigree number corresponding to the pedigree numbers used in the *Gun Dog Supreme*: Ped-1.

The headings for each test category are: A-Age (months), N-Nose, S-Search, W-Water, P-Pointing, T-Tracking, D-Desire to Work, C-Cooperation, T-Total points, PR-classification. NAVHDA does not assign a number to a dog for conformation, or for coat. Therefore, unless there is a major conformation problem, no mention is made. T-Temperament.

	Age (A)	Nose (N)	Search (S)	Water (W)	Pointing (P)	Tracking (T)	Desire to Work (W)	Cooperation (C)	Total Points (TP)	Classification (PR)	Conformation (C)	Coat (C)	Temperament (T)
NAV-1 (1976-77 and GR Ped 8) (Taquin du Bois Follet x Huckle Hill Patty)													
(See page 366, for 16 additional dogs from this breeding.) (3 litters)													
++HEIDI OF RAMSEY	21	3	3	1	4	2	2	3	72		-	-	o
HUCKLE HILL DIAMOND	11	3	2	4	4	1	2	3	80	III	-	-	*
	butt bite												
HUCKLE HILL CALLIOPE	14	3	4	4	4	1	4	4	100	III	-	-	o
HUCKLE HILL CALLIOPE	14	3	4	4	4	2	3	3	96	II	-	-	o
	butt bite, ectropic												
NAV-2 (1975) (Earls Stiefels x Ingwer v Pommorregon)													
VON EARLS TEDDY	11	2	3	2	3	2	3	2	69		-	-	o
NAV-3 (1977) (Rockymount Happy x Hardrock Mountain Floosie)													
SCHULTZ OF KAROWSKI	7	3	3	1	4	1	2	3	70		-	-	o
	overshot												
NAV-4 (1977) (Don v.d. Neuburg x Beaver v Schnaps)													
BARRY V.D. NEUBURG	10	1	2	0	1	2	2	2	36		-	-	o
INGA OF BLUE MOUNTAIN	10	1	3	4	4	1	3	3	77		-	-	o
MORGEN V NEUBURG	10	1	1	0	1	0	1	1	21		-	-	*
NAV-5 (1977 and GR Ped 83) (Tonik du Bois Follet x Bent Pine's Aberdeen)													
DUCKPOND DERAFIN	15	2	2	4	4	0	2	3	72		entropic*		
DUCKPOND DE POCO	16	4	4	4	4	2	4	3	106	II	-	-	o
NAV-6 (1978 and GR Ped 91) (Boss v Wolfsberg x Duckpond De Poco)													
DIABLO RIDGE TESON	5	3	3	4	3	1	3	3	85	III	-	-	o
DIABLO RIDGE TRUCKO	13	3	2	4	4	3	3	3	88	III	-	-	o
DIABLO RIDGE TRUCKO	16	2	2	4	4	1	2	2	72		-	-	o
NAV-7 (1978) (Bent Pine's Angus x First Frost Unipac)													
FIRST FROST AMIE DE MYSTIQUE	12	3	2	4	4	1	4	2	86	III	-	-	o
FIRST FROST AMANDA	13	4	1	2	3		1	1	57				*
	(shy, gunshy, cowhock)												
NAV-8 (1978-79) (Bent Pine's Angus x First Frost Yetta)													
SMOKE CREEK BRANDY	6	4	4	3	4	4	3	4	103	II	-	-	o
SMOKE CREEK BISKO	14	2	2	0	0	1	1	2	32		-	-	o
SMOKE CREEK BABE DE MYSTIQUE	15	3	2	4	3	4	4	2	88	III	-	-	o

	A	N	S	W	P	T	D	C	T	PR	C	C	T
NAV-9 (1979) (Axel v Ulrichsquell x Freya v Bibertal)													
FREYA V. D. NEUBURG	16	3	3	3	2	3	2	3	76	III	-	-	o
FURST V. D. NEUBURG	16	2	4	4	0	0	3	3	70		-	-	o
NAV-10 (1978) (Rockymount Happy x Happy Vantage Home)													
FLATHEAD JAGDHUND GRETEL	13	3	3	4	1	3	3	2	79		-	-	o
NAV-11 (1977-78 and GR Ped 86) (Whisky du Pironec x Huckle Hill Angela)													
SUNNY BRANCH'S FREYA	5	4	2	4	4	4	4	3	100	III	-	-	o
SUNNY BRANCH'S FREYA	14	3	3	4	4	4	3	3	95	II	-	-	o
**HUCKLE HILL BOOMER	14	3	4	4	4	1	4	3	98	III	-	-	o
HUCKLE HILL IRONWOOD SAM	14	3	4	3	4	3	2	3	89	III	-	-	o
NAV-12 (1978) (Hardrock Montana Talus x Spokane Princess)													
BARON BRISTLEFACE D LAMONA	13	2	2	1	4	4	2	3	65		-	-	o
HARDROCK MONTANA JAKE II	13	4	4	4	4	4	4	4	112	I	-	-	o
NAV-13 (1979) (Billy v Tana x Sacks Gerta v Oasis)													
++GRIZLEY COLORADO II	17	4	4	0	4	4	2	2	80		-	-	o
NAV-14 (1979 and GR Ped 108) (Barry v.d. Neuburg x Bent Pine's Aberdeen)													
DUCKPOND ESCAPADE V JADEE	12	3	2	2	4	1	2	3	70	III	-	-	o
DUCKPOND ESCAPADE V JADEE	12	3	2	4	4	2	3	3	86	III	-	-	o
DUCKPOND EAGER BARON	13	3	1	4	4	4	3	1	81		-	-	o
DUCKPOND ERIKA	13	3	1	4	4	2	3	2	79		-	-	o
DUCKPOND EBULLIENT KASY	13	3	4	4	4	3	4	4	104	II	-	-	o
NAV-15 (1979 & 81 and GR Ped 84) (Lucas of Hunters Creek x Victoria du Bois Follet) (See WPGCA NAT test results above, for these dogs and littermates.)													
++BON CHASSEUR DE LA COTE	+18	4	3	4	4	4	3	4	103		-	-	o
++CORDILEA DE LA COTE	+19	3	4	0	4	3	1	2	68		-	-	o
NAV-16 (1980 and GR Ped 113) (Taquin du Bois Follet x Zest Du Montmagny)													
ANNABELLE DU FEU FOLLET	4	3	2	4	4	4	3	4	92	III	-	-	o
ABBEY DU FEU FOLLET	7	3	2	4	4	4	3	3	90	III	-	-	o
++ABBEY DU FEU FOLLET	16	3	3	4	4	1	2	4	87		-	-	o
NAV-17 (1980) (Smoke Creek Bisko x Duckpond De Poco)													
DIABLO RIDGE SALINA	12	**No scores given: "...Dog is gunshy will not work"**											
DIABLO RIDGE SALSA	15	2	2	3	1	4	2	3	63		-	-	*
DIABLO RIDGE SETA ARROW	15	3	3	2	3	1	2	3	71	III	-	-	o
NAV-18 (1980, 1981 and GR Ped 104) (Sunny Branch's Beau Brokk x Huckle Hill Calliope) (2 litters)													
ALDERS EDGE AMUNDSEN	9	4	3	0	4	4	3	3	81		-	-	o
ALDERS EDGE ANHEUSER BUSCH	9	3	1	4	4	4	2	3	81		-	-	o
ALDERS EDGE ANHEUSER BUSCH	12	4	3	4	4	4	4	3	105	II	oversize		o
ALDERS EDGE ATTAGIRL	9	4	3	4	4	3	4	4	105	II	-	-	o

	A	N	S	W	P	T	D	C	T	PR	C	C	T
NAV-18 (1980, 1981 and GR Ped 104)f(Continued)													
ALDERS EDGE ATTAGIRL	12	4	4	4	4	4	4	3	110	I	-	-	o
ALDERS EDGE ATTATURK	9	3	4	4	3	2	4	3	96	II	-	-	o
ALDERS EDGE BEAUREGARD	12	3	4	4	4	2	4	4	102	II	-	-	o
ALDERS EDGE BIRD	12	4	2	4	3	3	2	3	86	III	-	-	o
ALDERS EDGE BOZO	12	4	2	4	4	3	3	2	92	III	-	-	o
ALDERS EDGE BRUTUS	12	3	3	4	4	3	3	3	93	II	-	-	o
ALDERS EDGE BUFFY CHERCHER	12	4	4	4	4	4	4	4	112	I	-	-	o
ALDERS EDGE BRISTOL	15	3	4	4	4	3	4	4	104	II	-	-	o
NAV-19 (1982) (Arn v Hamandel x Diablo Ridge Salina)													
E SMOKEN JOE	13	4	3	4	4	2	3	3	97	II	-	-	o
NAV-20 (1983) (Sunny Branch's Beau Brokk x Duckpond Froelich)													
DUCKPOND GARP	13	3	3	4	4	3	2	3	89	III	-	-	o
DUCKPOND GENERAL	13	2	2	2	2	0	1	1	46		-	-	o
DUCKPOND GORGEOUS GIRL	13	4	4	4	4	4	4	4	112	I	-	-	o
DUCKPOND GINGER	16	4	4	4	4	4	3	4	108	II	-	-	o
NAV-21 (1983) (Beaver Dam Kiowa x Jez-A-Bell)													
BEAVER DAM MICHELEEN O'FLYNN	6	3	1	4	3	3	2	2	73		-	-	o
BEAVER DAM MICHELEEN O'FLYNN	9	3	4	4	4	1	4	3	98	III	-	-	o
NAV-22 (1983 and GR Ped 164) (Ilk v Bibertal x Tasha v Snake River)													
TAWNA'S CHELSEA MORNING	12	4	4	4	4	4	4	4	112	I	-	-	o
NAV-23 (1983) (Bent Pines Blitz x Alders Edge Attagirl)													
ALDERS EDGE CALL COLLECT	12	3	3	4	0	4	3	2	77		-	-	*
ALDERS EDGE CHAUNTICLEER	12	3	2	0	4	4	2	2	64		-	-	o
ALDERS EDGE CHARLIE	14	2	3	4	3	0	2	2	71		-	-	o
ALDERS EDGE COFAIN	14	3	3	3	4	2	2	3	82	III	-	-	o
ALDERS EDGE CRICKET	14	3	2	4	3	4	3	3	86	III	-	-	o
ALDERS EDGE CHADOW	15	4	3	4	4	4	3	4	103	II	-	-	o
ALDERS EDGE CHARDONNAY	16	2	2	2	0	2	2	2	48		-	-	o
NAV-24 (1984 and GR Ped 142) (Cacei de la Cote x Anka v Fuchsberg)													
++FREEWINDS ANGEL	16	3	2	3	3	4	2	3	77		-	-	o
NAV-25 (1985 and GR Ped 175) (Liberty's Flag Wiskers x Alders Edge Attagirl)													
ALDERS EDGE DANCER	12	4	4	4	4	2	4	3	106	II	-	-	o
ALDERS EDGE DEBA	12	3	1	4	4	4	1	2	75		-	-	o
ALDERS EDGE DEBA	15	4	4	4	4	4	3	4	108	II	-	-	o
ALDERS EDGE DESIREE	12	3	3	4	4	4	3	4	97	II	**ectropic**		o
ALDERS EDGE DESTRY	12	4	2	4	4	4	2	3	92	III	**gun sensitive**		
ALDERS EDGE DIABLOTAN	12	4	4	4	4	3	4	4	110	I	-	-	o
ALDERS EDGE DIRK	12	2	2	4	3	1	2	2	68		-	-	o
ALDERS EDGE DIRK	15	4	4	4	0	4	4	3	94		-	-	o
ALDERS EDGE DUKE	12	4	4	4	4	3	4	3	108	I	-	-	o

	A	N	S	W	P	T	D	C	T	PR	C	C	T
NAV-25 (1985 and GR Ped 175) (Continued)													
ALDERS EDGE DAISY	13	4	2	4	4	3	3	3	94	III	-	-	o
ALDERS EDGE DOMINO	16	4	3	4	4	4	4	3	105	II	-	-	o
NAV-26 (1985 and GR Ped 152) (Fritz v Becker x Duchess v.d. Umpqua Park) (2 litters)													
BARON V HERRENHAUSEN	14	3	3	4	4	2	2	2	85	III	-	-	o
GRETA V HERRENHAUSEN	10	3	3	4	3	1	2	3	81	III	-	-	*
NAV-27 (1983, 1984, 1986 and GR Ped 144) (Furst v.d. Neuburg x Flatheads Jagdhund Gretel) (3 litters)													
SAM'S MONTANA DREAM	7	3	3	4	4	1	3	3	89	III	-	-	o
BARON V REIMER	11	4	4	4	4	4	4	4	112	I	-	-	o
PLUMCREEK PURKEY	11	4	4	4	4	2	3	4	104	II	-	-	o
HAMPTONS FUSILEHEIN DARNE	9	3	3	3	3	2	3	3	82	II	-	-	o
TIDEWATER ACCENT ASA	14	4	4	4	0	3	4	3	92		-	-	o
NAV-28 (1984) (Baron v Budd x Roci's Nellie Belle)													
ADOLPH V DUFFER	12	4	3	4	4	4	3	3	101	II	-	-	*
SASHA V BUDD	12	4	2	0	4	3	2	2	68		**butt bite**		*
NAV-29 (1985 and GR Ped 156) (Amos van Jagershort x Point's Pewter Tip)													
POINT'S SHOT	5	4	4	0	4	4	3	3	86			**ectropic**	o
TROY BOY'S SAGE	13	3	4	4	3	2	3	4	94	II	-	-	o
NAV-30 (1985 and GR Ped 180)(Bevs Beau Davis Boy x Davids Tiffney Girl Davis)(2 litters)													
SILLE GRAVEL GERTTI	15	3	2	0	3	4	2	2	60		-	-	o
NAV-31 (1985) (Brownie of Walden x Sugar Baby)													
BROWN SUGAR KITTY	16	4	4	4	4	4	4	4	112	I	-	-	o
NAV-32 (1985) (Claus v Gleissenberg x Zest du Montmagny)													
DANDOLA DU FEU FOLLET	14	3	3	4	4	1	3	3	89	III	-	-	o
NAV-33 (1986 and GR Ped 158) (Ranger des Chaumes de L'Aure D'Or x Urfe de la Valle Bertier)													
AXEL DE ST LANDRY	9	4	3	4	4	4	3	4	103	II	-	-	o
NAV-34 (1986-87 and GR Ped 165) (Erik od Jezerak x Mahaska's Merry Susan)													
AMOS OF IAMONIA	6	4	4	4	2	4	4	4	104	III	-	-	o
AVAJ OF IAMONIA	13	4	4	4	4	4	4	4	112	I	-	-	o
NAV-35 (1987 and GR Ped 153) (Furst v.d. Neuburg x Bar-Mi's Gretchen)													
BECKER'S GREY GRIFFON	15	3	2	4	4	3	4	3	92	III	-	-	o
NAV-36 (1987) (Sunny Branch's Beau Brokk x Alders Edge Dancer)													
ALDERS EDGE ELESSAR	8	4	4	4	4	4	4	4	112	I	-	-	o
ALDERS EDGE EPITOME	8	3	3	4	4	1	3	3	89	III		**entropic**	o
ALDERS EDGE ELLIE	11	3	3	4	4	3	3	3	93	II	-	-	o

	A	N	S	W	P	T	D	C	T	PR	C	C	T
NAV-37 (1987 and GR Ped 200) (Duckpond Garp x Duckpond Suzanne)													
DUCKPOND JOYEUX	16	4	3	4	4	4	3	4	103	II	-	-	o
NAV-38 (1987 and GR Ped 181) (Furst v.d. Neuburg x Flatheads Jagdhund Geri)													
MAX V D BUTTES	8	4	3	4	4	4	3	3	101	II	-	-	o
NAV-39 (1986 and GR Ped 157) (Duckpond Eager Baron x Duckpond Ginger) (2 litters)													
FIELD MASTER RALPH	14	3	4	4	3	3	4	3	98	II	-	-	o
GRAYS DUCKPOND SNOWBALL	15	2	0	2	1	3	1	1	38		-	-	*
SPRINGCREEK'S BARON HUBERT	8	3	3	4	3	3	3	3	89	II	-	-	o
NAV-40 (1988) (Loys du Tedelou x Alders Edge Attagirl)													
ALDERS EDGE FAYME	12	3	3	4	3	1	3	3	85	III	-	-	o
ALDERS EDGE FRITZ	12	2	2	4	3	1	2	3	70		-	-	o
ALDERS EDGE FROSTY DELITE	12	3	4	4	4	2	3	3	96	II	-	-	o
ALDERS EDGE FEU FOLLET	14	3	4	4	4	2	3	3	96	II	-	-	o
ALDERS EDGE FIRST FROST	14	3	2	3	4	3	3	2	81	III	-	-	o
ALDERS EDGE FETICHE	14	4	4	4	4	2	3	3	102	II	-	-	o
ALDERS EDGE FALCON	15	2	3	4	4	0	2	2	75	**buttbite**			*
ALDERS EDGE FABULAR	15	3	3	4	1	4	3	3	83	**ectropic**			o
NAV-41 (1988-89 and GR Ped 177) (Loys du Tedelou x Alders Edge Dancer)													
ALDERS EDGE GAMINE	5	4	3	4	4	4	3	3	101	II	-	-	o
ALDERS EDGE GAMINE	14	4	4	4	4	2	4	4	108	II	-	-	o
ALDERS EDGE GUSTO	6	3	2	4	2	4	3	3	82	III	-	-	o
ALDERS EDGE GUSTO	14	4	4	4	4	4	4	2	108	II	-	-	o
ALDERS EDGE GRISELDA	14	3	4	4	4	1	4	4	100	III	-	-	o
ALDERS EDGE GLEANER	14	3	4	4	4	2	3	3	96	II	-	-	o
ALDERS EDGE GAIA	15	3	3	2	4	0	2	2	71		-	-	o
NAV-42 (1988) (Alders Edge Blaze x Duckpond Froelich)													
DUCKPOND KEILLOR	14	3	3	4	2	2	3	3	83	III	-	-	o
DUCKPOND KEILLOR	15	3	2	4	2	1	3	2	74	III	-	-	o
NAV-43 (1988) (Chipeau de L'Oiselier x Raven de L'Oiselier)													
THEO DE L'ETHANG	15	3	2	4	0	2	2	2	64	**cross bite**			o
NAV-44 (1988 and GR Ped 192) (Baron v Herrenhausen x Roosters Copper Penny)													
SOPHIA V HERRENHAUSEN	6	4	4	4	4	4	4	4	112	I	-	-	o
SAMPSON V HERRENHAUSEN	11	3	3	4	3	1	3	3	85	III	-	-	o
WING MASTER'S TURK	8	3	3	4	4	4	3	3	95	II	-	-	*
NAV-45 (1989 and GR Ped 185) (Royal Hunts Reward x Grays Duck Pond Snowball)													
MEDOMAK VALLEY VANILLA	14	3	2	4	3	3	3	2	82	III	-	-	o
NAV-46 (1989 and GR Ped 182) (Fellow of Reininghaus x Nancy v.d. Koorndijk)													
ANNA OF BEAR'S CREEK	8	4	3	2	2	3	3	3	81	III	-	-	o

	A	N	S	W	P	T	D	C	T	PR	C	C	T
NAV-47 (1990) (Alders Edge Blaze x Armada's Georgia Brown)													
PRAIRIE LEK'S AKONA	12	4	3	4	4	4	3	4	103	II	**ectropic**		o
PRAIRIE LEK'S GERTA	13	4	4	4	4	3	4	4	110	I	-	-	o
RAIRIE LEK'S TIALINA	13	4	4	4	4	3	4	4	110	I	**entropic**		o
NAV-48 (1990 and GR Ped 201A) (Owyhee Canyon Deke x Chuckar Hill Tess)													
MEDOMARK VALLEY KATARINA	14	4	4	2	4	4	3	3	96	III	-	-	o
NAV-49 (1990) (Rexford v Abram x Eloise Vandaan Ely)													
GUNNY MON AMIE DE L'AVENTURE	9	3	1	4	4	2	2	2	75		-	-	o
NAV-50 (1990 and GR Ped 193) (Baron v Herrenhausen x Miss Amanda v Bleck)													
GINA V HERRENHAUSEN	14	4	2	2	4	4	2	3	82	III	-	-	o
FRITZ BARON HOGE	14	4	4	4	4	4	4	4	112	I	-	-	o
NAV-51 (1990 and GR Ped 188) (Erik od Jezerak(CF) x Patches v Ripoff)													
+AYLA OF WHITE WATER	13	4	4	4	4	4	4	4	112	I	-	-	o
NAV-52 (1990 and GR Ped 194) (Sharon's Mt John Reggie x Point's Pewter Tip)													
ASPEN POINT'S BARREL	9	2	2	4	2	2	3	3	72		-	-	o
ASPEN POINT'S BARREL	13	3	2	4	2	3	3	3	80	III	-	-	o
ASPEN POINT'S BREECH	10	4	3	3	4	4	3	4	98	II	-	-	o
ASPEN POINT'S BREECH	13	3	4	3	4	3	3	2	91	II	-	-	o
ASPEN POINT'S BOLT	14	3	4	4	3	2	4	3	96	II	-	-	o
NAV-53 (1990) (Ex v Ulrichsquell x Hilka v Kempter Wald)													
KARLO V KEMPTER WALD	13	4	3	2	4	1	3	3	85	III			*
(Dog growled during conformation examination. Jaws misaligned.)													
NAV-54 (1991) (Good Time Grady's Boy x Flatheads Heidi)													
VON BAUGHMAN'S KEDA	6	3	2	4	4	4	3	3	90	III	-	-	o
VON BAUGHMAN'S KEDA	15	4	4	4	4	3	4	4	110	I	-	-	o
NAV-55 (1991) (Cesar v Erlenbruch x Point's Pewter Tip)													
ASPEN POINT'S CASSANDRA	15	4	4	4	4	4	4	4	112	I	-	-	o
NAV-56 (1991 and GR Ped 203) (Dino de L'Etang x Alders Edge Feu Follet)													
ACAJOU DU FEU FOLLET	13	3	3	4	4	1	3	3	89	III	-	-	o
ACAJOU DU FEU FOLLET	15	3	4	4	4	0	3	3	92		-	-	o
AMBERGRIS DU FEU FOLLET	16	4	4	4	3	3	4	3	104	I	**undershot**		o
NAV-57 (1991 and GR Ped 201) (Boss of the Cascades(CF) x Avaj of Iamonia)													
+BRITTANY OF DUTCHMAN'S HOLLOW	13	4	4	4	4	4	4	4	112	I	-	-	o
NAV-58 (1990-91 and GR Ped 204) (Sampson v Herrenhausen x Kalispell Ingo v Glacier)													
FALCON V HERRENHAUSEN	6	4	4	4	4	2	3	4	104	II	-	-	o
FRAULEIN V HERRENHAUSEN	7	3	2	4	3	4	3	3	86	III	-	-	*
FARLEY V HERRENHAUSEN	14	3	3	4	4	4	4	3	99	II	-	-	o

	A	N	S	W	P	T	D	C	T	PR	C	C	T
NAV-59 Not used.													
NAV-60 (1991) (Fritz v Herrenhausen x Rikki v Ruetz)													
ROVER FIDO BLEU	15	4	3	4	4	4	4	3	105	II	-	-	o
(very aggressive toward other dogs)													
NAV-61 (1990 and GR Ped 216) (Point's Algernon Biff x Royal Hunt's Dinah)													
ASTRA V NUMMELHOF	13	4	4	4	4	4	4	4	112	I	-	-	o
AUGUSTUS V NUMMELHOF	15	3	2	4	3	4	3	4	88	III	-	-	o
++DORA V NUMMELHOF	17	3	3	0	4	4	2	3	71		-	-	o
NAV-62 (1991 and GR Ped 193) (Baron v Herrenhausen x Sophia v Herrenhausen)(2 litters)													
GRACE V HERRENHAUSEN	8	3	4	4	3	1	3	3	90	III	-	-	o
GRANT V HERRENHAUSEN	8	2	2	2	3	2	1	2	56		-	-	o
GALAHAD V HERRENHAUSEN	9	2	1	4	2	3	2	2	63		-	-	*
sensitive throughout test													
GALAHAD V HERRENHAUSEN	13	3	2	4	2	2	2	3	74	III	**sensitive**		*
++EZCHIEL V HERRENHAUSEN	32	3	2	4	1	4	3	3	78		-	-	o
NAV-63 (1988, 90, 91 and GR Ped 179) (Ingo vom Kastanienhain x Glac[i]er Cool Deecee) (3 litters)													
KALISPELL INGO V GLACIER	11	3	4	4	4	1	3	3	94	III	-	-	o
ALDERS EDGE INGOS COOL ALPHA	8	4	4	4	3	3	4	2	102	II	-	-	o
CAMAS INGO V GLACIER	9	2	1	4	4	4	2	2	73		-	-	o
GOOD TIME NATTIE	9	3	4	3	3	3	3	3	89	II	-	-	o
INGO'S IMAGE V GLACIER	9	3	4	4	4	3	4	4	104	II	-	-	o
NAV-64 (1992 and GR Ped 213) (Alders Edge Ingos Cool Alpha x Alders Edge Grieselda)													
ALDERS EDGE HARLEQUIN	13	3	2	4	3	4	3	3	86	III	-	-	o
ALDERS EDGE HONCO	14	4	3	4	3	3	3	3	95	II	**entropic**		o
ALDERS EDGE HAGAR	15	4	4	4	4	4	3	4	108	II	-	-	o
ALDERS EDGE HULLABALOU	15	3	2	3	4	4	2	3	81	III	**entropic**		o
ALDERS EDGE HEATHER	15	2	2	4	0	1	2	2	56		-	-	o
NAV-65 (1992) (Cesar v Erlenbruch x Aspen Point's Boxlock)													
ASPEN POINT'S DANCER	8	3	2	4	0	3	3	2	70		-	-	o
ASPEN POINT'S DANCER	8	3	2	4	4	1	2	3	80	III	-	-	o
ASPEN POINT'S DUBAY	8	3	4	4	4	0	2	3	88		-	-	o
ASPEN POINT'S DUSK	8	3	4	4	4	1	3	2	92	III	-	-	o
NAV-66 (1992-93 and GR Ped 231)(Cesar v Erlenbruch x Aspen Point's Buttstock)(1 litter)													
EJ'S GABE	7	3	3	4	3	0	2	2	77		-	-	o
EJ'S GABE	16	3	4	4	4	2	3	3	96	II	-	-	o
UPLAND'S PURDY SCHATZE	7	2	2	4	4	0	2	2	70		-	-	o
UPLAND'S PURDY SCHATZE	8	3	3	4	4	2	3	3	91	II	-	-	o
VALKYRIES SHADOW	7	3	3	4	4	4	3	4	97	II	-	-	o
UPLAND KENNELS ACTIVATOR	8	3	4	4	4	2	3	3	96	II	-	-	o
UPLAND KENNELS ACTIVATOR	9	4	4	4	4	4	4	4	112	I	-	-	o
UPLAND'S TANGLES	9	4	3	4	4	3	3	4	101	II	-	-	o

	A	N	S	W	P	T	D	C	T	PR	C	C	T
NAV-66 (1992-93 and GR Ped 231) (Continued)													
UPLAND'S TANGLES	16	3	3	4	3	2	3	3	87	II	-	-	o
UPLAND'S TIMBERLINE WALKER	16	4	4	3	4	4	3	4	103	II	-	-	o
UPLAND'S KENNELS ANGELINE	16	2	1	2	4	1	1	2	53		-	-	o
NAV-67 (1992 and GR Ped 212)(Andy of Perkins Corner x Cindy of Perkins Corner)													
BREO OF PERKINS CORNER	15	4	4	4	4	4	3	4	108	II	-	-	o
NAV-68 (1992 and GR Ped 230) (Welch's Sir Timothy x Beavers Dams Massie May)													
WELCH'S SIR BENJY	9	4	2	4	3	4	3	4	94	III	-	-	
WELCH'S SIR BENJY	16	4	4	4	4	4	4	4	112	I	-	-	o
BLUE GROUSE CACHE	16	3	2	0	4	2	1	2	56		-	-	o
NAV-69 (1990, 91, 92 and GR Ped 190) (Duckpond Dustin x Duckpond Joyeux)(2 litters)													
DUCKPOND LADY	12	3	4	4	3	2	3	3	92	II	-	-	o
DUCKPOND LUCKY LADY	15	3	3	4	2	1	2	3	77	III	-	-	o
DUCKPOND LIEDERKRANZ	14	3	2	4	3	3	3	3	84	III	-	-	o
DUCKPOND NIXIE	5	4	3	4	4	2	3	4	99	II	-	-	o
DUCKPOND NARRAGUAGUS	13	3	2	4	4	4	3	3	90	III	-	-	o
DUCKPOND NICATOUS	14	4	4	4	4	4	4	3	110	I	-	-	o
DUCKPOND NORRIDGEWOCK	14	4	4	4	4	3	4	4	110	I	-	-	o
DUCKPOND NIXIE	14	3	3	4	2	4	3	3	87	III	-	-	o
DUCKPOND NEQUASSET	15	4	4	4	4	4	4	3	110	I	-	-	o
++DUCKPOND NASKEAG	16+	2	2	4	3	1	2	2	68		-	-	o
NAV-70 (1992) (Duckpond Dustin x Duckpond Kossuth)													
DUCKPOND MADAWASKA	13	4	4	2	4	3	3	3	94	III	-	-	*
DUCKPOND MEDDYBEMPS	15	3	3	4	1	1	2	2	71		-	-	o
NAV-71 (1990, 91, 92 and GR Ped 191) (Sampson v Herrenhausen x Greta v Herrenhausen) (4 litters)													
DRUMMER V HERRENHAUSEN	14	4	2	4	4	4	3	4	98	III	-	-	o
DUCHESS V HERRENHAUSEN	14	3	2	3	3	4	2	3	77	III	**crossbite**		o
HESHKA V HERRENHAUSEN	13	2	1	4	1	1	2	2	55		**butt bite**		o
JASMINE V HERRENHAUSEN	13	3	1	4	3	2	2	2	71		**butt bite**		*
JEROME V HERRENHAUSEN	13	4	3	4	4	4	4	3	105	II	-	-	*
JR RILEY V HERRENHAUSEN	13	4	4	4	4	3	4	4	110	I	**butt bite**		o
MALETA V HERRENHAUSEN	6	4	4	3	4	4	4	4	107	I	-	-	o
MEMPHIS BELLE V HERRENHAUSEN	6	4	4	1	4	4	3	3	91		-	-	o
MEMPHIS BELLE V HERRENHAUSEN	10	3	3	4	4	1	3	3	89	III	**butt bite**		o
JANELLE V HERRENHAUSEN	14	4	4	4	4	3	4	4	110	I	**butt bite**		o
++JULES V HERRENHAUSEN	17+	3	4	4	3	1	2	3	86		-	-	o
MIEKA HERRENHAUSEN	10	3	1	4	4	2	2	2	75		**crossbite**		o
NAV-72 (1992) (Duke v Herrenhausen x Gina v Herrenhausen)													
KARMEN M V HERRENHAUSEN	10	4	3	0	4	4	3	3	81		-	-	o
KATARINA V HERRENHAUSEN	10	2	1	0	2	3	1	1	37		-	-	*

(shy to birds and noise, gunshy)

	A	N	S	W	P	T	D	C	T	PR	C	C	T
NAV-72 (1992) (Continued)													
KATIE V HERRENHAUSEN	10	3	2	4	3	4	2	2	80	III	-	-	o
LARA V HERRENHAUSEN	10	2	1	4	2	1	1	1	53		-	-	*
	(sensitive, gun sensitive, spooks at cow, stumps & ducks)												
KORKY V HERRENHAUSEN	10	3	1	0	3	2	1	1	45		*	-	*
	(Gunshy and sensitive to people and surroundings)												
NAV-73 (1992) (Fritz Baron Hoge x Sophia v Herrenhausen)(2 litters)													
LACY V HERRENHAUSEN	8	2	1	4	2	4	1	2	61		-	-	*
	(gun sensitive, shy to people, and bird shy)												
NORA WINDRUCH V HERRENHAUSEN	14	3	3	4	3	0	3	2	81		-	-	o
NAV-74 (1992) (Fritz v Herrenhausen x Helga v Rooster)													
ROOSTERS KEEN POINT TO POINT	10	3	3	3	4	4	3	3	90	II	-	-	o
NAV-75 (1992 and GR Ped 221) (Grif v Pointer x Tucker's Spooky Hollow)													
VINDTHEIM'S HELLZAPOPPIN	9	1	1	2	1	1	1	1	33		-	-	o
WAYFARER'S NEWLINE	14	4	4	4	4	4	4	3	110	I	-	-	o
NAV-76 (1992 and GR Ped 238) (Friedrich v Trendelburg x Kalispell Ingo v Glacier)													
WAYFARER'S A PARKER	9	1	1	4	2	0	1	1	45		-	-	*
	(shy, spooked by people and sounds, undershot)												
WAYFARER'S A REMINGTON	9	3	3	4	4	1	3	3	89	III	-	-	o
WAYFARER'S A WINCHESTER	9	4	3	2	3	4	2	2	81	III	-	-	o
WAYFARER'S TRENDELBURG AURA	9	3	2	4	2	3	3	3	80	III	-	-	o
NAV-77 (1992) (Flinn & Feathers Paddy O'Shea x Fireside's Animation)													
FIRESIDE'S WET ACRES JALAPENO	10	2	1	2	2	2	2	2	51		-	-	o
NAV-78 (1993, 94 and GR Ped 232) (Grif von Pointer x Camas Hot Springs Suzie)(2 litters)													
++NORTH LIGHT'S KACHINA DOLL	17+	4	4	4	4	3	4	4	110		-	-	o
ALEXIS KC SCHATTANHAIN	15	2	3	4	1	2	2	2	67		-	-	o
NAV-79 (1993) (Echo de St Landry x Alders Edge Fetiche)													
DE LOREE D'AULNES ARGUS	12	4	4	4	4	4	4	4	112	I	-	-	o
DE LOREE D'AULNES ACE	15	3	2	4	0	1	2	2	62		-	-	o
DE LOREE D'AULNES ANA	15	4	4	4	4	4	4	4	112	I	-	-	o
NAV-80 (1993 and GR Ped 228) (Aspen Point's Barrel x Cindy of Perkins Corners)													
CHINA DOLL OF PERKINS CORNER	13	3	2	4	2	4	3	3	82	III	-	-	o
COCOA BLAZE OF PERKINS CORNER	14	3	1	4	4	4	2	3	81		-	-	o
COCOA BLAZE OF PERKINS CORNER	14	3	2	4	3	4	3	4	88	III	-	-	o
NAV-81 (1993) (Point's Algernon Biff x Duckpond Joyeux)													
DUCKPOND OSSIPEE	11	3	2	0	4	1	2	2	58		-	-	o
DUCKPOND OSPREY	14	3	3	4	1	4	4	3	87		**overshot**		o
DUCKPOND ORION	14	3	3	4	4	4	3	3	95	II	**undershot**		o

	A	N	S	W	P	T	D	C	T	PR	C	C	T
NAV-82 (1993) (Aspen Point's Bolt x Duckpond Lady)													
PRAIRIE POND ATTILA	13	3	3	4	4	3	3	4	95	II	-	-	o
PRAIRIE POND ALEX	14	2	2	3	4	4	2	2	73		-	-	o
PRAIRIE POND ANNA	14	3	2	4	4	2	2	3	82	III	-	-	o
NAV-83 (1993) (Royal Hunts GDB Charlemage x Elsy de St Landry)													
GOOSE CREEKS AMIGO	14	3	2	4	4	4	3	3	90	III	-	-	o
GOOSE CREEKS ADVANTAGE	14	2	1	4	3	1	2	2	63		-	-	*
	sensitive, shy to judges and handlers												
GOOSE CREEKS ALI	15	4	4	4	4	4	4	4	112	I	-	-	o
NAV-84 (1993 and GR Ped 243) (Ingo v Kastanienhain x Flatheads Georgia)													
ECKER ABBY VON SCHATTANHAIN	12	3	3	4	3	4	3	3	91	II	**butt bite**		o
HERR FLINT VON SCHATTHAIN	12	3	1	4	4	2	2	2	75		-	-	*
NAV-85 (1993) (Fritz v Herrenhausen x Flicka's Griffitti)													
LINBLADE'S BOLD GRIF	6	1	1	4	0	1	2	2	45		-	-	o
LINBLADE'S BOLD GRIF	14	3	1	4	4	3	2	2	77		**teeth faults**		o
NAV-86 (1993 and GR Ped 236) (Friedrich v Trendelburg x Fraulein v Herrenhausen)													
WAYFARER'S BRUTUS	11	3	3	4	4	4	3	4	97	II	-	-	o
WAYFARER'S BRETA	12	4	3	4	4	4	4	3	105	II	**teeth**		o
WAYFARER'S BOSKO	12	4	4	4	4	4	4	4	112	I	-	-	o
WAYFARER'S BREWMASTER	12	2	3	4	3	0	2	2	71		-	-	o
NAV-87 (1993 and GR Ped 235) (Falcon v Herrenhausen x Gina v Herrenhausen)													
PENNY V HERRENHAUSEN	10	4	3	4	4	3	4	4	105	II	-	-	o
PATTON V HERRENHAUSEN	10	3	3	4	4	2	3	4	93	II	-	-	o
POTPOURRI V HERRENHAUSEN	10	4	3	4	4	4	4	3	105	II	-	-	o
PRIMA STORMNVN V HERRENHAUSEN	11	3	3	4	4	1	3	3	89	III	-	-	o
PANDORA V HERRENHAUSEN	14	2	1	4	4	1	1	2	63		-	-	o
NAV-88 (1993 and GR Ped 229) (Welch's Sir Timothy x Mac's Maggie)													
WELCH'S LADY CASSIDY	12	3	4	4	3	2	3	3	92	II	-	-	o
NAV-89 (1993) (Friedrich v Trendelburg x Travelin's Grady's Girl)													
HANS V SCHATTANHAIN	9	3	2	4	4	3	3	3	88	III	-	-	o
CIGO V SCHATTANHAIN	10	2	3	4	1	1	3	2	69		-	-	o
NAV-90 (1993) (Von Baxter Jakes Gunner x Von Bailey's Azel Gunner) (2 litters)													
BRIARSTONE'S NEBRASKA LADY	13	4	3	4	4	4	3	4	103	II	-	-	o
NAV-91 (1992-93-94) (Aspen Point's Bolt x Alders Edge Dancer) (2 litters)													
ALDERS EDGE IMPULSE	7	3	3	4	4	3	4	4	99	II	-	-	o
ALDERS EDGE IMPULSE	7	3	3	4	4	3	3	4	95	II	-	-	o
ALDERS EDGE IKE	7	3	4	4	3	1	3	3	90	III	-	-	o
ALDERS EDGE IAN	16	4	4	4	4	4	4	4	112	I	-	-	o
ALDERS EDGE JOLIE	7	4	4	4	4	2	3	3	102	II	-	-	o

	A	N	S	W	P	T	D	C	T	PR	C	C	T
NAV-91 (1992-93-94) (Continued)													
ALDERS EDGE JASPER	15	3	4	4	4	1	3	4	96	III	-	-	o
ALDERS EDGE JESTER	15	3	1	4	4	0	2	3	73		-	-	o
ALDERS EDGE JOKER	16	3	2	4	4	1	2	2	78	III	-	-	o
NAV-92 (1993-94) (Duckpond Dustin x Medomak Valley Katrina)													
CROCKYS V BARON	7	3	2	4	1	3	3	3	76		-	-	o
CROCKYS V BARON	15	4	4	4	4	4	4	4	112	I	**crossbite**		o
NAV-93 (1994) (Alders Edge Deba x Acajou du feu Follet)													
ITASCA WINGS ADAM	13	2	3	4	4	0	3	3	81		-	-	o
ITASCA WINGS ABBIGALE	13	3	1	2	2	2	2	2	57		-	-	o
ITASCA WINGS ACADIAN	14	3	4	4	4	0	3	3	92		-	-	o
ITASCA WINGS ALICE	14	3	2	4	4	4	3	4	92	III	-	-	o
ITASCA WINGS ARGUS	14	3	2	4	2	4	3	3	82	III	-	-	o
ITASCA WINGS AJ	15	3	3	4	3	1	3	2	83	III	-	-	o
ITASCA WINGS ATTABABY	15	4	3	4	4	3	3	3	99	II	-	-	o
NAV-94 (1994) (Junior Kamouraska x Alders Edge Feu Follet)													
DONNEZ FEU FOLLET	12	4	4	4	3	2	4	4	104	II	**teeth**		o
NAV-95 (1994) (Alders Edge Deba x Aspen Point's Buttstock)													
WISCONSIN PATRIOT GUNNER	14	4	3	4	4	4	3	4	103	II	**undershot**		o
NAV-96 (1994) (Aspen Point's Barrel x Astra v Nummelhoff)													
GREYLOCK GLEN'S ABBY	13	3	2	4	2	4	3	3	82	III	-	-	o
GREYLOCK GLEN'S AURORA	14	2	1	4	3	1	2	3	65		-	-	o
GREYLOCK GLEN'S ABBY	14	4	4	4	2	3	4	3	100	III	-	-	o
GREYLOCK GLEN'S ANDY	14	2	2	4	2	2	2	2	66		-	-	o
NAV-97 (1994) (Falcon v Herrenhausen x Autumn v Herrenhausen)													
QUINTESSA V HERRENHAUSEN	14	4	3	4	4	1	3	3	95	III	-	-	o
NAV-98 (1993, 94) (Grif von Pointer x Camas Hot Springs Gabaral) (2 litters)													
GRETA V GLACIER	6	2	2	3	3	1	2	2	63		**gun sensitive**		*
GRETA V GLACIER	14	3	2	4	3	3	2	2	78	III	-	-	o
BRET VON SHATTANHAIN	8	2	1	4	1	4	2	3	63		-	-	o
NAV-99 (1994) (Echo de st Landry x Diana v Herrenhausen)													
NACON DU CHASSEUR	15	3	4	4	1	1	3	2	80		-	-	o
NAV-100 (1994) (Duckpond Maranacook x Duckpond Nequasset)													
DUCKPOND PALERMO	10	3	2	3	3	0	2	2	67		-		o
	(short coat, no furnishings)												
DUCKPOND PEMIGEWASSETT	12	3	1	4	4	4	2	3	81				*
	(butt bite, shy, gunshy)												
DUCKPOND PALMYRA	16	3	2	0	3	2	1	2	52		-	-	o
DUCKPOND PORTLAND	16	4	3	4	3	4	3	4	99	II	-	-	o

	A	N	S	W	P	T	D	C	T	PR	C	C	T
NAV-101 (1994 and GR Ped 241) (Her Zech von Breicht x Edeltraut v Herrenhausen)													
DIGGER DINKUM VOM HAMPTON	13	3	2	4	3	4	3	4	88	III	-	-	o
SCHATZE FAIR DINKUM	13	3	2	4	2	3	3	3	80	III	-	-	o
NAV-102 (1994) (Bramble Bush Anchor Gauge x Elsy de St Landry)													
GOOSE CREEKS BOUTEEN-TRAIN	14	3	3	4	4	4	3	4	97	II	-	-	o
GOOSE CREEKS BRISE	15	3	2	4	4	2	3	2	84	III	-	-	o
NAV-103 (1994) (Axius x Faribole de Cornilly)													
IRIS	10	2	1	3	3	1	2	2	58		-	-	o
NAV-104 (1994) (Firesides Rollicking Ruckus x Firesides Wet Acres Jalpeno)													
WET ACRES ABERCROMBY & FETCH	8	4	4	4	0	4	4	3	94				*
	(sensitive, sensitive to shot echo and sudden noise)												
WET ACRES AGATHA FRISKY	8	4	4	4	4	4	4	4	112	I	-	-	o
NAV-105 (1994) (Fritz v Herrenhausen x Flicka's Griffitti)													
LINBLADE'S BOLD GRIFF	14	3	1	4	4	3	2	2	77				o
	(teeth misaligned)												
NAV-106 (1994) (Drummer v Herrenhausen x Gina v Herrenhausen)													
ROOSTER V HERRENHAUSEN	15	3	3	4	4	3	3	4	95	II	-	-	o
NAV-107 (1994) (Roosters Weed Waker Bruno x Helga von Rooster)													
ROOSTERS BANER MAKE YOUR POINT	8	3	2	4	3	1	2	3	76	III	-	-	o
ROOSTERS SHADOW PRANCER	12	3	3	4	3	4	2	3	87	III	-	-	o
NAV-108 (1994) (Bramble Bush's Tag A Long x Janelle Herrenhausen)													
BARBET'S BONAMI TAG-A-LONG	9	3	2	4	4	2	3	3	86	III	-	-	o
BARBET'S BEE FIFTY TWO	9	3	4	4	2	1	3	3	86	III	**butt bite**		o
BARBET'S BANDIT	9	4	4	4	3	2	3	3	98	II	-	-	o
NAV-109 (1994) (Echo de St Landry x Misty's Bristled Brie)													
BARBET'S ACE IN THE HOLE	11	3	4	4	1	0	3	3	80		-	-	o
BARBET'S ACHIEVER	11	4	4	4	3	4	4	4	108	I	**overshot**		o
BARBET'S AIRBOURNE RANGER	11	4	4	4	4	4	4	4	112	I	-	-	o
BARBET'S AUTUMN MIST	11	2	1	4	3	0	1	3	59		-	-	o
BARBET'S AIRBOURNE AVIATOR	12	2	2	4	3	0	3	3	72			-	*
	(sensitive, dog snapped at judge, teeth not judged)												
BARBET'S AIRBOURNE AVIATOR	15	3	4	4	1	2	3	3	84		-	-	*
NAV-110 (1994) (Cers Axel Friff Liveried x Princess Mandee Larouge)													
MAIDEN MEGAN LAROUGE	13	4	4	4	4	3	4	4	110	I	-	-	o
ROOSTER'S HIGH ROLLING HEIDI	13	4	3	4	4	4	4	4	107	II	-	-	o
NAV-111 (1994) (Roosters Gurbert Getam x Roxys Fox Rooster)													
NORTONS HEIDI	12	4	3	4	4	4	3	3	101	II	-	-	o

	A	N	S	W	P	T	D	C	T	PR	C	C	T
NAV-112 (1994) (Duke v Herrenhausen x Sophia v Herrenhausen)													
THEODORA V HERRENHAUSEN	11	3	2	2	3	1	2	3	66	III	-	-	o
NAV-113 (1994) (Falcon v Herrenhausen x Vindtheim's Hellzapoppin)													
VINDTHEIM'S WIRED TO THE MAX	12	3	3	4	4	1	3	3	89	III	-	-	o
NAV-114 (1994) (Von Baxter Jakes Gunner x Von Alexandra Bef Gunner)													
BRIARSTONES FRAZIER BRILLO	13	3	3	4	0	0	2	3	67		-	-	o

WPGCA INTERMEDIATE HUNTING DOG TEST

RESULTS 1976 THROUGH 1994

The Intermediate Hunting Dog Test (IHDT) uses an index for each category of the test, to weight some categories more than others. Like the Natural Ability tabulations, the IHDT tabulations are presented in chronological order, beginning in the fall of 1976 when the test was inaugurated by the WPGCA. Sometimes a pedigree number appears to be out of order, but because the tabulations are listed *chronologically* **the pedigrees do not always follow in chronological order. Listing is by** *year, not by pedigree.*

The categories are listed in the following order with the index following the category:

WATER	FIELD	JUDGED THROUGHOUT
Track Duck-5	**Searching-5**	**Nose-6**
Retrieve Duck Water-3	**Pointing-4**	**Attitude Toward Work-4**
	Retrieve Dragged Game-3	**Cooperation-3**
	Tracking Live Bird-3	**Obedience-3**

KEY TO HEADINGS: TD-Tracking Duck, RD-Retrieve of Duck, S-Searching, P-Pointing, D-Retrieve From Drag Track, TB-Tracking Live Bird, N-Nose, A-Attitude Toward Work, C-Cooperation, O-Obedience, TO-Total Points, PR-Prize Classification, CO-Conformation, CT-Coat, T-Temperament ("o" stands for "ok" meaning no defects in temperament were observed during the test.)

*** Indicates dog has temperament problem.**
**** Dog is dysplastic.**
***** Test is optional.**
+ Indicates breeding is from WPGCA Breeding Program.
++ Indicates dog was over age for IHDT (24 months) and was run under OHDT (Older Hunting Dog Test) and is expected to be further along with training.

PEDIGREE NUMBER refers to the pedigree number assigned each litter tested in WPGCA field tests and used in *The Gun Dog Supreme*. The same pedigree number is used whenever the dog is tested. For example, the first dog listed below--ROLF VON PHILOHELA--has Ped # 1, and that was used in both NAT and IHDT. These pedigree numbers DO NOT correspond with the pedigree numbers used in Part One and Two of this book.
Year indicates the year in which the dog was tested.

	Water		Field				Judged Throughout								
	Tracking Duck (TD)	Retrieve of Duck (RD)	Searching (S)	Pointing (P)	Retrieve from Drag Track (D)	Tracking Live Bird (TB)	Nose (N)	Attitude Toward Work (A)	Cooperation (C)	Obedience (O)	Total Points (TP)	Prize Classification (PR)	Conformation (CO)	Coat (CT)	Temperament (T)
Index	5	3	5	4	3	3	6	4	3	3					
Ped 1 (1976) (Barry v.d. Neuburg x Gretel v Altenburg)															
**ROLF V PHILOHELA, 6 YRS	1	4	4	4	4	4	4	4	4	4	141		2	2	o
Ped 2 (1976) (Barry v.d. Neuburg x Tina de la Reote)															
HUCKLE HILL BARBI, 4 YRS	1	0	3	4	0	4	3	3	2	2	90		3	4	*
Ped 7 (1976) (Pipo des Vieilles Rouches x Lorene de Ronciers de Clavieres)															
TONIK DU BOIS FOLLET, 6 YRS	3	2	2	4	0	4	4	3	2	2	107		4	4	o
Ped 8 (1977-78) (Taquin du Bois Follet x Huckle Hill Patty)															
BAYWATER SHAG, 2 YRS	2	2	3	2	0	1	3	2	2	2	80		3	2	o
BAYWATER SHAG, 3 YRS	2	2	3	3	0	4	4	2	2	2	99		3	3	o
WINGMASTERS TROUBLE MAKER, 2 YRS	2	4	4	1	4	4	3	3	3	3	118		3	4	o
HUCKLE HILL MISTY, 2 YRS	1	3	3	2	3	4	3	2	3	2	104		4	4	o
Ped 9 (1977-78) (Taquin du Bois Follet x Bent Pine's Brigette)															
BENT PINE'S ABERDEEN, 3 YRS	4	4	4	3	0	4	3	3	3	3	124		3	4	o
BENT PINE'S ABERDEEN, 3 YRS	3	4	4	4	0	2	3	4	2	2	115		2	4	o
BENT PINE'S ASTRID, 3 YRS	2	2	3	3	0	4	3	3	3	3	103		3	3	o

	TD	RD	S	P	D	TB	N	A	C	O	TO	PR	CO	CT	T
Ped 14 (1977) (Sacha de St Landry x Agate d'Argent)															
SNOW QUEUE BLANC, 5 YRS	2	4	4	4	4	3	4	4	3	3	137	II	4	3	o
Ped 19 (1976) (Bonzo of Copper Valley x Miska vom Schlemmkreide)															
**KIRK D'OASIS, 6 YRS	2	2	3	4	0	4	3	3	2	2	101		-	-	o
Ped 34 (1977) (Hardrock Montana Rip x Koko)															
MEYEN'S MOUNTAIN MAN, 3 YRS	1	0	2	1	0	1	2	1	1	2	47		4	2	*
+Ped 46 (1977-78) (Boss vom Wolfsberg x Snow Queue Blanc)															
LADY DAWN OF GLENAIRE, 3 YR	2	0	4	4	0	4	4	3	2	3	109		3	2	*
LADY DAWN OF GLENAIRE, 4 YR	3	4	4	4	4	4	4	4	4	4	151	I	4	3	o
SIEGREICH JAGER OF GLENAIRE,4YR	3	3	4	4	4	3	4	4	4	4	145	I	3	2	o
GLENAIR'S PECOS GYPSY, 3 YR	3	3	4	3	3	2	3	3	3	3	119	II	3	3	o
GLENAIR'S PECOS GYPSY, 4 YR	3	3	4	4	3	3	4	3	3	4	135	II	3	3	o
GLENAIRE'S DAK, 4 YRS	3	3	4	3	4	2	4	3	2	3	125	III	3	2	o
Ped 47 (1977-1980)(Don v.d. Neuburg x Juniper Heather Hen)															
KELLY OF SUTTER BUTTES,3 YR	1	2	4	3	3	3	3	3	3	3	109		3	3	o
++WYOMING'S LUCKY, 6 YRS	3	4	4	4	4	2	3	3	3	4	132		2	3	o
(Dog was overage, and under rules of that time could not qualify.)															
Ped 57 (1977) (Sacha de St Landry x Sweet Molly Malone)															
ADRIENNE, 3 YRS	1	0	4	4	0	1	2	2	2	2	76		3	2	o
+Ped 60 (1978-80) (Tonik du Bois Follet x Ulla de St Landry)															
LUCAS OF HUNTER'S CREEK, 18 MO	3	0	2	4	0	3	3	3	2	3	95		4	4	o
LUCAS OF HUNTER'S CREEK ,2 YR	2	0	4	4	0	2	3	2	2	3	93		4	4	o
LUCAS OF HUNTER'S CREEK,3 YR	1	1	4	4	0	3	3	3	2	3	95		4	4	o
LUCAS OF HUNTER'S CREEK,4 YR	1	4	4	4	4	3	3	3	3	3	122		4	4	o
LUCAS OF HUNTER'S CREEK,5 YR	2	2	4	4	2	2	3	3	3	3	112	III	4	4	o
LINUS OF HUNTER'S CREEK, 3 YR	2	3	3	4	0	2	3	3	2	3	95		4	4	o
+Ped 66 (1977-1978) Don v.d. Neuburg x Bent Pine's Alda)															
DREAMER OF DUSTY HILLS,18 MO	1	3	2	3	0	1	2	2	2	2	71		3	2	o
DREAMER OF DUSTY HILLS,30 MO	1	3	4	4	0	3	3	3	2	2	101		3	2	o
DUSTY HILLS DEMON, 30 MOS	1	0	4	3	-	0	2	2	2	3	72		3	2	o
Ped 70 (1976) (Billy vom Tana x Miss Penny Lane)															
WHITNEY'S TALLY HO, 17 MOS	1	0	-	-	-	-	2	1	1	1			-	-	*
Ped 77 (1977) (Dirk von Meierloh x Kortney v Meierloh)															
PUNKIN V MEIRLOH, 15 MOS	3	3	3	3	0	4	3	3	2	3	108		2	3	o
Ped 78 (1978) (Ulrich ("Ulysse") de St Landry x Valy de L'Alverne)															
MOUSTIQUE DE LA POINTE D'ARGENT, 2 YRS	2	4	4	4	3	3	4	3	3	3	130	II	4	2	o

	TD	RD	S	P	D	TB	N	A	C	O	TO	PR	CO	CT	T
+Ped 82 (1978) (Boss vom Wolfsberg x Birchwood Manor's Inga Igiture)															
ASHVIEW'S AUGIE D, 2 YRS	3	3	4	4	4	2	3	3	3	3	126	II	3	2	o
ASHVIEW'S K.C. GIESTESBLITZ, 2 YR	2	3	3	4	0	2	2	2	3	3	94		3	3	o
ANNA ASHVIEW KARENINA,2 YRS	2	4	3	4	0	4	3	3	3	3	113		2	1	o
ASHVIEWS DUTCH, 3 YRS	3	4	3	2	0	4	4	3	3	3	116		3	2	o
+Ped 83 (1978) (Tonik du Bois Follet x Bent Pine's Aberdeen)															
DUCKPOND DE POCO, 2 YRS	2	4	4	4	4	3	3	3	3	3	131	II	-	-	o
+Ped 84 (1980-84) (Lucas of Hunters Creek x Victoria du Bois Follet) (3 litters)															
ARRAS DE LA COTE, 3 YRS	3	4	4	4	3	3	4	4	4	4	145	I	3	3	o
BEAU JANGLES DE LA COTE,2 YR	2	3	3	3	2	4	3	3	2	3	109	III	3	2	o
BON CHASSEUR DE LA COTE,2 YR	4	4	4	4	4	4	4	4	4	4	156	I	4	4	o
BRISETTE DE LA COTE, 2 YRS	2	4	4	4	3	4	4	3	3	3	133	II	3	2	o
BRIDGETTE DE LA COTE, 2 YR	4	4	4H	4	0	3	4	4	3	3	135		4	4	o
CACEI DE LA COTE, 21 MOS	2	4	4	4	4	2	3	3	3	3	124	II	3	3	o
CZAR DE LA COTE, 20 MOS	3	4	4	4	0	4	4	3	3	3	129		3	3	o
CAROLINA DE LA COTE, 2 YRS	1	2	3	4	0	1	2	2	2	3	77		3	4	o
CAROLINA DE LA COTE, 4 YRS	1	3	3	3	0	3	3	2	2	2	88		3	4	o
Ped 85 (1979) (Bent Pine's Angus x First Frost Unipac)															
FIRST FROST AXEL-SMAX, 2 YR	4	3	4	3	0	4	4	3	3	3	127		4	3	o
FIRST FROST AXEL-SMAX, 3 YR	3	2	3	1	0	-	3	3	2	2	82		3	4	o
+Ped 92 (1980) (Linus of Hunter's Creek x Baywater Pepper)															
MINDY OF ST MARY'S, 21 MOS	2	1	3	3	0	2	3	3	2	2	88		2	3	o
Ped 96 (1983) (Gilead Lake's Boomer x Gretchen von Keefer)															
CARA VAN DE JAGER, 5 YRS	3	4	4	4	2	4	4	4	3	4	142	II	3	2	o
Ped 98 (1979) (Ruff vom Tana II x Ginger vom Vantage Home)															
BIRCHWOOD MANOR'S MISTY,3 YR	1	2	3	2	0	2	2	2	2	2	76		3	2	o
Ped 100 (1979) (Ucky du Ruisseau du Massacre x Urfe des Cheveches)															
MIRKA DES DAUPHINS DU FOREZ, 3 YR	3	4	4	4	3	4	4	3	4	4	133	II	4	2	o
Ped 101 (1979) (Dolf vom Geeste-Moor x Birchwood Manor's Melissa)															
BIRCHWOOD MANOR'S INGA IGITURE, 9 YRS	2	4	4	3	0	4	3	2	3	3	110		2	2	*
Ped 102 (1979) (Falk vom Waldpark x Mighty Heide)															
MOSES, 9 YRS	2	2	4	4	1	4	4	3	4	3	124		3	2	o
Ped 117 (1981) (Pleasant Valley Ozark x First Frost Heidi)															
CROSSWINDS GRIZZLY, 6 YRS	3	4	4	3	4	4	4	3	4	3	144	II	2	2	o

	TD	RD	S	P	D	TB	N	A	C	O	TO	PR	CO	CT	T
Ped 118 (1981) (Winterwinds Tail Wagger x Ixia du Bois de la Comme)															
WINTERWIND'S MR GRIFFITHS, 2 YRS	1	2	4	2	0	1	2	2	2	2	74		3	2	o
Ped 119 (1981) (Sacky des Matines x Bent Pine's Ahna)															
THREE RIVERS SAM, 3 YRS	2	3	4	4	4	0	3	3	3	3	106		2	2	o
Ped 108 (1982) (Barry v.d. Neuburg x Bent Pine's Aberdeen) (2 litters)															
DUCKPOND EBULLIENT KASY,2 YR	2	4	2	2	4	4	3	3	3	3	112	III	3	3	o
DUCKPOND FREDRICK V BISMARK, 22 MOS	1	0	2	3	0	2	2	2	1	1	59		3	4	o
DUCKPOND FREDA, 3 YRS	4	3	4	4	1	3	4	3	3	3	131		4	3	o
DUCKPOND FROELICH, 3 YRS	3	3	4	4	4	3	3	3	3	3	129	II	3	3	o
Ped 109 (1982) (Smoke Creek Bisko x Duckpond de Poco)															
DIABLO RIDGE SACTO ARROW, 2 YRS	3	3	2	2	1	2	3	2	2	2	89		3	3	o
DIABLO RIDGE SENA, 2 YRS	4	3	2	2	4	4	4	3	2	2	119	III	-	-	*
+Ped 111 (1982) (Lucas of Hunter's Creek x Happy Hilda Hunter)															
DE LA COTE'S DELIVERANCE, 2 YR	2	3	4	4	2	2	3	3	3	3	115	III	3	3	o
DESIREE DE LA COTE, 2 YRS	3	3	3	1	0	2	3	3	3	3	97		4	4	o
DUKE DE LA COTE, 2 YRS	4	2	4	2	0	4	4	2	1	1	104		3	3	o
DRYADES DE LA COTE, 2 YRS	1	3	3	2	0	0	2	2	2	2	69		3	3	o
+Ped 112 (1982) (Bent Pine's Biff x Bridgette de la Cote)															
EMBER DE LA COTE, 21 MOS	3	4	2	4	1	0	2	2	2	3	91		3	4	o
ENCORE DE LA COTE, 22 MOS	2	3	4	4	0	0	3	3	2	2	97		4	4	o
ENCORE DE LA COTE, 4 YRS	3	4	3	4	4	3	4	4	3	3	137	II	4	4	o
Ped 113 (1982) (Taquin du Bois Follet x Zest du Montmagny)															
**ABBEY DE FEU FOLLET, 2 YRS	2	3	4	4	3	0	3	3	3	3	112		2	2	o
Ped 114 (1982) (Gotz vom Bibertal x Diana vom Ramsberg)															
AMARA V FUCHSBERG, 2 YRS	1	1	2	4	4	4	3	2	2	2	94		2	2	*
ABBA V FUCHSBERG, 2 YRS	2	0	4	4	2	4	4	4	3	2	112		3	2	o
+Ped 120 (1983) (Bent Pine's Biff x Brisette de la Cote)															
ANJA V MAYERHOF, 2 YRS	2	1	3	4	0	4	4	2	2	3	106		4	4	o
AJAX V MAYERHOF, 2 YRS	3	3	4	4	0	3	3	3	3	3	117		4	3	o
AJAX V MAYERHOF, 3 YRS	3	4	3	4	3	2	3	3	4	4	127	II	3	3	o
ASTOR V MAYERHOF, 3 YRS	3	4	3	3	4	3	3	3	3	3	123	II	3	3	o
+Ped 121 (1982-85) (Bon Chasseur de la Cote x Alice b Toklias) (2 litters)															
MOLLY B TOKLIAS, 2 YRS	1	4	3	4	3	2	2	2	3	3	101		3	2	o
EIGHT BALL TOKLIAS, 2 YRS	1	3	4	4	0	1	3	1	2	2	87		4	4	o
MAHASKA'S MERRY SUSAN, 20 MOS	2	4	3	4	4	4	3	3	3	3	125	II	4	3	o

	TD	RD	S	P	D	TB	N	A	C	O	TO	PR	CO	CT	T
Ped 121 (Continued)															
BON CHASSEUR DE LA CHAMP, 19 MO	4	0	4	4	0	3	4	3	1	1	107		4	3	o
LARUE'S JASPER GREY, 19 MO	3	4	2	1	4	1	3	2	2	3	97		4	3	*
LARUE'S JASPER GREY, 32 MO	1	4	3	4	4	3	3	3	3	3	117		4	4	*
MISSEY OF OAK RIDGE, 32 MO	2	4	4	4	0	1	2	3	2	2	97		4	4	*
Ped 122 (1983) (Tracy A'Moustaches x Huckle Hill Angela)															
HUCKLE HILL ALFALFA, 23 MO	1	4	3	4	3	1	3	3	3	3	108		3	3	o
Ped 125 (1983) (Hardrock Montana Jeep x Bisquit McDuck)															
ROCKY MONTANA KNUT, 22 MOS	4	4	3	0	2	3	3	3	3	3	110		4	2	o
Ped 126 (1983) (Ilk vom Bibertal x Flatheads Jagdhund Gretel)															
SUZIE V HUNTER, 19 MOS	2	2	3	3	2	2	3	3	2	3	100	III	4	3	*
Ped 129 (1983) (Bar-Mi's Elmo at Rocin x J V's Gilda Griffon)															
QUAIL QUEEN BARMI'S PEPPER, 2 YRS	4	4	3	2	4	4	4	3	3	4	136	II	3	3	o
JV'S LITTLE RED LA-VITT, 2 YR	2	3	4	4	2	3	3	4	3	3	122	II	3	3	o
R S'S GRETCHEN GRIFFON,3 YR	2	4	3	4	0	1	3	3	3	3	98		4	2	o
Ped 131 (1983) (Winterwind's Mr. Griffiths x Winerwind's Waldschloss Suzy)															
WINTERWIND'S FEATHER FINDER, 21 MOS	3	3	4	4	3	3	4	3	3	3	132	II	3	2	o
+Ped 132 (1984-85) (Bent Pine's Biff x Desiree de la Cote)															
AMOS VAN JAGERSHORST, 21 MOS	2	4	4	4	4	4	3	3	4	4	136	II	4	3	o
ACKER VAN JAGERSHORST, 21 MO	2	0	4	4	0	2	3	3	2	2	94		3	4	o
ACKER VAN JAGERSHORTS, 33 MO	1	2	4	4	0	4	3	2	2	2	97		4	3	*
ADI VAN JAGERSHORST,20 MO	1	2	3	2	2	3	3	3	2	2	91		4	3	o
AMBER VAN JAGERSHORST, 20 MO	1	0	4	4	0	2	3	3	2	2	89		4	3	o
ASTRA VAN JAGERSHORST, 21 MOS+++		0	3	4	0	2	3	2	2	2	75		4	3	o
(+++-Dog was withdrawn, not tested at the water.)															
Ped 135 (1984) (Arn v Hammandel x Diabloe Ridge Salina)															
SMOKEN JOE, 28 MOS	1	4	2	2	4	1	2	2	2	2	82		3	2	o
Ped 139 (1984) (Magic Valley's Griff x Magic Valley's Beni)															
SWEET COCO, 2 YRS	1	3	2	3	2	2	2	2	2	2	80		3	3	o
Ped 140 (1986) (Sunwheel Buzz x Lady Coco of Hunter's Creek)															
TEAL OF ROCK CREEK, 4 YRS	1	4	3	4	4	3	3	2	3	3	113		2	2	o
PINCH OF THYME OF ROCK CREEK, 4 YRS	2	4	2	4	4	4	3	2	3	3	108	III	3	3	*
Ped 141 (1983) (Ilk vom Bibertal x Magic Valley's Dolly)															
LOLA, 2 YRS	3	3	4	4	3	4	3	3	3	3	129	II	3	1	o

	TD	RD	S	P	D	TB	N	A	C	O	TO	PR	CO	CT	T
+Ped 142 (1985) (Cacei de la Cote x Anka vom Fuchsberg)															
FREEWINDS ALAMANCE, 2 YR	4	4	3	4	4	4	4	4	3	3	145	II	3	2	o
FREEWINDS ABBRECOT, 2 YRS	3	4	4	4	4	3	3	4	4	4	142	II	3	2	o
FREEWINDS ALBERTA, 3 YRS	+++	0	4	4	0	3	3	2	2	2	83		3	1	o
(+++ Dog was withdrawn, not tested in the water.)															
Ped 144 (1985-88) (Furst v.d. Neuburg x Flatheads Jagdhund Gretel) (2 litters)															
HAMTON'S FUSILCHEIN DARNE, 17 MO	4	4	4	4	0	2	3	4	3	3	126		3	2	o
TIDEWATER ACCENT'S ASA, 22 MO	4	4	4	4	2	3	3	3	3	3	131	II	3	3	o
GRIFF FRANCOIS DE PERRAULT, 19 MO	3	2	2	4	0	2	3	2	3	3	97		3	2	*
(See below for an additional dog from this Ped 144.)															
Ped 145 (1985) (Magic Valley Rafe x Magic Vally Heidi)															
GREEN MOUNTAINS GRIFF, 22 MO	2	3	3	3	4	4	3	2	2	3	99	III	3	3	o
Ped 149 (1984) (Magic Valley Rafe x Amagot Getchurgun)															
THREE OAKS LONKA, 32 MOS	4	4	3	4	4	4	4	4	4	4	151	II	3	3	o
THREE OAKS LONKA, 44 MOS	4	4	4	4	4	4	4	4	4	4	156	I	3	3	o
+Ped 150 (1986) (Lucas of Hunter's Creek x Abba vom Fuchsberg)															
BUTZ VOM MAYERHOF, 2 YRS	2	2	3	0	0	3	3	2	2	3	81		3	3	*
Ped 151 (1986) (Alders Edge Amundsen x Koele's Meggen)															
ANDY (OF PERKINS CORNER), 2 YR	4	4	3	3	4	3	3	3	3	3	128	II	3	3	o
Ped 152 (1986) (Fritz von Becker x Duchess v.d. Umpqua Park)															
BARON V HERRENHAUSEN, 21 MOS	2	3	3	4	3	4	3	3	3	3	119	II	4	2	o
++BEAUX VON LINK, 34 MOS	3	3	2	4	3	3	3	2	2	4	112		2	2	o
Ped 153 (1986) (Furst v.d. Neuburg x Bar-Mi's Gretchen)															
SHARON'S MT JOHN REGGIE, 2 YRS	3	4	4	4	4	4	4	4	4	4	151	I	4	3	o
BECKER'S GRAY GRIFFON, 16 MOS	3	2	4	4	4	2	3	3	3	3	123	II	3	1	o
Ped 155 (1986) (Beaver Dam's Kiowa x Jez-A-Belle)															
DEIDRA OF POINT LOOKOUT, 22 MO	2	4	3	3	4	1	2	3	3	3	106		3	3	o
+Ped 156 (1986-87) (Amos Van Jagershorst x Point's Pewter Tip)															
POINT'S SHOT, 18 MOS	3	2	4	4	2	3	3	2	2	3	113	III	2	-	*
POINT'S SHOT, 2 YRS	4	4	4	4	4	4	4	4	3	4	153	II	2	1	o
POINT'S ALGERNON BIFF, 2 YR	4	4	4	4	2	4	4	3	3	3	140	II	3	3	*
(Growled and snapped at judges, would not allow conformation examination.)															
MAX-A-MILLION, 2 YRS	2	3	4	4	0	4	3	2	2	2	105		3	1	o
**DACOTA'S PICC OF THE TIP, 2 YRS	-	2	2	0	4	-	-	-	-						
(Dog withdrawn in middle of test.)															

	TD	RD	S	P	D	TB	N	A	C	O	TO	PR	CO	CT	T
Ped 157 (1987) (Duckpond Eager Baron x Duckpond Ginger)															
MAJESTIC KOKO WINFIELD,21 MOS	1	4	4	4	0	3	3	2	2	2	100		3	3	o
DUCKPOND SWEET SUZETTE,26 MO	1	3	4	4	0	2	2	3	3	2					
(Two dogs from this litter were tested under revised IHDT rules in 1989.)															
Ped 158 (1987) (Ranger des Chaumes de L'Aure D'or x Urfe de la Vallee Bertier)															
AXEL DE ST LANDRY, 20 MOS	1	4	4	1	0	1	2	2	2	2	76		3	3	o
Ped 162 (1987) (Lucas of Hunter's Creek x Trebeau Sue)															
TREBEAU ABBY, 2 YRS	2	3	3	4	3	1	3	2	2	3	103		4	4	o
+Ped 163 (1986) (Alan od Vejrice x Elsa z Trocnovskeho luhu) (CF)															
JISKRA Z TROCNORSKEHO LUHU, 26 MOS	2	4	4	4	2	4	4	4	3	3	134	II	3	2	o
+Ped 165 (1987-88) (Erik od Jezerak(CF) x Mahaska's Merry Susan)															
AVAJ OF IAMONIA, 19 MOS	4	3	4	4	4	4	4	4	4	3	150	I	4	3	o
AMBER OF IAMONIA, 19 MOS	4	3	4	4	3	4	4	4	3	3	144	II	2	2	o
ALF OF IAMONIA, 19 MOS	1	4	4	4	2	4	3	3	3	2	116		2	2	*
AUBIE OF IAMONIA, 19 MOS	0	0	4	4	0	4	3	2	2	2	86		3	3	*
AVIANA KATRINA OF IAMONIA, 24 MO	4	3	4	2	3	2	3	2	2	3	113	III	3	4	o
AUNATURAL OF IAMONIA, 25 MO	0	0	4	4	0	3	3	2	1	1	77		4	4	*
+Ped 166 (1987-88) (Erik od Jezerak(CF) x Freewinds Alamance)															
AMADEUS OF HOFFMAN MILL, 15 MOS	1	0	2	4	4	4	3	2	3	3	99		2	1	o
AUTUMN OF HOFFMAN MILL,20 MO	4H	4	4	4	4	4	4	4	4	4	156	I	4	3	o
AKRISTIFF OF HOFFMAN MILL,20 MO	3	3	4	4	4	4	4	4	4	4	148	I	4	3	o
AMBRA OF HOFFMAN MILL, 22 MO	0	0	4	4	3	0	2	2	1	1	71		4	2	*
Ped 167 (1988) ("Jaik" x Theresa Mantua vom Hasenhof)															
SATCH TOPALCH VOM KALKOFEN,26 MO	1	2	3	4	0	1	2	2	2	2	77		3	2	*
Ped 168 (1987) (Excaliber Jebadiah x Vancouver Anastasia)															
SIR DONZI MONOHULL, 18 MO	4	2	3	4	0	4	4	3	2	2	117		3	2	*
Ped 169 (1987) (Adolph von Duffer x Cora von Glantz)															
WELCH'S SIR TIMOTHY, 18 MO	3	4	4	4	0	4	4	4	3	3	133		-	-	o
WELCH'S SIR TIMOTHY, 23 MO	4	4	4	4	3	4	4	4	4	3	150	I	3	2	o
Ped 170 (1988) (Finnigan von Ripoff x Peppermint Patty von Carter)															
PATCHES VON RIPOFF, 16 MOS	3	4	3	4	4	3	3	3	3	4	130	II	2	3	o
PATCHES VON RIPOFF, 21 MOS	4	4	4	4	4	4	4	4	4	4	156	I	4	3	o
Ped 171 (1988) (Alder's Edge Blaze x Quail Queen Bar-mi's Pepper)															
LES FONDS DU WAPSIPINICON, 15 MO	4	4	4	4	3	4	4	4	3	4	150	I	3	3	o

	TD	RD	S	P	D	TB	N	A	C	O	TO	PR	CO	CT	T
+Ped 174 (1988) (Cagan z Dracina x Hela Z Dobrovska) (CF)															
BLITZEN OF THE CASCADES,16 MO	4	4	3	4	4	4	4	4	3	3	145	II	3	3	o
BLADE OF THE CASCADES,16 MO	3	4	3	4	4	2	3	3	3	3	127	II	4	3	o
BLISS OF THE CASCADES,16 MO	1	4	4	4	4	4	4	3	3	3	131		4	4	o
BOSS OF THE CASCADES,17 MO	3	3	3	1	3	4	4	4	3	3	122		4	3	o
BRIDGET OF THE CASCADES,17 MO	0	4	2	2	4	4	3	2	2	2	92		4	4	*
BREEZY OF THE CASCADES,16 MO	0	0	2	4	3	0	2	1	1	2	60		3	3	*
(See below under revised rules for more results from this litter.)															
Ped 179 (1988-91) (Ingo vom Kastanienhain x Glac[i]er Cool Deecee) (3 litters)															
BLUE MOUNTAIN BREW,19 MO	3	3	3	0	0	4	3	3	3	3	99		3	4	o
(See below under revised rules for more results from this litter.)															
Ped 181 (1988) (Furst v.d. Neuburg x Flatheads Geri)															
MAX VON DER BUTTES, 23 MO	4	3	4	4	3	4	4	4	3	3	144	II	2	3	o

REVISED INTERMEDIATE HUNTING DOG TEST RULES 1989

In the spring of 1989 we began using a revised, updated IHDT. See Chapter 23 for changes. This meant 4 new categories to be judged, 3 of the 4 to be optional. The additions were: ***Blind Retrieve from Reeds, ***Retrieve of Dragged Dead Game (Fur), ***Tracking Live Game (Fur), and Manner of retrieving. Also, dogs over 24 months were now judged under the Older Hunting Dog Test requirements, and noted thus in the tabulations with ++ before their name.

CATEGORIES with their index following, are listed as follows:

WATER	FIELD	JUDGED THROUGHOUT
TD-Tracking Duck-5	S-Searching-5	N-Nose-6
RD-Retrieve Duck-3	P-Pointing-4	A-Attitude Toward Work-4
BR-***Blind Retrieve-4	D-Retrieve Dragged Game-3	C-Cooperation-3
	TB-Tracking Live Bird-3	O-Obedience-3
	TF-***Tracking Live Fur-3	M-Manner of Retrieving-3
	RF-***Retrieve Dragged Fur-3	

	TD	RD	*BR	S	P	D	TB	*TF	*RF	N	A	C	O	M	TO	PR	CO	CT	T
Ped 144 (1989-91) (See above for other dogs tested before 1989 in IHDT.)																			
++FRIEDRICH VON TRENDELBURG, 2 YRS, 10 MOS	1	2		3	4	0	4			3	3	2	2	1	99		3	4	o
++FRIEDRICH VON TRENDELBURG, 4 YRS	2	3		3	4	0	4			3	3	2	2	2	110		3	4	o
Ped 157 (1989) (See above for other dogs from this breeding tested earlier.)																			
++LADY GINGER OF MEDOMAK VALLEY, 2 YRS	2	3		4	2	4	4			4	3	3	3	4	137	III	3	3	o
++DUCKPOND DUSTIN, 2 YRS	3	4		4	4	4	2			3	4	3	3	4	145	II	3	3	o
+Ped 173 (1991) (CF) (See above for dogs tested before 1990 in IHDT.)																			
BLITZEN OF THE CASCADES, 22 MOS	4	4	4	4	4	4	4		4	4	4	4	4	4	196	I	4	3	o
BOSS OF THE CASCADES, 19 MOS	3	3	4	4	3	4	4		4	4	4	3	3	3	175	II	4	4	o
BREEZE OF THE CASCADES, 22 MOS	4	3		3	4	4	4			4	4	4	4	4	160	II	3	4	o
BLISS OF THE CASCADES, 22 MOS	2	3		4	4	4	4			4	3	3	3	4	145	II	4	3	o
++BLADE OF THE CASCADES, 3 YRS	3	3		4	4	4	4			4	4	4	3	3	154	I	4	3	o
Ped 178 (1990) (Baron v Herrenhausen x Greta v Herrenhausen) (2 litters)																			
AUTUMN V HERRENHAUSEN, 24 MOS	4	3	`3	4	4	2	1			3	2	2	2	2	130		3	2	o
BELLE V HERRENHAUSEN,23 MO	1	3		3	4	3	2			3	2	3	3	3	114		3	2	o
Ped 179 (1991) (Ingo vom Kastanienhain x Glac[i]er Cool Deecee) (3 litters) (See above for dogs tested before 1990)																			
TINA OF PERKINS CORNER,23 MO	2	0		4	4	4	4			4	3	3	3	3	133		3	4	o
CINDY OF PERKINS CORNER, 21 MOS	4	2		3	4	4	3			4	3	3	3	2	138	II	3	3	o
INGO'S IMAGE VOM GLACIER, 16 MOS	3	2		4	4	0	3			4	2	2	2	1	113		4	4	o
++INGO'S IMAGE VOM GLACIER,31 MO	3	4		4	4	4	4		4	4	4	4	4	4	163	I	4	3	o
KALISPELL INGO VOM GLACIER,18 MO	3	3		4	4	4	4		4	4	4	4	4	4	172	I	4	3	o
VON BAILEY'S AXEL GUNNER, 18 MOS	2	4		4	4	0	0			3	2	2	2	2	102		4	4	*
Ped 182 (1990) (Fellow x Nancy v.d. Koorndijk)																			
ANNA OF BEARS CREEK, 20 MOS	4	4		3	4	0	4			4	3	3	3	2	135		3	3	o
+Ped 186 (1990-92) (Boss of the Cascades(CF) x Autumn of Hoffman Mill)																			
AUGUST OF AUGER FALLS, 16 MOS	3	2		4	4	3	3			4	3	3	3	2	135	III	3	4	o

	TD	RD	*BR	S	P	D	TB	*TF	*RF	N	A	C	O	M	TO	PR	CO	CT	T
A COOTER'S NIECE OF AUGER FALLS, 23 MO	4	4		4	4	4	4			4	4	4	4	4	168	I	4	3	o
ALEXANDRIA OF AUGER FALLS,23 MO	1	2		3	2	3	2			3	2	2	2	3	96		4	2	o
ALEXANDRIA OF AUGER FALLS,23 MO	2	2		4	2	4	4			4	3	3	3	3	131	III	4	2	o
ALPHA OF AUGER FALLS, 22 MOS	4	4		3	3	1	4			4	3	2	2	2	125		3	3	o
+Ped 187 (1990-92) (Blue Mountain Brew x Avaj of Iamonia) (2 litters)																			
ARROW OF DUTCHMAN'S HOLLOW, 16 MO	4	4		4	4	4	4			4	4	4	4	4	168	I	4	4	o
AVIAN OF DUTCHMAN'S HOLLOW, 16 MOS	4	3		4	4	2	4			4	4	3	3	3	150	II	3	4	o
ASAHEL OF DUTCHMAN'S HOLLOW, 16 MOS	4	2		3	4	4	4			4	3	3	3	3	144	II	3	2	o
ABBOT OF DUTCHMAN'S HOLLOW, 16 MOS	4	4		3	4	1	2			4	4	3	2	2	133		4	4	o
ABBOT OF DUTCHMAN'S HOLLOW, 23 MOS	4	4		4	4	4	4			4	4	4	4	4	168	I	4	4	o
AMY OF DUTCHMAN'S HOLLOW,16 MO	4	1		4	4	0	4			4	3	2	2	0	119		4	4	o
ASPEN OF DUTCHMAN'S HOLLOW, 16 MOS	4	2		3	3	1	3			4	3	2	2	1	116		4	4	o
ASPEN OF DUTCHMAN'S HOLLOW, 23 MOS	4	3		4	4	4	4			4	3	3	3	3	152	II	4	4	o
ABSAROKA OF DUTCHMAN'S HOLLOW, 23 MOS	3	1		4	4	4	2			3	2	3	3	2	122		3	4	o
CHAMPAGNE BLAZE OF DUTCHMAN'S HOLLOW, 17 MOS	4	4		4	4	4	4			4	4	4	4	4	168	I	3	4	o
CASSIE OF DUTCHMAN'S HOLLOW, 23 MOS	4	4		4	4	4	4			4	4	4	4	4	168	I	4	4	o
CERA OF DUTCHMAN'S HOLLOW,17 MO	4	4		3	4	4	4			4	4	4	4	3	160	II	4	4	o
CALLAJ OF DUTCHMAN'S HOLLOW, 17 MOS	4	4		4	4	4	4			4	4	3	3	3	159	II	3	4	o
CHEWBACCA OF DUTCHMAN'S HOLLOW, 17 MOS	2	4		3	3	4	4			4	4	3	3	4	143	II	3	4	o
CASIMIR LORING OF DUTCHMAN'S HOLLOW, 17 MOS	4	3		4	4	3	1			4	3	3	3	2	137		3	-	o
CASIMIR LORING OF DUTCHMAN'S HOLLOW, 24 MOS	2	4		4	4	4	4			4	4	4	3	3	152	II	3	2	o
CURSE OF DUTCHMAN'S HOLLOW, 24 MOS	1	1		3	2	0	4			3	2	2	3	3	93		3	4	*
+Ped 188 (1990-91) (Erik od Jezerak(CF) x Patches von Rippoff)																			
AYLA OF WHITE WATER, 17 MOS	4	4		4	4	4	4			4	4	4	4	4	168	I	4	2	*
ARO OF WHITE WATER, 18 MOS	4	0		4	3	4	2			3	2	2	3	1	114		3	1	o
ANKA OF WHITE WATER, 17 MOS	1	2		3	3	4	4			3	2	2	2	4	112		4	3	*

	TD	RD	*BR	S	P	D	TB	*TF	*RF	N	A	C	O	M	TO	PR	CO	CT	T
Pedigree 188 (Continued)																			
AMIE OF WHITE WATER, 17 MOS	1	0		4	4	4	4			3	1	2	2	2	105		3	3	*
Ped 192 (1990) (Baron v Herrenhausen x Rooster's Copper Penny)																			
SOPHIA V HERRENHAUSEN, 23 MOS	2	3		4	4	3	4			3	3	3	3	3	133	II	3	4	o
Ped 194 (1991) (Duckpond Dustin x Duckpond Joyeux)																			
GABRIELLE DUCK POND LARABEE, 22 MOS	4	2		3	4	4	2			3	3	3	3	2	129	III	4	4	o
Ped 196 (1991) (Bert's Venatic Kyle x Princess Lisa McDuck)																			
++JOSEPHINE QUEEN MCDUCK, 4 YRS	2	2		3	4	0	4			4	3	3	2	2	112		3	2	o
+Ped 199 (1991-92) (Erik od Jezerak x Hela Z Dobrovaka) (CF) (3 litters. There were a total of six dogs from the 3 litters. See Part One for explanation.)																			
ARIKO VOM ERIK, 23 MOS	4	2		2	4	0	2			3	2	2	2	1	99		4	3	o
++ARIKO VOM ERIK, 30 MOS	4	3		4	4	4	4			4	4	4	4	4	165	I	4	3	o
BECI VOM ERIK, 24 MOS	4H	4	4	4	4	4	4		4	4	4	4	4	4	196	I	3	3	o
BLUMELEIN VOM ERIK, 18 MOS	2	3		3	4	4	4			3	2	2	2	4	124	III	3	1	o
CHANEL VOM ERIK, 22 MOS	4	4		3	2	4	4			4	4	3	3	3	146	III	4	3	o
++CHANEL VOM ERIK, 34 MOS	4	3		3	3	4	4			4	3	3	3	2	140	III	3	3	o
COMMANDER VOM ERIK, 17 MOS	3	2		4	4	1	3			3	3	3	3	2	123		4	2	o
Ped 200 (Duckpond Garp x Duckpond Suzanne) (1990)																			
++DUCKPOND JOYEUX, 4 YRS	2	3		4	4	4	4			4	4	3	3	4	146	II	4	2	o
+Ped 201 (1990) (Boss of the Cascades(CF) x Avaj of Iamonia (1990)																			
BUCKINGHAM OF DUTCHMAN'S HOLLOW, 17 MOS	4	3		4	4	4	1			3	3	3	3	3	137		3	4	o
BUCKINGHAM OF DUTCHMAN'S HOLLOW, 23 MOS	4	4		4	4	4	3			4	4	4	4	4	165	I	3	3	o
BROOK OF DUTCHMAN'S HOLLOW, 17 MOS	2	3		4	2	1	3			3	3	2	2	2	107		3	3	o
BROOK OF DUTCHMAN'S HOLLOW, 23 MOS	3	4		4	4	4	4			4	4	4	3	4	160	I	3	3	o
BIRKLEY BELLE OF DUTCHMAN'S HOLLOW, 23 MOS	3	3		4	4	3	4			4	4	3	3	3	140	II	4	3	o

	TD	RD	*BR	S	P	D	TB	*TF	*RF	N	A	C	O	M	TO	PR	CO	CT	T
Pedigree 201 (Continued)																			
BRANDY OF DUTCHMAN'S HOLLOW, 17 MO	4	2		4	4	0	3			4	3	2	1	1	119		4	4	o
++BRANDY OF DUTCHMAN'S HOLLOW,29 MO	4	3		4	4	3	3			4	4	3	3	3	150	II	3	4	o
++BRITTANY OF DUTCHMAN'S HOLLOW, 29 MOS	4	3		4	4	2	4			4	4	3	3	2	150	III	3	4	o
BABETTE OF DUTCHMAN'S HOLLOW, 17 MOS	1	0		4	4	0	3			4	2	2	2	1	97		4	3	o
BABETTE OF DUTCHMAN'S HOLLOW, 23 MOS	2	3		4	4	3	4			4	3	2	3	2	125	III	4	3	o
BUCKEYE OF DUTCHMAN'S HOLLOW, 23 MOS	4	3		4	4	0	4			4	4	3	3	2	141		3	3	o
RUBY OF DUTCHMAN'S HOLLOW, 23 MOS	4	3		4	4	0	2			4	4	3	2	2	124		3	3	o
Ped 201A (1990) (Owyhee Canyon Deke x Chukar Hill Tess) (1990)																			
MEDOMAK VALLEY KATRINA, 17 MOS	4	0		3	3	4	4			4	3	3	3	3	146		3	4	*
(Reacted negatively to shot during water work.)																			
Ped 203 (1992) (Dino De L'Etang x Alders Edge Feu Follet)																			
AMBERGRIS DU FEU FOLLET, 23 MOS	3	3		4	4	4	4			4	4	4	4	3	157	I	2	4	o
Ped 205 (1992) (Duck v Herrenhausen x Sophia v Herrenhausen)																			
EDELTRAUT V HERRENHAUSEN, 27 MOS	1	0		2	3	0	2			2	2	1	1	0	59		3	3	o
+Ped 208 (1991-92) (Erik od Jezerak x Axa OD Pastejriko) (CF)																			
AMBROSE DE LOS ALTOS, 17 MOS	2	4	4	4	4	4	4		4	4	4	4	4	4	183	II	4	2	o
++AMBROSE DE LOS ALTOS, 29 MOS	4	4	4	4	4	4	4			4	4	4	4	4	196	I	4	3	o
Ped 215 (1991) (Bosko vom Rhonblick x Hexe vom Kempter Wald)																			
ALF VOM SUDMERBERG, 19 MOS	4	4	4	4	4	4	4		0	4	4	3	3	3	175	II	3	3	o
Ped 216 (1991) (Point's Algernon x Royal Hunts Dinah)																			
++ASTRA V NUMMELHOF,29 MO	2	4		4	3	4	3			3	3	4	3	4	138	II	4	4	o

	TD	RD	*BR	S	P	D	TB	*TF	*RF	N	A	C	O	M	TO	PR	CO	CT	T
Ped 217 (1991) (Fritz v Herrenhausen x Misty Rose Rooster)																			
++MISTY'S BRISTLED BRIE, 3 YRS	1	1		3	4	3	3			3	3	3	3	2	111		4	2	o
+Ped 218 (1992) (Arrow of Dutchman's Hollow x Autumn of Hoffman Mill)																			
BRENNA OF AUGER FALLS, 16 MOS	4H	4		4	4	4	4			4	4	4	4	4	177	I	4	4	o
BOBETT'S MEAGGAN OF AUGER FALLS, 22 MOS	4	3		4	4	3	4			4	4	4	3	2	153	III	3	3	o
BRANDISH OF AUGER FALLS, 22 MOS	1	4		4	4	4	4			3	3	2	2	4	131		4	?	o
BUCK OF AUGER FALLS, 22 MOS	1	4		4	4	1	4			3	3	2	2	3	119		4	3	o
++BIENE OF AUGER FALLS, 28 MOS	3	2	2	4	4	3	4			4	3	3	3	2	148	III	4	3	o
+Ped 219 (1992) (Erik od Jezarek(CF) x Amy of Dutchman's Hollow)																			
ANNIE OF OCEAN HOUSE, 15 MOS	2	2		4	3	3	3			3	3	2	2	2	114	III	3	3	*
AMOS OF OCEAN HOUSE, 23 MOS	3	2		4	4	2	4			4	3	3	2	2	132	III	4	3	o
AJAX OF OCEAN HOUSE, 23 MOS	1	3		4	4	4	4			3	3	3	3	4	134		4	4	o
ALEX OF OCEAN HOUSE, 23 MOS	1	3		3	4	3	4			3	3	3	3	3	123		4	4	o
+Ped 222 (1993-94) (Dan Cerniky x Axa od Pastejriko) (CF) (2 litters)																			
BRYANNA DE LOS ALTOS, 18 MOS	3	3	3	4H	4	4	4	4	4	4	4	3	3	3	187	II	4	3	o
BRIANNA DE LOS ALTOS, 21 MOS	2	3		4	4	4	4			4	4	3	3	3	146	II	4	3	o
BARTON DE LOS ALTOS, 18 MOS	2	4	4	3	4	2	2		4	3	3	2	2	3	144	III	4	4	o
COLFA DE LOS ALTOS, 19 MOS	3	4		4	4	3	4			4	4	3	3	3	147	II	3	3	o
(Remainder of "C" litter will be tested spring 1995.)																			
Ped 223 (1993) (Korky v Herrenhausen x Patches von Ripoff)																			
++EMMYLOU OF WHITE WATER, 24 MOS	2	2		3	4	0	4			4	2	1	1	0	97		3	3	*
+Ped 224 (1993) (Dan Cerniky x Borka z Kolodev) (CF)																			
ARCHIBALD OF DRUMMER'S RIDGE, 20 MOS	4	3		4	4	4	4			4	4	3	3	3	156	II	?	4	o
ALLIE OF DRUMMER'S RIDGE, 20 MOS	1	3		3	4	3	2			2	3	2	3	2	105		4	4	*

	TD	RD	*BR	S	P	D	TB	*TF	*RF	N	A	C	O	M	TO	PR	CO	CT	T
+Ped 226 (1993-94) (Dan Cerniky(CF) x Amy of Dutchman's Hollow) (1993-94)																			
BAILEY OF OCEAN HOUSE,18 MOS	4	4		4	4	4	4			4	4	4	4	4	168	I	4	3	o
BOSUN OF OCEAN HOUSE, 22 MOS	4	3		4	4	4	4			4	4	4	3	3	165	I	3	4	o
BUDDY OF OCEAN HOUSE, 18 MOS	4	3		4	4	3	4			4	4	3	3	3	153	II	3	3	o
BELL OF OCEAN HOUSE, 18 MOS	0	0		4	4	3	4			3	3	2	2	2	105		3	4	o
++BELL OF OCEAN HOUSE,30 MOS	4	3		4	4	4	4			4	4	3	3	2	150	II	3	4	o
++BOWLINE OF OCEAN HOUSE,31 MO	2	4		4	4	3	2			3	3	3	3	2	127	III	3	2	o
++BARNACLE OF OCEAN HOUSE,25 MO	2	4		4	4	0	4			4	3	3	3	2	130		4	3	o
BEACON OF OCEAN HOUSE, 24 MOS	1	4		2	4	0	3			3	2	2	2	1	93		4	3	*
+Ped 227 (1993-94) (Dan Cerniky(CF) x Autumn of Hoffman Mill)																			
COUNTESS OF AUGER FALLS, 23 MOS	4	3	4	3	4	4	4			4	4	4	4	4	176	II	4	2	*
COVEY OF AUGER FALLS, 17 MOS	4	2		4	2	3	4			4	4	3	2	2	136	III	3	3	*
CLEO OF AUGER FALLS, 17 MOS	1	2		4	3	2	2			3	3	2	2	2	103		3	3	*
CALLY OF AUGER FALLS, 17 MOS	2	1		4	4	2	3			3	3	2	1	1	106		?	3	*
CHARLEY OF AUGER FALLS, 23 MOS	0	4		3	4	3	4			4	3	3	3	3	127		4	2	*
Ped 228 (1993) (Aspen Point's Barrel x Cindy of Perkins Corner)																			
CHINA DOLL OF PERKINS CORNER, 18 MOS	4	3		3	3	3	2			3	3	2	2	2	119	III	3	4	o
CRISSI OF PERKINS CORNER, 24 MOS	4	2		4	4	1	4			4	3	2	2	1	128		4	4	o
Ped 232 (1993) (Grif von Pointer x Camas Hot Springs Suzie)																			
NORTH LIGHTS KACHINA DOLL, 19 MOS	4	4		4	0	4	4			4	4	3	3	4	146		4	3	o
Ped 233 (1993) (Good Time Furst Griff x Flatheads Magic Dolly)																			
++TRINA, 26 MOS	2	0		3	4	0	4			4	2	1	1	1	94		4	4	o
Ped 238 (1994) (Friedrich von Trendelburg x Kalispell Ingo vom Glacier)																			
WAYFARER'S TRENDELBURG AURA, 21 MOS	2	4		4	0	4	1			3	2	2	3	4	110		2	3	*

Ped 243 (1994) (Ingo vom Kastanienhain x Flatheads Georgia)
HERR FLINT VON SCHATTANHAIN, 18 MOS

TD	RD	*BR	S	P	D	TB	*TF	*RF	N	A	C	O	M	TO	PR	CO	CT	T
1	1		?	4	0	3			?	?	?	?	?			3	4	*

(Dog was too spooky and gun-shy to be able to judge in most categories)

NAVHDA UTILITY PREPARATORY TEST RESULTS FOR GRIFFONS FROM 1988 TO 1994

In 1988 NAVHDA began offering a test called the Utility Preparatory Test (UPT), which was designed to be exactly what the name says: a test to prepare a versatile hunting dog for the full Utility Field Test. Most of the categories tell how well the dog is trained for each task. It is not similar to the Intermediate Hunting Dog Test, which judges both inherited natural abilities, as well as how well the dog takes to training.

As explained in Part II, the IHDT is fashioned after the European Fall Breeding Test, and is one of the primary tools used in making breeding decisions. Dogs are nearly always tested between the ages of 18 and 24 months, before all their inherited abilities--good and bad--have been covered up (masked) by exposure and conditioning. The UPT and IHDT are not the same and one cannot compare results from each. One is an orange, the other is an apple. But the UPT results are part of our breed's testing record and therefore should be available. KEEP IN MIND THAT THE UPT DOES NOT TEST ANY TRACKING, not on a duck, not on a pheasant, nor on fur.

Following are the test categories, headings, and indexes:

WATER	FIELD	JUDGED THROUGHOUT
WS-Water Search-4	S-Search-5	N-Nose-6
H-Walk at Heel-2	P-Pointing-4	D-Desire to Work-5
B-Steady at Blind-2	SG-Steadiness on Game	C-Cooperation-3
RD-Retrieve Duck-3	RB-Retrive Shot Bird-3	O-Obedience-3
D-Retrieve from Drag-3		

In the tabulations below, additional information categories are: TP- Total Points, PR-Prize Classification, C-Coat and C-Conformation (unless major fault, this is left blank), and T-Temperament.

	WS	H	B	RD	S	P	SG	RB	D	N	D	C	O	TP	PR	C	C	T
NAV-40 (1988) (Loys du Tedelou x Alders Edge Attagirl)																		
ALDERS EDGE FETICHE, 24 MOS	3	4	4	4	4	3	3	4	4	3	3	3	3	156	II	-	-	o
NAV-56 (1992) (Dino de L'Etang x Alders Edge Feu Follet)																		
ACAJOU DU FEU FOLLET, 28 MOS	4	4	4	4	4	4	4	4	3	3	4	4	4	175	II	-	-	o
NAV-64 (1992) (Alders Edge Ingos Cool Alpha x Alders Edge Griselda)																		
ALDERS EDGE HAGAR, 18 MOS	1	4	4	4	3	4	2	3	3	4	2	2	3	136		-	-	o
NAV-47 (1990) (Alders Edge Blaze x Armada's Georgia Brown)																		
PRAIRIE LEK'S GERTA, 16 MOS	4	4	4	4	3	2	2	1	0	4	2	2	2	122			ectrop.	o
PRAIRIE LEK'S GERTA, 24 MOS	1	4	4	4	4	3	3	3	4	4	3	3	3	151			ectrop.	o
NAV-66 (1993) (Cesar v Erlenbruch x Aspen Point's Buttstock)																		
SUPER EMMA DUCHASSEUR, 20 MOS	4	4	4	4	4	4	3	4	4	4	4	4	4	181	I	-	-	o
NAV-69 (1991 and GR Ped #190) (Duckpond Dustin x Duckpond Joyeux) (2 litters)																		
DUCKPOND LIEDERKRANZ, 24 MOS	1	4	0	1	3	3	0	2	0	3	2	1	1	82		-	-	o
DUCKPOND LADY, 28 MOS	2	4	4	4	2	2	1	4	4	3	1	2	2	116		-	-	*
DUCKPOND NORRIDGEWOCK, 26 MOS	4	3	0	4	3	3	2	1	3	4	3	1	2	127		-	-	o
NAV-37 (1989 and GR-200) (Duckpond Garp x Duckpond Suzanne)																		
DUCKPOND JOYEUX, 40 MOS	4	4	4	4	4	4	3	2	4	4	4	3	3	169	II	-	-	o
NAV-54 (1991-92) (Good Time Grady Boy x Flatheads Heidi)																		
VON BAUGHMAN'S KEDA, 18 MOS	1	4	4	0	3	3	0	2	4	4	2	2	2	111		-	-	o
VON BAUGHMAN'S KEDA, 31 MOS	1	4	4	4	2	3	2	4	4	2	2	2	3	121		-	-	o
NAV-63 (1989, 1993 and GR Ped 179 (Ingo v Kastanienhain x Glac[i]er Cool Deecee) (3 litters)																		
KALISPELL INGO V GLACIER, 23 MOS	3	2	4	4	4	4	2	4	3	4	4	3	3	161	II	-	-	o
GOOD TIME NATTIE, 29 MOS	3	4	4	4	3	3	3	3	4	4	4	3	3	159	II	-	-	o
INGO'S IMAGE V GLACIER, 29 MOS	2	4	4	4	4	3	3	4	4	3	3	3	3	152	III	-	-	o

	WS	H	B	RD	S	P	SG	RB	D	N	D	C	O	TP	PR	C	C	T
NAV-115 (1991 and GR Ped 191) (Sampson v Herrenhausen x Greta v Herrenhausen)																		
DUCHESS V HERRENHAUSEN, 21 MOS	3	3	1	3	4	4	1	4	4	4	3	3	2	146	III	**butt bite**		o
DRUMMER V HERRENHAUSEN, 4 YRS	1	2	3	4	3	3	1	3	4	4	3	3	2	131		-	-	o
NAV-116A (1992 and GR Ped 217) (Fritz v Herrenhausen x Misty Rose Rooster)																		
MISTY'S BRISTLED BRIE, 36 MOS	1	2	4	0	2	1	0	2	0	2	1	1	2	62		-	-	o
MISTY'S BRISTLED BRIE, 44 MOS	3	3	4	2	4	1	0	3	3	4	2	2	2	120		-	-	o
NAV-46 (1990 and GR Ped 188) (Fellow of Reininghaus x Nancy v.d. Koorndijk)																		
ANNA OF BEAR'S CREEK, 22 MOS	1	4	4	2	4	2	1	2	0	3	2	1	2	100		-	-	o
NAV-51 (1991 and GR Ped 188) (Erik od Jezerak(CF) x Patches von Rippoff)																		
AYLA OF WHITE WATER, 17 MOS	2	4	4	2	3	0	0	2	3	3	0	2	2	90		-	-	o
NAV-52 (1990 and GR Ped 194) (Sharon's Mt John Reggie x Point's Pewter Tip)																		
ASPEN POINT'S BUTTSTOCK, 13 MOS	2	3	4	4	3	4	4	4	4	3	2	3	4	150	III	-	-	o
NAV-117 (1993 and GR Ped 214) (Fritz v Herrenhausen x Rosys Foxs Rooster)																		
ROOSTER'S GOOD TIME TALLY HO, 37 MOS	1	4	4	1	3	2	1	3	4	3	2	3	3	116		-	-	o
																(Jaw: prognathism)		
NAV-62 (1992) (Baron v Herrenhausen x Sophia v Herrenhausen)																		
GRACE V HERRENHAUSEN, 20 MOS	1	4	4	4	2	1	1	3	2	3	2	2	2	104		**butt bite**		o
NAV-118 (1994) (Echo de St Landry x Alders Edge Fetiche)																		
DE LOREE D'AULNES ANA, 27 MOS	1	3	4	3	3	2	0	2	4	4	2	2	2	114		-	-	o
NAV-119 (1994) (Flinn & Feathers Paddy O'Shea x Belle Archer)																		
PAYAK PINESIS DAMASCUS, 12 MOS	2	3	3	4	2	4	2	1	0	3	2	2	2	107		**entropic**		o
NAV-78 (1994 and GR Ped 232) (Grif von Pointer x Camas Hot Springs Suzie)																		
NORTH LIGHT'S KACHINA DOLL, 29 MOS	2	3	4	4	3	3	1	4	0	4	3	2	2	127		-	-	o

UTILITY FIELD TEST RESULTS

WPGCA & NAVHDA 1969 through 1976

From 1969 through 1976 Griffons were tested in NAVHDA sponsored tests, which were sanctioned by the WPGCA. In fact, a number of tests were put on by regional chapters of the WPGCA.

The categories for testing were divided into three major groups with sub categories and their index:

WATER	FIELD	JUDGED THROUGHOUT
4-Search for a Duck(Tracking)	5-Search	6-Use of Nose
2-Walking at Heel	4-Pointing	5-Desire to Work
2-Remaining by Blind	3-Steadiness to Wing & Shot	3-Stamina
2-Steadiness by Blind	3-Retrieve of Shot Bird	3-Cooperation
3-Retrieve of a Duck	3-Retrieve of Dragged Game	3-Obedience

The index indicates the weight (or importance) that is given to that category.

Test results are listed in *chronological* order, not by *pedigree number*.

No conformation and coat listed unless major faults. Last column is for temperament: o = okay, * = temperament problem.

Index	Search for Duck {Tracking} (TD)	Walking at Heel (H)	Remaining by Blind (RB)	Steadiness by Blind (SB)	Retrieve of a Duck (RD)	Search (S)	Pointing (P)	Steady to Wing & Shot ((W/S)	Retrieve of Shot Bird (RB)	Retrieve of dragged Game (RD)	Use of Nose (N)	Desire to Work (D)	Stamina (S)	Cooperation (C)	Obedience (O)	Total Points (TP)	Prize Classification (PR)	Temperament (T)
	4	2	2	2	3	5	4	3	3	3	6	5	3	3	3			
NAV-120 (1971-72) (Erwin v.d. Brech x Crissi v Altenburg)																		
HANSEL ZU DEN BERGEN GEHEN,7 YR	2	3	0	1	0	2	3	1	1	0	3	3	2	2	2	94		o
	(Overshot)																	
HANSEL ZU DEN BERGEN GEHEN,8 YR	2	3	3	2	2	2	2	1	1	3	3	3	2	2	2	113	III	o
	(Conformation: undershot, ectropic, back too long)																	
NAV-121 (1971) (Hansel Zu Den Bergen Gehen x Miss Tempest Nellagram)																		
HANSEL VOM HOHENWIND, 5 YR, 6 M	0	3	0	3	0	2	4	1	3	0	4	3	4	4	4	126		o
NAV-122 (1972) (Ohio du Sarrot x Roxanne du Nemtaye)																		
TRISTAN DU NEMTAYE, 2 YRS, 3 MOS	0	4	4	2	0	2	4	4	0	0	3	3	3	1	2	109		o
NAV-123 (1971) (Als Ledaren v Bitterroot x Kelly v Kastanienhain)																		
MISS HEIDI V ALLEN, 2 YRS 5 MOS	3	3	3	3	0	2	2	0	2	0	2	2	3	3	2	101		o
MISS HEIDI V ALLLEN, 3 YRS, 8 MOS	1	2	0	0	0	3	3	0	1	0	3	2	2	1	1	78		o
NAV-124 (1972) (Ohio du Sarrot x Pythie du Grand Dormen)																		
UTO DU NEMTAYE, 20 MOS	0	3	2	2	0	2	2	1	0	0	2	2	2	1	1	69		o

	TD	H	RB	SB	RD	S	P	WS	RB	RD	N	D	S	C	O	TP	PR	T
NAV-125 (1974-75 and GR Ped 7) (Pipo des Vieilles Rouches x Lorene de Ronciers de Clavieres)																		
VICTORIA DU BOIS FOLLET, 2 Y, 8 M	2	1	4	4	3	3	4	1	4	0	3	4	4	2	2	143		o
VICTORIA DU BOIS FOLLET, 3 YRS	3	4	4	4	2	4	4	1	3	4	3	4	4	3	3	170	III	o
VICTORIA DU BOIS FOLLET, 3 Y, 9 M	4	4	4	4	4	4	4	2	4	2	4	4	4	3	2	183	II	o
NAV-126 (1974) (Pyram x Patty des Vieilles Rouches)																		
SACKY DES MATINES, 4 YRS, 4 MOS	3	3	4	4	0	2	4	3	4	3	3	2	3	2	3	143		o
NAV-127 (1973-75 and GR Ped 14) (Sacha de St Landry x Agate de Agent)																		
SNOW QUEUE BLANC, 22 MOS	1	2	0	3	3	3	1	0	2	0	3	4	4	2	2	110		o
SNOW QUEUE BLANC, 3 YRS	3	1	4	1	2	4	3	0	3	2	4	4	4	3	2	148		o
SNOW QUEUE BLANC, 3 YRS, 9 MOS	4	4	0	2	2	4	4	1	2	4	4	4	4	4	3	168		o
SNOW QUEUE BLANC, 4 YRS, 6 MOS	2	4	4	2	2	3	3	0	3	0	4	2	3	2	2	126		o
SNOW QUEUE BLANC, 5 YRS, 4 MOS	2	4	3	4	3	4	4	0	3	3	3	3	4	3	3	157		o
NAV-128 (1976 and GR Ped 12) (Kentucky v Griff x Awatobi of Windy Hills)																		
DIRK V MEIERLOH, 4 YRS	2	2	4	3	3	4	3	3	2	3	3	3	3	2	3	148	III	o
NAV-129 (1976 and GR Ped 17) (Sacky des Matines x Miska v Schlemmkreide)																		
CHRISTIE D'OASIS, 23 MOS	2	4	4	4	4	2	3	3	4	4	2	3	3	4	4	159		o
CHRISTIE D'OASIS, 3 YRS	1	4	4	4	4	3	4	3	3	0	3	4	4	3	4	160		o
NAV-130 (1975-1977 and GR Ped 9) (Taquin du Bois Follet x Bent Pine's Brigette)																		
BENT PINES ALDA, 19 MOS	2	4	2	4	0	3	2	0	4	4	4	2	4	2	2	135		o
BENT PINES ABERDEEN, 4 YRS, 1 MO	1	4	4	4	4	3	2	0	3	1	2	3	4	2	2	127		*
NAV-131 (1976-77 and GR Ped 2) (Barry v.d. Neuburg x Tina de la Reote)																		
BENT PINES BRIGETTE, 21 MOS	1	3	0	0	0	2	4	1	2	0	3	3	3	2	2	99		o
BENT PINES BRIGETTE, 23 MOS	2	4	4	4	0	4	3	1	3	4	4	3	4	3	2	155		o
BENT PINES BRIGETTE, 2 YRS, 9 MOS	0	4	1	3	0	3	0	0	2	0	3	2	4	1	1	85		o
BENT PINES BRIGETTE, 4 YRS, 7 MOS	0	3	4	3	0	4	3	1	3	3	3	2	4	2	2	127		*
PELUDO VAN DUEZEN, 2 YRS, 9 MOS	1	2	0	0	1	3	2	0	0	0	3	2	3	2	2	84		*
NAV-132 (1974 and GR Ped 18) (Sacky des Matines x Birchwood Manors Inga Igiture)																		
BOUCHES DU RHONE, 3 YRS, 2 MOS	1	1	2	1	0	2	2	0	0	0	3	2	3	2	2	80		o

	TD	H	RB	SB	RD	S	P	WS	RB	RD	N	D	S	C	O	TP	PR	T
NAV-133 (1973-74) (Baron v Dunkel x Crissi v Bitterroot)																		
**HEIDI VON LINK, 3 YRS, 9 MOS	1	3	4	4	4	4	3	1	4	2	3	3	3	1	3	145		o
**HEIDI VON LINK, 4 YRS, 9 MOS	3	3	4	4	4	3	3	2	4	4	3	4	3	2	3	164	II	o
**HEIDI VON LINK, 5 YRS, 4 MOS	3	4	4	4	3	4	3	4	4	4	4	4	4	4	3	190	II	o
NAV-134 (1974 and GR Ped 4) (Ajax v Culm x Diana v Neuburg)																		
BOSS VOM WOLFSBERG, 2 YRS	1	4	4	4	4	4	2	0	3	4	3	4	4	3	3	157		o
BOSS VOM WOLFSBERG, 2 YRS, 7 MOS	3	4	4	4	4	4	4	1	4	4	4	4	4	3	3	185	III	o
BOSS VOM WOLFSBERG, 3 YRS 7 MOS	1	4	4	4	4	4	3	2	4	4	3	3	4	3	3	166		o
NAV-135 (1973) (Mike v Hessling x Geri Vantage Home)																		
MISS GEM OF VANTAGE HOME, 4 YRS	0	2	4	3	0	3	2	0	3	0	3	3	4	1	3	108		o
NAV-136 (1973) (Schnapps x Geri Vantage Home)																		
MISS MEG OF VANTAGE HOME, 2Y,1M	1	0	0	0	0	2	2	0	0	0	3	3	4	1	1	74		o
(Conformation: hindquarters slightly weak.)																		
NAV-137 (1974 and GR Ped 1) (Barry v.d. Neuburg x Gretel v Altenburg)																		
GHOSTS SHADOW, 4 YRS	3	4	4	4	2	3	4	0	4	0	3	3	4	2	3	146		o
NAV-138 (1974) (Pollux des Ajoncs de Neung x Puce du val de Veude)																		
SALINE DU VAL DE VEUDE, 4 Y, 7 M	0	3	0	0	0	3	3	0	3	0	3	3	4	2	2	100		o
NAV-139 (1973-79 and GR Ped 20) (Oscar des Vieux Grisards x Quiche de St Landry)																		
**ULRICH DE ST LANDRY, 2 YRS, 1 MO	1	3	4	4	0	3	1	0	0	0	2	3	3	1	2	90		o
**ULRICH DE ST LANDRY, 6 YRS, 1 MO	3	1	0	3	4	3	1	0	4	4	4	3	4	2	2	139		o
**ULRICH DE ST LANDRY, 7 YRS, 1 MO	3	1	1	4	4	2	2	2	3	4	3	3	3	2	3	138	III	o
(Right eye loose.)																		
**ULRICH DE ST LANDRY, 8 YRS, 1 MO	3	3	0	0	4	3	4	4	3	4	3	3	4	3	2	155		o
NAV-140 (1975 and GR Ped 16) (Sacha de St Landry x Riki v Tana)																		
MARGUERTIE DU MARECAGE, 3 Y, 6 M	3	2	4	4	2	4	3	1	4	3	3	3	4	2	3	155	III	o

	TD	H	RB	SB	RD	S	P	WS	RB	RD	N	D	S	C	O	TP	PR	T
NAV-141 (1975-1980 and GR Ped 8) (Taquin du Bois Follet x Huckle Hill Patty) (3 litters)																		
HUCKLE HILL ANGELA, 2 YRS, 4 MOS	2	3	4	4	0	3	3	3	2	2	3	3	4	3	3	142		o
HUCKLE HILL ANGELA, 2 YRS, 11 MOS	4	2	4	4	4	3	3	1	3	4	3	4	4	4	3	170	III	o
HUCKLE HILL ANGELA, 3 YRS 5 MOS	1	3	4	4	3	3	4	4	3	0	3	3	4	2	3	148		o
WINGMASTER'S TROUBLE MAKER, 3 Y, 2 M	3	4	4	4	4	4	1	1	3	4	4	4	4	3	3	170		o
WINGMASTER'S TROUBLE MAKER, 5 Y, 1 M	4	3	4	4	4	4	4	3	4	4	4	4	4	4	4	199	I	o
WINGMASTER'S TROUBLE MAKER, 5 Y, 10 M	1	3	4	4	4	3	2	3	4	4	2	3	4	2	3	149		o

WPGCA UTILITY FIELD TEST RESULTS OF GRIFFONS

1982 THROUGH 1994

In 1982 the W.P.G.C.A. Board of Directors did a major revision of our Utility Field Test (UFT), which up to that time was practically identical to the NAVHDA UFT. The revision enabled us to begin incorporating more of the tracking aspects of versatile hunting dogs. We took most of these additional testing categories straight from the German Testing Organizations. (See the scoring system and division of work in Chapter 23.)

Of special note was the incorporation of the following tests:

WATER:
1. Search without a Duck.
2. Blind Retrieve.

FIELD:
3. Whoa or Down.

WOODS: We added the "WOODS" group, and there we included:

4. Search in Woods
5. ***Find and Retrive Dead Game
6. ***Blood Track

*** - optional. Both these tests are required in Europe, and perhaps some day we will require them here.

We moved Walking at Heel to the woods portion, and usually test that in the woods, using the trees and bushes as obsticals for the dog and handler to walk around. It tries to simulate a hunter and dog sneaking up on some ducks in a pond or creek, a situation where the dog must heel quietly if any game is to get in the bag.

CATEGORIES AND THEIR INDEXES

WATER
T-Tracking Duck-5
S-Search w/o Duck-3
B-Blind Retrieve-3
SB-Steadiness at Blind-2
R-Retrieve Marked Fall-3

FIELD
S-Searching-5
P-Pointing-4
WS-Steady Wing/Shot-3
R-Retrieve Shot Bird-3
W-Whoa or Down-3
T-Track Live Bird-4

WOODS
S-Search in Woods-4
W-Walk at Heel-2
D-Retrieve Dragged Game-3
*****F-Find/Retrieve Dead Game-3**
*****BT-Blood Track-4**

JUDGED THROUGHOUT
N-Nose-6
A-Attitude Toward Work-4
C-Cooperation-4
O-Obedience-3

Maximum number of points possible 284

INDEXES APPEAR UNDER THE HEADINGS

+-Litter is from WPGCA Breeding Program.

Here then are the Griffons who were tested under these revised rules, since 1982 through 1994, ***listed chronologically, not by pedigree number***.

	T	S	B	SB	R	S	P	WS	R	W	T	S	W	D	*F	*B	N	A	C	O	TP	PR	C	C	T
INDEX	5	3	3	2	3	5	4	3	3	3	4	4	2	3	3	3	6	4	4	3					
+ GR 120 (1985-86) (Bent Pine's Biff x Brisette de la Cote)																									
AJAX VOM MAYERHOFF, 4 YRS	2	4	4	4	4	3	2	3	3	0	2	3	4	4	4		3	3	3	3	198		3	3	o
AJAX VOM MAYERHOFF, 5 YRS	3	4	4	4	4	4	4	4	4	4	4	4	4	4			4	4	4	4	251	II	3	3	o
GR 129 (1985-86) (Bar-Mi's Elmor at Rocin x J V's Gilda Griffon)																									
QUAIL QUEEN BARMI'S PEPPER, 4 Y	4	4	4	4	4	4	4	4	4	2	3	4	4	4			4	4	4	4	246	II	3	3	o
J.V.'S LITTLE RED LA-VITT,	4	4	4	2	4	4	1	4	3	4	4	4	4	4			4	4	3	3	231	III	3	3	o
+GR 132 (1985) (Bent Pine's Biff x Desiree de la Cote)																									
AMOS VAN JAGERSHORST, 2 Y, 9 M	2	4	3	4	1	4	4	4	3	4	4	2	3	2			3	3	3	3	201		4	4	o
AMOS VAN JAGERSHORST, 3 Y	3	4	4	4	4	4	4	4	3	4	2	4	4	0			3	4	3	3	215		4	4	o
AMOS VAN JAGERSHORST, 3 Y	3	4	4	4	4	4	4	4	3	4	2	4	4	0			3	4	3	3	215		4	4	o
+GR 121 (1986) (Bon Chasseur de la Cote x Alice B Toklias)																									
POINT'S PEWTER TIP, 5 YRS	2	3	2	4	4	4	4	3	4	4	4	4	4	2	3		4	4	3	3	230	III	4	3	o
GR 145 (1986) (Magic Valley Rafe x Magic Valley Heidi)																									
GREEN MOUNTAINS GRIFF, 2 Y	3	3	3	2	3	3	4	1	2	3	4	3	3	3			4	3	2	2	188	III	3	3	o
GR 155 (1986) (Beaver Dam's Kiowa x Jez-A-Belle)																									
DIEDRA OF POINT LOOKOUT, 3 Y	2	2	3	4	4	4	2	1	3	1	4	3	3	3			3	3	2	2	175	III	3	3	o
GR 164 (1986) (Ilk v Bibertal x Tasha v Snake River)																									
TAWNA'S CHELSEA MORNING, 4 Y	2	3	4	4	2	4	4	4	3	3	3	3	4	4			4	3	3	3	212	III	4	4	o
TAWNA'S CHELSEA MORNING, 7 Y	4	4	4	4	4	4	4	2	2	2	4	4	4	4			4	3	3	3	227	II	4	4	o

	T	S	B	SB	R	S	P	WS	R	W	T	S		D	*F	*B	N	A	C	O	TP	PR	C	C	T
GR 149 (1986) (Magic Valley Rafe x Amargot Getchurgun)																									
THREE OAKS LONKA, 5 Y	4	4	3	4	4	4	4	4	4	4	2	4	4	4			4	4	4	4	245	III	3	3	o
THREE OAKS LONKA, 5 Y	4	4	3	4	3	4	4	4	4	4	4	4	4	4			4	4	4	4	250	I	3	3	o
GR 153 (1987, 1988) (Furst v.d. Neuburg x Bar-Mi's Gretchen)																									
SHARON'S MT JOHN REGGIE, 3 Y	2	2	3	4	3	3	1	0	2	4	4	3	4	4			3	3	2	3	178		4	3	o
SHARON'S MT JOHN REGGIE, 4 Y	4	3	4	4	4	3	3	3	4	3	4	4	4	4	4		4	4	3	3	243	II	4	3	o
+GR 156 (1987) (Amos van Jagershorst x Point's Tewter Tip)																									
POINT'S SHOT, 2 Y, 6 M	4	4	4	4	4	4	4	4	3	2	4	3	3	4	4		4	4	3	3	246	II	2	1	o
GR 144 (1987) (Furst v.d. Neuburg x Flatheads Jagdhund Gretel)																									
TIDEWATER ACCENT'S ASA, 4Y, 6 M	4	3	2	4	4	3	0	0	1	3	4	2	3	0			3	2	2	2	152		3	3	*
GR 172 (1987) (Pepper v Snake River x Plum Creek's Muffin)																									
EVITA PERRONCITA JUNIPERS, 4Y,6M	0	-	-	-	-	1	-	-	-	4	0	1	2	-			-	-	-	-	-	-	-	-	
+GR 163 (1987) (Alan od Verjrice x Elsa z Trocnovskeho luhu) (CF)																									
JISKRA Z TRONCHOVSKEHO LUHU, 3Y,6M	4	4	4	4	4	4	4	2	3	4	2	4	3	4	4		3	3	3	3	232	III	3	2	o
GR 169 (1988) (Adolph von Duffer x Cora von Glantz)																									
WELCH'S SIR TIMOTHY, 2 Y, 6 M	2	4	4	4	0	4	4	2	3	4	4	4	4	4			4	3	2	2	207		3	3	o

	T	S	B	SB	R	S	P	WS	R	W	T	S	W	D	*F	*B	N	A	C	O	TP	PR	C	C	T
GR 175 (1988) (Liberty's Flag Wiskers x Alders Edge Attagirl)																									
ALDERS EDGE DIABLOTAN, 4 Y	3	4	4	4	4	4	4	4	3	4	4	4	4	4			4	4	2	4	240	III	3	4	o
+GR 176 (1988) (Alan od Ditetu x Brita z Bilych skal) (CF)																									
HELA Z DOBROWSKA (CF), 4 Y	2	4	4	4	4	4	4	2	2	1	4	4	4	4	2		4	4	3	3	224	III	4	3	o
GR 151 (1988) (Alders Edge Amundsen x Koele's Meggen)																									
ANDY, 4 YRS, 6 MOS	3	4	4	4	3	4	4	2	3	4	3	4	3	4			3	3	3	3	219	II	3	3	o
GR 152 (1988) (Fritz von Becker x Duchess v.d. Umpqua Park)																									
BARON VON HERRENHAUSEN,4Y,6M	3	3	2	3	1	2	2	0	2	2	4	4	3	3			3	2	1	1	149		4	2	o
+GR 166 (1989) (Erik od Jezerak x Freewinds Alamance)																									
AUTUMN OF HOFFMAN MILL, 4 Y	4	4	4	4	4	4	4	3	3	4	4	4	3	4			4	4	4	3	245	I	4	3	o
GR 179 (1990) (Ingo v Kastanienhain x Glac[i]er Cool Deecee)																									
KALISPELL INGO VOM GLACIER, 3 Y	4	4	4	4	4	3	3	2	4	4	4	3	4	4			4	3	3	3	226	II	4	2	o
GR 179A (1990) (Furst v.d. Neuburg x Flathead's Geri)																									
GOOD TIME GRADY BOY, 3 Y, 9 M	4	3	4	4	2	4	4	2	3	4	4	4	4	4			4	4	3	3	231	II	4	4	o
+GR 188 (1991) (Erik od Jezerak x Patches von Rippoff)																									
ALYA OF WHITE WATER, 2 Y	4	3	3	4	3	4	2	1	3	2	4	4	4	4	4	3	4	3	3	3	234	III	4	2	o
ALYA OF WHITE WATER, 2 Y, 6 M	4	4	4	4	4	4	4	4	2	4	3	4	4	1			4	3	3	2	235	III	4	2	*
AMIE OF WHITE WATER, 4 Y, 4 M	4	3	2	4	4	4	4	3	2	4	4	4	3	4			4	3	3	2	222	III	3	3	*

	T	S	B	SB	R	S	P	WS	R	W	T	S	W	D	*F	*B	N	A	C	O	TP	PR	C	C	T
+GR 210 (1991) (Bojar z Burdovny x Cila ze Strazneho kopeo) (CF)																									
AXA OD PASTEJRIKO (CF), 3 Y, 6 M	4	3	3	3	3	4	4	2	4	4	4	4	4	3	3		4	4	3	3	238	II	4	4	o
+GR 187 (1992, 93, 94) (Blue Mountain Brew x Avaj of Iamonia) (2 litters)																									
ABBOT OF DUTCHMAN'S HOLLOW,3Y,5M	4	2	3	2	0	4	4	2	3	4	4	4	4	4			4	3	3	2	208		4	4	o
ABBOT OF DUTCHMAN'S HOLLOW,5Y,6M	3	1	0	4	1	4	4	1	4	4	2	4	4	1			3	2	2	2	167		4	4	o
ARROW OF DUTCHMAN'SHOLLOW,5Y,6M	4	2	3	4	4	4	3	4	4	4	4	4	4	3			4	3	3	3	229	II	4	4	o
CHAMPAGNE BLAZE OF DUTCHMAN'S HOLLOW, 3 Y, 5 M	3	3	4	4	3	4	4	0	3	4	2	3	3	3			4	3	2	2	145		3	4	o
GR 194 (1992) (Sharon's Mt John Reggie x Point's Pewter Tip)																									
ASPEN POINT'S BARREL, 3 Y	4	4	4	4	4	4	4	3	4	4	4	4	4	4			4	4	4	4	253	I	4	4	o
+GR 225 (1992) (Beno z Nolkopu x Ara Cerniky) (CF)																									
DAN CERNIKY, 4 YRS	2	1	2	4	4	4	4	3	2	4	4	4	4	4			3	3	3	3	205	III	4	4	o
+GR 186 (1993) (Boss of the Cascades x Autumn of Hoffman Mill)																									
A COOTER'S NIECE OF AUGER FALLS, 3 Y, 10 M	4	4	4	4	4	4	4	0	4	4	4	4	4	4			4	4	3	3	237		4	3	o
+GR 208 (1993) (Erik od Jezerak x Axa od Pastejriko) (CF)																									
AMBROSE DE LOS ALTOS, 3 Y, 5 M	3	4	4	4	4	4	4	3	4	4	4	4	4	4	3		4	4	4	3	244	II	4	2	o

	T	S	B	SB	R	S	P	WS	R	W	T	S	W	D	*F	*B	N	A	C	O	TP	PR	C	C	T
GR 201 (1994) (Boss of the Cascades x Avaj of Iamonia)																									
BUCKINGHAM OF DUTCHMAN'S HOLLOW, 4 YR	4	3	4	4	0	2	4	0	4	4	3	4	4	4			4	3	2	2	197		3	3	o
GR 203 (1994) (Dino De L'Etang x Alders Edge Feu Follet)																									
AMBERGRIS DU FEU FOLLET,4Y,4M	3	4	3	4	4	3	3	1	3	4	4	3	4	4			4	3	3	3	212	III	2	4	o
+GR 226 (1994) (Dan Cerniky x Amy of Dutchman's Hollow)																									
BAILEY OF OCEAN HOUSE, 2Y,6M	4	3	3	4	4	4	4	2	4	4	4	4	4	4			4	4	3	3	237	II	4	3	o

CONTINUATION OF NAVHDA UFT RESULTS 1977-1994

(NOTE that in the water portion, Search for a Duck has been changed, the dog is no longer required to demonstrate tracking ability. It may track, but it is not required. After the duck is hidden in some cover, "...A judge will indicate to the handler the general direction in which the duck was tossed. The handler will fire one blank shot over the water in the general direction of the duck. ...The capable dog will systematically search likely cover and, if conditions are appropriate, will find and follow the scent path left as the duck moves through the aquatic cover and over short stretches of open water. If the scent is lost, the dog should not mill around aimlessly at the spot, but should start a systematic search to relocate the scent.")

(See page 423 for test categories)

HEADINGS AND INDEXES:

	SD	H	RB	SB	RD	S	P	WS	RB	RD	N	D	S	C	O	TP	PR	T
Index	2	2	2	3	3	5	4	3	3	3	6	5	3	3	3			
NAV-142 (1976-1982 and GR Ped 47) (Don v.d. Neuburg x Juniper Heather Hen)																		
WYOMINGS LUCKY, 2 YRS	3	4	4	4	4	3	3	4	4	0	3	3	3	3	4	162		o
WYOMINGS LUCKY, 2 YRS, 5 MOS	4	4	4	4	4	2	3	3	4	4	4	4	3	4	4	183	III	o
(Conformation: large, slight cowhock, rounded back.)																		
WYOMINGS LUCKY, 4 YRS, 5 MOS	1	4	4	4	0	1	2	0	2	4	1	2	2	3	2	96		o
(Conformation: oversized, rear crosses over, cowhock.)																		
SUNNY BRANCHS BEAU BROKK, 4 YRS	1	4	4	4	3	2	2	1	3	0	2	2	3	2	2	111		o
SUNNY BRANCHS BEAU BROKK,4Y,2M	4	2	4	4	4	3	4	3	3	4	3	4	3	3	3	173	II	o
SUNNY BRANCHS BEAU BROKK,5Y,5M	4	4	2	4	3	4	3	2	3	4	4	4	4	4	3	181	II	o
SUNNY BRANCHS BEAU BROKK,6Y,2M	3	3	3	4	4	4	3	2	4	4	3	4	4	2	3	171	II	o
(Conformation: oversized.)																		
SUNNY BRANCHS BEAU BROKK,6Y,5M	4	4	3	4	4	4	4	4	4	4	4	4	4	4	4	202	I	o
SUNNY BRANCHS BEAU BROKK, 8 Y	4	4	4	4	4	3	2	1	4	4	4	3	4	2	3	169	III	o
(Conformation: large for breed, cowhock.)																		
NAV 143 (1978) (Hardrock Montana Talus x Spokane Princess)																		
HARDROCK MONTANA JAKE II, 17 M	4	3	2	4	0	3	2	1	2	2	3	3	4	2	2	130		o

	SD	H	RB	SB	RD	S	P	WS	RB	RD	N	D	S	C	O	TP	PR	T
NAV-144 (1975-76) (Turck de la Vieille Oise x Tanya du Nemtaye)																		
IGOR DU HAUT BLAINVILLE, 2 YRS	3	2	3	4	4	3	3	0	3	3	3	3	3	3	3	147		o
(Conformation: excessive height and length.)																		
IGOR DU HAUT BLAINVILLE, 3 YRS	2	2	4	2	4	3	3	2	3	4	3	4	3	3	3	154	III	o
NAV-145 (1980) (Whiskey du Pironec x Huckle Hill Angela)																		
SUNNY BRANCH'S FREYA, 3 YRS, 5 M	0	4	4	4	0	3	4	4	2	0	3	2	3	2	2	123		o
NAV-23 (1984) (Bent Pines Blitz x Alders Edge Attagirl)																		
ALDERS EDGE COFAIN, 2 YRS	0	4	0	4	0	3	2	1	3	0	2	1	2	1	1	81		o
NAV BB (1986-87)) (Ranger des Chamumes de L'Aure D'or x Perle di San Germano)																		
VALINA DI SAN GERMANO, 2 Y, 6 M	4	4	4	4	0	4	3	4	3	0	3	3	4	2	2	151		o
VALINA DI SAN GERMANO, 3 Y, 6 M	2	4	4	4	0	3	3	2	2	4	3	2	3	3	2	135		o
VALINA DI SAN GERMANO, 3 Y, 6 M	4	4	4	3	4	4	4	4	2	4	4	4	4	4	3	193	III	o
NAV AA (1988) (GR Ped 153) (Furst v.d. Neuburg x Bar-Mi's Gretchen)																		
SHARON'S MT JOHN REGGIE, 4 YRS	4	4	4	4	4	4	2	2	3	4	4	4	4	3	3	181	III	o
SHARON'S MT JOHN REGGIE, 4 YRS	2	4	4	4	4	3	3	4	3	4	3	3	4	3	3	167	III	o
NAV-25 (1987-1991) (Liberty's Wiskers x Alders Edge Attagirl)																		
ALDERS EDGE DUKE, 2 YRS, 3 MOS	4	3	0	3	2	3	2	3	3	4	3	3	4	3	2	148		o
(Conformation: eyes ectropic)																		
ALDERS EDGE DIABLOTAN, 3 YRS	3	4	2	4	2	3	3	1	2	0	4	3	4	2	2	137		o
ALDERS EDGE DIABLOTAN, 3 Y, 3 M	4	3	4	4	2	2	4	3	3	3	3	2	3	3	3	152	III	o
ALDERS EDGE DIABLOTAN, 3 YRS, 3 M	3	3	4	4	4	3	2	4	3	4	3	3	4	2	3	162	III	o
ALDERS EDGE DIABLOTAN, 3 YRS, 4 M	4	2	4	4	4	2	4	4	4	4	3	3	3	3	3	170	III	o
ALDERS EDGE DIABLOTAN, 4 YRS	4	3	4	4	4	3	3	3	3	4	4	3	4	2	3	173	II	*
ALDERS EDGE DIABLOTAN, 4 Y, 11 M	4	2	3	4	4	4	3	3	3	4	4	4	4	3	3	182	II	o
ALDERS EDGE DIABLOTAN, 6 Y, 9 M	3	4	2	4	4	2	3	4	3	3	4	2	3	3	2	154	III	*
ALDERS EDGE DEBA, 3 YRS, 3 MOS	4	3	4	4	4	3	3	0	2	4	4	3	4	2	2	158		o
ALDERS EDGE DEBA, 3 YRS, 4 MOS	3	3	4	0	4	2	3	1	1	4	2	3	4	2	2	129		o
ALDERS EDGE DEBA, 4 YRS, 3 MOS	4	4	4	4	4	3	3	1	4	0	4	2	4	2	2	152		o
ALDERS EDGE DANCER, 5 YRS, 3 MOS	3	4	4	4	3	4	3	2	4	4	3	3	4	3	3	170	II	o

	SD	H	RB	SB	RD	S	P	WS	RB	RD	N	D	S	C	O	TP	PR	T
NAV-14 (1981-86) (Barry v.d. Neuburg x Bent Pine's Aberdeen)																		
DUCKPOND EBULLIENT KASY, 3 YRS	3	3	4	4	0	2	3	1	3	0	3	2	2	3	2	117		o
DUCKPOND EBULLIENT KASY, 4 YRS	3	4	4	4	2	4	4	3	3	4	4	4	4	4	3	185		o
DUCKPOND FROELICH, 6 YRS	4	3	4	4	3	2	2	0	4	4	3	3	4	3	3	153		o
DUCKPOND FROELICH, 7 YRS	1	4	4	1	2	3	3	0	4	4	3	3	4	3	2	140		o
NAV-146 (1984-85) (Furst v.d. Neuburg x Rocky Mountain Happy Kim)																		
JAMI OF WHITMAN, 2 YRS, 4 MOS	4	4	4	3	4	3	1	1	4	4	3	4	4	3	3	164		o
JAMI OF WHITMAN, 3 YRS, 4 MOS	4	4	4	4	4	3	4	4	4	0	4	3	4	3	3	177		o
JAMI OF WHITMAN, 3 YRS, 5 MOS	4	4	4	4	4	3	4	2	2	4	4	4	4	3	3	181	II	o
+NAV 147 (1985 and GR Ped 120) (Bent Pines Biff x Brisette de la Cote)																		
AJAX V MAYERHOF, 4 YRS	4	4	4	4	3	3	4	1	3	4	4	3	3	3	2	167	III	o
+NAV 148 (1985 and GR Ped 132) (Bent Pine's Biff x Desiree de la Cote)																		
AMOS V JAGERSHORST, 2 Y, 10 M	4	4	4	4	1	3	2	2	2	0	3	3	4	2	2	136		o
(Conformation: butt bite)																		
AMOS V JAGERSHORST, 3 YRS	2	4	4	4	1	4	3	4	1	0	3	2	4	1	2	133		o
NAV 31 (1985) (Brownie of Walden x Sugar Baby)																		
BROWN SUGAR KITTY, 22 MOS	2	2	4	4	0	3	2	0	1	4	2	2	3	2	2	110		o
NAV-18 (1983-86) (Sunny Branch's Beau Brokk x Huckle Hill Calliope)																		
ALDERS EDGE ATTAGIRL, 4 YRS	3	4	4	2	4	3	2	0	4	0	2	3	4	2	2	131		o
ALDERS EDGE ATTAGIRL, 5 YRS	2	4	4	4	2	3	3	2	4	0	3	3	3	2	2	137		o
ALDERS EDGE ATTAGIRL, 5 YRS, 8 M	4	4	4	4	4	4	4	0	4	4	4	4	4	3	3	186		o
ALDERS EDGE ATTAGIRL, 5 YRS, 9 M	4	4	4	4	2	4	2	1	2	4	3	3	4	2	3	156	III	o
(Dog mutilated bird.)																		
ALDERS EDGE ATTAGIRL, 6 YRS, 8 M	3	4	4	4	3	4	3	1	3	4	4	4	4	3	3	175	III	o
NAV 149 (1983-85 and GR Ped 129)(Barmi's Elmo at Rocin x JV's Gilda Gr.)																		
QUAIL QUEEN BARMI'S PEPPER, 2 YRS, 5 M	4	2	4	4	4	3	3	1	1	0	4	3	3	0	2	135		o
QUAIL QUEEN BARMI'S PEPPER, 3 YRS	4	4	4	4	0	2	3	2	4	4	3	3	3	2	2	146		o
QUAIL QUEEN BARMI'S PEPPER, 3 YRS, 5 M	3	4	4	4	4	3	3	4	3	0	2	3	3	1	2	141		o
(Mutilated pheasant on drag.)																		

	SD	H	RB	SB	RD	S	P	WS	RB	RD	N	D	S	C	O	TP	PR	T
NAV 149 (Continued)																		
QUAIL QUEEN BARMI'S PEPPER, 4 YRS, 2 M	3	4	4	4	4	4	3	4	4	4	3	3	4	3	4	183	II	o
QUAIL QUEEN BARMI'S PEPPER, 4 YRS, 3 MOS	2	4	4	4	4	3	3	4	4	4	4	3	3	3	3	173	III	o
NAV 150 (1984-89 and GR Ped 122) (Tracy a Moustaches x Huckle Hill Angela)																		
HUCKLE HILL ALFALFA, 3 YRS, 3 MOS	3	4	4	4	2	3	3	0	2	4	2	3	4	3	2	142		o
(Spooky at water.)																		
HUCKLE HILL ALFALFA, 3 YRS, 4 MOS	2	4	4	2	4	2	3	1	1	4	3	3	4	3	2	141	III	o
HUCKLE HILL ALFALFA, 8 YRS, 4 MOS	4	4	2	4	4	4	3	4	4	4	4	4	4	4	3	193	II	o
NAV 22 (1985-86 and GR Ped 164) (Ilk v Bibertal x Tasha v Snake River)																		
TAWNA'S CHELSEA MORNING, 3 Y, 3 M	3	4	4	4	4	4	4	0	3	4	4	4	4	3	3	179		o
TAWNA'S CHELSEA MORNING, 4 YRS, 3 M	3	4	4	4	3	4	4	4	4	3	4	4	4	4	3	191	II	o
NAV 151 (1986) (Achille du feu Follet x Zest du Montmagny)																		
CHEIK DU FEU FOLLET, 3 YRS, 6 MOS	3	2	1	3	4	3	3	2	1	4	3	3	4	3	2	145	III	o
+NAV 151A and GR Ped 121 (1986-1987) (Bon Chasseur de la Cote x Alice B. Toklias)																		
POINT'S PEWTER TIP, 5 YRS, 1 MO	2	4	4	4	4	4	4	4	4	4	3	4	4	4	4	190	III	o
POINT'S PEWTER TIP, 5 YRS, 3 MOS	4	4	4	4	4	4	4	4	4	3	3	3	4	4	4	191	II	o
POINT'S PEWTER TIP, 6 YRS, 1 MO	4	4	4	4	4	4	4	4	4	3	4	4	4	3	3	195	I	o
POINT'S PEWTER TIP, 6 YRS, 5 MOS	3	4	4	4	3	4	4	4	4	4	4	1	4	3	3	176		o
NAV 29 (1988 and GR Ped 156) (Amos v Jagershorst x Point's Pewter Tip)																		
POINT'S SHOT, 3 YRS	4	3	4	4	4	4	4	2	2	4	4	4	4	3	2	181	II	o
(ectropic eyes)																		
POINT'S ALGERNON BIFF, 3 YRS, 2 M	4	4	4	4	4	2	3	4	0	3	3	2	3	2	2	144		o
POINT'S ALGERNON BIFF, 3 YRS, 4 M	2	4	4	4	3	3	3	4	3	4	2	2	3	3	3	150		o
(Testes: one small, one large and fatty tissue mass.)																		
POINT'S ALGERNON BIFF, 3 YRS, 4 M	4	4	4	4	4	3	3	3	4	4	4	4	4	4	4	192	II	o
(Testes-epididymis enlarged)																		
NAV 40 (1989-91) (Loys du Tedelou x Alders Edge Attagirl)																		
ALDERS EDGE FETICHE, 2 YRS	3	3	4	4	0	3	3	3	4	4	3	3	4	3	3	157		o
ALDERS EDGE FETICHE, 3 YRS	1	3	4	4	0	4	4	3	4	4	3	3	4	3	3	158		o

	WS	H	B	RD	S	P	SG	RB	D	N	D	C	O	TP	PR	C	C	T
NAV-40 (1988) (Loys du Tedelou x Alders Edge Attagirl)																		
ALDERS EDGE FETICHE, 24 MOS	3	4	4	4	4	3	3	4	4	3	3	3	3	156	II	-	-	o
NAV-56 (1992) (Dino de L'Etang x Alders Edge Feu Follet)																		
ACAJOU DU FEU FOLLET, 28 MOS	4	4	4	4	4	4	4	4	3	3	4	4	4	175	II	-	-	o
NAV-64 (1992) (Alders Edge Ingos Cool Alpha x Alders Edge Griselda)																		
ALDERS EDGE HAGAR, 18 MOS	1	4	4	4	3	4	2	3	3	4	2	2	3	136		-	-	o
NAV-47 (1990) (Alders Edge Blaze x Armada's Georgia Brown)																		
PRAIRIE LEK'S GERTA, 16 MOS	4	4	4	4	3	2	2	1	0	4	2	2	2	122		**ectropic**		o
PRAIRIE LEK'S GERTA, 24 MOS	1	4	4	4	4	3	3	3	4	4	3	3	3	151		**ectropic**		o
NAV-66 (1993) (Cesar v Erlenbruch x Aspen Point's Buttstock)																		
SUPER EMMA DUCHASSEUR, 20 MOS	4	4	4	4	4	4	3	4	4	4	4	4	4	181	I	-	-	o
NAV-69 (1991 and GR Ped #190) (Duckpond Dustin x Duckpond Joyeux) (2 litters)																		
DUCKPOND LIEDERKRANZ, 24 MOS	1	4	0	1	3	3	0	2	0	3	2	1	1	82		-	-	o
DUCKPOND LADY, 28 MOS	2	4	4	4	2	2	1	4	4	3	1	2	2	116		-	-	*
DUCKPOND NORRIDGEWOCK, 26 MOS	4	3	0	4	3	3	2	1	3	4	3	1	2	127		-	-	o
NAV-37 (1989 and GR-200) (Duckpond Garp x Duckpond Suzanne)																		
DUCKPOND JOYEUX, 40 MOS	4	4	4	4	4	4	3	2	4	4	4	3	3	169	II	-	-	o
NAV-54 (1991-92) (Good Time Grady Boy x Flatheads Heidi)																		
VON BAUGHMAN'S KEDA, 18 MOS	1	4	4	0	3	3	0	2	4	4	2	2	2	111		-	-	o
VON BAUGHMAN'S KEDA, 31 MOS	1	4	4	4	2	3	2	4	4	2	2	2	3	121		-	-	o
NAV-63 (1989, 1993 and GR Ped 179 (Ingo v Kastanienhain x Glac[i]er Cool Deecee) (3 litters)																		
KALISPELL INGO V GLACIER, 23 MOS	3	2	4	4	4	4	2	4	3	4	4	3	3	161	II	-	-	o
GOOD TIME NATTIE, 29 MOS	3	4	4	4	3	3	3	3	4	4	4	3	3	159	II	-	-	o
INGO'S IMAGE V GLACIER, 29 MOS	2	4	4	4	4	3	3	4	4	3	3	3	3	152	III	-	-	o

	SD	H	RB	SB	RD	S	P	WS	RB	RD	N	D	S	C	O	TP	PR	T
NAV 64 (1992 and GR Ped 213) (Alders Edge Ingos Cool Alpha x Alders Edge Griselda)																		
ALDERS EDGE HAGAR, 3 YRS, 7 MOS	4	4	4	4	4	3	3	3	2	4	4	4	4	3	3	180	II	o
NAV 66 (1994) (Cesar v Erlenbruch x Aspen Point's Buttstock)																		
UPLAND'S PURDY SCHATZE, 2 Y, 7 M	3	4	4	4	2	4	4	4	4	4	4	3	4	3	3	183	II	o
SUPER EMMA DUCHASSEUR, 20 MOS	1	3	3	4	1	4	4	4	4	4	3	3	4	3	3	162		o
NAV 83 (1994) (Royal Hunts GDB Charlemage x Elsy de St Landry)																		
GOOSE CREEKS AMIGO, 2 YRS, 2 MOS	3	4	4	4	2	3	4	4	2	4	4	3	4	3	2	169	II	o
NAV 116A (1994) (Sampson v Herrenhausen x Greta v Herrenhausen)																		
DRUMMER V HERRENHAUSEN, 5 YRS	4	3	1	1	4	2	3	2	4	3	3	3	4	3	2	147	III	o
NAV 61 (1994 and GR Ped 216) (Point's Algernon Biff x Royal Hunt's Dinah)																		
ASTRA V NUMMELHOF, 5 YRS, 5 MOS	4	4	4	4	4	4	3	4	4	4	3	3	3	4	4	186	II	o

Appendix B

Original Constitution (1951)
Wirehaired Pointing Griffon Club of America

Article I. Name and purpose

Section 1. The name of this organization shall be the Wirehaired Pointing Griffon Club of America.

Section 2. The purpose of the Club is to improve the Wirehaired Pointing Griffon creed by such activities as:

a. Sponsoring sanction matches, shows, field trials, and obedience trials in accordance with the rules of the American Kennel Club and the Field Dog Stud Book.

b. Sponsoring the organization of local chapters of the Club.

c. Cooperating with all other agencies devoted to the betterment and advancement of dogs.

d. Developing recommended breeding programs.

e. Affiliating with foreign clubs and stud books devoted to the Wirehaired Pointing Griffon.

f. Acquainting the American public, particularly sportsmen, with the breed and its characteristics.

Section 3. The Club is a non-profit organization.

Section 4. For the purpose of complying with AKC regulations relative to dog shows, Missoula, Montana is designated as the place at which shows, matches, and trials conducted by the Club will be held. This limitation does not prevent the Club from supporting the entry at any AKC approved show held anywhere in the United States.

Article II. Activation and Membership

Section 1. The Club shall become active upon the payment of annual dues by ten or more persons on the attached list of suggested charter members. All persons on the attached list who do pay their dues prior to six months after the Club is activated shall be charter members.

Section 2. Persons residing in the United States, of good standing, who either own or have owned a Wirehaired Pointing Griffon, nominated by a member of the Club, and approved by two-thirds of the ballots received, shall become members of the Club upon payment of annual dues. Active members are those who have paid their annual dues for the current year.

Section 3. The Club may elect to honorary membership any person making an outstanding contribution to the purpose of the Club. Honorary members are not entitled to vote.

Article III. Officers

Section 1. The officers of the club shall consist of the President, Vice President, Secretary-Treasurer, and (when appropriate) American Kennel Club delegate. All officers serve for one year and without pay.

Section 2. The President of the Club shall monitor all voting (see Article V below), shall appoint acting officers to fill any vacancy occurring between elections, and shall appoint members to such committees as may be established by the Club.

Section 3. The Secretary-Treasurer is the executive agent of the Club. His duties include maintaining all records of the Club, conducting all correspondence, publishing a quarterly news bulletin, and conducting the business of the Club within the policies of this constitution, its by-laws, AKC regulations, and motions carried by the Club. See also Article V below.

Article IV. Elections

Section 1. The pro term officers at the time of activation of the Club shall remain in office until after the first annual election.

Section 2. Nominations for office may be made by any active member of the club by mail to the Secretary-Treasurer. Nominations should reach the Secretary-Treasurer prior to 31 December each year.

Section 3. Prior to 31 January of the following year the Secretary-Treasurer will mail to each member a slate of all nominees along with postcard ballots in duplicate. Marked ballots will be returned both the President and to the Secretary-Treasurer prior to 1 March. Nominees receiving the greatest number of votes become elected except that no person may occupy two officer positions. New officers take office 10 March each year.

Article V. Conduct of Parliamentary Business

Section 1. The parliamentary business of the Club shall be conducted by mail. To the extent practicable, Robert's Rules of Order will apply.

Section 2. The general procedure to be followed requires that the Secretary-Treasurer periodically canvass opinions of club members, receive their recommendations, and frame appropriate motions to be submitted to all active members on a duplicate ballot. Ballots are to be marked and returned, one copy to the President, and one copy to the Secretary-Treasurer within 30 days of their receipt. For a quorum ballots must be received from fifty percent of the active Club membership. A simple majority of all votes cast carries a motion, except for motions to amend the constitution or to admit a new member, which motions require a two-thirds majority.

Section 3. During the month of April the Secretary-Treasurer shall submit for vote a recommended annual budget. During the month of March the Secretary-Treasurer will prepare and distribute to members the annual financial statement.

Article VI. Dues.

Section 1. The annual dues are $5.00 per member per year, payable 1 January for the ensuing year, except for those members who enter the Club after 1 July of any year in which case their initial dues entitle them to membership during the entire following year.

Section 2. Honorary members are not required to pay dues.

Section 3. The initial payment of annual dues by charter members entitles them to membership until 31 December 1952.

Appendix C

Constitution of the Wirehaired Pointing Griffon Club of America (Revised 1994)

Article I. Name and Purpose

Section 1. The name of this organization is the Wirehaired Pointing Griffon Club of America.

Section 2. The purpose of the Club is to protect, promote, and improve the Wirehaired Pointing Griffon breed in accordance with the principles originated by E.K. Korthals, by such activities as:

a. developing recommended breeding programs based on performance and type, as outlined in the breed standards.
b. sponsoring and participating in field tests which are designed to evaluate the versatile hunting qualities of the Wirehaired Pointing Griffon.
c. sponsoring regional chapters of the Wirehaired Pointing Griffon Club of America.
d. affiliating with foreign clubs and stud books devoted to the advancement and protection of hunting dogs.
e. cooperating with all other clubs and organizations devoted to the advancement and protection of hunting dogs; and
f. acquainting hunters with the characteristics of the Wirehaired Pointing Griffon.

Section 3. The Club is a non-profit organization.

Article II. Activation and Membership

Section 1. The Club was activated in 1951 and has been active since that date. (This revision of the constitution becomes effective with a two-thirds majority of the vote in the affirmative by paid-up Club members.

Section 2. Persons of good standing interested in the Wirehaired Pointing Griffon and approved by the Board of Directors become members upon payment of annual dues. Active members are those who have paid their annual dues for the current year.

Section 3. Expulsion of a member may be made by the Board of Directors at the discretion of the Board of Directors, by a majority vote, for any action that they believe to be detrimental to the Club. Expulsion shall not be contestable, except that the expelled member may apply for membership in any succeeding year.

Section 4. The Club may elect to lifetime honorary membership, without payment of dues, any person who makes an outstanding contribution to the purpose of the Club.

Section 5. Should membership fees not be paid within two months of the due date, the delinquent member is subject to expulsion from the Club.

Article III. Officers and Committees

Section l. The officers of the club are the President, Vice-President, Secretary, and Treasurer. Officers serve for three years and without pay.

Section 2. The President appoints acting officers to fill vacancies occurring between elections, and appoints regional chairs and committee chairs as may be required. The President, in consultation with the other officers, appoints a member of the Club to serve as Editor of the club news bulletin, and a member to serve as Registrar.

Section 3. The Secretary is the executive agent of the Club. He or she maintains records of the Club, conducts Club correspondence, and conducts the business of the Club in accordance with its constitution and motions adopted by the Club.

Section 4. The Treasurer receives all Club membership fees and other monies for the Club, except monies directed elsewhere by the President. The Treasurer mails membership cards to paid-up Club members. He or she maintains the club bank accounts as directed by the President. He or she pays Club bills as directed by the President. He or she maintains a record of all Club monies. Once per year, he or she prepares the Annual Treasurer's Report for publication in the December issue of the Club news bulletin, *The Gun Dog Supreme*. This annual financial report must be submitted to the Board of Directors (via the Secretary) prior to publication in the Club news bulletin. The Treasurer also processes all new member applications, which are then mailed to the Secretary.

Section 5. The Editor of the club news bulletin, *The Gun Dog Supreme*, publishes the news bulletin six times per year under the direction of the Board of Directors. He or she mails a copy to each paid-up Club member.

Section 6. The Registrar maintains the Griffon Club Registry, called Griffon Registry Book (GRB), and related items, such as certified pedigrees, litter and individual registrations, Breeders Agreements, and reports directly to the Secretary. He or she also presents an annual report of the Registry to the Board of Directors.

Article IV. Elections

Section 1. Nominations for office are mailed by any paid-up member to the Secretary prior to November 1 of an election year. The Secretary will publish in the December *The Gun Dog Supreme* of an election year nominations received. All votes mailed to the designated vote counter, prior to December 31 of that year, after publication of the slate of nominees, are counted, and election is by a majority.

Article V. Parliamentary Procedure

Section 1. The parliamentary business of the Club is conducted by mail. To the extent practicable, Robert's Rules of Order apply.

Section 2. Normal procedure requires the Secretary, by correspondence and through the medium of *The Gun Dog Supreme*, to canvas the opinions of the Club members and to frame appropriate motions to be presented to Club members either by mail or by publication in *The Gun Dog Supreme*. A simple majority of votes cast by paid-up members within thirty days carries a motion, except for motions to revise or amend the constitution, which motions require a two-thirds majority.

Article VI. Dues

Section 1. The annual dues are thirty dollars ($30.00) unless changed by a vote of the membership by a simple majority, payable on January 1 of each year.

Appendix D

Breeding Rules of the Wirehaired Pointing Griffon Club of America Breeding Program

I. Philosophy.

The basic concepts used in the WPGCA Breeding Program are:

A. Genetic compatibility.
B. Performance.
C. Conformation.
D. Control. Every breeding must be approved by the WPGCA Breeding Committee.

II. Bitches.

In order to be used for breeding a bitch must have received a Prize II in Intermediate Hunting Dog Test (IHDT) (or its equivalent) approved by the WPGCA Breeding Committee.

The bitch must have received a 4 (or its equivalent) in Nose; at least a 3 in conformation; and at least a 3 in coat from a conformation judge approved by the WPGCA Breeding Committee.

The bitch must be certified by OFA as having at least the category of "good" in the hip evaluation.

The bitch must have received an evaluation in an IHDT (or its equivalent) in the category of "temperament" of: "no defects observed." The test must be approved by the WPGCA Breeding Committee.

The following physical defect eliminate a bitch from breeding: ectropic or entropic overshot or undershot.

In brief:

A. Prize II, IHDT.
B. Nose, 4.
C. Conformation, 3.
D. Coat, 3.
E. OFA, good.
F. Temperament, no defects observed.

Exceptions may be made in special cases by the WPGCA Breeding Committee.

III. Males.

In order to be used for breeding a male dog must have received a Prize I in IHDT (or its equivalent) approved by the WPGCA Breeding Committee.

The male must also have received at least a Prize III in a Utility Field Test (UFT) approved by the WPGCA Breeding Committee.

The male must have received a 4 (or its equivalent) in Nose in IHDT, and at least a 3 (or its equivalent) in UFT, both tests approved by the WPGCA Breeding Committee.

The male must have received, in IHDT or UFT a 3 in conformation; and at least a 3 in coat, by a conformation judge approved by the WPGCA Breeding Committee.

The male must be certified by OFA as having at least the category of "good" in the hip evaluation.

The male must have received an evaluation in an IHDT (or its equivalent) in the category of "temperament" of: "no defects observed." The test must be approved by the WPGCA Breeding Committee.

The following physical defects eliminate a male from breeding:

Ectropic or entropic.
Overshot or undershot.
Monorchidism or cryptorchidism.

In brief:

A. Prize I, IHDT.
B. Prize III, UFT.
C. Nose, 4 (IHDT).
D. Conformation, 3.
E. Coat, 3.

F. OFA, good.
G. Temperament, no defects observed.

Exceptions may be made in special cases by the WPGCA Breeding Committee.

IV. Breeders' Fees.

A. Each puppy in a litter shall be sold for not more than $500.00. This fee to be evaluated in November-December each year by the WPGCA Board of Directors.

B. $100.00 of that price is held by the breeder for eventual rebate to the buyer once the following obligations have been met:

1. $50.00 rebate when proof of 24 month hip x-ray evaluation by OFA is received by the breeder.
2. $25.00 rebate when proof of results of Natural Ability Test (NAT) is received by the breeder.
3. $25.00 rebate when proof of results of IHDT is received by the breeder.

C. $50.00 of the purchase price of each pup must be paid by the breeder to the WPGCA Breeding Program at the time of the sale of each pup.

V. Sale and placement of puppies.

A. All puppies from every breeding approved by the WPGCA Breeding Committee must be sold to someone who has been approved by the WPGCA Breeding Committee. This selection of puppy purchasers will be done in close consultation between the breeder and the Breeding Committee. The Breeding Committee will offer to any breeder who has an approved breeding all information available on any prospective puppy buyer.

VI. Other Obligations of the Breeder.

A. In any approved breeding the breeder is obligated to keep all pups in the litter to the age of at least 10 weeks. Permission to release pups to their new owners earlier than 10 weeks of age must be obtained from the WPGCA Breeding Committee.

B. In any approved breeding in the case of a pup that is born dead, or any puppy that dies from the time of birth up until the puppy is transferred to its new owner, an autopsy must be performed by a licensed DVM and the report must be sent to the WPGCA Breeding Committee. In the case of multiple deaths it may be necessary to have an autopsy performed on only one pup in an effort to cut costs. In such cases the breeder should check with a member of the Breeding Committee. Whenever in doubt dead puppies should be frozen at the time of death for possible autopsy at a later date.

VII. Stud fees.

A. Stud fees for any breeding approved by the WPGCA Breeding Committee shall not exceed the price of one pup, less the deposit requirements listed in IV.B and IV. C.

B. If the owner of the stud elects to take a pup in lieu of a fee he must pay the breeder $150 to be used for the requirements listed in IV. B and IV C. And, this pup must also be sold with the WPGCA Breeder's Agreement.

C. The owner of the stud does not necessarily have the right of "pick of the litter." However, the breeder will try to provide the owner of the stud with the pup of his choice, if at all possible.

VIII. Breeder's Agreement.

A. Every pup sold from a breeding approved by the WPGCA Breeding Committee shall be sold with the WPGCA Breeder's Agreement, which is signed by the breeder, the purchaser of the pup, and by the members of the WPGCA Breeding Committee.

Appendix E
Wirehaired Pointing Griffon Club of America
Breeder's Agreement

I agree to sell one healthy Griffon pup to

for the sum of____________which includes $100.00 deposited in good faith with the breeder for later reimbursement to the buyer upon completion of articles of this agreement. The buyer will pay shipping costs.

This pup was sired by ______________________________

Reg. No. ___________ out of ______________________

Reg. No. ___________
whelped____.

I agree to reimburse the buyer $25 upon publication in The Gun Dog Supreme of the dog's Natural Ability Test results (sanctioned by the WPGCA).

I also agree to reimburse the buyer $25 upon publication in *The Gun Dog Supreme* of the dog's Intermediate Hunting Dog Test results (sanctioned by the WPGCA).

At 24 months of age, upon receipt of the report from OFA, I agree to reimburse the buyer $50.

If the dog is diagnosed dysplastic by the OFA at 12 months of age, or at 24 months, I agree to send the buyer a replacement pup if I have one available. Or, I agree to refund half the purchase price of the dog, less any portion of the $100.00 previously refunded if the buyer does not want a replacement pup.

If the dog qualifies in its NAT evaluation and in its IHDT evaluation, or does well enough to satisfy the member of the WPGCA Breeding Committee; is evaluated as having no mental defects; no major faults in conformation and in coat as determined by the Breeding Committee; and is certified by OFA as being free of hip dysplasia at 24 months of age, I agree to register the dog in the buyer's name in the Griffon Registry Book (GRB) at no charge to the buyer.

If the dog is dysplastic; and/or does not qualify in its NAT evaluation and/or IHDT for reasons of poor nose; or is evaluated as having an unstable temperament; or is evaluated as having major faults in conformation and/or coat; the dog will not be registered in the buyer's name. If the dog is not going to be registered in the buyer's name because of one or more of the reasons stated above I agree to offer a replacement pup, or refund half the purchase price less any portion of the $100.00 previously refunded, whichever the buyer wishes. If the buyer wishes to keep a dog with one or more of the above faults, the dog must be sterilized and a letter from the attending veterinarian on his letterhead must be sent to the secretary of the WPGCA. Only when this requirement has been met will I refund one-half the purchase price to the buyer.

If the dog should die by an accident or natural causes before it reaches 12 months of age I agree to refund to the buyer $100.00 less any part of the purchase price previously refunded. This refund will be made only upon receipt of a statement from the attending Veterinarian on his letterhead as to the cause of death.

The breeder and the buyer hereby agree that this document is a bill of sale and the breeder is not legally responsible for any damage caused by this dog to any persons or any property.

Date Breeder's Signature

Date Buyer's Signature

This breeding was approved by the WPGCA Breeding Committee. This approval does not constitute a guarantee of any specific quality of dog, nor does the Breeding Committee guarantee any financial actions.

The purpose of the WPGCA Breeder's Agreement is to protect the breed by imposing controls to prevent indiscriminate breeding of dogs of inferior hunting ability or dogs not meeting breed standards.

Any alterations to this document are done without the consent and agreement of the Breeding Committee.

Warren Webster

Joan Bailey

Joseph Nadeker

Appendix F

Griffon Registry Book (GRB)
Explanations of Abbreviations in Griffon Certified Pedigrees
Wirehaired Pointing Griffon Club of America

A. American and Canadian dogs in pedigrees.

1.GRB. Griffon Registry Book of the WPGCA.

2.FPR. Field Performance Record number. Any dog with as FPR number means that the dogs has qualified in a field test sanctioned by WPGCA. (Before 1976, NAT was included. After 1976, a FPR number is only assigned to dogs that have qualified in IHDT, and/or UFT.)

3.AKC. American Kennel Club.

4.CKC. Canadian Kennel Club.

5.FDSB. Field Dog Stud Book registration of the American Field Publishing Company.

6.NAT. Natural Ability Test.

7.IHDT. Intermediate Hunting Dog Test.

8.UFT. Utility Field Test.

9.Pr. Prize classification.

10.c/c. Conformation and coat evaluation based on 1 through 4: 1-poor, 2-fair, 3-good, 4-very good. Conformation and coat evaluation on dogs under 24 months is tentative pending final evaluation at maturity.

11.OFA. Orthopedic Foundation for Animals. OFA number with dog's name indicates that dog's hip x-ray was certified by OFA as not having hip dysplasia.

B. French dogs.

1.A dog bred in France is designated by (F) to the right of dog's name.

2.LOF. Livre des Origines du Francais (French Lineage Book) registration number in the French Lineage Book.

French dogs may have one or more of the following abbreviations in front of or below their names:

a.TR. Abbreviation for "Trialer." It means the dog qualified in a field trial. It signifies a qualification in "work," meaning work in the field.

b.CH.T. Means Champion of Work. The dog has earned this by placing in several trials.

c.CH.T. S/GT. Abbreviation for Champion Trialer on Live Game.

d.CH.B. Champion of Beauty. The dog has placed in several expositions for conformation, under several different conformation judges. (The "exhibition" is what we call here a dog show.)

e.CH.I.B. Champion of International Beauty. The dog has won at expositions in France and other countries.

3.French Canadian dogs. Dogs of French bloodlines, but bred in Quebec, Canada, will be designated by (FQ) to right of dog's name.

C. German dogs.

1. A dog bred in Germany is designated by (G) to right of dog's name.

2.GSB. Griffon Stammbuch. (German Griffon Club Registry Book).

3.DGSt.B. Deutsches Gebrauchshundestammbuch (German All Purpose Hunting Dog Registry Book). Dogs with a DGSt.B number have qualified in the full Utility Field Test. Such dogs may have one or more of the following symbols marked on their pedigrees, usually in red:

a. /. This line means that the dog passed the sharpness test, and has killed a fox or a cat.

b. \. This means that the dog when searching in the forest on a track, or behind the game, bays, or gives tongue.

c. __. This line signifies that when the dog has tracked a wounded deer (or a blood track laid by a judge), and found the deer, he barks beside the deer until the hunter arrives. This is called in German, Totverbeller.

d. Vbr. An abbreviation that means when a dog finds a wounded rabbit which has run hundreds of meters, he retrieves it.

e. Btr. Signifies that when a dog is searching in a woods or field and finds a dead piece of game, he brings it without command to his master.

f. Suchensieger. This title is given to the most outstanding dog in a Utility Field Test.

g. HD frei. Means the hip x-ray shows no signs of hip dysplasia.

D. Belgian dogs.

1.LOSH. These letters followed by a registration number, signify that the dog was bred in Belgium.

E. Dutch dogs.

1. GSTB. Signify the dog was bred in The Netherlands.

F. Gunshy Test.

1. NGS. The dog exhibited no signs of being gunshy during a field test.

2. GS. The dog exhibited behavior to be classified as gunshy during a test.

3. GSS. The dogs exhibited behavior to be classified as gun sensitive.

G. Other abbreviations:

1. CACIB. Recognized world-wide as a candidate for international conformation champion.

2. CACIT. Recognized world-wide as a candidate for international working champion.

Appendix G

Breed Standards For German and French Griffon Clubs, and for AKC

German Griffon Club, Revised 1968

Head: Big and long, wirehair, but not long with well developed moustache and eyebrows. Skull not very wide. Muzzle long and square. Bridge of nose to the front slightly convex. Angle of forehead not too pronounced.

Ears: Medium, flat to the head. Tapered to bottom, not rounded and set too low. The smooth hair on them is mixed with longer hair.

Nose: Always brown.

Neck: Fairly long, without dewlap.

Chest: Deep, slightly rounded, showing strength and stamina.

Height: Males 19 1/2 inches to 23 1/2 inches. Females 19 1/2 inches to 21 1/2 inches. The judge should be allowed some leeway regarding height. Height can be slightly under or over the standard without disqualifying the dog. The height is a standard or guide. Normally the Griffon should be medium height and not too high on the legs (10% longer than high).

Shoulders: Fairly long in a well pronounced angle, or slope.

Ribs: Slightly bowed.

Front legs: Straight, strong, well set under and with wirehair.

Hind legs: Wirehair, shanks long and well developed. Hock well angled.

Feet: Round, strong and toes tightly closed.

Tail: Held straight or slightly up. Wirehair, but without feathers. (One third up to nearly one half of the tail is docked.)

Color: Most preferably blue-grey, grey with brown markings, or solid brown, quite often ticked with grey. White with brown is acceptable too.

Coat: Wirehair and harsh. Should feel like fine wire or the hair of the wild boar. Never curly or wooly. Under the rough wirehair, longer coat, is thick, soft undercoat.

The Following Should Be Recognized as Faults

Head: Too small or two wide with soft or wooly hair. Pointed muzzle. Too straight or flat forehead., Strong developed cheek bones.

Jaw: Overshot or undershot. Poorly developed teeth.

Ears: If you pull the ears to the front of the dogs face they should end on the middle of the bridge of the nose. Fault would be round, curly hair, too low or too high set ears, or ears that are not flat to the body.

Eyes: Too small, too light, hidden by eyebrows. Open eyes. Vicious looks. Ungriffon like expression.

Nose: Black or pink.

Chest: Too narrow. Too wide. Not deep.

Height: Too small and light, or too high and heavy, dogs with a build not useful for their work.

Shoulders: Too straight.

Ribs: High pulled ribs.

Legs: Short haired. Open feet. Bad angles. Cowhocked.

Back: Too short. Form too square. Straight falling rump.

Tail: Not docked. Brush or feathers.

Color: Bad, washed out colors. Dry leaf colors. Black-brown with white spot on chest.

Coat: Fine, soft, wooly or curly hair. Not enough undercoat. Short haired dogs will not be registered anymore in the G.S.B.

French Standard

Head: Large and long, with tuft abundant but not too long hair with well defined moustache and eyebrows, skull not too wide, nose long and square, sloping slightly convex, facial angle not too pronounced.

Ears: Medium size, flat, lying against the head, set not too low, the short hair covering them may be mixed with some longer ones.

Eyes: Wire, not covered by the eyebrows, very intelligent expression, never yellow, can be all shade of brown. Shape of eye must not be too round, nor too slitted.

Muzzle: Always brown.

Neck: Quite long, without dewlap.

Chest: Deep, but not too large, not like boxer dog.

Height: 21 1/2 - 23 1/2 inches for males, 19 1/2 - 21 1/2 inches for females.

Shoulders: Quite long and very oblique or sloping.

Rib Cage: Slightly curved, convex.

Front legs: Straight, vigorous, well in the line of the shoulder. Coat with hard hair.

Back: Must be strong, well developed in lower region, or kidney region.

Hind legs: Coat stiff. Thigh long with good muscles. Well developed angulation at knee and hock. Coat tufted.

Feet: Round, solid, toes together and a little up on the toes.

Tail: Tufted, not too long and carried straight, or slightly up. Cut 1/4 to 1/3 off.

Coat: Steel grey with brown markings, either brown and chestnut, white and orange, white and brown. The hair hard, coarse, reminding on of wild boar. Never curly or wooly. Under the outer coat, small down, thick and tight.

American and Canadian Kennel Clubs

The Wirehaired Griffon is a dog of medium size, fairly short-backed, rather a little low on his legs, he is strongly limbed, everything about him indicates strength and vigor.

His coat is harsh like the bristles of wild boar and his appearance, notwithstanding his short coat, is as unkempt as that of the long-haired Griffon, but on the other hand he has a very intelligent air.

Head: Long, furnished with a harsh coat, forming a moustache and eyebrows, skull long and narrow, muzzle square.

Eyes: Large, open, full of expression, iris yellow or light brown.

Ears: Of medium size, flat or sometimes lightly curled, set rather high, very lightly furnished with hair.

Nose: Always brown.

Neck: Rather long, no dewlap.

Shoulders: Long, sloping.

Ribs: Slightly rounded.

Forelegs: Very straight, muscular, furnished with rather short wire hairs.

Hind Legs: Furnished with rather short stiff hair, the thighs long and well developed.

Feet: Round, firm and well formed.

Tail: Carried straight or gaily, furnished with hard coat without plume, generally cut to a third of its length.

Coat: Hard, dry, stiff, never curly, the undercoat downy.

Color: Steel gray with chestnut splashes, gray white with chestnut splashes, chestnut, dirty white mixed with chestnut, never black.

Height: 21 1/2 to 23 1/2 inches for males, and 19 1/2 to 21 1/2 inches for females.

NOTE: See Chapter 27 for updated (1995) breed standard for WPGCA.

Appendix H

Awards From the Dog Writers of America Association to the WPGCA and Its Club Members

1971 Best National Breed Club Bulletin, *The Gun Dog Supreme*, editor Joan Bailey

1971 Best Article in a National Breed Club Bulletin, "*Raising a Litter of Pups*," by Joan Bailey.

1973 Best Article in a National Breed Club Bulletin, "*Breeders, We Have Not Been Keeping the Trust*," by Joan Bailey.

1977 Best Article in a National Breed Club Bulletin, "*How to Train Your New Griffon Pup -Don't! Let it be a Pup*," by Joan Bailey.

1980 Honorable Mention, article in National Breed Club Bulletin, "*The Breeder's Agreement - The Best Incentive for Having Dogs Tested*," by Joan Bailey.

1981 National Breed Club Publication, other than Bulletin, "*Wirehaired Pointing Griffon, It's History, Description and Use*," edited by Joan Bailey.

1981 Honorable Mention, National Breed Club Bulletin, *The Gun Dog Supreme*, editor Joan Bailey.

1981 Best Article in a National Breed Club Bulletin, "*Natural Ability Dog, What Does it Mean?*," by Joan Bailey.

1984 Honorable Mention, Black and White Photo, National Breed Club Bulletin, by Joan Bailey.

1984 Best National Breed Club Publication, *The Gun Dog Supreme*, edited by Joan Bailey.

1984 Best Article in National Breed Club Publication, "*Restoration of the Griffon on the North American continent*," by Joan Bailey.

1986 Special Publication other than National Club Bulletin, edited by Joan Bailey.

1986 Honorable Mention, Best Article, "*Intermediate Test For Versatile Hunting Dogs - Purpose and Importance,*" by Dr. Rolf Benseler.

1987 Honorable Mention, Black and White Photograph, National Breed Club Bulletin.

1992 Honorable Mention, Black and White Photograph, National Breed Club Bulletin.

1994 Best Article in Multi-Breed or Hunting Magazines, Ed Bailey, "*The Forty-ninth Day*," in ***GUN DOG*** magazine.

Appendix I

Hello, Wired Dog - Goodbye, Cooperation
By Ed Bailey

(Reprinted with kind permission from the author, from *Gun Dog Magazine,* June/July 1993.)

In the fall, the local Thursday afternoon weeklies always carry ads like:

Lost. Brittany spaniel, Cedar County. Dog's name-Hurrykane's Flash. Phone (somewhere out of state), or: *German shorthair, Blitz, lost in Knox County opening week of pheasant season. Phone(somewhere else out of state).* And missing wirehairs are listed too (the ad likely says Drahthaar), as well as pointers and setters, all lost the opening week of pheasant season.

Now, how can a Brittany—a breed originally close working, obedient, dependent, designed for the poacher sneaking onto the shooting grounds of Henry (the Fourteenth, or so)—be a lost dog? Or how about that skin-draped-over-bones, solid-liver shorthair that I saw on Al Niederklein's farm the third week of November last fall when I stopped to renew an acquaintance and reaffirm permission to hunt on some land he farmed? He said the dog had appeared a week earlier. He had been feeding it, but the animal just wouldn't calm down.

Or the exhausted shorthair I found sleeping beside a pheasant pen on a research area; I returned it to a field trial going on four miles away. The dog really broke away on the break away. But a four-mile cast is a bit much for a shorthair that was originally bred for affinity with handler, for cooperation. Whatever happened to the poacher's Brittany or the do-all-that-is-necessary shorthair or wirehair? Mostly, these lost dogs are the pointing breeds, rarely a retriever or springer. So why are so many dogs of the pointing breeds so fired they go at speeds and distances far out of proportion for the breed and for individual well being, so uncooperative that they become lost dogs? How did we get these wired dogs that must be vigorously exercised several hours before hunting for us rather than for themselves? Like one fellow I noticed driving twice around a section with his shorthair running flat out behind the pickup. I asked him why he did it. "It's the only way to keep him inside the same section I'm hunting." he said. These are not the dogs portrayed on the old Remington calendars.

At home or in a kennel, these dogs often pace constantly in a circle or they may be chewers, even chewing on themselves. With this hyperactive behavior, they are impossible to have as house dogs. Yet, these breeds were selectively bred originally to be the dog for the hunter, the dog that lived at or in the house of its owner. How did we come up with so many dogs, nearly whole breeds in some cases, so wired that professional trainer is required to make the dog do what it was purportedly bred to do? The ultimate cause or evolutionary pressure for hot-wired dogs is competition. The proximate or functional cause is we breed them that way, selecting against cooperation so the dogs are better competitors.

Before you whack me with your flushing whip, let me explain. It is not the competition per se, but what constitutes competition, that is the driving force, and we, in satisfying the vagaries of competition, are the driven. Add our need to exceed the normal expectations (our interpretation of competition) to our historical propensity for vicarious participation in the competition, and we have our dogs pushed to the limit. Our dogs become our champions, much like a professional athlete whom we pay megabucks to take up our cause, whatever it might be. Just as we push our kid into Little League and reward him or her with praise if he hammers another kid's pitching or, in midget hockey, cheer as our kind high sticks or body checks the neighbor's kid, so it is with our dogs. To win is all.

We enter the arena through or dogs, the field trial, the show ring or any other competition under various names or acronyms. Nothing wrong with a little friendly competition? This is a contradiction in terms, like a friendly war. The goal in entering competition is to win, to be the best. The price we pay: our dogs' cooperation.

But trials, tests, shows by any other euphemism are intended, indeed designed, to bring out the best, to shake the jar and see what rises to the top. The rules are made to select the best and the judges presumably are the best people to interpret the rules.

Through competition we select the best, and the best are bred to the best to produce better. Better must exceed the criteria that made a dog's parents best. We then must upgrade the criteria by which the best is chosen. So what are those criteria?

Pointing, for example, is judged. The criteria: a point must be staunch, convincing, productive and a few other subjective adjectives. The judge tries to be objective and defines staunch as absolute granite; convincing is tail at 12 o'clock, eyes abulge, an obvious arrested explosion; productive means a bird (usually a dizzied, planted bird) is there to be flushed. The dog that best fits the definitions or most exceeds them gets highest marks for pointing.

But here's a typical scenario: Joe Hunter has his pointing dog, probably one of the versatile breeds, with about a ton of field experience on wild game. He knows he has the best hunting dog in the world and perhaps the universe and wants to prove it in a trial. The dog finally gets into the bird field miles behind his field trial bracemate, gets wind of a dizzied pen-reared bird deep in shock, points momentarily, steps in, picks up the bird and dutifully, joyfully returns it to his handler—a losing performance. To the experienced field dog that's had hundreds of wild birds shot over it, this bird smells like a cripple and the dog did exactly the right thing for hunting: cooperated with the boss in finding and retrieving a crippled bird.

Search is another area that is judged. Criteria: forward going, aggressively independent style, desire for game contact, hits the objectives (my personal favorite trial jargon). Translation: fast, far, independent (dog neither knows nor cares where the handler is), out to the front. These will be scored highest. But our experienced, cooperative hunting dog that retrieved the dizzied bird quarters the open homogeneous cover seldom beyond MOD/IC range, carefully uses the wind along the fencerow, closes to 20 to 25 yards in tall weeds and brushy or wooded cover, checks out every possible scent, every clump of weeds where experience has taught him a bird might be and always maintains contact with the handler. The dog fits none of the criteria for search and doesn't win. NO one want pups from a loser, so the dog is excluded from breeding programs. The genetic complement for cooperation is shelved. Cooperation in which the dog excelled costs points. Selection pressure in breeding programs will be against cooperation in favor of more competitive, independent dogs.

This type of selection pressure means the average dog of each generation is faster, more independent, less cooperative and, in the hands of the average hunter, less controllable than the previous generation. But this selection pressure will produce dogs that win trials, or get prize one in the tests as indeed they should because they satisfy or exceed the established criteria. And such is the stuff our dreams of great dogs are made of.

A good trainer can take uncooperative dogs and hack them in, can steady them, can make them totally obedient. But no one can make them cooperative hunting dogs. The average hunter who buys one of these competitive, winning-line dogs—but has neither the time nor the expertise not the desire to haul in a wired dog—will be placing an ad in the lost and found section of Thursday's paper, usually in the dog's second season, or the dog will simply be left to become the hide-over-bones boarder at a farmer's place, trying to scarf a meal from a pig trough.

But what is this cooperation that is so badly overlooked in trials and tests? First, cooperation is the single most important characteristic of a hunting dog. A cooperative dog can be an exceptional hunting companion with a modicum of exposure and even less formal training, even though it might have just average scenting ability, desire, obedience, range, speed or anything else that is currently judged. Yet the concept of cooperation is foreign to most North Americans.

If considered at all, most will say it is obedience or biddability.

Biddability is the ability to do the handler's bidding, i.e., to be obedient. A recent issue of a versatile dog club newsletter carried a dog food ad wrongly defining cooperation as biddability. The tests sponsored by this club include judgement of cooperation, yet allowed cooperation to be equated with biddability. Cooperative dogs will appear obedient and biddable, but being obedient or biddable does not equate with being cooperative. Obedience or biddability can be trained in; cooperation must be bred in.

Cooperation is not easily understood; being uncooperative is a more easily grasped concept. A dog that eats or buries a bird rather than give it up to the handler is being uncooperative and, if being scored for cooperation, would lose some points unless the judge mistakes it for disobedience—and many do.

Obedience is a trained characteristic which can be instilled in any dog.

Cooperation, however, is a genetically transmitted quality or potential for the quality of developing total rapport with the handler. No amount of training can make a dog cooperative; cooperation is in the genetic complement to a greater or lesser degree. Cooperation, this tendency for developing rapport with a human, can often be seen in pups by ten weeks of age (another reason why dogs should not be taken from the litter at the "magical" age of seven weeks). To have a pup demonstrate its cooperation, all one need do is sit on the lawn with a group of ten-week-olds and a few squeaky toys, or some dead frogs or small sticks or anything pups will play with. The pup that repeatedly brings the playthings to you in a show-an-tell manner is the cooperative one. Everything cooperative pups do tells you they want to share it with you and not keep it for themselves or share it with their brothers and sisters. A pup like this has the potential to be an outstanding hunting dog.

There won't be any need to spend months force-training to retrieve, to walk by our knee on or off leash, to handle in the field. You won't need check cords or shock collars to get control. There is little need for strict training, only some positive reinforcement to show that you are pleased when the dog works correctly. A cooperative dog will be reading you and responding to your thought at about the same time you start thinking it. Everything the dog does is for the benefit of the handler. It is altruism shown by an individual of one species for the benefit of an individual of another species. The cooperative dog modifies its search to maximize production of game for the tuner; it retrieves everything it finds, whether told to or not. However, the dog does not discriminate between very dead, cold things and freshly shot things as though whatever the dog might eat will also please dog's best friend. The cooperative dog will hold point until you get there. But if the situation is such that you can't step in for the flush, it will leap in for you, yet will never leap in before you are ready for the shot. Some of this can be taught to the uncooperative dog by a very good trainer with labor-intensive techniques. Moderately cooperative dogs can be trained to do them with relative ease. The most cooperative dogs will require only exposure to the situation. They do it because they work for you; they like the job and do everything to keep it.

Cooperation then is not obedience, not biddability, not tractability, though these are very much affected by cooperation. How obedient, how biddable, how tractable a dog is are the results of cooperation, but cooperation in a dog is not the result of obedience or biddability or tractability, all of which mean how well the dog responds to a command. Cooperation is much more; it is a mindset and the potential for this mindset is genetically determined. Again, it cannot be created by training, only by selective breeding.

So why are increasing numbers of these wired dogs appearing in the lost-and-found section or as strays on pheasant country farms or lost from the game fields? A major reason is that we have overlooked cooperation in the breeding programs. We can't blame it on competition rules. The blame is on us and our need to exceed, to get the rush of winning even when done vicariously. Cooperation is overlook partly because it is not understood. It is a behavioral phenomenon and is measured by behavioral parameters. Few understand dog behavior well enough to read cooperation even when it's written in capital letters. Partly it is overlook because it interferes with reaching the heights of pointing dog stardom in the competition fields, in the arena. Independence and cooperation are inversely related. Independence is an absolute requirement for pointing dog competition. We select for it and we are the best selectors ever created. We easily exceed natural selection. We do in a few generations what natural selection works at for millennia.

We select for competitive dogs by taking advantage of their competitive nature as well. What dog does not run faster and farther when braced up with another fast, far-ranging dog. But competition between dogs is not the major problem. Competition between dog and handler is. And, the competitive dog, like any competitive athlete, does not discriminate between sources of competition. It competes against its handler as against another dog. A non-competitive dog does not win in competitions any more than a non-competitive athlete winds Olympic medals. Selection for competition is selection against cooperation by default.

As we select against cooperation, however inadvertently, we increase the probability of Flash or Blitz becoming the subject of a classified ad and decrease the probability of a Belle or a Blue warming our gray-stockinged feet while we run an oily rag over gun barrels of an evening after a perfect day of relaxed hunting. Like an old Remington calendar, a collector's item.

Bibliography

Bailey, Joan. *How To Help Gun Dogs Train Themselves.* Hillsboro, Oregon, Swan Valley Press, 1992.

Bailey, Edward D. "Hello, Wired Dog - Goodbye, Cooperation," *Gun Dog*, June/July 1993.

Bylandt, Count Henry de, "Griffons-Korthals," *Dogs of All Nations*, Volume I, K. Paul, T. Trubner & Co., Ltd., London. (Out of print.)

Castaing, Jean. *Le Griffon d'Arret.* Nouvelles Editions de la Toison d'Or. Paris, 1949.

Corley, Dr. E.A. "Hip Dysplasia - Statement of the Problem," and "Rationale for Selective Breeding," *A Monograph for Dog Breeders and Owners.* O.F.A., 1983.

Corley, Dr. E.A. "Memorandum to Breed Club Representatives." O.F.A., January 1994.

Corley, Dr. E.A. "Memorandum," O.F.A., February 2, 1994.

van Dam, A. several articles in the *clubblad van de nederlandse griffonclub.* (Mr. van Dam's pen name is "Partout.")

Derr, Mark, "The Politics of Dogs," *The Atlantic Monthly*, March 1990.

Falk, John R., *The Practical Hunter's Dog Book.* Second edition. Voyaguer Press, Stillwater, Minnesota, 1991.

Griffon-Club e.V. Club-Mitteilungen [news bulletin] 1950 through January 1995.

Griffon Stammbuch (GSB). 1889 to 1992.

Gun Dog Supreme, The, 1951-1995.

Hegewald, "What Counts In Judging Working Dogs," *Deutsche Jager-Zeitung*, Vol. XI, No. 12.

Hochwalt, A.F., *Bird Dogs: Their History and Achievements.* 1922. A.F. Hochwalt Co. Dayton, Ohio.

Hutchinson's Dog Encyclopaedia, Volume II, pages 842-850, Hutchinson & Co., Ltd., London, 1934-1935. (Out of print.)

Hutt, Frederick B. *Genetics For Dog Breeders.* San Francisco. W.H. Freeman & Company, 1979. (Out of print.)

I.C.G. News [International Canine Genetics], June, 1994.

75 Jahre Griffon-Club E.V., 1963, Mannheim.

Der Jagdgebrauchshund, April 1975, October 1993, Munich.

Kantz, W., "Origin and History of the Griffon," *Das Waidwerk.*

Kirkelie, Kirk, letter to Marg Allen, November 27, 1970.

Kirkelie Kennel Book.

Koessler, Barbara. Verification of manuscript. Telephone: July, August, 1994.

Korthals Kennel Book, 1872-1888.

Large Munsterlander News, Fall/Winter 1994. "A Loss to the Hunting Dog World," Joe Schmutz.

Lemonick, Michael D. "A Terrible Beauty." *Time*. December 12, 1994.

Livre des Origines du Griffon a Poil Dur (LOG). (1919) Club Francais du Griffon a poil dur (Korthals).

Lorenz, Konrad. *Man Meets Dog*. Kodansha Globe. 1994. (This is a new edition of the Nobel Laureate Lonrenz's classic book on dogs.)

Monografie Ceskeho Fouska, MVDr. Josef Kuhn, Cesky Myslivecky Svaz, Klub Chovatelu Ceskych Fousku, n.d., circa 1980's.

Mueller, Larry. "How To Improve a Breed." *Outdoor Life*. January, 1988.

Mueller, Larry. "Self-help Shorthairs," *Outdoor Life*. June 1992.

North American Versatile Hunting Dog Assoc. Newsletter, 1969-1995.

Rogers, General Thomas DeF. Rogers. Letter to Douglas Fethers, Secretary WPGCA (circa 1960).

Rosseau, Percival L. *Extracts from the History of the Wirehaired Pointing Griffon*, [by Leliman, President of the Dutch Griffon Club]. Translated from French by Percival L. Rosseau. n.d. Printed by Press of 40 Nassau St., New York.

Rosseau, Percival L. "The Pointing Griffon," *Forest and Stream*. April 1917.

Smith, Steve. "Profile," *Missoulian*. April 7, 1980.

Speece, Roy. "Wintering Quail," *Hunting Dog*. April 1970.

Tabel, Carl. *Der Jagdgebrauchshund*. BLV Jagdbuch. circa 1963.

Toepoel, P.M.C. Toepoel's Honden Encyclopaedie. (circa 1952)

The Gun Dog Supreme. Volumes I through 70, covering 1951 through June 1995.

Ward, Russell. Missoula, Montana. Manuscript confirmation in letter dated April 4, 1994.

Winterhelt, Sigbot. "The German Wirehaired Pointer." *The Pointing Dog Journal*. July/August 1993.

Winterhelt, Sigbot & Bailey, Ed. The Training and Care of The Versatile Hunting Dog. 1973. Puslinch, Ontario

Above: ***ATTICA V.D. PAARTENBURGH****, in Holland, summer of 1992, photo by John Pitlo. Below: A very young* ***CHIPPER DE LOS ALTOS****, who grew up and received a Prize I NAT, Pr. II IHDT, and turned out to be a very handsome fellow who is easy to see in the grouse and woodcock coverts of Pennsylvania and Maine, where his owner, Tim Schwager hunts him. He is one of the males we hope to use for breeding.*

BOSUN OF OCEAN HOUSE *and owner Scott Davis, at the KDK annual test on Grizzley Island, California, January 1994, where this fine team earned a Prize I in IHDT.*

In Germany, March 1990, at a special retrieving field test, Maria Zumbaum's ***HILKA VOM KEMPTER WALD****, completing the retrieve of the dead fox.*